Projects, Programs, and Project Teams

Advanced Program Management

Edited by

James Hiegel

Roderick James

Frank Cesario

Keller
Graduate School
of Management
of DeVry University

WILEY
CUSTOM SERVICES

To order books or for customer service, please call 1(800)-CALL-WILEY (225-5945).

Printed in Mexico

ISBN-13   978-0-470-03736-2
ISBN-10   0-470-03736-9

10 9 8 7 6

Contents _____

Preface   ix

Unit 1: Project Portfolio Management   1

1   INTRODUCTION   3

**2   WHAT IS PROJECT PORTFOLIO MANAGEMENT,
AND WHY DO WE NEED IT?   9**

2.1   Why Do We Need Project Portfolio Management?   10
2.2   What is Project Portfolio Management?   14

Notes   17

**3   THE FUNDAMENTALS OF A PROJECT
PORTFOLIO MANAGEMENT PROCESS   19**

3.1   Selecting Projects for the Pipeline?   21
3.2   Maintaining the Pipeline   26
3.3   Executing Project Portfolio Management   32
3.4   Tools for Project Portfolio Management   35
3.5   Implementing Project Portfolio Management   47

Notes   51

4.   THE FINER POINTS OF PROJECT PORTFOLIO MANAGEMENT   53

4.1   Defining PPM: A Bridge or a Hub?   54
4.2   A Prequalification Process for Selecting Projects for the Portfolio   57
4.3   The Impact of Uncertainty on Projects and the Portfolios   61
4.4   Is There a Gorilla in Your Portfolio? Turning Opportunity Into Value   66

4.5   Work Breakdown Structures for Risk and Strategies 69

4.6   An Introduction to Earned Value Analysis 75

Notes 80

5   PPM APPLICATIONS: NEW PRODUCT DEVELOPMENT 81

5.1   A Stage-Gate® Idea-to-Launch Framework for Driving New Products to Market 81

5.2   Portfolio Management for Product Innovation 106

Notes 135

Unit 2: Managing High-Technology Programs and Projects 137

6   ORGANIZING THE PROJECT MANAGEMENT FUNCTION AND OFFICE 139

6.1   Organizational Alternatives for Project Management 140

6.2   Reporting Relationships of Project Managers 141

6.3   Project Management Office 142

6.4   Staffing Projects: The Project Office and Project Team 147

6.5   Product and Project Support Services 151

6.6   Charting Organizational Relationships and Responsibilities 154

7   MANAGING PROJECT PORTFOLIOS, PROGRAMS, AND MULTIPLE PROJECTS 163

7.1   Managing Project Portfolios 164

7.2   Project Selection 167

7.3   Establishing and Controlling Project Priorities 172

7.4   Managing Multiproject Programs 174

7.5   Managing Multiple Projects 175

7.6   Resource Management for Projects 177

7.7   Multiproject Operations Planning and Control 178

8   PROJECT INTERFACE MANAGEMENT 185

8.1   Why Project Interface Management 185

8.2   The Concept: The Project Manager as the Project Interface Manager 186

8.3   Project Interface Management in Action 187

8.4   Product and Project Interfaces 188

8.5   Project Interface Events 190

8.6   The Five Steps of Project Interface Management 190

8.7   Conclusion 192

Unit 3: Project Management 193

9   ORGANIZING AND STAFFING THE PROJECT OFFICE AND TEAM 195

9.0   Introduction   195
9.1   The Staffing Environment   196
9.2   Selecting the Project Manager: An Executive Decision   198
9.3   Skill Requirements for Project and Program Managers   202
9.4   Special Cases in Project Manager Selection   208
9.5   Selecting the Wrong Project Manager   208
9.6   Next Generation Project Managers   212
9.7   Duties and Job Descriptions   213
9.8   The Organizational Staffing Process   217
9.9   The Project Office   223
9.10 The Functional Team   229
9.11 The Project Organizational Chart   230
9.12 Special Problems   233
9.13 Selecting the Project Management Implementation Team   235
9.14 Studying Tips for the PMI® Project Management Certification Exam   238

Problems   240

10   MANAGEMENT FUNCTIONS   247

10.0   Introduction   247
10.1   Controlling   249
10.2   Directing   249
10.3   Project Authority   254
10.4   Interpersonal Influences   262
10.5   Barriers to Project Team Development   265
10.6   Suggestions for Handling the Newly Formed Team   270
10.7   Team Building as an Ongoing Process   272
10.8   Leadership in a Project Environment   273
10.9   Life-Cycle Leadership   274
10.10 Organizational Impact   277
10.11 Employee–Manager Problems   279
10.12 Management Pitfalls   282
10.13 Communications   285
10.14 Project Review Meetings   294
10.15 Project Management Bottlenecks   295
10.16 Communication Traps   296
10.17 Proverbs and Laws   297
10.18 Management Policies and Procedures   300
10.19 Studying Tips for the PMI® Project Management Certification Exam   300

Problems   305

Case Studies
The Trophy Project   315
Leadership Effectiveness (A)   317
Leadership Effectiveness (B)   322
Motivational Questionnaire   328

11   MANAGEMENT OF YOUR TIME AND STRESS   335

11.0   Introduction   335
11.1   Understanding Time Management   336
11.2   Time Robbers   336
11.3   Time Management Forms   338
11.4   Effective Time Management   339
11.5   Stress and Burnout   340
11.6   Studying Tips for the PMI® Project Management Certification Exam   342

Problems   343

Case Study
The Reluctant Workers   344

12   CONFLICTS   345

12.0   Introduction   345
12.1   Objectives   346
12.2   The Conflict Environment   347
12.3   Conflict Resolution   350
12.4   Understanding Superior, Subordinate, and Functional
         Conflicts   351
12.5   The Management of Conflicts   353
12.6   Conflict Resolution Modes   354
12.7   Studying Tips for the PMI® Project Management Certification Exam   356

Problems   358

Case Studies
Facilities Scheduling at Mayer Manufacturing   361
Telestar International   362
Handling Conflict in Project Management   363

13 SPECIAL TOPICS **369**

13.0 Introduction 369
13.1 Performance Measurement 370
13.2 Financial Compensation and Rewards 377
13.3 Effective Project Management in the Small Business Organization 383
13.4 Mega Projects 385
13.5 Morality, Ethics, and the Corporate Culture 386
13.6 Professional Responsibilities 389
13.7 Internal Partnerships 392
13.8 External Partnerships 393
13.9 Training and Education 395
13.10 Integrated Product/Project Teams 397
13.11 Studying Tips for the PMI® Project Management Certification Exam 400

Problems 406

14 MODERN DEVELOPMENTS IN PROJECT MANAGEMENT **409**

14.0 Introduction 409
14.1 The Project Management Maturity Model (PMMM) 410
14.2 Developing Effective Procedural Documentation 414
14.3 Project Management Methodologies 418
14.4 Continuous Improvement 419
14.5 Capacity Planning 424
14.6 Competency Models 425
14.7 Managing Multiple Projects 428
14.8 End-of-Phase Review Meetings 429

15 CRITICAL CHAIN PROJECT MANAGEMENT **431**

15.0 Introduction 431
15.1 Anatomy of a Task Estimate 433
15.2 Task Execution 437
15.3 Protection in a Critical Chain Project 438
15.4 Buffer Management 443
15.5 Managing the Execution of a Critical Chain Project 444
15.6 Critical Chain Multiproject Problem and Solution 445
15.7 Implementing Multiproject Critical Chain 448
15.8 How Critical Chain Extends Critical Path 448

Problems 450

Case Studies
Lucent Technologies 451
Elbit Systems LTD. 453
Seagate Technology 456

Unit 4: The Discipline of Teams   459

16   DISCIPLINE IS WISDOM   461

17   MASTERING TWO DISCIPLINES—NOT ONE   467

17.1   The Single-Leader Discipline   469
17.2   The Team Discipline   470
17.3   Linking Work Products to Performance   473

18   VIRTUAL TEAMING   481

18.1   Virtual Teaming: Same Disciplines in New Context   483
18.2   Groupwork Technology: Key Features and Functionality   484

19   OUTCOMES—NOT ACTIVITIES—SHAPE YOUR CHOICE   491

19.1   Articulating Outcome-Based Performance Goals   493
19.2   Make Your Outcome-Based Goals Smart   495

20   PERFORMANCE AGENDAS FOR APPLYING BOTH DISCIPLINES   503

20.1   Performance Agendas for Leadership Teams   506

21   APPLYING THE TEAM DISCIPLINE   517

21.1   Resistance to Integration   518
21.2   Building a Sense of Mutual Accountability   518

22   OBSTACLES AND OPPORTUNITIES FOR VIRTUAL TEAMING   527

22.1   Expanded Access   528
22.2   Asynchronous Participation and Disembodied Communication   530
22.3   Bias Toward the Single-Leader Discipline—
The Distortion of "Working Together"   533
22.4   What To Do: Practical Pointers on Virtual Teaming and Virtual Work   534

Appendix A. Solutions to the Project Management Conflict Exercise   541
Appendix B. Solution to Leadership Exercise   547

Index   553

Preface

In today's world, most successful companies have multiple concurrent projects in different stages of their respective development life cycles. Some of these projects may be related in an integrated program, and others might be independent. In either case, all projects compete for limited financial resources, project and management staff, and capital equipment. All projects/programs, no matter how refined planning and execution may be, are subject to random, unexpected events that will test and challenge the project team's ability to keep each project on track. As far as project management is concerned, application of both hard (i.e., technical) skills and soft (i.e., people) skills are necessary ingredients in achieving acceptable outcomes.

We are learning that it is cogent to manage multiple projects as we would manage an investment portfolio. We must continually monitor and assess the project mixture to be sure that it is supporting the organization's goals and objectives as might be embodied, say, in the strategic plan. Even existing projects approved and in progress must be continually evaluated against new ones that will compete for the limited resources. That is to say, project and program benefits, costs, and risks must be continuously compared to the plan and decisions made about the project portfolio must be based upon a formalized process.

Developing projects and programs on time, within budget, at or above quality standards, is more important than ever in achieving corporate growth and success in the fast-moving competitive environment of the 21st Century. The same may be said of government operations. Achieving this difficult challenge is also critical to the growth and success of the individuals who undertake development and management roles required for these endeavors. Project teams, guided and led by highly trained cross-functional project managers, constitute the critical human capital necessary for the realization of any substantial project or program and nearly always are the critical ingredient for project/program success or failure. Technology and project management process maturity play key roles as well. However, it is truly people who make the difference between success and failure.

Successfully executing the role of project or program manager requires individuals who are capable of getting things accomplished through others, many times others over whom they have limited control or influence. To be highly effective in the role of project or program manager, one needs to have strong technical skills in not only the product or service under development by the project team, but also the discipline of the project management process per se. This paradigm is fundamental to commanding the respect and trust of the project team. Project managers must have a strong sense of self and must exhibit considerable confidence in all that they do. They must have the capacity for recognizing and dealing with their own emotions and those of others, and for effectively managing themselves in their relations with other people. Project managers must have a strong set of interpersonal skills because, most often, the problems and challenges they face involve the human issues of a project, namely; team conflict, team decision-making, rallying a team at its darkest moment, keeping morale at a high level, setting the operational and behavioral examples, helping to keep people focused on the end result, and operating as the conscience for the project, while at the same time acting as the lightning rod. As opposed to the "hard skills" that are exemplified by mastery over planning processes, scheduling, risk assessment, and so on, these people-oriented management examples are what might best be considered as "soft skills." It is fair to say that the most successful project and program managers are those individuals who have learned to balance the hard skills and the soft skills in the most effective ways.

Within this context, *Projects, Programs, and Project Teams* attempts to capture, in a single source, the critical technical aspects of planning and managing projects in a multi-project environment as well as the key project manager soft skills necessary to effectively build and lead project teams.

The book is organized into four Units, each being a collection of chapters from books that are considered leaders in their respective specialized fields. Unit 1 is a collection of chapters from *Project Portfolio Management* (2005) by Harvey A. Levine. These chapters focus on business practices that serve to integrate projects within the context of overall company or government operations. Unit 2 assembles key chapters from the 3d edition of *Managing High-Technology Programs and Projects* (2005) authored by Russell D. Archibald. This evolving text has been a classic in the field of multi-project management for many years. Unit 3 is from the 9th edition of *Project Management: A System Approach to Planning, Scheduling, and Controlling* (2005) written by Harold Kerzner. This text is widely considered to present some of the most up-to-date thinking on both hard and soft skills that are available currently. Finally, Unit 4 contains extracts from *The Discipline of Teams: A Mindbook-Workbook for Delivering Small Group Performance* (2005) by Jon R. Katzenbach and Douglas K. Smith. This relatively new book focuses on team performance and ways of enhancing it.

We considered many alternatives in compiling this collection of materials. To insure timeliness of concepts as well as continuity in subject areas, we have tried to present a comprehensive and balanced approach using the minimum number of up-to-date book selections as possible. Updating these selections will be an ongoing process.

This book may be used as a reader or as a reference by professionals in the field of project management, or it may be used as a text in project management instructional courses. When used in the latter way, instructors can "pick and choose" the selections that would be most appropriate for the course objectives that are germane. For example, a course that has as its focus team-building concepts would be oriented toward Units 3 and 4, while courses that were geared more to portfolio and program management per se would find the most applicable material to be in Units 1 and 2.

The motivation for putting this book together was to supply material to support the learning objectives of Keller Graduate School of Management's graduate-level Advanced Program Management course in which portfolio analysis, multi-project management and team development serve as the central themes. We were unable to locate a single source that contained all of what was needed. Hence, we resorted to this compilation approach.

We would like to thank Jay Beck for so effectively utilizing his hard and soft editorial skills as the Wiley project manager in completing this publication on time, on budget, and well above the minimum expectation of quality.

JH, FC, RJ
Keller Graduate School of Management
DeVry University

UNIT 1
Project Portfolio Management

The material within this unit has been excerpted from the following textbook:

Harvey A. Levine
Project Portfolio Management
A Practical Guide to Selecting Projects, Managing Portfolios, and Maximizing Benefits

Copyright 2005 by John Wiley & Sons, Inc.
ISBN: 0-7879-7754-3

Introduction

Project portfolio management is a set of business practices that brings the world of projects into tight integration with other business operations. It brings projects into harmony with the strategies, resources, and executive oversight of the enterprise and provides the structure and processes for project portfolio governance.

I have never been one to jump on the bandwagon. Much to the contrary, I tend to resist and question new trends and fads, finding that many of them are only a flash in the pan—short on substance and practical use. However, when it comes to PPM, I eagerly join the stampede. PPM is more than an expanded application of project management. The emergence of PPM as a recognized set of practices may be considered the biggest leap in project management technology since the development of Program Evaluation and Review Technique and Critical Path Method in the late 1950s. However, it is important to recognize that this newer technique goes way beyond the simple expansion of project management practices. PPM revolutionizes the way that we look at projects, the impact that projects have on the health of the business, and even the governance of projects.

Understanding What PM Is Not

Don't confuse PPM recent popular concepts, such as enterprise project management and professional services automation. These are an expansion of project management, but in a totally different direction. And neither addresses the alignment of projects with strategies or the science of selecting the right projects. Neither of these provides for project portfolio governance.

Another key misconception is to think of PPM as the management of multiple projects. Yes, PPM does address this. But the primary and unique aspect of PPM is what it does to formalize and assist in the selection of projects.

We talk about why we need PPM in Section.2.1 and about what PPM is and is not in Section.2.2. But here's a brief look.

The What and Why of PPM   PPM is a set of business practices that brings the world of projects into tight integration with other business operations. In the past, the absence of this integration has resulted in a large disconnect between the projects' function and the rest of the operations of the enterprise. Without this essential connectivity, a lot of effort goes into doing projects right—even if they are not the right projects.

We have projects proposed and approved that do not deliver the promised benefits. We have projects that are wrong; they are not in sync with the goals of the enterprise. We have projects that have excessive risk, yet the risk is set aside when the project is considered for approval. We have projects that get approved solely because of the political power of the project sponsor. These projects drain valuable and scarce resources from more beneficial projects.

We have projects that are failing at an early stage. Yet they are continued until total failure is recognized and the team admits that the product cannot be delivered. We have projects that are designed to generate income (or cost savings), but because of various kinds of failures, they become a burden instead. We have projects that slip so badly in time that they miss the window of opportunity. Yet they are continued when they should be terminated.

So what we have here are two distinct and costly problems:

- Projects that should not have been selected to be in the pipeline
- Projects that remain in the pipeline even after they no longer serve the company's best interests

The result is that many projects are not delivering on their promises or are not supporting the goals of the enterprise.

The Impact of PPM   Fortunately, as widespread and as costly as these problems are, the solution is simple and inexpensive: it requires very little in the way of acquisitions and has very little impact on head count. It does require a few new skills and some small additions to management software. Moving to a PPM culture will require a top-level commitment and a mature and cooperative environment for the project and governance teams.

For this small investment, you can have a significant impact on the way that the organization deals with projects and business initiatives. PPM will push the corporate culture in a new direction—one in which it really wants to go if it could only articulate it.

Success will require the development and implementation of new practices. While the new process flow will be comprehensive, it will actually streamline the selecting and managing of projects. The new processes will be executed primarily with current staffing.

Perhaps the biggest change will be in communication and decision making. And these changes will be for the better.

Do you remember the Six Sigma movement? It propelled us ever closer to zero defects. The PPM process will move us closer to zero failed projects. The objective is to reduce terminated projects to zero. It's hard to argue with the premise that the earlier that you can weed out a bad project, the better. Best yet is not wasting any time on such a project in the first place.

The Components of PPM   The PPM process starts with a rational prioritization and selection procedure. By evaluating a proposed project against a set of selection criteria, bad projects get weeded out (or modified to meet the criteria). If a proposed project can't pass the minimal criteria, there is no need even to rank it for selection. If we don't let the wild horse out of the corral, we don't have to go and chase it back.

PPM is about having the right information so you can make the right decisions to select the right projects. It's about bridging the gap between projects and operations. It's about communicating and connecting the business strategy to the project selection process. It's about making sure that intended opportunities are real opportunities. By evaluating value and benefits, by modifying benefit calculations on the basis of risk, and by forcing such analyses to take place under structured and consistent procedures, we prevent problem projects from sneaking in with real opportunities. (See Section 4.2 on project prequalification.)

By evaluating benefits, risks, alignment, and other business and project factors, we can prioritize candidate projects and select the higher-ranking ones to get first crack at the organization's limited economic and human resources. This is the set of practices associated with project prioritization and selection, addressed in Section 3.1.

By monitoring performance of active projects against both the project goals and the selection criteria, we can adjust the portfolio to maximize return. This means being willing to restructure, delay, or even terminate projects with performance deficiencies. The ability to monitor such performance exists in all traditional project management systems. All we add in PPM is the routine to do so and the ability to feed these data into the PPM system. This is the set of practices associated with maintaining the project pipeline (Section 3.2).

The Voice of the Skeptic   This book does not profess to have all of the answers. Early adopters of PPM, an emerging art and science, are reporting phenomenal results. Nevertheless, as proven in the Hawthorne experiments, almost any kind of change can bring about initial improvements. Do we need more time to be sure that the improvements that have been experienced are directly related to the adoption of PPM practices? I think not. The first decade of PPM development and application has produced numerous stories of enormous success. We present four of these success stories in the case studies in Section Nine.

If there is any doubt about the value of PPM, it is whether PPM is equally effective across all project environments. In Section 4.2 on project prequalification, we look at three typical classifications of projects and discuss the applicability of PPM to each of these.

Nevertheless, there are those who believe that some of the processes offer a simple formula for a complex condition. Some of these processes deal with financial valuations of the proposed projects, such as benefits, return on investment, or net present value without directing much effort toward how these values can be determined. Many PPM tools offer extended abilities to display such values without support for creating valid data. Other tools, such as analytic hierarchy process (AHP), are specifically designed to assist in simplifying the prioritization of complex issues and data. AHP is widely recognized and employed as an aid to the decision-making process. Still, the skeptic in me pauses to ask whether even this admirable technique might focus too much on the details and miss the big picture.

And then there is the other extreme: where supposedly very precise data are displayed with attractive, advanced graphic techniques. These techniques, such as the increasingly popular bubble chart, are superb vehicles for presenting extensive, multidimensional data in intelligent, usable formats. They are so impressive as to allow us to overlook the possibility that the data displayed may not sit on a solid foundation.

In a recent discussion, a colleague raised this question:

I find my skepticism to be directly proportional to the PPM software hype curve. The root of my skepticism lies in the benefit and benefit-risk side of PPM. I see bubble charts and Web forms as too simple and shallow to support the depth needed to analyze significant undertakings. Significant undertakings require in-depth business plans with market positioning, detailed financial models, trade-off studies, and competitive analysis. This analysis takes place well before any projects are initiated and continues throughout the life cycle. The approval process is interactive and face-to-face with many PowerPoint briefings. Now, one could argue that the PPM discipline embraces all this, but this embracing is more a declaration of hoped-for ownership rather than value-added.

Because PPM software is limited to simple projects, it is relatively well positioned for internal work like information technology projects. I don't think I will ever see the day when Ford executives look at a project portfolio bubble chart to pick which cars to build. I do think that an IT exec could decide on a Web-based expense report over an upgrade to Office 2999 or vice versa using the PPM tools (but maybe not even here).

One message that we can derive from my colleague's declaration is that (as in any other discipline) we need to understand the available processes and tools and be prepared to apply them where practicable—but not blindly. Every data-based process is subject to somebody fouling up the numbers. Diligence and dutiful wariness must be built into the process.

Nothing in the PPM process precludes preparing traditional business plans and analyses. In fact, they are strongly endorsed. Where PPM helps is in dealing with multiple business plans and opportunities.

Remember also that portfolio planning is based extensively on forecasting. I once read that forecasting is like driving an automobile while blindfolded and taking directions from someone who is looking out of the back window. You certainly want to be careful in betting the future of the company on data such as these.

To avoid falling into the trap of accepting faulty assumptions and data, everyone involved in PPM should become a devil's advocate. By this, I mean that we need to question things that look too good. Someone has to ask the difficult and probing questions. We need to be careful not to get swept up in the current of popular opinion. It may not take you where you want to go.

Even having said this, I am confident of the value of PPM as the best means of addressing the issues of aligning projects with strategies and attempting to select the best projects for the health of the business.

This book presents the many sides of PPM. The other authors and I offer an extensive overview of the fundamentals and why and where they can be employed. We provide several discussions of specific issues and techniques. Throughout the process, we maintain a skeptic's eye so as not to overly promote any part of this emerging discipline. We have noted that PPM is already delivering positive benefits and results. This book does not offer the final word on PPM because it is a work in progress. Still, it is fully ready for prime time, and we sincerely recommend that you consider putting these practices into action. We will also be maintaining a watchful eye on these applications, ever ready to report and implement improvements based on such feedback.

An Executive's Guide to Project Portfolio Management

As you read through the Contents and this Introduction, you may notice that there is considerable mention of projects. We also discuss the project management office, the management of projects in general, and some popular techniques that we use in managing projects.

However, the real focus of this book is how to ensure that projects contribute to a successful enterprise, so the target readership goes well beyond the project management community. In fact, it is the business executive who will gain the most from this material. If you are a senior manager, such as a chief executive officer, chief operations officer, chief financial officer, chief information officer, or a strategic planner, you are surely concerned about picking the right projects and getting the most out of your resources. The answers are in PPM. If you are an executive charged with the responsibility for information technology, application development, or new product development, this book was written for you.

Perhaps your executive duties limit the time that you have to read everything. For a comprehensive look at PPM, I suggest that you read all of Chapters 2 and 3. Then you can select other chapters that attract your interest. Among these I recommend Sections 4.1, 4.3, and 4.4. Chapter 5 is a must for new product development managers.

PPM brings the projects community and the operations community together to achieve business success. We hope that this book will facilitate a better partnership.

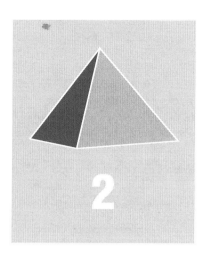

What Is Project Portfolio Management, and Why Do We Need It?

The project portfolio life span extends well beyond the project life cycle to include identification of needs and opportunities on the front end and the realization of benefits at the other end. PPM recognizes this, bridging the traditional gap between the projects and operations functions and delivering maximum value from limited resources. Every executive should demand that PPM practices be put in place, and they should lead in their development and execution.

The next three chapters of this book cover the topic of PPM in increasing detail. Chapter 2 introduces PPM, discussing why it is so valuable and providing an overview of what PPM is. Chapter 3 goes into the meat of PPM, providing complete coverage of what it takes to create a PPM capability and to implement it. Chapter 4 covers some of the finer points pertinent to PPM.

When you read Section 2.1, it should become readily apparent that something has been missing in how we view the place of projects in the enterprise. It will also come as no surprise that PPM is growing exceptionally fast and that virtually all of the software vendors that support the project management discipline have revamped their offerings to support PPM.

I'll introduce you to the project portfolio life span. You'll learn why PPM is much more than just an extension to project management. You'll start to question whether your firm is working on the right projects. You'll discover that there is a significant gap between the projects function and the operations functions of most firms, and I'll show how to use PPM as a means to bridge that gap.

In Section 2.2, you'll see specifics on how to do just that. You'll get your first look at the things that you can accomplish with PPM and the processes that support these accomplishments. In addition, you'll find an overview of how to organize for PPM.

After four decades of being completely engrossed in project management, I thought that I fully understood its power and value. But as I learned about PPM, it opened an entirely new world of capabilities to exponentially increase our ability to use projects to build business value and fully integrate the projects environment with the ongoing business. After reading this section, I hope that you will feel the same way.

2.1 WHY DO WE NEED PROJECT PORTFOLIO MANAGEMENT?

> Do traditional measures of project success miss the true business objectives? Scope, Time, Cost and Quality are only components of the objective, rather than independent measures of success.
>
> Harvey Levine, June 2000

Could what I said five years ago be considered blasphemous? Imagine going against conventional wisdom at a time when project portfolio management (PPM) was just emerging as a body of thought. Project management was finally getting its well-deserved recognition, and everyone was focusing on spreading the gospel of bringing projects in on time, within budget, and meeting scope and quality objectives. Well, almost everyone.

Why would anyone want to shoot holes in the acceptance of project management? No one is suggesting that project management is wrong. However, limiting our focus to the critical measures of project success confuses the means to an end with the end itself.

Almost everything written about measurements of project success dwells on the four pillars of success: scope, time, cost, and quality. We have been taught to identify the goals for success in each of these areas and then to create plans that balance these objectives. Then we implement practices and use computer-based tools to measure how well we are accomplishing these objectives. When we meet these objectives and satisfy the project stakeholders, we consider the project to have been successful.

However, most executives are not interested in these areas of measurement. Instead, they talk about profitability, return on investment, delivery of benefits, and taking advantage of windows of opportunity. We used to say that executives are interested in just two things about projects: when they will be finished and what they will cost. Not anymore. Now (in the for-profit arena) they ask:

- What mix of potential projects will provide the best utilization of human and cash resources to maximize long-range growth and return on investment for the firm?
- How do the projects support strategic initiatives?
- How will the projects affect the value of corporate shares (stock)?

Similar issues apply to the nonprofit and government operations where optimizing the use of limited funds and resources and support of missions and strategies is vital. While

PPM can be effectively applied to both the public and private sectors, most of the examples in this book use a for-profit enterprise as the model. With minor adjustments, PPM can be adapted to nonprofit and government operations.

Perhaps this is an oversimplification. However, if we start with this premise and examine its meaning, we can begin to realize the tremendous impact of this observation on the way that we conduct project management and even in the way that we select and implement project management tools.

The Emergence of Project Portfolio Management

Certainly it is not news to anyone that the basic concept of project management has evolved to what we call *enterprise project management*. At first, many people in the PM community thought that this shift was more of a way of aggrandizing project management—sort of a pompous elevating of project management to a higher level of importance. Later we came to realize that enterprise project management was a reflection of the importance of consolidating and integrating all of the organization's projects—for universal access and evaluation. Now we come to find that enterprise project management entails consideration of potential projects as well as approved projects. We also find that the emphasis has shifted from traditional project-centric objectives to higher-level operational objectives.

Projects, executives have come to realize, are the basis for the future profitability of the firm. Hence, they have a growing interest in how projects are selected and managed. They are precipitating an increased demand for more standardization and automation of project management. But what they are asking for is different from the requests from traditional project management sources. And what they are calling this emerging project management protocol has also changed. It is no longer just project management or even *enterprise project management*. It is now called *project portfolio management*.

Bridging the Gap Between Operations Management and Projects Management

Project portfolio management is the bridge between traditional operations management and project management (see Section 4.1). For organizations that will be depending on project success for the success of the overall enterprise, a well-structured bridge, built on a good foundation, is the preferred way to overcome the traditional gap between operations and projects management.

In PPM, it is assumed that the enterprise positions itself for increased strength and profitability through its selection and execution of projects and ensures that it continues to thrive in a world of constant change and the threat of competition.

The basic elements of PPM are not new, nor is the environment in which it is applied. However, before the emergence of PPM as a defined discipline, these elements were the responsibility of two distinct groups: operations management and projects management, each with its specific role:

Operations Management	Projects Management
Strategies	Schedule/time
Objectives, goals	Project cost
Business performance	Project performance
Stockholder satisfaction	Stakeholder satisfaction
Project selection and mix	Scope/change control
Resource availability	Resource utilization
Cash flow, income	Cash usage

The Traditional Organization   When the execution of projects is a normal part of the organization's business, typically the organization establishes, in parallel with the operations function, a function to manage the projects. This normally includes a central project office or project management office (PMO) and specialized personnel to manage projects. The PMO, under a chief project officer (or similar title), develops standards and practices directed at the effective execution of projects and the attainment of schedule, cost, scope, and quality objectives. In doing so, a project management planning and information system is put in place, and periodic measurements of project progress and performance are conducted.

In traditional organizations, responsibility for determining and achieving the organization's goals is assigned to the operations function. Senior managers with titles such as chief operating officer, chief technology officer, chief information officer, chief financial officer, and strategic planner establish objectives and goals and develop strategies to achieve these. When there are projects associated with these goals, these senior managers are expected to select from a menu of proposed and pending projects. The objective is to create the mix of projects most likely to support the achievement of the organization's goals within the preferred strategies and within the organization's resource (people and funding) constraints.

A problem common to many organizations is that there is no connection between the operations and projects functions and no structured, consistent, and meaningful flow of information between these two groups. The organization's objectives (enterprise-level goals) are hardly ever communicated to the project office, and the periodic measurements made by the projects group cannot be related to these objectives.

What a waste! Both groups are off in their own world, working to do the best that they can but not knowing if their efforts are effective or efficient. Are the projects that are being worked on (assuming that they were properly selected in the first place) still the best ones to support the objectives? How well are they supporting the objectives? Are there performance issues associated with meeting the objectives? How would the operations people know?

And over in the project office, when the project performance data is evaluated, what knowledge is available to influence the corrective action decisions? If the individual project objectives are in danger, what should the project manager know to work on balancing schedule, cost, scope, and quality parameters? Can this be effectively done in the absence of operations inputs?

Bridging the Gap Between Portfolio Planning and Portfolio Management

There is a second gap with which to contend. Our traditional approach is to separate the function of project selection from that of managing the project pipeline. The traditional assumption is that once a project is approved, it is separated from the parental umbilical cord. The criteria on which the selection was based are lost. The only criteria remaining for monitoring project performance are specific to the individual project goals rather than the portfolio as a whole.

And how shall we deal with project and portfolio assessment? Is a project a static item or a dynamic system? If a project is dynamic in nature (its scope, timing, and cost are subject to change), then what effect does this have on the project portfolio? The typical project has a range of possible outcomes and costs. There is the base case and potential upside and downside. If the project was selected on the basis of a set of assumptions (stated in the base case), does that project still belong in the portfolio when its attributes change? Periodically we need to review the project to test assumptions, update givens, and monitor progress; examine alternatives; and consider remodeling the portfolio.

Thus, we can see that there are potential weaknesses in the typical project management implementation:

- The organization's objectives and goals, as supported by the project portfolio, are not communicated to the people responsible for project performance.
- The project performance, as monitored by the project managers, is not communicated to the portfolio managers, strategic planners, and senior managers.
- The gap that exists between these two groups, in both communication and available information, prevents active management of the portfolio based on the current, changing status of the component projects.

What is needed is a basis for addressing project selection issues, deciding on project termination, facilitating reallocation of resources, changing of priorities, and evaluating alternatives. Without this capability, there is no project portfolio management.

The Project Portfolio Life Span

Perhaps the strongest way to delineate the differences between project management and PPM is to look at the true life span of projects within the PPM environment. We usually consider the life span of a project to be from authorization to delivery. In some models, we start earlier, with a proposal.

With PPM, this life span is expanded, on both ends. According to Max Wideman, the project portfolio life span (PPLS) consists of the following phased components (see Figure 2–1):[1]

1. Identification of needs and opportunities
2. Selection of best combinations of projects (the portfolios)
3. Planning and execution of the projects (project management)
4. Product launch (acceptance and use of deliverables)
5. Realization of benefits

Looking at this model, you can see that the purview of the project office is concentrated on item 3. The expansion of the life span and scope to include all five items requires the involvement and leadership of the executive side of the organization and the development of a portfolio governance culture, processes and tools.

Furthermore, the measurement of success does not stop with project delivery. The project was designed to deliver certain defined benefits. The true measure of success must extend to the evaluation of whether these benefits were in fact obtained.

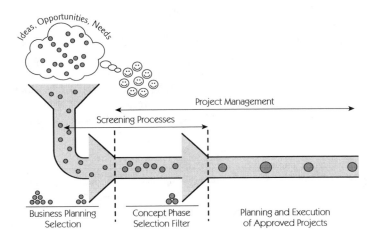

FIGURE 2–1. First Three Steps of the Project Portfolio Life Span

Source: R. M. Wideman, *A Management Framework for Project, Program and Portfolio Integration* (New Bern, N.C.: Trafford Publishing 2004), p. 169.

2.2 WHAT IS PROJECT PORTFOLIO MANAGEMENT?

Project portfolio management is the management of the project portfolio so as to maximize the contribution of projects to the overall welfare and success of the enterprise.

Now that organizations have discovered the importance of projects and project management, the next logical step is to move toward the recognition of PPM. However, it is a very big mistake to think that PPM is merely an extension of project management. These two equally important functions are not alike at all.

As more and more firms adopt project management central office or project management office (PMO) methods, it would not surprise me to see responsibility for PPM thrust fully into the hands of the chief project officer (CPO). This too would be a mistake.

This section presents an overview of what PPM is as well as what it is not. Each of these topics is discussed in greater detail in Chapter 3.

Project Portfolio Management Is Not Just Enterprise Project Management

A critical mistake is to think that PPM is fundamentally the management of multiple projects. This is not so. PPM is the management of the project portfolio so as to maximize the contribution of projects to the overall welfare and success of the enterprise. This means that:

- Projects must be aligned with the firm's strategy and goals.
- Projects must be consistent with the firm's values and culture.
- Projects must contribute (directly or indirectly) to a positive cash flow for the enterprise.
- Projects must effectively use the firm's resources—both people and other resources.
- Projects must not only provide for current contributions to the firm's health but must help to position the firm for future success.

This cannot be accomplished solely within the projects domain. PPM, to be fully effective, requires the participation of several core components of the firm. Furthermore, it requires the integration of several systems within the organization. Let's look at each of these first from an organizational point of view and then from a systems point of view.

What Processes Comprise PPM?

We can subdivide PPM into two primary phases: the first focusing on the prioritization and selection of projects for the portfolio and the second dealing with managing the projects within the portfolio. Although these two components require different practices and are separate in nature, each affects the other, so they must be integrated.

PHASE 1: SELECTING PROJECTS FOR THE PIPELINE

This phase deals with proposed projects and provides a structured process to:

- Guide the preparation of project proposals (business case) so that they can be evaluated.
- Evaluate project value and benefits.
- Appraise the risks that might modify these benefits.
- Align candidate projects with enterprise strategies.
- Determine the most favorable use of resources.
- Rank projects according to a set of selection criteria.
- Select projects for the portfolio.

In order to perform the ranking and selection of projects, it will also be necessary to:

- Execute a strategic plan and subsequent tactical planning guidelines.
- Maintain an inventory of available resources.

● Establish budget buckets for the portfolios.
● Decide on an optimum or acceptable size of the project pipeline.
● Establish a set of weighted scoring criteria.
● Set some boundaries or guidance for acceptable risk.

Details of the prioritization and selection phase are presented in Section 3.1.

PHASE 2: MAINTAINING THE PROJECT PIPELINE

After selecting projects, we manage these projects with an eye toward achieving two sets of objectives: to meet the *project* objectives (this is the traditional project tracking and control process that we used even before we implemented PPM) and to meet the *portfolio* (business) objectives.

When we execute the ranking and selection phase, we match the characteristics of the proposed projects with a set of selection criteria. Then when we execute the projects, we need to monitor and evaluate any conditions that might alter either of these (project characteristics or selection criteria). Periodically we need to update or confirm the criteria used for project selection. On a regular basis, we evaluate the status and performance of each project. If the performance will change the values that we assumed at the proposal stage (in the business case), we need to consider whether the project should remain in the portfolio. Although delaying or terminating an active project may not always be possible or prudent, we should always consider those options as part of managing the portfolio.

To facilitate the periodic evaluation of project status and performance, we can rely on two well-known techniques: earned value analysis and the Stage-Gate® process.[1] (Both techniques are discussed in Section 3.2. In addition, Section 4.6 is devoted to earned value analysis and Section 5.1 to the Stage-Gate® Process.

Organizing for PPM

The responsibility for leading the PPM function falls to the person responsible for operations management within the firm. In most organizations, this is the individual who brings together the strategies, measurements, and cash management. It may be someone with the title of chief operating officer (COO) or vice president of operations. It also could be the chief executive officer or president. Also playing key roles on the PPM team are the chief financial officer or vice president of finance, and the CPO, or vice president of projects. While the project management office would have the major role in operating and supporting the PPM practices, it would not own the final decision role. In a firm where information technology is the primary business, the chief information officer would certainly have a significant role. Rounding out the PPM team are representatives of the various functional operations and the marketing function.

Here, we are assuming that the functional departments own the critical resources that will be used on projects. Hence, the importance of their participation on the PPM team. In addition, because the management of the projects portfolio will require consideration of future engagements and resource demands, the marketing operation will have to contribute forecasting data to the PPM function.

Note that there are no new functional positions defined for PPM. Rather, we are viewing PPM as a *process,* to be supported by the PMO and senior personnel already in place in the firm. The PPM process will be added to the responsibilities of these senior members, who will function as a team to manage the projects portfolio under the leadership of the COO (or equivalent). It's not as if these newly defined (or redefined) responsibilities are changed. What is different within the PPM process is that the individual responsibilities for the project portfolio are executed within a structured, integrated PPM team.

A growing popular term for the process of guiding the port-folio is *governance*. This is especially so in the information technology area, where the term *IT governance* is becoming synonymous with PPM. Further discussion of organization and roles is presented in Section 3.3.

Supporting Processes
So far we have brought several functions together under the umbrella of PPM: projects, operations, financial, functional departments and resources, and marketing. Each of these is supported by automated information systems. A challenge under PPM is to bring these computer-based systems together. Furthermore, extended capabilities must be added to support the intended benefits of PPM and to support integration of the individual systems.

If you have an enterprise resource management (ERP) system or a multifunction project management system, you probably have the underlying structure to move in the desired direction. But even then, new processes and functions will be needed. We look at the tools for PPM and tool integration in Section 3.4.

NOTES

Section 2.1

1. R. M. Wideman, *A Management Framework for Project, Program and Portfolio Integration* (New Bern, N.C.: Trafford Publishing, 2004), chap. 13.

Section 2.2

1. Stage-Gate® is a registered term.

The Fundamentals of a Project Portfolio Management Process

3

Executives expect projects to be aligned with strategies, make effective use of limited resources, and deliver certain benefits. The processes associated with PPM bring the operations and projects functions together to fulfill these expectations.

We started this book with a discussion of why we need PPM, followed by an overview of what PPM is and what PPM is not. To really appreciate PPM, we need to take a good look at the fundamentals.

The five chapters in this section provide a complete review of PPM that will help you decide if PPM is for you. If the answer is yes, it will help you understand what you need to do to set up a PPM capability. Once you buy into the process, you can move on to detailed discussions of specific PPM areas in the sections that follow.

In this chapter, we will assume that you can accept certain key premises and conditions:

- A basic project management capability is in place, managed and supported by a professional staff. It is preferable that this function be centralized (for standardization and consistency). In our discussion, we will refer to such a function as the project management office (PMO).
- There is a desire to develop a structured approach to selecting projects, based on a fair and balanced ranking system. The projects that are selected will be aligned with business strategies and placed in portfolios that represent the tactical imple-

mentation of such strategies. (Any discussion in this book about a portfolio may also apply to one of several portfolios or subportfolios that are created to support the strategies.)

- After projects are selected for the portfolio, they will be managed to achieve two sets of objectives. One set consists of objectives that are associated with specific project goals and commitments. The second set consists of evaluating project performance so as to assess the ability of the project to continue to meet the original selection criteria (that is, to realize the expected benefits). A culture and practices will be developed to consider delaying or terminating projects that no longer represent adequate value or efficient use of resources.
- New roles will be created to support PPM. This would include the naming of a team responsible for portfolio governance. This team will be able to act for senior executives (or may include the executives) to oversee the portfolios. In this section, the governance team is referred to as the *governance council.*
- The PMO will review its current project management tool set for support of the new PPM functions. If the existing tool set has not added such support, the PMO will evaluate additional software capabilities to be integrated with the project management tools.

Discussion of a PPM process must consider five major areas:

- Selecting projects for the pipeline, that is, what goes in the pipeline
- Maintaining the pipeline, that is, what stays in the pipeline
- Executing PPM, that is, who does it
- Tools for data gathering and analysis and other PPM processes
- Implementing PPM

Where Do We Start?

Getting started in implementing a PPM process is a bit like the chicken-and-egg question. Do we first attack the existing portfolio and then implement an improved project selection process? Or do we accept the current portfolio and go right after the selection of new projects? There is no prescribed order. However, reports from the field indicate that many firms have first reviewed their current portfolio, eliminating a significant portion of their project load (due to redundancy, nonalignment with strategies, poor value, or inefficient use of resources), thus making room to add more valuable projects.

In reality, the two phases are inseparable. The processes form a loop: build the project portfolio; manage the project portfolio; adjust the project pipeline, if indicated, based on project performance and reevaluation; consider proposed projects to fill availabilities due to completed, delayed, or terminated projects; update the project portfolio; and so on. Since we cannot address all of these parts at once, we will look at the process for selecting new projects first. Then we'll look at managing the pipeline, followed by discussion of issues of PPM execution, including adjustments to organizational roles and responsibilities.

Purpose and Types of Projects

When we talk about "projects" in a portfolio, what do we mean by *projects?* The flavor of a project portfolio management process will depend somewhat on the kinds of projects involved. Although most firms are now heavily involved in projects, the purposes and types of projects vary—for instance:

- The project is for the benefit of an external client. The primary benefit to the project producer is income (profit). Secondary benefits may include making use of surplus resources, building a reputation in a new area, or creating reusable technology or knowledge. Examples of these are architectural, engineering, and construction projects; consulting; temporary labor sources; and professional services organizations.
- The project is for the benefit of the performing company: to create new products and services that will be sold (at a profit). Examples are manufacturing and process companies, software developers, and pharmaceutical firms.
- The project is for the benefit of the performing company: to improve or maintain capabilities required to operate the business effectively. These would include internal information technology projects, manufacturing processes, facilities improvements, or expansions.
- The project is for the benefit of the performing company: to improve a competitive position. All of the previous examples apply here.

We can see that a project portfolio management process for Bechtel or Halliburton, involved in architectural, engineering, and construction work, would have a different focus from the internal IT department at Citicorp.

Just as traditional project management can be effectively applied to all types of industries and technologies, PPM has a universal applicability. There will be variations in the process and the roles, but the fundamentals are similar. What follows here is equally applicable to new product development, information technology, and dozens of other business areas. With some modification, it is equally applicable to nonprofits and the public sector.

We can also see that the funnel of proposed projects could be filled from many sources. Project requests may come in through the firm's opportunity management program, product managers or other internal requests, or senior management (to support strategic initiatives). The challenge of PPM is to filter the project requests so that the projects that pass through the funnel into the pipeline best serve the long-term interests of the firm.

3.1 SELECTING PROJECTS FOR THE PIPELINE

> The objective is to create the mix of projects most likely to support the achievement of the organization's goals, aligned with the preferred strategies, and within the organization's resource (people and funding) constraints.

There are thousands of true stories that illustrate what is wrong with how most organizations determine which projects to approve. It is obvious that the pointy-haired guy (Dilbert's boss in the cartoon *Dilbert*) has gotten around. Here's an example of just one of these situations:

> The company was a major manufacturer of paper goods. When it added a new project to the pipeline, the process began when a client of the paper company called her sales rep and asked if the company could provide a product to a new specification. The sales rep called the product line manager, who in turn called the development engineer responsible for that technology. The engineer decided whether he would like to work on creating a version of the product to the new specification. He has the option (solely on his own) to accept or decline the product line manager's solicitation. If he decides to work on the project, he has the right to draw on several of the firm's resources.
>
> Here is what is wrong with this picture:
>
> ● The engineer has no idea how this modified product fits into the firm's strategies.
> ● He has no data on marketability or profitability.
> ● He has no process for performing a value/benefits evaluation.
> ● He probably hasn't considered the capability to support the revised specification.
> ● He has not considered risk issues.
> ● He is committing other resources, which may be needed for higher-priority projects.
> ● There really isn't a practice for determining project priorities.

What about the customer? Is she really serious about the revised product? Will she buy it at a price that is not yet determined? Will she take her business elsewhere if the current supplier does not deliver a new version? Can she get a product to the new spec from someone else? A development engineer would be unlikely to ask these questions or have the answers. Yet this information is essential in making the project decision and should be an integral part of the project selection process.

The project pipeline for this firm was a disaster. Resources were shifted from project to project, many of which should never have been in the pipeline in the first place. Resources were diverted from high-value, low-risk, strategically aligned projects to someone's pipe dream. Many of these projects never reached completion. Meanwhile, opportunities were lost and money was wasted.

Evaluating Candidate Projects

We'll assume that the objective of the PPM process is to prioritize work that brings the most value to the firm. The definition of *value* will certainly differ in accordance with the firm's focus, strategies, and types of projects. Regardless of these differences, a project portfolio management process should address the following:

● A ranking of value and benefits
● An appraisal of risk (in achieving these benefits)

- An inventory of resource availability and allocation
- An idea of an optimum or acceptable size of the project pipeline

The criteria for each of these factors will have to be customized by the firm that is implementing the PPM process. This definition will be driven by the firm's strategic focus. The project portfolio is one of the layers of tactical planning that are executed in support of the strategic plan. So we must add to the list above:

- Publication of the strategic plan to the project portfolio management governance council. (In defining the PPM process, we assume that the process will involve some type of governance council, usually a team of senior people designated by top management to make decisions about the project portfolio. The roles and organization for PPM are addressed in Section 3.3.)
- Development of tactical plans that would involve projects in support of the strategic plan
- Definitions of value and benefits as they apply to the tactical plans
- Some boundaries on acceptable risk parameters
- A long-range projection of resource strategies

RANKING VALUE AND BENEFITS

Assuming that the number of potential projects exceeds the number that can be effectively executed in a reasonable time, there must be a means of prioritizing each project. This process must be structured and conducted by a team in order to eliminate the tendency to select projects by political means, power plays, or emotion.

Conceptually this ranking process is simple, although the individual parameters will vary according to strategies, resources, profit motive, and other categories. The process is not unlike that used in selecting items for an investment portfolio. In fact, this is an investment portfolio: you are investing in projects with the objective of maximizing the return.

One of the primary ranking factors will be expected return on investment (ROI). However, there are qualifiers associated with this process. You can't prioritize projects using ROI alone. You need to also consider:

- Alignment with strategic and tactical plans
- Balance between maintenance projects and investment projects
- Allocation of R&D expenditures and resources
- Allocation of marketing expenditures and resources
- Effective use of resources
- Probability of delivering the project on time, within budget, and with the designed work scope
- Ancillary benefits (nonfinancial)

The ranking practice should use a balanced scorecard approach, with each of the factors listed and weighted. As each factor is rated, an aggregate score for each project is obtained. The rating of each factor can be prompted by a series of questions, with the answers noted in a narrative format and then converted to a numerical score based on the level of the answer against a guideline. (For additional discussion and details on ranking and prioritization of projects, see Section 5)

RISK

The value/benefits ranking may be modified by risk: the risk that the perceived benefits might not be realized. A potential million-dollar return with a 10 percent chance of happening is probably not as desirable as a potential quarter of a million-dollar return with a 90 percent probability. A new technology with a 20 percent chance of success may not fit with the strategy. A project that is vulnerable to critical delays might be a lower-ranked candidate than one that is certain to be delivered in time to produce the expected benefit.

A typical value formula takes the expected benefits, minus the total cost of ownership, divided by the risk. The risk factor takes time into consideration, acknowledging that a longer duration to ROI increases the potential risk. (See Section 4 for more on risk and uncertainty.)

A common practice is to display the value/benefit ranking and the risk ranking on a grid (Figure 3–1). Preference would be given to projects that appear in the high value–low risk quartile.

As the typical project environment moves away from repetitive-type projects to unique and original challenges, risk assessment and management becomes an essential part of PPM.

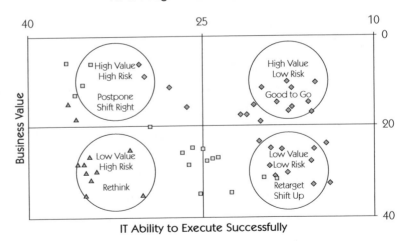

FIGURE 3–1 Risk-Benefits Ranking Grid Diagram

Source: Don Kingsberry, Hewlett-Packard.

RESOURCES

If we acknowledge that the availability of resources is a constraint on the number of projects in the pipeline, then why can't we just increase resources as we need them? There are a number of obvious answers to this question:

● Resources cost money. They have an impact on cash flow. In a well-managed organization, the size of a firm's labor force is dictated by the firm's revenue. In a growing organization, the amount of resources are increased incrementally as the revenues increase, usually by a set proportion. They are not increased just because there are more projects in the pipeline than can be supported by current resources.

● Effective and efficient use of resources calls for a stable workforce—a group of people who understand how the organization works and communicates and who fit the organization's culture and can work well as teams on projects. Although there are times when temporary or transient resources can be used to meet specific needs, it is best to avoid this as a standard source of resources. The cost of supervision, coordination, and learning curve issues will often negate the benefits.

● One of the key objectives of a managed portfolio is balance. This is a well-respected strategy in investment portfolios and should also be an objective in project portfolios. Resource balancing is one aspect of a balanced project portfolio. This is a bidirectional process. The mix of projects and the mix of resources should be manipulated to best use the firm's resources on work that is well matched to the available strengths and skills.

SIZE OF THE PIPELINE

How much project work is enough? How much is too much? If we proceed on the basis that projects generate value and benefits, then doesn't it follow that the more projects that we have in the pipeline, the better off we will be? *Ridiculous!* you say! Well, of course, it is. But that doesn't stop many organizations from shooting at everything that moves.

The opportunities (or demand) for projects usually exceed the capacity to execute them all. We all have stories in which project deliverables were significantly delayed because the pipeline was overloaded. In almost every case, the delays eroded the value and benefits of the venture (as well as alienated the client).

There is significant feedback from successful firms that tends to show that doing fewer projects actually improves the bottom line. Committed resources are staying on the assigned job and doing the assigned work in support of established target dates. The income or benefits start earlier, and everyone is happier. Furthermore, because the projects are not drawn out, new projects can be added sooner, and just as many projects may eventually find their way into the pipeline and under improved conditions.

The message here is very clear: limiting the amount of work in the pipeline so that the projects can be completed as quickly as possible results in increased profits or savings and more satisfied clients, and it leads to executing more projects without increasing resources.

Adding an Approved Project to the Pipeline

A structured approach toward project initiation is critical to managing a successful portfolio of projects. Here are some critical first steps.

ISSUE A PROJECT CHARTER

Although often omitted from the project process, there should be a formal project authorization practice. This is best instituted by means of a project charter document that contains much of the early description of project content, objectives, and budget. It is both a starting point for the project initiation process and the basis for guidance and measurement during execution. It specifies the project sponsor, the intended benefits and benefactors, and the source of funding. The project charter serves as the spending authorization. Time or expenses should not be charged to a project until such charges are authorized. The authorization document should specify who may charge and to what accounts the charges can go. Spending authorizations may be granted by phases. The project team should set up the Stage-Gate® criteria for the specific project, based on the established life cycle standard.[1] These are used to evaluate project progress before proceeding to the next major phase. (We introduce Stage-Gates in Section 3.2. Stage-Gate developer Robert Cooper describes the process in even greater detail in Section 5.1.)

ESTABLISH CRITICAL PARAMETERS

This includes targets, limits, and thresholds. The basis for these parameters is the values that were used to evaluate the project during the selection phase. For instance, what is the target delivery date? What amount of time extension can be tolerated? When do projected delays dictate that continuation of the effort be evaluated? Milestone dates may also be important and can help to identify out-of-tolerance conditions earlier in the project. Target and limit values should also be established for cost items, technology accomplishments, window-of-opportunity issues, and any area where performance is critical to supporting the criteria associated with the original goals. This process is crucial to prevent wishful-thinking projects from sapping the resources of the firm.

DETERMINE WHAT IS TO BE MEASURED AND BY WHOM

What gets measured to monitor the targets, limits, and thresholds? What is the mechanism for making the measurements? Who makes the measurements, who evaluates them against the measurement parameters, and who reports out-of-tolerance situations?

In Section 3.2, we'll look at the fundamentals of managing the pipeline with respect to maintaining the optimal portfolio.

3.2 MAINTAINING THE PIPELINE

> The identification of opportunities and the selection of the best projects are only the beginning. It is the realization of benefits that is the end objective. The portfolio must be managed to deliver those benefits.

Due to our effective application of the project selection process, we have established a portfolio of projects that are aligned with the firm's strategies, maximize potential benefits, and make the most effective use of the firm's resources. At least that was the situation when the projects were chosen and initiated. Now that the projects are underway, has anything happened that would lead us to want to change these decisions?

In the practice of PPM, one fundamental is to treat projects as if their selection was conditional. That's not to say that every project is on continual probation. We plan and execute each project with the intention of bringing it to a successful completion. But there is no blank check. There are numerous conditions that could warrant a reevaluation of a project's position in the portfolio.

This being the case, the normal process of project control must undergo some change in order to recognize the increased importance of the project status and performance as a part of the PPM process. In this chapter, we look at the fundamentals of maintaining the project pipeline (that is, what stays in the pipeline):

- Periodic measurement of status and performance
- Evaluation of status and performance against critical parameters
- Reporting of items that don't support targets, limits, or thresholds
- Stage-Gate® and bounding box concepts[1]

Modern Project Management (Past Its Prime?)

For about the past forty-five years (the era of modern project management), the focus of project management was on successfully completing projects, delivering project content, and satisfying project stakeholders. We paid significant attention to issues of schedule, resource use, cost, and quality. We employed specialized computer-based tools such as critical path scheduling, critical chain, risk analysis, resource allocation and leveling, and multiproject reporting engines. Project management grew from an arcane practice to a widespread and respected profession. And we took these scattered project management practitioners and brought them into centralized project management offices (PMO).

While those of us in the project management discipline were joyful when we helped to achieve project management success, we were dismayed to learn that project success did not always equate to business success. Across the hall from the PMO, senior operating personnel were often disconnected from the projects scene, as if the hallway were the Maginot Line. "Why," they would ask, "are so many projects not contributing to the firm's bottom line?" "Why," they would query, "are critical and scarce resources being allocated to work that is not aligned with strategic objectives?" They searched to find the "value" in these projects.

Across the hall in the PMO, they would ask, "What strategic objectives?" "Value? That's not in our purview. Isn't it enough to bring the project in on schedule and within budget? How can we perform so well and still fail to produce the results that senior management demands?"

The schism is even greater than that. What about the projects that don't make it to the end? Or the projects that do make it all the way through but deliver an unusable product? Finally, we have begun to question whether the projects should have been approved or continued past a point of limited value. So it is time to enter the era of postmodern project management, or what we now call project portfolio management (PPM).

**PPM Is More Than
Selecting Projects**

PPM is primarily the process of determining which projects should be in the firm's project portfolio. In Section 3.1, we discussed the process of selecting projects for the portfolio. In this chapter, we turn to maintenance of the portfolio.

During the selection process, we make assumptions about the value of candidate projects. We look at the opportunities and balance them against potential risks. We predict the effect of the project on revenue and cash flow and consider the costs of the project. We make many assumptions about key criteria at the completion of the project (and major segments of the project) according to a forecasted time line.

But the project and business environments are not cast in concrete. These are not static environments. Projects don't always go as planned. The assumptions may become less valid with time. Windows of opportunity close, and sometimes unpredictably.

Managing the Pipeline

During the project selection process, we match the assumptions about the project with the assumptions about the business needs and opportunities. Once the projects are in the pipeline, we update both sets of assumptions. On the projects side, we periodically measure project status and performance. On the business side, we periodically validate or adjust strategies and the assumptions about value, risk, resources, budgets, opportunity, and need.

Two popular and proven techniques that are available to support management of the project pipeline are (1) earned value analysis and (2) the Stage-Gate process. Each of these processes is introduced in this chapter to provide an overview of their contribution to PPM. (For a more detailed discussion of earned value analysis, see Section 4.6, and of the Stage-Gate process, see Section 5.1.)

Earned Value Analysis

How can we tell if a project is proceeding according to plan? If we are employing critical path scheduling techniques (CPM), diminishing float or slack is an indication of schedule slippage. However, with its focus on the critical path activities, this doesn't always reveal how badly the entire scope of work is falling behind. It also doesn't measure the actual costs against the amount of work that has been accomplished. The bottom line is that monitoring float or slack is not an adequate device for evaluating project performance.

A better way is the earned value analysis technique (EVA). EVA can even be used in the absence of a critical path schedule, but it works best in conjunction with the CPM. To use EVA, there should be a list of the work to be performed, a weight factor for each item on the list, and a planned schedule of accomplishment. When we use a CPM, these items become a natural part of the process. The weight factor can be the budget in either cost or labor-hours. This budget is expressed as the budget at completion (BAC). When the work is scheduled, we can generate the budgeted cost of work scheduled (BCWS), which is the planned effort at any point in time.

In order to track status and performance, we need to periodically provide two pieces of information for each work item. The first is the item percent complete (%C). By multiplying the %C times the BAC, we can compute the budgeted cost of work performed (BCWP).

This is the earned value. I prefer to call it the earned value of the work performed. By comparing the value of the work performed (BCWP) to the value of the work that we had planned to accomplish (BCWS), we can calculate the schedule variance (SV) at any point in time. If we had planned to do 50 percent of the work item and accomplished only 20 percent, then we can clearly tell that the item is behind. By using the budget values in the calculation, we are able to roll up the SV to any level of the work breakdown structure (WBS). By dividing the BCWP by the BCWS, we produce the schedule performance index (SPI). In this example, the SPI would indicate that we are making only 40 percent of the progress that we had planned. (The acronyms used here are the traditional terms for EVA. A simplified set of terms is gaining popularity and is introduced in Section 4.6.)

To repeat, the first progress data item is BCWP (based on the %C). The second progress item is actual cost for work performed (ACWP). With these two data items (synchronized time-wise), we can evaluate cost performance. To generate a cost variance (CV), we compare what we have spent (the ACWP) to the budget for the work that we actually accomplished (BCWP). This is an important improvement over older accounting methods. Before we had earned value data, it was common to compare actual costs to planned costs. But this can produce a misleading story when the progress has not kept up with the plan. In the example, if we had actually spent 30 percent of the budget to accomplish 20 percent of the defined work, we are really overspent by 50 percent. By dividing the BCWP by the ACWP, we produce the schedule performance index (SPI).

For a more detailed discussion on EVA techniques, see Section 4.6. It's really much more straightforward than it sounds.

Updating Critical Parameters

The EVA data provides information about project performance against the plan. With this information, the team can evaluate whether certain deficient performance warrants consideration of terminating the project prior to completion, changing the priority of the project, or reallocating resources to other work.

However, there will generally be an additional set of factors to consider. Has there been any change in the need for this project? Is the window of opportunity still open? Has critical technology changed? Have the firm's strategies changed? On a periodic basis, all of the criteria that were examined when putting a value on the project should be validated and updated.

The project management office (PMO) will publish reports indicating where defined targets, limits, and thresholds have been violated. The PPM governance council will consider this information, together with the updated critical parameters, to evaluate all projects for continuation or termination.

There is a special case where a structured reevaluation of the projects in the portfolio against the selection criteria is of paramount importance. This is when there is a major departure from the published strategic plan, such as when there is a merger of two firms. In this situation, the newly merged entity will publish a revised strategic plan and the PMO and GC will review the entire portfolio for alignment with the new plan. It would not be surprising to find cause to eliminate 5 to 25 percent of the project volume due to duplication of efforts or nonalignment with emerging strategies.

The Stage-Gate Process   If you hang around with some new product development (NPD) people, it won't be very long before someone reverently invokes the name "Cooper." This is a reference to Robert G. Cooper, widely recognized as an NPD guru, and father of the Stage-Gate process, who has much to contribute to the discipline of PPM.

The typical NPD project consists of a series of steps starting with project conception and leading to product delivery/launch. These steps can usually be grouped into a series of phases. Each phase will have a number of activities, possibly performed in multiple disciplines, leading to an interim milestone or goal.

The Stage-Gate concept was developed primarily to enhance the efforts involved in new product development. It is a natural practice to apply to PPM. (In Section 5.1, Cooper thoroughly covers this topic as originally developed for NPD and technology development.)

In the Stage-Gate process, each phase (called a *stage*) is separated by a decision point (called a *gate*). As described by Cooper for the NPD environment, Stage-Gate is applied across the entire project life cycle. Conditions for passing through a gate are defined. At the end of a stage, a cross-functional team evaluates the status against the pass/no-pass conditions.

I believe that the process can be expanded in the development and testing stages to improve management of projects during those phases. This would entail declaring development milestones as mini-gates that would be monitored by the PMO. In this way, the project doesn't have to wait until development is completed before evaluating it for a kill or delay decision.

Therefore, active projects within the portfolio continue to be subject to a Stage-Gate control process. Just as there is a set of criteria for determining if the project is to be selected for the active portfolio, each gate will have a set of metrics by which the project can be evaluated. The PMO reviews each project at each gate, before making a go/no-go recommendation to the governance council. Funding may be cut off or the project put on hold if the evaluation data shows that the project performance is not supporting the original plan or is no longer making sound use of limited resources. Other reasons for killing the project include technical limitations or failure, a change in financial considerations, or inability to meet the allowable time window.

The governance council is the gatekeeper. The council is made up of senior representatives of the functions responsible for business success. Evaluations are made against predetermined criteria and decisions are made by comparing the metrics to those criteria. Gut feelings or territorial protectionism should be resisted.

Stage-Gate techniques need not be limited to NPD projects. These practices can be applied effectively to any type of project that has identifiable phases.

**The Bounding
Box Approach**   What if your project doesn't fit well into a phased mode? Perhaps there are significant overlaps between basic phases. Or the project contains some looping components, as might be found in pure research projects.

In this case, you might want to pass up the Stage-Gate process for the *bounding box approach.* This process calls for setting selected critical parameters (boundaries) and is a type of management-by-exception technique. The governance council approves a set of targets or limits, such as delivery dates, cash flow, projected returns, and performance metrics. As long as the project stays within the boundaries, the project team will control most of the action and decisions. However, if a critical target or limit is compromised, then the situation must be identified by the PMO and brought to the attention of the governance council. The PMO and governance council then review the project to consider project termination or continuation with reset targets and limits.

Managing Projects with a High Degree of Uncertainty

We have acknowledged that two of the primary application candidates for PPM are the fields of information technology and NPD. These two fields share a common challenge: they often have projects with a high degree of uncertainty.

These high-uncertainty projects create two distinct problems in regard to PPM. The first is a high and complex risk condition, which we address at length in Section 4.3. The second problem is that of setting performance targets and metrics for projects where what is learned from each phase defines the succeeding phase. This issue is addressed by establishing two sets of targets by phase. One set consists of long-range soft targets, based on the business case that was presented with the project proposal. As with the bounding box, we look for project performance issues that would indicate that the project might not be delivering the benefits that were expected as a condition of selection. The second set is shorter-term hard targets that would be used for the EVA. These targets would be updated at the end of each phase. As each phase clarifies the efforts and objectives of the next phase, a set of specific target metrics is produced. What we avoid by this method is having the project being measured against an obsolete set of metrics. (For discussion on phased baselining and other aspects of managing the EVA baseline and scope changes, see Practical Project Management: Tips, Tactics, and Tools, Section 5.1.)[2]

Success Stories

Organizations can benefit in several ways by employing a structured termination process—for example:

- During the first ninety days of the merger between HP and Compaq, the global project management office stopped over one hundred projects or programs that were not aligned with the emerging strategy or made poor use of resources.)
- In 2003, AOL built an entirely new project management culture around its implementation of PPM. It set up seven portfolio management teams, each centered on a line of business. For the 2004 planning cycle, AOL was able to achieve a 40 percent reduction in demand hours (from the initial portfolio), allowing it to balance resource capacity versus demand without additional head count.
- There are reported claims that the best-performing companies averaged 40 percent early cancellation of projects using Stage-Gate techniques to review value against risk.
- Critical resources are freed up for higher-value projects.
- Projects that are not performing well, whether due to technical, schedule, cost, or scope problems, do not continue to drain resources and dollars.

3.3 EXECUTING PROJECT PORTFOLIO MANAGEMENT

> PPM is an enterprise-wide process involving a wide range of participants. It is also an extremely visible and sensitive process. How well this process is executed will have the greatest possible impact on the viability and success of the firm for an extended time.

Any implementation of a PPM capability needs strong and visible sponsorship of the defined processes by the senior executives and new or revised roles and responsibilities for the people who will make it happen. In this chapter, we discuss the execution of PPM, focusing on who does what.

Extending the Boundaries　　The process for PPM extends well beyond the scope of traditional project management. Consider, for example, some of the following functions that are usually beyond the typical purview of project managers or the project management office (PMO) in the traditional project management process:

- Identifying opportunities and needs
- Selecting which projects are to be undertaken
- Selecting which projects are to be terminated or deferred
- Establishing project priorities
- Projecting revenue and effect on cash flow
- Aligning projects with strategic objectives
- Evaluating the value and benefits of the project to the firm
- Making a determination as to whether there are adequate benefits from the opportunity to overcome predicted risks
- Ensuring balance among various types of projects (maintenance, opportunity, competitive edge) so as to protect and enhance the firm's future

These are primarily the purview of financial managers, strategic planners, operations executives, and other senior officers. The processes listed above may also warrant inputs and participation from the marketing, purchasing and outsourcing, and human resource departments, as well as the various functional departments.

PPM is an enterprise-wide process involving a wide range of participants. It is also an extremely visible and sensitive process. How well this process is executed will have the greatest possible impact on the viability and success of the firm for an extended time.

Level of Participation　　PPM not only has a wide breadth across the organization, requiring a wide range of participation, it also extends deeply into the hierarchy. At the upper end, the leadership and direction must come from the very highest levels of the enterprise: the chief executive officer (CEO), chief operating officer (COO), and chief financial officer (CFO). In an organization where information technology (IT) is a primary business, we can expect the chief information officer (CIO) to play a significant role. Certainly the vice president of projects or chief projects officer is a key player.

Depending on the type of business, there might be participation by the director of manufacturing, the chief chemist, the chief engineer, or the director of construction. In the pharmaceutical industry, the director of regulatory affairs should be involved. The key factor here is to identify the parts of the organization that have major stakeholder responsibility and make sure that their leaders are part of the PPM leadership.

PPM Governance Council

One of the impediments to having a PPM process is that most of the people mentioned above have their specific territories to oversee. They typically are not motivated to spend their time on PPM and are unlikely to have the specific skills, practices, and tools to participate fully in this important function.

Although this senior management group must carry full responsibility for PPM and approve all major decisions, the process can be centered just below this level, at the PPM governance council. (In information systems organizations, this group is often called the *IT governance council* or the *IT business management team.*) The governance council can consist of any of the senior positions noted above or high-level designated representatives of these officer-level people. It is the PPM governance council that is charged with the responsibility for the key decisions that affect the project portfolio.

The senior officers, in adopting a PPM process, must provide the overall leadership of the process. In this regard, the CEO, with the support and participation of other key officials, will announce the implementation of the PPM process. A PPM charter declaration will be issued, explaining the need for and purpose of the PPM process, the roles of all participants, and the makeup of the initial governance council. The PPM charter declaration will spell out the specific responsibilities of the governance council and note when the council must elevate issues and decisions to senior management. PPM orientation sessions will be conducted to present the new PPM processes and answer questions about each defined role.

The governance council, working with the PMO, will meet and communicate regularly to ensure that the information needed to select projects and manage the pipeline is available and that decisions are made based on this data.

Project Management Office

PPM is a process that brings together the projects and operations sides of the enterprise. The operations side, consisting of the general business departments, plus the financial, and strategic and tactical planning functions, is represented by the PPM governance council. The projects side is represented by the PMO.

The PMO is responsible for the oversight of all projects. This includes monitoring project accomplishments against established criteria and advising the governance council of status and issues that would affect the planned benefits of any project. The placement of any project in the portfolio was based on a set of expectations of the value of the project, the potential contribution of the project to the welfare of the enterprise, and the expected impact on and use of the firm's resources. Whenever any of these expectations is compromised due to poor schedule or cost performance, technical impediments, reduced technical performance, and so forth, the PMO prepares a report and recommendations for consideration by the governance council.

The governance council, coordinating with the PMO, will need to reevaluate the effect of the situation on revenues and cash flow, as well as reviewing risk issues, project priority, and support for strategic initiatives. It is the governance council that then has the responsibility to decide if the affected project should be terminated, delayed, or continued under a revised set of expectations.

Although most PPM implementations have a PMO and a governance council, the balance of power and responsibility between the two will vary from organization to organization. In some implementations, the PMO carries most of the evaluation and decision responsibility, escalating to the governance council only in critical situations. In other implementations, the PMO prepares all of the analytical data, but the governance council makes all of the selection, delay, and termination decisions. In either case, it is important that both groups remember that they are not the owners of the projects or the portfolios. There are clients or sponsors who fill this bill. The challenge to the PPM team is to balance the needs of the owners with the strategies of the firm.

Integration

PPM is a way of facilitating the integration of several critical enterprise functions. Without PPM, the business of managing projects is conducted with the sense that the ultimate objective is to achieve project success. That is, if the schedule, cost, technical, scope, and quality objectives of a project have been met, then it is assumed that the project is of value. Yet early implementers of PPM have frequently found that many projects that are approved and allocated scarce resources do not fit very well with the strategic objectives of the firm, do not contribute (as well as other projects) to the cash flow, and do not represent the best use of resources.

The project portfolio represents part of the tactical planning that is implemented to support the strategic plan. Therefore, the governance council, in selecting projects for the portfolio and in managing what stays in the portfolio, is in fact an integral part of the strategic and tactical planning process.

The projects that comprise the project portfolio have a significant impact on the financial condition of the firm. Most projects incur costs during their execution and generate revenue (or reduce costs) on completion (or during execution, in the case of progress payments). Projects thus have an impact on the cash flow and the projection of financial condition. Today's regulatory atmosphere demands that financial reports represent a current and true picture of the asset value of projects.

Traditionally, project reporting has focused on costs (ignoring other financial items such as revenue and cash flow). Therefore, the PMO has to integrate with the financial function to update revenue and cash flow data based on project status and performance. The tools employed to support the PPM process either have to add revenue and cash flow capabilities or be integrated with tools that can fill the void.

Decisions on the makeup of the project portfolio should take into consideration not only the projects at hand but also prospective projects, which may be represented by marketing initiatives or as a result of top-down initiatives coming out of the strategic plan. Forecasting, based on data furnished by the strategic planning committee and the opportunities management system, should be integrated with the PPM process.

Project Managers and Executives Don't Speak the Same Language

In this new world of PPM, we are looking not only for projects that are managed well but also for projects that are right for the firm. So we have formed a partnership between the project-oriented people in the PMO and the business-oriented people, represented by the governance council. My experience has been that the design and implementation of a PPM capability has often been derailed for the simple reason that the two groups do not speak the same language (as well as having a different focus).

To illustrate this, picture yourself as working within the PMO. When you report to others about how your project is going, do you focus on schedule and costs? Do you talk about resource utilization or scope changes? Surely these are important items. As project managers, we are taught to communicate these key items to management as a measure of whether the project is progressing successfully. They still are important—a gauge of project health. But they don't always reflect the project's true impact on the business.

When communicating to executives, you need to focus on the terms that reflect how the project is contributing to the larger set of objectives of the enterprise. How is the project contributing to growth, competitive advantage, revenue and cash flow, effective use of all resources, and key strategic initiatives? Focus more on benefits, revenue, and return on investment than on costs. The project end date may not be as important as the window of opportunity.

For each person with whom you communicate, think about how that person gets measured and views success. Then design custom communications for each in the language that he or she uses. One of the first tasks of the governance council will be to develop a set of terms and metrics that will form the basis of the communication stream that supports the PPM process.

Summary

Implementation of the PPM process involves three groups of people:

- Senior management, for providing leadership and direction and designating their representatives to the PPM governance council
- The members of the PPM governance council, who will manage the selection of projects for the portfolio and review projects for possible deselection
- The project management office, which monitors approved projects and advises the governance council where projects are deviating from expected benefits and value

The PPM process leads to improved integration of projects with strategic and tactical plans, financial projections and reporting, and opportunity management.

3.4 TOOLS FOR PROJECT PORTFOLIO MANAGEMENT

PPM extends traditional project management practices and tools to situations beyond the planning and control of approved projects. It requires the development and application of some new practices and tools. Effective integration of new and existing practices and tools is essential to PPM success.

Project portfolio management is a set of processes, usually supported by a set of tools (software). Support for PPM requires some supplementary tool support, in addition to the tools that you are already using for traditional project management. But don't throw away the tools that you have been using. You'll still need them. PPM integrates traditional project and business functions. You'll need to integrate your support tools as well.

We start with a brief summary of the preceding three sections as a review of the PPM processes and a guide for our evaluation of software requirements for support of PPM. We then use this framework to look at how PPM fits in with other project management practices. Finally, we look at how the various project management and PPM tools work together to support project portfolio management.

An Overview of the Project Portfolio Management Processes

PPM is more than an extension of project management to deal with multiple projects. Although it addresses different needs, it is very important to have full integration with traditional project management capabilities.

As more and more firms adopt project management office (PMO) methods, it would not surprise us to see responsibility for PPM thrust fully into the hands of the chief project officer. This, too, would be a mistake. *PPM requires governance at the executive level.* And the tools need to be optimized to support these changing roles.

The core mistake is to think that PPM is fundamentally the management of multiple projects. This definitely is not so. PPM is the management of the project portfolio so as to maximize the contribution of projects to the overall welfare and success of the enterprise. What this means is:

- Projects must be aligned with the firm's strategy and goals.
- Projects must be consistent with the firm's values and culture.
- Projects must contribute to a positive cash flow for the enterprise.
- Projects must effectively use the firm's resources—both people and other resources.
- Projects must not only provide for current contributions to the firm's health but must help to position the firm for future success.

We repeat this list here so that we can think about the impact of these attributes of PPM on tool support for the process. Our application of traditional project management processes and tools has focused on managing projects. Now we need to extend our practices and tools to support project prioritization and selection. We also have to integrate the project management tools with the portfolio management tools.

Extending Management Processes to Include PPM

There are two primary components of the PPM process. Although they are intertwined, each has its specific objectives and practices:

- Prioritization and selection of candidate projects for the portfolio
- Maintaining the pipeline: continuing, delaying, or terminating approved projects

Both of these segments of PPM compel us to apply structured, repeatable, proactive practices to the selection and continuance of projects:

- PPM extends traditional project management practices and tools to situations beyond the planning and control of approved projects.
- PPM requires the development and application of new practices and tools.

If you already have processes and tools to support planning and scheduling, earned value management, risk management, and communication, you are well on your way to having a PPM capability. But you will need additional capabilities to complete your PPM arsenal.

Defining the New PPM Processes
This section reviews the workings of the PPM processes, to describe the tools that are available to support these processes and to explain the interrelationships between the core planning and control components and newer facilities needed for PPM.

PHASE ONE: PRIORITIZATION AND SELECTION OF CANDIDATE PROJECTS

In this phase, we identify and evaluate candidate projects. The evaluation requires us to consider the opportunity (value and benefits) as well as the risks (which modify the expected benefits). We also have to consider our ability to handle the project loads, much of which is dependent on resource availability.

Evaluating Candidate Projects. We'll assume that the objective of the PPM process is to prioritize work that brings the most value to the firm. The definition of *value* will certainly differ in accordance with the firm's focus, strategies, and types of projects. Regardless of these differences, a project portfolio management process will have to address the following:

- A ranking of value and benefits
- An estimate of the total costs
- An appraisal of risk (in achieving these benefits)
- An inventory of resource availability and allocation (capacity planning)
- An idea of an optimum or acceptable size of the project pipeline

While we will have a defined process specifically designed to guide and support the evaluation of candidate projects, we may rely on established tools to aid in some of these steps—for instance:

- Your standard planning and control tool would be a convenient source of the resource availability and allocation data.
- Your risk management tool would be used to address the risk component of the evaluation.
- Your enterprise resource planning (ERP) tools would cover financial and human resources (HR) functions, and possibly opportunity management.

- Using an integrated collection of project management tools, where available, minimizes redundancy (and conflicting data) and provides efficient, seamless flow of information.

However, most PM tools were not designed to hold the ranking data or to display it in ways that facilitate portfolio decisions by the governance team (although such capabilities are being added to some). For this, you will need a specifically designed PPM tool. In addition, some recognized decision support tools have been optimized for application to PPM.

Ranking Value and Benefits. Assuming that the number of potential projects exceeds the number that can be effectively executed in a reasonable time, there must be a means of prioritizing each project. Conceptually, this ranking process is simple, although the individual parameters will vary according to strategies, resources, profit motive, and other categories. Earlier, we noted that the process is not unlike that used in selecting items for an investment portfolio. In fact, this *is* an investment portfolio: you are investing in projects with the objective of maximizing the return.

One of the primary ranking factors will be expected return on investment (ROI) or net present value (NPV), or some variation of these traditional financial measurements. However, there are qualifiers associated with this process. You can't prioritize projects using ROI or NPV alone. You also need to consider:

- Alignment with strategic and tactical plans
- Balance between maintenance projects and investment projects
- Allocation balance of R&D or marketing expenditures and resources
- Effective use of resources
- Probability of delivering the project on time, within budget, and with the designed work scope
- Ancillary benefits (nonfinancial)
- Impact of potential risk
- Cost of performing the project

The last two items are often considered in a formula such as: Value = NPV × probability of technical success/costs. (See Section 5.2 for additional examples.) There are almost endless approaches toward developing a value figure. Your software should support your preferences in this area.

Risk. Risk is a modifier of opportunity. (See Section 4.3 for detailed discussion of risk.) Any estimate of the benefits of a project must be adjusted for the consideration of risk. There is always the issue of technical risk. What is the probability that the technical objectives won't be met? What are the consequences of that happening? Can anything be done to mitigate or otherwise contain the risk? If so, what is the impact of the mitigation action on benefits and costs? If the project is intended to generate income, what is the probability that the commercial objectives won't be met? If the project deliverables are targeted for a specific window of opportunity, what is the probability that the time objective will be missed? Again, there are the questions of mitigation and effect on benefits and costs.

This is a lot of information and data to keep in one's head or on the back of an envelope. As with any other project management and PPM processes, it is best to have a standardized, repeatable process for evaluating and managing risk, supported by appropriate software. And it is preferable to integrate the risk software with the other PPM tools.

Balanced and Weighted Ranking. The ranking practice should use a balanced scorecard approach, where each of the factors is listed and weighted. As each factor is rated, an aggregate score for each project is obtained. The rating of each factor can be prompted by a series of questions, with the answers noted in a narrative format and then converted to a numerical score based on the level of the answer against a guideline.

A common practice is to evaluate the value/benefit ranking and the risk ranking on a grid. Preference would be given to projects that appear in the high-value/low-risk quartile.

Analytic Hierarchy Process. The issue of ranking has brought an established, mathematics-based, decision-making process called analytic hierarchy process (AHP) to the PPM tool market. AHP involves the use of voting groups using paired comparisons to create weighted rankings for multiple objectives. For instance, the group may compare the importance of short-range income to long-range income, and then long-range income to technical standing, and so on. AHP software tallies all of the results to derive weight factors for each objective. Then the group may use the pairwise comparisons to judge how well each project matches up with the objectives. The result is a fairly weighted prioritization of the projects.

While the AHP method might appear (to some) to be overkill, it allows everyone to have an equal and complete voice in the ranking and selection process and minimizes the effect of personal biases.

In addition to the formal application of AHP, other vendors have adopted similar capabilities aimed at optimizing the decision-making process. These include the use of pairwise comparison matrices, efficient frontier, and other structured decision analysis methodologies.

Displaying the Ranking and Selection Data. Regardless of the techniques employed to weigh the selection criteria and prioritize the candidate projects, you will eventually have to display and communicate these data to the decision makers. This capability is supported by almost all PPM software solutions. In some cases, it is the primary PPM-specific feature in products that were developed with a PPM focus.

Common display mechanisms are bubble charts, spreadsheets, four-quadrant grids, X-Y charts, bar charts, matrix comparison charts, executive dashboards (see Figure 3–2), and an interesting graph called the Efficient Frontier, a portfolio optimization tool. They all support multidimensional analysis of data to provide multidimensional presentations. Through the use of axes, variable bubble size, colors, and shapes, some bubble charts can display as many as six different variables on one chart. Many products allow you to display multiple charts on a single page or screen.

Most of these display methods support "what-if" analysis to test various scenarios. There is tremendous power and utility in these display methods. But a little caution is called for. The quality of the display is not a direct indication of the quality of the data.

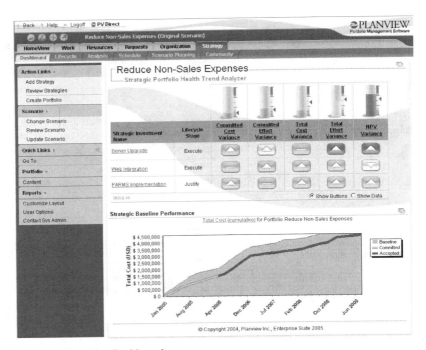

FIGURE 3–2 An Executive Dashboard

Note: The figure displays summary information about the projects in a portfolio. Typically, colored "traffic lights" (green, yellow, red) call attention to the health (schedule and cost) of the projects. Thresholds for yellow and red are established by the user.

Without a meticulous, structured approach toward developing the data, you might be manipulating and displaying only junk.

One way to reduce the likelihood of bad data is to have a seamless connection from the data generators to the data displays. That is, the data is developed using accepted practices that provide an audit trail back to the source. You can be assured that the selection committee will frequently look at the data in a display and say, "Where did that come from?" Will you be able to answer?

PHASE TWO: MAINTAINING THE PIPELINE

The old conventional wisdom was that once a project has been initiated, it is active until completion (or failure). The new conventional wisdom is that a project is active as long as it continues to support the criteria that were established for its selection and acceptable performance. In this respect, projects are periodically evaluated against these criteria.

The evaluation considers two basic aspects of the project: project performance and an updating of the project critical parameters. Some of the things that we want to know are:

- Is the project still aligned with the strategies?
- What is the current probability that the project will be technically successful?

- What is the current probability that the project will be commercially successful?
- How is the project performing against the target criteria?
- What are the performance trends? Improving or worsening?
- Does the project still represent effective use of the firm's resources?

Measuring Project Performance. If you are directly involved with project management, you have been working with most of the project tracking practices. If we have a critical path (CPM) schedule, we maintain the project progress in the CPM software and monitor schedule milestones and float. Diminishing float is an indication of schedule slippage, but that value doesn't always reveal how much the work is falling behind. It focuses on the most critical schedule items.

A better way to look at performance is with earned value analysis (EVA), a process for evaluating schedule and cost performance on a project. It produces schedule variance data by comparing actual accomplishment to planned accomplishment. It produces cost variance data by comparing the actual cost for the work that has actually been accomplished to the budgeted cost for that quantity of work. EVA usually generates these values at a detailed level and then rolls the data up to summary levels for evaluation.

EVA provides an early warning system for schedule and cost overruns. When the EVA data indicates that certain work is not keeping up with the schedule target or is running over budget, the project team is expected to investigate the problem and, if possible, recommend corrective action. When the data (after considering corrective action) indicates that schedule or cost overruns jeopardize achievement of the project objectives, the PMO will communicate this to the portfolio governance council.

EVA capabilities are available in almost all conventional project management software. If you have planned a project using such software, the core data for EVA is already in place. If you use this software for project tracking, entering percent complete values will provide the data needed for automatic calculation of schedule variance (SV). If you track actual costs, you'll have what you need for calculation of cost variance (CV). (For a more detailed discussion of EVA, see Section 4.6.)

Updating Critical Parameters. The EVA data provides information about project performance against the plan. When the results show that project performance is deficient, the team should conduct an evaluation to consider terminating the project prior to completion, changing the priority of the project, or reallocating resources to other work.

There are generally additional factors to consider. Has there been any change in the need for this project? Is the window of opportunity still open? Has critical technology changed? Have the firm's strategies changed? On a periodic basis, all of the criteria that were examined when putting a value on the project should be validated and updated.

The PMO publishes reports indicating where defined targets, limits, and thresholds have been violated. As part of the periodic project selection cycle, it makes recommendations regarding rescheduling or terminating projects with deteriorating performance or that no longer rank well against the selection criteria. The PMO, as part of these recommendations, identifies funding and resources that could be freed up for new, more beneficial projects. The PPM software must be able to process and publish all of these data.

The PPM governance council considers this information, together with the updated critical parameters, to evaluate all projects for continuation or termination.

Defining PPM and the Tools for PPM

Getting a clear, unified definition of PPM and PPM tools is virtually impossible. Consider this statement from a leading consulting firm (one of many on this topic):

> We define PPM as software that streamlines outward functions and inward processes of project-intensive departments, industries and organizations. Integrating multiple business processes and point solutions into one application suite, PPM features integrated management of pipeline, scope, time, resource, skills, cost, procurement, communication, reporting and forecasting, and risk management functions.

I propose a different definition:

> PPM is a set of *processes,* supported by people and tools, to guide the enterprise in selecting the right projects and the right number of projects, and in maintaining a portfolio of projects that will maximize the enterprise's strategic goals, efficient use of resources, stakeholder satisfaction, and the bottom line.

Although PPM does not directly encompass the traditional PM processes and tools mentioned in the first statement, they are part of the process flow. PPM is integrated with these processes and tools and relies on inputs from them for its success.

First, we note that PPM is a set of processes, supported by tools, rather than being the tools themselves. Second, the PPM tool set (in my definition) includes software that helps us to automate specific PPM processes. There are many other tools used in the process of managing projects or the business operations of the enterprise that would also be used in conjunction with PPM tools to serve the entire operations and projects needs. That these various tools work together is a major objective of implementing a PPM capability.

In discussing the software for PPM, we describe several configurations of tool sets. Although each category contains powerful and valuable capabilities, none of them offers every capability that could be used to support PPM. Yet most of these are being advertised as PPM solutions.

Software for Project Management and PPM. Tools for PPM are being offered in many varieties and from various vendors who have focused on different needs. Among the traditional offerings (before adding support for PPM) are the following:

- *Critical Path Scheduling (CPM) programs.* These are the basic tools for scheduling and tracking projects. They allow you to define the project work items, define task relationships, assign task durations, assign resources, and calculate base critical path schedules and resource-constrained schedules. These programs also usually have excellent support for work breakdown structures (WBS) and simple applications of EVA. All offer multiple means of reporting plans and status. Additional features may include simplified risk planning and tracking, issue tracking, and time keeping.
- *Critical chain project management (CCPM).* This is a variation on traditional CPM methods, focusing on methods for sharing contingency. CCPM has created almost a cult

following of adopters who praise its benefits. As with the traditional CPM advocates, CCPM supporters are also moving to embrace PPM.

● *Earned value method (EVM) programs.* These support advanced EVA applications, especially for defense system projects and other programs where EVM is mandated. These EVM programs have a strong focus on cost control and strong support for multiple WBS's (used for directed cost buckets).

● *Risk management programs.* These usually go well beyond the skeleton risk capabilities in traditional CPM programs. These are valuable where a highly structured, proactive risk-management culture is required. There are two quite different foci to risk management. One is often called the PERT approach. It addresses only schedule risk and uses three time estimates per task and Monte Carlo simulation to determine project durations and probability of meeting specified completion dates. Currently more in vogue is the risk assessment and management approach. This calls for identification of potential risk events, an assessment of the probability that the event will occur, and the probable impact of the event if it does occur. The user is then expected to consider mitigation options to contain the risks.

● *Slice-and-dice software.* Originally created as separate software, these capabilities are commonly found in most project management tools. The objective is to access and present large volumes of data in meaningful ways. Many of these use online analytical processing techniques.

● *Enterprise resource planning (ERP) tools.* ERP software combines integrated support for project management and many business operations. The most common components (for project management applications) are accounting and human resource software. Customer relations management (CRM) and opportunities management modules can also be integrated with the PM systems.

● *Professional services automation (PSA) tools.* This is another integration of project management and business components. Developed primarily for firms that provide outsourced IT services, PSA components include project management, billing, time accounting, CRM, engagement management, and cross-charging. There are several terms being used for this class of tools, including enterprise services automation (ESA).

● *Structured objectives planning software.* This is an unusual program that helps to structure a statement of strategic objectives. Starting with the strategic plan, you can build down to individual objectives and align them with projects or parts of projects. When integrated with traditional project planning software, the project work can be associated with specific strategy-based objectives.

● *Analytic hierarchy process (AHP).* AHP is a mathematics-based decision-making process. It has been used in a wide variety of applications and is now being applied to PPM. It uses voting groups using pairwise comparisons to create weighted rankings for multiple objectives.

Adding PPM Software to the Mix. Do you remember the old story about a group of blind people attempting to describe an elephant? Each person surveyed a different area of the elephant by feel, and each came up with a different description.

Trying to describe PPM software is not unlike describing the elephant. In this case, the vast majority of PPM tool vendors had already been market players with tools that provided capabilities as noted above. In some cases, PPM capabilities were added to the existing tool sets. In other cases, the product line was revamped and refocused to center on PPM.

So what we have are CPM vendors offering PPM tools, ERP vendors offering PPM tools, PSA vendors offering PPM tools, AHP vendors offering PPM tools, data presentation (slice-and-dice) vendors offering PPM tools, and so on. No single vendor is providing 100 percent of the functions that are available for PPM. But many come very close and offer an extensive set of capabilities.

The primary additions to the capabilities (to support PPM) include:

- A repository for proposed and active projects
- Guidelines for presenting project proposals for ranking and selection
- Project selection criteria
- Decision engines to develop weight factors for selection criteria
- A repository for financial and resource allocation data
- Tools to assist in computing potential project benefits, including the ability to incorporate the impact of costs and risks
- Tools to support project prioritization and ranking
- Tools to display ranking results
- Tools to aid in project selection
- What-if capabilities to explore alternatives
- The ability to integrate these capabilities with other operations and projects tools

EXAMPLES OF AN INTEGRATED TOOL SET

From the various configurations noted earlier, I have selected a few representative vendor offerings for the purpose of providing illustrations of integrated tool sets. The selection of any of the vendors for these illustrations is not an indication of my preference for any specific solution. Each firm should evaluate and choose software to meet its specific needs.

The Welcom Family of Tools. Welcom offers a suite of five tools that support the PPM process. These are two recent additions, WelcomPortfolio and WelcomRisk, which join WelcomHome, Open Plan, and Cobra. In addition, Microsoft Project can be substituted for Open Plan (for planning and control). The complete PPM process uses all five tools, with WelcomPortfolio serving as the primary repository for the portfolio data.

Projects to be considered for the portfolio would be initiated in WelcomPortfolio, and capabilities within this tool are designed to facilitate data collection and manipulation leading to evaluation-based rankings. Additional capabilities will display this information to facilitate selection decisions.

WelcomRisk can produce risk scores for the candidate projects and feed this data into WelcomPortfolio. However, risk values can also be determined outside WelcomRisk and entered directly into WelcomPortfolio.

Open Plan (or Microsoft Project) can be used in two ways to support portfolio planning. It can help with capacity planning by calculating and holding data relative to the maximum project pipeline size and the available resource pool. It can also be used to produce preliminary, high-level plans to compute schedule, resource, and cost data needed for the portfolio evaluation process.

WelcomHome can be used throughout any of the processes as a global communication tool. WelcomHome facilitates collaboration by supporting bidirectional communication among all parties. It would be used to publish the project charter and to officially open the project to all interested parties.

Once a project is approved, detailed planning would begin, using Open Plan (or Microsoft Project). Project plans would be maintained, and data affecting capacity planning would be fed back to WelcomPortfolio.

Once the project is in progress, we will need to monitor project performance as well as reviewing the criteria used for selection. A key performance measuring technique is EVA, supported in its simplest form by Open Plan (and Microsoft Project) and at an advanced level by Cobra. The PMO monitors project performance with these tools and feeds information and recommendations to the governance council when such information indicates that the status of the project should be reexamined.

Coming full circle, recommendations regarding active projects will be routed back into WelcomPortfolio to produce an updated list of ranked projects.

The entire process is dynamic and ongoing. All Welcom components are used as needed to support the process, with periodic WelcomPortfolio outputs being provided to the governance council for portfolio decisions.

Oracle, SAP, and PeopleSoft. Leading ERP vendors Oracle, SAP, and PeopleSoft have added PPM attributes to support project ranking and selection, skills analysis and resource deployment, collaboration, and the popular dashboard and bubble chart display modes. These capabilities are integrated with all of the other previously integrated functions for projects and business management that are typical in the ERP models.

Niku and Other PSA Vendors. Niku is one of the original providers of PSA software. Its package featured integration of several business components linked to the Workbench Results Management package (project management) that it acquired from ABT. It was developed primarily for firms that provide outsourced IT services. Niku 6 components included a collection of project management and financial management modules, resource management, demand management, opportunity management, and work flow and collaboration facilities. Niku 6 also introduced Niku's first portfolio manager module.

Upgraded and rebadged as Clarity 7 in 2004, it covers a wide span of capabilities with eight modules. Portfolio Manager, upgraded and moved up to anchor the system, is a repository for project evaluation data and is used to develop and display data for ranking and selection. There are three choices for project management: a new Web-based Project Manager module and the ability to use Workbench or Microsoft Project. The Resource Planner is used to help assign resources, balance capacity and demand, and identify and track skills information. The Financial Manager handles charge backs, billing and invoicing, cost and rate management, and financial reporting. The Process Manager features a work flow capability to automate business processes and standardize them.

Similar integrated offerings are available from vendors such as Lawson and Changepoint (now called "Compuware IT Governance by Changepoint").

IT Governance. Several project management and PPM vendors have specifically focused on IT applications. It is not that their offerings could not be used for other applications. However, these have been packaged and advertised for the IT market. Many of these choose to label their solutions as IT governance solutions, containing PPM and allied functions. Niku and Changepoint fall into this group. Others are ProSight, Mercury Interactive, and PlanView. Even PeopleSoft, with a wide market, has packaged its integrated PPM solution as ESA (Enterprise Services Automation) for IT.

ProSight. The centerpiece of ProSight is a portfolio analysis and prioritization tool that provides strong data manipulation and presentation. This is an example of a PPM product that is not attempting to cover a wide range of project management and PPM capabilities. Rather, it prefers to act as a hub for data that it then processes to support portfolio analysis. Any project management functionality is provided through a bridge to Microsoft Project Server.

Expert Choice and United Management Technologies. United Management Technologies (UMT) and Expert Choice go deeper into mathematical engines to assist with assigning collaborated weights to the selection criteria and supporting prioritization and selection. In Expert Choice, this is accomplished through the use of the analytic hierarchy process, an effective decision support tool.

These capabilities are integrated with components that help to optimize resource use and to evaluate and select projects. Strong presentation components are featured. Neither product has a project scheduling engine. UMT has a gateway connection to Microsoft Project Server. Expert Choice connects through Microsoft Access or SQL Server.

Project Management with Expanded PPM Processing and Displays. Primavera, PlanView, and Sciforma are long-time key players in traditional project and resource management software systems. PlanView has added an extensive set of PPM functions anchored by its PRISMS for IT Governance and Resource Management process set. Primavera and Sciforma offer extensive user configuration of database and computational functions that effectively support PPM needs. Their key strengths (as with Welcom) are strong traditional scheduling and resource engines and good support for EVA, risk analysis, resource allocation, and reporting.

Implementing a PPM Capability

PPM is a valuable process to aid in the selection of projects that will best further the organization's mission considering risks, capacity limits, and project value. In order to implement such a capability, the firms must:

- Develop a PPM process.
- Establish a governance team.
- Acquire PPM and other project management support tools.
- Integrate the PPM process and tools with other project management processes and tools.

3.5 IMPLEMENTING PROJECT PORTFOLIO MANAGEMENT _____

> The first step in the new PPM process is to evaluate the existing project inventory. Excising nonaligned, redundant, or nonbeneficial projects will release scarce resources for better opportunities.

Do you remember the chicken-or-egg question? Now that we're ready to implement a PPM capability, which should we do first? Do we use the portfolio planning process to prioritize or select projects for the portfolio? Or do we evaluate the currently active projects?

In most cases, the firm will already have a portfolio of projects (or multiple portfolios), although they might not call it by that name. Field experience has shown that this is a good place to start. New implementers of PPM have found that a structured review and evaluation of the existing portfolio can turn up numerous instances of deficiencies in that portfolio. In taking inventory of current project activity, they found projects that should never have been approved and projects that were failing to the point that they would not deliver anything close to their expected benefits.

We mentioned the HP/Compaq inventory of their combined project loads and their decision to eliminate over one hundred projects. This reduced the overall cost burden of the projects and opened up resources for more beneficial opportunities. AXA Financial reports a similar success:

> When I took an as-is snapshot of what the lay of the land looked like, I discovered there were a number of projects behind schedule and over budget and, more important, that all projects were created equal. There was no hierarchy of improvement. There was no sense of how these projects related to our vision, mission, long-term, short-term—any kind of objective you wanted to define.
>
> I bet we saved $5 million to $10 million in the first year alone, on projects that would have automatically gone through before. But, now the business units knew what could get killed, so they killed it first. It just became immediately apparent how much junk we weeded out of the system.[1]

Evaluating the Current Portfolio

It would certainly appear that a good place to start is by taking an inventory of the current project burden. It is not unlikely that the results of such an inventory will more than pay for the efforts invested in implementing the new PPM capability.

As noted in Section 3.2, the evaluation process for projects in the pipeline has two dimensions. The first is performance of the project. Here, we evaluate the project performance against targets that have been set for the project, normally including metrics regarding schedule, resource utilization, costs, deliverables, and quality. The data would include planned status, current status, and forecast performance. Indications of poor performance would be a cause of concern, but it's not the only condition to be considered.

The second dimension to be evaluated is the criteria that were used to select the project in the first place. Has anything changed? Are the project deliverables still needed? Can they be delivered in an acceptable time frame? Are the cost benefits still acceptable? Is the project still aligned with the strategies? Has a competitor beaten you to the punch? Has the market fizzled? Has the technology changed, making this design obsolete?

Actually, many of the projects currently in the pipeline probably were selected without a structured portfolio process, so there are no criteria to be evaluated. It will have to be constructed after the fact (sort of reverse-engineering).

So if the first step in the new PPM process is to evaluate the existing project inventory, the first job of the team is to establish the decision criteria, establish thresholds, and clarify responsibilities for the decisions.

Culture and Project Weeding

Developing a culture that supports the excising of poor projects is not easy. Sometimes you can try to impose a bogey (quota) for reductions, to give it a push. This works with forced personnel cutbacks. Why not for projects? As an alternative, you can impose some key pass-fail criteria associated with items like strategy alignment or budgetary resource or risk limits.

Project Prioritization and Selection

There are some essential steps for initiating the selection phase of PPM. A key step is to make sure that the governance council is in place and that its roles and responsibilities are clear. Another key item is to make sure that the governance council is fully aware of the firm's strategic plans and the tactical options to support the strategies.

There should be a standardized practice for submitting proposed projects to the system. Guidelines spelling out information required from the project sponsor should be published. (See Section 4.2.)

What are the optimum and maximum sizes of the project pipeline? This will be based in part on the availability of resources. You'll want to know these limits before you complete the selection process.

In Section 3.1, we described several options for ranking candidate projects. You can use any or all of these in your PPM system. The team will want to decide which methods to use and make sure that practices and tools are available to support these methods.

PPM Implementation Tips

Instead of deploying the new PPM system across the board all at once, try it out with a pilot program. Make sure that the initial people involved are adventurous supporters (and not reactionaries). Use the pilot to fine-tune the practices before you broadcast them as company standards.

When you're ready to implement the PPM process, the effort would be well served if you employ a checklist, perhaps similar to the questionnaire shown in Exhibit 3–1, prepared by United Management Technologies (UMT).

Executive Support

Finally, let's make sure that there is full executive support. There are several ways to validate that level of support. One is to have the top ex-

Exhibit 3–1 Program Management Questionnaire

Governance

- We have a formal procedure to review projects, approve (funding decisions) submitted project proposals and business case changes, as well as to rationalize our investment portfolio.

- We have clear lines of responsibility and accountability for the technical and financial performance of our projects.

- We use a consistent set of policies to guide the development of estimates (costs, benefits, etc.), to assess progress and to manage projects.

- Every project has a senior business manager/sponsor, who oversees the project definition and budget, and takes responsibility for its success.

Business Case

- Each project proposal identifies the specific business goals and objectives it will support.

- Each submittal includes a description of the scope (what's included, what's omitted) of the proposed effort and the approach (methodology) to be employed, as well as the identification of project overlaps and dependencies.

- We require that each proposal include a detailed work plan consisting of a task breakdown structure, timeline, resources, deliverables and milestones.

- We have a standard framework to quantify the benefits of proposed projects that includes non-financial elements

- A project proposal identifies and assesses all risks associated with the development plan as well as those associated with achieving the promised benefits.

Culture Compatible with Program Management

- We are accustomed to managing multiple projects across business units and/or the regular functional organizational structure.

- We have a recognized, documented standard procedure for capturing and formalizing project ideas from all stakeholders (IT, business, others).

- Our program management office is well-established and respected for its contributions to the organization.

- In our company, key decision makers have demonstrated the judgment and practical experience to interpret status reports, foresee obstacles and react in a timely fashion.

Infrastructure Supportive of Program Management

- We use standardized processes for key project management events—planning, initiation, change control, reporting, etc.

Exhibit 3–1 Program Management Questionnaire, Cont'd.

- Our financial system provides an infrastructure of accounts, internal pricing and resource cost transfer policies compatible with a multi-project environment.
- The projects in our portfolio are selected on the basis of their relative impact on our company's strategic goals and objectives.
- We employ automation tools for project status information collection, aggregation and portfolio analysis.
- We provide training for new project managers and program management office staff.

Analysis and Tracking Processes

- We have a clear strategy and process for the sources of information and the distribution of project portfolio status reports to appropriate decision-making levels.
- Our tracking process includes milestones, budget and resource usage against the approved project plan.
- At the portfolio level, we ensure that inter-project dependencies, overlaps and coordination do not generate scope, timing and resource conflicts.
- Our procedures are designed to ensure consistent quality of all project deliverables.
- We have a robust process for identifying, tracking, analyzing and escalating issues to the appropriate decision makers.
- We periodically replan the entire portfolio of projects to reflect changes in individual projects (scope, benefits, budget, timing) as well as overall business conditions.

Source: United Management Technologies.

ecutive authenticate all of the key role modifications. The roles and responsibilities should show up in revised position guides and in any management-by-objectives metrics. People so affected should receive a letter from the CEO acknowledging the importance of their role in the new PPM process.

Kick the process off with a bang, even if it's just a pilot program. Let people know that this is big. Make it clear to everyone (in a message from the CEO) that "PPM is a way of life in the organization and that support for PPM is a condition of employment."

Implementing PPM Is a Project   People often fail to realize that the development and implementation of a PPM capability is in itself a project and should be handled just like any other major project. Among the significant items and issues to be addressed within this project are these:

- Prepare and issue an approved project charter.
- Prepare and distribute the project plan.
- Prepare a responsibilities matrix, and clarify all roles.
- Develop the PPM processes.
- Select the support tools, and integrate them with existing tools.
- Conduct orientation and training.
- Provide mentoring and conduct implementation audits.
- Begin with pilot portfolios and then expand.

NOTES

Section 3.1

1. Stage-Gate® is a registered term.

Section 3.2

1. Stage-Gate® is a registered term.
2. H. A. Levine, *Practical Project Management: Tips, Tactics, and Tools* (New York: Wiley, 2002).

Section 3.5

1. "Case Study: The Efficient Frontier: AXA Financial Inc.," *CIO Insight,* June 1, 2004.

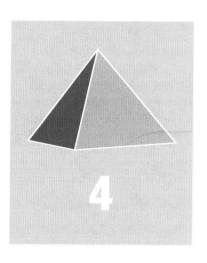

4

The Finer Points of Project Portfolio Management

Integrating operations and projects, fostering better proposals, dealing with risk and uncertainty, applying work breakdown structures to risks and strategies, and understanding earned value analysis: these are topics that will aid in the effective implementation of PPM.

Unit one presented the essentials of PPM without dwelling too long on any particular element. In the sections that follow, we delve into some of the finer points of PPM. Specifically, the six chapters in Section Three contain practical advice for optimizing the benefits that you are certain to gain from implementing a PPM methodology.

Earlier, we suggested that PPM is a way of bridging the gap between the projects and operations sides of the enterprise. In Section 4.1, we expand on that premise by considering that PPM is in reality a hub rather than a bridge. We see PPM as a means of eliminating the gap. We see PPM as the center of a process that brings these two diverse groups together in harmony and purpose to promote the health of the business.

One of the problems with selecting projects for the pipeline is that too many projects are proposed that shouldn't be. A casual meeting at the water cooler ends up producing a pet project for some executive. An innocent phone call from a client generates a request for a modified gizmo assembly. Proposals are instigated for some half-baked idea without prior thought to costs, schedules, impact on resources, value, alignment with strategies, technical feasibility, commercial feasibility, or risk.

Such proposals clog the funnel into the pipeline. Each proposal puts demands on the project management office and the governance council, requiring them to evaluate the proposal prior to rejecting it for any of the deficiencies noted above. In Section 4.2, we propose a process for project prequalification. This process helps to generate improved proposals and significantly reduce the submittal of proposals for bad projects. The use of the prequalification procedure often induces project sponsors to improve their project value and alignment. If they can't find such improvement, they may stop short of forwarding the proposal because they can see that it doesn't support the selection criteria.

Uncertainty and risk are constant companions for any project. We need not fear them, but we must respect them. Suggestions for dealing with uncertainty and risk are presented in Section 4.3. Risk will have an impact on value and benefits. If risk is not considered, the proposed project value and benefits will be erroneous. A project that would get a high priority may very well be rejected if the risk elements are honestly considered. Risk is especially present in development and transformation projects. We need not abandon a project because of high risk, but we will want to look into options to mitigate the risks.

Not all projects are equal. Three typical classifications of projects are utility or maintenance, growth or enhancement, and transformation. The latter is a project for which the goal is to capture a new market or a leap ahead in technology. It has the potential of yielding monumental benefits but requires very special handling. We discuss this in Section 4.4.

Have you been using work breakdown structures (WBSs)? They are extremely valuable and typically are used to develop hierarchies for tasks, resources, budgets, and so on. In Section 4.5, we expand the concept of WBSs to risk and to strategies.

In Section 3.2, we noted the importance of evaluating project performance. We mentioned the concept of earned value analysis and earned value management as practical and powerful methods to monitor project performance. For readers who are not familiar with EVA, we present a primer in Section 4.6.

4.1 DEFINING PPM: A BRIDGE OR A HUB?

> If embraced and supported by senior management, PPM becomes the core of a set of combined business and projects processes, leading to much improved effectiveness in the use of limited cash and human resources.

Some six years ago, I started writing about PPM. With some of my early-adapter colleagues, I recognized the potential power and benefits of this emerging art and science. I then saw PPM as a bridge, connecting the world of projects with the world of business operations.

As I noted in Section 2.1, the basic elements of PPM and the environment in which it is applied are not new. However, before the emergence of PPM as a defined discipline, these elements were the responsibility of two distinct groups, operations management and projects management, each with its specific role:

Operations Management	*Projects Management*
Strategies	Schedule/time
Objectives/goals	Project cost
Business performance	Project performance
Stockholder satisfaction	Stakeholder satisfaction
Project selection and mix	Scope/change control
Resource availability	Resource utilization
Cash flow/income	Cash usage

The gap between these two worlds was very apparent. The projects world was diligently pursuing excellence in project performance, virtually totally oblivious to the strategies of the enterprise and whether its projects were in line with these strategies. The operations side of the business was called on to support these projects with funding and resources, not understanding how or whether these were really the projects that it wanted or needed. There was no way of knowing this.

In the absence of a repeatable structure, neither group could communicate with the other in a meaningful way to make the connection. Communication was further hampered by the lack of a common language. A bridge was needed.

Today I see PPM not as a bridge but as a hub (Figure 4–1). PPM is the nucleus of a system that brings projects and operations together. It is the core of an integrated collection of processes that represent both operations and projects functions. It is also the engine that drives the production of project deliverables to enhance the total health of the enterprise.

Building a bridge between these two functions will not do the job. A bridge acknowledges that a gap exists and does nothing to eliminate the gap. A connection between these two entities is not enough. They must be brought together in unity as distinct roles working in harmony, within a shared system and for a common cause.

PPM ties these distinct functions into an efficient business machine that increases the value and purpose of projects so as to contribute to the overall health and success of the enterprise. It does much more than bridge a gap. It eliminates the gap by bringing these diverse functions together.

The basis for PPM is a rational decision system with these components:

- Having all of the information
- Having analytical processes for effective use of the information
- Having means of communicating with all stakeholders in their language
- Aligning opportunities with objectives
- Conditioning opportunities by assessing and controlling risk
- Eliminating or minimizing office politics and personal favoritism
- Getting all of the disciplines of the enterprise on the same page
- Promoting the use of common sense

PPM as a BRIDGE

OPERATIONS	PROJECTS
Strategies	Schedule, time
Objectives, goals	Project cost
Business performance	Project performance
Stockholder satisfaction	Stakeholder satisfaction
Project selection and mix	Scope, change control
Resource availability	Resource use
Cash flow, income	Cash use

PPM as a HUB

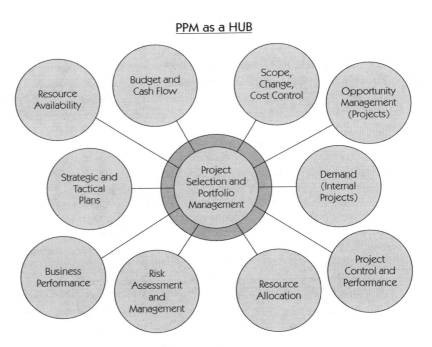

FIGURE 4–1 Project Portfolio Management as a Hub

PPM provides the motivation and the vehicle for all of this. If embraced and supported by senior management, PPM becomes the core of a set of combined business and projects processes, leading to much improved effectiveness in the use of limited cash and human resources. With PPM as the hub for these linked processes, better project portfolios are developed, affording greater opportunities for increased benefits. Feeding the results of project status and performance back into the portfolio management system provides a loop ensuring that the project selection process encompasses both proposed and active projects.

All of these processes have to be connected. The PPM hub is a means to accomplish this. It serves as a place holder for proposed and active projects. It serves as a database for PPM data and a link to other associated data. It serves as a reporting and communication system for information regarding projects and business items. It contains the engines to support rational analysis and decision making.

PPM encompasses several project and operations management processes. It is not just a new piece of the project management picture (a common misconception) or an extension of project management. It is an entirely new discipline that includes project management as an important component. PPM is the hub of a system that makes all of this happen, and it is the glue that holds it all together.

4.2 A PREQUALIFICATION PROCESS FOR SELECTING PROJECTS FOR THE PORTFOLIO

> The prequalification process provides a structured routine that guides the sponsor through the preparation of the proposal, for ranking. Once this is done, the proposal or business case must pass certain tests before the project can get on the candidate list.

The process for prioritizing and selecting projects for inclusion in one or more project portfolios requires the development of a set of data for each project, representing an appraisal of value, benefits, risk, and impact on resources. These data should also consider alignment with strategies, technical feasibility, and miscellaneous other ranking items. This is a lot of work to be performed before a project is even proposed and considered for approval. The project management office (PMO) and the governance council (GC) then invest additional effort in reviewing these data.

All of this effort is for a good cause: building a good portfolio of projects or, better yet, weeding out the bad proposals. Even so, wouldn't it be better to minimize the submission of poor projects and reduce the preparation and review effort for candidate projects? Wouldn't it be better to guide people to consider the critical criteria before running the projects up the flagpole to see if they get a salute?

Prequalification An effective way to accomplish these goals is using a prequalification process. The idea is to follow a structured routine that guides the sponsor through the preparation of the ranking material. Once this is done, the proposal or business case must pass certain tests before the project can get on the candidate list.

As part of the development of the PPM process, the PMO creates a prequalification template. This template has a section for each subject area of the proposal to be considered with questions to guide the sponsor's responses. Periodically (in conjunction with the strategic planning cycle) the prequalification template is updated with the current ranking and selection criteria to reflect the latest thinking relative to strategic buckets, risk philosophy, and financial and resource constraints.

As each project is conceived, a proposal (or business case) is prepared that will include the response to the current prequalification questionnaire. The first objective is one of self-regulation. It is expected that many inappropriate proposals will be withdrawn before being issued because the sponsor will recognize that it doesn't meet the acceptance criteria, or it will be ranked so low as not to make the cut.

At this juncture, projects should be withdrawn for these reasons:

● Not in line with available resources, mission, or other criteria
● Not sound politically, socially, or for business relationships
● Feasible technologically but not economically
● Feasible economically but not technologically
● Involve excessive risk or are not within the risk culture

The prequalification criteria should not be rigid. However, if there are exceptions, the business case must present arguments to pass the prequalification criteria.

Because the prequalification criteria have been published and distributed, sponsors are obligated to address potential issues early. The result is a reduction in the number of bad proposals.

Proposals that are not withdrawn are now reviewed within the PMO for pass-fail against prequalification criteria. The PMO may reject proposals that do not meet the criteria or may pass on recommendations to the GC. The project sponsor may appeal the PMO decision to the GC. A review team will judge whether anyone has a reason to override the prequalification criteria for a particular proposal. They will have to convince others on the committee. The committee may recommend modifications to the proposed project to allow it to pass the prequalification test.

Once the proposed project passes the prequalification test, it is placed in the hopper for the ranking review, the next step. Failed proposals may be fully withdrawn or placed in a second-tier group as backups.

This prequalification routine will save the time and effort to rank proposed projects that don't really have a chance. It will also help to make the number of proposed projects more manageable. Figure 4–1 is a flow diagram of the prequalification process within a PPM system.

The Prequalification Criteria   I suggest that a prequalification template be designed that can be updated with specific values and conditions in accordance with the latest strategies, tactical plans, and corporate culture.

Actually, most operations will have multiple prequalification models. As an example, let's consider an organization that manages three types of projects: maintenance and utility projects, growth or enhancement projects, and transformation projects. It therefore has a portfolio for each type of project and a separate prequalification model for each category.

MAINTENANCE OR UTILITY PROJECTS

Maintenance or utility projects generally support ongoing products and services. When we prioritize these, they might not register as high on the benefits-value scale as some other types of projects. Nevertheless, most organizations earmark funding and resources for these projects. But which ones shall be undertaken?

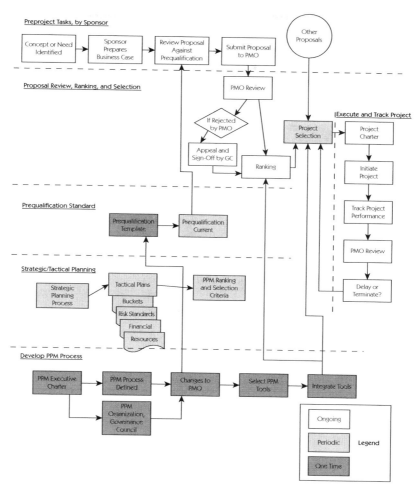

FIGURE 4–2 The Prequalification Process

We can't use the same selection evaluation criteria because these projects will be evaluated to a different standard and set of objectives than the other types of projects. For instance, there may not be a directly measurable value for return on investment (ROI) or net present value (NPV). If we set a single threshold for NPV, maintenance projects might never pass the prequalification test. The strategic plan probably doesn't show anything for maintenance and utility efforts, although we would certainly expect the tactical plans to allocate resources and a budget.

For this category, the prequalification criteria consist more of need and justification data as opposed to cash-based benefits and alignment to strategies. The prequalification questionnaire might ask for evidence of what would suffer if the project were bypassed. It might look for data that shows interdependence with other projects. Some statement of benefits is certainly called for. Alignment criteria cannot be totally ignored. Would we want to select a maintenance project to make improvements to a product or capability that is no longer supported by the firm's strategies? Even for this group, the general PPM practices apply.

GROWTH OR ENHANCEMENT PROJECTS

Growth or enhancement projects are likely to fall nicely into medium-to-high benefit and high-alignment segments of the ranking criteria. By design, these should be projects that support strategic initiatives and represent increasing value. Such projects are needed to keep the firm in a solid competitive position.

For most organizations that employ PPM techniques, the growth or enhancement projects will comprise the bulk of the projects. You can expect serious competition among the proposed projects, making the portfolio planning process critical to efficient and effective project selection. The development of sound prequalification guidelines will help to keep the project sponsors focused on the business objectives and the selection criteria. It will also make it more difficult for them to get carried away with desired benefits, mistaking them for carefully evaluated benefits.

Setting thresholds and ranges that are aligned with the strategies and the tactical plans will be helpful. These should reflect budget and resource allocation objectives, as well as risk guidelines. The process requires that the high-level strategies be transformed into specific tactical plans, with clearly stated objectives and constraints.

TRANSFORMATION PROJECTS

Transformation projects are the opportunities to move the firm to a new level or to introduce new products or services that will dominate the marketplace. This category requires extraordinary diligence starting at the proposal phase. A prequalification model can also be used here, but only as part of the evaluation process. Assuming that the proposed project is aligned with the strategies and guidelines, it will require the preparation of a full business case, complete with three scenarios: most likely, potential upside, and potential downside.

We can expect these projects to exhibit a higher risk profile. However, the potential benefits can be so great as to place the project off the scale when we plot NPV or ROI. There is also a greater sensitivity to the benefits and risk data for transformation projects, especially when there is an indefinite window of opportunity. Multiple scenarios, as presented in the business case, will produce considerably different values for benefits and risk. The range of these values is in itself a value to be considered. A conservative strategy, if that is the culture, would have you rank the more sensitive projects (those with a higher differential between case extremes) a bit lower than a project that has less uncertainty. You can't mix transformation-type projects with growth projects or use the same prequalification criteria for both types of projects.

Transformation projects may be "bet the firm's future" projects. Failure to select the right projects in this category will lead not only to failure of the project, but will also waste the monetary and human resources that could have been used for a better opportunity. It is difficult to sustain business growth without periodic transformation projects. To choose wisely is to protect the future of the enterprise.

4.3 THE IMPACT OF UNCERTAINTY ON PROJECTS AND THE PORTFOLIOS _____

> Uncertainty is an element of all projects. Risk in projects must be recognized, evaluated, and considered as part of the project prioritization and selection process, as well as during the execution of selected projects. In managing risk, the goal is to minimize the potential for failure to achieve the project's benefits.

When we execute any of the ranking and prioritization schemes, we are basing our decisions on data that is assumed to be precise. In fact, almost all of the data is fraught with uncertainty.

Uncertainty is part of the definition of a project. We are either doing something for the first time or are inventing or developing or designing or experimenting. We are operating in a variable environment, where some of the conditions are beyond our direct control. We are depending on the contributions of others. A slight delay, a change in the exchange rate, a failure of an experiment, an act of nature: each of these can turn a promising project into a disappointment.

Disregarding all of this, we take the assumed values and submit the data to a very exacting routine, generating a set of numerical values that we take to the bank. What we are likely to have is erroneous because it assumes results that are based on a specific set of circumstances that have little chance of occurring exactly as planned. Then we extend this data to four decimal places, based on the assumed results, which will only give us a very precise error.

Developing a Range of Values

So what are we to do? I would not for a moment suggest abandoning the effort to quantify the value of proposed projects. But we do have to look at this data as a function of the surrounding environment. We have to recognize that uncertainty exists. We have to evaluate the source and degree of uncertainty. We have to attempt to reduce uncertainty and contain the effects of risk events. We have to look at the data as a range of values rather than a single precise value.

Throughout this book, there are references to viewing a project portfolio as we would an investment portfolio. In the world of investments, we acknowledge that there are risks. We usually choose investments with some recognition of the events that can affect the results and what the acceptable range of results is. Many business decisions require the preparation of a business case. Each case will contain three scenarios: a most likely, a best case (potential upside), and a worst case (potential downside). A wise decision is based on considering all three scenarios. The proposal may be rejected if the potential downside has more than a remote probability and the worst-case results would make the business opportunity too unattractive.

We need to apply a similar approach to proposed projects—for instance:

1. Conduct a formal risk evaluation of the project and all of its segments.
2. Identify potential risk events.

3. Weigh the probability of the risk event occurrence.
4. Estimate the impact of the risk event, should it occur.
5. Identify possible ways to reduce risk (mitigation).
6. Calculate the cost of mitigation actions and the effect of these actions on the risk impact.
7. Incorporate the variables into the project valuation.
8. Extend the valuation to a range of expected results.
9. Consider each of the scenarios.

Defining a Policy for Uncertainty

The consideration of risk is a normal component of the portfolio-planning process. But we have to be careful about how the risk is factored in. For instance, some of the formulas call for modifying the expected benefits by the risk percentage. This can be misleading. Let's use the *Titanic* for an example. We'll say that the net present value (NPV) of the investment is calculated as $50 million. There is a 10 percent chance that the ship will hit an iceberg during the first year and sink. Is it reasonable to modify the NPV to $45 million?

No! What we have here is a case where the risk event would totally eliminate any return on the investment. The issue is not how much to modify the benefit. It is whether the governance council is willing to consider a project that might fail entirely.

This is an issue that has to be addressed by those responsible for implementing the tactical plans in support of the strategic plan. If we recognize that uncertainty is part of the game and that in some cases the degree of uncertainty can seriously negate the expected benefits, then surely a risk policy is needed.

At the executive level, guidance should be provided relative to how much risk is acceptable. The guidelines might spell out a risk balance, with a mix of high-risk and low-risk projects within a portfolio or a limit to one (or a specified number) of high-risk projects.

Getting back to the *Titanic* illustration, what if we mitigate the risk? We insure the ship. Certainly that is an option. But now we have to consider the effect of the mitigation on the income model. First, there is the cost of the insurance. If it is $2 million, we have to factor that cost into the NPV for the base case. We still have to have a figure for the effect of destruction of the ship from collision with an iceberg. The insurance is not likely to cover the income that would be lost, only the loss of the property. So we would still have a risk-based income odel that is substantially below the $50 million.

Dealing Honestly with Risk

Uncertainty is an ever-present element of the project environment. Risk is not necessarily bad. In fact, many of the best opportunities have considerable risk. The key is to make sure that the risk is fully disclosed and considered. This can be ensured only if there is a proactive culture to address risk, backed up by mandated and audited practices. There is considerable danger that enthusiastic or biased project sponsors will hide potential risks or discount the impact of potential risks.

Here's a scene played out regularly in the corporate world. The project case is presented. There is a most likely scenario, plus a potential upside and a potential downside.

The sponsor then says to ignore the downside because the downside won't happen. No one can will the downside to go away. You not only have to be honest enough to recognize the risk. You also have to acknowledge the necessity to deal with risk.

Remember the saying, "If you can't stand the heat, then stay out of the kitchen"? For projects, it can be reworded as, "If you can't stand uncertainty, then stay out of the projects business." But don't let the uncertainty be an enemy. Recognize it and deal with it.

Dealing with Uncertainty and Change in the Active Portfolio

Think about digital photography for a moment. There are two types. One is the still shot, a photograph of something taken at a specific point in time. The other is the video, a continual photograph taken over a span of time.

What does this have to do with PPM? Diagnostic and reporting tools essentially take snapshots. They provide a view of projects and portfolios at a single point in time. Yet projects and portfolios are not stagnant. They are dynamic and ever changing. In a perfect world, we would toss out our still camera and replace it with a video camera. But this is not practical.

What we can do is to recognize the dynamics and be prepared to deal with change and uncertainty. Uncertainty is a by-product of change and exists in every project. We make plans and generate estimates, then make decisions based on these plans and estimates.

If you look at an active portfolio, it consists of projects that were selected based on data that was available before the projects were activated. Once the project is initiated, the uncertainties start to move us in directions that were not planned. Periodically, we have to ask, "Would we have made the same decision on the basis of the data that we have now?"

So the first few things to acknowledge are these:

● The projects selected will have risk and uncertainty.
● This risk and uncertainty will result in change, either unplanned or corrective.
● The changes (including performance issues) may negate the basis for the original selection decision.
● Our picture is changing. Are we satisfied with the direction that it is taking us?

What About Projects with High Uncertainty?

Many projects, especially in the new product development area (this includes software development), have a high degree of uncertainty. It is the very nature of these types of projects to exhibit increased uncertainty in the later phases. That is, it is the objective of the earlier phases to define the later ones. As the project moves through the phases, the degree of uncertainty should diminish. At the proposal phase, can the technical or commercial success be ensured, or is this just the desired objective, subject to risk?

The worse thing we can do in this case is to say that "the project is too uncertain" to apply risk assessment techniques. In fact, it is these types of projects that need risk assessment the most. The challenge is not so much in identifying potential risks as it is in quantifying them with any precision.

So rather than ignoring the matter, we can best address the problem by processing the risk assessment in stages. At the proposal stage, we need to identify as many of the potential risks as possible. For each, we rough out a potential range of probability and impact, specifically noting the risk areas that can ruin the project. We also note if there are any options to contain these risks and when we would have to know to implement these options. Once the project is initiated, the risk items should be revisited at the end of each phase, especially as each phase helps to define the succeeding phases.

Managing Risk Mitigation Options

Before we address the effect of change on decisions, I want to stay a bit longer with the discussion of risk and uncertainty. We addressed this earlier when we evaluated risk on proposed projects and took into account the impact of risk on the benefits model. If we did not reject the project outright due to unacceptable risk, we identified potential risk events and potential risk mitigation options. Some of these options will have been chosen prior to project selection. Others may have been backup mitigation options, to be employed sometime during the project execution, based on risk events.

Therefore, managing risk in the active portfolio requires:

- Identifying the points in time where decisions regarding mitigation options should be made. These should be noted in the project schedule.
- Allowing some lead time just prior to the decision point for the review and decision process.
- Incorporating the effect of the risk/mitigation decision issue into the project valuation data to allow reconsideration of the selection decision.
- Repeatedly asking, "Are we satisfied with the direction that the project is taking?"

Three Levels of Review and Action

Now let's visit the issue of evaluating changes in timing, costs, resource demand, benefits, or deliverables. When do we do this? We can't do it on a continuing basis, as with a video camera. So how often should we take a snapshot? There is no single right answer to this question. However, we can let three levels of review and decision making serve as a guide.

LEVEL 1: PERIODIC PROJECT STATUS REVIEW

The first level, the periodic project status review, will probably be performed monthly, but it should be performed more often for short-duration or highly sensitive (critical) projects. At this level, the typical review consists of comparing current status to the plan. Have key milestones been met? Are technical or design issues threatening project success? Variances to schedule and cost will be evaluated. Trend data showing a continuing degradation of performance should be highlighted. The effect of excessive variances (outside a declared tolerance level) should be evaluated, and, if warranted, brought to the attention of higher management. The project manager should maintain an awareness of the decision criteria on which the project selection was based. However, unless there is an obvious indication of a critical degradation, the portfolio selection process is not invoked at this time. (See Section 4.6 for a description of the earned value analysis method for evaluating project performance.)

LEVEL 2: PHASE-LEVEL REVIEW

Most projects should be broken down into segments called phases or stages. The end point of each phase usually represents a point where the entire project should undergo review of all aspects. For instance, a typical early project phase is the feasibility study. The deliverable of this phase is an appraisal of the likelihood that the defined project objectives will be met. If the result is a recommendation that the project objectives are unattainable, then the decision is simple. But in all likelihood, the results are that the objectives can be met with some higher degree of difficulty, or that part of the solution is not feasible, or that the technical objectives can be met but at a higher cost.

This is a critical point in the PPM process. If the results of any phase-level review indicate that the original business case for the project is no longer supported, then the business case needs to be amended and reevaluated. This process of evaluating projects at the end of each phase is often called Stage-Gate® or phase-gate.[1] (See Section 5.1 for more on this process.)

The Stage-Gate reviews should also include a checklist of all associated risk mitigation option items. We are managing projects with uncertainty. We need to maintain vigilance over performance and risk issues.

LEVEL 3: PERIODIC PROJECT SELECTION REVIEW

This is a regular review of proposed projects and the selection of projects for the portfolio. During this review process, all ongoing projects that are in danger of not meeting set objectives should be put through the review. It is at this time that current projects (those that have not previously been paused or dropped as a result of the Stage-Gate review) may be considered for delay or termination, and replaced by proposed projects that better support the business goals.

Summary

Uncertainty is an element of all projects. Risk in projects must be recognized, evaluated, and considered as part of the project prioritization and selection process, as well as during the execution of selected projects. In managing risk, the goal is to minimize the potential for failure to achieve the project's benefits. The risk-based process has these key elements:

- Evaluate proposed projects against the selection criteria using each business case scenario: once with the base case and again with the potential upside and downside case data.
- Consider bypassing a proposed project that has excessive risk. Make sure that there is a clear policy for risk, and then adhere to it.
- Reduce the ranking of a proposed project where the range of risk-based results is large. A high level of uncertainty is not a desirable condition.
- Where risk is large enough to demote a project, consider risk mitigation options to contain such risk.
- Add the cost of mitigation actions (if any) to the project proposal data.
- Balance risk, that is, don't put too many high-risk projects in a portfolio.
- Don't stop with project selection. Consider the effect of risk and change in ongoing projects.

- Conduct periodic project status reviews. Note any items that can influence the decision to have that project in the portfolio. Consider delay or termination where warranted.
- Conduct periodic Stage-Gate reviews. Include significant risk milestones.
- Consider active projects as well as proposed projects when conducting the periodic ranking, selection, and resource allocation exercises.

4.4 IS THERE A GORILLA IN YOUR PORTFOLIO? TURNING OPPORTUNITY INTO VALUE

> Gorillas are products that dominate a market, placing the company in an extraordinarily powerful position. Companies with gorilla products or services can experience 30 to 40 percent growth per quarter. Gorilla projects require special handling.

Most discussions of the project portfolio describe several different types of projects for the makeup of portfolios. In Section 4.2, we introduced three general types: maintenance or utility projects, growth or enhancement projects, and transformation projects.

These discussions suggested that the typical portfolio consists of a balance of these types of projects. The nature of the business will dictate the proper makeup and balance of its portfolio. Balance does not mean that the portfolios are equal. For instance, the three examples stated here have a considerably different effect on the business, with the potential impact of the transformation projects being higher than the other types.

Maintenance or utility projects generally support ongoing products and services. When we prioritize these, they might not register as high on the benefits-value scale as some other type of projects. Yet they can be important even if they are not especially attractive or exciting. These types of projects are essential to maintaining current capabilities even if they don't show a direct return on investment (ROI).

Growth or enhancement projects are likely to fall into medium- to high-benefit and high-alignment segments of the ranking criteria. By design, these should be the projects that support strategic initiatives and represent increasing value. Such projects are needed to keep the firm in a solid competitive position. In today's technological environment, no business can succeed by maintaining the status quo.

Therefore, the typical business will have at least two project portfolios (or divisions of their portfolio): one for utility projects and another for enhancement projects. Strategy buckets will be established with goals and budgets attached to each, as well as resources allocated to each.

A third bucket will often be established for transformation projects. These are the opportunities to move the firm to a new level or to introduce new products or services that will dominate the marketplace. Although the projects in this category might exhibit a higher risk profile, the potential benefits can be so great as to place the project off the scale when plotting net present value or ROI. However, these numbers are extremely sensitive to market timing and success and must be treated with some skepticism.

Transformation projects require special handling. When we compute a benefits number for these projects, we are assuming a particular return based on a specific market position. Whether this assumed market position is attained depends on several factors, and whether this assumed market position is attained will have a monumental effect on benefits. I refer to these as gorilla projects, based on research conducted and reported by Geoffrey Moore.[1]

What Is a Gorilla?

According to Moore, gorillas are products that dominate a market, placing the company in an extraordinarily powerful position. Companies with gorilla products (or gorilla services) can experience 30 to 40 percent growth per quarter. Gorillas can be so strong as to force any potential competitor to search for a niche market instead.

Managing the Gorilla Project

The gorilla project, if it is to be successful, requires every possible advantage that can come from superior project management diligence. Here are some special characteristics to consider.

PLANNING

Although it is quite possible that the plans will change, it is essential at least to start with a plan. However, the planning process must be very dynamic. The gorilla project will often be based on leading-edge technology. As the project moves along, we may find that we must deviate from the initially preferred path and should be ready to select alternate strategies. The ability to have alternate plans and to perform what-if evaluations quickly and frequently is essential in this environment.

TIMING

For the gorilla project, speed is of the essence. The second firm to offer the new product or service does not become the gorilla. Only the first gets to claim that title and the spoils that go with it. The plan must consider every possible way to shorten the time-to-market cycle. Every exception to the defined plan or any delay must be evaluated for effect on the opportunity to be first to market. Therefore, the plan must be carefully monitored, and pressure must be maintained to prevent loss of critical time.

DECISION POINTS

The gorilla project has a finite time window. If the window of opportunity is missed, even the most successful and advanced technical accomplishment may lose out to a lesser product or service that makes it to the market first. This overall time window must be broken down into smaller units, marking key decision points along the way. The plan must identify these decision points. The team must be aware of upcoming decision points (or gates) and be prepared to make the decisions that are required to keep the project on track.

RISK

Significant risk is a normal component of the gorilla project. However, such risk can be managed. To do so, the potential risks must first be identified and then quantified as to probability of occurrence and consequence of occurrence. For all high-impact risks, a mitigation plan should be prepared. After these tasks have been performed (risk identification, quantification, and mitigation), we evaluate whether the risk is acceptable (for example, are there less risky approaches to the same objective?). Finally, we monitor all risk areas, being prepared to apply mitigation strategies where warranted.

SCHEDULE RISK

Schedule risk is especially sensitive for the gorilla project. Tools are available to evaluate critical path schedules for the probability of meeting calculated project completion dates. Traditional critical path scheduling techniques will deliver a plan having 50 percent or less probability of being executed by the dates calculated. If your project can't accept this low confidence factor, you can use Monte Carlo scheduling techniques to develop and evaluate schedules having a higher degree of safety. (Monte Carlo–based risk software is available from several companies, including Pertmaster, Palisade, and C/S Solutions.) A common alternative is to insert selective schedule contingency elements. These are dummy tasks, placed in strategic paths that represent a shared contingency for the work along that path. Avoid adding contingency to individual tasks. It will be construed to mean that there is additional time available to complete these tasks. An alternate scheduling technique (employing shared contingency) is the critical chain method, based on the theory of constraints.

COMMUNICATION

Communication is the greatest in importance. Communication, especially for the gorilla project, will have great impact on project success. Frequent communication among all stakeholders, in formats that convey essential information and in ways that promote and facilitate the desired responses to action items, must be the foundation of any project management system for gorilla projects. Decisions can't be made in a vacuum. Nor can they be made if no one knows that the decision is required. A system of alarms and alerts that highlight items needing attention and that are distributed promptly to the proper parties is a part of such a system.

Time-to-Market

You might be thinking, *Aren't these things that should be done for all projects?* Of course, they are. However, on many projects, you might get away without being very diligent in applying these basic project management principles. When it comes to the gorilla project, there is no room for being casual about it.

Getting back to the significance of being the first to market, Moore has some interesting figures to offer on this. He says that when a new product is created for a new market, the first one getting to market is most likely to garner at least 50 percent of the total market. The remaining 50 percent is all that will remain for all of the other players. No wonder that there is so much pressure on new developments (and perhaps why some developers are willing to skimp on quality rather than chance delays).[2]

There's more. If the first vendor to the market garners 50 percent of possible sales, while vendor 2 picks up, say, 20 percent, that is not the probable ratio for income. That is because vendor 1 sets the price, which, without competition, allows maximizing profits and return on investment. By the time the other vendors join the battle, profit margins will drop (but only after vendor 1 has made its killing). Moore figures that vendor 1 will garner at least 70 percent of the profits pie in this model.

Is that enough motivation to drive schedule compression and management?

Every day that can be squeezed out of the schedule improves the developer's chances of grabbing the lion's share of the market. Every day of slippage that is avoided due to diligent management of the project can bring the spoils of being the gorilla closer to home. The new product developer must not only invest effort in creating fast-track schedules, but must also continually tweak the schedule looking for ways to shorten the time cycles. The payoff for getting there first can be monumental.

Gorillas in the Portfolio

Recognizing the extreme sensitivity of time-to-market, we have to be very careful of the values that we declare for the potential benefits from transformation projects. If we assume that we will be first-to-market (the gorilla), the declared benefits will be exceedingly higher than not being the leader. If we do use the higher figures, we have to make sure that the project has enough visibility and priority to meet the window of opportunity. As long as the project remains on track to be a gorilla, it should rate the highest priority for critical resources.

We have to continually monitor the position of the project against the window of opportunity. If it looks as if the window will be missed and corrective actions are not available, the benefit calculations will have to be revised. This may change the ranking of the project.

The gorilla portfolio should have continual executive attention. The success of its component projects represents the highest benefit-to-cost potential among all projects and portfolios. Time-to-market is a critical aspect of these projects. The one who scores first almost always wins.

4.5 WORK BREAKDOWN STRUCTURES FOR RISK AND STRATEGIES ⎯⎯⎯⎯⎯⎯

> Work breakdown structures are popular mechanisms for creating hierarchical arrangements for project tasks, resources, cost buckets, and organizations. In this chapter, we expand the WBS concept to risk and strategies.

Most practitioners of project management are familiar with work breakdown structures (WBS). We use the WBS format to create a hierarchical structure of the work in a project. We have also adapted WBS technology to organizations (OBS), resources (RBS), and finances. Let's look at applying WBS concepts to aligning projects with strategies.

A WBS for Strategies

Figure 4–3 presents a matrix-style WBS for strategies. In this example, we show a one-layer vertical WBS and a one-layer horizontal WBS. (There can be additional layers, but we've tried to keep this example simple.)

FIGURE 4–3 Strategies Work Breakdown Structure in a Matrix Format

Alignment Matrix	STRATEGIC INITIATIVES			
	Generate Income	Reduce Costs	Reduce Head Count	Establish New Market Beachhead
Desktop and Notebook Computers	Add build-to-order capability	Outsource customer support to India	Outsource customer support to India	Add build-to-order capability
Specialty Computers (PDA, Pocket PC)				New leading-edge pocket PC
Servers and Networks		Move European plants to China		
Printers		Outsource customer support to India	Outsource customer support to India	
Displays	Add plasma line	Build new plant in Mexico		
Other	Develop new advertising program	R&D for packaging	Outsource surveys and marketing research	

S T R A T E G I C   B U S I N E S S   U N I T

The vertical WBS represents strategic business units (SBUs) or product lines. Here it is assumed that each SBU will be aligning its projects with the various strategic buckets. The horizontal WBS represents four business strategies.

Each proposed project is placed in the matrix to show alignment with an SBU and a strategic bucket. Note that it is possible to have a project support more than one strategy. In this example, we show two SBUs with plans to outsource customer support. This tactical initiative (to be conducted jointly by the two SBUs) supports two strategies: "Reduce Costs" and "Reduce Head Count."

The strategies WBS serves as a visual display of how projects are aligned with SBUs and strategic buckets. If desired, the project boxes can be color-coded to distinguish proposed projects from approved projects, and additional data can be added (for example, ranking scores, internal or external client, or internal or external resources).

The matrix-style display also provides a visual indication of which strategies are not being supported and which SBUs are not participating.

Figure 4–4 presents the strategies WBS in a bubble chart format. This chart contains all of the information as the matrix in Figure 4–3, plus data on the size (net present value) of each of the candidate projects. Through the use of bubble sizing and color, such a chart can present up to four aspects of the data (x-axis, y-axis, bubble size, and bubble color).

A WBS for Risk

Using the WBS approach for risk works even better than the SBS. In the example provided in Figure 4–5, we use the WBS primarily as a structured checklist.

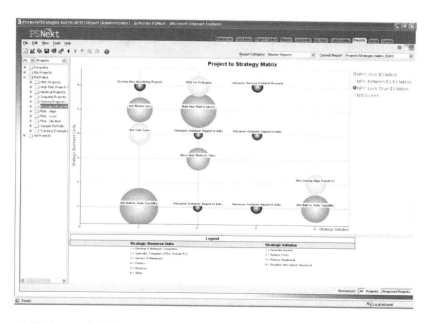

FIGURE 4–4 Strategies Work Breakdown Structure as a Bubble Chart

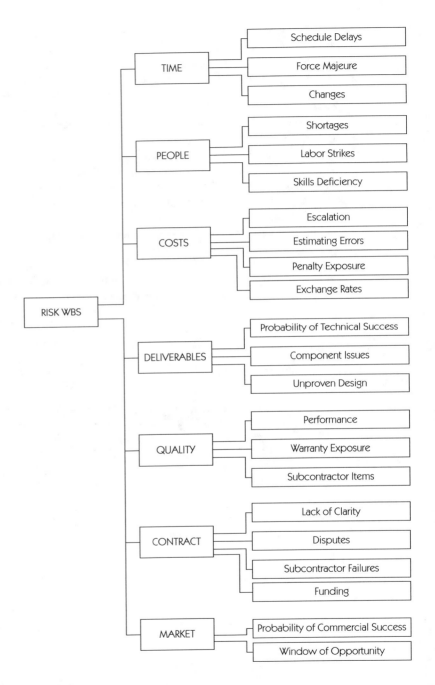

FIGURE 4–5 Risk Breakdown Structure Diagram

At the first level of the risk WBS, we list seven categories for risk consideration: time, people, costs, deliverables, quality, contract, and market. (Obviously there can be others.) For each of these categories, we list any areas where there could be a risk issue. For instance, under the category of cost, we might ask, "Are there any risk issues associated with escalation, estimating errors, penalty exposure, or exchange rates?" These are the areas where issues often arise that can upset the cost projections developed to support the project proposal.

In developing a cost figure, we assume a number for escalation. In the risk assessment exercise, we have to ask, "What is the range of possible escalation on items that are sensitive to such escalation?" Then we ask, "What is the effect on cost?" We would also probe the project estimating data, looking for areas that might be sensitive to an estimating error. Is this a risk item?

Is there a penalty condition in the contract? What risks to cost (or income) does this present? Are we dealing with multiple currencies? Is there a risk to cost (or income) because of unexpected exchange rate changes? I have experienced a major international project where all aspects of the project were completed with great success and the firm lost money on it because of significant and damaging changes in the exchange rate.

Using the WBS as a Checklist   There's a good chance that your project does not have exchange rate or penalty exposure. No problem! You just cross that off the checklist that the risk WBS represents. It is much easier to start with a list of all possible items and to delete those that do not apply rather than start out with a blank sheet of paper (or a blank screen) and try to think of risk items.

Templates can be developed for each type of common project. The proposal manager deletes items that don't apply and adds items that are unique to that project. Actually, even better than deleting nonapplicable items is to mark them *N/A*. This serves as an audit trail, showing that the item was considered.

Some of the second-level items can easily belong in more than one place. This is not important. What is important is that they show up somewhere and are not overlooked.

Assessing and   On each of these second-level items, the first question is, "Does it ap-
Mitigating Risk   ply?" If the answer is yes, then describe the potential risk event. For each event, you then need to assess the potential effect on schedule, cost, resources, deliverables, technical objectives, and commercial objectives. The potential effect is the product of two estimates. First, what is the probability that the event will occur? Second, what is the impact of the event if it does happen?

Finally, you consider options for containing the risks. Look for options to reduce the probability of risk occurrence and minimize the impact of risk events should they occur.

Steps in Dealing with Risk Issues

1. Determine the probability of the event.
   - Consider the ability to reduce probability.
   - Can you insure, find an alternative, or reduce the risk?
2. Determine the impact of the event.
   - Consider the ability to reduce the impact.
   - Can you insure, find an alternative, or reduce the risk?
3. What is the cost to mitigate the risk?
4. What is the ability to absorb the impact?
   - Consider schedule contingency, cost contingency, and the design margin, for example.
5. Can the impact be shifted to others?
   - Consider cost plus, extras, or that the client or sponsor might accept a lesser product.

Summary

- More people have written about risk management than have practiced it. Risk management is a way of dealing with uncertainty in projects. Every project has some degree of uncertainty. Therefore, every project requires risk management.
  - ➤ Risk assessment and management (RAM) requires a structured, proactive approach.
  - ➤ A risk WBS is a valuable element of a structured RAM system.
- An "accurate estimate" is an oxymoron.
  - ➤ How reliable is your information?
- How sensitive is the project to the risks?
  - ➤ What is the ability to absorb impacts? For example, being late for a dinner reservation can be tolerated. Being late for a cruise ship departure cannot.
- Avoid redundant or cumulative contingency.
  - ➤ Contingency is important. Without it, you will finish late and over budget. However, there is a tendency to pile on contingencies so that they are redundant. To avoid this, consider shared contingency. Apply contingency to groups rather than individual items. For instance, apply schedule contingency for a string of tasks rather than to each task. Apply cost contingency to work packages, not individual line items.
- A guarantee against all risk may not be practical or economically feasible.
- Risk is dynamic.
  - ➤ The probability and impact of risk can change as the project progresses. Consider the time dimensions of risk and when to address the risk issues.
- Maintain a risk issues directory.
  - ➤ Log all risk items. Identify a responsible party for each risk issue. Maintain an audit trail of all communications and actions. Flag open risk items.

- Don't forget the big picture.
  - ➤ Consider risk issues at the project level. How well is the organization situated to do this project? What is the organization's risk culture? What risk guidelines have been established at the strategic level?

4.6 AN INTRODUCTION TO EARNED VALUE ANALYSIS

> A key component of PPM is improved management of the project pipeline. We conduct performance reviews of active projects with the objective of considering termination of projects that no longer support the conditions on which approval was granted. An essential capability for such performance reviews is the process of Earned Value Analysis. The ability to monitor schedule and cost variances in a consistent, structured manner provides key data for performance reviews and removes personal biases from the evaluation.

Do you cringe when someone brings up the subject of Earned Value Management (EVM) or Earned Value Analysis (EVA)? Do you see yourself drowning in torrents of seemingly obscure data, generated by some space age software that has run amok? And what about all that alphabet soup? What the heck are BCWS, SPI, and ACWP?

If you're into project management, you've probably heard of EVA and maybe even tinkered with it. Unfortunately, there is a widespread misconception that EVA is only for the big aerospace and defense jobs, where the customer is the government. If you're working on these kinds of projects, you've probably read up on earned value, perhaps the highly recognized text by EVM guru Quentin Fleming, which is crammed with 560 pages of really good stuff on "Cost/Schedule Control Systems Criteria" (the Department of Defense's version of EVM).[1] Or maybe you are familiar with the downsized discussion on "Earned Value Project Management," published by Project Management Institute (PMI), still inviting the reader to digest 140 pages.[2]

The good news is that you can pick up the essentials of EVA in about five pages, and you don't have to use all of the available EVA features in order to benefit from EVA.

EVA Made Easy
I am a real believer in EVA. Although I fully understand its intricacies and power, I can also sympathize with the novice project management practitioner who feels overwhelmed by the seemingly complicated EVA concepts. I also have found through actual field experience that the concepts of EVA can be effectively applied in virtually every project situation, from very complex to the absurdly simple.

There are two things that you should know about learning and using EVA. First, there are just a few basic concepts, which you can learn in an hour or less. Second, you can use and benefit from EVA without applying the entire set of capabilities. The basic application of EVA is an easy and practical way to monitor and evaluate project performance. So I offer here a stripped-down version of an EVA (Earned Value Analysis) primer.

The entire EVA practice essentially consists of about six key measurement values. We actually use these values in the planning and tracking of a project, even though we often don't give them names or structure.

ESTABLISHING A BASELINE

If we are going to evaluate project performance by measuring cost and schedule variance, then we have to have a *baseline* to measure against. So the first two values that we use actually show up in the project plan before we track progress. First, there is the *BAC (Budget at Completion),* which is a value that we assign to a task or any part of the project. The most common budgets are based on cost, but in place of an actual dollar value, it can also be a labor value (such as planned hours) or any other value that provides a weight factor for the task. For example, if you are tracking spent time rather than actual money expenditures, you can set the BAC values based on the labor estimates for the tasks.

The second plan value is the *BCWS (Budgeted Cost of Work Scheduled).* The BCWS is the weighted value of the task at a specific point in time during its planned execution. For instance, if a task with a budget of $5,000 were scheduled to be executed between February 15 and March 15, the BCWS on March 1 would be $2,500 (50% of the BAC). The BCWS on March 15 is $5,000. We'll use the BCWS to determine the schedule variance.

The PMI Exposure Draft for EVM offers alternative (more sensible) terms for three basic EVA nomenclature items. For example, it suggests PV (Planned Value) as an alternative for BCWS. In addition, it substitutes EV (Earned Value) for the traditional term "Budgeted Cost of Work Performed" (BCWP), and AC (Actual Cost) for the traditional term "Actual Cost of Work Performed" (ACWP).

For readers who are new to the earned value concepts, I feel that it is easier to work with the newer terms. Therefore, in this section, we will use the following:

PV = Planned Value = BCWS = Budgeted Cost of Work Scheduled
EV = Earned Value = BCWP = Budgeted Cost of Work Performed
AC = Actual Cost = ACWP = Actual Cost of Work Performed

CALCULATING EARNED VALUE

The next two values are created when we track the project. Both of these are periodic values. That is, they relate to a specific date during the life of the project (as does the PV). The key component of the entire EVA process is the *BCWP (Budgeted Cost of Work Performed).* Does this term confuse you? Then we will call it the *"Earned Value" (EV),* which is what it is.

Computation of EV couldn't be more elementary. It is the percent complete (%C) of a task times the budget (BAC). If on March 1, our $5,000 task is declared to be 40% complete, then the EV is $2,000. How simple can it get? EV = %C × BAC. 40% × $5,000 = $2,000. Stating this once more, *the earned value is the percent complete times the budget.*

If you're using resource hours instead of costs, the process is the same. If the BAC is 200 hours and the percent complete is 40%, then the EV is 80 hours.

The second tracking item is actual cost. In EVA-land, it is called *ACWP (Actual Cost of Work Performed).* We'll be calling it *AC.* If as of March 1 our subject task has accumulated $2,400 in costs, then the AC is $2,400. Still simple, right?

THE FOUR BASIC MEASUREMENTS

Reviewing what we have learned thus far, there are four basic measurements. As part of the plan, we have the item budget (BAC) and the planned value of the work to be performed at a specified time (PV). As part of the tracking, we add the earned value (EV) and the actual cost to date (AC). With these measurements, we can evaluate project performance using variance and trend analysis. *It all comes down to Cost Variance and Schedule Variance.*

Measuring Cost Performance: Cost Variance and Cost Performance Index

For cost performance evaluation, we need only two pieces of data: earned value and the actual cost. We use these data to compute the cost variance. The *CV (Cost Variance)* is the earned value minus the actual cost. The calculation is: EV – AC = CV. Using our example, it is 2,000 –2,400 = –400.

Again, although we use the term *cost,* it also works with labor hours (or any other weight factor). If the EV is 80 hours and the AC is 96 hours, the CV is –16.

It is actually more useful to express this variance as a fraction. The *CPI (Cost Performance Index)* is the EV *divided* by the AC, or 2,000/2,400 = 0.8333. We are looking for a CPI that is 1.000 or greater, so this 0.8333 signifies subpar cost performance. We spent $2,400 to do $2,000 worth of work (or 96 hours to do 80 hours of work).

Measuring Schedule Performance: Schedule Variance and Schedule Performance Index

The process is similar for computing the schedule variance. The *SV (Schedule Variance)* is the earned value minus the planned value. The calculation is: EV – PV = SV. Using our example, it is 2,000 – 2,500 = -500.

Again, the more useful expression is the *SPI (Schedule Performance Index),* which is EV *divided* by PV. Here, our SPI is 2,000/2,500 = 0.800. Looking at the SPI, we can easily see that we are behind schedule. The SPI indicates that we are executing the work at a rate of 80% of the planned rate.

That's essentially all that there is to this whole EVA mystique. Table 4–1 provides a quick review.

You Don't Have to Do Both CV and SV

Let's make it even simpler. Let's say that you are not tracking actual costs or actual hours. Obviously, you cannot compute the cost variance. But that doesn't stop you from tracking the progress and computing the schedule variance. All that you need is a plan, as represented by the BAC and PV, and the periodic tracking of the percentage complete, expressed as the EV. With these data, you can determine the SV and the SPI.

A similar option applies to cost. You don't even have to have a baseline plan to process cost variances. What you must have is (1) a budget (or weight factor), (2) a measurement of percent complete (which is used to determine the EV [EV = %C × budget]), and (3) the actual cost (AC). You just need to compare what you spent to the value of what you accomplished.

Table 4–1. A Glossary of EVA Terms

Term	Explanation
BAC (Budget at Completion)	The budget
BCWS (Budgeted Cost of Work Scheduled) (a.k.a. PV)	Planned accomplishment (at any point in time)
BCWP (Budgeted Cost of Work Performed) (a.k.a. EV)	Earned value or accomplishment value (at any point of time)
ACWP (Actual Cost of Work Performed) (a.k.a. AC)	Actual cost to date
SV (Schedule Variance)	Difference between planned accomplishment and EV
CV (Cost Variance)	Difference between actual cost and EV
SPI (Schedule Performance Index)	Earned value divided by planned value
CPI (Cost Performance Index)	Earned value divided by actual cost

A Common Cost Measurement Mistake

There is a common mistake made in traditional cost performance analysis (non-EVA) where the actual cost is compared to the planned cost. This is fundamentally wrong. Just look at our example. Following this flawed practice, the accountants might report that the cost performance is favorable (spent $2,400 against the plan of $2,500). However, only $2,000 of work has actually been accomplished. The ugly truth is that the item is both behind schedule and over budget. Without earned value, there is no valid performance analysis.

Trends Are the Most Revealing

A report of a negative CV or SV should easily get our attention but may not always be a matter of great concern. What should sound the alarm is a continuing negative value or a CV or SV that is moving in the wrong direction. That's why I like to use the CPI and SPI. I plot these values against a time line (Figure 4–6). If the values are below 1.0 and fail to move back to this par value, then corrective action is indicated (or we acknowledge that the targets won't be met).

Summarize to Any Level

Although the data can be collected at the task level of detail, analysis is usually performed at a higher level. This is why it is so important to be able to summarize the data. We usually use a WBS to define the summarization hierarchy.

In the practical application of EVA, we roll up the data to a reasonable higher level of detail. When there are areas of unsatisfactory SV or CV, we can drill down to the details of the suspect area to pinpoint the cause.

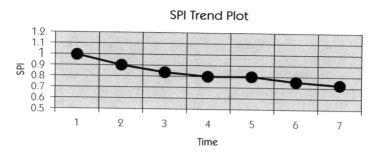

FIGURE 4–6 SPI Trend Plot

Segregate by Any Classification

Most project management software supports EVA for multiple WBSs. The WBS and other task coding can also be used to segregate the data by any interest area. For instance, we can evaluate performance by location, performing craft, responsible manager, cost accounts, or any other classification that has been defined to the system.

We can roll up by classification and then drill down in the poorly performing areas. This supports a management-by-exception approach. By identifying areas that are outside the performance targets, we can focus on finding causes and correcting such nonperforming areas. This permits us to apply resources where they will do the most good.

EVA: The Easy Way

That's it for a quick overview of earned value. Just these few measurements, processed within a structured and consistent policy, can deliver significant benefits, even in a limited application of EVA capabilities.

Almost all critical path method software has this EVA capability built in. You enter the basic planning and tracking data, and all calculations and reporting are already programmed and available. If you are already entering such data, the EVA process takes no further effort.[3]

EVA and PPM

A key component of PPM is improved management of the project pipeline. That is, we strive to review the performance of active projects against several criteria with the objective of considering termination of those projects that no longer support the conditions on which approval was granted. An essential capability for such performance reviews is the process of EVA. The ability to monitor schedule and cost variances in a consistent, structured manner provides key data for performance reviews and removes personal biases from the evaluation.

NOTES ————————————————————————————————————

Section 4.3

1. Stage-Gate® is a registered term.

Section 4.4

1. G. A. Moore, *Crossing the Chasm* (New York: HarperCollins, 1991), and *Inside the Tornado* (New York: HarperCollins, 1995).
2. Moore, *Inside the Tornado.*

Section 4.6

1. Q. W. Fleming, *Cost/Schedule Control Systems Criteria: The Management Guide to C/SCSC* (Burr Ridge, Ill.: Irwin, 1992).
2. Q. W. Fleming and J. M. Koppelman, *Earned Value Project Management* (Newtown Square, Pa.: : Project Management Institute, 1996).
3. For additional pragmatic approaches to earned value analysis, see H. A. Levine, *Practical Project Management: Tips, Tactics, and Tools* (New York: Wiley, 2002).

PPM Applications:
New Product Development

5

I have noted that the two most significant application areas for PPM are information technology and new product development (NPD). In the NPD area, there is one standout expert who has earned the title of guru. Indeed, it is virtually impossible to read anything on the application of PPM to NPD without a reference to Robert G. Cooper. Thanks to Cooper's generosity, you will not have to locate the Cooper references. He has written two chapters for this book that cover the core of his groundbreaking work.

Cooper is the author of the Stage-Gate® concept and techniques, which provide structure, order, and control to the entire NPD process.[1] Stage-Gate is a valuable tool for developing ideas into projects and maintaining the portfolio pipeline. It is a highly structured yet practical method of managing a project through its life cycle, ensuring that (from proposal to launch), the project is viable and in support of the organization's strategies and objectives. I first mentioned Stage-Gate in Section 3.2 and promised a more detailed treatment of the subject. In Chapter 5.1, we get the details from the developer of the concept. In Section 5.2, Cooper continues his thorough and perceptive exploration of portfolio management for product innovation. This section provides complete guidance for implementing a set of processes to support the evaluation, prioritization, and selection of projects for the portfolio.

There are significant and obvious reasons that PPM is a natural for NPD. In NPD, we are dealing with investment, innovation, opportunity, limited resources, and risk. Whether we evaluate these elements properly, employing a structured, repeatable methodology, can determine the success or failure of an enterprise. It's that important.

5.1 A STAGE-GATE® IDEA-TO-LAUNCH FRAMEWORK FOR DRIVING NEW PRODUCTS TO MARKET

Robert G. Cooper

New products are critical for the survival and prosperity of the modern corporation. New products launched in the previous three years now account for about 40 percent of companies' sales revenues and are seen as a major instrument of company growth. Innovation is no longer an optional investment, according to a recent executive survey: almost half of senior executives rate innovation as "very critical" to their future business success.[1]

The term *new product* is defined as anything that the organization offers to its marketplace for use or consumption and is new to the selling organization—that is, something it had not previously sold or made. This definition includes tangible goods as well as service products.

Product innovation is not so easy, however. Indeed, new products fail at an alarming rate (about one in ten new product concepts succeeds); 44 percent of new product projects fail to meet their profit objectives, and 49 percent are launched late to market.[2] Thus, many senior managers seek ways to improve their new product success, profitability, and speed to market and to build best practices into their product innovation methodology.

A Stage-Gate® framework is one solution that many leading companies have adopted to drive new product projects to market quickly and effectively.[3] The analogy of a North American football game helps to explain the concept. Imagine a football team without a game plan. The coach urges his players to "go out there and play hard . . . play to win." These are wonderful words of encouragement, but without a playbook or game plan, there's likely to be chaos on the football field.

A Stage-Gate new product process or idea-to-launch framework is simply a playbook or game plan to guide new product projects from beginning to end. In this section, we look at what a Stage-Gate framework is and then at ten best practices that top-performing businesses have built into their frameworks or playbooks. The section also provides the details of a best-in-class Stage-Gate idea-to-launch framework via a walk through the process. And the section ends with a look at how Stage-Gate methods have been applied to other types of development projects and some tips on how to implement Stage-Gate.

Necessary for Effective Product Development

Almost every top-performing company has implemented a Stage-Gate framework to drive new product projects through to commercialization, according to the American Productivity and Quality Center (APQC) benchmarking study on product innovation management best practices.[4] A solid idea-to-launch process is the strongest best practice observed among the sample of businesses and was embraced by virtually every top-performing business in the study. The Product Development and Management Association's (PDMA) best practices study concurs: "Nearly 60 percent of the firms surveyed use some form of Stage-Gate process."[5]

Stage-Gate methods work. According to the PDMA best practices study, "The Best [companies] are more likely to use some type of formal NPD process than the rest. They are more likely to have moved from simpler Stage-Gate processes to more sophisticated

---

Section 5.1 is taken from two books by the author: *Product Leadership: Pathways to Profitable Innovation,* 2nd edition (Reading, Mass.: Perseus Books, 2005), and *Winning at New Products: Accelerating the Process from Idea to Launch,* 3rd ed. (Reading, Mass: Perseus Books, 2001). It also draws on other writings by the author: "Doing It Right—Winning with New Products," *Ivey Business Journal,* July-Aug. 2000, pp. 54–60; "Stage-Gate New Product Development Processes: A Game Plan from Idea to Launch," in E. Verzuh (ed.), *The Portable MBA in Project Management* (New York: Wiley, 2003); and even earlier publications such as "Stage-Gate Systems: A New Tool for Managing New Products," *Business Horizons,* 1990, 33(3).

Stage-Gate® is a registered trademark of Product Development Institute, Inc.

facilitated or third-generation processes."[6] And the APQC benchmarking study found that many of the practices that businesses had embedded within their idea-to-launch process have a very strong positive impact on performance: they separate the best performers from the rest.

Structure of the Stage-Gate® Framework

The Stage-Gate new product approach is a conceptual and operational model for moving a new product project from idea to launch. Stage-Gate methods break the innovation process into a predetermined set of stages, each stage consisting of a set of prescribed, cross-functional, and parallel activities (Figure 5–1). The entrance to each stage is a gate, which controls the process and serves as the quality control and go/kill checkpoints. This stage-and-gate format leads to the name *Stage-Gate process.*

The Stage-Gate method is based on the experiences, suggestions, and observations of a large number of managers and firms and on my own and others' research in the field. In short, it is a game plan or playbook based on how winning project teams and winning business consistently win the game. Since this method first appeared in print, it has been implemented in whole or in part in hundreds of leading firms worldwide, many of which have provided an excellent laboratory setting to refine and improve the process.[7]

The Stages

Stages are where the action occurs. They are analogous to the plays in a North American football game. The players on the project team undertake key tasks in order to gather information needed to advance the project to the next gate or decision point.

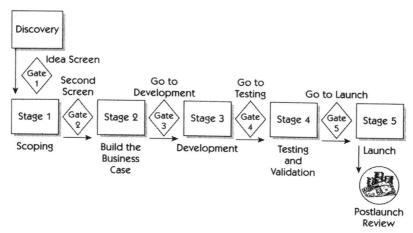

FIGURE 5–1 Overview of the Stage-Gate Idea-to-Launch Framework

Source: R. G. Cooper, Winning at New Products: Accelerating the Process from Idea to Launch, 3rd ed. (Reading, Mass.: Perseus Books, 2001).

The stages are defined by the activities within them, and there is usually a fairly standard or prescribed list of actions for each stage. Specifying the activities within a stage amounts to answering the questions:

- What does management need to know at the end of this stage in order to make an informed decision to move forward?
- Therefore, what actions are required in order to get this information?

For example, in Stage 2, Build the Business Case, a number of key actions may be required to deliver a solid business case, for example, undertaking voice-of-customer research, doing a competitive analysis, defining the product, and doing a source-of-supply assessment. These required or prescribed actions are mapped out within each stage of the Stage-Gate framework.

Stages include best practices. It's not just enough to map out a process that contains only current practices; there's no improvement in simply doing that. Later in this section, the success drivers, which must be built into each stage, are outlined.

Stages are also cross-functional. There is no R&D or marketing stage. Rather, each stage consists of a set of parallel activities undertaken by people from different functional areas within the firm, working together as a team and led by a project team leader. And these actions within each stage occur rapidly and in parallel—a rugby approach.

In order to manage risk using the Stage-Gate method, the parallel activities in each stage must be designed to gather vital information—technical, market, financial, operations—in order to drive down both the technical and business risks of the project. Each stage costs more than the preceding one, so that the game plan is based on incremental commitments. As uncertainties decrease, expenditures are allowed to mount. Risk is managed.

From Idea to Launch: An Overview

The general flow of the typical Stage-Gate model is shown pictorially in Figure 5–1. Here the key stages are:

- **Discovery:** Prework designed to discover opportunities and generate new product ideas.
- **Scoping:** A quick, preliminary investigation and scoping of the project. This stage provides inexpensive information, based largely on desk research, to enable the field of projects to be narrowed before Stage 2.
- **Build the Business Case:** A much more detailed investigation involving primary research, both market and technical, leading to a business case. This is where the bulk of the vital homework is done and most of the market studies are carried out. These result in a business case: the product definition, the project justification, and a project plan.
- **Development:** The actual detailed design and development of the new product, along with some product testing work. The deliverable at the end of Stage 3 development is an alpha-tested or lab-tested product. Full production and market launch plans are also developed in this potentially lengthy stage.
- **Testing and Validation:** Tests or trials in the marketplace, lab, and plant to verify

and validate the proposed new product and its marketing and production/opera-tions: field trials or beta tests, test market or trial sell, and opera-tions trials.
● **Launch:** Commercialization—the beginning of full operations or production, marketing, and selling. Here the market launch, production/operations, distribu-tion, quality assurance, and postlaunch monitoring plans are executed.

At first glance, this overview portrays the stages as relatively simple steps in a logical process. But don't be fooled: this is only a high-level view of a generic process, that is, the concept of the process. In a real company process, drilling down into the details of each stage reveals a much more sophisticated and complex set of activities: a detailed list of ac-tivities within a stage, the how-to's of each activity, best practices that the project team ought to consider, and even the required deliverables from each activity in that stage (for example, in the format of templates). In short, the drill-down provides a detailed and op-erational playbook for the project team—everything they need to know and do in order to complete that stage of the process and project successfully.

The Gates   Preceding each stage is an entry gate or a go/kill decision point. The gates are the scrums or huddles on the rugby or football field. They are the points during the game where the team converges and all new information is brought together. Effective gates are central to the success of a fast-paced new product process:

● Gates serve as quality control checkpoints. Is this project being executed in a qual-ity fashion?
● Gates also serve as go/kill and prioritization decision points. They provide the fun-nels where mediocre projects are culled out at each successive gate.
● Gates are where the action plan for the next stage is decided, along with resource commitments.

Gate meetings are usually staffed by senior managers from different functions—the gatekeepers—who own the resources required by the project leader and team for the next stage.

Gates Format. Gates have a common format (Figure 5–2):

● A set of required *deliverables*: What the project leader and team must bring to the gate decision point (such as the results of a set of completed activities). These de-liverables are visible, are based on a standard menu for each gate, and are decided at the output of the previous gate. Management's expectations for project teams are thus made very clear.
● *Criteria* against which the project is judged in order to make the go/kill and prior-itization decisions.
● Defined *outputs*: for example, a decision (go/kill/hold/recycle), an approved action plan for the next stage (complete with people required, money and person-days com-mitted, and an agreed time line), and a list of deliverables and date for the next gate.

FIGURE 5–2 Common Format of Gates

Types of Gate Criteria. Each gate has it own list of criteria for use by the gatekeepers. There are three types of gate criteria:

- Readiness-Check: These are yes/no questions that check whether the key tasks have been completed, and that all deliverables are in place for that gate—in effect, a quality check. A no answer can signal a recycle to the previous stage: the project is not ready to move on. Checklists are the usual format for these readiness items—for example:
  Is the product definition complete? Yes ☐   No ☐
  Fact based? Signed off by project team? Yes ☐   No ☐
- Must-Meet: These are yes/no or "knock-out" questions that include the minimum criteria that a project must meet in order to move forward. A single no signals a kill decision. Again, checklists are the usual format for must-meet items—for example:
  Is the project within our business's mandate? Yes ☐   No ☐
  Does the project meet our policies on values and ethics? Yes ☐   No ☐
  Is the project technically feasible (better than 50 percent)? Yes ☐   No ☐
- Should-Meet: These are highly desirable project characteristics (so a no on one question won't kill the project). They are used to distinguish between superb projects and the minimally acceptable ones. These should-meet items are typically in a scorecard format (see Chapter 5.2). And the resulting project attractiveness score is used to make go/kill decisions and also to help prioritize projects at gates.

Using the Gate Criteria. Gate criteria are designed to be used by the leadership team at the gate meeting. After the project is presented and debated, each criterion is discussed. The readiness-check and must-meet questions are displayed on a video projector and debated openly by the gatekeepers. A single consensus no is enough to kill or recycle the project.

The should-meet questions are best handled on a physical scorecard. These criteria are scored by the gatekeepers independently of each other at the gate meeting (paper and pen or computer-assisted scoring). Scores are tallied and displayed (for example, on a video projector) and the differences debated. A consensus go/kill and prioritization decision is reached, and if go, the action plan is approved and resources committed to the project team.

Building In Best Practices: The Key Success Drivers   A number of best practices must be built into the idea-to-launch framework in order to yield superlative results. Many insights have been gained over the years into what makes for successful product innovation. The challenge now is to take all of these lessons learned and integrate them into the Stage-Gate playbook.

SHARPER FOCUS, BETTER PROJECT PRIORITIZATION

Most businesses' new product efforts suffer from a lack of focus: too many projects and not enough resources to execute them well.[8] Adequate resources are a principal driver of businesses' new product performance, but a lack of resources plagues too many development efforts.[9] Sometimes this lack is simply that management has not devoted the needed people and money to the company's new product effort. But often this resource problem stems from trying to do too many projects with a limited set of resources—that is, from a lack of focus, the result of inadequate project evaluations. The root cause of this lack of focus is management's failure to set priorities and make tough go/kill decisions. In short, the gates are weak.

The need is for a new product funnel rather than tunnel. A new product funnel builds in tough go/kill decision points in the form of gates; the poor projects are weeded out; scarce resources are directed toward the truly deserving projects; and more focus is the result (Figure 5–3). The expectation is that a certain percentage of projects will be killed at each gate, especially at the earlier ones (gates 1, 2, and 3 in Figure 5–1). These gates are thus the bailout points where the question is, "Are you still in the game?" They are the quality control checkpoints in the new product process and check the quality, merit, and progress of the project.

PRODUCTS WITH COMPETITIVE ADVANTAGE: DIFFERENTIATED PRODUCTS, UNIQUE BENEFITS, SUPERIOR VALUE FOR THE CUSTOMER

Top-performing businesses build in product superiority at every opportunity, and they look for the "wow!" factor. This is one key to new product success, yet all too often, when redesigning their new product processes, too many firms fall into the trap of repeating current, often faulty practices. There's no attempt to seek truly superior products, and so the results are predicable: more ho-hum, tired, vanilla products that don't make much money.

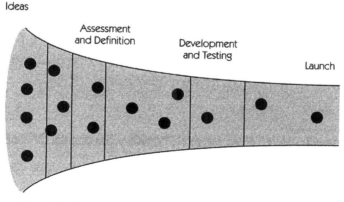

Ideas and projects should be successively screened or culled out at each gate, leaving only the best projects in the pipeline—a funneling approach. Once into Development, most of the poor projects have been weeded out, so the funnel begins to resemble a tunnel.

FIGURE 5–3 A Funnel Leading to a Tunnel to Weed Out Poor Projects Early

Here's how to drive the quest for product advantage:

- Ensure that at least some of the criteria at every gate focus on product superiority. Questions such as, "Does the product have at least one element of competitive advantage?" "Does it offer the user new or different benefits?" and "Is it excellent value for money for the user?" become vital questions to rate and rank potential projects.
- Require that certain key customer actions designed to deliver product superiority be included in each stage of the process. Examples are given in the "strong market orientation" item below.
- Demand that project teams deliver evidence of product superiority to gate reviews, and make product superiority an important deliverable and issue at such gate meetings.

EXEMPLARY QUALITY OF EXECUTION

A common theme throughout the Stage-Gate process is the emphasis on quality of execution: doing it right the first time. The argument that the proponents of Total Quality Management make is this: The definition of quality is precise: It means meeting all the requirements all the time. It is based on the principle that all work is a process. It focuses on improving business processes to eliminate errors.[10] The concept is perfectly logical and essentially simple, and the same logic can be applied to new product development.

A quality-of-execution crisis exists, however, in the product innovation process. Figure 5–4 shows assessments of sample activities from idea generation through to the postlaunch review. Note how poorly most are executed (the gray bars). For example, only 19 percent of businesses undertake effective idea generation, only 18 percent do a first-rate job on the market research, and only 26 percent do business case development well.[11] Note also how much better the top-performing businesses execute these activities (the black versus white bars). For example, 57 percent of top-performing businesses do excellent market research in new product projects; by contrast, only 23 percent of poor performers do excellent market research. Similar differences are noted for most of the activities in the figure.

Clearly there is a need for a more systematic and quality approach to the way firms conceive, develop, and launch new products. The way to deal with the quality-of-execution problem is to visualize product innovation as a process and apply process management and quality management techniques to this process. Note that any process in business can be managed, and managed with a view to quality. Get the details of the process right, practice discipline to the process, and the result will be a high-quality output.

A STRONG MARKET ORIENTATION WITH VOICE-OF-CUSTOMER INPUTS

If positive new product performance is the goal, then a market orientation (executing the key marketing activities in a quality fashion) must be built into the new product process as a matter of routine rather than by exception. Marketing inputs must play a decisive role from the beginning to the end of the project. Here are six best-practice marketing actions that should be built into an idea-to-launch process:

- Customer-focused ideation to gain insights into customer problems
- Preliminary market assessment in the very early phases of the new product project to assess the market opportunity

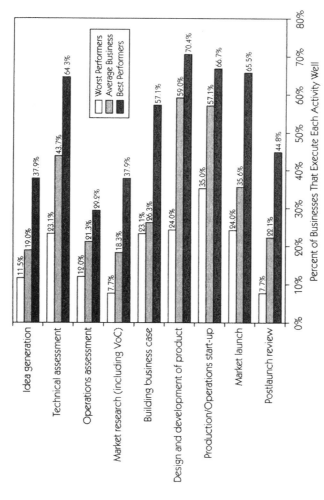

FIGURE 5–4 Quality of Execution of Key Activities: Impact on Performance

Note: This shows that 19 percent of businesses do an excellent job on idea generation. This is a key but weak activity. Note that 37.9 percent of best performers (and only 11.5 percent of poor performers) handle idea generation proficiently.

Source: American Productivity and Quality Center, *New Product Development Best Practices Study: What Distinguishes the Top Performers* (Houston: American Productivity and Quality Center, 2002).

- Voice-of-customer research to identify unmet or unarticulated needs, that is, what the winning new product must be and do
- Competitive product analysis, that is, figuring out what competitors' strategy is and how to beat them
- Value-in-use analysis to determine the economic value of the product to the customer or user
- Concept and *protocept* tests, preference tests and trial sells, that is, constant iterations with customers from Stage 1 through to launch using a series of build-test-and-redo loops or spirals

In order for these marketing actions to be undertaken proficiently, adequate marketing resources must available to project teams; often these are noticeably absent on project teams. Note that much more marketing and sales resources and people are available to new product project teams in top-performing businesses according to the APQC study.[12]

BETTER UP-FRONT HOMEWORK AND SHARP, EARLY, AND STABLE PRODUCT DEFINITION

New product success or failure is largely decided in the first few plays of the game—in those crucial steps and tasks that precede the actual development of the product. The up-front homework defines the product and builds the business case for development. The ideal new product process ensures that these early stages are carried out and that the product is fully defined before the project is allowed to become a full-fledged development project.

The need for solid upfront homework parallels the case for a stronger market orientation. Top performers ensure that the new product process does indeed include solid homework (Stages 1 and 2 in Figure 5–1) and stable, fact-based product definition. For example, they build in a product definition check point at Gate 3 in the process. And they halt projects if the homework and product definition aren't in place.

A TRUE CROSS-FUNCTIONAL TEAM APPROACH

The new product process is cross-functional: it requires the inputs and active participation of players from many different functions in the organization. The multifunctional nature of innovation coupled with the desire for parallel processing means that a cross-functional team approach is mandatory. It has these essential ingredients:

- A cross-functional team with committed players from the different functional areas
- A defined team captain or leader, championing the entire project from beginning to end and with formal authority (co-opting authority from the functional heads)
- A fluid team structure, with new members joining or dropped as work requirements demand
- A small core group of responsible and committed team players from beginning to end
- Most important, a team that is accountable for the entire project's end results (not just team members responsible for their part of the project)

A FAST-PACED GAME PLAN VIA PARALLEL PROCESSING

These new product teams face a dilemma. On the one hand, they are urged by senior management to compress the cycle time: that is, to shorten the elapsed time from idea to launch.

On the other hand, they are urged to improve the effectiveness of product development: cut down the failure rate: to do it right, which suggests a more thorough, longer process.

Parallel processing is one solution to the need for a complete and quality process, yet one that meets the time pressures of today's fast-paced business world. Traditionally, new product projects have been managed using a series approach: one task strung out after another in sequence. The analogy is that of a relay race, with each department running with the project for its 100-meter lap. Phrases such as "handoff" or "passing the project on," and even "dropping the ball" or "throwing it over the wall," are common in this relay race approach to new products.

In marked contrast to the relay race or sequential approach, with parallel processing many activities are undertaken concurrently rather than in series. The appropriate analogy is that of a rugby match rather than a relay race.[13] A team (not a single runner) appears on the field. A scrum or huddle ensues, after which the ball emerges. Players run down the field in parallel with much interaction, constantly passing the ball laterally. After 25 meters or so, the players converge for another scrum, huddle, or gate review, followed by another stage of activities.

With parallel processing, the game is far more intense than a relay race and more work gets done in an elapsed time period: three or four activities are done simultaneously and by different members on the project team. Second, there is less chance that an activity or task will be overlooked or handled poorly because of lack of time: the activity is done in parallel, not in series, and hence does not extend the total elapsed project time. Moreover, the activities are designed to feed each other (the metaphor of the ball being passed back and forth across the field). And finally, the entire new product process becomes cross-functional and multidisciplinary. The whole team—marketing, R&D, engineering, sales, manufacturing—is on the field together, participates actively in each play, and takes part in every gate review or scrum.

AN EFFICIENT PROCESS WITH TIME WASTERS REMOVED

The idea-to-launch framework must be built for speed. This means eliminating all the time wasters and work that add no value in the current new product process. Go through the process end to end and look at every required procedure, form to be filled out, or paperwork that must completed. There's probably a lot of unnecessary work that does not add any value to anyone. If it does not add value, get rid of it. And look at every committee that must sit and review projects or facets of projects. Again, if they're not really needed, get rid of them.

A DYNAMIC, FLEXIBLE, AND SCALABLE PROCESS

The idea-to-launch framework must be flexible and dynamic, responsive to changing conditions and varying circumstance of projects. It cannot be a rigid, lockstep process. Smart companies have built maneuvers into their processes in the interest of flexibility and speed:

- Ask the project team to map out the best path forward for their project, using the standard process as a guide, but not every stage activity or gate deliverable is mandatory.
- Permit combining gates and collapsing stages, or even going back to a previous gate or stage (see Stage-Gate Express later in this section).
- Move long-lead-time items forward (for example, instead of awaiting a specific

gate approval to order production equipment, certain long-lead-time items can be ordered in advance as long as the risk is recognized).

- Allow overlapping stages. A project team can begin the next stage before the entrance gate even occurs (although taking this practice too far can lead to chaos).
- Use self-managed gates, where the project team makes its own gate decisions rather than wait for senior management to call a meeting.
- Allow fuzzy gates or conditional gates, where projects can be moved ahead conditional on certain future events or future information.[14]

In addition, recognize that not all development projects are the same size and risk. Lower-risk projects do not need all the activities and stages that higher-risk ones do.

PERFORMANCE METRICS IN PLACE

The idea-to-launch framework must feature solid performance metrics, so that senior management can assess how well new product development and the process is working, and, most important, so that project teams are held accountable for results. According to the APQC study, putting metrics in place is indeed a best practice with a strong positive impact, a distinguishing feature of top-performing businesses.[15]

How does one establish new product performance metrics? For individual new product projects, success metrics often include:

- First-year sales (versus the sales forecast in the business case at Gate 3)
- Product profitability (for example, NPV) versus that forecast in the business case
- On-time performance: actual versus promised launch date[16]

Top performers build in a postlaunch review point twelve to eighteen months after launch, as in Figure 5.1-1, where these metrics are used to gauge the ultimate success of the project. Here the project's actual results are assessed versus those results promised back when the project was approved at Gate 3. In addition, sales, profits, and on-time performance results for individual projects can be aggregated or averaged to yield performance metrics for the business's entire new product effort.

A Walk Through the Stage-Gate Framework: Idea to Launch

Now that the key success drivers have been identified, let's have a more detailed look at the Stage-Gate framework—what's involved at each stage and gate. Let's do a walk-through of the model, stage by stage, as in Figure 5–1.

DISCOVERY STAGE

Ideas are the feedstock or trigger to the process, and they make or break the process. Don't expect a superb new product process to overcome a shortage of good new product ideas. The need for great ideas coupled with high attrition rate of ideas means that the idea generation stage is pivotal: the goal is great ideas and lots of them!

Many companies consider ideation so important that they handle this as a formal stage in the process, called Discovery. They build in a defined, proactive idea generation and capture system (Figure 5–5). Ideas are fed to a focal person, who then gets a decision at

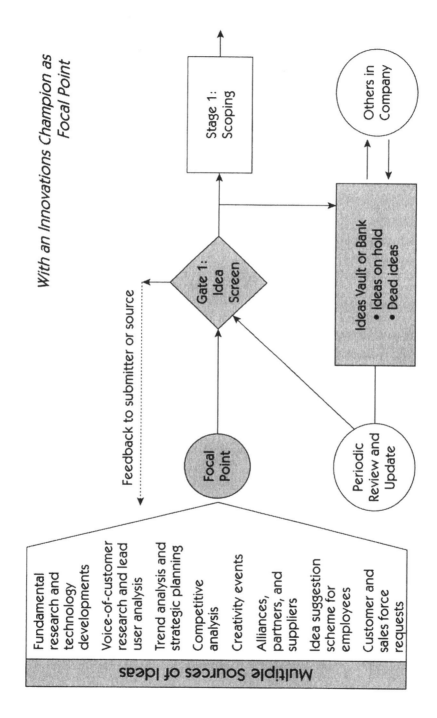

FIGURE 5–5 A System for Idea Capture and Handling

Gate 1. Go or kill ideas are archived in an idea vault, while teams are assigned go ideas to move forward into Stage 1.

Many activities can be built into the Discovery stage in order to stimulate the creation of great new product ideas. Such activities include undertaking fundamental but directed technical research, seeking new technological possibilities, working with lead or innovative users[17] or undertaking product value analysis with customers,[18] using voice-of-customer research to capture unarticulated needs and customer problems,[19] competitive analysis and reverse-brainstorming competitive products, installing an idea suggestion scheme to stimulate ideas from your own employees, and using your strategic planning exercise to uncover disruptions, gaps and opportunities in the marketplace.

GATE 1: IDEA SCREEN

Idea screening is the first decision to commit resources to the project. The project is born at this point. If the decision is go, the project moves into the scoping or preliminary investigation stage. Thus, Gate 1 signals a preliminary but tentative commitment to the project: a flickering green light.

Gate 1 is a "gentle screen" and amounts to subjecting the project to a handful of key must-meet and should-meet criteria. Financial criteria are typically not part of this first screen, since relatively little reliable financial data is available here. A checklist for the must-meet criteria and a scorecard or scoring model (point count rating scales) for the should-meet criteria are used to help focus the discussion and rank projects in this early screen.

STAGE 1: SCOPING

This first and inexpensive homework stage has the objective of determining the project's technical and marketplace merits. Stage 1 is a quick scoping of the project, involving desk research or detective work; little or no primary research is done here. Stage 1 is often done in less than one calendar month's elapsed time and five to ten person-days' work effort.

A preliminary market assessment is one facet of Stage 1 and involves a variety of relatively inexpensive activities: an Internet search; a library search; contacts with key users, distributors, and salespeople; a survey of competitors' Web pages or literature; focus groups; and even a quick concept test with a handful of potential users. The purpose is to

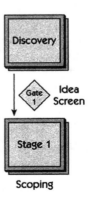

determine market size, market potential, and likely market acceptance and also to begin to shape the product concept.

Concurrently a preliminary technical assessment is carried out, involving a quick and preliminary in-house appraisal of the proposed product. The purpose is to assess development and manufacturing routes (or source of supply), technical and manufacturing/operations feasibility, possible times and costs to execute, and technical, legal, and regulatory risks and roadblocks.

Stage 1 thus provides for the gathering of both market and technical information, at a low cost and in a short time, to enable a cursory and first-pass financial and business analysis as input to Gate 2. Because of the limited effort and depending on the size of the project, very often Stage 1 can be handled by a team of a few people, usually from marketing and from a technical group.

GATE 2: SECOND SCREEN

The project next proceeds to a second and somewhat more rigorous screen at Gate 2. This gate is essentially a repeat of Gate 1: the project is reevaluated in the light of the new information obtained in Stage 1. If the decision is go at this point, the project moves into a heavier spending stage.

At Gate 2, the project is subjected to a list of readiness check questions and also a set of must-meet and should-meet criteria similar to those used at Gate 1. Here additional should-meet criteria may be considered, dealing with sales force and customer reaction to the proposed product and potential legal, technical, and regulatory "killer variables," the result of new data gathered during Stage 1. Again, a checklist and scoring model facilitate this gate decision. The financial return is assessed at Gate 2, but only by a quick and simple financial calculation (for example, the payback period).

STAGE 2: BUILD THE BUSINESS CASE

The business case is constructed in Stage 2, a detailed investigation stage that clearly defines the product and verifies the attractiveness of the project prior to heavy spending. It is also the critical homework stage, which is so often weakly handled.

Stage 2 sees voice-of-customer research undertaken to determine the customer's needs, wants, and preferences, that is, to help define a superior, differentiated, and winning new product. Competitive analysis is also a part of this stage. Another market activity is concept testing. A representation of the proposed new product is presented to potential customers, their reactions are gauged, and the likely customer acceptance of the new product is determined.

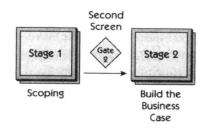

A detailed technical appraisal at Stage 2 focuses on the technical feasibility of the project. That is, the customer needs and "wish list" are translated into a technically and economically feasible solution on paper. This translation might even involve some preliminary design or laboratory work, but it should not be construed as a full-fledged development project. A manufacturing (or operations) appraisal is often a part of building the business case, where issues of manufacturability, source of supply, costs to manufacture, and investment required are investigated. If appropriate, detailed legal, patent, and regulatory assessment work is undertaken in order to remove risks and map out the required actions.

Finally, a detailed business and financial analysis is conducted as part of the justification facet of the business case. The financial analysis typically involves a net present value (NPV) calculation, complete with sensitivity analysis to look at possible downside risks.

The result of Stage 2 is a business case for the project: the product definition, a key to success, is agreed to, and a thorough project justification and detailed project plan are developed.

Stage 2 involves considerably more effort than Stage 1 and requires the inputs from a variety of sources. Stage 2 is best handled by a team consisting of cross-functional members, the core group of the eventual project team.

GATE 3: GO TO DEVELOPMENT

This is the final gate prior to the development stage, the last point at which the project can be killed before entering heavy spending. Once past Gate 3, financial commitments are substantial. In effect, Gate 3 means "go to a heavy spend." Gate 3 also yields a sign-off of the product and project definition. Because of the substantial resource commitments here, Gate 3 is usually staffed by the leadership team of the business for major projects.

This Gate 3 evaluation involves a review of each of the activities in Stage 2, checking that the activities were undertaken, the quality of execution was sound, and the results were positive. Next, Gate 3 subjects the project once again to the set of readiness-check, must-meet, and should-meet criteria similar to those used at Gate 2. Finally, because a heavy spending commitment is the result of a go decision at Gate 3, the results of the financial analysis are an important part of this screen.

If the decision is go, Gate 3 sees commitment to the product definition and agreement on the project plan that charts the path forward. The development plan and the preliminary operations and market launch plans are reviewed and approved at this gate. The full project team—an empowered, cross-functional team headed by a leader with authority—is designated.

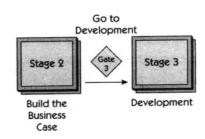

STAGE 3: DEVELOPMENT

Stage 3 witnesses the implementation of the development plan and the physical development of the product. Lab tests, in-house tests, or alpha tests ensure that the product meets requirements under controlled conditions. Also, the production, operations, or source-of-supply process is mapped out.

For lengthy projects, numerous milestones and periodic project reviews are built into the development plan. These are not gates per se: go/kill decisions are not made here. Rather, these milestone check points provide for project control and management. Extensive in-house testing, alpha tests, or lab testing usually occurs at this stage as well. The deliverable at the end of Stage 3 is a lab-tested or alpha prototype of the product.

The emphasis in Stage 3 is on technical work, but marketing and operations activities also proceed in parallel. For example, market analysis and customer feedback work continue concurrently with the technical development, with constant customer opinion sought on the product as it takes shape during development. These activities are back-and-forth or iterative, with each development result (for example, rapid prototype, working model, first prototype) taken to the customer for assessment and feedback: spiral or iterative development. Meanwhile, detailed test plans, market launch plans, and production or operations plans, including production facilities requirements, are developed. An updated financial analysis is prepared, while regulatory, legal, and patent issues are resolved.

GATE 4: GO TO TESTING

This postdevelopment gate is a check on the progress and the continued attractiveness of the product and project. Development work is reviewed and checked, ensuring that the work has been completed in a quality fashion and that the developed product is consistent with the original definition specified at Gate 3.

This gate also revisits the economic question using a revised financial analysis based on new and more accurate data. The test or validation plans for the next stage are approved for immediate implementation, and the detailed market launch and operations plans are reviewed for probable future execution.

STAGE 4: TESTING AND VALIDATION

This stage tests and validates the entire viability of the project: the product itself, the production process, customer acceptance, and the economics of the project. It also begins extensive external validation of the product and project. A number of activities are undertaken at Stage 4:

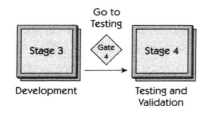

- In-house product tests: Extended lab tests or alpha tests to check on product quality and product performance under controlled or lab conditions
- User, preference, or field trials of the product: To verify that the product functions under actual use conditions and also to gauge potential customers' reactions to the product and establish purchase intent
- Trial, limited, or pilot production/operations: To test, debug, and prove the production or operations process and to determine more precise production costs and throughputs
- Pretest market, test market, or trial sell: To gauge customer reaction, measure the effectiveness of the launch plan, and determine expected market share and revenues
- Revised business and financial analysis: To check on the continued business and economic viability of the project, based on new and more accurate revenue and cost data

Sometimes Stage 4 yields negative results, and it's back to Stage 3.

GATE 5: GO TO LAUNCH

This final gate opens the door to full commercialization: market launch and full production or operations start-up. It is the final point at which the project can still be killed. This gate focuses on the quality of the activities in the testing and validation stage and their results. Criteria for passing the gate focus largely on the expected financial return, the project's readiness for launch, and the appropriateness of the launch and operations start-up plans. The operations and market launch plans are reviewed and approved for implementation in Stage 5.

STAGE 5: LAUNCH

This final stage involves implementing both the market launch plan and the production or operations plan. Production equipment is acquired, installed and commissioned (sometimes this is done earlier in Stage 4, as part of the Stage 4 production trials); the logistics pipeline is filled; and selling begins. Barring any unforeseen events, it should be clear sailing for the new product—another new product winner!

POSTLAUNCH REVIEW

Two postlaunch reviews are typical. The first, an interim review, occurs about two to four months after launch, when initial launch results are available. Here, a postaudit is done while the details of the project are still fresh in team members' minds. This postaudit as-

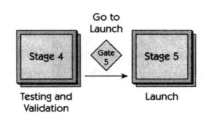

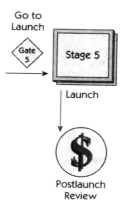

sesses the project's strengths and weaknesses, identifies what can be learned from the project, and provides key learnings on how to do the next project even better. In addition, interim commercial results (initial sales and production costs, for example) are reviewed, and needed course corrections are made.

The final review is held once the project is stable and commercial results are known, typically twelve to eighteen months into market. Here the project team is disbanded, and the product becomes a "regular product" in the firm's product line. This is also the point where the project and product's performance is reviewed. The latest data on revenues, costs, expenditures, profits, and timing is compared to projections made at Gates 3 and 5 to gauge performance. Project team accountability is a central issue here: Did the team deliver the results it promised or forecast? This review marks the end of the project. Note that the project team and leader remain responsible for the success of the project through this postlaunch period, right up to the point of the postlaunch review.

Stage-Gate Express for Lower-Risk Projects

Stage-Gate frameworks are scalable, with different versions to handle different types of projects. The full-fledged Stage-Gate model in Figure 5–1 is designed for larger, higher-risk new product projects with much at stake and many unknowns. But many projects are much smaller than this. They include product modifications, extensions, improvements, simple sales requests, and single-customer projects. Forcing such smaller projects through the full five-stage model only creates frustration, unneeded work, and the impression of added bureaucracy, a sure way to cause people to circumvent an otherwise excellent framework.

When the project risk is low, use an abbreviated version of Stage-Gate: the three-stage Stage-Gate Express framework in Figure 5–6.[20] Here's how the three-stage version works:

- Stages 1 and 2 in Figure 5–1 are combined into a single "homework" stage. The usual Stage 1 activities are then merged with Stage 2 tasks. In lower-risk projects, often much of the needed information is readily available, and so the work effort required for the homework phase in Stage-Gate Express is considerably less than in the full five-stage process.

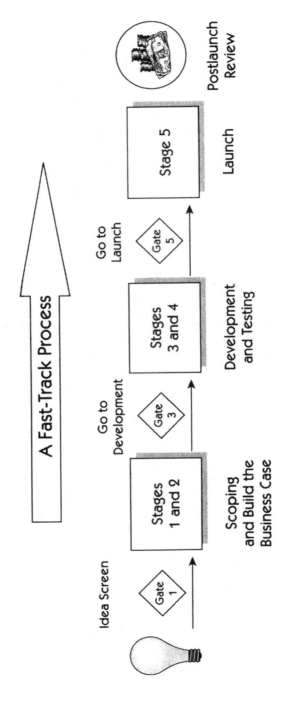

FIGURE 5–6 Stage-Gate Express: A Three-Stage Version for Lower-Risk Projects

Source: R. G. Cooper, *Winning at New Products: Accelerating the Process from Idea to Launch,* 3rd ed. (Reading, Mass.: Perseus Books, 2001).

- Stage 3 (Development) is merged with Stage 4 (Testing and Validation) in Figure 5–1. The project team reviews the activities normally undertaken in Stages 3 and 4 and decides which are relevant to the smaller project and which should be omitted or abbreviated.
- Because stages are combined, Gates 2 and 4 are eliminated (often the project team conducts a "self-check" or "self-managed gate" prior to moving ahead).

The result is a fast-track process suitable to facilitate product development for low-risk projects.

Stage-Gate for Technology and Platform Developments

Technology development or technology platform projects promise to open up new strategic opportunities to the business.[21] A limited number of businesses that engage in such innovative developments have successfully employed a different type of Stage-Gate process to drive these special projects through to fruition. ExxonMobil Chemicals has even published a synopsis of its special process to handle the company's technology projects.[22]

First, here are some definitions:

- Technology development (TD) projects are those where the deliverable is new knowledge and a technological capability (also called "science projects" and "fundamental" or "basic research projects"). This new capability or new knowledge may spawn a number of specific new product projects (and thus may overlap with the notion of a platform project—a technology platform). When the TD project begins, there may be no specific new product (or new manufacturing process) well defined. Rather, the scientist initiates some experiments with the hope of finding some technical possibilities and discoveries that might yield ideas for commercial products or processes.
- Disruptive technologies and radical innovations yield projects that are a special subcategory of technology developments What is a disruptive technology? Most new technologies result in improved performance, which can come from incremental innovations or from those that are more radical in character. Most technological advances in industry are sustaining, but "occasionally disruptive technologies emerge: innovations that result in worse performance, at least in the near term."[23] These innovations may be inferior to the existing technology when measured on traditional performance metrics, but they bring a new performance dimension or a new value proposition to the market. For example, the first digital cameras produced a poorer picture (lower resolution) than traditional 35mm film cameras and were considered inferior products by most camera users. But for a handful of users, most notably those who wanted the picture in digital format so that they could modify or electronically transmit the photo, such as real estate agents, there was new value in the digital camera.
- Platform projects are defined in the PDMA handbook to be "design and components that are shared by a set of products in a product family. From this platform, numerous derivatives can be designed."[24] Thus, Chrysler's engine transmission from its K-car was a platform that spawned other vehicles, including the famous Chrysler minivan.

The notion of platforms has since been broadened to include technological capabilities. For example, ExxonMobil's Metallocene platform is simply a catalyst that has yielded an entirely new generation of polymers. Thus, a platform is like an oil drilling platform in the ocean, which you invest heavily in. From this platform, you can drill many holes relatively quickly and at low cost. Thus, the platform establishes the capability, and this capability spawns many new product projects much more quickly and cost-effectively than starting from scratch each time. A platform project could be based on a new technology or a technology development (above) and is called a *technology platform project.*

The main difference between these and a typical new product project, for which Stage-Gate in Figure 5–1 is designed, is that technology and platform developments are often much broader, more vaguely defined, and more difficult to predict at the outset than is the typical new product project. For example, in a technology development project designed to ultimately yield new products, it may take months of technical research before it's even clear what might be technically possible. So undertaking a market analysis in Stage 1 in Figure 5–1 and detailed market studies in Stage 2 makes little sense because the product hasn't even been defined or characterized. And the criteria for project selection are clearly different here than they are for a very tangible, well-defined new product project simply because so little is known about the commercial possibilities early in the life of such projects.

STAGE-GATE-TD

The methodology for handling such technology platform and technology developments is shown in Figure 5–7. The method is called *Stage-Gate-TD,* where "TD" stands for "technology development." The top part of the schematic shows the three stages of the process:

1. Scoping: A relatively inexpensive stage involving literature search, secondary research, and detective work. Its purpose is to lay the foundation and define the scope of the project.
2. Technical assessment: A more extensive stage designed to demonstrate technical feasibility—in other words, that something is worth pursuing further.
3. Detailed investigation: The full experimental effort to take the technology to the point where you can start working on specific new product projects or perhaps on a new manufacturing process. During this stage, commercial possibilities (for example, some possible new products) are identified and defined, and preliminary market and business analyses are conducted on each.

The Applications Pathway gate is where senior management meets to decide what do with this new technology or capability. Very often, multiple new product projects are defined, which then enter the standard five-stage Stage-Gate framework (across the bottom of Figure 5–7) at Gate 1, 2, or 3, depending on how far along and how defined the project already is.

The TD gates are similar to those in the traditional Stage-Gate framework, except that the gatekeepers usually include a strong contingent of technology people, as well as senior people from key businesses within the corporation, that is, businesses where this new technology will eventually be commercialized. Readiness-check, must-meet and should-meet

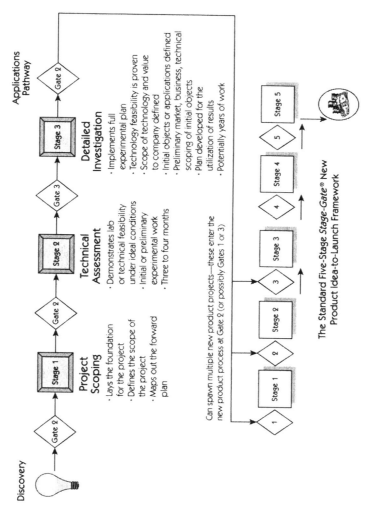

FIGURE 5–7 Stage-Gate-TD Framework for Technology Developments and Technology Platforms

Source: R. G. Cooper, *Winning at New Products: Accelerating the Process from Idea to Launch*, 3rd ed. (Reading, Mass.: Perseus Books, 2001).

questions (in the form of a scorecard) are used to focus the discussions and make more effective go/kill decisions, but the specific criteria are different from those in the gates of a regular process in Figure 5–1.[25]

Some Tips on Implementing Stage-Gate

Designing and successfully implementing a Stage-Gate framework is no small task. When it is done well, the rewards are significant: faster to market by about 30 percent, higher success rates, and more projects on time and on target.

To achieve these enviable results, an investment is required. Let's assume that the business's leadership team has decided to move forward and implement a Stage-Gate framework for new products (or perhaps for technology developments). Step 1 is preparatory (see Figure 5–8 for a step-by-step approach to implementing a Stage-Gate framework). First, establish a cross-functional, cross-business task force with strong leadership and executive sponsors in place. Next, find out what's working and what needs fixing in the current product development methods: conduct an audit of the current process; do some retrospective reviews of recent past projects to find out how well or poorly they were handled; hold some town hall meetings to better understand the problems and challenges faced by product developers in the organization; and do some internal and external benchmarking (including a solid literature search).[26] Most firms get some outside help and expertise so that they don't repeat many of the same mistakes that slowed other businesses down in their efforts to adopt a Stage-Gate framework.

Step 2 is the physical design of the Stage-Gate framework (Figure 5–8). This step usually proceeds in a series of off-site meetings, whereby the task force crafts the process stage-by-stage and gate-by-gate. Note that multiple iterations of the process are developed,

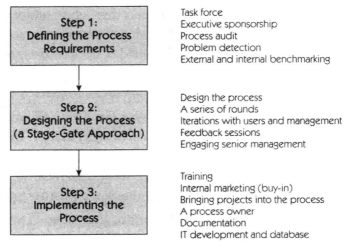

Figure 5–8 Key Steps in Implementing a Stage-Gate New Product Framework

Source: R. G. Cooper, Winning at New Products: Accelerating the Process from Idea to Launch, 3rd ed. (Reading, Mass.: Perseus Books, 2001).

and each should be tested with the user community within the business. Often what the task force thought was an excellent model receives anything but rave reviews from the potential user group. So seek feedback many times in an iterative design effort, and build the feedback into the proposed Stage-Gate framework. Some task forces shorten this step considerably by purchasing an off-the-shelf version of Stage-Gate such as SG-Navigator™.[27]

The final step, implementation, is by far the most difficult and time-intensive. Figure 5–8 lists the many activities that firms undertake when implementing Stage-Gate. The challenge here is to get people in the organization, from senior executives on down, to understand, support, and live the process. Here are the key actions:

- Assign a process manager to shepherd the process and its implementation. This person and position is key. No process, no matter how clever, ever implemented itself.
- Train everyone from the gatekeepers through to junior technicians. Although the newly developed process may seem simple to the task force that designed it, the process is quite foreign to everyone else in the company. Don't underestimate the communication and training job required here.
- Get existing projects into the process fast. Don't sit around for months waiting for new projects to enter Gate 1. Instead, shoe-horn existing projects into the new process right away. Better yet, as soon as the task force starts designing the process (Step 2 in Figure 5–8), start piloting some existing projects.
- Develop user-friendly documentation, and put an IT support system in place. IT helps users adopt, use, and embrace the process quickly (there are many solid IT support tools around, such as the Accolade™ and SG-Navigator™ decision support systems).[28]

Doing It Right

Product innovation is one of the most important endeavors of the modern corporation. The message from both Wall Street and Main Street is "innovate or die!" Customers as well as shareholders seek a steady stream of innovative new products. Customers want innovative products because they demand value for money, and shareholders seek the organic and profitable growth that innovations provide. Without a systematic new product process, however, the product innovation effort often is a shambles—a chaotic, hit-and-miss affair. The Stage-Gate framework is an enabler or guide, building in best practices and ensuring that key activities and decisions are done better and faster. But Stage-Gate is considerably more complex than the simple diagram in Figure 5–1 suggests; there are many intricacies in the details—both the "what's" and the "how-to's." And implementing the process is also a major challenge. Many leading companies nevertheless have taken the necessary step and designed and implemented a world-class idea-to-launch Stage-Gate framework, and the results have been positive: better, faster and more profitable new product developments.

Robert G. Cooper is professor of marketing at the School of Business, McMaster University in Ontario, Canada, and ISBM Distinguished Research Fellow at Penn State University's Smeal College of Business Administration. He is the father and developer of the Stage-Gate process, now widely used around the world to drive new products to market. He is a prolific researcher and thought leader in the field of product innovation management, with more than ninety articles in leading journals on new product management and six books.

5.2 PORTFOLIO MANAGEMENT FOR PRODUCT INNOVATION _____

Robert G. Cooper

Much like a stock market portfolio manager, senior executives who manage to optimize their R&D investments will win in the long run.[1] Management in successful businesses in product innovation focuses resources on the right arenas, select winning new product projects, and strive for the ideal balance and mix of projects. That is what portfolio management is all about: resource allocation and investment decisions to achieve the business's new product objectives.

Portfolio Management Defined

Portfolio management is formally defined as a dynamic decision process, whereby a business's list of active new product (and development) projects is constantly updated and revised. In this process, new projects are evaluated, selected, and prioritized; existing projects may be accelerated, killed, or deprioritized; and resources are allocated and reallocated to active projects. The portfolio decision process is characterized by uncertain and changing information, dynamic opportunities, multiple goals and strategic considerations, interdependence among projects, and multiple decision makers and locations.[2]

The portfolio decision process encompasses or overlaps a number of decision-making processes within the business, including periodic reviews of the total portfolio of all projects (looking at all projects holistically and against each other), making go/kill decisions on individual projects on an ongoing basis, and developing a new product strategy for the business, complete with strategic resource allocation decisions.

New product portfolio management sounds like a fairly mechanistic exercise of decision making and resource allocation. But there are many unique facets of the problem that make it perhaps the most challenging decision making faced by the modern corporation in business today:

- New product portfolio management deals with future events and opportunities; thus, much of the information required to make project selection decisions is at best uncertain and at worst very unreliable.
- The decision environment is a highly dynamic one. The status of and prospects for projects in the portfolio are ever changing as markets change and new information becomes available.

Section 5.2 is based on R. G. Cooper, *Product Leadership: Pathways to Profitable Innovation,* 2nd ed. (Reading, Mass.: Perseus Books, 2005); R. G. Cooper, S. J. Edgett, and E. J. Kleinschmidt, *Portfolio Management for New Products,* 2nd ed. (Reading, Mass: Perseus Books, 2002); and R. G. Cooper, *Winning at New Products: Accelerating the Process from Idea to Launch,* 3rd ed. (Reading, Mass: Perseus Books, 2001).

- Projects in the portfolio are at different stages of completion, yet all projects compete against each other for resources, so comparisons must be made between projects with different amounts and quality of information.
- Resources to be allocated across projects are limited. A decision to fund one project may mean that resources must be taken away from another, and resource transfers between projects are not totally seamless.

The Importance of Portfolio Management

Portfolio management and the prioritization of new product projects is a critical management task. Roussel, Saad, and Erickson claim in their widely read book that "portfolio analysis and planning will grow to become the powerful tool that business portfolio planning became in the 1970s and 1980s."[3]

Here's why portfolio management, that is, the ability to pick the right projects and make the right investments, is vital to winning the product innovation war.

First, a successful product innovation effort is fundamental to business success. This logically translates into portfolio management: the ability to select today's projects that will become tomorrow's new product winners.

Second, new product development is the manifestation of the business's strategy. One of the most important ways of implementing strategy is through the new products one develops. If the business's new product initiatives are wrong—the wrong projects or the wrong balance—then it fails at implementing its business strategy.

Third, portfolio management is about resource allocation. In a business world preoccupied with value to the shareholder and doing more with less, technology and marketing resources are simply too scarce to allocate to the wrong projects. The consequences of poor portfolio management are evident: scarce resources are squandered on the wrong projects, and as a result, the truly deserving ones are starved.

Specific reasons for the importance of portfolio management, cited by managers in a survey of 205 firms and derived from a best practices portfolio study, are set out in Exhibit 5–1.[4]

There are essentially three main goals that an effective portfolio management system should achieve. Management should set its sights on at least some of these goals (according to benchmarking results, very few companies achieve all three):

- *To ensure strategic alignment.* The main goal here is to ensure that regardless of all other considerations, the final portfolio of projects truly reflects the business's strategy: that all projects are on strategy, support the strategy, or are critical components of the strategy; and that the breakdown of spending across projects, areas, markets is directly tied to the business strategy (for example, to areas of strategic focus that management has previously delineated).
- *To maximize the value of the portfolio.* Here the goal is to allocate resources so as to maximize the value of the portfolio for a given spending level. That is, one selects projects so as to maximize the sum of the values or commercial worths of all active projects in the pipeline in terms of some business objective, such as NPV (net present value), EVA (earned value analysis), return on investment, likelihood of success, or some other strategic objective).

Exhibit 5–1 Key Reasons That Portfolio Management Is a Vital Management Task

1. Financial—to maximize return, maximize R&D productivity, and achieve financial goals.

2. To maintain the competitive position of the business—to increase sales and market share.

3. To properly and efficiently allocate scarce resources.

4. To forge the link between project selection and business strategy. The portfolio is the expression of strategy; it must support the strategy.

5. To achieve focus—not doing too many projects for the limited resources available and providing resources for the great projects.

6. To achieve balance—the right balance between long- and short-term projects, and high-risk and low-risk ones, consistent with the business's goals.

7. To better communicate priorities within the organization vertically and horizontally.

8. To provide better objectivity in project selection and weed out bad projects.

Source: R. G. Cooper, S. J. Edgett, and E. J. Kleinschmidt, "New Product Portfolio Management: Practices and Performance," *Journal of Product Innovation Management,* 1999, 16, 333–351; and R. G. Cooper, S. J. Edgett, and E. J. Kleinschmidt, "Portfolio Management for New Product Development: Results of an Industry Practices Study," *R&D Management,* 2001, 31, 361–380.

● *To seek the right balance of projects.* The goal of seeking the right balance flows logically from the first goal, strategic alignment. Here the principal concern is to achieve the desired balance of projects in terms of a number of parameters—for example, the right balance in terms of long-term projects versus short-term ones or high-risk versus lower-risk projects and across various markets, technologies, product categories, and project types (for example, new products, improvements, cost reductions, maintenance and fixes, and fundamental research).

Although the focus here is on portfolio management for new products, because technology resources used in new products are also required for other types of projects, portfolio management also includes process developments, extensions and modifications, cost reduction projects, platform developments, and even fundamental research projects.

Strategic Portfolio Management

Portfolio management and resource allocation can be treated as a hierarchical process, with two levels of decision making. This hierarchical approach simplifies the decision challenge somewhat (see Figure 5–9):[5]

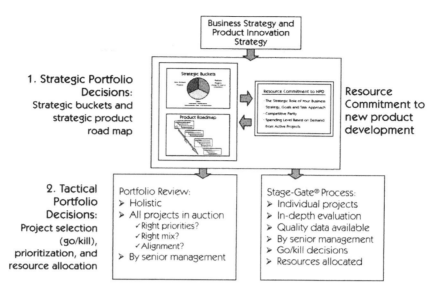

FIGURE 5–9 The Portfolio Management System and Its Elements: The Two Levels of Decision Making

Source: R. G. Cooper, *Product Leadership: Pathways to Profitable Innovation,* 2nd ed. (Reading, Mass: Perseus Books, 2005).

● **Level 1: Strategic portfolio management.** Strategic portfolio decisions answer the question, "Directionally, where should the business spend its new product development resources (people and funds)?" How should resources be split across projects types, markets, technologies, or product categories? And on what major initiatives or new platforms should the business concentrate its resources? Establishing strategic buckets and defining strategic product road maps are effective tools.

● **Level 2: Tactical portfolio decisions (individual project selection).** Tactical portfolio decisions focus on individual projects but obviously follow from the strategic decisions. They address the question, "What specific new product projects should the business undertake?" Such decisions are shown at the bottom part of Figure 5–9.

THE STRATEGIC PRODUCT ROAD MAP

The product road map is a strategically driven resource allocation method (middle right part of Figure 5–9). This top-down approach is designed to ensure that the list of projects (at least the major ones) contributes to or is essential for the realization of the business's strategy and goals.[6] A strategic product road map is an effective way to map out this series of assaults in an attack plan.

A road map is simply management's view of how to get where they want to go or to achieve their desired objective.[7] The strategic road map is a useful tool that helps senior management ensure that the capabilities to achieve their objective are in place when needed. There are different types of road maps: the product road map and the technology road map.

Let's use a military analogy. The term *strategy* was first used in a military context, and much of what we know about strategy comes from the military field. You are a five-star general and are at war. You have clearly specified goals: presumably to win the war or achieve certain ends. You may have identified certain key strategic arenas—fronts, major battlefields, or arenas on a map—where you hope to attack and win. But as you chart your strategy, you see that there are some key assaults or initiatives along the way—individual battles that you must fight in order to see your strategy succeed.

Now let's translate this into a new product context:

- **Goals:** What goals your business has, including specific new product goals. For example, what percentage of your business's growth over the next three years will come from new products?
- **Arenas, fronts, and major battlefields:** These are the stra-tegic arenas defined in your business and new product strategy. Which markets, technologies, and product types does the business plan to attack? Where will it focus its development efforts?
- **Deployment:** How many troops will the business place on each battlefield or front (or strategic buckets, later in this section)?
- **Assaults and initiatives:** The major developments that you must undertake in order to implement your strategy: the major new product, technology, or platform developments, that is, your strategic road map.

Your strategic product road map defines the business's major new product and platform developments along a time line, establishes place marks for these major initiatives, and tentatively commits or reserves resources for them. An example is in Figure 5–10 for an equipment manufacturer. Here the product road map not only maps out the various major product introductions and their timing; it also defines the platforms and platform extensions needed to develop these new products.[8]

The technology road map is derived from the product road map but also specifies how you will get there. That is, it lays out the technologies and technological competencies that are needed in order to implement (develop and source) the products and platforms in the product road map. The technology road map is a logical extension of the product road map and is closely linked to it. Indeed, at Lucent Technologies, the two are combined into a product-technology road map as a tool to help management link business strategy, product plans, and technology development.[9]

Most often, the specification of projects on the product road map is left fairly general and high level. For example, designations such as "a low-carb beer for the Atkins diet market" or "ceramic-coated tooling for the aerospace industry" or "low-power petroleum blenders" are often the way these projects are shown on the product road map time line. That is, place marks for projects yet to be defined are the norm. The road map is meant to be directional and strategic, but not provide detailed product and project definitions. As each project progresses through the idea-to-launch process, however (the Stage-Gate® process in Section 5.1), increasingly the project and product becomes specified and defined.

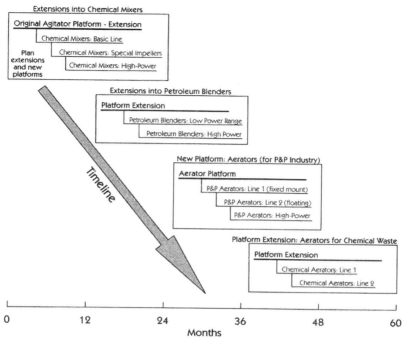

FIGURE 5–10 Strategic Product Road Map: New Platforms and Major Products

Source: Based on work in M. H. Meyer and A. P. Lehnerd, *The Power of Platforms* (New York: Free Press, 1997).

DEVELOPING THE STRATEGIC PRODUCT ROAD MAP

The development of a product road map flows logically from the product innovation strategy. Delineating the major initiatives required as part of the product road map is a multifaceted task:

● *Strategic assessment.* Sometimes the mere specification of a strategic arena as top priority leads logically to a list of those products and projects that are necessary to enter and be successful in that arena. For example, a major health products company identified "wound care" as a priority strategic arena (the company already sold a few products in this health care sector but was a minor player). However, once "wound care" was made top priority, the specific products the company needed to be a force in this sector became evident, and the development programs to generate these products fell into a logical sequence in a product road map.

● *Portfolio review of existing products.* Here, one takes a hard look at the business's current product offerings and decides which are tired and should be pruned and which should be replaced. Forecasts of products' life cycles often reveal the need and timing for replacement products or perhaps even a new platform. In addition, gaps in the product line are identified. In this way, place marks are inserted in the product road map for these required developments. Such an exercise is undertaken periodically in order to keep the product line fresh, current, and complete.

● *Competitive analysis.* Where are the business's products and product lines relative to those of its competitors? Here one assesses competitors' current and probable future offerings and where they have advantage, and then assesses the gaps. This exercise often points to the need for new products either immediately or in the foreseeable future.

● *Technology trend assessment.* Here one forecasts technology and what new technologies, and hence new platform developments, will be required and their timing. For example, each new cell phone technology signals a host of development projects within cell phone manufacturing firms and also within service providers.

● *Market trends assessment.* This is a forecasting exercise and looks at major market trends and shifts. In this exercise, often one is able to pinpoint specific initiatives that must be undertaken in response to these evident trends; for example, in the food business, "the development of a line of nutriceutical 'good-for-you' foods."

STRATEGIC BUCKETS

A second strategic resource allocation approach is strategic buckets, which can be used alongside or instead of the product road map. When translating the business's strategy into strategic portfolio decisions (the middle left part of Figure 5–9), a major challenge is spending breakdown or deployment. Where does senior management wish to spend its resources when it comes to product innovation: on what types of projects and in what product, market, or technology areas? And how much do they wish to spend in each area?

The strategic buckets model operates from the simple principle that implementing strategy equates to spending money on specific projects. (Note that "resources" includes dollars as well as people time; hence, resource or money allocation is for both fiscal expenditures and person-months allocation.) Thus, operationalizing strategy really means setting spending targets.

The method begins with the business's strategy and requires senior management to make forced choices along each of several dimensions—choices about how they wish to allocate their scarce resources. This enables the creation of "envelopes of resources" or "buckets." Existing projects are categorized into buckets; then senior management determines whether actual spending is consistent with desired spending for each bucket. Finally, projects are prioritized within buckets to arrive at the ultimate portfolio of projects—one that mirrors management's strategy for the business.

A rather simple breakdown is used at Honeywell: the Mercedes Benz star method of allocating resources (Figure 5–11). The leadership team of the business begins with the business's strategy and uses the Mercedes emblem (the three-point star) to help divide up the resources. There are three buckets:

● Platform development projects, which promise to yield major breakthroughs and new technology platforms
● New product developments
● Others, which include extensions, modifications, product improvements, and cost reductions

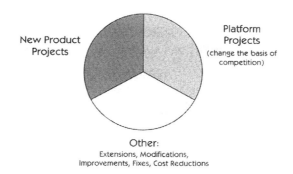

The business's strategy dictates the split of resources into buckets; projects are rank ordered within buckets, but using different criteria within each bucket.

FIGURE 5–11 Strategic Buckets: The Mercedes Benz Star Method of Portfolio Management

Source: R. G. Cooper, S. J. Edgett, and E. J. Kleinschmidt, Portfolio Management for New Products, 2nd ed. (Reading, Mass.: Perseus Book, 2002).

Management divides the R&D funds into these three buckets. Next, the projects are sorted into each of the three buckets; management then ranks projects against each other within each bucket. In effect, three separate portfolios of projects are created and managed, and the spending breakdown across buckets and project types mirrors strategic priorities.

What dimensions should be used in the strategic buckets splits? One leading R&D planning executive identified them as "whatever dimensions the leadership team of the business find most relevant to describe their own strategy." In other businesses, such as ITT Industries, the dimensions used in each business unit are prescribed. ITT uses two dimensions: project types and business areas. And Honeywell uses only the single-dimension project types as in Figure 5–11. Some common dimensions to consider are:

● *Strategic goals:* Management splits resources across the specified strategic goals. For example, what percentage will be spent on defending the base? On diversifying? On extending the base?

● *Across arenas:* The most obvious spending split is across the strategic arenas defined in the business strategy (arenas are generally product, market, or technology areas where the business wishes to focus its new product efforts). That is, once management has defined the arenas of strategic focus and the priorities of each, they then move to deployment and decide how many resources each arena or battlefield should receive (see Figure 5–12, left).

● *Product lines:* Resources are split across product lines: For example, how much to spend on product line A? On product line B? On C? A plot of product line locations on the product life cycle curve is used to help determine this split.

● *Types of projects:* Decisions or splits can be made in terms of the types of projects (as in Figures 5–11 or 5–12, right).

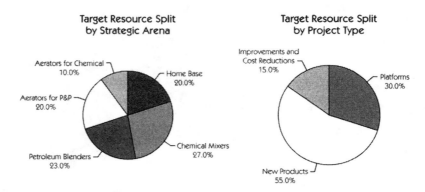

FIGURE 5–12 Deciding the Spending Splits: Strategic Buckets by Strategic Arena and Product Type

As an example, given its aggressive product innovation strategic stance, EXFO Engineering (a manufacturer of fiber-optic test equipment) targets 65 percent of R&D spending to genuine new products, another 10 percent to platform developments and research (technology development for the future), and the final 25 percent to incrementals (the "supportfolio," that is, product modifications, fixes, and improvements).[10]

● *Technologies or technology platforms:* Spending splits can be made across technology types (for example, base, key, pacing, and embryonic technologies) or across specific technology platforms.

● *Familiarity matrix:* What should be the split of resources to different types of markets and different technology types in terms of their familiarity to the business? Some companies use the popular familiarity matrix (technology newness versus market newness) to help split resources (see Figure 5–13).[11]

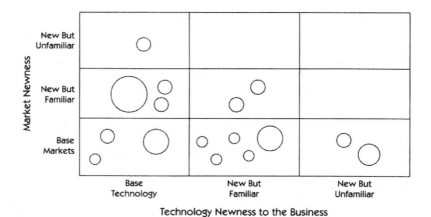

FIGURE 5–13 Familiarity Matrix Bubble Diagram: Resources Split Across Market and Technology Newness Categories

Note: Projects are shown as bubbles, with bubble size denoting the resources being spent on each project.

Source: Reported for Bayer in Cooper, Edgett, and Kleinschmidt, *Portfolio Management for New Products.*

● *Geography:* What proportion of resources should be spent on projects aimed largely at North America? At Latin America? At Europe? At Asia-Pacific? Or globally?

● *By stage or phase of development*: Some businesses distinguish between early-stage projects and projects in development and beyond. Two buckets are created: one for development projects and the other for early-stage projects. One division at GTE allocates seed corn money to a separate bucket for early-stage projects.

THE OPTIMAL SPLIT IN PROJECT TYPES

A major strategic question is, "What's the best mix or balance of development projects—for example, incremental developments versus true innovations?" Certainly, a business's new product strategy ideally should be reflected in the breakdown of types of product developments it undertakes—that is, where the funds are invested. In addition, breakdowns of new products and projects by type are a predictor of the business's new product development performance. For example, too much emphasis on short-term small projects might point to an underachieving business. Table 5–1 shows the breakdown results from the APQC benchmarking study. Incremental product changes is the dominant category, representing 32.7 percent of all projects on average. Next are new products to the business,

TABLE 5–1. Breakdown of Projects by Project Types: Best versus Worst

	Average Business	Best Performers	Worst Performers
Promotional developments and package changes	9.45%	5.89%	12.31%
Incremental product improvements and changes	32.74	28.21	40.42
Major product revisions	21.97	25.00	19.15
New to the business products	24.16	24.11	20.00
New to the world products	10.23	15.89	7.42

Note: Columns do not add up to 100 percent due to a small percentage of other types of products.

Sources: R. G. Cooper, S. J. Edgett, and E. J. Kleinschmidt, *Best Practices in Product Innovation: What Distinguishes Top Performers* (Product Development Institute, 2003) [www.prod-dev.com]; R. G. Cooper, S. J. Edgett, and E. J. Kleinschmidt, *New Product Development Best Practices Study: What Distinguishes the Top Performers* (Houston: American Productivity and Quality Center, 2002) [www.apqc.org].

accounting for 24.2 percent of projects. Then are major product revisions, making up 21.9 percent of projects. There is an even balance among projects across these three most popular categories. And on average, fairly noninnovative products—incrementals, revisions, and promotional developments—together account for about 64 percent of projects. By contrast, new-to-the-world products—true innovations—represent a minority of development projects (10.2 percent).

Do the best performers adopt a different mix of project types, and is there an optimal portfolio of project types? Consider how the average business compares to the best- and worst-performing businesses in Table 5–1. What is noteworthy is the shift toward much more innovative and bolder projects as one moves from worst to best performers. For example, more than half (53 percent) of worst businesses' projects are the small, incremental ones—promotional or package changes or incremental product improvements and changes. By contrast, just over one-third (34 percent) of best performers' projects are these small, incremental ones. Top performers take on a higher proportion of larger, more innovative projects: 40 percent of best performers' projects are either new to the business or true innovations (new to the world). By contrast, only 27 percent of worst performers' projects are these bolder projects. Best performers undertake twice as large a proportion of true innovations (new-to-the-world products) than do worst performers: 15 percent of their projects are true innovations (versus 7 percent).

Tactical Decisions: Picking the Right Development Projects

Tactical portfolio decisions focus on projects and address the questions: What specific new product and development projects should the business undertake? What are their relative priorities? And what resources should be allocated to each? These tactical decisions are shown at the bottom part of Figure 5–1.

To make effective tactical decisions, two project selection processes should be installed (gates and portfolio review), both working in harmony, as in Figure 5–1 (bottom).

Project decisions are made at *gates* (bottom right of Figure 5–1). Embedded within the idea-to-launch new product framework are go/kill decision points called gates (see Stage-Gate® in Section 5.1). Gates provide an in-depth review of individual projects, and render go/kill, prioritization, and resource allocation decisions; hence, gates must be part of the portfolio management system.

Many companies already have a gating process in place and confuse that with a comprehensive portfolio management system. Doing the right projects is more than simply individual project selection at gate meetings; it's about the entire mix of projects and new product or technology investments that the business makes. Project selection deals only with the fingers: go/kill decisions are made on individual projects, each judged individually and on its own merits. Portfolio management deals with the fist: it is holistic and looks at the entire set of project investments together.

The second decision process is the periodic *portfolio review* (bottom left of Figure 5–1). Senior management meets perhaps two to four times per year to review the portfolio of all projects. Here, senior management also makes go/kill and prioritization decisions, where all projects are considered on the table together, and all or some could be up for auction. Key issues and questions are:

- Are all projects strategically aligned (fit the business's strategy)?
- Does management have the right priorities among projects?
- Are there some projects on the active list that should be killed or perhaps accelerated?
- Is there the right balance of projects? The right mix?
- Are there enough resources to do all these projects?
- Is there sufficiency? If one does these projects, will the business achieve its stated business goals?

Both decision processes, gating and portfolio reviews, are needed. Note that the gates are project specific and provide a thorough review of each project in depth and in real time. By contrast, portfolio reviews are holistic: they look at all projects together, but in much less detail on each project. In some businesses, if the gates are working, not too many decisions or major corrective actions are required at the portfolio review. Some companies indicate that they don't even look at individual projects at the portfolio review, but consider projects only in aggregate. But in other businesses, the majority of decisions are made at these quarterly or semiannual portfolio reviews.

Tools to Use for Effective Gates and Portfolio Reviews

Within these gates and portfolio reviews, a number of tools can be used to help achieve portfolio goals: maximize the portfolio's value, achieve the right balance and mix or projects, and ensure strategic alignment yet not overload the development pipeline.[12]

MAXIMIZING THE VALUE OF THE PORTFOLIO

The methods used to achieve this goal range from financial tools to balanced scorecard models. Each has its strengths and weaknesses. The end result of each is a rank-ordered or prioritized list of "go" and "hold" projects, with the projects at the top of the list scoring highest in terms of achieving the desired objectives: the portfolio's value in terms of that objective is thus maximized.

Rank Projects Using Their Economic Value or Net Present Value. The simplest approach is merely to calculate the NPV (net present value) of each project on a spreadsheet. Most businesses already require the NPV and a financial spreadsheet as part of the project's business case, so the NPV number is already available for each project.

The NPV, a proxy for the economic value of the project to the business, can be used in two ways. First, go/kill decisions at gates are based on NPV. Project teams should use the minimum acceptable financial return or hurdle rate (as a percentage) for projects of this risk level as the discount rate when calculating their projects' NPVs. If the NPV is positive, the project clears the hurdle rate. So NPV is a key input to go/kill decision at gates. A best practice here is for the business's finance department to develop a standardized spread-sheet for this calculation so all project teams produce a consistently calculated NPV. Also, the finance people should develop a table of risk-adjusted discount rates for project teams to use for different risk levels of projects: low risk (such as a cost reduction project) to high risk (a genuine new product, first of its kind).

Second, at portfolio reviews, all projects are ranked according to their NPVs. The go projects are those that are at the top of the list. One continues to add projects down the list until resources run out. The result is a prioritized list of projects, which logically should maximize the NPV of the portfolio. In the example in Table 5–2, the top four projects are Foxtrot, Beta, Echo, and Alpha, but there is a resource limit of $15 million in the development budget. Thus, only two projects are go: Foxtrot and Beta (they consume almost all of the $15 million budget). The value of the portfolio is $115 million from these two projects.

This method is fine in theory, but there are some problems. The NPV method assumes that financial projections are accurate for development projects (they usually are not); it assumes that only financial goals are important, for example, that strategic considerations are irrelevant; it ignores probabilities of success and risk (except by using risk-adjusted discount rates); and it fails to deal with constrained resources, that is, the desire to maximize the value for a limited resource commitment, or getting the most bang for the limited buck. A final objection is more subtle: the fact that NPV assumes an all-or-nothing investment decision, whereas in new product projects, the decision process is an incremental one, more like buying a series of options on a project.[13]

This NPV method has a number of attractive features, however. First, it requires the project team to submit a financial assessment of the project. That means they must do some research, make some fact-based projections, and think through the commercial implications of the project before development begins. Second, a discounted cash flow method is used, which is the correct way to value investments, as opposed to EBIT (earnings before interest and taxes), ROI (return on investment), or payback period. Finally, all monetary amounts are discounted to today (not just to launch date), thereby appropriately penalizing projects that are years away from launch.

Rank Projects Using the Productivity Index Based on the NPV. Here's an important modification to the NPV ranking approach that recognizes that resources are limited. The problem is that some projects (for example, Foxtrot and Beta in Table 5–2) are great projects and have huge NPVs, but they consume many resources, thus making it impossible to do other less attractive but far less resource-intensive projects. Other projects, although having lower NPVs, are quite efficient: they can be done using relatively few resources. How does one decide?

Simple. The goal is to maximize the bang for buck, and the way to do this is to take the ratio of what one is trying to maximize (in this case, the NPV) divided by the constraining resource (the R&D dollars required). (This decision rule of rank order according to the ratio of what one is trying to maximize divided by the constraining resource seems to be an effective one. Simulations with a number of sets of projects show that this decision rule works very well, truly giving "maximum bang for buck.") One may choose to use R&D people or work-months or the total dollar cost remaining in the project (or even capital funds) as the constraining resource. This bang-for-buck ratio or "productivity index" is shown in column 4 in Table 5–3: Productivity index = NPV of the project/Total resources remaining to be spent on the project.

Now it's time to re-sort the list of projects. But first consider the constraint: the R&D spending constraint is $15 million for new products in this business (the resources required to do all the projects in Table 5–3 adds up to $26 million). To select the go projects, one

TABLE 5–2. Using NPV to Rank and Prioritize Projects

Project	PV (present value of future earnings)	Development Cost	Commercialization Cost	NPV (net present value)	Ranking Based on NPV	Decision
Alpha	30	3	5	22	4	Hold
Beta	64	5	2	57	2	Go
Gamma	9	2	1	6	5	Hold
Delta	3	1	0.5	1.5	6	Hold
Echo	50	5	3	42	3	Hold
Foxtrot	66	10	2	58	1	Go

Note: All figures are in millions of dollars

TABLE 5-3 Ranking Projects According to the NPV-Based Productivity Index

Project	NPV	Development Cost	Productivity Index = NPV/ Development Cost	Sum of Development Costs
Beta	57	5	11.4	5
Echo	42	5	8.4	10
Alpha	22	3	7.3	13
				Limit reached
Foxtrot	58	10	5.8	23
Gamma	6	2	3.0	25
Delta	1.5	1	1.5	26

Note: The Productivity Index is used to rank projects until out of resources. The horizontal line shows the limit: the $15 million in development costs is reached. Go projects are now Beta, Echo, and Alpha. Foxtrot drops off the list. The value of the portfolio is NPV = $121M from these three projects.

simply reorders the project list, ranking projects according to the productivity index (this reordering is shown in Table 5–3). Then one goes down the list until out of resources. Note that column 6 shows the cumulative resource expenditure. One runs out of resources (that is, hits the $15 million limit) after project Alpha.

The point to note here is that introducing the notion of constrained resources, which every business has, dramatically changes the ranking of projects. Compare the ranked list in Table 5–2 with that in Table 5–3. Note that Foxtrot, the number one project in Table 5–2, drops off the list entirely using the productivity index in Table 5–3; the resulting portfolio contains more projects; and its overall economic value is higher.

This NPV productivity index method yields benefits in addition to those inherent in the straight NPV approach above. By introducing the productivity index ratio, the method favors those projects that are almost completed and have little cost remaining in them (the denominator is small, hence the productivity index is high). And the method deals with resource constraints, yielding the best set of projects for a given budget or resource limit.

Introduce Risk by Using Expected Commercial Value. This method seeks to maximize the commercial value of the portfolio, subject to certain budget constraints, but introduces the notion of risks and probabilities. The expected commercial value (ECV) method determines the probability-adjusted value of each project to the corporation, namely, its expected commercial value. The calculation of the ECV, based on a decision tree analysis, considers the future stream of earnings from the project, the probabilities of both commercial success and technical success, along with both commercialization costs and development costs (see Figure 5–14 for the calculation and definition of terms). Because the

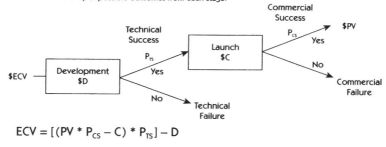

A model of a two-stage investment decision process. First, invest $D in development, which may yield a technical success with probability P_T. Then invest $C in commercialization, which may result in a commercial success with proability P_CS. If successful, the project yields an income stream whose present value is $PV. More sophisticated versions of this model entail more stages than the two shown here and an array of possible outcomes from each stage.

$$ECV = [(PV * P_{CS} - C) * P_{TS}] - D$$

ECV = Expected commercial value of the project
P_{TS} = Probability of technical success
P_{CS} = Probability of commercial success (given technical success)
D = Development costs remaining in the project
C = Commercialization (launch) costs
PV = Net present value of project's future earnings (discounted to today)

FIGURE 5–14 Determining the Expected Commercial Value of a Project

Source: Cooper, Edgett, and Kleinschmidt, Portfolio Management for New Products.

method treats new product development investment decisions in a series of stages, the solution a close proxy for options pricing theory or real options.

The ECV can be used at gate meetings as an input to the go/kill decision, much like the NPV, except risk and probabilities are built in. For portfolio reviews, in order to arrive at a prioritized list of projects, what resources are scarce or limiting are identified, much like the NPV productivity index example above. Then the productivity index ratio is computed: what one is trying to maximize (the ECV) divided by the constraining resource. Projects are rank-ordered according to this new productivity index until the resource limit is reached. Projects at the top of the list are go, and those at the bottom (beyond the resource limit) are placed on hold. The method thus ensures the greatest bang for the buck—that the ECV is maximized for a given resources limit.

This ECV model has a number of attractive additional features. It includes probabilities and risk, which are inherent in any new product project; it recognizes that the go/kill decision process is an incremental one (the notion of purchasing options, a stage-wise decision process); and it deals with the issue of constrained resources and attempts to maximize the value of the portfolio in the light of this constraint.

Use a Simulation Financial Model for Major Projects. Another way to introduce risk and probabilities is the use of a computer-based Monte Carlo simulation model, such as $^@$Risk. Here's how these models are used. Instead of merely imputing a point estimate for each financial variable in the spreadsheet, such as year 1 sales, year 2 sales, and so on, one inputs three estimates for each variable: a best case, a worst case, and a likely case. A probability curve (much like a bell-shaped curve) is drawn through each set of estimates. So each financial estimate (sales, costs, investment, and others) has a probability distribution.

The model begins by calculating multiple scenarios of possible financial outcomes, all based on the probability distributions. Tens of thousands of scenarios are quickly generated by the computer, each yielding a financial outcome such as the NPV. The distribution of the NPVs generated in these thousands of scenarios becomes the profit distribution—an expected NPV as well as a probability distribution of NPVs.

One can use the NPV and its distribution to help make the go/kill decision at gates, much as in the method for ranking projects using their economic value or NPV; take the expected NPV and divide by the costs remaining in the project; and rank the projects according to this probability-adjusted NPV, much as in ranking projects using the productivity index based on the NPV.

These simulation models, such as $^@$Risk, are commercially available and relatively easy to use. But there are a few quirks or assumptions in the model that cause problems. For example, the model fails to deal with the options notion of a new product project, and it permits the generation of all-but-impossible scenarios. Nonetheless, it's a solid method and particularly appropriate for projects that involve large capital expenditures and where probability distributions of input variables can be estimated.

Score Projects Using a Balanced Scorecard Approach. Scoring models or balanced scorecards are based on the premise that a more balanced approach to project selection is desirable—that not everything can be reduced to a single NPV or ECV metric. Thus, a variety of criteria are used to rate the project. These criteria are based on research into what makes new product projects successful, and hence are proven proxies for success and profitability.

In a scorecard system, each senior manager rates the project on a number of criteria on 1–5 or 0–10 scales. Typical criteria include:

- Strategic alignment
- Product and competitive advantage
- Market attractiveness
- Ability to leverage core competencies
- Technical feasibility
- Reward versus risk

The scores from the various senior managers at the gate review are tallied and combined, and the project attractiveness score is computed: the weighted or unweighted addition of the item ratings. This attractiveness score is the basis for making the go/kill decision at gates, and can also be used to develop a rank-ordered list of projects for portfolio reviews. A sample scoring model for well-defined new product projects is shown in Table 5–4. (Different scorecards with different criteria should be used for different types of projects: one scorecard for simple projects such as line extensions and modifications; another scorecard for true new products, as in Table 5–4; and yet another scorecard for major platform projects.)

Scoring models generally are praised in spite of their limited popularity. Research into project selection methods reveals that scoring models produce a strategically aligned portfolio and one that reflects the business's spending priorities; they yield effective and efficient decisions better than the financial tools outlined above; and they result in a portfolio of high-value projects.[14]

Seeking the Right Balance of Projects

A major portfolio goal is a balanced portfolio: a balanced set of development projects in terms of a number of key parameters. The analogy is that of an investment fund, where the fund manager seeks balance in terms of high-risk versus blue-chip stocks and balance across industries and geographies in order to arrive at an optimum investment portfolio.

Visual charts effectively display balance in new product project portfolios. These visual representations include portfolio maps or bubble diagrams (see the example in Figure 5–15), an adaptation of the four-quadrant BCG (stars, cash cows, dogs, and wildcats) diagrams that have seen service since the 1970s as strategy models, as well as more traditional pie charts and histograms.

A casual review of portfolio bubble diagrams will lead some readers to observe that "these new models are nothing more than the old strategy bubble diagrams of the 1970s!" *Not so.* Recall that the BCG strategy model and others like it (such as the McKinsey-GE model) plot business units on a "market attractiveness" versus "business position" grid. Note that the unit of analysis is the business unit: an existing business whose performance, strengths, and weaknesses are all known. By contrast, today's new product portfolio bubble diagrams, which may appear similar, plot individual new product projects—that is, fu-

Table 5–4 A Typical Balanced Scorecard for New Product Project Selection

Factor 1: Strategic Fit and Importance

- Alignment of project with our business's strategy
- Importance of project to the strategy
- Impact on the business

Factor 2: Product and Competitive Advantage

- Product delivers unique customer or user benefits
- Product offers customer/user excellent value for money
- Competitive rationale for project
- Positive customer/user feedback on product concept (concept test results)

Factor 3: Market Attractiveness

- Market size
- Market growth and future potential
- Margins earned by players in this market
- Competitiveness—how tough and intense competition is

Factor 4: Core Competencies Leverage

- Project leverages our core competencies and strengths in:
  - Technology
  - Production/operations
  - Marketing
  - Distribution/sales force

Factor 5: Technical Feasibility

- Size of technical gap
- Familiarity of technology to our business
- Newness of technology (base to embryonic)
- Technical complexity
- Technical results to date (proof of concept?)

Factor 6: Financial Reward versus Risk

- Size of financial opportunity
- Financial return (NPV, ECV)
- Productivity index
- Certainty of financial estimates
- Level of risk and ability to address risks

- Projects are scored by the gatekeepers (senior management) at the gate meeting using these six factors on a scorecard (0–10 scales).
- The scores are tallied, averaged across the evaluators, and displayed for discussion.
- The project attractiveness score (PAS) is the weighted or unweighted addition of the scores, taken out of 100.
- A PAS score of 60/100 is usually required for a go decision.

Sources: R. G. Cooper, Product Leadership: Pathways to Profitable Innovation, 2nd ed. (Reading, Mass.: Perseus Books, 2005); R. G. Cooper, S. J. Edgett, and E. J. Kleinschmidt, Portfolio Management for New Products, 2nd ed. (Reading, Mass.: Perseus Books, 2002).

ture businesses, or what might be. As for the dimensions of the grid, here too the "market attractiveness" versus "business position" dimensions used for existing business units may not be as appropriate for new product possibilities, so other dimensions or axes are extensively used.

What are some of the parameters that should be plotted on these portfolio diagrams in order to seek balance? Different pundits recommend various parameters and lists and even suggest the best plots to use.

Risk-Reward Bubble Diagrams. The most popular bubble diagram is the risk-return chart (see Figure 5–15). About 44 percent of businesses with a systematic portfolio management scheme in place use this bubble diagram or one like it.[15] Here, one axis is some measure of the reward to the company and the other is a success probability.

One approach is to use a qualitative estimate of reward, ranging from "modest" to "excellent."[16] The argument here is that too heavy an emphasis on financial analysis can do serious damage, notably in the early stages of a project. The other axis is the probability of overall success (probability of commercial success times probability of technical success).

In contrast, other firms rely on very quantitative and financial gauges of reward, namely, the probability-adjusted NPV of the project.[17] Here the probability of technical success is the vertical axis, as probability of commercial success has already been built into the NPV calculation.

A sample bubble diagram is shown in Figure 5–15 for a business unit of a major chemical company. Here the size of each bubble shows the annual resources committed to each project (dollars per year; it could also be people or work-months allocated to the project). The four quadrants of the portfolio model are:

- *Pearls* (upper-left quadrant): These are the potential star products: projects with a high likelihood of success and that are also expected to yield a very high reward. Most businesses desire more of these. There are two such Pearl projects, and one of them has been allocated considerable resources (denoted by the sizes of the circles).

- *Oysters* (lower-left quadrant): These are the long-shot projects: those with a high expected payoff but with low likelihoods of technical success. They are the projects where technical breakthroughs will pave the way for solid payoffs. There are three of these; none is receiving many resources.

- *Bread and Butter* (upper-right quadrant): These are small, simple projects with a high likelihood of success but low reward. They include the many fixes, extensions, modifications, and updating projects of which most companies have too many. More than 50 percent of spending is going to these projects.

- *White Elephants* (lower-right quadrant): These are the low-probability and low-reward projects. Every business has a few white elephants; they inevitably are difficult to kill, but this company has far too many. One-third of the projects and about 25 percent of spending fall in this quadrant.

Given that this chemical business is in a specialty area and a star business seeking rapid growth, a quick review of the portfolio map in Figure 5–15 reveals many problems.

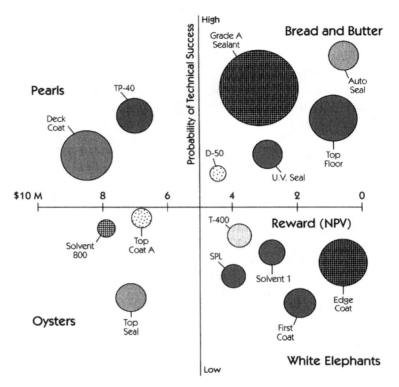

FIGURE 5–15 A Risk-Reward Bubble Diagram

Note: Projects are plotted as bubbles, with bubble size denoting the resources committed to each project. The shading or cross-hatching shows the product line that each project is associated with.

Source: Cooper, Edgett, and Kleinschmidt, *Portfolio Management for New Products.*

There are too many White Elephant projects (it's time to do some serious project pruning), too much money spent on Bread and Butter low-value projects, not enough Pearls, and heavily underresourced Oysters.

One feature of this bubble diagram model is that it forces senior management to deal with the resource issue. Given finite resources, the sum of the areas of the circles must be a constant. That is, if one adds one project to the diagram, another must be subtracted; alternatively, one can shrink the size of several circles. The elegance here is that the model forces management to consider the resource implications of adding one more project to the list: some other projects must pay the price.

Also shown in this bubble diagram is the product line that each project is associated with (the shading or cross-hatching). A final breakdown is timing, indicated by color (not shown in the black-and-white figure). Thus, this apparently simple risk-reward diagram shows a lot more than risk and profitability data. It also conveys resource allocation, timing, and spending breakdowns across product lines.

Bubble Diagrams That Capture Newness to the Firm. Two key dimensions that senior managers should consider when mapping their development portfolio are:

- Market newness—how new or "step-out" the markets are for projects underway
- Technology newness—how new the development and manufacturing technology is to the business

Both dimensions are proxies for risk and aggressiveness.[18] Here, development projects are plotted on these two axes in order to help management view the current portfolio and whether it has the right balance and mix of step-out versus close-to-home projects (similar to the newness diagram in Figure 5–13). Again, circle sizes denote resources allocated to each project. This is the second most popular bubble diagram used for NPD portfolio management by industry.

Traditional Charts to Display Resource Breakdowns. There are numerous other parameters, dimensions, or variables across which one might wish to seek a balance of projects. As a result, there is an endless variety of histograms and pie charts that help to portray portfolio balance—for example:

- Resource breakdown by project types is a vital concern. What is the spending on genuine new products versus product renewals (improvements and replacements), or product extensions, or product maintenance, or cost reductions and process improvements? And what should it be? Pie charts effectively capture the spending split across project types—actual versus desired splits, shown in italics in Figure 5–16. Pie charts that show the resource breakdown by project types are a particularly useful sanity check when the business has already established strategic buckets. Now one can compare the current resource split (the "what is") to the target split ("what should be") as defined by strategic buckets, as in Figure 5–16. Note in this figure that the market sector splits are almost on target, but the project types are too heavily weighted toward cost reductions and fixes.
- Markets, products, and technologies provide another set of dimensions across which managers seek balance. The question is: Does the business have the appropriate split in R&D spending across its various product lines? Or across the markets or market segments in which it operates (see Figure 5–16)? Or across the technologies it possesses? Pie charts are again appropriate for capturing and displaying these types of data. And once again, these pie charts close the loop on the strategic buckets exercise, revealing the "what is" versus the "what should be."
- Timing is a key issue in the quest for balance. One does not wish to invest strictly in short-term projects or totally in long-term ones. Another timing goal is for a steady stream of new product launches spread out over the quarters, that is, constant "new news" and no sudden logjam of product launches all in one quarter. A histogram captures the issue of timing and portrays the distribution of resources to specific projects according to quarters or years of launch.
- Another timing issue is *cash flow*. Here the desire is to balance projects in such a way that cash inflows are reasonably balanced with cash outflows in the business. Some companies produce a timing histogram that portrays the total cash flow per year from all projects in the portfolio over the next three to five years.

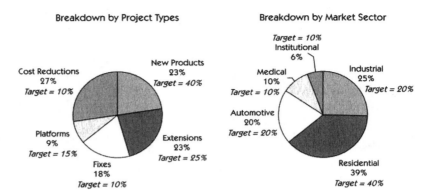

FIGURE 5–16 Pie Charts: Actual versus Targeted Resource Allocation in the Portfolio

Note: The targets are shown in italics, and the pie chart slices show expenditure breakdowns to date.

Popularity and Effectiveness of Portfolio Methods

Which methods are the most popular, and which work the best? In practice, not surprisingly, the financial methods dominate portfolio management, according to a portfolio best practices study.[19] Financial methods include various profitability and return metrics, such as NPV, ECV, ROI, EV, or payback period—metrics that are used to rate, rank-order, and ultimately select projects. A total of 77.3 percent of businesses use such a financial approach in portfolio management (see Figure 5–17). For 40.4 percent of businesses, this is the dominant method.

Other methods are also quite popular:

- *Strategic approaches:* Letting the strategy dictate the portfolio is a popular approach and includes strategic buckets, product road mapping, and other strategically driven methods. A total of 64.8 percent of businesses use a strategic approach; for 26.6 percent of businesses, this is the dominant method.
- *Bubble diagrams or portfolio maps:* Slightly more than 40 percent of businesses use portfolio maps, but only 8.3 percent use this as their dominant method. The most popular map is the risk-versus-reward map in Figure 5–15, but many variants of bubble diagrams are used.
- *Scoring or scorecard models:* Scaled ratings are obtained by using scorecards at gates and are added to yield a project attractiveness score. These models are used by 37.9 percent of businesses; in 18.3 percent, this is the dominant decision method.
- *Checklists:* Projects are evaluated on a set of yes-no questions. Each project must achieve either all yes answers or a certain number of yes answers to proceed. The number of yes answers is used to make go/kill and/or prioritization (ranking) decisions. Only 17.5 percent of businesses use checklists, and in only 2.7 percent is this the dominant method.

Popularity does not necessarily equate to effectiveness, however. When the performance of businesses' portfolios was rated on six metrics in our study, those businesses that

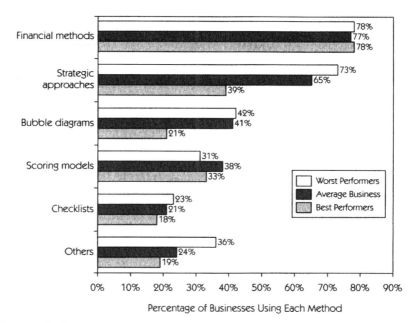

FIGURE 5–17 Popularity of Portfolio Methods

Source: Cooper, Edgett, and Kleinschmidt, Portfolio Management for New Products.

relied heavily on financial tools as the dominant portfolio selection model fared the worst. Financial tools yield an unbalanced portfolio of lower-value projects and projects that lack strategic alignment. By contrast, strategic methods produce a strategically aligned and balanced portfolio. And scorecard models appear best for selecting high-value projects and also yield a balanced portfolio. Finally, businesses using bubble diagrams obtain a balanced and strategic aligned portfolio.

It is ironic that the most rigorous techniques—the various financial tools—yield the worst results, not so much because the methods are flawed but simply because reliable financial data are often missing at the very point in a project where the key project selection decisions are made. Often, reliable financial data (expected sales, pricing, margins, and costs) are difficult to estimate in many cases because the project team simply has not done its homework. As one executive exclaimed as he referred to his business's sophisticated financial model being applied to projects with very soft data, "We're trying to measure a soft banana with a micrometer." In other cases, an overzealous project leader makes highly optimistic projections in order to secure support for his project.

**Implementing a
Systematic Portfolio
Management Process**

Having a portfolio management approach in place seems to be more important than the details of which tools and metrics one chooses. Any portfolio system seems to be better than no system at all. The research shows clearly that businesses that feature a systematic portfolio management process, regardless of the specific approach, outperform the rest (Figure 5–18).[20]

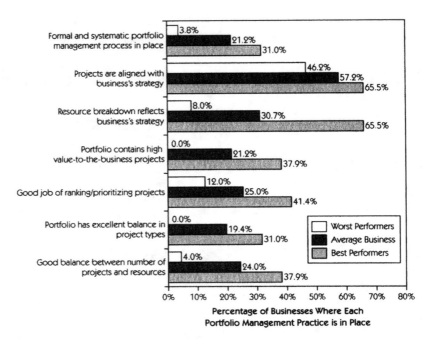

Reads: 21.2% of businesses have a systematic portfolio management process in place
(meaning that 79% do not!). Best performers are better here, with 31.0% having such
a system, while only 3.8% of poor performers do.

FIGURE 5–18 Impact of Portfolio Management Practices on Performance

Sources: Cooper, Edgett, and Kleinschmidt, Best Practices in Product Development, and Cooper,
Edgett, and Kleinschmidt, New Product Development Best Practices Study.

Top-performing businesses in product development have implemented a systematic portfolio management approach; they have achieved strategic alignment of projects with their
innovation strategy; they prioritize and rank their projects effectively so that their portfolios contain high value-to-the-corporation projects; and they seek and achieve the right
balance and mix of projects. Portfolio management pays off.

Robert G. Cooper is professor of marketing at the School of Business, McMaster
University in Ontario, Canada, and ISBM Distinguished Research Fellow at Penn State
University's Smeal College of Business Administration. He is the father and developer of
the Stage-Gate™ process, now widely used around the world to drive new products to
market. He is a prolific researcher and thought leader in the field of product innovation
management, with more than ninety articles in leading journals on new product management and six books.

NOTES _____

Chapter 5

1. Stage-Gate® is a registered term.

Section 5.1

1. "Fast, Focused, Fertile: The Innovation Evolution, Cheskin and Fitch: Worldwide, 2003." [www.fitchworldwide.com].
2. See new product performance results in R. G. Cooper, *Winning at New Products: Accelerating the Process from Idea to Launch,* 3rd ed. (Reading, Mass.: Perseus Books, 2001); American Productivity and Quality Center, *New Product Development Best Practices Study: What Distinguishes the Top Performers* (Houston: American Productivity and Quality Center, 2002).
3. The term *Stage-Gate*® was coined by the author in the 1980s and is a trademark of the Product Development Institute, www.prod-dev.com.
4. The APQC benchmarking study is a major study into new product performance and practices by the premier benchmarking institute in the United States. For more details on the benchmarking study, see American Productivity and Quality Center, *New Product Development Best Practices Study,* and R. G. Cooper, S. J. Edgett, and E. J. Kleinschmidt, *Best Practices in Product Innovation: What Distinguishes Top Performers* (Newtown Square, Pa.: Product Development Institute, 2003). The APQC benchmarking results cited in this chapter have also appeared in recent journal articles; see, for example, R. G. Cooper, S. J. Edgett, and E. J. Kleinschmidt, "Benchmarking Best NPD Practices—Part I: Culture, Climate, Teams and Senior Management Roles," *Research Technology Management,* 2003, *47*(1), 31–43; R. G. Cooper, S. J. Edgett, and E. J. Kleinschmidt, "Benchmarking Best NPD Practices—Part II: Strategy, Resource Allocation and Portfolio Management," *Research Technology Management,* 2004, *47*(3), 50–59; and R. G. Cooper, S. J. Edgett, and E. J. Kleinschmidt, "Benchmarking Best NPD Practices—Part III: The NPD Process and Decisive Idea-to-Launch Practices," *Research Technology Management,* 2004, *47*(6).
5. See A. Griffin, *Drivers of NPD Success: The 1997 PDMA Report* (Chicago: Product Development and Management Association, 1997).
6. Griffin, *Drivers of NPD Success.*
7. The term *Stage-Gate*® first appeared in print in R. G. Cooper, "The New Product Process: A Decision Guide for Managers," *Journal of Marketing Management,* 1988, *3*(3), 238–255. An earlier version was outlined in previous works; see, for example, R. G. Cooper, *Winning at New Products* (Reading, Mass: Addison Wesley, 1986). *Stage-Gate*® is now a legally registered trade name in a number of countries.
8. Problems and challenges in project selection and portfolio management were uncovered in several studies. See Cooper, Edgett, and Kleinschmidt, "Portfolio Management in New Product Development: Lessons from the Leaders—Part I"; Cooper, Edgett, and Kleinschmidt, "Portfolio Management in New Product Development: Lessons from the Leaders—Part II"; and R. G. Cooper, S. J. Edgett, and E. J. Kleinschmidt, "Best Practices for Managing R&D Portfolios," *Research-Technology Management,* 1998, *41*(4), pp.

20–33. A second major benchmarking study, undertaken with the Industrial Research Institute, into portfolio management practices probed portfolio management practices and performance. Results are in R. G. Cooper, S. J. Edgett, and E. J. Kleinschmidt, "New Product Portfolio Management: Practices and Performance," *Journal of Product Innovation Management,* 1999, *16*(4), 333–351; and R. G. Cooper, S. J. Edgett, and E. J. Kleinschmidt, "Portfolio Management for New Product Development: Results of an Industry Practices Study," *R&D Management,* 2001, *31,* 361–380.

9. American Productivity and Quality Center, *New Product Development Best Practices Study*; Cooper, Edgett, and Kleinschmidt, *Best Practices in Product Innovation: What Distinguishes Top Performers*; Cooper, Edgett, and Kleinschmidt, "Benchmarking Best NPD Practices—Part I: Culture, Climate, Teams and Senior Management Roles"; Cooper, Edgett, and Kleinschmidt, "Benchmarking Best NPD Practices—Part II: Strategy, Resource Allocation and Portfolio Management"; Cooper, Edgett, and Kleinschmidt, "Benchmarking Best NPD Practices—Part III: The NPD Process and Decisive Idea-to-Launch Practices."

10. Parts of this section are taken from R. G. Cooper, "Overhauling the New Product Process," *Industrial Marketing Management,* 1996, *25,* 465–482.

11. The assessments are from American Productivity and Quality Center, *New Product Development Best Practices Study: What Distinguishes the Top Performers.* Similar results have been reported in other studies. See, for example, S. Mishra, D. Kim, and D. H. Lee, "Factors Affecting New Product Success: Cross Country Comparisons," *Journal of Product Innovation Management,* 1996, *13,* 530–550; X. M. Song and M. E. Parry, "What Separates Japanese New Product Winners from Losers," *Journal of Product Innovation Management,* 1996, *13,* 422–439; X. M. Song and M. M. Montoya-Weiss, "Critical Development Activities for Really New Versus Incremental Products," *Journal of Product Innovation Management,* 1998, *15,* 124–135; C. A. Di Benedetto, "Identifying the Key Success Factors in New Product Launch," *Journal of Product Innovation Management,* 1999, *16,* 530–544. For a comprehensive review of factors that lead to success in new product development, see R. G. Cooper, *The PDMA Handbook of New Product Development,* 2nd ed. (New York: Wiley, 2004).

12. American Productivity and Quality Center, *New Product Development Best Practices Study*; Cooper, Edgett, and Kleinschmidt, *Best Practices in Product Innovation: What Distinguishes Top Performers*; Cooper, Edgett, and Kleinschmidt, "Benchmarking Best NPD Practices—Part I: Culture, Climate, Teams and Senior Management Roles"; Cooper, Edgett, and Kleinschmidt, "Benchmarking Best NPD Practices—Part II: Strategy, Resource Allocation and Portfolio Management"; Cooper, Edgett, and Kleinschmidt, "Benchmarking Best NPD Practices—Part III: The NPD Process and Decisive Idea-to-Launch Practices."

13. The rugby analogy was first introduced in B. Uttal, "Speeding New Ideas to Market," *Fortune,* Mar. 1987, pp. 62–66.

14. Some of these practices are explained in Cooper, *Winning at New Products*; Cooper, *The PDMA Handbook of New Product Development*; R. G. Cooper "Third-Generation New Product Processes," *Journal of Product Innovation Management,* 1994, *11*(1), 3–14.

15. American Productivity and Quality Center, *New Product Development Best Practices Study*; Cooper, Edgett, and Kleinschmidt, *Best Practices in Product Innovation: What

Distinguishes Top Performers; Cooper, Edgett, and Kleinschmidt, "Benchmarking Best NPD Practices—Part I: Culture, Climate, Teams and Senior Management Roles"; Cooper, Edgett, and Kleinschmidt, "Benchmarking Best NPD Practices—Part II: Strategy, Resource Allocation and Portfolio Management"; Cooper, Edgett, and Kleinschmidt, "Benchmarking Best NPD Practices—Part III: The NPD Process and Decisive Idea-to-Launch Practices."

16. American Productivity and Quality Center, *New Product Development Best Practices Study*; Cooper, Edgett, and Kleinschmidt, *Best Practices in Product Innovation: What Distinguishes Top Performers*; Cooper, Edgett, and Kleinschmidt, "Benchmarking Best NPD Practices—Part I: Culture, Climate, Teams and Senior Management Roles"; Cooper, Edgett, and Kleinschmidt, "Benchmarking Best NPD Practices—Part II: Strategy, Resource Allocation and Portfolio Management"; Cooper, Edgett, and Kleinschmidt, "Benchmarking Best NPD Practices—Part III: The NPD Process and Decisive Idea-to-Launch Practices."

17. For more information on the use of lead users in idea generation, see E. A. Von Hippel, S. Thomke, and M. Sonnack, "Creating Breakthroughs at 3M," *Harvard Business Review,* Sept.-Oct. 1999, pp. 47–57.

18. R. Sears and M. Barry, "Product Value Analysis—Product Interaction Predicts Profits," *Innovation,* Winter 1993, pp. 13–18.

19. For voice of-customer methods and idea generation, see P. Lindstedt and J. Burenius, *The Value Model: How to Master Product Development and Create Unrivalled Customer Value* (Sweden: NIMBA AB, 2003).

20. For more information on fast-track versions of Stage-Gate®, see Cooper, *Product Leadership,* and Cooper, *Winning at New Products.*

21. For more information on Stage-Gate® for technology and platform developments, see Cooper, *Product Leadership,* and Cooper, *Winning at New Products.*

22. L. Yapps-Cohen, P. W. Kamienski, and R. L. Espino, "Gate System Focuses Industrial Basic Research," *Research-Technology Management,* July-Aug. 1998, pp. 34–37.

23. The concept of disruptive technologies (or radical innovations) was first developed by MIT researchers in the 1960s and later popularized by Christensen. See C. M. Christensen, *The Innovator's Dilemma* (New York: HarperCollins, 2000).

24. Milton D. Rosenau Jr. (ed.), *PDMA Handbook for New Product Development* (New York: Wiley, 1996).

25. For a sample scorecard for technology development projects, see R. G. Cooper, S. J. Edgett, and E. J. Kleinschmidt, *Portfolio Management for New Products,* 2nd ed. (Reading, Mass: Perseus Book, 2002).

26. Cooper, *Winning at New Products,* has become the authority for task forces in designing a Stage-Gate® framework.

27. SG-Navigator™ is available from Stage Gate Inc. at www.stage-gate.com.

28. Accolade™ is a comprehensive decision support system for Stage-Gate®. It was developed and is sold by Sopheon Inc. See www.sopheon.com. SG-Navigator™ is a somewhat simpler electronic version of Stage-Gate®, available from Stage Gate Inc. at www.stage-gate.com.

Section 5.2

1. This chapter also draws on R. G. Cooper, S. J. Edgett, and E. J. Kleinschmidt, "Portfolio Management in New Product Development: Lessons from the Leaders—Part I," *Research-Technology Management,* Sept.-Oct. 1997, pp. 16–28; R. G. Cooper, S. J. Edgett, and E. J. Kleinschmidt, "Portfolio Management in New Product Development: Lessons from the Leaders—Part II," *Research-Technology Management,* Nov.-Dec. 1997, pp. 43–57; R. G. Cooper, S. J. Edgett, and E. J. Kleinschmidt, "New Problems, New Solutions: Making Portfolio Management More Effective," *Research-Technology Management,* 2000, *43*(2), 18–33; and R. G. Cooper, S. J. Edgett, and E. J. Kleinschmidt, "Portfolio Management: Fundamental to New Product Success," in P. Beliveau, A. Griffin, and S. Somermeyer (eds.), *The PDMA Toolbox for New Product Development* (New York: Wiley, 2002).

2. Portfolio management is defined in Cooper, Edgett, and Kleinschmidt, "Portfolio Management in New Product Development: Lessons from the Leaders—Part I."

3. P. Roussel, K. N. Saad, and T. J. Erickson, *Third Generation R&D: Managing the Link to Corporate Strategy* (Boston: Harvard Business School Press and Arthur D. Little, 1991).

4. Some statistics cited in this chapter are from a major study on portfolio management practices and performance study. See R. G. Cooper, S. J. Edgett, and E. J. Kleinschmidt, "New Product Portfolio Management: Practices and Performance," *Journal of Product Innovation Management,* 1999, *16,* 333–351; and R. G. Cooper, S. J. Edgett, and E. J. Kleinschmidt, "Portfolio Management for New Product Development: Results of an Industry Practices Study," *R&D Management,* 2001, *31,* 361–380.

5. Parts of this section are taken from R. G. Cooper, "Maximizing the Value of Your New Product Portfolio: Methods, Metrics and Scorecards," *Current Issues in Technology Management,* 2003, *7*(1).

6. R. G. Cooper, S. J. Edgett, and E. J. Kleinschmidt, *Portfolio Management for New Products,* 2nd ed. (Reading, Mass.: Perseus Book, 2002).

7. Much of this section on road mapping is taken from Lucent Technologies. See R. E. Albright, "Roadmaps and Roadmapping: Linking Business Strategy and Technology Planning," in *Proceedings, Portfolio Management for New Product Development, Institute for International Research and Product Development and Management Association* (Fort Lauderdale, Fla., Jan. 2001). See also M. H. Meyer and A. P. Lehnerd, *The Power of Platforms* (New York: Free Press, 1997).

8. For more information on platforms, see Myer and Lehnerd, *The Power of Product Platforms.*

9. Cooper, Edgett, and Kleinschmidt, *Portfolio Management for New Products.*

10. The example is taken from a case study in the American Productivity and Quality Center (APQC) benchmarking study on new product best practices. R. G. Cooper, S. J. Edgett, and E. J. Kleinschmidt, *Best Practices in Product Innovation: What Distinguishes Top Performers* (Product Development Institute, 2003) [www.prod-dev.com]; R. G. Cooper, S. J. Edgett, and E. J. Kleinschmidt, *New Product Development Best Practices Study: What Distinguishes the Top Performers* (Houston: American Productivity and Quality Center, 2002) [www.apqc.org].

11. E. Roberts and C. Berry, "Entering New Businesses: Selecting Strategies for Success," *Sloan Management Review,* Spring 1983, pp. 3–17.

12. More detail on the methods outlined in this section can be found in Cooper, *Product Leadership*; and Cooper, Edgett, and Kleinschmidt, *Portfolio Management for New Products.*

13. T. Faulkner, "Applying 'Options Thinking' to R&D Valuation," *Research-Technology Management,* May-June 1995, pp. 50–57.

14. R. G. Cooper, S. J. Edgett, and E. J. Kleinschmidt, *R&D Portfolio Management Best Practices Study, Industrial Research Institute* (Washington, D.C.: Industrial Research Institute, 1997); R. G. Cooper, S. J. Edgett, and E. J. Kleinschmidt, "Best Practices for Managing R&D Portfolios," *Research-Technology Management,* 1998, *41*(4), 20–33.

15. Cooper, Edgett, and Kleinschmidt, "New Product Portfolio Management: Practices and Performance." Cooper, Edgett, and Kleinschmidt, "Portfolio Management for New Product Development: Results of an Industry Practices Study." Faulkner, "Applying 'Options Thinking' to R&D Valuation."

16. Bubble diagrams with "value" measured qualitatively are recommended in Roussel, Saad, and Erickson, *Third Generation R&D.*

17. P. Evans, "Streamlining Formal Portfolio Management," *Scrip Magazine,* Feb. 1996; and D. Matheson, J. E. Matheson, and M. M. Menke, "Making Excellent R&D Decisions," *Research Technology Management,* Nov.-Dec. 1994, pp. 21–24.

18. Based on Roberts and Berry, "Entering New Businesses: Selecting Strategies for Success."

19. Cooper, Edgett, and Kleinschmidt, "New Product Portfolio Management: Practices and Performance." Cooper, Edgett, and Kleinschmidt, "Portfolio Management for New Product Development: Results of an Industry Practices Study." Faulkner, "Applying 'Options Thinking' to R&D Valuation."

20. Cooper, Edgett, and Kleinschmidt, "Best Practices in Product Development: What Distinguishes Top Performers" and "Improving New Product Development Performance and Practices."

UNIT 2
Managing High-Technology Programs and Projects

The material within this unit has been excerpted from the following textbook:

Russell D. Archibald
Managing High-Technology Programs & Projects
Third Edition

Copyright 2003 by Russell D. Archibald
ISBN: 0-471-26557-8

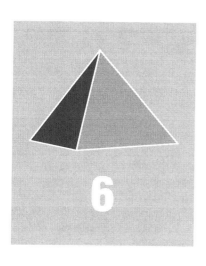

Organizing the Project Management Function and Office

Creating the proper organizational setting for project management must be accomplished in the absence of well-known principles such as those that apply when organizing a traditional, functionally oriented structure. No single organizational pattern has yet emerged to answer the following organizational questions:

Organizing to Manage Individual Projects
- How will the project manager and other integrative responsibilities be assigned and interrelated?
- To whom should project managers report? At what level, and within which part of the organization?
- Who should be assigned as full-time project office members reporting directly to a given project manager, and who should contribute as project participants while remaining in their functional departments?
- How are specialist staff skills in project planning and control, contract administration, finance, legal, and so on, best provided to project managers and teams?

Management of Multiple Projects
- Who is responsible for development and operation of multiproject, integrated project planning and control systems?
- Who should hold what specific responsibilities for multiproject management and to whom should they report?

Overall Project Management Function for the Enterprise
- Where will the manager of project management be located organizationally?
- How will this important position relate to the project portfolio steering group, the sponsors assigned to major projects, and the various program and project managers?
- Should there be established a project management office (PMO) and/or center of project management excellence at the corporate or lower level to provide a home for the project management function and for the manager of project management?

In this chapter, the underlying factors influencing the answers to these questions are discussed and where possible some basic guidelines are set forth. Illustrations are provided of various organizational arrangements used by a number of different companies.

6.1 ORGANIZATIONAL ALTERNATIVES FOR PROJECT MANAGEMENT

Three basic alternative forms of organization have been used for the planning and execution of projects: (1) purely functional, (2) function/project matrix, and (3) purely project (that is, a functional organization devoted solely to one project). Each of these has its strengths and weaknesses. Each can be made to work, with varying degrees of effectiveness, depending upon the characteristics of the basic organization (size, degree of rigidity, nature of the business, culture, and habits) and of the projects (number, size, complexity, degree of uniqueness, duration, and other factors).

Companies and agencies typically evolve their approach to managing their projects through some combination of these basic forms. Initially, most organizations are structured along the classic functional pyramid lines, with separate departments for marketing, engineering, financial, manufacturing or other operations, and staff specialists for legal, treasury, human resources, administration, and so on. Product lines, geography, technologies, and customers are often also represented in the pyramidal structure. As projects within the functional organization become more numerous, larger, and more complex, and as schedule and/or cost performance becomes more critical, the managers introduce changes which lead them either to a functional/project matrix solution or to establish essentially stand-alone, "projectized" organizations.

Often, a series of failures in the purely functional organization forces the senior managers to look for a better way. It is rarely possible to establish a completely separate organization for each and every project due to the cost of duplicating all the needed specialized skills and facilities. The result is that most organizations find themselves in a function/project matrix of some kind.

The Functional/Project Matrix Organization

Operating in a functional/project matrix organization is well known to be rife with difficulties. It is not an easy task to introduce the role of the project manager into a long-established, highly bureaucratic functional structure, and then to achieve the proper balance of responsibility and authority between functional and project managers. The crux of the problem is that at some level people within the functional departments must receive direction from two sources: functional and project. They view this as "having two bosses," and that is thought to be a violation of good management practice. Without the proper understanding of the difference between functional direction on one hand and project direction on the other, this situation will produce substantial, undesirable, and costly conflict.

There is a broad range of organizational possibilities in designing a matrix organization. Figure 6–1 illustrates the matrix continuum from weak to strong between a fully functional and fully separate project organization. Many organizations can trace their continuing maturity in project management along this continuum.

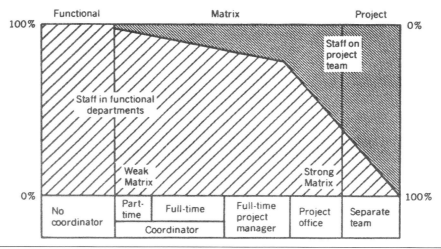

FIGURE 6–1   Organizational Continuum 1.

Source: Robert, Youker, "Organizational Alternatives for Project Management," *Project Management Quarterly,* 8, no. 1 (March 1975). Used by permission.

The Project Taskforce   Frequently organizations find it useful to physically locate a large part of the project team in one place to enhance communication, control, and teamwork. Large engineering/construction companies often use this approach. Some may view this as a "projectized" organization, but many times it is still a matrix, since the functional contributors are not always transferred formally (especially for performance reviews and pay increases) from their home departments to the project department. However the physical proximity of most if not all team members overcomes some of the problems of a matrix situation and usually improves the team efficiency.

6.2 REPORTING RELATIONSHIPS OF PROJECT MANAGERS _____

After a major project has been identified and the decision made to assign a project manager, the next decisions regarding the level in the organization and the specific part of the organization in which she will be placed are crucial to the manager's effectiveness.

Reporting Location of   The project manager must report to the line executive or manager who
a Project Manager   will actually resolve essentially all of the conflicts within and between
    the projects to be managed. Thus, a project manager could properly report to the manager of a department, division, product line, or to the general manager or managing director of a company. For very large projects involving several companies, he would probably report to the managing director of the "lead house" that has prime contractual responsibility.

The size, scope, and nature of the project are key factors in determining where the project manager should report. The number of projects within the organization and the existence or absence of a project management office or other formalized multiproject responsibility will also influence the decision. The executive rank, seniority, experience, and personality of the project manager will also have a direct effect on the final decision regarding the reporting location.

Project managers typically feel that their job would be easier if they reported to the highest executive in the organization. Experience indicates that this is not always the case. A reporting level that is too high can be as ineffective as one that is too low, for different reasons. If the reporting level is too high, the result can be serious and unneeded conflict with senior line managers, impeded communication with functional managers contributing to the project, or unresponsiveness to the project manager caused by the separation of several levels of organization, causing him to resort to using the power of his reporting position, further increasing conflict and retarding communication. If too low, as for instance reporting to a department (or lower) manager when four other departments are contributing significantly to the project, the result can be inability of the project manager to get needed cooperation from the other departments, or inability to evaluate critically and objectively the contribution of the department to which he is assigned. In either case, the project will suffer because the project manager is not located at the level commensurate with the needs of the project.

6.3 PROJECT MANAGEMENT OFFICE

One measure of the maturity of an organization in project management is the recognition that it must establish a home for the project management function—the project management office (PMO), or some similar title—at an appropriate level and reporting to an appropriate senior executive.

The term *project office* is sometimes used for this project management office. It is recommended that the project office title be used only to refer to a specific, individual project (or program) office, that is, the office of one project (or program) manager, as described in Chapter 7. The project management office has distinctly broader and different responsibilities than an individual project/program office.

An additional possible organizational entity must be recognized that impacts the project management capabilities of an organization. That is what can be termed generically a *multiproject operations planning and control* function that provides planning, scheduling, and control for a large number of smaller projects. None of these smaller projects can justify the assignment of a full-time project manager or the full application of systematic project management planning and control. However, in the aggregate, these projects can comprise a significant portion of the organization's overall business. This function is discussed in some detail in Chapter 7. Conceivably, this function could be included within the responsibilities of a PMO that are described next.

Alternative Charters for the Project Management Office

Current project management literature describes a wide range of alternative charters for PMOs at various levels in an organization. A PMO can be designed to meet the needs of a total enterprise or corporation, a business unit, an operating division, a project portfolio, or a multiproject program.

The organizational scope and services to be performed for the organization by the PMO can vary widely as indicated by the following possible alternatives:

Range of Organizational Scope
- Corporate/enterprise-wide.
- Business unit/operating division.
- Product line.
- Project portfolio.
- Multiproject program.
- Individual projects (replacing or overlapping with the individual project office).

Range of Responsibilities
- Design, develop, implement, operate, and continually improve the enterprise-wide project management system.
- Design, develop or acquire, implement, operate and continually improve (through appropriate management research and development) the organization's project management processes, systems and tools:
  —The project portfolio management process.
  —The project life-cycle management process (PLCMS) for each category of projects in the organization.
  —Project management computer software applications in support of the PLMCS for each project category and the enterprise-wide project management system.
- Acquire, disseminate, and apply project management knowledge (the PM Center of Excellence):
  —Identify best project management and related practices within the organization's industrial or other sector.
  —Capture, document, archive, retrieve and promulgate the organization's project management experiences, good and bad, within the organization for use with continual improvement efforts.
  —Disseminate this information throughout the organization in practical, useful ways to all affected persons.
  —Assure that the available information and knowledge is actually being applied appropriately within the organization.
- Provide project management training and indoctrination:
  —Design and deliver, in close cooperation with and through the appropriate training departments, the manager and specialist training and indoctrination needed to properly implement and use the organization's project management processes, systems, and tools.
  —Evaluate and recommend the use of external training resources in project management as appropriate.

- Provide project management consulting and mentoring:
  —Conduct project risk assessments as requested using the most appropriate risk analysis and management approach for the situation.
  —Provide proposal assistance as required to assure that the project management aspects of proposals are adequately covered.
  —Provide facilitator/consulting assistance for project start-up planning workshops.
  —Conduct project performance audits of active projects as requested to identify opportunities for improvement and recommend corrective actions.
  —Provide on-the-job mentoring, training, and consultation to program and project managers and to project specialists as required in all aspects of project management, including the operation and use of project management software applications.
- Develop and supply project managers and project management specialists:
  —Develop and oversee the administration of career paths in project management for project managers and project planning and control specialists.
  —Establish through the appropriate human resources departments effective performance and salary review procedures for project and program managers and project management specialists.
  —Establish assignments within the PMO that provide useful experience to project management specialists and unassigned or potential project managers in preparation for their assignment to positions with greater responsibilities.
- Provide direct support to individual projects:
  —Provide administrative support to active project managers.
  —Provide specialist support to active project managers in risk management, project planning, resource estimating, project control, reporting, variance analysis, issue tracking, change control, contract administration, and other areas as required.
  —Establish and operate a project control center with appropriate graphic displays and audio/visual aids and equipment for use in conducting project review meetings with each project team.

It is not recommended that an organization attempt to establish a PMO overnight with all of these potential responsibilities. Rather a logical evolutionary plan must be established that builds on the existing situation and in a series of steps or phases extends the PMO responsibilities as its success is demonstrated through its performance to date.

Implementation and Evolution of the PMO

The development of an effective project management office is normally an evolutionary process in most organizations. Block (1998) presents a useful discussion of the range of services that can be provided by such offices at different organizational levels together with a plan for their implementation.

Knutson (1999) identifies three basic variations in the role of the project management office together with their primary responsibilities:

1. The PMO in a staff role:
   a. Keeper of the methodology.
   b. Mentoring/coaching.

   c. Librarian.

   d. Source of history.

   e. Prescreening of phase review reports.

  2. The PMO in an enterprise-administrative role; the above plus:

   a. Multiproject reporter.

   b. Priority-setting coordinator.

   c. Resource tracker.

   d. Administrator.

   e. Monitor.

   f. Change controller.

  3. The PMO in a line role; all of the above plus:

   a. Manager of projects.

   b. Leader.

Implementation of a PMO in an Information Technology (IT) Organization

Stratton (2001) describes how the PMO concept was used at two levels, the corporate (national) level and the program level, to implement "key operations engineering (OE) disciplines, which enable the perennially short-handed IT departments to function and scale to meet the demands of today's fast-paced business environment." He describes the responsibilities of the PMO at each of these levels and explains how the PMOs focus on basic processes that are simple and easy to use and prescribe how to accomplish tasks and roles on programs and projects. Their national level PMO is called the *3P PMO Process,* referring to *Process>Proposal>Project,* with a number of phases within each of these. Each phase is defined in detail with its required deliverables. They track all programs and projects through this 3P PMO Process and its subsidiary phases, and use qualified metrics at the national level to determine the profit margin on each program and project. Stratton (2001) also presents detailed illustrations of the program scorecards used to track and report on the programs and projects and their deliverables.

Benefits of a Project Management Office

Block (1998) lists the benefits of a PMO that matures into a full-service provider of project management as:

  Global recognition.

  Profitability improvement.

  Productive project teams.

  Organizational improvement.

  Culture shift to project management.

  Staff professionalism in project management.

  Predictable, reusable PM tools and techniques.

As a result, "The hidden benefit of the project [management] office is the gradual assimilation of project management into the entire organization" (Block, 1998). Indeed, this is the ultimate goal for creating the PMO organization.

**Problems and Pitfalls
with PMOs**

Not every attempt at establishing a PMO has been successful over the years. Many PMOs have been established, flourished for a time, and then have disappeared. The fundamental issue is one of centralization versus decentralization, coupled with the temptation that many practitioners have to build an empire.

The issue of how much centralization can be addressed by looking at the range of responsibilities of a PMO that were listed earlier. Some of these, having to do with the overall processes, methods, systems, and tools for the total organization, clearly should be centralized. Others, primarily those dealing with planning and control of individual programs and projects and the reporting relationships of the several program and project managers, are not so clear-cut.

One principle that is important to recognize is that the project planning and control support services provided to a major project manager should be directly controlled by that manager. Especially on larger projects that required full-time support specialists, these persons should report directly to the project (or program) manager. Attempts to centralize those support services and simply dish out the information to the various project managers usually are not very successful, for several reasons. The detailed knowledge of the schedule, budget, expenditures, and related forecasts are the life blood of the project and vital to every project manager. Having this information produced entirely by an independent centralized staff that knows the problems it reveals even before the project manager is aware of them is not acceptable to an experienced project manager. The result will often be that he will develop his own set of plans and schedules that he will use to manage the project, thus creating much duplication of effort and confusion in the various management reports that are being circulated.

The question of whether some or all project managers should report to the manager of project management in the PMO is also a difficult one. If all major project managers so report this results in the manager of project management becoming an extremely powerful position—and therefore a likely target to be "cut down to size" by political rivals in the organization. Depending on the reporting level of the PMO and its organizational scope, it may be much more effective to have the individual project managers report to various line executives. The manager of project management can still exert her staff authority in the project management discipline over all of the project managers, but would not have day-to-day line authority over all projects.

If the person given the job of manager of project management sees the assignment as an opportunity to build a PMO empire, and tries to capitalize on the interest in project management in that way, without considering all of the longer term ramifications and respecting the position and authority of the involved program and projects managers, then the PMO will probably not last very long.

Example of a Failed PMO

McMahon and Busse (2001) provide a useful and interesting description of the rise and fall of a project management office in the information system (IS) area. Some of the problems they describe that led to the fall of the PMO are:

- Staffing the PMO with PM experts with little knowledge of IS.
- Reluctance of the IS manager to spread the word about the benefits of PM and the PMO outside the IS department.

- The IS applications manager had several reservations about PM and the PMO concept, leading to dissension and mistrust in the leadership team, staff conflict, and some staff turnover.
- The Y2K effort was a primary driving force in setting up the PMO and when it was over the impetus for moving toward an enterprise-wide PMO was removed. After Y2K there was pressure to use the budget dollars on other initiatives.
- The PMO manager left the organization followed by the departure of the corporate champion for the PMO concept.
- A new IS director took over with a new set of initiatives, and this was the final blow for this PMO, which was disbanded.

McMahon and Busse list these recommendations for assuring the success of a PMO implementation:

- *Place it at the top.* It is critical that the PMO be placed at the highest operational level or reporting to a steering committee at the highest operational level.
- *Build deep roots.* The importance of building coalitions, enterprise level placement of the PMO, and recurring staff education all contribute to building deep organizational roots that cannot be pulled out by a change in personnel, no matter the level.
- *Communicate.* Establish a communication plan to the entire organization regarding the benefits of a PMO.
- *Demonstrate value added.* Implement easy-to-read reports distributed to the entire enterprise via company intranet or e-mail that describe successes and demonstrate the benefits of learning from failures.
- *Lessons learned sessions.* On completion of each project hold a lessons learned session open to all levels of participants, and build a knowledge management repository.
- *Build project manager professionalism.* Treat the project manager role as a professional one, develop formal staff training, encourage professional affiliations and certification.

These authors list a number of other actions that will continue to build professionalism in project managers and the project specialist staff.

6.4 STAFFING PROJECTS: THE PROJECT OFFICE AND PROJECT TEAM _____

Alternative Staffing Methods

The three basic alternatives (ordinarily used in combination) in staffing a project are:

1. Assign people directly to the individual project office, under the control of the project manager.
2. Assign tasks required for the project to specific functional departments or specialized staffs.
3. Contract for project tasks with outside organizations.

The project manager typically desires to have all the people contributing to his project assigned full-time to the project organization or office that he directly manages. In most situations, this is undesirable, if not impossible, because:

- Skills required by the project vary considerably as the project matures through each of its life-cycle phases.
- Building up a large, permanently assigned project office for each project inevitably causes duplication of certain skills (often those in short supply), carrying of people who are not needed on a full-time basis or for a long period, and causing personnel difficulties in reassignment.
- The project manager may tend to be diverted from his primary task and become the project engineer, for example, as well as having to become concerned with the supervision, administration, and personnel problems of a large office rather than concentrating on managing all aspects of the project itself.
- Professionally trained people often prefer to work within a group devoted to their professional area, with permanent management having qualifications in the same field, rather than to be isolated from their specialty peers by being assigned to and physically located with a project staff.
- Projects are subject to sudden shifts in priority or even to cancellation, and full-time members of a project office are thus exposed to potentially serious threats to their job security; this often causes reluctance on the part of some people to accept a project assignment requiring transfer to a project office.

All of these factors favor keeping the full-time project office staff as small as possible and depending on established functional departments and specialized staffs to the greatest extent possible for performance of the various tasks necessary to complete the project. This approach places greater emphasis on the planning and control procedures used on the project.

On the other hand, there are valid reasons for assigning particular persons with various specialties to the project office. These specialties usually include:

- Systems analysis and engineering (or equivalent technical discipline), and product quality and configuration control if the product requires such an effort.
- Project planning, scheduling, control, and administrative support.

Experience of many companies indicates that at least these specialties must be under the direct control of the project manager if he is to be able to carry out his assigned responsibilities effectively. Setting up a large project office staff by transferring people to it from the functional departments may be done to achieve better control of the work, in the absence of effective planning and control procedures or systems.

Organization of Project Participants

The team of project participants includes all persons to whom specific project tasks have been assigned, including those directly under the project manager in the project office, in functional departments, on specialized staffs, or in outside organizations.

Figure 6–2 illustrates a generalized organization for an industrial project showing all

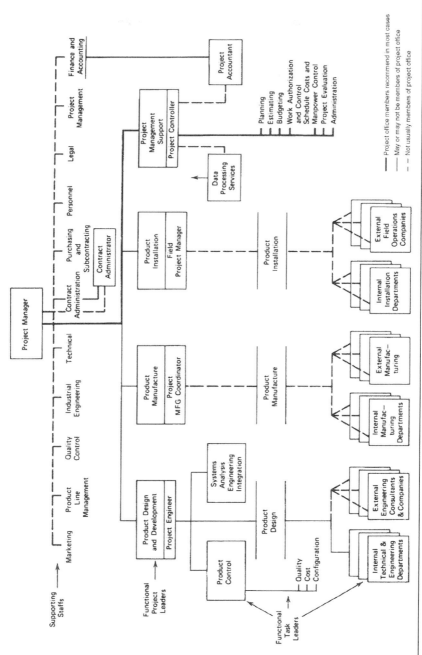

FIGURE 6–2 Generalized organization of the project team.

participants and indicating the persons and functions desirable to have in the project office (under the direct authority of the project manager), and those participants almost always indirectly related to the project manager. The persons and facilities that may vary in their reporting relationship, depending on the situation, are also indicated.

Some or all members of the product design group are justified in being assigned to the project office if:

- Continuous, close communication is required with other members of the project office.
- They are needed for extended periods of time (e.g., six months or more).
- There is otherwise a low confidence that they will be able to spend the agreed upon time and effort on the project. In other words, inadequate control of work assignment exists.

Extreme care is required to select only those persons who are definitely justified in being assigned to the project office before such transfers are made. A practical alternative is to identify those engineers and other specialists within the functional departments who are to perform the assigned project tasks, and physically group these people together, either within the functional department or within the project office. In this case, the people are not formally transferred to the project office but maintain their permanent relationships to their functional departments.

The manufacturing project coordinator should probably remain within the functional manufacturing organization because of the need for close coordination and contact with the manufacturing people.

The field project manager will probably retain a permanent relationship with the field organization, such as the installation or other field operations department, and report to the project manager on an indirect basis, especially if the project is relatively short or if the field project manager is involved with several projects at once. When this phase of the project covers an extended period (six months or more), it is recommended that the field project manager be assigned to the project office.

Effect of Staffing Method on the Project Manager's Authority

If all required people are placed directly under the project manager her role is quite similar to that of a multifunctional division manager. For the reasons discussed earlier, this rarely occurs except in very large, high priority projects.

In practice, much (and in many cases, most) of the work is performed for a project by people in various functional departments or outside the parent organization of the project. These people do not report organizationally to the project manager, but he must still integrate their efforts to achieve the project objectives. The result is the matrix situation discussed earlier, where task leaders are receiving direction from both a functional boss and a project boss. The authority of the project manager in this project/functional situation is changed considerably from that which he has on a fully autonomous project.

Under these conditions, effective project management requires that the project manager act as an "interface manager" and that adequate project support services be provided to the project manager to establish control of the project through integrated planning, scheduling, and evaluation.

Relationships between Project and Functional Managers: Interface Management

It is difficult to convey a good understanding of the project manager role to functional managers whose experience has been wholly within traditional, functional organizations. The project manager's responsibilities are integrative and relate to the interaction between the various contributing functions for his specific project. These responsibilities overlay those of the functional managers but do not change the basic accountability of each functional manager for his portion of the project.

If the general manager to whom all the functional managers report were to retain the project manager role himself, then the functional manager would readily understand and accept his role as project manager. But when responsibility for the project is assigned to someone other than the general manager, the functional managers may have difficulty accepting the idea.

The concept of the project manager as an *interface manager* is useful to clarify her relationships with functional managers and others outside her direct control. Within this concept, the project manager's prime responsibilities are to:

- Identify the various interfaces between functional departments and other elements of the project.
- Develop plans and schedules that incorporate these interface points.
- Communicate the current and future status of all interfaces to all affected functional contributors.
- Monitor progress in all areas and periodically evaluate the project to identify problems and initiate appropriate corrective action.

Interface management is described more fully in Chapter 8. Project managers who practice interface management find they do not need to invade the prerogatives of the functional managers, and their relations noticeably improve. By being helpful to the functional managers in this manner, her role will be welcomed enthusiastically.

6.5 PRODUCT AND PROJECT SUPPORT SERVICES

In addition to the people and facilities required to design, manufacture, and install (or otherwise put into use or operation) the product to be created, specialized project management support services are needed to assist the project manager in carrying out her responsibilities. These responsibilities include achieving the technical (product) objectives within the established limits of time and cost. The specialized support services relate to both the *product* and *project* planning and control functions described in more detail later. Figure 6–3 shows one example of the organization of the product support services for a major electronic project under contract.

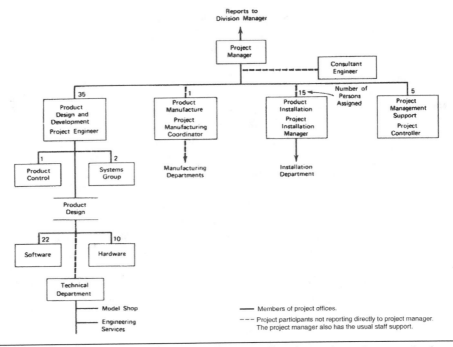

FIGURE 6–3   Example of organization for a major electronic project under customer contract.

Product Support Services   The services of greatest importance to the product, and which may be provided by assigned members of the project office, are:

Technical Management
● Direct the product design and development work.

Systems Analysis, Engineering, and Integration
● Analyze and specify product performance requirements and criteria.
● Evaluate and integrate detailed designs by all project participants.
● Design and specify the system tests and product functional tests, and evaluate test results.
● Carry out design review practices.

Product Control
● Establish detailed performance objectives and assure achievement in product quality, reliability, and maintainability.
● Document a baseline system and product configuration, and control and document any changes to that configuration.
● Establish detailed estimates of product cost and revise these as design changes or other revised information become available.

Project Management Support Services

These include specialized functions related to the following:

- *Contract administration,* usually performed by a contract administrator assigned to the project but usually not considered a member of the project office under the direct control of the project manager.
- *Project accounting,* performed by a member of the accounting department designated for the project, and usually reporting indirectly to the project controller (or equivalent).
- *Specialized project management support services,* usually performed by members of the project office under the direction of a project controller (or similar title). These are discussed in the following chapters.

The number of people required to carry out the management support functions will vary, depending on the size and complexity of the project, from one person (the project manager), perhaps with a secretary, to 10, 15, or more on very large projects. In general, it is desirable to hold the project office to a minimum number of people (see Chapter 9).

Centralized versus Decentralized Project Management Support Services

In situations involving a number of relatively small projects, it is not possible to provide a project manager and supporting project staff for each. In this case, a centralized project management support group is required to provide the planning and control services for whoever is responsible for the projects, whether this is a line manager, a project manager, or a multiproject manager.

As previously discussed, experience indicates that a centralized group is less effective in support of those major projects that could justify one or more full-time people performing support functions. Because these functions deal with vital information regarding the current health and ultimate success of the project, a project manager on a large effort often will not entrust the information to an outside group. If these services are offered or imposed from outside the project then the project manager will generally shield the outsiders from key information and ignore their efforts of assistance. This often results in developing internal methods for performing these functions, which may be less effective and more costly than if qualified specialists were placed within the project office.

Central Planning for Multiprojects

In most large companies, major projects exist together with numerous smaller projects. Thus, there is frequently a need for a centralized project support staff to plan and control the smaller projects, as well as for equivalent specialists assigned to the various major project offices. The central staff can be used as a training ground for persons to be assigned to major project offices and to coordinate development of improved methods, procedures, and systems, including multiproject planning, resource allocation, and control systems.

The concept of a full-blown operations planning and control function, supported by a computer-based operations planning and control system, is presented in Chapter 7. Where such a function exists, it can provide very effective planning and control support to the various project managers.

Figure 6–4 shows an example of this type of multiproject management support in a large telecommunications company.

Relationships between the Individual Project Office, Central Planning and Control, and Information Processing Services

Effective use of advanced project management software applications requires skilled information processing support services. These services must be made available as directly as possible to the project managers or project controllers within the project offices. Figure 6–5 illustrates the recommended relationships.

6.6 CHARTING ORGANIZATIONAL RELATIONSHIPS AND RESPONSIBILITIES _____

Because the project manager responsibilities and relationships do not conform to traditional organizational theory and practice, it is difficult to illustrate these relationships accurately using the familiar organizational charting methods. Organizations have prepared

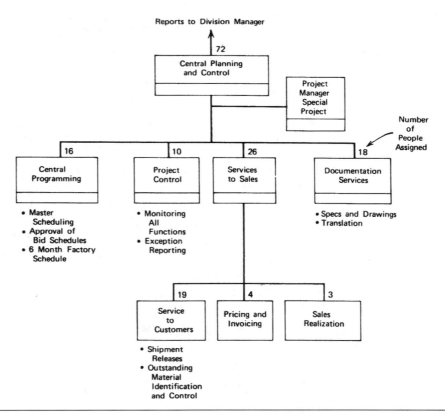

FIGURE 6–4   Example of central planning and control for a major division.

different kinds of charts in attempting to portray the project management situation graphically, to enable analysis and improved understanding.

Various alternative organizational arrangements have been and continue to be developed and used for the project management function. As previously discussed, most of these result in what is usually termed a *matrix* organization, wherein the project manager's relationships are overlaid on the basic organizational structure, forming a matrix of reporting, direction-giving, and coordinating lines of communication and linkage. The most common forms of the resulting organization are shown in Figures 6–6 through 6–9.

Responsibility Matrix   Traditional organization charts and position descriptions are necessary and valuable, but they do not show how the organization really works. Another approach that comes closer to this goal has evolved and is generally referred to as linear responsibility charting to produce a responsibility matrix. To be most effective, the members of a work group should actively participate in developing such a chart to describe their roles and relationships. Such development resolves differences and improves communications so that the organization works more effectively. The responsibility matrix is useful for analyzing and portraying any organization, but it is particularly effective in relating project responsibilities to the existing organization.

CEO DEMANDS: ORGANIZING THE PMO AND THE PM FUNCTION

To obtain the full benefits of project management for the entire organization the CEO must demand that:

1. Full-time program and project managers be appointed for each major program and project, each reporting to the most appropriate senior executive.

2. Multiproject managers be appointed for those minor projects that do not justify full-time project managers, with appropriate planning and control support provided as required in the form of a multiproject operations planning and control function (as described in Chapter 7).

3. An experienced manager of project management be appointed reporting to a senior executive.

4. An appropriate home for the project management function be established in the form of a PMO under the direction of the manager of project management.

5. The responsibilities of the PMO be defined in several stages of evolution and implemented according to plan commensurate with the organization's capacity to absorb the resulting changes.

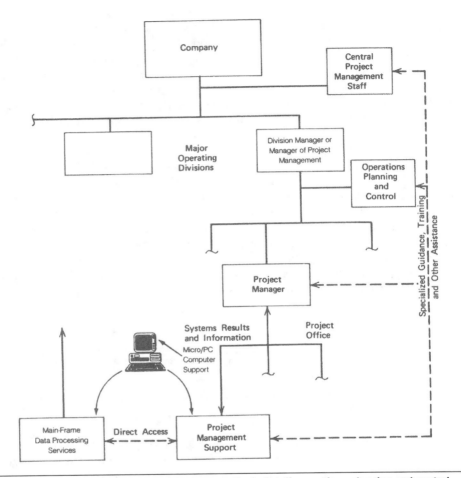

FIGURE 6–5 Recommended relationships between central staff, operations planning and control, project office, and data processing services.

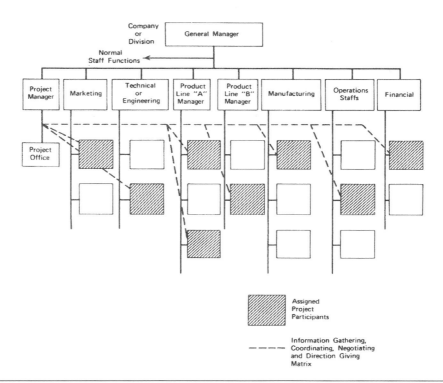

FIGURE 6–6 **Generalized organization chart with project responsibility delegated to full-time project manager. The matrix relationships include direction giving information to carry out decisions of the project manager, in addition ot the communicating and coordinating functions.**

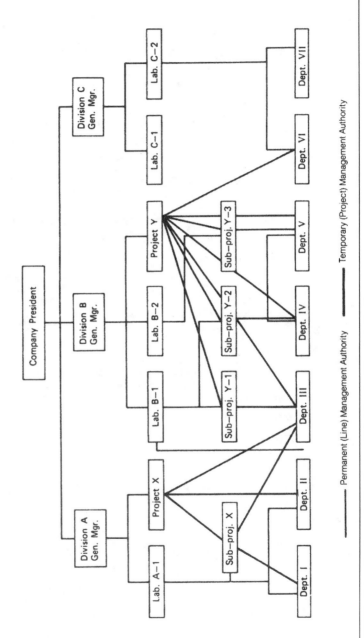

—— Permanent (Line) Management Authority   —— Temporary (Project) Management Authority

FIGURE 6–7   Generalized organization for a multidivisional, miltiproject situation.

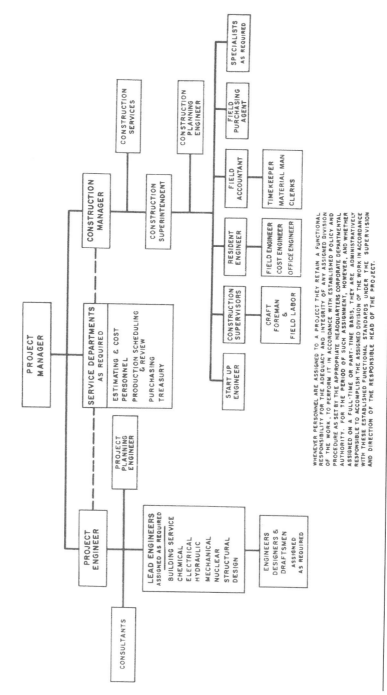

FIGURE 6–8 Typical organization chart for a large engineering-construction company.

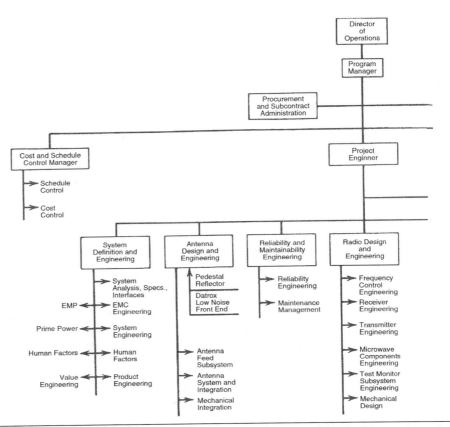

FIGURE 6–9 Program organization chart. This chart is typical of those submitted to a customer to emphasize the strength of the company's program/project management approach. However, in most cases, few of the people represented on the chart actually report to the program or project manager. The lines on such a chart must be clearly understood to represent project-related direction only, with team members reporting on a "hard-line" basis to their functional managers.

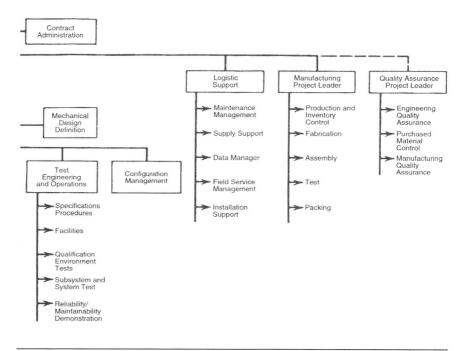

FIGURE 6–9 *(Continued)*

Managing Project Portfolios, Programs, and Multiple Projects

It is rare to find a project in any organization today that exists by itself without interaction with other projects. The reality is that projects must be managed as interrelated efforts at four levels in large organizations: project portfolio, multiproject program, multiple small/minor projects, and the individual major project levels.

The first three levels are discussed in this chapter. Some processes, systems, procedures, and tools for managing individual major projects are discussed in Chapter 8. These levels are not mutually exclusive: a major project can be within a program and a portfolio, for example, and if so it would require management at all three of these levels. A small project can be managed as one of a group as well as part of a project portfolio.

Multiproject Environment

The multiproject environment that exists in most large organizations imposes complications at each of these project levels and at each level of the functional organization. The basic problems result from competition between and within projects for resources and for management attention. Since no organization possesses completely unlimited resources, it is not possible simultaneously to plan and execute all the projects that can be conceived. In addition to resource constraints, many projects depend on the results and products from other projects. At appropriate levels in the organization, the multiproject requirements and priorities must be brought together to assure that all projects are completed to realize the maximum benefits for the entire organization.

The need for some means to integrate these multiproject requirements is frequently not fully recognized. The result is that a number of projects are individually managed from different parts of an organization with a great deal of effort being exerted by the various project managers to win available skills or other resources. A very strong project manager may thus be successful on one project but the company may suffer severely from the delays that result in other projects.

Multiproject Objectives   The higher order objectives of multiproject management, in comparison to managing a single project, include:

- Completing all projects to best achieve the overall strategic goals of the organization.
- Determining both long-term and short-range priorities between projects to enable appropriate decisions regarding allocation of limited resources.
- Identifying and understanding the comparative risks involved in each project, deciding which are acceptable to the organization, and managing the accepted risks proactively.
- Acquiring and maintaining an adequate supply of resources to support all projects, including people, facilities, material, and money; but at the same time assuring that these resources are gainfully and efficiently employed in approved, productive work required to complete the approved projects.
- Integrating these multiproject requirements with other ongoing activities and operations not directly related to projects (such as production of off-the-shelf products).
- Developing and using organizational patterns and management processes and systems to satisfy the ever-changing project needs, and to provide organizational stability, professional development, and administrative efficiency for persons managing and supporting various projects.

7.1 MANAGING PROJECT PORTFOLIOS

The development and application of the project portfolio management process must be planned as a management project. The most appropriate approach is to assign the manager of project management, assuming there is one, as the project manager. Persons who are obvious candidates to be members of the project portfolio steering group should be included on the project team with appropriate responsibilities. Other members of the team will be drawn from the project management office (PMO) staff and probably will also include experienced internal or external consultants in strategic and project management.

The project objective is to design, develop, and implement the project portfolio management process for the specified parts of the organization. The project scope defines exactly which parts of the organization are to be included in the implementation. During the initial implementation of the process, the senior members of the project team are transformed into the project portfolio steering group. This group is established formally when the process design has been approved and its implementation is authorized.

The project portfolio management process consists of the following twelve basic steps. Comments on each step indicate how the process is developed and applied.

1. *Define the* project portfolios *required within the organization.* This would normally be done as a part of the organization's strategic planning and management process. The defined portfolios would reflect the organization's growth strategies, reporting structure, geographic markets, product lines, and other significant factors.

2. *Define the* project categories *within each portfolio based on uniform criteria for the entire organization.* The list of project categories for the organization is prepared by the project team reflecting the factors.

3. *Identify and group all current and proposed projects within appropriate categories and programs.* Preparing the inventory of projects is a necessary prerequisite for this step. Grouping the currently approved projects by the team into their appropriate categories will generally be straightforward. Creating and selecting new projects is further discussed in a following section.

4. *Validate all projects with the organization's strategic objectives.* The implementation project team with the project portfolio steering group compares the objectives and scope of each project within a portfolio and ascertains that these are directly linked to one or more of the organization's strategic objectives. If not, higher level managers must decide if the project will be cancelled or retained in the portfolio after suitable modification.

5. *Prioritize projects within programs and portfolios.* The implementation project team designs and recommends the methods and procedures for prioritizing projects and programs within each portfolio. Further discussion of project prioritization methods is presented in a following section. The project portfolio steering group then applies these methods and establishes the current project priorities, with supporting assistance from the PMO staff.

6. *Develop the project portfolio master schedule.* The implementation team designs and develops the format for this master schedule and enters summary information for each project and program within each portfolio reflecting the currently approved project priorities. This can take the form of a large, graphic, time-scaled display showing the beginning and end of each project or program together with a few major milestones for each. This should also display any logical dependencies between projects or programs in each portfolio, and any such dependencies between projects in different portfolios. This display can be automated and Web-enabled using available project management software.

7. *Establish and maintain the key resources databank.* A significant element of the design of the project portfolio management process will be the selection of which key resources are to be included in this databank. The number of such resources should be kept small, at least initially. As experience is gained in the practicalities of maintaining and using such a databank, additional resources can be added to it.

8. *Allocate available key resources to programs and projects within portfolios.* This step requires development of fairly detailed plans and schedules for each active program and project within each portfolio. These initial project plans will include estimates of what key resources are required over time to plan and execute each project as scheduled. As resources are allocated, the project schedules will obviously be affected. When the projects are reprioritized (Step 5), these resource allocations are revised and the projects are then rescheduled.

9. *Compare financial needs (primarily cash flow) with availability.* This also requires fairly detailed plans and schedules for each program and project with cost estimates linked to schedules. Planning templates for newly conceived projects can be used until more detailed plans for them are available.

10. *Decide how to respond to shortfalls in money or other key resources and approve the list of funded projects and their priorities.* The steering group makes these decisions regarding allocation of funds. It then oversees the repetition of Steps 5 through 10 until available money and other key resources have been allocated on an optimum basis.

11. *Plan, authorize, and manage each program and project using the organization's project management process and supporting systems and tools for each project category.* The manager of project management and the supporting staff assigned to the PMO provide direction and assistance as required and reflecting the PMO charter (as discussed in Chapter 7) to carry out this step.

12. *Periodically reprioritize, reallocate resources to, and reschedule all programs and projects as required within each portfolio.* Repeat Steps 1 through 12 as required on a monthly or quarterly basis. Reflect changes in strategies, products, markets, competition, and technologies, as well as progress made to date (or the lack thereof) on each project. Add newly proposed and approved projects. As further discussed later in this chapter, the project portfolio steering group gives strategic direction to each project sponsor who interprets that direction and communicates it to the affected project manager(s).

Responsibilities of the Project Portfolio Steering Group   The project portfolio steering group responsibilities include:

- Approving the design of the project portfolio management process during its initial implementation, and any significant subsequent changes to it.
- Active participation in the operation of the project portfolio management process:
  —Integrating and validating the organization's strategic objectives with the programs and projects within the project portfolios over which the group has cognizance.
  —Establishing and integrating the relative priorities of projects within each portfolio at appropriate preestablished intervals and when required by major events or changes in the projects or their environments.
  —Approving new projects for inclusion in the assigned portfolios and reprioritizing all portfolio projects when such new projects are added.
  —Communicating the current project priorities to their sponsors and through the sponsors to the program and project managers, as well as to the functional management structure of the organization.
- Recommending to the CEO and other cognizant senior managers the acquisition of additional financial and other resources when required to plan and execute the projects needed to achieve the strategic objectives of the organization on a timely basis.
- Identifying opportunities for improvement and recommending improvements in the project portfolio management process and the other project management processes, systems and tools.

In large, complex organizations, there will usually be more than one project portfolio to be managed, and these may overlap and compete for available corporate resources and management attention. The CEO, general manager, or other senior executive or multiport-folio steering group may be required to resolve interportfolio conflicts—unless one port-folio steering group holds responsibility for all portfolios.

Relationships between the Project Portfolio Steering Group, Project Sponsors, the Project Management Office, and Project/Program Managers

The *project portfolio steering group* provides strategic direction for all programs and projects within the portfolios under its cognizance. The currently approved portfolio master schedule reflects the key resource allocations and project priorities that have been established by the steering group. This master schedule includes the currently agreed target dates for key milestones in each program and project. This information is transmitted to the project sponsors and the manager of project management.

The *project sponsors* assigned to major programs and projects inform the manager of project management, the cognizant program and project managers, and also the affected functional managers, of any changes to the resource allocations and priorities for their projects. The sponsors also communicate to those managers any other information (both internal and external to the organization) of a political, economic, technological or other pertinent nature that may have an effect—good or bad—on their programs or projects.

The *manager of project management* communicates the resource allocation, priority and milestone information contained in the portfolio master schedule to the managers of all programs and projects for which a sponsor has not been designated. Depending on the manager of project management's charter he may carry out the responsibilities of the sponsor for all such projects.

The *program and project managers,* both of individual major programs and projects and of multiple smaller projects, receive their strategic direction from either their project sponsors or the manager of project management. The manager of project management will provide operational support and professional project management guidance to the program and project managers if this is within the scope of his charter. Each program and project manager must reflect any resource, priority, schedule, or other strategic changes to their program or project in their plans, estimates and schedules, and quickly provide an assessment of the impact of such changes to their project sponsor and/or the manager of project management.

The project sponsors and the manager of project management immediately transmit these impacts to the project portfolio steering committee for inclusion in the next iteration of the project portfolio planning process.

7.2 PROJECT SELECTION

The complexities and processes involved in new project selection vary considerably depending on the category of projects in question. The four high-technology categories identified as the primary focus of this unit are:

1. Communication systems.
2. Information systems.

3. Product and service development.
4. Research and development.

Project selection within each of these categories is discussed next. Although each project category requires a somewhat different approach the selection process is focused in all of them on the three main goals of portfolio management, according to Cooper, Edgert, and Kleinschmidt (2001) in their reporting the results of their industry studies:

1. *Maximizing the value of the portfolio against an objective,* such as profitability, return on investment, or likelihood of success.
2. *Balance in the portfolio:* The most popular balancing dimensions used were risk versus reward, ease versus attractiveness, and breakdown by project type, market and product line.
3. *Link to strategy:* Strategic fit and resource allocation that reflects the business's strategy were the key issues here.

"Of the three, no one goal seemed to dominate; moreover, no one portfolio model or approach seemed capable of achieving all three goals" (Cooper et al., 1999, p. 29).

Dye and Pennypacker (1999) have compiled a very useful compendium of articles that discuss and present a wide range of industrial experience and practices relating to portfolio management in general and project selection and prioritization in particular. These articles focus primarily on the information system, new product, and R&D project categories.

Selecting New Communication Systems Projects

Selection of projects in this category will be made both by the buyers and the sellers of new communication systems. Only in rare cases will a supplier of these systems execute such a project for its own end use.

Selection by buyers of communication systems projects. For the buyer of a new communication system the decision to proceed with such a project is motivated by its growth strategies. Senior management must determine what the communication needs of the organization are now and will be at some point in the future, and allocate the required financial resources to meet those needs. The requirement for allocation of its internal key resources (such as communications and information technology specialists) to the planning and execution of the new project is also a consideration in the selection process. Buyers of communications systems are found in every industrial and governmental sector worldwide.

The most difficult part of the selection process for the buyer will generally be choosing between two or more competing proposals from the suppliers of such systems. The basic criteria for that choice include price, system features and performance, supplier reputation and previous experience, the technology involved and its compatibility with existing communications systems, delivery date, and performance and maintenance warranties. These criteria are the primary basis for the buyer's risk analysis on such new projects.

Selection by sellers of communication systems projects. The sellers or suppliers of such systems will use a rather different selection process. Since such projects are at least a major part (perhaps the entirety) of their primary business they are constantly looking for and encouraging potential buyers to issue requests for proposals (RFPs) of these projects, or better yet to sign a contract for them without competing proposals being submitted. When an RFP is received, the seller will examine it carefully to determine if they have the capabilities needed to respond with a proposal that will completely fill the stated need on schedule and at the same time be profitable for them.

The selection of new projects for which to submit proposals is the critical point in the seller's decision process. Their risk analysis must include not only the planning for and execution of the project itself, should their proposal be accepted, but the risk that perhaps several such proposals will be accepted by several buyers and the supplier will not have the resources needed to deliver all of them at the time that they have proposed. This could occur since the supplier must submit more proposals than will be accepted because no supplier can expect a 100 percent acceptance rate for their proposals. Successful suppliers of these projects have learned the hard way that effective project management must begin during the proposal stage. In other words, they apply the total project life-cycle management system (PLCMS) during preparation of their proposal.

Once a contract has been signed, there will be one project, and both the buyer and seller must collaborate in its planning and execution since for most projects in this category both will make significant contributions to the project. However, the supplier usually has the lead responsibility for managing such a project.

Selecting Information Systems Projects

In most organizations, there is a greater demand for information systems projects than can be met with available funding and specialized resources. The many users of the information systems within the organization continually submit requests for such new projects. The selection process must choose which of the many possible projects should be added to the portfolio and approved for funding and execution. Essentially all projects in this category are for improvement of internal business processes and performance or to offer new services to outside customers, although many such projects will use the services of outside software developers under contract for their planning and execution. New information systems projects that are intended to produce hardware and/or software products for sale to other users are considered to be in the category of new products and services, discussed later.

Miller (1997, p. 56) identifies four areas in which criteria have typically been established to help organizations choose between information technology projects:

1. *Customer:* Commitment in terms of need.
2. *Strategy:* Alignment with company goals and objectives:
   —Profitability: Measuring the IT project's cost savings.
   —Process improvement: Ability to improve business processes in a timely manner.
   —Employee satisfaction.
3. *Technology:* Ability to meet technical requirements:
   —Core competency: Organizational capability to perform the project.
   —Cost competitiveness: Ability to provide a competitive solution.
   —Integration: With existing technology.

4. *Delivery:* Ability to successfully deliver the project on schedule, within budget and meeting the quality specifications.

Bridges (1999) recommends establishing twelve to fifteen criteria based on these items to support IT decision making.

Selecting New Product and Service Projects

As with information systems projects, "There are far more new product ideas or projects conceived than resources to commercialize them. Moreover the great majority of these projects are unfit for commercialization. In an ideal new product process, management would be able to identify the probably new product winners in advance, and be able to allocate the firm's development resources to these projects. As a result, failure rates would be low, misallocated resources would be kept to a minimum, and the return would be maximized" (Cooper, 1985, p. 34).

Cooper (1985) lists the four models to initial screening of new product projects as benefit measurement, economic, portfolio selection, and market research models (p. 36).

The extensive industry research conducted by Cooper identified eight "factors or underlying dimensions" that were found to impact on new product outcomes:

1. Product superiority, quality, and uniqueness.
2. Overall product/company resource compatibility.
3. Market need, growth, and size.
4. Economic advantage of product to end user.
5. Newness to the firm (negative).
6. Technological resource compatibility.
7. Market competitiveness (negative).
8. Product scope.

A practical seven-step approach for organizations to develop their own new product screening model is given by Cooper (1985, p. 40). An example of a commercially available computer-based scoring model is NewProd™ 3000 (a registered trademark of R. G. Cooper and Associates Consultants, Inc; see www.prod-dev.com), which is "based on the profiles and outcomes of hundreds of past new product projects. It serves as both a diagnostic tool and a predictive model. It is premised on the fact that the profile of a new product project is a reasonable predictor of success" (p. 67). The profile characteristics used are shown in the list of eight factors.

Selecting New Research and Development Projects

This category includes a broad range of projects from exploratory, undirected research to very specific new or improved product, service, or process development. The obvious new product and service projects generally should be placed in that project category, discussed earlier.

Methods for screening and selecting research and development (R&D) projects will reflect the R&D phase that a particular idea or embryo project is in. Lambert (1993, pp. 388–389) identifies three major R&D phases:

1. Phase I research phase is exploring, or basic.
2. Phase II research phase is feasibility, or application.
3. Phase III—the development phase—can best be described as refinement, or optimization.

The product or result of Phase I is most often a research report or document, not a physical product. The typical product of Phase II is a prototype or laboratory scale test plus documentation. At some point in Phase III, the project becomes a new product or service development project and then must be moved to that category and managed accordingly.

Project selection occurs at the start of each of these phases. Hosley (1993, p. 386) recommends: "Compile as large list of possible projects that capitalizes on the company's strengths, together with an estimate of potential sales, required investment, and probably success." The next step is to "Prioritize items from the list so that the gap (between where the company is now and where it wants to be in ten years) is filled year-by-year." Since most R&D projects will mature into new product or service projects the methods used for selecting the latter can also be applied to selecting R&D projects.

General Rules for Selecting Projects

Frame (1999, p. 180) provides five general rules for project selection that, if followed, will lead to better choices:

1. Be explicit about what is important in choosing projects.
2. Identify explicit procedures for choosing projects, then stick to them.
3. Be prepared to rigorously challenge all assertions.
4. Prepare a project selection team whose members represent a broad array of stakeholders.
5. Involve key project personnel in the selection process.

Some Problems with Portfolio Management Models

The project portfolio management process is dynamic and deals with constantly changing, uncertain information. Cooper et al. (1999, p. 30) state that "Portfolio models suffer from imaginary precision. A universal weakness is that virtually every portfolio model we studied *implied a degree of precision far beyond people's ability to provide reliable data;* that is, the model's sophistication far exceeded the quality of the input data." Also, "Many portfolio models yield information overload" (p. 33). Care is obviously needed to keep the process as simple as possible while still achieving its objectives. As with product or process design it is far easier to produce a very complicated, impressive looking or sounding process that is ultimately unworkable than it is to produce an elegantly simple result that does the job.

7.3 ESTABLISHING AND CONTROLLING PROJECT PRIORITIES ─────────

When several projects are competing for limited resources, the need for a method of determining and communicating the relative priority of each project is easily recognized. However, developing a practical method to satisfy that need has proved to be a difficult job.

The Need for Project Prioritization

Effective planning of each project and forecasting of its resource needs will assist in predicting potential conflicts with other projects if all are similarly planned. Decisions can then be made whether to supply additional resources or to delay or otherwise replan one or more projects. Some measure of project priority is needed to make such decisions. Predicting such potential conflicts is the only way to enable effective management action that can avoid the actual conflict in a crisis atmosphere. Unfortunately, such planning is often impractical in the early conceptual phases of most projects, primarily because of the time and cost involved in preparing such detailed plans. The dilemma is that executives are reluctant to invest too much in the early phases when they know that a large percentage of projects in these phases will be killed. But without an adequate investment in planning during these early phases, truly informed decisions cannot be made.

Even in the most thoroughly planned projects unforeseen problems or needs can cause short-term conflicts. When these occur, the person allocating a limited resource to one or the other project must have accurate knowledge of their current relative priorities.

In the absence of an effective prioritizing method, decisions are made daily at the first-line management and supervisory levels regarding relative project priorities. It is conceivable that contradictory decisions are made on different parts of the same two projects, with the result that both projects suffer delay in the end.

In addition, it is often difficult to translate priorities established by management into appropriate action at, for example, the level where material is requisitioned. In spite of such difficulties, the need for current project priorities to penetrate to the lowest level of the organization is essential if management decisions are to be carried out effectively.

Factors Influencing Project Priorities

While the relative importance of these factors vary depending on the organization and the type of project involved, the following list includes most of the factors that affect project priorities (not necessarily in order of importance):

Completion or delivery date, and its proximity.
Penalty risks.
Customer importance.
Competitive risks.
Technical risks.
Regulatory agency risks.
Health and product liability risks.
Management sponsor.

Return on investment.
Magnitude of costs, investment, and/or profit, and related risks.
Impact on other projects.
Impact on other affiliated organizations.
Impact on a particular product line.
Political and visibility risks.

Such factors must be translated into some form of a model in order to be useful to management, as discussed in the next section.

Prioritization Models

Models for project prioritization range from simple to complex. There are two basic classifications: projects that are funded, and those that are on hold and not funded. A more useful approach is to create a three-tier list:

1. *Priority projects:* Those that take precedence over all others.
2. *Normal projects:* Those that are funded and active but do not bear the priority label.
3. *Back-burner projects:* Those that are on hold, waiting for funding or resources to become available.

Buss (1999, p. 188) describes the use of four priority grids with a common vertical axis of all four grids showing the level of investment (low, medium, high) and the horizontal axis of each separate grid showing a range of low, medium, and high for:

Financial benefits.
Intangible benefits.
Technical benefits.
Fit with business objectives.

All projects are placed in their respective positions on each of the four grids, and then a consensus is reached regarding their relative overall priority ranking.

At the complex end of the scale are prioritization models with quantified criteria weighting risk and return mathematical approaches. These often depend on subjectively prepared numbers to produce deceptively accurate looking results. For new product prioritization, the references provided earlier under project selection also deal extensively with new product prioritization models.

Lower Level Priority Rules to Resolve Interproject Schedule and Resource Conflicts

Only about 15 percent of the activities in any one project are truly critical to meeting its completion date. Thus, from a multiproject point of view, the overall project priorities discussed in the preceding sections should only be applied when conflicts occur between the truly critical activities of two or more projects.

For this approach to be used, it is necessary to plan and schedule each project in such a way that the critical 15 percent of the activities can be identified. The network planning discipline with resource information is the most effective method of doing this in a consistent manner. When two or more projects are planned in this way, information is provided that allows application of various lower level priority rules as shown in Table 7–1. Other similar priority rules may be developed and used.

7.4 MANAGING MULTIPROJECT PROGRAMS

As previously discussed, programs are defined as being comprised of two or more projects. Classic program management comes from large U.S. Department of Defense weapon systems efforts and NASA aerospace endeavors. Typically, these require a program manager at a high level of the governmental agency sponsoring the effort, with project managers identified within each of the private contractors that are carrying out the design, development, fabrication, assembly, test, and other required operations for the portion of the program for which they have executed contracts with the government. In some cases, these contracts are so large that they are actually multiproject programs with a number of subcontractors executing the projects.

In other economic and industrial sectors organizations have found it useful to group related projects within a program. Such projects might be related to a particular product line, operating division, or geographic area. Projects within a program are usually closely related in some way, in addition to using common resources. Such interrelationships include logical dependencies like a test result or product from one project that is required before a task or activity within another project can be started or completed. Programs could conceivably be considered as being synonymous with small portfolios.

Table 7–1   Rules for Resolving Conflicts between Projects without Resorting to Overall Project Priorities*

Conflict between Activities in Different Projects	Priority Given to:
Critical (from a schedule or resource viewpoint)	Project with highest overall current priority.
Critical versus noncritical	Critical activity (regardless of overall project priority).
Noncritical versus noncritical	Activity with least slack or shortest critical chain buffer (allowable delay); if equal slack, shortest, or longest activity; if same duration, use current project priority. Alternatively, give priority to activity using largest number of critical resources.

* Slack or float calculations must reflect resource constraints.

Program versus Project Managers

The similarities and differences between the program and project manager roles have been discussed.

Programs may not have a well-defined life cycle of their own since they are comprised of two or more projects that each have their own life cycles. Programs usually have longer durations than projects and may continue for indefinite periods of time as projects are completed and new projects added. As a result, the program manager assignment will typically be more permanent or longer in duration than that of a project manager. That may make it more difficult to maintain the continuity of responsibility in one program manager, and this in turn places more importance on establishing and maintaining adequate files and records for the program so that a newly assigned program manager will inherit the complete information needed for successfully completing the program.

7.5 MANAGING MULTIPLE PROJECTS

This book is directed primarily to situations involving a number of major projects. However, of equal importance in many organizations are the project management needs in the situation where a large number of relatively small projects exist. This is typical of many high technology companies that design, manufacture, and install complex products or systems.

To illustrate this point, consider the situation where one or more contracts with customers cover a large number of specific central office telephone exchanges or central telephone switches (PBXs) and related communication systems on a user's premises. Each of these contracts is in reality a project, requiring hardware engineering work, software modification, procurement, manufacturing, assembly, customer training, installation, and test. These overlapping projects flow through marketing, hardware and software engineering, one or more factories, and only emerge as clearly distinct projects during installation, where typically the installation department manages a number of geographically separate sites. In such situations, it is not possible or even desirable to appoint a project manager for each PBX with responsibility through engineering, manufacturing, and installation. In some cases, a project manager is appointed for a group of related exchanges for a single customer, or for a very large, complex PBX and system. The general practice is to appoint a supervisor for each exchange only during the installation phase, reporting to the installation department.

Even though project managers may not be appointed to every project in this situation, management of the projects on an integrated basis is still of vital importance to meeting the contract cut-over dates. Since a typical telephone switching equipment division is predominantly devoted to the execution of these somewhat repetitive (but never identical) projects, the division general manager typically retains the overall project management responsibilities. This places even greater emphasis on the need for organization, methods, and systems that enable truly integrated planning and control of all projects through all their life-cycle phases. This situation is very similar to a manufacturing "job shop" where each order flowing through the shop is for a similar but not identical product. Job shop scheduling software applications have existed for many years, and the approach discussed here for multiple small projects is simply an extension of that concept to include the functions of marketing, engineering, procurement, manufacturing, and installation.

Centralized planning and control offices have been established in some companies to provide the needed marketing-engineering-manufacturing- installation planning and master scheduling where this multiple small project situation exists. The planning manager, overseen by the division general manager, coordinates these plans and master schedules, and does the appropriate follow-up to assure compliance. These offices are useful in training and developing individuals with the special skills required for project management support personnel on major projects. Table 7–2 summarizes the key differences between these two commonly encountered situations.

PERT/CPM/PDM Network-Based Project Management Systems

Significant benefits are realized from the proper use of network-based systems in both the multiple major and multiple small project situations, including:

- Improved planning and scheduling of activities and forecasting of resource requirements.
- Identification of repetitive planning patterns that can be followed in a number of projects, thereby simplifying the planning process.
- Ability to reschedule activities to reflect interproject dependencies and resource limitations following known priority rules.
- Ability to use the computer effectively to produce timely, valid information for multiproject management purposes.

The concept of multiproject operations planning and control is discussed further in Section 7.7.

Table 7–2 Key Differences between Multiple Major and Small Projects

	Multiple Major Projects	**Multiple Small Projects**
Project manager role	Assigned to a manager who does not have a functional responsibility.	Retained within the line organization with integrated staff assistance in planning and coordination. Possibly several projects are assigned to a project (or program) manager or project coordinator.
Project team	Key team members may report to the project manager or may only be physically located together or may stay in their functional organizations.	Project work always assigned to functional departments; in field phase full-time team is assigned to each project.
Integrated planning and control	Each project planned and controlled on an integrated basis; multiproject conflicts resolved above project manager level. Different systems often used on different projects.	All projects must be planned and controlled on an integrated basis within one multiproject operations planning and control system; conflicts resolved by multiproject and/or functional managers.

Interdependencies between and within Projects

Projects and activities within projects can be interrelated in three basic ways:

1. *Result-of-action:* The results produced by completion of an activity in one project or task must be available before an activity in another project or task can begin.
2. *Common-unit-of-resource:* An engineer, for example, must complete an activity in one project or task before she can begin another activity in another project or task.
3. *Rate-of-use-of-common-resources:* Two or more projects or tasks are using one resource pool, such as a group of pipefitters; when the rate of use of the resource by the projects exceeds the supply, the projects or tasks become interdependent on each other through the limited resource pool.

The first two interdependencies can be represented by interface events as discussed in Chapter 8. The third interdependency is treated in more detail in the following section.

7.6 RESOURCE MANAGEMENT FOR PROJECTS

A common cause of project delays resulting in penalties and other undesirable effects is the overcommitment of the organization to contracts or projects with respect to available resources. Cost overruns can also occur when the limitations of available resources are not considered at the time of project commitment and during project execution. Resource management therefore becomes important to project managers, to those responsible for multiproject situations, and to functional managers contributing to projects. It involves:

● Estimating and forecasting the resource requirements by functional task for each project and summarized for all projects. This requires linking project action plans and schedules with resource estimates and actual expenditures.
● Acquiring, providing, and allocating the needed resources in a timely and efficient manner.
● Planning the work for accomplishment within the constraints of limited resources.
● Controlling the use of resources to accomplish the work according to the project plan.

An important difference has been observed in human resource management on one or a few large projects compared with multiple smaller projects. On a large project, the required resources usually will be obtained somehow, either through hiring additional people on a permanent or temporary basis, or by using contractors, consultants, or "body shops." On multiple smaller projects, the available, always limited resources usually must be carefully allocated to support all the projects and it is often more difficult to augment the resource pools with outsiders.

Resources to Be Managed   A variety of resources must be managed, including time, money, people, facilities, equipment, and material. Time is a fundamental resource that cannot be managed like the others. Time flows at a constant rate and time that is not used can never be recovered. It cannot be stored or accumulated for later use. Time is the element that interrelates all other resources with the project plan.

The other resources listed earlier are forecasted, provided, and controlled in accordance with established procedures in all organizations for the management of departments, divisions, and other organizational elements. However, procedures and tools for performing these resource management tasks on a project basis are frequently inadequate.

Procedures and Tools for Project Resource Management   Effective procedures for estimating, forecasting, allocating, and controlling the resources on one or many projects are described in Chapter 8. On major projects and in multiproject situations, computer-supported systems are frequently the only practical way to handle the dynamic need to replan, reschedule, and reallocate resources considering the large volume of detailed information involved.

7.7 MULTIPROJECT OPERATIONS PLANNING AND CONTROL

Situations involving multiple projects, large or small, frequently require the establishment of an operations planning and control function. This may be set up within a division, a product line, or for an entire company. Operations planning and control integrates and controls, on a master plan level and for all contracts and/or projects, the functions of marketing, engineering, procurement, manufacturing, and installation, usually within a specific product line or division. Such a function within a particular organization can provide significant benefits to the organization's project management capabilities and to the project management office, resulting in improved:

- Project planning and control support to each multiproject manager, with reduction in planning and control staff in each project office. (The risks of overcentralizing such support for major projects have been discussed earlier.)
- Ability to resolve conflicts between projects and to control relative priorities of projects, expecially for multiple smaller projects.
- Uniformity of project planning and control practices, enabling higher management to review all projects on a more consistent basis.
- Forecasting of resource requirements for all projects.

Nature of the Problem   The need exists for top management to have confidence that planning is directed toward optimum corporate and project performance. It must have adequate feedback on actual compared to forecasted achievement for functional, corporate, and customer performance goals to be able to evaluate the consequences of specific cost trade-offs and specific alternative business strategies, quickly and quantitatively.

Central planning functions tend to stop short of filling those management needs, because they usually lack the capability to:

- Monitor functional planning continuously at a manageable level of detail.
- Evaluate the corporate impact of forecasted functional achievement accurately and routinely.
- Carry out quantitative analyzes, within a reasonable time, of the consequences of alternative business strategies.
- Replan, on time, matching available resources with contract requirements.
- Issue top level schedules reflecting a balanced, coordinated load between engineering, manufacturing, and installation or field operations.

What is needed is a planning capability in a position to evaluate functional plans and their impact on corporate and project performance objectives, with tools powerful enough to evaluate the effect of discrete contract-oriented decisions on project performance, and so placed in the organizational structure to be able to offer solutions to problems transcending functional organizational boundaries.

Solution: Operations Planning and Control

The solution to this need is to establish an operations planning and control function with supporting system. The function would have the following charter:

- Optimization of corporate and project performance goals by coordination of planning activities in the marketing, engineering, manufacturing, and installation functions through generation of corporate master schedules.
- Coordination of functional planning by means of continuous workload versus capacity evaluation, recognizing functional dependencies in project execution, with a planning horizon extending as far as firm, proposed, and forecasted project activities will allow.
- Continuous evaluation of functional capabilities relative to requirements to (1) allow forecasting of performance against corporate and project goals and (2) highlight areas of deviation where management action is required to resolve cases of potential capacity shortage or surplus.
- Development and maintenance of supporting systems for simulation purposes: to evaluate the likely consequences of alternative business strategies in order to offer possible solutions to senior management.

Potential Benefits

The potential benefits of the operations planning and control function are:

- Improving cross-functional communications with a positive effect on functional performance.

● Improving overall contract and project performance.
● Improving corporate performance by improved resource planning and utilization.

Examples of specific benefits include:

● Reduction of project cycle time.
● Increased direct labor efficiency.
● Increased utilization of tools, test equipment, and other facilities.
● Reduction of gross inventory.
● Reduced exposure to contract penalties.

The final effect of all these benefits is to enable the company to handle more projects, and produce more sales revenue and net income without increasing total personnel and capital investment.

Operations Planning and Control Overview

Operations planning and control reflects the application of currently accepted management concepts combined with network-based systems. It is the result of viewing the problem outlined above from a management perspective, which recognizes that the proper organizational structure is requisite to the implementation of a planning and control system, and that an organization with inadequate systems and procedures will be ineffective. To solve the problem addressed by operations planning and control, both organizational considerations and systems development must be welded together.

Organizational Considerations

The operations planning and control function must report at a level that ensures complete objectivity and impartiality. The exact placement of the function in a given organization will depend on the company product line structure and its size. It is clear that the function must report at a director level with responsibility for overall corporate planning, or to the division or product line manager responsible for engineering, manufacturing, and installation.

In those companies with more than one product line, where normal product cycle time exceeds one year, and contributions from two or more functions are required to execute the project, then a separate operations planning and control organization should exist within each product line, and overall coordination should be supplied by a similar function reporting to a corporate level manager.

Operations planning and control performs a distinctly different corporate role from that usually associated with the management of large projects. Project managers are responsible for large one-of-a-kind projects. If they use a network-based system for controlling the project, it will be structured to reflect a great amount of detail and will generally not be related to other large projects. Operations planning and control on the other hand deals with contracts that reflect a high degree of similarity and are generally smaller than those found under the control of a project manager. The operations planning and control manager can, however, make a valuable contribution to project management by reserving capacity assigned to the project when preparing the master schedule; by providing an effective interface with the functions; and by providing most or all of the project planning and control information required for the major projects.

Supporting Systems

To perform the operations planning and control organization function, systems support will be required for operations scheduling and evaluation, planning evaluation, and resource allocation.

Organization and System Interface

The concept of operations planning and control and the interface between the involved organizational functions and the supporting systems are illustrated in Figure 7–1. The operations planning and control function plans, schedules, monitors, reports, and controls, *at the master schedule level,* all orders and contracts (projects) through all contributing functions.

The set of bridging networks integrates the functional plans and schedules for all projects. The networks are also linked to the supporting functional systems by the downward flow of master scheduling information, and the upward flow of progress and status information. This means that the bridging networks must incorporate milestone or interface events common to both the operations planning and control systems and the functional systems. These milestone/interface events must meet the needs of both types of systems.

Experience indicates that the two elements of operations planning and control—the organizational function and the system—must be developed and introduced concurrently. One element without the other simply will not work. Additionally, if one element is implemented prematurely less than desirable results will be produced.

Standard and Unique Milestones

Boznak (1987) describes a system for multiproject planning and control based on a four-phased project process (design, procure, build/test, and deliver/support) with a set of standardized milestone events that are scheduled and controlled by the project manager, and a set of project-unique milestones scheduled and controlled by the functional project leader or manager. The project manager controlled milestones in Boznak's approach are standardized, coordinative, business-level, and summary in nature.

The functional project leader controlled milestones are project unique, coordinative, functional-level, and detailed in nature.

This multiproject system produces several types and levels of reports, including customer satisfaction report; multiyear master plan, containing all projects; detail reports of various kinds; management action reports, listing all milestones not on schedule; and monthly performance summary, showing schedule compliance by project and functional organization.

There are a number of ways to plan, schedule, track, and control multiple projects within an organization. The key to success is to have a coherent, integrated, consistent system for doing this, and to make sure that everyone is using the same system.

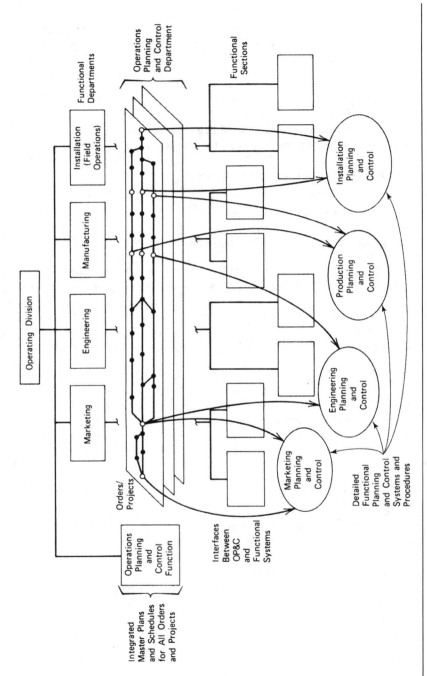

FIGURE 7–1 General illustration of operations planning and control concept.

CEO DEMANDS: PROJECT PORTFOLIO, PROGRAM, AND MULTIPROJECT MANAGEMENT

Regarding project portfolios and multiproject management the CEO must demand that:

1. A well-defined project portfolio management process be implemented on each defined project portfolio.

2. A project portfolio steering group be assigned the responsibilities described here to achieve effective operation of the portfolio management process for each portfolio in the organization.

3. Resources be managed in multiproject situations using available multiproject resource estimating and allocating methods and software applications.

4. Multiproject and multicontract operations planning and control systems be implemented within appropriate operating divisions of the organization.

Project Interface Management

8.1 WHY PROJECT INTERFACE MANAGEMENT

Planning and executing projects is challenging work for all persons involved: the project manager; the project planning and control staff (if any); the contributing functional managers, project leaders, and specialists (including outside contractors, consultants, vendors, and others); and the senior managers to whom these people report.

In spite of decades of experience in positioning the project manager within our organizations, and the availability of and experience in using powerful planning and control systems and procedures in project management, there are many areas that could be improved. Often there is too much conflict, too little acceptance of the role of the project manager, too little real use of the advanced planning and control systems that are available today, and projects that are not planned and controlled as effectively as they can and should be.

One approach to attacking these areas of need in project management can be found in the practice of *project interface management*. Experience in the application of this approach shows that it can lead to significant improvements in the following respects:

- Better definition of roles and responsibilities:
  —Improved understanding of the role of the project manager and better acceptance of the need for that role.
  —Clarification of the roles and responsibilities of the functional contributors to the project.
  —Reduction in conflicts between the project manager and the functional contributors, as well as among the individual functional managers, project leaders, and specialists.

- Project planning and control improvements:
  - —Provision of good, logical linkage points between the levels in the schedule hierarchy, and between subprojects and subnetwork plans.
  - —Better identification of the proper degree of detail at each schedule level.
  - —Wider acceptance and use of project planning and control systems.
- Teamwork and team building improvement:
  - —Improved teamwork through clear identification of the points of interaction between functional tasks.
  - —More effective team building through joint identification of the key project interface points.

8.2 THE CONCEPT: THE PROJECT MANAGER AS THE PROJECT INTERFACE MANAGER

The basic concept of interface management is that the project manager plans, schedules, and controls—in a word, manages—the key interface events on the project, while the responsible functional project leaders manage the tasks or work between these interface events. This is no more than recognition, systemization, and formalization of how the project manager and functional contributors should divide their responsibilities, and how they should work together on any given project. The project manager must plan, schedule, and control the project interfaces in close cooperation with the contributing functional project leaders.

Various Meanings of Interface

The word *interface* can mean different things to different people. Often you see *interface agreements* as part of the project procedures, especially on large engineering/construction projects. These agreements establish the ground rules governing the relationships between the owner, the project manager, the architect engineer firm, and major contractors. In other words, they deal with the ongoing organizational relationships (or interfaces) between the major parties involved in a project.

Another meaning relates to the interaction between phases of a project, and there are many references in the literature to the engineering/construction interface, for example. This is closer to the meaning of "project interface management" used in this book, but not exactly the same thing.

Project Interface Management

While the management of these kinds of *interfaces* could be considered a form of *interface management,* this term refers more specifically to managing the specific project interfaces, as defined next. As used here, it is therefore somewhat different from managing on-going interfaces between organizations in a general sense, or generally managing the interface between engineering and construction, or other *interphase* management activities.

8.3 PROJECT INTERFACE MANAGEMENT IN ACTION

For a specific project, implementation of project interface management involves these activities during project start-up, execution, and closeout:

- Project or new phase start-up planning.
  —During the initiation of the project, or of one of its major phases, the key project interface events are identified and described, planned, scheduled; outgoing and incoming responsibilities are assigned to specific individuals.
- Project or phase execution.
  —During project execution, the project interface events are monitored and controlled as part of the on-going procedures used to manage the project.
- Project closeout.
  —During the close-out phase, the project interface events that occur at the end of the project form important elements of the closeout checklists, and assist the project and functional managers in assuring that all the loose ends of the project are tied up so that the project can be completed cleanly.
- Identifying project interfaces through input-output analysis.
  —The key project team members, once they have studied and understood the project objectives and scope, can usually identify most if not all of the key interfaces by performing an input-output analysis of the tasks they will be responsible for on the project.

This analysis simply requires each task leader to think through two questions:

1. What inputs do we need (information, resources, approvals, other) to initiate and then complete this task, and who will provide these? This will identify the *incoming* interfaces for that task.
2. What intermediate and final outputs will we generate in the performance of this task, and who should receive these? This will identify the *outgoing* interfaces related to the task.

An effective practice is to ask the functional managers, project leaders, or task leaders to prepare a memorandum for each major task they are responsible for on the project, listing the identified incoming and outgoing interfaces, with the expected sources and recipients for each. These memos should then be distributed to all affected project team members. It is sometimes surprising, at least to some team members, to see what others are expecting of them. In other cases, a task leader may not be aware that a particular team member needs to receive the output from a given outgoing interface. By sharing these memos with the other team members, each person has the opportunity to verify who is expecting what input from whom, and who is planning to give what output to whom. Better teamwork, improved communications, and fewer omissions and mistakes are the result.

A useful form for task input-output analysis enabling a more rigorous approach to identifying key interface points is given in Figure 8–1.

This approach also helps to position the project manager as the project interface

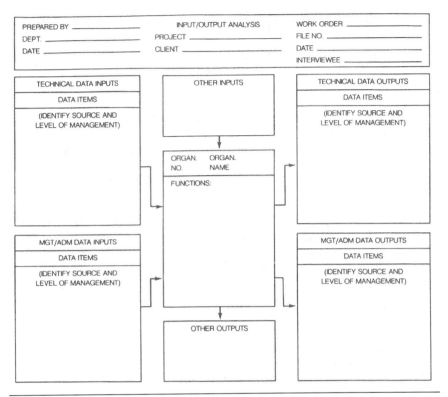

FIGURE 8–1 Input/output chart. *Source:* John Tuman Jr., "Development and Implementation of Project Management Systems," Chapter 27, *Project Management Handbook* (2nd ed.), David I. Cleland and William R. King (Eds.) (New York: Van Nostrand Reinhold, 1988), p. 666. Used by permission.

manager. In this role, she is seen by all members of the project team as fulfilling a vital function that will aid the entire team in achieving success.

8.4 PRODUCT AND PROJECT INTERFACES

It is useful to differentiate between product and product interfaces. *Product* interfaces deal specifically with the things being created by the project activities: the intermediate and final results or products of the project. *Project* interface deals with the process of creating these products.

Product interfaces fall into two categories: (1) *Performance interfaces,* which exist between product subsystems or components; and (2) *Physical interfaces,* which exist between interconnecting parts of the product.

Note that the products or results of the project can be hardware, software, services, new consumable products, physical facilities, documents, and information. Performance and physical interfaces exist in all of these types of products.

For engineering products, procedures for managing the product design, quality assurance, and product configuration will provide the required management of the product interfaces, both performance and physical. For other types of products, equivalent procedures must be provided.

Types of Project Interfaces   Six categories of project interfaces can be identified, although the lines of distinction between some of these can be rather hazy:

1. *Change of responsibility:* One task is completed and the task product is handed over to another team member or organization for further work. A large percentage of project interfaces are of this type.

   Example: Engineering completes a specification, then Purchasing initiates procurement of the items specified. Transmittal of the specification from Engineering to Purchasing is an interface event (outgoing for Engineering, incoming for Purchasing). This example is also an information interface.

2. *Result of action:* Results from one task are required before another task can begin.

   Example: Foundations must be completed by the concrete contractor before the process equipment can be set in place by the equipment erection contractor. This could also be considered a change of responsibility interface.

3. *Management:* Key decisions, approvals, and other management actions affecting other project interfaces, specific tasks, or the overall project.

   Example: Senior manager approval of the contract award for development of a software system needed for the project.

4. *Customer:* Actions similar to management interfaces, but involving the customer or client.

   Example: Customer approval of the conceptual system design in a software development project.

5. *Information:* Information or data developed in one task and needed by one or more other tasks.

   Example: Information on the soil conditions obtained during site investigations by the geologic survey engineering consultant is needed by the civil engineers designing the foundations.

6. *Material:* Equipment, supplies, facilities, or other physical items must be available at a specific location for work to proceed.

   Example: A mobile crane needed to hoist a major piece of equipment into place must be removed from another area of the project.

8.5 PROJECT INTERFACE EVENTS

All of these six types of project interfaces can be represented as *project interface events*. Events are points in time associated with specific dates (predicted, scheduled, or actual) that indicate when an action has taken place. Many project interface events represent doing something to a product interface, as for example, "Product XX Specification Released," or "System YY Design Approved." The specification released by engineering contains performance and physical information on a specific part of the product being created, enabling the purchasing department to procure the item in question so that it will perform and fit within the total project result and schedule.

Interface events are important elements of any comprehensive project plan. The most important ones must be included in the project master plan and schedule, and all key interface events must be included in the integrated project network plan. Interface events provide the means for integrating subnets at the second, third, or lower level planning tiers into the overall project plan and schedule. Many management milestone events are also interface events.

8.6 THE FIVE STEPS OF PROJECT INTERFACE MANAGEMENT

Project interface management consists of five steps:

1. Identification.
2. Documention.
3. Scheduling.
4. Communication.
5. Monitoring and controlling the key interface events.

Identification   The first step in interface management is to identify the key project interface events. Clear, unambiguous event identification is required. An event occurs at a point in time and is different from an activity or task, which consumes time. An event signifies the start or completion of one or more activities or tasks. Events must be identified and defined so that they are recognizable when they occur. Their identifying description should relate each event to an element of the project/work breakdown structure. Each interface event is "outgoing" for the originator (usually only one) and "incoming" for each receiver (of which there may be several).

Documention   On smaller projects, inclusion of well-identified interface events in the project plans and schedules is usually all that is required. However, on large, complex projects formal procedures are required to document and control interface events. These usually provide for three interface event lists:

1. *The Interface Event Coordination List,* covering new events not yet on the other lists.
2. *The Approved Interface Event List,* which includes all such events which have been coordinated with the affected organizations (originators and receivers) and approved by the project manager.
3. *The Interface Event Revision List,* which includes revisions made to the Approved Interface Event List during the past month (or reporting period).

When such formal procedures are required, due to the size or complexity of the project, number of organizations involved, or geographic dispersal of project contributors, the following basic information is provided:

- Codes: An event code number consistent with the network planning procedures in use on the project, plus an identifier indicating that this is an interface event.
- Description of the event.
- Organizations affected:
  —Originator.
  —Receiver(s).
- Project elements and tasks within the breakdown structure related to the event, and the subnetworks in which it appears.

Scheduling   The third step in interface management is to develop a scheduled date for each interface event, reflecting the current integrated project master schedule.

The top-level master project network must include the most important interface events, together with other milestone events of interest to top management. Initial estimates of the time required between the major interface events are made by the persons responsible for each outgoing interface event, and the master project network plan is then analyzed and revised until the key target dates appear to be achievable. At this stage, the second level, more detailed subnets are developed, incorporating the pertinent interface events, and adding detail for the functional tasks involved in each subnet. After each responsible functional manager approves his or her subnets, the results are incorporated into the integrated project network. The subnets can either be integrated into the project network, or the durations between interface events can be entered into the project network on a summary basis. On large projects, integration of all lower level subnets, with all their details, into one integrated project network may prove to be impractical, due to the large volume of information that would have to be updated.

It is not mandatory for lower level schedules to be in the form of network plans, depending on the complexity of the specific tasks involved. In many cases, functional tasks between interface events can be planned and controlled effectively using bar charts, process sheets, or checklists. However, the project manager must assure that the tasks are adequately planned and scheduled, so that there is a reasonable assurance that the future interface event dates that have been promised will, in fact, be met. Weekly or monthly revisions of the estimated time to complete each task (not a percent complete estimate) are required.

On smaller projects, all that may be required is an overall project master schedule that incorporates the key interface events.

Communication

Communication between members of the project team, with the customer and with upper management can be enhanced through the proper use of interface events. By using the interface event lists, with clear identification of each event, omissions, errors, and confusion can be avoided. Properly coded events lend themselves to accurate reference by electronic mail, telex, telefax, or telephone, for discussion, changes in planning, conflict resolution, and progress reporting.

Affected interfaces should be included in task work orders, contracts, subcontracts and purchase orders, with appropriate language to assure that they are properly planned, scheduled, monitored, and controlled.

Monitoring and Controlling the Key Interface Events

Interface events should be emphasized in normal project monitoring and control procedures. Progress reporting should require a statement of the estimated time remaining to reach each future interface, if their previously predicted completion dates have changed.

If all interface events are well controlled, the project will also be well-controlled. Interface event control is achieved through the procedures used to add events to the approved list, to revise them, and through the schedule review and control procedures. Control of the project is achieved jointly by the project and functional managers by:

- Controlling the interface events.
- Work authorization and control procedures and practices.
- Project directives.
- Project evaluation and review procedures.

8.7 CONCLUSION

Good project interface management practices will:

- Clarify roles and responsibilities, and reduce conflicts.
- Define who will provide what to each project team member, enhancing teamwork and communications.
- Improve project planning, scheduling, and control.
- Increase the effectiveness of the project team, thereby improving the changes of project success: Delivery of the specified results on time and within budget.

UNIT 3
Project Management

The material within this unit has been excerpted from the following textbook:

Harold Kerzner, Ph.D.
Project Management: A Systems Approach to Planning, Scheduling, and Controlling
Ninth Edition

Copyright 2006 by John Wiley & Sons, Inc.
ISBN: 0-471-74187-6

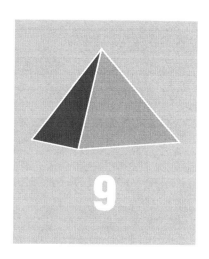

Organizing and Staffing the Project Office and Team

Related Case Studies (from Kerzner/*Project Management Case Studies,* 2nd Edition)	Related Workbook Exercises (from Kerzner/*Project Management Workbook and PMP®/CAPM® Exam Study Guide,* 9th Edition)	PMBOK® Guide, 3rd Edition, Reference Section for the PMP® Certification Exam
• Government Project Management • Falls Engineering • White Manufacturing • Martig Construction Company • Ducor Chemical • The Carlson Project	• The Bad Apple • Multiple Choice Exam	• Human Resource Management

9.0 INTRODUCTION

PMBOK® Guide, 2004
Chapter 9 Human Resource Management

Successful project management, regardless of the organizational structure, is only as good as the individuals and leaders who are managing the key functions. Project management is not a one-person operation; it requires a group of individuals dedicated to the achievement of a specific goal. Project management includes:

- A project manager
- An assistant project manager

- A project (home) office
- A project team

Generally, project office personnel are assigned full-time to the project and work out of the project office, whereas the project team members work out of the functional units and may spend only a small percentage of their time on the project. Normally, project office personnel report directly to the project manager, but they may still be solid to their line function just for administrative control. A project office usually is not required on small projects, and sometimes the project can be accomplished by just one person who may fill all of the project office positions.

Before the staffing function begins, five basic questions are usually considered:

- What are the requirements for an individual to become a successful project manager?
- Who should be a member of the project team?
- Who should be a member of the project office?
- What problems can occur during recruiting activities?
- What can happen downstream to cause the loss of key team members?

On the surface, these questions may not seem especially complex. But when we apply them to a project environment (which is by definition a "temporary" situation) where a constant stream of projects is necessary for corporate growth, the staffing problems become complex, especially if the organization is understaffed.

9.1 THE STAFFING ENVIRONMENT

PMBOK® Guide, 2004
9.1 Human Resource Planning

To understand the problems that occur during staffing, we must first investigate the characteristics of project management, including the project environment, the project management process, and the project manager.

Two major kinds of problems are related to the project environment: personnel performance problems and personnel policy problems. Performance is difficult for many individuals in the project environment because it represents a change in the way of doing business. Individuals, regardless of how competent they are, find it difficult to adapt continually to a changing situation in which they report to multiple managers.

On the other hand, many individuals thrive on temporary assignments because it gives them a "chance for glory." Unfortunately, some employees might consider the chance for glory more important than the project. For example, an employee may pay no attention to the instructions of the project manager and instead perform the task his own way. In this situation, the employee wants only to be recognized as an achiever and really does not care if the project is a success or failure, as long as he still has a functional home to return to where he will be identified as an achiever with good ideas.

The second major performance problem lies in the project–functional interface, where an individual suddenly finds himself reporting to two bosses, the functional manager and the project manager. If the functional manager and the project manager are in agreement about the work to be accomplished, then performance may not be hampered. But if conflicting directions are received, then the individual may let his performance suffer because of his compromising position. In this case, the employee will "bend" in the direction of the manager who controls his purse strings.

Personnel policy problems can create havoc in an organization, especially if the "grass is greener" in a project environment than in the functional environment. Functional organizations normally specify grades and salaries for employees. Project offices, on the other hand, have no such requirements and can promote and pay according to achievement. The difficulty here is that one can distinguish between employees in grades 7, 8, 9, 10, and 11 in a line organization, whereas for a project manager the distinction might appear only in the size of the project or the amount of responsibility. Bonuses are also easier to obtain in the project office but may create conflict and jealousy between the horizontal and vertical elements.

Because each project is different, the project management process allows each project to have its own policies, procedures, rules, and standards, provided they fall within broad company guidelines. Each project must be recognized as a project by top management so that the project manager has the delegated authority necessary to enforce the policies, procedures, rules, and standards.

Project management is successful only if the project manager and his team are totally dedicated to the successful completion of the project. This requires each team member of the project team and office to have a good understanding of the fundamental project requirements, which include:

- Customer liaison
- Project direction
- Project planning
- Project control
- Project evaluation
- Project reporting

Ultimately, the person with the greatest influence during the staffing phase is the project manager. The personal attributes and abilities of project managers will either attract or deter highly desirable individuals. Basic characteristics include:

- Honesty and integrity
- Understanding of personnel problems
- Understanding of project technology
- Business management competence
  - Management principles
  - Communications
- Alertness and quickness
- Versatility
- Energy and toughness
- Decision-making ability
- Ability to evaluate risk and uncertainty

Project managers must exhibit honesty and integrity to foster an atmosphere of trust. They should not make impossible promises, such as immediate promotions for everyone if a follow-on contract is received. Also, on temporarily assigned activities, such as a project, managers cannot wait for personnel to iron out their own problems because time, cost, and performance requirements will not be satisfied.

Project managers should have both business management and technical expertise. They must understand the fundamental principles of management, especially those involving the rapid development of temporary communication channels. Project managers must understand the technical implications of a problem, since they are ultimately responsible for all decision-making. However, many good technically oriented managers have failed because they have become too involved with the technical side of the project rather than the management side. There are strong arguments for having a project manager who has more than just an understanding of the necessary technology.

Because a project has a relatively short time duration, decision-making must be rapid and effective. Managers must be alert and quick in their ability to perceive "red flags" that can eventually lead to serious problems. They must demonstrate their versatility and toughness in order to keep subordinates dedicated to goal accomplishment. Executives must realize that the project manager's objectives during staffing are to:

- Acquire the best available assets and try to improve them
- Provide a good working environment for all personnel
- Make sure that all resources are applied effectively and efficiently so that all constraints are met, if possible

9.2 SELECTING THE PROJECT MANAGER: AN EXECUTIVE DECISION

PMBOK® Guide, 2004
9.2.1 Acquire Project Team
9.3.2 General Management Skills

Probably the most difficult decision facing upper-level management is the selection of project managers. Some managers work best on long-duration projects where decision-making can be slow; others may thrive on short-duration projects that can result in a constant-pressure environment. A director was asked whom he would choose for a key project manager position—an individual who had been a project manager on previous programs in which there were severe problems and cost overruns, or a new aggressive individual who might have the capability to be a good project manager but had never had the opportunity. The director responded that he would go with the seasoned veteran assuming that the previous mistakes would not be made again. The argument here is that the project manager must learn from his own mistakes so they will not be made again. The new individual is apt to make the same mistakes the veteran made. However, this may limit career path opportunities for younger personnel. Stewart has commented on the importance of experience[1]:

> Though the project manager's previous experience is apt to have been confined to a single functional area of business, he must be able to function on the project as a kind of general

---

1. John M. Stewart, "Making Project Management Work." Reprinted with permission from *Business Horizons,* Fall 1965, p. 63. Copyright © 1965 by the Board of Trustees at Indiana University.

manager in miniature. He must not only keep track of what is happening but also play the crucial role of advocate for the project. Even for a seasoned manager, this task is not likely to be easy. Hence, it is important to assign an individual whose administrative abilities and skills in personal relations have been convincingly demonstrated under fire.

The selection process for project managers is not easy. Five basic questions must be considered:

- What are the internal and external sources?
- How do we select?
- How do we provide career development in project management?
- How can we develop project management skills?
- How do we evaluate project management performance?

Project management cannot succeed unless a good project manager is at the controls. It is far more likely that project managers will succeed if it is obvious to the subordinates that the general manager has appointed them. Usually, a brief memo to the line managers will suffice. The major responsibilities of the project manager include:

- To produce the end-item with the available resources and within the constraints of time, cost, and performance/technology
- To meet contractual profit objectives
- To make all required decisions whether they be for alternatives or termination
- To act as the customer (external) and upper-level and functional management (internal) communications focal point
- To "negotiate" with all functional disciplines for accomplishment of the necessary work packages within the constraints of time, cost, and performance/technology
- To resolve all conflicts

If these responsibilities were applied to the total organization, they might reflect the job description of the general manager. This analogy between project and general managers is one of the reasons why future general managers are asked to perform functions that are implied, rather than spelled out, in the job description. As an example, you are the project manager on a high-technology project. As the project winds down, an executive asks you to write a paper so that he can present it at a technical meeting in Tokyo. His name will appear first on the paper. Should this be a part of your job? As this author sees it, you really don't have much of a choice.

In order for project managers to fulfill their responsibilities successfully, they are constantly required to demonstrate their skills in interface, resource, and planning and control management. These implicit responsibilities are shown below:

- Interface Management
  - Product interfaces
    - —Performance of parts or subsections
    - —Physical connection of parts or subsections
  - Project interfaces

- Customer
- Management (functional and upper-level)
- Change of responsibilities
- Information flow
- Material interfaces (inventory control)
- Resource Management
  - Time (schedule)
  - Manpower
  - Money
  - Facilities
  - Equipment
  - Material
  - Information/technology
- Planning and Control Management
  - Increased equipment utilization
  - Increased performance efficiency
  - Reduced risks
  - Identification of alternatives to problems
  - Identification of alternative resolutions to conflicts

Consider the following advertisement for a facilities planning and development project manager (adapted from *The New York Times*, January 2, 1972):

Personable, well-educated, literate individual with college degree in Engineering to work for a small firm. Long hours, no fringe benefits, no security, little chance for advancement are among the inducements offered. Job requires wide knowledge and experience in manufacturing, materials, construction techniques, economics, management and mathematics. Competence in the use of the spoken and written English is required. Must be willing to suffer personal indignities from clients, professional derision from peers in the more conventional jobs, and slanderous insults from colleagues.

Job involves frequent extended trips to inaccessible locations throughout the world, manual labor and extreme frustration from the lack of data on which to base decisions.

Applicant must be willing to risk personal and professional future on decisions based upon inadequate information and complete lack of control over acceptance of recommendations by clients. Responsibilities for the work are unclear and little or no guidance is offered. Authority commensurate with responsibility is not provided either by the firm or its clients.

Applicant should send resume, list of publications, references and other supporting documentation to. . . .

Fortunately, these types of job descriptions are very rare today.

Finding the person with the right qualifications is not an easy task because the selection of project managers is based more on personal characteristics than on the job description. In Section 9.1 a brief outline of desired characteristics was presented. Russell Archibald defines a broader range of desired personal characteristics[2]:

---

2. Russell D. Archibald, *Managing High-Technology Programs and Projects* (New York: Wiley, 1976), p. 55. Copyright © 1976 by John Wiley & Sons, Inc. Reprinted by permission of the publisher.

PMBOK® Guide, 2004
9.3 Develop Project Team

- Flexibility and adaptability
- Preference for significant initiative and leadership
- Aggressiveness, confidence, persuasiveness, verbal fluency
- Ambition, activity, forcefulness
- Effectiveness as a communicator and integrator
- Broad scope of personal interests
- Poise, enthusiasm, imagination, spontaneity
- Able to balance technical solutions with time, cost, and human factors
- Well organized and disciplined
- A generalist rather than a specialist
- Able and willing to devote most of his time to planning and controlling
- Able to identify problems
- Willing to make decisions
- Able to maintain proper balance in the use of time

This ideal project manager would probably have doctorates in engineering, business, and psychology, and experience with ten different companies in a variety of project office positions, and would be about twenty-five years old. Good project managers in industry today would probably be lucky to have 70 to 80 percent of these characteristics. The best project managers are willing and able to identify their own shortcomings and know when to ask for help.

The difficulty in staffing, especially for project managers or assistant project managers, is in determining what questions to ask during an interview to see if an individual has the necessary or desired characteristics. Individuals may be qualified to be promoted vertically but not horizontally. An individual with poor communication skills and interpersonal skills can be promoted to a line management slot because of his technical expertise, but this same individual is not qualified for project management promotion.

One of the best ways to interview is to read each element of the job description to the potential candidate. Many individuals want a career path in project management but are totally unaware of what the project manager's duties are.

So far we have discussed the personal characteristics of the project manager. There are also job-related questions to consider, such as:

- Are feasibility and economic analyses necessary?
- Is complex technical expertise required? If so, is it within the individual's capabilities?
- If the individual is lacking expertise, will there be sufficient backup strength in the line organizations?
- Is this the company's or the individual's first exposure to this type of project and/or client? If so, what are the risks to be considered?
- What is the priority for this project, and what are the risks?
- With whom must the project manager interface, both inside and outside the organization?

Most good project managers know how to perform feasibility studies and cost-benefit analyses. Sometimes these studies create organizational conflict. A major utility company begins each computer project with a feasibility study in which a cost-benefit analysis is performed. The project managers, all of whom report to a project management division, perform the study themselves without any direct functional support. The functional managers argue that the results are grossly inaccurate because the functional experts are not involved. The project managers, on the other hand, argue that they never have sufficient time or money to perform a complete analysis. Some companies resolve this by having a special group perform these studies.

Most companies would prefer to find project managers from within. Unfortunately, this is easier said than done.

There are also good reasons for recruiting from outside the company. A new project manager hired from the outside would be less likely to have strong informal ties to any one line organization and thus could be impartial. Some companies further require that the individual spend an apprenticeship period of twelve to eighteen months in a line organization to find out how the company functions, to become acquainted with the people, and to understand the company's policies and procedures.

One of the most important but often least understood characteristics of good project managers is the ability to know their own strengths and weaknesses and those of their employees. Managers must understand that in order for employees to perform efficiently:

- They must know what they are supposed to do.
- They must have a clear understanding of authority and its limits.
- They must know what their relationship with other people is.
- They should know what constitutes a job well done in terms of specific results.
- They should know where and when they are falling short.
- They must be made aware of what can and should be done to correct unsatisfactory results.
- They must feel that their superior has an interest in them as individuals.
- They must feel that their superior believes in them and wants them to succeed.

9.3 SKILL REQUIREMENTS FOR PROJECT AND PROGRAM MANAGERS

PMBOK® Guide, 2004
Human Resources Management
9.3.2 Develop Project Team

Managing complex programs represents a challenge requiring skills in team building, leadership, conflict resolution, technical expertise, planning, organization, entrepreneurship, administration, management support, and the allocation of resources. This section examines these skills relative to program management effectiveness. A key factor to good program performance is the program manager's ability to integrate personnel from many disciplines into an effective work team.

To get results, the program manager must relate to (1) the people to be managed, (2) the task to be done, (3) the tools available, (4) the organizational structure, and (5) the organizational environment, including the customer community.

With an understanding of the interaction of corporate organization and behavior elements, the manager can build an environment conducive to the working team's needs. The internal and external forces that impinge on the organization of the project must be reconciled to mutual goals. Thus the program manager must be both socially and technically aware to understand how the organization functions and how these functions will affect the program organization of the particular job to be done. In addition, the program manager must understand the culture and value system of the organization he is working with. Effective program management is directly related to proficiency in these ten skills:

- Team building
- Leadership
- Conflict resolution
- Technical expertise
- Planning
- Organization
- Entrepreneurship
- Administration
- Management support
- Resource allocation

It is important that the personal management style underlying these skills facilitate the integration of multidisciplinary program resources for synergistic operation. The days of the manager who gets by with technical expertise alone or pure administrative skills are gone.

Team-Building Skills
Building the program team is one of the prime responsibilities of the program manager. Team building involves a whole spectrum of management skills required to identify, commit, and integrate the various task groups from the traditional functional organization into a single program management system.

To be effective, the program manager must provide an atmosphere conducive to teamwork. He must nurture a climate with the following characteristics:

- Team members committed to the program
- Good interpersonal relations and team spirit
- The necessary expertise and resources
- Clearly defined goals and program objectives
- Involved and supportive top management
- Good program leadership
- Open communication among team members and support organizations
- A low degree of detrimental interpersonal and intergroup conflict

Three major considerations are involved in all of the above factors: (1) effective communications, (2) sincere interest in the professional growth of team members, and (3) commitment to the project.

Leadership Skills
A prerequisite for program success is the program manager's ability to lead the team within a relatively unstructured environment. It involves

dealing effectively with managers and supporting personnel across functional lines and the ability to collect and filter relevant data for decision-making in a dynamic environment. It involves the ability to integrate individual demands, requirements, and limitations into decisions and to resolve intergroup conflicts.

As with a general manager, quality leadership depends heavily on the program manager's personal experience and credibility within the organization. An effective management style might be characterized this way:

- Clear project leadership and direction
- Assistance in problem-solving
- Facilitating the integration of new members into the team
- Ability to handle interpersonal conflict
- Facilitating group decisions
- Capability to plan and elicit commitments
- Ability to communicate clearly
- Presentation of the team to higher management
- Ability to balance technical solutions against economic and human factors

The personal traits desirable and supportive of the above skills are:

- Project management experience
- Flexibility and change orientation
- Innovative thinking
- Initiative and enthusiasm
- Charisma and persuasiveness
- Organization and discipline

Conflict Resolution Skills   Conflict is fundamental to complex task management. Understanding the determinants of conflicts is important to the program manager's ability to deal with conflicts effectively. When conflict becomes dysfunctional, it often results in poor program decision-making, lengthy delays over issues, and a disruption of the team's efforts, all negative influences to program performance. However, conflict can be beneficial when it produces involvement and new information and enhances the competitive spirit.

To successfully resolve conflict and improve overall program performance, program managers must:

- Understand interaction of the organizational and behavioral elements in order to build an environment conducive to their team's motivational needs. This will enhance active participation and minimize unproductive conflict.
- Communicate effectively with all organizational levels regarding both project objectives and decisions. Regularly scheduled status review meetings can be an important communication vehicle.
- Recognize the determinants of conflict and their timing in the project life cycle. Effective project planning, contingency planning, securing of commitments, and

involving top management can help to avoid or minimize many conflicts before they impede project performance.

The accomplished manager needs a "sixth sense" to indicate when conflict is desirable, what kind of conflict will be useful, and how much conflict is optimal for a given situation. In the final analysis, he has the sole responsibility for his program and how conflict will contribute to its success or failure.

Technical Skills

The program manager rarely has all the technical, administrative, and marketing expertise needed to direct the program single-handedly. It is essential, however, for the program manager to understand the technology, the markets, and the environment of the business. Without this understanding, the consequences of local decisions on the total program, the potential growth ramifications, and relationships to other business opportunities cannot be foreseen by the manager. Further technical expertise is necessary to evaluate technical concepts and solutions, to communicate effectively in technical terms with the project team, and to assess risks and make trade-offs between cost, schedule, and technical issues. This is why in complex problem-solving situations so many project managers must have an engineering background.

Technical expertise is composed of an understanding of the:

- Technology involved
- Engineering tools and techniques employed
- Specific markets, their customers, and requirements
- Product applications
- Technological trends and evolutions
- Relationship among supporting technologies
- People who are part of the technical community

The technical expertise required for effective management of engineering programs is normally developed through progressive growth in engineering or supportive project assignments in a specific technology area. Frequently, the project begins with an exploratory phase leading into a proposal. This is normally an excellent testing ground for the future program manager. It also allows top management to judge the new candidate's capacity for managing the technological innovations and integration of solutions.

Planning Skills

Planning skills are helpful for any undertaking; they are absolutely essential for the successful management of large complex programs. The project plan is the road map that defines how to get from the start to the final results.

Program planning is an ongoing activity at all organizational levels. However, the preparation of a project summary plan, prior to project start, is the responsibility of the program manager. Effective project planning requires particular skills far beyond writing a document with schedules and budgets. It requires communication and information processing skills to define the actual resource requirements and administrative support necessary. It requires the ability to negotiate the necessary resources and commitments from key personnel in various support organizations with little or no formal authority.

Effective planning requires skills in the areas of:

- Information processing
- Communication
- Resource negotiations
- Securing commitments
- Incremental and modular planning
- Assuring measurable milestones
- Facilitating top management involvement

In addition, the program manager must assure that the plan remains a viable document. Changes in project scope and depth are inevitable. The plan should reflect necessary changes through formal revisions and should be the guiding document throughout the life cycle of the program. An obsolete or irrelevant plan is useless.

Finally, program managers need to be aware that planning can be overdone. If not controlled, planning can become an end in itself and a poor substitute for innovative work. It is the responsibility of the program manager to build flexibility into the plan and police it against misuse.

Organizational Skills

The program manager must be a social architect; that is, he must understand how the organization works and how to work with the organization. Organizational skills are particularly important during project formation and startup when the program manager is integrating people from many different disciplines into an effective work team. It requires defining the reporting relationships, responsibilities, lines of control, and information needs. A good program plan and a task matrix are useful organizational tools. In addition, the organizational effort is facilitated by clearly defined program objectives, open communication channels, good program leadership, and senior management support.

Entrepreneurial Skills

The program manager also needs a general management perspective. For example, economic considerations affect the organization's financial performance, but objectives often are much broader than profits. Customer satisfaction, future growth, cultivation of related market activities, and minimum organizational disruptions of other programs might be equally important goals. The effective program manager is concerned with all these issues.

Entrepreneurial skills are developed through actual experience. However, formal MBA-type training, special seminars, and cross-functional training programs can help to develop the entrepreneurial skills needed by program managers.

Administrative Skills

Administrative skills are essential. The program manager must be experienced in planning, staffing, budgeting, scheduling, and other control techniques. In dealing with technical personnel, the problem is seldom to make people understand administrative techniques such as budgeting and scheduling, but to impress on them that costs and schedules are just as important as elegant technical solutions.

Particularly on larger programs, managers rarely have all the administrative skills required. While it is important that program managers understand the company's operating procedures and available tools, it is often necessary for the program manager to free himself from administrative details regardless of his ability to handle them. He has to delegate considerable administrative tasks to support groups or hire a project administrator.

Some helpful tools for the manager in the administration of his program include: (1) the meeting, (2) the report, (3) the review, and (4) budget and schedule controls. Program managers must be thoroughly familiar with these available tools and know how to use them effectively.

Management Support Building Skills

The program manager is surrounded by a myriad of organizations that either support him or control his activities. An understanding of these interfaces is important to program managers as it enhances their ability to build favorable relationships with senior management. Project organizations are shared-power systems with personnel of many diverse interests and "ways of doing things." Only a strong leader backed by senior management can prevent the development of unfavorable biases.

Four key variables influence the project manager's ability to create favorable relationships with senior management: (1) his ongoing credibility, (2) the visibility of his program, (3) the priority of his program relative to other organizational undertakings, and (4) his own accessibility.

Resource Allocation Skills

A program organization has many bosses. Functional lines often shield support organizations from direct financial control by the project office. Once a task has been authorized, it is often impossible to control the personnel assignments, priorities, and indirect manpower costs. In addition, profit accountability is difficult owing to the interdependencies of various support departments and the often changing work scope and contents.

Effective and detailed program planning may facilitate commitment and reinforce control. Part of the plan is the "Statement of Work," which establishes a basis for resource allocation. It is also important to work out specific agreements with all key contributors and their superiors on the tasks to be performed and the associated budgets and schedules. Measurable milestones are not only important for hardware components, but also for the "invisible" program components such as systems and software tasks. Ideally, these commitments on specs, schedules, and budgets should be established through involvement by key personnel in the early phases of project formation, such as the proposal phase. This is the time when requirements are still flexible, and trade-offs among performance, schedule, and budget parameters are possible. Further, this is normally the time when the competitive spirit among potential contributors is highest, often leading to a more cohesive and challenging work plan.

9.4 SPECIAL CASES IN PROJECT MANAGER SELECTION

Thus far we have assumed that the project is large enough for a full-time project manager to be appointed. This is not always the case. There are four major problem areas in staffing projects:

- Part-time versus full-time assignments
- Several projects assigned to one project manager
- Projects assigned to functional managers
- The project manager role retained by the general manager

The first problem is generally related to the size of the project. If the project is small (in time duration or cost), a part-time project manager may be selected. Many executives have fallen into the trap of letting line personnel act as part-time project managers while still performing line functions. If the employee has a conflict between what is best for the project and what is best for his line organization, the project will suffer. It is only natural that the employee will favor the place the salary increases come from.

It is a common practice for one project manager to control several projects, especially if they are either related or similar. Problems come about when the projects have drastically different priorities. The low-priority efforts will be neglected.

If the project is a high-technology effort that requires specialization and can be performed by one department, then it is not unusual for the line manager to take on a dual role and act as project manager as well. This can be difficult to do, especially if the project manager is required to establish the priorities for the work under his supervision. The line manager may keep the best resources for the project, regardless of the priority. Then that project will be a success at the expense of every other project he must supply resources to.

Probably the worst situation is that in which an executive fills the role of project manager for a particular effort. The executive may not have the time necessary for total dedication to the achievement of the project. He cannot make effective decisions as a project manager while still discharging normal duties. Additionally, the executive may hoard the best resources for his project.

9.5 SELECTING THE WRONG PROJECT MANAGER

Even though executives know the personal characteristics and traits that project managers should possess, and even though job descriptions are often clearly defined, management may still select the wrong person because they base their decision on the following criteria.

Maturity

Some executives consider gray hair to be a sure indication of maturity, but this is not the type of maturity needed for project management. Maturity in project management generally comes from exposure to several types of projects in a variety of project office positions. In aerospace and defense, it is possible for a project manager to manage the same type of project for ten years or more. When placed on a new project, the individual may try to force personnel and project requirements to adhere to the same policies and procedures that existed on the ten-year project. The project manager may know only one way of managing projects.

Hard-Nosed Tactics

Applying hard-nosed tactics to subordinates can be very demoralizing. Project managers must give people sufficient freedom to get the job done, without providing continuous supervision and direction. A line employee who is given "freedom" by his line manager but suddenly finds himself closely supervised by the project manager will be very unhappy.

Line managers, because of their ability to control an employee's salary, need only one leadership style and can force the employees to adapt. The project manager, on the other hand, cannot control salaries and must have a wide variety of leadership styles. The project manager must adapt a leadership style to the project employees, whereas the reverse is true in the line organization.

Availability

Executives should not assign individuals as project managers simply because of availability. People have a tendency to cringe when you suggest that project managers be switched halfway through a project. For example, manager X is halfway through his project. Manager Y is waiting for an assignment. A new project comes up, and the executive switches managers X and Y. There are several reasons for this. The most important phase of a project is planning, and, if it is accomplished correctly, the project could conceivably run itself. Therefore, manager Y should be able to handle manager X's project.

There are several other reasons why this switch may be necessary. The new project may have a higher priority and require a more experienced manager. Second, not all project managers are equal, especially when it comes to planning. When an executive finds a project manager who demonstrates extraordinary talents at planning, there is a natural tendency for the executive to want this project manager to plan all projects.

Technical Expertise

Executives quite often promote technical line managers without realizing the consequences. Technical specialists may not be able to divorce themselves from the technical side of the house and become project managers rather than project doers. There are also strong reasons to promote technical specialists to project managers. These people often:

- Have better relationships with fellow researchers
- Can prevent duplication of effort
- Can foster teamwork
- Have progressed up through the technical ranks
- Are knowledgeable in many technical fields
- Understand the meaning of profitability and general management philosophy

- Are interested in training and teaching
- Understand how to work with perfectionists

Promoting an employee to project management because of his technical expertise may be acceptable if, and only if, the project requires this expertise and technical direction, as in R&D efforts. For projects in which a "generalist" is acceptable as a project manager, there may be a great danger in assigning highly technical personnel. According to Wilemon and Cicero[3]:

- The greater the project manager's technical expertise, the higher the propensity that he will overly involve himself in the technical details of the project.
- The greater the project manager's difficulty in delegating technical task responsibilities, the more likely it is that he will overinvolve himself in the technical details of the project. (Depending upon his expertise to do so.)
- The greater the project manager's interest in the technical details of the project, the more likely it is that he will defend the project manager's role as one of a technical specialist.
- The lower the project manager's technical expertise, the more likely it is that he will overstress the nontechnical project functions (administrative functions).

Customer Orientation

Executives quite often place individuals as project managers simply to satisfy a customer request. Being able to communicate with the customer does not guarantee project success, however. If the choice of project manager is simply a concession to the customer, then the executive must insist on providing a strong supporting team.

New Exposure

Executives run the risk of project failure if an individual is appointed project manager simply to gain exposure to project management. An executive of a utility company wanted to rotate his line personnel into project management for twelve to eighteen months and then return them to the line organization where they would be more well-rounded individuals and better understand the working relationship between project management and line management. There are two major problems with this. First, the individual may become technically obsolete after eighteen months in project management. Second, and more important, individuals who get a taste of project management will generally not want to return to the line organization.

Company Exposure

The mere fact that individuals have worked in a variety of divisions does not guarantee that they will make good project managers. Their working in a variety of divisions may indicate that they couldn't hold any one job. In that case, they have reached their true level of incompetency, and putting them into project man-

---

3. D. L. Wilemon and J. P. Cicero, "The Project Manager—Anomalies and Ambiguities," *Academy of Management Journal,* Vol. 13, 1970, pp. 269–282.

TABLE 9–1. METHODS AND TECHNIQUES FOR DEVELOPING PROJECT MANAGERS

I. Experiential training/on-the-job
   Working with experienced professional leader
   Working with project team member
   Assigning a variety of project management responsibilities, consecutively
   Job rotation
   Formal on-the-job training
   Supporting multifunctional activities
   Customer liaison activities
II. Conceptual training/schooling
   Courses, seminars, workshops
   Simulations, games, cases
   Group exercises
   Hands-on exercises in using project management techniques
   Professional meetings
   Conventions, symposia
   Readings, books, trade journals, professional magazines
III. Organizational development
   Formally established and recognized project management function
   Proper project organization
   Project support systems
   Project charter
   Project management directives, policies, and procedures

agement will only maximize the damage they can do to the company. Some executives contend that the best way to train a project manager is by rotation through the various functional disciplines for two weeks to a month in each organization. Other executives maintain that this is useless because the individual cannot learn anything in so short a period of time.

Tables 9–1 and 9–2 identify current thinking on methods for training project managers.

Finally, there are three special points to consider:

- Individuals should not be promoted to project management simply because they are at the top of their pay grade.
- Project managers should be promoted and paid based on performance, not on the number of people supervised.
- It is not necessary for the project manager to be the highest ranking or salaried individual on the project team with the rationale that sufficient "clout" is needed.

TABLE 9–2. HOW TO TRAIN PROJECT MANAGERS

Company Management Say Project Managers Can Be Trained in a Combination of Ways:

Experiential learning, on-the-job	60%
Formal education and special courses	20%
Professional activities, seminars	10%
Readings	10%

9.6 NEXT GENERATION PROJECT MANAGERS

The skills needed to be an effective, twenty-first century project manager have changed from those needed during the 1980s. Historically, only engineers were given the opportunity to become project managers. The belief was that the project manager had to have a command of technology in order to make all of the technical decisions. As projects became larger and more complex, it became obvious that project managers might need simply an understanding rather than a command of technology. The true technical expertise would reside with the line managers, except for special situations such as R&D project management.

As project management began to grow and mature, the project manager was converted from a technical manager to a business manager. The primary skills needed to be an effective project manager in the twenty-first century are:

● Knowledge of the business
● Risk management
● Integration skills

The critical skill is risk management. However, to perform risk management effectively, a sound knowledge of the business is required. Figure 9–1 shows the changes in project management skills needed between 1985 and 2006.

As projects become larger, the complexities of integration management become more pronounced. Figure 9–2 illustrates the importance of integration management. In 1985, project managers spent most of their time planning and replanning with their team. This was necessary because the project manager was the technical expert. Today, line managers

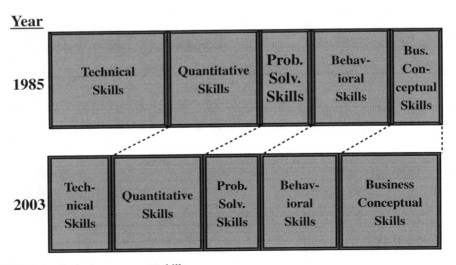

FIGURE 9–1. Project management skills.

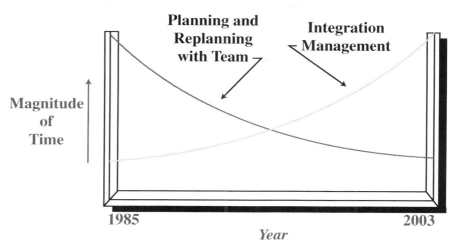

FIGURE 9–2. How do project managers spend their time?

are the technical experts and perform the majority of the planning and replanning within their line. The project manager's efforts are now heavily oriented toward integration of the function plans into a total project plan. Some people contend that, with the increased risks and complexities of integration management, the project manager of the future will become an expert in damage control.

9.7 DUTIES AND JOB DESCRIPTIONS

Since projects, environments, and organizations differ from company to company as well as project to project, it is not unusual for companies to struggle to provide reasonable job descriptions of the project manager and associated personnel. Below is a simple list identifying the duties of a project manager in the construction industry[4]:

- Planning
  - Become completely familiar with all contract documents
  - Develop the basic plan for executing and controlling the project
  - Direct the preparation of project procedures
  - Direct the preparation of the project budget
  - Direct the preparation of the project schedule
  - Direct the preparation of basic project design criteria and general specifications

4. Source unknown.

- Direct the preparation of the plan for organizing, executing, and controlling field construction activities
- Review plans and procedures periodically and institute changes if necessary
- Organizing
  - Develop organization chart for project
  - Review project position descriptions, outlining duties, responsibilities, and restrictions for key project supervisors
  - Participate in the selection of key project supervisors
  - Develop project manpower requirements
  - Continually review project organization and recommend changes in organizational structure and personnel, if necessary
- Directing
  - Direct all work on the project that is required to meet contract obligations
  - Develop and maintain a system for decision-making within the project team whereby decisions are made at the proper level
  - Promote the growth of key project supervisors
  - Establish objectives for project manager and performance goals for key project supervisors
  - Foster and develop a spirit of project team effort
  - Assist in resolution of differences or problems between departments or groups on assigned projects
  - Anticipate and avoid or minimize potential problems by maintaining current knowledge of overall project status
  - Develop clear written strategy guidelines for all major problems with clear definitions of responsibilities and restraints
- Controlling
  - Monitor project activities for compliance with company purpose and philosophy and general corporate policies
  - Interpret, communicate, and require compliance with the contract, the approved plan, project procedures, and directives of the client
  - Maintain personal control of adherence to contract warranty and guarantee provisions
  - Closely monitor project activities for conformity to contract scope provisions. Establish change notice procedure to evaluate and communicate scope changes
  - See that the plans for controlling and reporting on costs, schedule, and quality are effectively utilized
  - Maintain effective communications with the client and all groups performing project work

A more detailed job description of a construction project manager (for a utility company) appears below:

DUTIES

Under minimum supervision establishes the priorities for and directs the efforts of personnel (including their consultants or contractors) involved or to be involved on project controlled tasks to provide required achievement of an integrated approved set of technical, manpower, cost, and schedule requirements.

1. Directs the development of initial and revised detailed task descriptions and forecasts of their associated technical, manpower, cost, and schedule requirements for tasks assigned to the Division.
2. Directs the regular integration of initial and revised task forecasts into Divisional technical, manpower, cost, and schedule reports and initiates the approval cycle for the reports.
3. Reviews conflicting inter- and extra-divisional task recommendations or actions that may occur from initial task description and forecast development until final task completion and directs uniform methods for their resolution.
4. Evaluates available and planned additions to Division manpower resources, including their tasks applications, against integrated technical and manpower reports and initiates actions to assure that Division manpower resources needs are met by the most economical mix of available qualified consultant and contractor personnel.
5. Evaluates Divisional cost and schedule reports in light of new tasks and changes in existing tasks and initiates actions to assure that increases or decreases in task cost and schedule are acceptable and are appropriately approved.
6. Prioritizes, adjusts, and directs the efforts of Division personnel (including their consultants and contractors) resource allocations as necessary to both assure the scheduled achievement of state and federal regulatory commitments and maintain Divisional adherence to integrated manpower, cost, and schedule reports.
7. Regularly reports the results of Divisional manpower, cost, and schedule evaluations to higher management.
8. Regularly directs the development and issue of individual task and integrated Project programs reports.
9. Recommends new or revised Division strategies, goals, and objectives in light of anticipated long-term manpower and budget needs.
10. Directly supervises project personnel in the regular preparation and issue of individual task descriptions and their associated forecasts, integrated Division manpower, cost, and schedule reports, and both task and Project progress reports.
11. Establishes basic organizational and personnel qualification requirements for Division (including their consultants or contractors) performance on tasks.
12. Establishes the requirements for, directs the development of, and approves control programs to standardize methods used for controlling similar types of activities in the Project and in other Division Departments.
13. Establishes the requirements for, directs the development of, and approves administrative and technical training programs for Divisional personnel.
14. Approves recommendations for the placement of services or material purchase orders by Division personnel and assures that the cost and schedule data associated with such orders is consistent with approved integrated cost and schedule reports.
15. Promotes harmonious relations among Division organizations involved with Project tasks.
16. Exercises other duties related to Divisional project controls as assigned by the project manager.

TABLE 9–3.   PROJECT MANAGEMENT POSITIONS AND RESPONSIBILITIES

Project Management Position	Typical Responsibility	Skill Requirements
• Project Administrator • Project Coordinator • Technical Assistant	Coordinating and integrating of subsystem tasks. Assisting in determining technical and manpower requirements, schedules, and budgets. Measuring and analyzing project performance regarding technical progress, schedules, and budgets.	• Planning • Coordinating • Analyzing • Understanding the organization
• Task Manager • Project Engineer • Assistant Project Manager	Same as above, but stronger role in establishing and maintaining project requirements. Conducting trade-offs. Directing the technical implementation according to established schedules and budgets.	• Technical expertise • Assessing trade-offs • Managing task implementation • Leading task specialists
• Project Manager • Program Manager	Same as above, but stronger role in project planning and controlling. Coordinating and negotiating requirements between sponsor and performing organizations. Bid proposal development and pricing. Establishing project organization and staffing. Overall leadership toward implementing project plan. Project profit. New business development.	• Overall program leadership • Team building • Resolving conflict • Managing multidisciplinary tasks • Planning and allocating resources • Interfacing with customers/sponsors
• Executive Program Manager	Title reserved for very large programs relative to host organization. Responsibilities same as above. Focus is on directing overall program toward desired business results. Customer liaison. Profit performance. New business development. Organizational development.	• Business leadership • Managing overall program businesses • Building program organizations • Developing personnel • Developing new business
• Director of Programs • V.P. Program Development	Responsible for managing multiprogram businesses via various project organizations, each led by a project manager. Focus is on business planning and development, profit performance, technology development, establishing policies and procedures, program management guidelines, personnel development, organizational development.	• Leadership • Strategic planning • Directing and managing program businesses • Building organizations • Selecting and developing key personnel • Identifying and developing new business

QUALIFICATIONS

1. A Bachelor of Science Degree in Engineering or a Business Degree with a minor in Engineering or Science from an accredited four (4) year college or university.
2. a) (For Engineering Graduate) Ten (10) or more years of Engineering and Construction experience including a minimum of five (5) years of supervisory experience and two (2) years of management and electric utility experience.

    b) (For Business Graduate) Ten (10) or more years of management experience including a minimum of five (5) years of supervisory experience in an engineering and construction related management area and two (2) years of experience as the manager or assistant manager of major engineering and construction related projects and two (2) recent years of electric utility experience.
3. Working knowledge of state and federal regulations and requirements that apply to major design and construction projects such as fossil and nuclear power stations.
4. Demonstrated ability to develop high level management control programs.
5. Experience related to computer processing of cost and schedule information.
6. Registered Professional Engineer and membership in appropriate management and technical societies is desirable (but not necessary).
7.[5] At least four (4) years of experience as a staff management member in an operating nuclear power station or in an engineering support on- or off-site capacity.
8.[5] Detailed knowledge of federal licensing requirement for nuclear power stations.
9.[5] Reasonably effective public speaker.

Because of the potential overlapping nature of job descriptions in a project management environment, some companies try to define responsibilities for each project management position, as shown in Table 9–3.

9.8 THE ORGANIZATIONAL STAFFING PROCESS

PMBOK® Guide, 2004
Chapter 9 Human Resources
    Management
9.2 Acquire Project Team

Staffing the project organization can become a long and tedious effort, especially on large and complex engineering projects. Three major questions must be answered:

- What people resources are required?
- Where will the people come from?
- What type of project organizational structure will be best?

To determine the people resources required, the types of individuals (possibly job descriptions) must be decided on, as well as how many individuals from each job category are necessary and when these individuals will be needed.

---

5. Qualifications 7 through 9 apply only for Nuclear Project Directors.

Consider the following situation: As a project manager, you have an activity that requires three separate tasks, all performed within the same line organization. The line manager promises you the best available resources right now for the first task but cannot make any commitments beyond that. The line manager may have only below-average workers available for the second and third tasks. However, the line manager is willing to make a deal with you. He can give you an employee who can do the work but will only give an average performance. If you accept the average employee, the line manager will guarantee that the employee will be available to you for all three tasks. How important is continuity to you? There is no clearly definable answer to this question. Some people will always want the best resources and are willing to fight for them, whereas others prefer continuity and dislike seeing new people coming and going. The author prefers continuity, provided that the assigned employee has the ability to do the up-front planning needed during the first task. The danger in selecting the best employee is that a higher-priority project may come along, and you will lose the employee; or if the employee is an exceptional worker, he may simply be promoted off your project.

Sometimes, a project manager may have to make concessions to get the right people. For example, during the seventh, eighth, and ninth months of your project you need two individuals with special qualifications. The functional manager says that they will be available two months earlier, and that if you don't pick them up then, there will be no guarantee of their availability during the seventh month. Obviously, the line manager is pressuring you, and you may have to give in. There is also the situation in which the line manager says that he'll have to borrow people from another department in order to fulfill his commitments for your project. You may have to live with this situation, but be very careful—these employees will be working at a low level on the learning curve, and overtime will not necessarily resolve the problem. You must expect mistakes here.

Line managers often place new employees on projects so they can be upgraded. Project managers often resent this and immediately go to top management for help. If a line manager says that he can do the work with lower-level people, then the project manager must believe the line manager. After all, the line manager, not the assigned employees, makes the commitment to do the work, and it is the line manager's neck that is stuck out.

Mutual trust between project and line managers is crucial, especially during staffing sessions. Once a project manager has developed a good working relationship with employees, the project manager would like to keep those individuals assigned to his activities. There is nothing wrong with a project manager requesting the same administrative and/or technical staff as before. Line managers realize this and usually agree to it.

There must also be mutual trust between the project managers themselves. Project managers must work as a team, recognize each other's needs, and be willing to make decisions that are in the best interest of the company.

Once the resources are defined, the next question must be whether staffing will be from within the existing organization or from outside sources, such as new hires or consultants. Outside consultants are advisable if, and only if, internal manpower resources are being fully utilized on other programs, or if the company does not possess the required project skills. The answer to this question will indicate which organizational form is best for achievement of the objectives. The form might be a matrix, product, or staff project management structure.

Not all companies permit a variety of project organizational forms to exist within the main company structure. Those that do, however, consider the basic questions of classical management before making a decision. These include:

- How is labor specialized?
- What should the span of management be?
  - How much planning is required?
  - Are authority relationships delegated and understood?
  - Are there established performance standards?
  - What is the rate of change of the job requirements?
- Should we have a horizontal or vertical organization?
  - What are the economics?
  - What are the morale implications?
- Do we need a unity-of-command position?

As in any organization, the subordinates can make the superior look good in the performance of his duties. Unfortunately, the project environment is symbolized by temporary assignments in which the main effort put forth by the project manager is to motivate his (temporary) subordinates toward project dedication and to make them fully understand that:

- Teamwork is vital for success.
- Esprit de corps contributes to success.
- Conflicts can occur between project and functional tiers.
- Communication is essential for success.
- Conflicting orders may be given by the:
  - Project manager
  - Functional manager
  - Upper-level manager
- Unsuccessful performance may result in transfer or dismissal from the project as well as disciplinary action.

Earlier we stated that a project operates as a separate entity but remains attached to the company through company administration policies and procedures. Although project managers can establish their own policies, procedures, and rules, the criteria for promotion must be based on company standards. Project managers should be careful about making commitments they can't keep. After unkept promises on previous projects, a project manager will find it very difficult to get top-quality personnel to volunteer for another project. Even if top management orders key individuals to be assigned to his project, they will always be skeptical about any promises that he may make.

Selecting the project manager is only one-third of the staffing problem. The next step, selecting the project office personnel and team members, can be a time-consuming chore. The project office consists of personnel who are usually assigned as full-time members of the project. The evaluation process should include active project team members, functional team members available for promotion or transfer, and outside applicants.

Upon completion of the evaluation process, the project manager meets with upper-level management. This coordination is required to assure that:

- All assignments fall within current policies on rank, salary, and promotion.
- The individuals selected can work well with both the project manager (formal reporting) and upper-level management (informal reporting).
- The individuals selected have good working relationships with the functional personnel.

Good project office personnel usually have experience with several types of projects and are self-disciplined.

The third and final step in the staffing of the project office is a meeting between the project manager, upper-level management, and the project manager on whose project the requested individuals are currently assigned. Project managers are very reluctant to give up qualified personnel to other projects, but unfortunately, this procedure is a way of life in a project environment. Upper-level management attends these meetings to show all negotiating parties that top management is concerned with maintaining the best possible mix of individuals from available resources and to help resolve staffing conflicts. Staffing from within is a negotiation process in which upper-level management establishes the ground rules and priorities.

The selected individuals are then notified of the anticipated change and asked their opinions. If individuals have strong resentment to being transferred or reassigned, alternate personnel may be selected to avoid potential problems.

Figure 9–3 shows the typical staffing pattern as a function of time. There is a manpower buildup in the early phases and a manpower decline in the later stages. This means

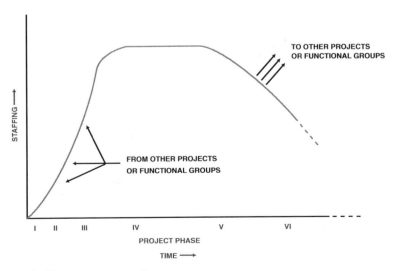

FIGURE 9–3. Staffing pattern versus time.

that the project manager should bring people on board as *needed* and release them as *early* as possible.

There are several psychological approaches that the project manager can use during the recruitment and staffing process. Consider the following:

- Line managers often receive no visibility or credit for a job well done. Be willing to introduce line managers to the customer.
- Be sure to show people how they can benefit by working for you or on your project.
- Any promises made during recruitment should be documented. The functional organization will remember them long after your project terminates.
- As strange as it may seem, the project manager should encourage conflicts to take place during recruiting and staffing. These conflicts should be brought to the surface and resolved. It is better for conflicts to be resolved during the initial planning stages than to have major confrontations later.

It is unfortunate that recruiting and retaining good personnel are more difficult in a project organizational structure than in a purely traditional one. Clayton Reeser identifies nine potential problems that can exist in project organizations[6]:

- Personnel connected with project forms of organization suffer more anxieties about possible loss of employment than members of functional organizations.
- Individuals temporarily assigned to matrix organizations are more frustrated by authority ambiguity than permanent members of functional organizations.
- Personnel connected with project forms of organization that are nearing their phase-out are more frustrated by what they perceive to be "make work" assignments than members of functional organizations.
- Personnel connected with project forms of organization feel more frustrated because of lack of formal procedures and role definitions than members of functional organizations.
- Personnel connected with project forms of organization worry more about being set back in their careers than members of functional organizations.
- Personnel connected with project forms of organization feel less loyal to their organization than members of functional organizations.
- Personnel connected with project forms of organization have more anxieties in feeling that there is no one concerned about their personal development than members of functional organizations.
- Permanent members of project forms of organization are more frustrated by multiple levels of management than members of functional organizations.
- Frustrations caused by conflict are perceived more seriously by personnel connected with project forms of organization than members of functional organizations.

---

6. Clayton Reeser, "Some Potential Human Problems of the Project Form of Organization," *Academy of Management Journal,* Vol. XII, 1969, pp. 462–466.

Employees are more likely to be motivated to working on a project if the employee had been given the right to accept or refuse the assignment. Although employees usually do not refuse assignments, there is still the question of how much permissiveness should be given to the worker. The following would be a listing or possible degrees of permissiveness:

- The line manager (or project manager) explains the project to the worker and the worker has the right to refuse the assignment. The worker does not need to explain the reason for refusing the assignment and the refusal does not limit the worker's opportunity for advancement or assignment to other project teams.
- With this degree of permissiveness, the worker has the right to refuse the assignment but must provide a reason for the refusal. The reason could be due to personal or career preference considerations such as having to travel, relocation, health reasons, possibly too much overtime involved, simply not an assignment that is viewed as enhancing the individual's career, or the employee wants an assignment on some other project.
- With this degree of permissiveness, the worker has no choice but to accept the assignment. Only an emergency would be considered as a valid reason for refusing the assignment. In this case, refusing the assignment might be damaging to the employee's career.

Grinnell and Apple have identified four additional major problems associated with staffing[7]:

- People trained in single line-of-command organizations find it hard to serve more than one boss.
- People may give lip service to teamwork, but not really know how to develop and maintain a good working team.
- Project and functional managers sometimes tend to compete rather than cooperate with each other.
- Individuals must learn to do more "managing" of themselves.

Thus far we have discussed staffing the project. Unfortunately, there are also situations in which employees must be terminated from the project because of:

- Nonacceptance of rules, policies, and procedures
- Nonacceptance of established formal authority
- Professionalism being more important to them than company loyalty
- Focusing on technical aspects at the expense of the budget and schedule
- Incompetence

There are three possible solutions for working with incompetent personnel. First, the project manager can provide an on-the-spot appraisal of the employee. This includes

---

7. S. K. Grinnell and H. P. Apple, "When Two Bosses Are Better Than One," *Machine Design,* January 1975, pp. 84–87.

identification of weaknesses, corrective action to be taken, and threat of punishment if the situation continues. A second solution is reassignment of the employee to less critical activities. This solution is usually not preferred by project managers. The third and most frequent solution is the removal of the employee.

Although project managers can get project office people (who report to the project manager) removed directly, the removal of a line employee is an indirect process and must be accomplished through the line manager. The removal of the line employee should be made to look like a transfer; otherwise the project manager will be branded as an individual who fires people.

Executives must be ready to cope with the staffing problems that can occur in a project environment. C. Ray Gullett has summarized these major problems[8]:

● Staffing levels are more variable in a project environment.
● Performance evaluation is more complex and more subject to error in a matrix form of organization.
● Wage and salary grades are more difficult to maintain under a matrix form of organization. Job descriptions are often of less value.
● Training and development are more complex and at the same time more necessary under a project form of organization.
● Morale problems are potentially greater in a matrix organization.

9.9 THE PROJECT OFFICE

PMBOK® Guide, 2004
1.6.4 Project Management Office

The project team is a combination of the project office and functional employees as shown in Figure 9–4. Although the figure identifies the project office personnel as assistant project managers, some employees may not have any such title. The advantage of such a title is that it entitles the employee to speak directly to the customer. For example, the project engineer might also be called the assistant project manager for engineering. The title is important because when the assistant project manager speaks to the customer, he represents the company, whereas the functional employee represents himself.

The project office is an organization developed to support the project manager in carrying out his duties. Project office personnel must have the same dedication toward the project as the project manager and must have good working relationships with both the project and functional managers. The responsibilities of the project office include:

● Acting as the focal point of information for both in-house control and customer reporting
● Controlling time, cost, and performance to adhere to contractual requirements
● Ensuring that all work required is documented and distributed to all key personnel

---

8. C. Ray Gullett, "Personnel Management in the Project Environment," *Personnel Administration/Public Personnel Review,* November–December 1972, pp. 17–22.

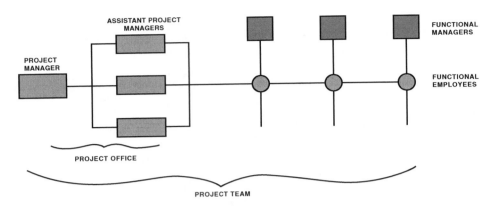

FIGURE 9–4. Project organization.

- Ensuring that all work performed is both authorized and funded by contractual documentation

The major responsibility of the project manager and the project office personnel is the integration of work across the functional lines of the organization. Functional units, such as engineering, R&D, and manufacturing, together with extra-company subcontractors, must work toward the same specifications, designs, and even objectives. The lack of proper integration of these functional units is the most common cause of project failure. The team members must be dedicated to all activities required for project success, not just their own functional responsibilities. The problems resulting from lack of integration can best be solved by full-time membership and participation of project office personnel. Not all team members are part of the project office. Functional representatives, performing at the interface position, also act as integrators but at a closer position to where the work is finally accomplished (i.e., the line organization).

One of the biggest challenges facing project managers is determining the size of the project office. The optimal size is determined by a trade-off between the maximum number of members necessary to assure compliance with requirements and the maximum number for keeping the total administrative costs under control. Membership is determined by factors such as project size, internal support requirements, type of project (i.e., R&D, qualification, production), level of technical competency required, and customer support requirements. Membership size is also influenced by how strategic management views the project to be. There is a tendency to enlarge project offices if the project is considered strategic, especially if follow-on work is possible.

On large projects, and even on some smaller efforts, it is often impossible to achieve project success without permanently assigned personnel. The four major activities of the project office, shown below, indicate the need for using full-time people:

- Integration of activities
- In-house and out-of-house communication

- Scheduling with risk and uncertainty
- Effective control

These four activities require continuous monitoring by trained project personnel. The training of good project office members may take weeks or even months, and can extend beyond the time allocated for a project. Because key personnel are always in demand, project managers should ask themselves and upper-level management one pivotal question when attempting to staff the project office:

Are there any projects downstream that could cause me to lose key members of my team?

If the answer to this question is yes, then it might benefit the project to have the second- or third-choice person selected for the position or even to staff the position on a part-time basis. Another alternative, of course, would be to assign the key members to activities that are not so important and that can be readily performed by replacement personnel. This, however, is impractical because such personnel will not be employed efficiently.

Program managers would like nothing better than to have all of their key personnel assigned full-time for the duration of the program. Unfortunately, this is undesirable, if not impossible, for many projects because[9]:

- Skills required by the project vary considerably as the project matures through each of its life-cycle phases.
- Building up large permanently assigned project offices for each project inevitably causes duplication of certain skills (often those in short supply), carrying of people who are not needed on a full-time basis or for a long period, and personnel difficulties in reassignment.
- The project manager may be diverted from his primary task and become the project engineer, for example, in addition to his duties of supervision, administration, and dealing with the personnel problems of a large office rather than concentrating on managing all aspects of the project itself.
- Professionally trained people often prefer to work within a group devoted to their professional area, with permanent management having qualifications in the same field, rather than becoming isolated from their specialty peers by being assigned to a project staff.
- Projects are subject to sudden shifts in priority or even to cancellation, and full-time members of a project office are thus exposed to potentially serious threats to their job security; this often causes a reluctance on the part of some people to accept a project assignment.

All of these factors favor keeping the full-time project office as small as possible and dependent on established functional departments and specialized staffs. The approach places great emphasis on the planning and control procedures used on the project. On the

9. Russell D. Archibald, *Managing High-Technology Programs and Projects* (New York: Wiley, 1976), p. 82. Copyright © 1976 by John Wiley & Sons, Inc. Reprinted by permission of the publisher.

other hand, there are valid reasons for assigning particular people of various specialties to the project office. These specialties usually include:

- Systems analysis and engineering (or equivalent technical discipline) and product quality and configuration control, if the product requires such an effort
- Project planning, scheduling, control, and administrative support

Many times a project office is staffed by promotion of functional specialists. This situation is quite common to engineering firms with a high percentage of technical employees, but is not without problems.

> In professional firms, personnel are generally promoted to management on the basis of their professional or technical competence rather than their managerial ability. While this practice may be unavoidable, it does tend to promote men with insufficient knowledge of management techniques and creates a frustrating environment for the professional down the line.[10]

There is an unfortunate tendency for executives to create an environment where line employees feel that the "grass is greener" in project management and project engineering than in the line organization. How should an executive handle a situation where line specialists continually apply for transfer to project management? One solution is the development of a dual ladder system, as shown in Figure 9–5, with a pay scale called "consultant." This particular company created the consultant position because:

- There were several technical specialists who were worth more money to the company but who refused to accept a management position to get it.
- Technical specialists could not be paid more money than line managers.

Promoting technical specialists to a management slot simply to give them more money can:

- Create a poor line manager
- Turn a specialist into a generalist
- Leave a large technical gap in the line organization

Line managers often argue that they cannot perform their managerial duties and control these "prima donnas" who earn more money and have a higher pay grade than the line managers. That is faulty reasoning. Every time the consultants do something well, it reflects on the entire line organization, not merely on themselves.

The concept of having functional employees with a higher pay grade than the line manager can also be applied to the horizontal project. It is possible for a junior project manager suddenly to find that the line managers have a higher pay grade than the project manager. It is also possible for assistant project managers (as project engineers) to have a

---

10. William P. Killian, "Project Management—Future Organizational Concept," *Marquette Business Review,* 1971, pp. 90–107.

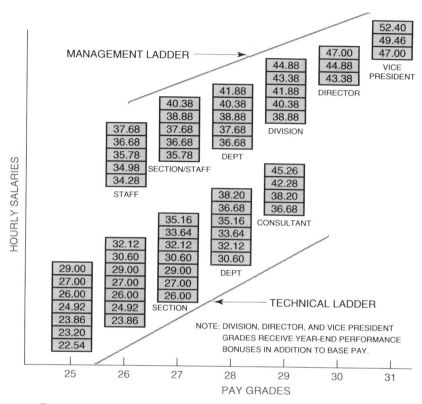

FIGURE 9–5. Exempt, upper-level pay structure.

higher pay grade than the project manager. Project management is designed to put together the best mix of people to achieve the objective. If this best mix requires that a grade 7 report to a grade 9 (on a "temporary" project), then so be it. Executives should not let salaries, and pay grades, stand in the way of constructing a good project organization.

Another major concern is the relationship that exists between project office personnel and functional managers. In many organizations, membership in the project office is considered to be more important than in the functional department. Functional members have a tendency to resent an individual who has just been promoted out of a functional department and into project management. Killian has described ways of resolving potential conflicts[11]:

> It must be kept in mind that veteran functional managers cannot be expected to accept direction readily from some lesser executive who is suddenly labelled a Project Manager. Management can avoid this problem by:

11. William P. Killian, "Project Management—Future Organizational Concept," *Marquette Business Review,* 1971, pp. 90–107.

- Selecting a man who already has a high position of responsibility or placing him high enough in the organization.
- Assigning him a title as important-sounding as those of functional managers.
- Supporting him in his dealings with functional managers.

If the Project Manager is expected to exercise project control over the functional departments, then he must report to the same level as the departments, or higher.

Executives can severely hinder project managers by limiting their authority to select and organize (when necessary) a project office and team. According to Cleland[12]:

> His [project manager's] staff should be qualified to provide personal administrative and technical support. He should have sufficient authority to increase or decrease his staff as necessary throughout the life of the project. The authorization should include selective augmentation for varying periods of time from the supporting functional areas.

Many executives have a misconception concerning the makeup and usefulness of the project office. People who work in the project office should be individuals whose first concern is project management, not the enhancement of their technical expertise. It is almost impossible for individuals to perform for any extended period of time in the project office without becoming cross-trained in a second or third project office function. For example, the project manager for cost could acquire enough expertise eventually to act as the assistant to the assistant project manager for procurement. This technique of project office cross-training is an excellent mechanism for creating good project managers.

We have mentioned two important facts concerning the project management staffing process:

- The individual who aspires to become a project manager must be willing to give up technical expertise and become a generalist.
- Individuals can be qualified to be promoted vertically but not horizontally.

Once an employee has demonstrated the necessary attributes to be a good project manager, there are three ways the individual can become a project manager or part of the project office. The executive can:

- Promote the individual in salary and grade and transfer him into project management.
- Laterally transfer the individual into project management without any salary or grade increase. If, after three to six months, the employee demonstrates that he can perform, he will receive an appropriate salary and grade increase.
- Give the employee a small salary increase without any grade increase or a grade increase without any salary increase, with the stipulation that additional awards will be forthcoming after the observation period, assuming that the employee can handle the position.

---

12. David I. Cleland, "Why Project Management?" Reprinted with permission from *Business Horizons,* Winter 1964, p. 85. Copyright © 1964 by the Board of Trustees at Indiana University.

Many executives believe in the philosophy that once an individual enters the world of project management, there are only two places to go: up in the organization or out the door. If an individual is given a promotion and pay increase and is placed in project management and fails, his salary may not be compatible with that of his previous line organization, and now there is no place for him to go. Most executives, and employees, prefer the second method because it actually provides some protection for the employee.

Many companies don't realize until it is too late that promotions to project management may be based on a different set of criteria from promotions to line management. Promotions on the horizontal line are strongly based on communicative skills, whereas line management promotions are based on technical skills.

9.10 THE FUNCTIONAL TEAM

PMBOK® Guide, 2004
Chapter 9 Human Resources
Management

The project team consists of the project manager, the project office (whose members may or may not report directly to the project manager), and the functional or interface members (who must report horizontally as well as vertically for information flow). Functional team members are often shown on organizational charts as project office team members. This is normally done to satisfy customer requirements.

Upper-level management can have an input into the selection process for functional team members but should not take an active role unless the project and functional managers cannot agree. Functional management must be represented at all staffing meetings because functional staffing is directly dependent on project requirements and because:

- Functional managers generally have more expertise and can identify high-risk areas.
- Functional managers must develop a positive attitude toward project success. This is best achieved by inviting their participation in the early activities of the planning phase.

Functional team members are not always full-time. They can be full-time or part-time for either the duration of the project or only specific phases.

The selection process for both the functional team member and the project office must include evaluation of any special requirements. The most common special requirements develop from:

- Changes in technical specifications
- Special customer requests
- Organizational restructuring because of deviations from existing policies
- Compatibility with the customer's project office

A typical project office may include between ten and thirty members, whereas the total project team may be in excess of a hundred people, causing information to be shared slowly. For large projects, it is desirable to have a full-time functional representative from each major division or department assigned permanently to the project, and perhaps even to the project office. Such representation might include:

- Program management
- Project engineering
- Engineering operations
- Manufacturing operations
- Procurement
- Quality control
- Cost accounting
- Publications
- Marketing
- Sales

Both the project manager and team members must understand fully the responsibilities and functions of each other team member so that total integration can be achieved rapidly and effectively. On high-technology programs the chief project engineer assumes the role of deputy project manager. Project managers must understand the problems that the line managers have when selecting and assigning the project staff. Line managers try to staff with people who understand the need for teamwork.

When employees are attached to a project, the project manager must identify the "star" employees. These are the employees who are vital for the success of the project and who can either make or break the project manager. Most of the time, star employees are found in the line organization, not the project office.

As a final point, project managers can assign line employees added responsibilities within the scope of the project. If the added responsibilities can result in upgrading, then the project manager should consult with the line manager before such situations are initiated. Quite often, line managers (or even personnel representatives) send "check" people into the projects to verify that employees are performing at their proper pay grade. This is very important when working with blue-collar workers who, by union contractual agreements, must be paid at the grade level at which they are performing.

Also, project managers must be willing to surrender resources when they are no longer required. If the project manager constantly cries wolf in a situation where a problem really does not exist, the line manager will simply pull away the resources (this is the line manager's right), and a deteriorating working relationship will result.

9.11 THE PROJECT ORGANIZATIONAL CHART

One of the first requirements of the project startup phase is to develop the organizational chart for the project and determine its relationship to the parent organizational structure. Figure 9–6 shows, in abbreviated form, the six major programs at Dalton Corporation. Our concern is with the Midas Program. Although the Midas Program may have the lowest pri-

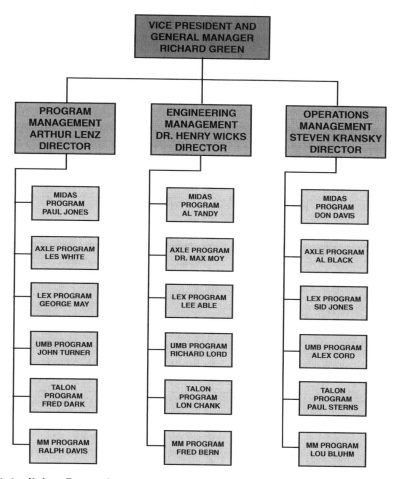

FIGURE 9–6. Dalton Corporation.

ority of the six programs, it is placed at the top, and in boldface, to give the impression that it is the top priority. This type of representation usually makes the client or customer feel that his program is important to the contractor.

The employees shown in Figure 9–6 may be part-time or full-time, depending upon the project's requirements. Perturbations on Figure 9–6 might include one employee's name identified on two or more vertical positions (i.e., the project engineer on two projects) or the same name in two horizontal boxes (i.e., for a small project, the same person could be the project manager and project engineer). Remember, this type of chart is for the customer's benefit and may not show the true "dotted/solid" reporting relationships in the company.

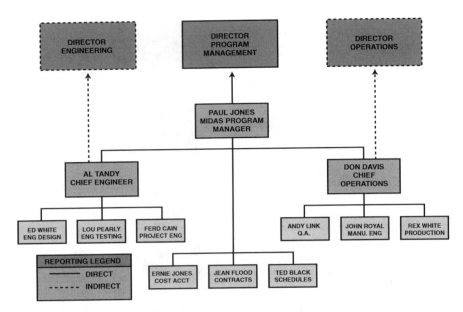

FIGURE 9–7. Midas Program office.

The next step is to show the program office structure, as illustrated in Figure 9–7. Note that the chief of operations and the chief engineer have dual reporting responsibility; they report directly to the program manager and indirectly to the directors. Again, this may be just for the customer's benefit with the real reporting structure being reversed. Beneath the chief engineer, there are three positions. Although these positions appear as solid lines, they might actually be dotted lines. For example, Ed White might be working only part-time on the Midas Program but is still shown on the chart as a permanent program office member. Jean Flood, under contracts, might be spending only ten hours per week on the Midas Program.

If the function of two positions on the organizational chart takes place at different times, then both positions may be shown as manned by the same person. For example, Ed White may have his name under both engineering design and engineering testing if the two activities are far enough apart that he can perform them independently.

The people shown in the project office organizational chart, whether full-time or part-time, may not be physically sitting in the project office. For full-time, long-term assignments, as in construction projects, the employees may be physically sitting side by side, whereas for part-time assignments, it may be imperative for them to sit in their functional group. Remember, these types of charts may simply be eyewash for the customer.

Most customers realize that the top-quality personnel may be shared with other programs and projects. Project manning charts, such as the one shown in Figure 9–8, can be used for this purpose. These manning charts are also helpful in preparing the management volume of proposals to show the customer that key personnel will be readily available on his project.

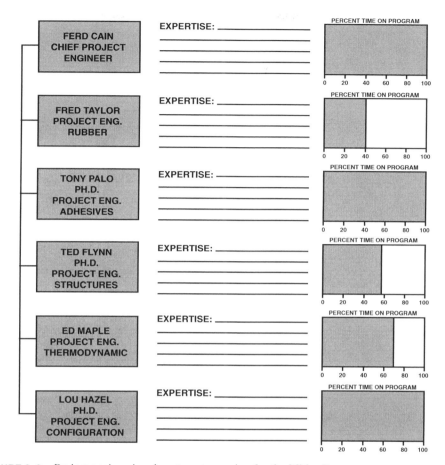

FIGURE 9–8. Project engineering department manning for the Midas Program.

9.12 SPECIAL PROBLEMS

There are always special problems that influence the organizational staffing process. For example, the department shown in Figure 9–9 has a departmental matrix. All activities stay within the department. Project X and project Y are managed by line employees who have been temporarily assigned to the projects, whereas project Z is headed by supervisor B. The department's activities involve high-technology engineering as well as R&D.

The biggest problem facing the department managers is that of training their new employees. The training process requires nine to twelve months. The employees become familiar with the functioning of all three sections, and only after training is an employee assigned to one of the sections. Line managers claim that they do not have sufficient time to supervise training. As a result, the department manager in the example found staff person

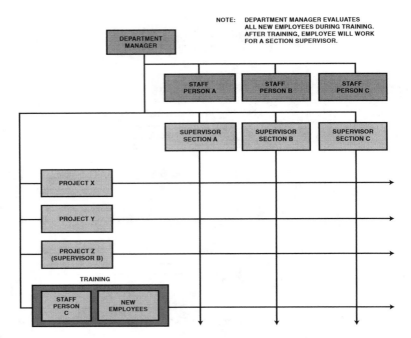

FIGURE 9–9. The training problem.

C to be the most competent person to supervise training. A special department training project was set up, as shown in Figure 9–9.

Figure 9–10 shows a utility company that has three full-time project managers controlling three projects, all of which cut across the central division. Unfortunately, the three full-time project managers cannot get sufficient resources from the central division because the line managers are also acting as divisional project managers and saving the best resources for their own projects.

The obvious solution to the problem is that the central division line managers not be permitted to wear two hats. Instead, one full-time project manager can be added to the left division to manage all three central division projects. It is usually best for all project managers to report to the same division for priority setting and conflict resolution.

Line managers have a tendency to feel demoted when they are suddenly told that they can no longer wear two hats. For example, Mr. Adams was a department manager with thirty years of experience in a company. For the last several years, he had worn two hats and acted as both project manager and functional manager on a variety of projects. He was regarded as an expert in his field. The company decided to incorporate formal project management and established a project management department. Mr. Bell, a thirty-year-old employee with three years of experience with the company, was assigned as the project manager. In order to staff his project, Bell asked Adams for Mr. Cane (Bell's friend) to be assigned to the project as the functional representative. Cane had been with the company for two years. Adams agreed to the request and informed Cane of his new assignment, closing with the remarks, "This project is yours all the way. I don't want to have anything

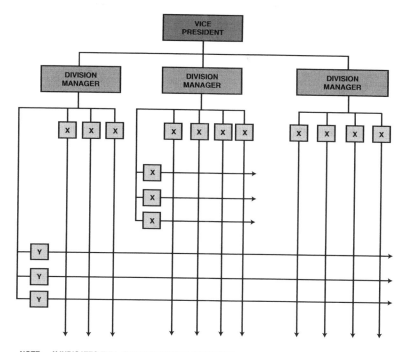

NOTE: X INDICATES FULL–TIME FUNCTIONAL MANAGERS
        Y INDICATES FULL–TIME PROJECT MANAGERS

FIGURE 9–10. Utility service organization.

to do with it. I'll be busy with paperwork as a result of the new organizational structure. Just send me a memo once in a while telling me what's happening."

During the project kickoff meeting, it became obvious to everyone that the only person with the necessary expertise was Adams. Without his support, the duration of the project could be expected to double.

The real problem here was that Adams wanted to feel important and needed, and was hoping that the project manager would come to him asking for his assistance. The project manager correctly analyzed the situation but refused to ask for the line manager's help. Instead, the project manager asked an executive to step in and force the line manager to help. The line manager gave his help, but with great reluctance. Today, the line manager provides poor support to the projects that come across his line organization.

9.13 SELECTING THE PROJECT MANAGEMENT IMPLEMENTATION TEAM

PMBOK® Guide, 2004
Chapter 9 Human Resources
  Management
9.2 Acquire Project Team

The implementation of project management within an organization requires strong executive support and an implementation team that is dedicated to making project management work. Selecting the wrong team players can either lengthen the implementation process or reduce

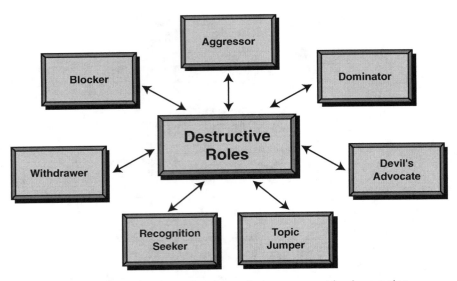

FIGURE 9–11. Roles people play that undermine project management implementation.

employee morale. Some employees may play destructive roles on a project team. These roles, which undermine project management implementation, are shown in Figure 9–11 and described below:

- The aggressor
  - Criticizes everybody and everything on project management
  - Deflates the status and ego of other team members
  - Always acts aggressively
- The dominator
  - Always tries to take over
  - Professes to know everything about project management
  - Tries to manipulate people
  - Will challenge those in charge for leadership role
- The devil's advocate
  - Finds fault in all areas of project management
  - Refuses to support project management unless threatened
  - Acts more of a devil than an advocate
- The topic jumper
  - Must be the first one with a new idea/approach to project management
  - Constantly changes topics
  - Cannot focus on ideas for a long time unless it is his/her idea
  - Tries to keep project management implementation as an action item forever
- The recognition seeker
  - Always argues in favor of his/her own ideas
  - Always demonstrates status consciousness

- Volunteers to become the project manager if status is recognized
- Likes to hear himself/herself talk
- Likes to boast rather than provide meaningful information
- The withdrawer
  - Is afraid to be criticized
  - Will not participate openly unless threatened
  - May withhold information
  - May be shy
- The blocker
  - Likes to criticize
  - Rejects the views of others
  - Cites unrelated examples and personal experiences
  - Has multiple reasons why project management will not work

These types of people should not be assigned to project management implementation teams. The types of people who should be assigned to implementation teams are shown in Figure 9-12 and described below. Their roles are indicated by their words:

- The initiators
  - "Is there a chance that this might work?"
  - "Let's try this."
- The information seekers
  - "Have we tried anything like this before?"
  - "Do we know other companies where this has worked?"
  - "Can we get this information?"

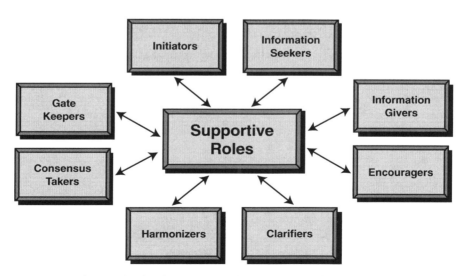

FIGURE 9–12.   Roles people play that support project management implementation.

- The information givers
  - "Other companies found that . . ."
  - "The literature says that . . ."
  - "Benchmarking studies indicate that . . ."
- The encouragers
  - "Your idea has a lot of merit."
  - "The idea is workable, but we may have to make small changes."
  - "What you said will really help us."
- The clarifiers
  - "Are we saying that . . . ?"
  - "Let me state in my own words what I'm hearing from the team."
  - "Let's see if we can put this into perspective."
- The harmonizers
  - "We sort of agree, don't we?"
  - "Your ideas and mine are close together."
  - "Aren't we saying the same thing?"
- The consensus takers
  - "Let's see if the team is in agreement."
  - "Let's take a vote on this."
  - "Let's see how the rest of the group feels about this."
- The gate keepers
  - "Who has not given us their opinions on this yet?"
  - "Should we keep our options open?"
  - "Are we prepared to make a decision or recommendation, or is there additional information to be reviewed?"

9.14 STUDYING TIPS FOR THE PMI® PROJECT MANAGEMENT CERTIFICATION EXAM

This section is applicable as a review of the principles to support the knowledge areas and domain groups in the PMBOK® Guide. This chapter addresses:

- Human Resources Management
- Planning
- Project Staffing

Understanding the following principles is beneficial if the reader is using this text to study for the PMP® Certification Exam:

- What is meant by a project team
- Staffing process and environment
- Role of the line manager in staffing
- Role of the executive in staffing

- Skills needed to be a project manager
- That the project manager is responsible for helping the team members grow and learn while working on the project

The following multiple-choice questions will be helpful in reviewing the principles of this chapter:

1. During project staffing, the *primary* role of senior management is in the selection of the:
   A. Project manager
   B. Assistant project managers
   C. Functional team
   D. Executives do not get involved in staffing.

2. During project staffing, the *primary* role of line management is:
   A. Approving the selection of the project manager
   B. Approving the selection of assistant project managers
   C. Assigning functional resources based upon who is available
   D. Assigning functional resources based upon availability and the skill set needed

3. A project manager is far more likely to succeed if it is obvious to everyone that:
   A. The project manager has a command of technology.
   B. The project manager is a higher pay grade than everyone else on the team.
   C. The project manager is over 45 years of age.
   D. Executive management has officially appointed the project manager.

4. Most people believe that the best way to train someone in project management is through:
   A. On-the-job training
   B. University seminars
   C. Graduate degrees in project management
   D. Professional seminars and meeting

5. In staffing negotiations with the line manager, you identify a work package that requires a skill set of a grade 7 worker. The line manager informs you that he will assign a grade 6 and a grade 8 worker. You should:
   A. Refuse to accept the grade 6 because you are not responsible for training
   B. Ask for two different people
   C. Ask the sponsor to interfere
   D. Be happy! You have two workers.

6. You priced out a project at 1000 hours assuming a grade 7 employee would be assigned. The line manager assigns a grade 9 employee. This will result in a significant cost overrun. The project manager should:
   A. Reschedule the start date of the project based upon the availability of a grade 7
   B. Ask the sponsor for a higher priority for your project
   C. Reduce the scope of the project
   D. See if the grade 9 can do the job in less time

7. As a project begins to wind down, the project manager should:
   A. Release all nonessential personnel so that they can be assigned to other projects
   B. Wait until the project is officially completed before releasing anyone
   C. Wait until the line manager officially requests that the people be released
   D. Talk to other project managers to see who wants your people

ANSWERS

1. A
2. D
3. D
4. A
5. D
6. D
7. A

PROBLEMS

9–1 From S. K. Grinnell and H. P. Apple ("When Two Bosses Are Better Than One," *Machine Design,* January 1975, pp. 84–87):

- People trained in single-line-of-command organizations find it hard to serve more than one boss.
- People may give lip service to teamwork, but not really know how to develop and maintain a good working team.
- Project and functional managers sometimes tend to compete rather than cooperate with each other.
- Individuals must learn to do more "managing" of themselves.

The authors identify the above four major problems associated with staffing. Discuss each problem and identify the type of individual most likely to be involved (i.e., engineer, contract administrator, cost accountant, etc.) and in which organizational form this problem would be most apt to occur.

9–2 David Cleland ("Why Project Management?" Reprinted from *Business Horizons,* Winter 1964, p. 85. Copyright © 1964 by the Foundation for the School of Business at Indiana University. Used with permission) made the following remarks:

His [project manager's] staff should be qualified to provide personal administrative and technical support. He should have sufficient authority to increase or decrease his staff as necessary throughout the life of the project. This authorization should include selective augmentation for varying periods of time from the supporting functional areas.

Do you agree or disagree with these statements? Should the type of project or type of organization play a dominant role in your answer?

9–3 The contractor's project office is often structured to be compatible with the customer's project office, sometimes on a one-to-one basis. Some customers view the contractor's project organization merely as an extension of their own company. Below are three statements concerning this relationship. Are these statements true or false? Defend your answers.

- There must exist mutual trust between the customer and contractor together with a close day-to-day working relationship.

- The project manager and the customer must agree on the hierarchy of decision that each must make, either independently or jointly. (Which decisions can each make independently or jointly?)
- Both the customer and contractor's project personnel must be willing to make decisions as fast as possible.

9–4 C. Ray Gullet ("Personnel Management in the Project Organization," *Personnel Administration/Public Personnel Review,* November–December 1972, pp. 17–22) has identified five personnel problems. How would you, as a project manager, cope with each problem?

- Staffing levels are more variable in a project environment.
- Performance evaluation is more complex and more subject to error in a matrix form of organization.
- Wage and salary grades are more difficult to maintain under a matrix form of organization. Job descriptions are often of less value.
- Training and development are more complex and at the same time more necessary under a project form of organization.
- Morale problems are potentially greater in a matrix organization.

9–5 Some people believe that a project manager functions, in some respects, like a physician. Is there any validity in this?

9–6 Paul is a project manager for an effort that requires twelve months. During the seventh, eighth, and ninth months he needs two individuals with special qualifications. The functional manager has promised that these individuals will be available two months before they are needed. If Paul does not assign them to his project at that time, they will be assigned elsewhere and he will have to do with whomever will be available later. What should Paul do? Do you have to make any assumptions in order to defend your answer?

9–7 Some of the strongest reasons for promoting functional engineers to project engineers are:

- Better relationships with fellow researchers
- Better prevention of duplication of effort
- Better fostering of teamwork

These reasons are usually applied to R&D situations. Could they also be applied to product life-cycle phases other than R&D?

9–8 The following have been given as qualifications for a successful advanced-technology project manager:

- Career has progressed up through the technical ranks
- Knowledgeable in many engineering fields
- Understands general management philosophy and the meaning of profitability
- Interested in training and teaching his superiors
- Understands how to work with perfectionists

Can these same qualifications be modified for non-R&D project management? If so, how?

9–9 W. J. Taylor and T. F. Watling (*Successful Project Management,* London: Business Books, 1972, p. 32) state:

It is often the case, therefore, that the Project Manager is more noted for his management technique expertise, his ability to "get things done" and his ability to "get on with people" than for his sheer technical prowess. However, it can be dangerous to minimize this latter talent when choosing Project Managers dependent upon project type and size. The Project Manager should preferably be an expert either in the field of the project task or a subject allied to it.

How dangerous can it be if this latter talent is minimized? Will it be dangerous under all circumstances?

9–10 Frank Boone is the most knowledgeable piping engineer in the company. For five years, the company has turned down his application for transfer to project engineering and project management stating that he is too valuable to the company in his current position. If you were a project manager, would you want this individual as part of your functional team? How should an organization cope with this situation?

9–11 Tom Weeks is manager of the insulation group. During a recent group meeting, Tom commented, "The company is in trouble. As you know, we're bidding on three programs right now. If we win just one of them, we can probably maintain our current work level. If, by some slim chance, we were to win all three, you'll all be managers tomorrow." The company won all three programs, but the insulation group did not hire anyone, and there were no promotions. What would you, as a project manager on one of the new projects, expect your working relations to be with the insulation group?

9–12 You are a project engineer on a high-technology program. As the project begins to wind down, your boss asks you to write a paper so that he can present it at a technical meeting. His name goes first on the paper. Should this be part of your job? How do you feel about this situation?

9–13 Research has indicated that the matrix structure is often confusing because it requires multiple roles for people, with resulting confusion about these roles (Keith Davis, *Human Relations at Work,* New York: McGraw-Hill, 1967, pp. 296–297). Unfortunately, not all program managers, project managers, and project engineers possess the necessary skills to operate in this environment. Stuckenbruck has stated, "The path to success is strewn with the bodies of project managers who were originally functional line managers and then went into project management" (Linn Stuckenbruck, "The Effective Project Manager," *Project Management Quarterly,* Vol. VII, No. 1, March 1976, pp. 26–27). What do you feel is the major cause for this downfall of the functional manager?

9–14 For each of the organizational forms shown below, who determines what resources are needed, when they are needed, and how they will be employed? Who has the authority and responsibility to mobilize these resources?

    a. Traditional organization
    b. Matrix organization
    c. Product line organization
    d. Line/staff project organization

9–15 Do you agree or disagree that project organizational forms encourage peer-to-peer communications and dynamic problem-solving?

9–16 The XYZ Company operates on a traditional structure. The company has just received a contract to develop a new product line for a special group of customers. The company has decided to pull out selected personnel from the functional departments and set up a single product organizational structure to operate in parallel with the functional departments.

    a. Set up the organizational chart.

    b. Do you think this setup can work? Does your answer depend on how many years this situation must exist?

9–17 You are the project engineer on a program similar to one that you directed previously. Should you attempt to obtain the same administrative and/or technical staff that you had before?

9–18 A person assigned to your project is performing unsatisfactorily. What should you do? Will it make a difference if he is in the project office or a functional employee?

9–19 You have been assigned to the project office as an assistant project engineer. You are to report to the chief project engineer who reports formally to the project manager and informally to the vice president of engineering. You have never worked with this chief project engineer before. During the execution of the project, it becomes obvious to you that the chief project engineer is making decisions that do not appear to be in the best interest of the project. What should you do about this?

9–20 Should individuals be promoted to project management because they are at the top of their functional pay grade?

9–21 Should one functional department be permitted to "borrow" (on a temporary basis) people from another functional department in order to fulfill project manning requirements? Should this be permitted if overtime is involved?

9–22 Should a project manager be paid for performance or for the number of people he supervises?

9–23 Should a project manager try to upgrade his personnel?

9–24 Why should a functional manager assign his best people to you on a long-term project?

9–25 A coal company has adopted the philosophy that the project manager for new mine startup projects will be the individual who will eventually become the mine superintendent. The coal company believes that this type of "ownership" philosophy is good. Do you agree?

9–26 Can a project manager be considered as a "hired gun"?

9–27 Manufacturing organizations are using project management/project engineering strictly to give new employees exposure to total company operations. After working on one or two projects, each approximately one to two years in duration, the employee is transferred to line management for his career path and opportunities for advancement. Can a situation such as this, where there is no career path in either project management or project engineering, work successfully? Could there be any detrimental effects on the projects?

9–28 Can a project manager create dedication and a true winning spirit and still be hated by all?

9–29 Can anyone be trained to be a project manager?

9–30 A power and light company has part-time project management in which an individual acts as both a project manager and a functional employee at the same time. The utility company claims that this process prevents an employee from becoming "technically obsolete," and that when the employee returns to full-time functional duties, he is a more well-rounded individual. Do you agree or disagree? What are the arrangement's advantages and disadvantages?

9–31 Some industries consider the major criterion for promotion and advancement to be gray hair and/or baldness. Is this type of maturity advantageous?

9–32 In Figure 9–9 we showed that Al Tandy and Don Davis (as well as other project office personnel) reported directly to the project manager and indirectly to functional management. Could this situation be reversed, with the project office personnel reporting indirectly to the project manager and directly to functional management?

9–33 Most organizations have "star" people who are usually identified as those individuals who are the key to success. How does a project manager identify these people? Can they be in the project office, or must they be functional employees or managers?

9–34 Considering your own industry, what job-related or employee-related factors would you wish to know before selecting someone to be a project manager or a project engineer on an effort valued at:

    a. $30,000?
    b. $300,000?
    c. $3,000,000?
    d. $30,000,000?

9–35 One of the major controversies in project management occurs over whether the project manager needs a command of technology in order to be effective. Consider the following situation:

You are the project manager on a research and development project. Marketing informs you that they have found a customer for your product and that you must make major modifications to satisfy the customer's requirements. The engineering functional managers tell you that these modifications are impossible. Can a project manager without a command of technology make a viable decision as to whether to risk additional funds and support marketing, or should he believe the functional managers, and tell marketing that the modifications are impossible? How can a project manager, either with or without a command of technology, tell whether the functional managers are giving him an optimistic or a pessimistic opinion?

9–36 As a functional employee, you demonstrate that you have exceptionally good writing skills. You are then promoted to the position of special staff assistant to the division manager and told that you are to assume full responsibility for all proposal work that must flow through your division. How do you feel about this? Is it a promotion? Where can you go from here?

9–37 Government policymakers content that only high-ranking individuals (high GS grades) can be project managers because a good project manager needs sufficient "clout" to make the project go. In government, the project manager is generally the highest grade on the project team. How can problems of pay grade be overcome? Is the government's policy effective?

9–38 A major utility company is worried about the project manager's upgrading functional employees. On an eight-month project that employs four hundred full-time project employees, the department managers have set up "check" people whose responsibility is to see that functional employees do not have unauthorized (i.e., not approved by the functional manager) work assignments above their current grade level. Can this system work? What if the work is at a position below their grade level?

9–39 A major utility company begins each computer project with a feasibility study in which a cost-benefit analysis is performed. The project managers, all of whom report to a project management division, perform the feasibility study themselves without any functional support. The functional personnel argue that the feasibility study is inaccurate because the functional "experts" are not involved. The project managers, on the other hand, stipulate that they never have sufficient time or money to involve the functional personnel. Can this situation be resolved?

9–40 How would you go about training individuals within your company or industry to be good project managers? What assumptions are you making?

9–41 Should project teams be allowed to evolve by themselves?

9–42 At what point or phase in the life cycle of a project should a project manager be appointed?

9–43 Top management generally has two schools of thought concerning project management. One school states that the project manager should be used as a means for coordinating activities that cut across several functional departments. The second school states that the project management position should be used as a means of creating future general managers. Which school of thought is correct?

9–44 Some executives feel that personnel working in a project office should be cross-trained in several assistant project management functions. What do you think about this?

9–45 A company has a policy that employees wishing to be project managers must first spend one to one-and-a-half years in the functional employee side of the house so that they can get to know the employees and company policy. What do you think about this?

9–46 Your project has grown to a point where there now exist openings for three full-time assistant project managers. Unfortunately, there are no experienced assistant project managers available. You are told by upper-level management that you will fill these three positions by promotions from within. Where in the organization should you look? During an interview, what questions should you ask potential candidates? Is it possible that you could find candidates who are qualified to be promoted vertically but not horizontally?

9–47 A functional employee has demonstrated the necessary attributes of a potentially successful project manager. Top management can:

- Promote the individual in salary and grade and transfer him into project management.
- Laterally transfer the employee into project management without any salary or grade increase. If, after three to six months, the employee demonstrates that he can perform, he will receive an appropriate salary and grade increase.
- Give the employee either a grade increase without any salary increase, or a small salary increase without any grade increase, under the stipulation that additional awards will be given at the end of the observation period, assuming that the employee can handle the position.

If you were in top management, which method would you prefer? If you dislike the above three choices, develop your own alternative. What are the advantages and disadvantages of each choice? For each choice, discuss the ramifications if the employee cannot handle the project management position.

Management Functions

Related Case Studies (from Kerzner/*Project Management Case Studies,* 2nd Edition)	Related Workbook Exercises (from Kerzner/*Project Management Workbook and PMP®/CAPM® Exam Study Guide,* 9th Edition)	PMBOK® Guide, 3rd Edition, Reference Section for the PMP® Certification Exam
• Wynn Computer Equipment (WCE) • The Trophy Project*	• The Communication Problem • Meetings, Meetings, and Meetings • The Empowerment Problem • Project Management Psychology • Multiple Choice Exam • Crossword Puzzle on Human Resource Management • Crossword Puzzle on Communications Management	• Human Resource Management • Communications Management

10.0 INTRODUCTION

PMBOK® Guide, 2004
1.5.4 General Management Skills
1.5.5 Interpersonal Skills
2.3.4 Role of the PMO

As we have stated, the project manager measures his success by how well he can negotiate with both upper-level and functional management for the resources necessary to achieve the project objective. Moreover, the project manager may have a great deal of delegated authority but very little

*Case Study also appears at end of chapter.

power. Hence, the managerial skills he requires for successful performance may be drastically different from those of his functional management counterparts.

The difficult aspect of the project management environment is that individuals at the project–functional interface must report to two bosses. Functional managers and project managers, by virtue of their different authority levels and responsibilities, treat their people in different fashions depending on their "management school" philosophies. There are generally five management schools, as described below:

- *The classical/traditional school:* Management is the process of getting things done (i.e., achieving objectives) by working both with and through people operating in organized groups. Emphasis is placed on the end-item or objective, with little regard for the people involved.
- *The empirical school:* Managerial capabilities can be developed by studying the experiences of other managers, whether or not the situations are similar.
- *The behavioral school:* Two classrooms are considered within this school. First, we have the human relations classroom in which we emphasize the interpersonal relationship between individuals and their work. The second classroom includes the social system of the individual. Management is considered to be a system of cultural relationships involving social change.
- *The decision theory school:* Management is a rational approach to decision making using a system of mathematical models and processes, such as operations research and management science.
- *The management systems school:* Management is the development of a systems model, characterized by input, processing, and output, and directly identifies the flow of resources (money, equipment, facilities, personnel, information, and material) necessary to obtain some objective by either maximizing or minimizing some objective function. The management systems school also includes contingency theory, which stresses that each situation is unique and must be optimized separately within the constraints of the system.

In a project environment, functional managers are generally practitioners of the first three schools of management, whereas project managers utilize the last two. This imposes hardships on both the project managers and functional representatives. The project manager must motivate functional representatives toward project dedication on the horizontal line using management systems theory and quantitative tools, often with little regard for the employee. After all, the employee might be assigned for a very short-term effort, whereas the end-item is the most important objective. The functional manager, however, expresses more concern for the individual needs of the employee using the traditional or behavioral schools of management.

Modern practitioners still tend to identify management responsibilities and skills in terms of the principles and functions developed in the early management schools, namely:

- Planning
- Organizing
- Staffing
- Controlling
- Directing

Although these management functions have generally been applied to traditional management structures, they have recently been redefined for temporary management positions. Their fundamental meanings remain the same, but the applications are different.

10.1 CONTROLLING

Controlling is a three-step process of measuring progress toward an objective, evaluating what remains to be done, and taking the necessary corrective action to achieve or exceed the objectives. These three steps—measuring, evaluating, and correcting—are defined as follows:

- *Measuring:* determining through formal and informal reports the degree to which progress toward objectives is being made.
- *Evaluating:* determining cause of and possible ways to act on significant deviations from planned performance.
- *Correcting:* taking control action to correct an unfavorable trend or to take advantage of an unusually favorable trend.

The project manager is responsible for ensuring the accomplishment of group and organizational goals and objectives. To effect this, he must have a thorough knowledge of standards and cost control policies and procedures so that a comparison is possible between operating results and preestablished standards. The project manager must then take the necessary corrective actions. Later chapters provide a more in-depth analysis of control, especially the cost control function.

Project managers must understand organizational behavior in order to be effective and must have strong interpersonal skills. This is especially important during the controlling function. Line managers may have the luxury of time to build up relationships with each of their workers. But for a project manager time is a constraint, and it is not always easy to predict how well or how poorly an individual will interact with a group, especially if the project manager has never worked with this employee previously. Understanding the physiological and social behavior of how people perform in a group cannot happen overnight.

10.2 DIRECTING

Directing is the implementing and carrying out (through others) of those approved plans that are necessary to achieve or exceed objectives. Directing involves such steps as:

- *Staffing:* seeing that a qualified person is selected for each position.
- *Training:* teaching individuals and groups how to fulfill their duties and responsibilities.
- *Supervising:* giving others day-to-day instruction, guidance, and discipline as required so that they can fulfill their duties and responsibilities.
- *Delegating:* assigning work, responsibility, and authority so others can make maximum utilization of their abilities.
- *Motivating:* encouraging others to perform by fulfilling or appealing to their needs.

- *Counseling:* holding private discussions with another about how he might do better work, solve a personal problem, or realize his ambitions.
- *Coordinating:* seeing that activities are carried out in relation to their importance and with a minimum of conflict.

Directing subordinates is not an easy task because of both the short time duration of the project and the fact that employees might still be assigned to a functional manager while temporarily assigned to your effort. The luxury of getting to "know" one's subordinates may not be possible in a project environment.

Project managers must be decisive and move forward rapidly whenever directives are necessary. It is better to decide an issue and be 10 percent wrong than it is to wait for the last 10 percent of a problem's input and cause a schedule delay and improper use of resources. Directives are most effective when the KISS (keep it simple, stupid) rule is applied. Directives should be written with one simple and clear objective so that subordinates can work effectively and get things done right the first time. Orders must be issued in a manner that expects immediate compliance. Whether people will obey an order depends mainly on the amount of respect they have for you. Therefore, never issue an order that you cannot enforce. Oral orders and directives should be disguised as suggestions or requests. The requestor should ask the receiver to repeat the oral orders so that there is no misunderstanding.

> **PMBOK® Guide, 2004**
> Chapter 9 Human Resources
>   Management
> 9.4 Manage the Team

Project managers must understand human behavior in order to motivate people toward successful accomplishment of project objectives. Douglas McGregor advocated that most workers can be categorized according to two theories.[1] The first, often referred to as Theory X, assumes that the average worker is inherently lazy and requires supervision. Theory X further assumes that:

- The average worker dislikes work and avoids work whenever possible.
- To induce adequate effort, the supervisor must threaten punishment and exercise careful supervision.
- The average worker avoids increased responsibility and seeks to be directed.

The manager who accepts Theory X normally exercises authoritarian-type control over workers and allows little participation during decision-making. Theory X employees generally favor lack of responsibility, especially in decision-making.

According to Theory Y, employees are willing to get the job done without constant supervision. Theory Y further assumes that:

- The average worker wants to be active and finds the physical and mental effort on the job satisfying.
- Greatest results come from willing participation, which will tend to produce self-direction toward goals without coercion and control.
- The average worker seeks opportunity for personal improvement and self-respect.

---

1. Douglas McGregor, *The Human Side of Enterprise* (New York: McGraw-Hill, 1960), pp. 33–34.

The manager who accepts Theory Y normally advocates participation and a management–employee relationship. However, in working with professionals, especially engineers, special care must be exercised because these individuals often pride themselves on their ability to find a better way to achieve the end result regardless of cost. If this happens, project managers must become authoritarian leaders and treat Theory Y employees as though they are Theory X.

William Ouchi has identified a Theory Z that emphasizes the Japanese cultural values and the behavior of the Japanese workers.[2] According to Theory Z, there exist significant differences between the Japanese and American cultures and how the workers are treated. The Japanese focus on lifetime employment whereas the Americans look at short-term employment. The Japanese focus on collective decision-making such as in quality circles whereas Americans focus on individual decision-making. The Japanese emphasize informal administrative control whereas the Americans lean toward a more formal control. Japanese companies place workers on nonspecialized career paths with slow evaluation and promotion whereas Americans prefer specialized career path opportunities with rapid evaluation and promotion. Finally, Japanese managers have more of an interest in the personal life of their workers than do American managers.

> **PMBOK® Guide, 2004**
> Chapter 9 Human Resources
>   Management
> 9.3.2 Develop the Team

Many psychologists have established the existence of a prioritized hierarchy of needs that motivate individuals toward satisfactory performance. Maslow was the first to identify these needs.[3] Maslow's hierarchy of needs is shown in Figure 10–1. The first level is that of the basic or physiological needs, namely, food, water, clothing, shelter, sleep, and sexual satisfaction. Simply speaking, human primal desire to satisfy these basic needs motivates him to do a good job.

After an employee has fulfilled his physiological needs, he turns to the next lower need, safety. Safety needs include economic security and protection from harm, disease, and violence. Safety can also include security. It is important that project managers realize this because these managers may find that as a project nears termination, functional employees are more interested in finding a new role for themselves than in giving their best to the current situation.

The next level contains the social needs, including love, belonging, togetherness, approval, and group membership. At this level, the informal organization plays a dominant role. Many people refuse promotions to project management (as project managers, project office personnel, or functional representatives) because they fear that they will lose their "membership" in the informal organization. This problem can occur even on short-duration projects. In a project environment, project managers generally do not belong to any informal organization and, therefore, tend to look outside the organization to fulfill this need. Project managers consider authority and funding to be very important in gaining project support. Functional personnel, however, prefer friendship and work assignments. In other words, the project manager can use the project itself as a means of helping fulfill the third level for the line employees (i.e., team spirit).

---

2. W. G. Ouchi and A. M. Jaeger, "Type Z Organization: Stability in the Midst of Mobility," *Academy of Management Review,* April 1978, pp. 305–314.

3. Abraham Maslow, *Motivation and Personality* (New York: Harper and Brothers, 1954).

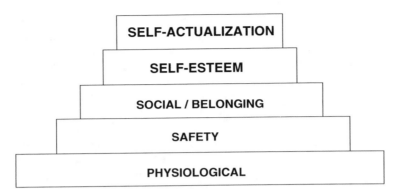

FIGURE 10–1. Maslow's hierarchy of needs.

The two lowest needs are esteem and self-actualization. The esteem need includes self-esteem (self-respect), reputation, the esteem of others, recognition, and self-confidence. Highly technical professionals are often not happy unless esteem needs are fulfilled. For example, many engineers strive to publish and invent as a means of satisfying these needs. These individuals often refuse promotions to project management because they believe that they cannot satisfy esteem needs in this position. Being called a project manager does not carry as much importance as being considered an expert in one's field by one's peers. The lowest need is self-actualization and includes doing what one can do best, desiring to utilize one's potential, full realization of one's potential, constant self-development, and a desire to be truly creative. Many good project managers find this level to be the most important and consider each new project as a challenge by which they can achieve self-actualization.

Frederick Herzberg and his associates conducted motivational research studies.[4] Herzberg concluded that Maslow's lower three levels (physiological, safety, and social needs) were hygiene factors that were either satisfied or dissatisfied. The only real motivational factors were the self-esteem and self-actualization needs. Herzberg believed that the physiological needs were hygiene factors and were extremely short-term needs. Self-esteem and self-actualization were more long-term needs and could be increased through job rotation, which includes job enrichment.

Another motivational technique can be related to the concept of expectancy theory (also referred to as the immature–mature organization), which was developed by the behaviorist Chris Argyis. Expectancy theory says that when the needs of the organization and the needs of the individual are congruent, both parties benefit and motivation increases. When there is incongruence between the needs of the individual and the needs of the organization, the individual will experience:

● Frustration
● Psychological failure
● Short-term perspectives
● Conflict

4. F. Herzberg, B. Mausner, and B. B. Snyderman, *The Motivation to Work* (New York: John Wiley & Sons, 1959).

Project managers must motivate temporarily assigned individuals by appealing to their desires to fulfill the lowest two levels, but not by making promises that cannot be met. Project managers must motivate by providing:

- A feeling of pride or satisfaction for one's ego
- Security of opportunity
- Security of approval
- Security of advancement, if possible
- Security of promotion, if possible
- Security of recognition
- A means for doing a better job, not a means to keep a job

Understanding professional needs is an important factor in helping people realize their true potential. Such needs include:

- Interesting and challenging work
- Professionally stimulating work environment
- Professional growth
- Overall leadership (ability to lead)
- Tangible rewards
- Technical expertise (within the team)
- Management assistance in problem-solving
- Clearly defined objectives
- Proper management control
- Job security
- Senior management support
- Good interpersonal relations
- Proper planning
- Clear role definition
- Open communications
- A minimum of changes

Motivating employees so that they feel secure on the job is not easy, especially since a project has a finite lifetime. Specific methods for producing security in a project environment include:

- Letting people know why they are where they are
- Making individuals feel that they belong where they are
- Placing individuals in positions for which they are properly trained
- Letting employees know how their efforts fit into the big picture

Since project managers cannot motivate by promising material gains, they must appeal to each person's pride. The guidelines for proper motivation are:

- Adopt a positive attitude
- Do not criticize management

- Do not make promises that cannot be kept
- Circulate customer reports
- Give each person the attention he requires

There are several ways of motivating project personnel. Some effective ways include:

- Giving assignments that provide challenges
- Clearly defining performance expectations
- Giving proper criticism as well as credit
- Giving honest appraisals
- Providing a good working atmosphere
- Developing a team attitude
- Providing a proper direction (even if Theory Y)

10.3 PROJECT AUTHORITY

PMBOK® Guide, 2004
9.1.3 Human Resource Planning

Project management structures create a web of relationships that can cause chaos in the delegation of authority and the internal authority structure. Four questions must be considered in describing project authority:

- What is project authority?
- What is power, and how is it achieved?
- How much project authority should be granted to the project manager?
- Who settles project authority interface problems?

One form of the project manager's authority can be defined as the legal or rightful power to command, act, or direct the activities of others. Authority can be delegated from one's superiors. Power, on the other hand, is granted to an individual by his subordinates and is a measure of their respect for him. A manager's authority is a combination of his power and influence such that subordinates, peers, and associates willingly accept his judgment.

In the traditional structure, the power spectrum is realized through the hierarchy, whereas in the project structure, power comes from credibility, expertise, or being a sound decision-maker.

Authority is the key to the project management process. The project manager must manage across functional and organizational lines by bringing together activities required to accomplish the objectives of a specific project. Project authority provides the way of thinking required to unify all organizational activities toward accomplishment of the project regardless of where they are located. The project manager who fails to build and maintain his alliances will soon find opposition or indifference to his project requirements.

The amount of authority granted to the project manager varies according to project size, management philosophy, and management interpretation of potential conflicts with functional managers. There do exist, however, certain fundamental elements over which the project manager must have authority in order to maintain effective control. According to Steiner and Ryan[5]:

> The project manager should have broad authority over all elements of the project. His authority should be sufficient to permit him to engage all necessary managerial and technical actions required to complete the project successfully. He should have appropriate authority in design and in making technical decisions in development. He should be able to control funds, schedule and quality of product. If subcontractors are used, he should have maximum authority in their selection.

Generally speaking, a project manager should have more authority than his responsibility calls for, the exact amount of authority usually depending on the amount of risk that the project manager must take. The greater the risk, the greater the amount of authority. A good project manager knows where his authority ends and does not hold an employee responsible for duties that he (the project manager) does not have the authority to enforce. Some projects are directed by project managers who have only monitoring authority. These project managers are referred to as influence project managers.

Failure to establish authority relationships can result in:

● Poor communication channels
● Misleading information
● Antagonism, especially from the informal organization
● Poor working relationships with superiors, subordinates, peers, and associates
● Surprises for the customer

The following are the most common sources of power and authority problems in a project environment:

● Poorly documented or no formal authority
● Power and authority perceived incorrectly
● Dual accountability of personnel
● Two bosses (who often disagree)
● The project organization encouraging individualism
● Subordinate relations stronger than peer or superior relationships
● Shifting of personnel loyalties from vertical to horizontal lines
● Group decision-making based on the strongest group
● Ability to influence or administer rewards and punishment
● Sharing resources among several projects

The project manager does not have unilateral authority in the project effort. He frequently negotiates with the functional manager. The project manager has the authority to

---

5. Reprinted from George A. Steiner and William G. Ryan, *Industrial Project Management* (1968), p. 24. Copyright © 1968 by the Trustees of Columbia University in the City of New York. Reprinted with permission of The Free Press, a division of Simon and Schuster.

determine the "when" and "what" of the project activities, whereas the functional manager has the authority to determine "how the support will be given." The project manager accomplishes his objectives by working with personnel who are largely professional. For professional personnel, project leadership must include explaining the rationale of the effort as well as the more obvious functions of planning, organizing, directing, and controlling.

Certain ground rules exist for authority control through negotiations:

- Negotiations should take place at the lowest level of interaction.
- Definition of the problem must be the first priority:
  - The issue
  - The impact
  - The alternative
  - The recommendations
- Higher-level authority should be used if, and only if, agreement cannot be reached.

The critical stage of any project is planning. This includes more than just planning the activities to be accomplished; it also includes the planning and establishment of the authority relationships that must exist for the duration of the project. Because the project management environment is an ever-changing one, each project establishes its own policies and procedures, a situation that can ultimately result in a variety of authority relationships. It is therefore possible for functional personnel to have different responsibilities on different projects, even if the tasks are the same.

During the planning phase the project team develops a responsibility assignment matrix (RAM) that contains such elements as:

- General management responsibility
- Operations management responsibility
- Specialized responsibility
- Who must be consulted
- Who may be consulted
- Who must be notified
- Who must approve

The responsibility matrix is often referred to as a linear responsibility chart (LRC) or responsibility assignment matrix (RAM). Linear responsibility charts identify the participants, and to what degree an activity will be performed or a decision will be made. The LRC attempts to clarify the authority relationships that can exist when functional units share common work. As described by Cleland and King[6]:

> The need for a device to clarify the authority relationships is evident from the relative unity
> of the traditional pyramidal chart, which (1) is merely a simple portrayal of the overall

6. From David I. Cleland and William Richard King, *Systems Analysis and Project Management* (New York: McGraw-Hill), p. 271. Copyright © 1968, 1975 McGraw-Hill Inc. Used with permission of McGraw-Hill Book Company.

functional and authority models and (2) must be combined with detailed position descriptions and organizational manuals to delineate authority relationships and work performance duties.

Figure 10–2 shows a typical linear responsibility chart. The rows, which indicate the activities, responsibilities, or functions required, can be all of the tasks in the work breakdown structure. The columns identify either positions, titles, or the people themselves. If the chart will be given to an outside customer, then only the titles should appear, or the customer will call the employees directly without going through the project manager. The symbols indicate the degrees of authority or responsibility existing between the rows and columns.

Another example of an LRC is shown in Figure 10–3. In this case, the LRC is used to describe how internal and external communications should take place. This type of chart can be used to eliminate communications conflicts. Consider a customer who is unhappy about having all of his information filtered through the project manager and requests that his line people be permitted to talk to your line people on a one-on-one basis. You may

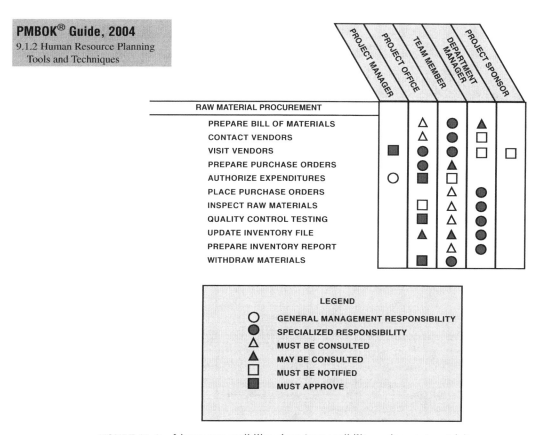

FIGURE 10–2. Linear responsibility chart (responsibility assignment matrix).

INITIATED FROM	REPORTED TO													
	INTERNAL							EXTERNAL (CUSTOMER)**						
	PROJECT MANAGER	PROJECT OFFICE	TEAM MEMBER	DEPARTMENT MEMBERS	FUNCTIONAL EMPLOYEES	DIVISION MANAGER	EXECUTIVE MANAGEMENT	PROJECT MANAGER	PROJECT OFFICE	TEAM MEMBER	DEPARTMENT MEMBERS	FUNCTIONAL EMPLOYEES	DIVISION MANAGER	EXECUTIVE MANAGEMENT
PROJECT MANAGER	▨	O	◆	△	▲	▲	◆	O	O	■	■	■	■	△
PROJECT OFFICE	O	▨	O	O	▲	▲	▲	O	O	△	△	■	■	△
TEAM MEMBER	◆	O	▨	◆	⬡	■	■	■	■	▲	▲	▲	■	■
DEPARTMENT MEMBERS	▲	△	O	▨	O	◆	■	△	△	△	△	△	■	■
FUNCTIONAL EMPLOYEES	▲	▲	O	O	▨	■	■	▲	▲	▲	▲	▲	■	■
DIVISION MANAGERS	△	▲	▲	▲	▲	▨	△	■	■	■	■	■	△	△
EXECUTIVE MANAGEMENT	△	▲	▲	▲	▲	▲	▨	△	△	▲	▲	■	△	△

*CAN VARY FROM TASK TO TASK AND CAN BE WRITTEN OR ORAL
** DOES NOT INCLUDE REGUARLY SCHEDULED INTERCHANGE MEETINGS

LEGEND
O DAILY
◆ WEEKLY
◇ MONTHLY
▲ AS NEEDED
△ INFORMAL
■ NEVER

FIGURE 10–3. Communications responsibility matrix.*

have no choice but to permit this, but you should make sure that the customer understands that:

- Functional employees cannot make commitments for additional work or resources.
- Functional employees give their own opinion and not that of the company.
- Company policy comes through the project office.

Figures 10–4 and 10–5 are examples of modified LRCs. Figure 10–4 is used to show the distribution of data items, and Figure 10–5 identifies the skills distribution in the project office.

The responsibility matrix attempts to answer such questions as: "Who has signature authority?" "Who must be notified?" "Who can make the decision?" The questions can only be answered by clear definitions of authority, responsibility, and accountability:

- *Authority* is the right of an individual to make the necessary decisions required to achieve his objectives or responsibilities.
- *Responsibility* is the assignment for completion of a specific event or activity.
- *Accountability* is the acceptance of success or failure.

DATA ITEM DISTRIBUTION MATRIX		CUSTOMER AND CONTRACTOR'S PERSONNEL				
DATA ITEM	REPORT DESCRIPTION	PROJECT MANAGER	PROJECT OFFICE	TEAM MEMBER	LINE MANAGER	EXECUTIVE MANAGEMENT
1	MONTHLY COST SUMMARIES	X	X			X
2	MILESTONE REPORTS	X	X	X	X	X
3	MANPOWER CURVES	X	X		X	
4	INVENTORY UTILIZATION	X	X			
5	PRESSURE TEST REPORT	X	X		X	
6	HUMIDITY TESTS	X	X		X	
7	HOTLINE REPORTS	X	X	X	X	X
8	SCHEDULING SUMMARIES	X	X	X	X	

FIGURE 10–4. Data distribution matrix.

The linear responsibility chart, although a valuable tool for management, does have a weakness in that it does not describe how people interact within the program. The LRC must be considered with the organization for a full understanding of how interactions between individuals and organizations take place. As described by Karger and Murdick, the LRC has merit[7]:

> Obviously the chart has weaknesses, of which one of the larger ones is that it is a mechanical aid. Just because it says that something is a fact does not make it true. It is very difficult to discover, except generally, exactly what occurs in a company—and with whom. The chart tries to express in specific terms relationships that cannot always be delineated so clearly; moreover, the degree to which it can be done depends on the specific situation. This is the difference between the formal and informal organizations mentioned. Despite this, the Linear Responsibility Chart is one of the best devices for organization analysis known to the authors.

Linear responsibility charts can result from customer-imposed requirements above and beyond normal operations. For example, the customer may require as part of its quality control that a specific engineer supervise and approve all testing of a certain item or that another individual approve all data released to the customer over and above program office

7. D. W. Karger and R. G. Murdick, *Managing Engineering and Research* (New York: Industrial Press, 1963), p. 89.

FUNCTIONAL AREAS OF EXPERTISE \ PROJECT TEAM	ABLE, J.	BAKER, P.	COOK, D.	DIRK, L.	EASLEY, P.	FRANKLIN, W.	GREEN, C.	HENRY, L.	IMHOFF, R.	JULES, C.	KLEIN, W.	LEDGER, D.	MAYER, O.	NEWTON, A.	OLIVER, G.	PRATT, L.
ADMINISTRATIVE MANAGEMENT		a				a		a			a	a			a	
COST CONTROL		b	b		b	b	b				b	b		b	b	
ECONOMIC ANALYSIS	c			c				c	c				c			c
ENERGY SYSTEMS		d	d		d		d			d			d		d	d
ENVIRONMENTAL IMPACT ASSESSMENT	e	e	e						e		e		e			
INDUSTRIAL ENGINEERING	f				f					f						
INSTRUMENTATION	g			g		g					g				g	
PIPING AND DESIGN LAYOUT	h		h		h	h				h			h			
PLANNING AND SCHEDULING		i		i	i	i		i				i		i		i
PROJECT MANAGEMENT	j			j		j					j				j	
PROJECT REPORTING		k	k		k			k	k			k		k		k
QUALITY CONTROL		l	l			l	l	l	l							
SITE EVALUATION		m				m			m	m				m		
SPECIFICATION PREPARATION			n	n			n				n		n			n
SYSTEM DESIGN		o	o		o		o	o		o		o			o	

FIGURE 10–5. Personal skills matrix.

approval. Such customer requirements necessitate LRCs and can cause disruptions and conflicts within an organization.

Several key factors affect the delegation of authority and responsibility, both from upper-level management to project management and from project management to functional management. These key factors include:

- The maturity of the project management function
- The size, nature, and business base of the company
- The size and nature of the project
- The life cycle of the project
- The capabilities of management at all levels

Once agreement has been reached as to the project manager's authority and responsibility, the results must be documented to clearly delineate his role in regard to:

- His focal position
- Conflict between the project manager and functional managers
- Influence to cut across functional and organizational lines
- Participation in major management and technical decisions
- Collaboration in staffing the project
- Control over allocation and expenditure of funds
- Selection of subcontractors
- Rights in resolving conflicts
- Voice in maintaining integrity of the project team
- Establishment of project plans
- Providing a cost-effective information system for control
- Providing leadership in preparing operational requirements
- Maintaining prime customer liaison and contact
- Promoting technological and managerial improvements
- Establishment of project organization for the duration
- Cutting red tape

Perhaps the best way to document the project manager's authority is through the project charter, which is one of the three methods, shown in Figure 10–6, by which project managers attain authority. Documenting the project manager's authority is necessary because:

- All interfacing must be kept as simple as possible.
- The project manager must have the authority to "force" functional managers to depart from existing standards and possibly incur risk.
- The project manager must gain authority over those elements of a program that are not under his control. This is normally achieved by earning the respect of the individuals concerned.
- The project manager should not attempt to fully describe the exact authority and responsibilities of his project office personnel or team members. Instead, he should encourage problem-solving rather than role definition.

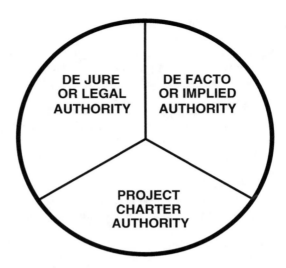

FIGURE 10–6. Types of project authority.

10.4 INTERPERSONAL INFLUENCES

PMBOK® Guide, 2004
9.1.2 Human Resource Planning
Tools and Techniques

There exist a variety of relationships (although they are not always clearly definable) between power and authority. These relationships are usually measured by "relative" decision power as a function of the authority structure, and are strongly dependent on the project organizational form. Consider the following statements made by project managers:

- "I've had good working relations with department X. They like me and I like them. I can usually push through anything ahead of schedule."
- "I know it's contrary to department policy, but the test must be conducted according to these criteria or else the results will be meaningless" (remark made to a team member by a research scientist who was temporarily promoted to project management for an advanced state-of-the-art effort).

Project managers are generally known for having a lot of delegated authority but very little formal power. They must, therefore, get jobs done through the use of interpersonal influences. There are five such interpersonal influences:

- *Legitimate power:* the ability to gain support because project personnel perceive the project manager as being officially empowered to issue orders.
- *Reward power:* the ability to gain support because project personnel perceive the project manager as capable of directly or indirectly dispensing valued organizational rewards (i.e., salary, promotion, bonus, future work assignments).

● *Penalty power:* the ability to gain support because the project personnel perceive the project manager as capable of directly or indirectly dispensing penalties that they wish to avoid. Penalty power usually derives from the same source as reward power, with one being a necessary condition for the other.
● *Expert power:* the ability to gain support because personnel perceive the project manager as possessing special knowledge or expertise (that functional personnel consider as important).

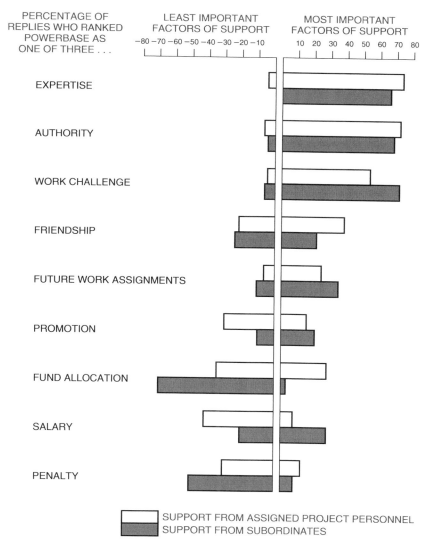

FIGURE 10–7. Significance of factors of support to project management. *Source: Seminar in Project Management Workbook,* © 1979 by Hans J. Thamhain. Reproduced by permission.

● *Referent power:* the ability to gain support because project personnel feel personally attracted to the project manager or his project.

The following six situations are examples of referent power (the first two are also reward power):

● The employee might be able to get personal favors from the project manager.
● The employee feels that the project manager is a winner and the rewards will be passed down to the employee.
● The employee and the project manager have strong ties, such as the same foursome for golf.
● The employee likes the project manager's manner of treating people.
● The employee wants identification with a specific product or product line.
● The employee has personal problems and believes that he can get empathy or understanding from the project manager.

Figure 10–7 shows how project managers perceive their influence style.

Like relative power, interpersonal influences can be identified with various project organizational forms as to their relative value. This is shown in Figure 10–8.

For any temporary management structure to be effective, there must exist a rational balance of power between functional and project management. Unfortunately, a balance of equal power is often impossible to obtain because each project is inherently different from others, and the project managers possess different leadership abilities.

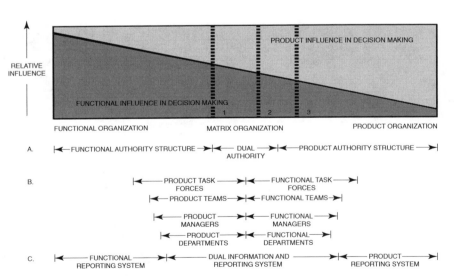

FIGURE 10–8. The range of alternatives. *Source:* Jay R. Galbraith, "Matrix Organization Designs." Reprinted with permission from *Business Horizons,* February 1971, p. 37. Copyright © 1971 by the Board of Trustees at Indiana University.

Achievement of this balance is a never-ending challenge for management. If time and cost constraints on a project cannot be met, the project influence in decision-making increases, as can be seen in Figure 10–8. If the technology or performance constraints need reappraisal, then the functional influence in decision-making will dominate.

Regardless of how much authority and power a project manager develops over the course of the project, the ultimate factor in his ability to get the job done is usually his leadership style. Developing bonds of trust, friendship, and respect with the functional workers can promote success.

10.5 BARRIERS TO PROJECT TEAM DEVELOPMENT

PMBOK® Guide, 2004
9.3 Develop Project Team

Most people within project-driven and non–project-driven organizations have differing views of project management. Table 10–1 compares the project and functional viewpoints of project management. These differing views can create severe barriers to successful project management operations.

The understanding of barriers to project team building can help in developing an environment conducive to effective teamwork. The following barriers are typical for many project environments.

Differing outlooks, priorities, and interests. A major barrier exists when team members have professional objectives and interests that are different from the project objectives. These problems are compounded when the team relies on support organizations that have different interests and priorities.

Role conflicts. Team development efforts are thwarted when role conflicts exist among the team members, such as ambiguity over who does what within the project team and in external support groups.

Project objectives/outcomes not clear. Unclear project objectives frequently lead to conflict, ambiguities, and power struggles. It becomes difficult, if not impossible, to define roles and responsibilities clearly.

Dynamic project environments. Many projects operate in a continual state of change. For example, senior management may keep changing the project scope, objectives, and resource base. In other situations, regulatory changes or client demands can drastically affect the internal operations of a project team.

Competition over team leadership. Project leaders frequently indicated that this barrier most likely occurs in the early phases of a project or if the project runs into severe problems. Obviously, such cases of leadership challenge can result in barriers to team building. Frequently, these challenges are covert challenges to the project leader's ability.

Lack of team definition and structure. Many senior managers complain that teamwork is severely impaired because it lacks clearly defined task responsibilities and reporting structures. We find this situation is most prevalent in dynamic, organizationally unstructured work environments such as computer systems and R&D projects. A common pattern is that a support department is charged with a task but no one leader is clearly delegated the responsibility. As a consequence, some personnel are working on the

TABLE 10–1. COMPARISON OF THE FUNCTIONAL AND THE PROJECT VIEWPOINTS

Phenomena	Project Viewpoint	Functional Viewpoint
Line–staff organizational dichotomy	Vestiges of the hierarchical model remain: the line functions are placed in a support position. A web of authority and responsibility exists.	Line functions have direct responsibility for accomplishing the objectives; line commands, and staff advises.
Scalar principle	Elements of the vertical chain exist, but prime emphasis is placed on horizontal and diagonal work flow. Important business is conducted as the legitimacy of the task requires.	The chain of authority relationships is from superior to subordinate throughout the organization. Central, crucial, and important business is conducted up and down the vertical hierarchy.
Superior–subordinate relationship	Peer-to-peer, manager-to-technical expert, associate-to-associate, etc., relationships are used to conduct much of the salient business.	This is the most important relationship; if kept healthy, success will follow. All important business is conducted through a pyramiding structure of superiors and subordinates
Organizational objectives	Management of a project becomes a joint venture of many relatively independent organizations. Thus, the objective becomes multilateral.	Organizational objectives are sought by the parent unit (an assembly of suborganizations) working within its environment. The objective is unilateral.
Unity of direction	The project manager manages across functional and organizational lines to accomplish a common interorganizational objective.	The general manager acts as the one head for a group of activities having the same plan.
Parity of authority and responsibility	Considerable opportunity exists for the project manager's responsibility to exceed his authority. Support people are often responsible to other managers (functional) for pay, performance reports, promotions, etc.	Consistent with functional management; the integrity of the superior–subordinate relationship is maintained through functional authority and advisory staff services.
Time duration	The project (and hence the organization) is finite in duration.	Tends to perpetuate itself to provide continuing facilitative support.

Source: David I. Cleland, "Project Management," in David I. Cleland and William R. King, eds., *Systems Organizations, Analysis, Management: A Book of Readings* (New York: McGraw-Hill, Inc., 1969), pp. 281–290. © 1969 by McGraw-Hill Inc. Reprinted with permission of the publisher.

project but are not entirely clear on the extent of their responsibilities. In other cases, problems result when a project is supported by several departments without interdisciplinary coordination.

Team personnel selection. This barrier develops when personnel feel unfairly treated or threatened during the staffing of a project. In some cases, project personnel are assigned to a team by functional managers, and the project manager has little or no input into the selection process. This can impede team development efforts, especially when the project leader is given available personnel versus the best, hand-picked team members. The assignment of "available personnel" can result in several problems (e.g., low motivation levels, discontent, and uncommitted team members). We've found, as a rule, that the more power the project leader has over the selection of his team members, and the more negotiated agreement there is over the assigned task, the more likely it is that team-building efforts will be fruitful.

Credibility of project leader. Team-building efforts are hampered when the project leader suffers from poor credibility within the team or from other managers. In such cases, team members are often reluctant to make a commitment to the project or the leader. Credibility problems may come from poor managerial skills, poor technical judgments, or lack of experience relevant to the project.

Lack of team member commitment. Lack of commitment can have several sources. For example, the team members having professional interests elsewhere, the feeling of insecurity that is associated with projects, the unclear nature of the rewards that may be forthcoming upon successful completion, and intense interpersonal conflicts within the team can all lead to lack of commitment.

Lack of team member commitment may result from suspicious attitudes existing between the project leader and a functional support manager, or between two team members from two warring functional departments. Finally, low commitment levels are likely to occur when a "star" on a team "demands" too much effort from other team members or too much attention from the team leader. One team leader put it this way: "A lot of teams have their prima donnas and you learn to live and function with them. They can be critical to overall success. But some stars can be so demanding on everyone that they'll kill the team's motivation."

Communication problems. Not surprisingly, poor communication is a major enemy to effective team development. Poor communication exists on four major levels: problems of communication among team members, between the project leader and the team members, between the project team and top management, and between the project leaders and the client. Often the problem is caused by team members simply not keeping others informed on key project developments. Yet the "whys" of poor communication patterns are far more difficult to determine. The problem can result from low motivation levels, poor morale, or carelessness. It was also discovered that poor communication patterns between the team and support groups result in severe team-building problems, as does poor communication with the client. Poor communication practices often lead to unclear objectives and poor project control, coordination, and work flow.

Lack of senior management support. Project leaders often indicate that senior management support and commitment is unclear and subject to waxing and waning over the project life cycle. This behavior can result in an uneasy feeling among team members and lead to low levels of enthusiasm and project commitment. Two other common problems are that senior management often does not help set the right environment for the project team at the outset, nor do they give the team timely feedback on their performance and activities during the life of the project.

Project managers who are successfully performing their role not only recognize these barriers but also know when in the project life cycle they are most likely to occur. Moreover, these managers take preventive actions and usually foster a work environment that is conducive to effective teamwork. The effective team builder is usually a social architect who understands the interaction of organizational and behavior variables and can foster a climate of active participation and minimal conflict. This requires carefully developed skills in leadership, administration, organization, and technical expertise on the project. However, besides the delicately balanced management skills, the project manager's sensitivity to the basic issues underlying each barrier can help to increase success in developing an effective project team. Specific suggestions for team building are advanced in Table 10–2.

TABLE 10–2. BARRIERS TO EFFECTIVE TEAM BUILDING AND SUGGESTED HANDLING APPROACHES

Barrier	Suggestions for Effectively Managing Barriers (How to Minimize or Eliminate Barriers)
Differing outlooks, priorities, interests, and judgments of team members	Make effort early in the project life cycle to discover these conflicting differences. Fully explain the scope of the project and the rewards that may be forthcoming on successful project completion. Sell "team" concept and explain responsibilities. Try to blend individual interests with the overall project objectives.
Role conflicts	As early in a project as feasible, ask team members where they see themselves fitting into the project. Determine how the overall project can best be divided into subsystems and subtasks (e.g., the work breakdown structure). Assign/negotiate roles. Conduct regular status review meetings to keep team informed on progress and watch for unanticipated role conflicts over the project's life.
Project objectives/outcomes not clear	Assure that all parties understand the overall and interdisciplinary project objectives. Clear and frequent communication with senior management and the client becomes critically important. Status review meetings can be used for feedback. Finally, a proper team name can help to reinforce the project objectives.
Dynamic project environments	The major challenge is to stabilize external influences. First, key project personnel must work out an agreement on the principal project direction and "sell" this direction to the total team. Also educate senior management and the customer on the detrimental consequences of unwarranted change. It is critically important to forecast the "environment" within which the project will be developed. Develop contingency plans.

(*continues*)

TABLE 10–2. BARRIERS TO EFFECTIVE TEAM BUILDING AND SUGGESTED HANDLING
APPROACHES (*Continued*)

Barrier	Suggestions for Effectively Managing Barriers (How to Minimize or Eliminate Barriers)
Competition over team leadership	Senior management must help establish the project manager's leadership role. On the other hand, the project manager needs to fulfill the leadership expectations of team members. Clear role and responsibility definition often minimizes competition over leadership.
Lack of team definition and structure	Project leaders need to sell the team concept to senior management as well as to their team members. Regular meetings with the team will reinforce the team notion as will clearly defined tasks, roles, and responsibilities. Also, visibility in memos and other forms of written media as well as senior management and client participation can unify the team.
Project personnel selection	Attempt to negotiate the project assignments with potential team members. Clearly discuss with potential team members the importance of the project, their role in it, what rewards might result on completion, and the general "rules of the road" of project management. Finally, if team members remain uninterested in the project, then replacement should be considered.
Credibility of project leader	Credibility of the project leader among team members is crucial. It grows with the image of a sound decision-maker in both general management and relevant technical expertise. Credibility can be enhanced by the project leader's relationship to other key managers who support the team's efforts.
Lack of team member commitment	Try to determine lack of team member commitment early in the life of the project and attempt to change possible negative views toward the project. Often, insecurity is a major reason for the lack of commitment; try to determine why insecurity exists, then work on reducing the team members' fears. Conflicts with other team members may be another reason for lack of commitment. It is important for the project leader to intervene and mediate the conflict quickly. Finally, if a team member's professional interests lie elsewhere, the project leader should examine ways to satisfy part of the team member's interests or consider replacement.
Communication problems	The project leader should devote considerable time communicating with individual team members about their needs and concerns. In addition, the leader should provide a vehicle for timely sessions to encourage communications among the individual team contributors. Tools for enhancing communications are status meetings, reviews, schedules, reporting system, and colocation. Similarly, the project leader should establish regular and thorough communications with the client and senior management. Emphasis is placed on written and oral communications with key issues and agreements in writing.

(*continues*)

TABLE 10–2. BARRIERS TO EFFECTIVE TEAM BUILDING AND SUGGESTED HANDLING APPROACHES (*Continued*)

Barrier	Suggestions for Effectively Managing Barriers (How to Minimize or Eliminate Barriers)
Lack of senior management support	Senior management support is an absolute necessity for dealing effectively with interface groups and proper resource commitment. Therefore, a major goal for project leaders is to maintain the continued interest and commitment of senior management in their projects. We suggest that senior management become an integral part of project reviews. Equally important, it is critical for senior management to provide the proper environment for the project to function effectively. Here the project leader needs to tell management at the onset of the program what resources are needed. The project manager's relationship with senior management and ability to develop senior management support is critically affected by his own credibility and the visibility and priority of his project.

10.6 SUGGESTIONS FOR HANDLING THE NEWLY FORMED TEAM

A major problem faced by many project leaders is managing the anxiety that usually develops when a new team is formed. The anxiety experienced by team members is normal and predictable, but is a barrier to getting the team quickly focused on the task.

This anxiety may come from several sources. For example, if the team members have never worked with the project leader, they may be concerned about his leadership style. Some team members may be concerned about the nature of the project and whether it will match their professional interests and capabilities, or help or hinder their career aspirations. Further, team members can be highly anxious about life-style/work-style disruptions. As one project manager remarked, "Moving a team member's desk from one side of the room to the other can sometimes be just about as traumatic as moving someone from Chicago to Manila."

Another common concern among newly formed teams is whether there will be an equitable distribution of the workload among team members and whether each member is capable of pulling his own weight. In some newly formed teams, members not only must do their own work, but also must train other team members. Within reason this is bearable, but when it becomes excessive, anxiety increases.

Certain steps taken early in the life of a team can minimize the above problems. First, we recommend that the project leader talk with each team member one-to-one about the following:

1. What the objectives are for the project.
2. Who will be involved and why.
3. The importance of the project to the overall organization or work unit.

4. Why the team member was selected and assigned to the project. What role he will perform.
5. What rewards might be forthcoming if the project is successfully completed.
6. What problems and constraints are likely to be encountered.
7. The rules of the road that will be followed in managing the project (e.g., regular status review meetings).
8. What suggestions the team member has for achieving success.
9. What the professional interests of the team member are.
10. What challenge the project will present to individual members and the entire team.
11. Why the team concept is so important to project management success and how it should work.

Dealing with these anxieties and helping team members feel that they are an integral part of the team can yield rich dividends. First, as noted in Figure 10–9, team members are more likely to openly share their ideas and approaches. Second, it is more likely that the team will be able to develop effective decision-making processes. Third, the team is likely to develop more effective project control procedures, including those traditionally used to monitor project performance (PERT/CPM, networking, work breakdown structures, etc.) and those in which team members give feedback to each other regarding performance.

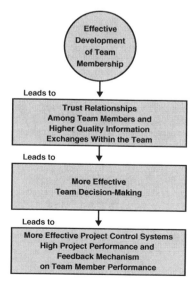

FIGURE 10–9. Team-building outcomes.

10.7 TEAM BUILDING AS AN ONGOING PROCESS _____

While proper attention to team building is critical during early phases of a project, it is a never-ending process. The project manager is continually monitoring team functioning and performance to see what corrective action may be needed to prevent or correct various team problems. Several barometers (summarized in Table 10–3) provide good clues of potential team dysfunctioning. First, noticeable changes in performance levels for the team and/or for individual team members should always be investigated. Such changes can be symptomatic of more serious problems (e.g., conflict, lack of work integration, communication problems, and unclear objectives). Second, the project leader and team members must be aware of the changing energy levels of team members. These changes, too, may signal more serious problems or that the team is tired and stressed. Sometimes changing the work pace or taking time off can reenergize team members. Third, verbal and nonverbal clues from team members may be a source of information on team functioning. It is important to hear the needs and concerns of team members (verbal clues) and to observe how they act in carrying out their responsibilities (nonverbal clues). Finally, detrimental behavior of one team member toward another can be a signal that a problem within the team warrants attention.

We highly recommend that project leaders hold regular meetings to evaluate overall team performance and deal with team functioning problems. The focus of these meetings can be directed toward "what we are doing well as a team" and "what areas need our team's attention." This approach often brings positive surprises in that the total team is informed of progress in diverse project areas (e.g., a breakthrough in technology development, a subsystem schedule met ahead of the original target, or a positive change in the client's be-

TABLE 10–3. EFFECTIVENESS–INEFFECTIVENESS INDICATORS

The Effective Team's Likely Characteristics	The Ineffective Team's Likely Characteristics
• High performance and task efficiency • Innovative/creative behavior • Commitment • Professional objectives of team members coincident with project requirements • Team members highly interdependent, interface effectively • Capacity for conflict resolution, but conflict encouraged when it can lead to beneficial results • Effective communication • High trust levels • Results orientation • Interest in membership • High energy levels and enthusiasm • High morale • Change orientation	• Low performance • Low commitment to project objectives • Unclear project objectives and fluid commitment levels from key participants • Unproductive gamesmanship, manipulation of others, hidden feelings, conflict avoidance at all costs • Confusion, conflict, inefficiency • Subtle sabotage, fear, disinterest, or foot-dragging • Cliques, collusion, isolation of members • Lethargy/unresponsiveness

havior toward the project). After the positive issues have been discussed the review session should focus on actual or potential problem areas. The meeting leader should ask each team member for his observations and then open the discussion to ascertain how significant the problems really are. Assumptions should, of course, be separated from the facts of each situation. Next, assignments should be agreed on for best handling these problems. Finally, a plan for problem follow-up should be developed. The process should result in better overall performance and promote a feeling of team participation and high morale.

10.8 LEADERSHIP IN A PROJECT ENVIRONMENT

Leadership can be defined as a style of behavior designed to integrate both the organizational requirements and one's personal interests into the pursuit of some objective. All managers have some sort of leadership responsibility. If time permits, successful leadership techniques and practices can be developed.

Leadership is composed of several complex elements, the three most common being:

- The person leading
- The people being led
- The situation (i.e., the project environment)

Project managers are often selected or not selected because of their leadership styles. The most common reason for not selecting an individual is his inability to balance the technical and managerial project functions. Wilemon and Cicero have defined four characteristics of this type of situation[8]:

- The greater the project manager's technical expertise, the higher his propensity to overinvolve himself in the technical details of the project.
- The greater the project manager's difficulty in delegating technical task responsibilities, the more likely it is that he will overinvolve himself in the technical details of the project (depending on his ability to do so).
- The greater the project manager's interest in the technical details of the project, the more likely it is that he will defend the project manager's role as one of a technical specialist.
- The lower the project manager's technical expertise, the more likely it is that he will overstress the nontechnical project functions (administrative functions).

There have been several surveys to determine what leadership techniques are best. The following are the results of a survey by Richard Hodgetts[9]:

---

8. D. L. Wilemon and John P. Cicero, "The Project Manager: Anomalies and Ambiguities," *Academy of Management Journal,* Vol. 13, pp. 269–282, 1970.

9. Richard M. Hodgetts, "Leadership Techniques in Project Organizations," *Academy of Management Journal,* Vol. 11, pp. 211–219, 1968.

- Human relations–oriented leadership techniques
  - "The project manager must make all the team members feel that their efforts are important and have a direct effect on the outcome of the program."
  - "The project manager must educate the team concerning what is to be done and how important its role is."
  - "Provide credit to project participants."
  - "Project members must be given recognition and prestige of appointment."
  - "Make the team members feel and believe that they play a vital part in the success (or failure) of the team."
  - "By working extremely closely with my team I believe that one can win a project loyalty while to a large extent minimizing the frequency of authority-gap problems."
  - "I believe that a great motivation can be created just by knowing the people in a personal sense. I know many of the line people better than their own supervisor does. In addition, I try to make them understand that they are an indispensable part of the team."
  - "I would consider the most important technique in overcoming the authority-gap to be understanding as much as possible the needs of the individuals with whom you are dealing and over whom you have no direct authority."
- Formal authority–oriented leadership techniques
  - "Point out how great the loss will be if cooperation is not forthcoming."
  - "Put all authority in functional statements."
  - "Apply pressure beginning with a tactful approach and minimum application warranted by the situation and then increasing it."
  - "Threaten to precipitate high-level intervention and do it if necessary."
  - "Convince the members that what is good for the company is good for them."
  - "Place authority on full-time assigned people in the operating division to get the necessity work done."
  - "Maintain control over expenditures."
  - "Utilize implicit threat of going to general management for resolution."
  - "It is most important that the team members recognize that the project manager has the charter to direct the project."

10.9 LIFE-CYCLE LEADERSHIP

PMBOK® Guide, 2004
9.3 Develop Project Team

In the opinion of the author, Hersey and Blanchard developed the best model for analyzing leadership in a project management environment.[10] The model, which has been expanded by Paul Hersey and is shown in Figure 10–10, is the life-cycle theory of leadership. The model contends that leadership

---

10. Paul Hersey and Kenneth Blanchard, *Management of Organizational Behavior* (Englewood Cliffs, New Jersey: Prentice-Hall, 1979), p. 165.

TASK BEHAVIOR—
The extent to which the leader engages in defining roles, i.e., telling what, how, when, where, and if more than one person, who is to do what in:
• Goal Setting
• Organizing
• Establishing Time Lines
• Directing
• Controlling

RELATIONSHIP BEHAVIOR—
The extent to which a leader engages in two-way (multi-way) communication, listening, facilitating behaviors, socioemotional support:
• Giving Support
• Communicating
• Facilitating Interactions
• Active Listening
• Providing Feedback

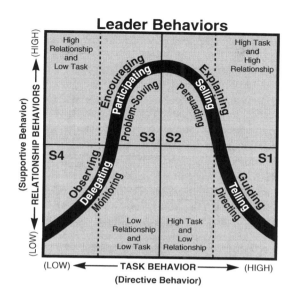

DECISION STYLES

1
Leader-Made Decision

2
Leader-Made Decision with Dialogue and/or Explanation

3
Leader & Follower-Made Decision or Follower-Made Decision with Encouragement from Leader

4
Follower-Made Decision

ABILITY: has the necessary knowlege, experience, and skill

WILLINGNESS: has the necessary confidence, commitment, motivation

FOLLOWER READINESS

HIGH	MODERATE		LOW
R4	**R3**	**R2**	**R1**
Able and Willing and Confident	Able but Unwilling or Insecure	Unable but Willing or Confident	Unable and Unwilling or Insecure

FIGURE 10–10. Expanded Situational Leadership Model. Adapted from Paul Hersey, *Situational Selling* (Escondido, California: Center for Leadership Studies, 1985), p. 35. Reproduced by permission of the Center for Leadership Studies.

styles must change according to the readiness of the employees, with readiness defined as job-related experience, willingness to accept job responsibility, and desire to achieve. This definition of readiness is somewhat different from other behavioral management definitions, which define readiness (and maturity) as age or emotional stability.

As shown in Figure 10–10, the subordinates enter the organization in quadrant S1, which is high task and low relationship behavior. In this quadrant, the leadership style is almost pure task-oriented behavior and is an autocratic approach, where the leader's main concern is the accomplishment of the objective, often with very little concern for the employees or their feelings. The leader is very forceful and relies heavily on his own abilities and judgment. Other people's opinions may be of no concern. In the initial stage, there is anxiety, tension, and confusion among new employees, so that relationship behavior is inappropriate.

In quadrant S2, employees begin to understand their tasks and the leader tries to develop strong behavioral relationships. The development of trust and understanding between the leader and subordinates becomes a driving force for the strong behavioral relationships. However, although the leader begins utilizing behavioral relationships, there still exists a strong need for high task behavior as well, since employees may not have achieved the level of competency to assume full responsibility.

Quadrant S3 is often regarded as pure relationship behavior, where the leader is perhaps more interested in gaining the respect of the employees than in achieving the objectives. Referent power becomes extremely important. This behavior can be characterized by delegation of authority and responsibility (often excessive), participative management, and group decision-making. In this phase, employees no longer need directives and are knowledgeable enough about the job and self-motivated to the extent that they are willing to assume more responsibility for the task. Therefore, the leader can try to strengthen his relationships with subordinates.

In quadrant S4, employees are experienced in the job, confident about their own abilities, and trusted to handle the work themselves. The leader demonstrates low task and low relationship behavior as the employees "mature" into a high degree of readiness.

This type of leadership model also has specific titles associated with specific quadrants.

- **Democratic or Participative Leadership:** This leadership style encourages workers to communicate with one another and get involved with decision-making either by himself or herself or with assistance of the project manager. A great deal of authority is delegated to the team members, and they are encouraged to take an active role in the management of the project. This leadership style is often found in quadrants S3 and S4.
- **Laissez-Faire Leadership:** With this leadership style, the project manager turns things over to the workers. The project manager may make an occasional appearance just to see how things are going, but for the main part there is no active involvement by the project manager. This leadership style is found in quadrant S3.
- **Autocratic Leadership:** With this leadership style, the project manager focuses very heavily upon the task, with little concern for the workers. With autocratic leadership, all authority is in the hands of the project manager and the project manager has the final say in any and all decisions. This leadership style is found in quadrant S1.

This type of life-cycle approach to leadership is extremely important to project managers, because it implies that effective leadership must be dynamic and flexible rather than static and rigid (see Figure 10–11). Effective leaders are neither pure task or relationship behavioralists, but maintain a balance between them. However, in time of crisis, a leader may be required to demonstrate a pure behavioral style or a pure task style.

In pure project management, the situation is even more complex. Line managers have *sufficient time* to develop a meaningful relationship with subordinates to the point that they get to know each other quite well. The line manager can then "train" his subordinates to adapt to the line manager's leadership style.

Project managers, on the other hand, are under a severe time constraint and may have to develop a different leadership style for each team member. To illustrate this graphically, the quadrants in Figure 10–10 should be three-dimensional, with the third axis being the

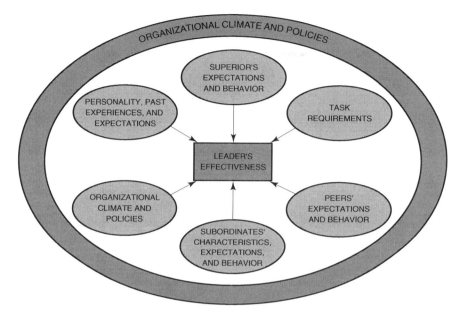

FIGURE 10–11. Personality and situational factors that influence effective leadership. *Source:* James A. F. Stoner, *Management,* 2nd ed. (Englewood Cliffs, New Jersey: Prentice-Hall Inc., 1982) Used by permission.

life-cycle phase of the project. In other words, the leadership style is dependent not only on the situation, but on the life-cycle phase of the project.

10.10 ORGANIZATIONAL IMPACT

In most companies, whether or not project-oriented, the impact of management emphasis on the organization is well known. In the project environment there also exists a definite impact due to leadership emphasis. The leadership emphasis is best seen by employee contributions, organizational order, employee performance, and the project manager's performance:

- Contributions from People
  - A good project manager encourages active cooperation and responsible participation. The result is that both good and bad information is contributed freely.
  - A poor project manager maintains an atmosphere of passive resistance with only responsive participation. This results in information being withheld.

- Organizational Order
  - A good project manager develops policy and encourages acceptance. A low price is paid for contributions.
  - A poor project manager goes beyond policies and attempts to develop procedures and measurements. A high price is normally paid for contributions.
- Employee Performance
  - A good project manager keeps people informed and satisfied (if possible) by aligning motives with objectives. Positive thinking and cooperation are encouraged. A good project manager is willing to give more responsibility to those willing to accept it.
  - A poor project manager keeps people uninformed, frustrated, defensive, and negative. Motives are aligned with incentives rather than objectives. The poor project manager develops a "stay out of trouble" atmosphere.
- Performance of the Project Manager
  - A good project manager assumes that employee misunderstandings can and will occur, and therefore blames himself. A good project manager constantly attempts to improve and be more communicative. He relies heavily on moral persuasion.
  - A poor project manager assumes that employees are unwilling to cooperate and therefore blames subordinates. The poor project manager demands more through authoritarian attitudes and relies heavily on material incentives.

Management emphasis also impacts the organization. The following four categories show this management emphasis resulting for both good and poor project management:

- Management Problem-Solving
  - A good project manager performs his own problem-solving at the level for which he is responsible through delegation of problem-solving responsibilities.
  - A poor project manager will do subordinate problem-solving in known areas. For areas that he does not know, he requires that his approval be given prior to idea implementation.
- Organizational Order
  - A good project manager develops, maintains, and uses a single integrated management system in which authority and responsibility are delegated to the subordinates. In addition, he knows that occasional slippages and overruns will occur, and simply tries to minimize their effect.
  - A poor project manager delegates as little authority and responsibility as possible, and runs the risk of continual slippages and overruns. A poor project manager maintains two management information systems: one informal system for himself and one formal (eyewash) system simply to impress his superiors.
- Performance of People
  - A good project manager finds that subordinates willingly accept responsibility, are decisive in attitude toward the project, and are satisfied.

- ● A poor project manager finds that his subordinates are reluctant to accept responsibility, are indecisive in their actions, and seem frustrated.
- ● Performance of the Project Manager
  - ● A good project manager assumes that his key people can "run the show." He exhibits confidence in those individuals working in areas in which he has no expertise, and exhibits patience with people working in areas where he has a familiarity. A good project manager is never too busy to help his people solve personal or professional problems.
  - ● A poor project manager considers himself indispensable, is overcautious with work performed in unfamiliar areas, and becomes overly interested in work he knows. A poor project manager is always tied up in meetings.

10.11 EMPLOYEE–MANAGER PROBLEMS

The two major problem areas in the project environment are the "who has what authority and responsibility" question, and the resulting conflicts associated with the individual at the project–functional interface. Almost all project problems in some way or another involve these two major areas. Other problem areas found in the project environment include:

- ● The pyramidal structure
- ● Superior–subordinate relationships
- ● Departmentalization
- ● Scalar chain of command
- ● Organizational chain of command
- ● Power and authority
- ● Planning goals and objectives
- ● Decision-making
- ● Reward and punishment
- ● Span of control

The two most common employee problems involve the assignment and resulting evaluation processes. Personnel assignments were discussed in Chapter 9. In summary:

- ● People should be assigned to tasks commensurate with their skills.
- ● Whenever possible, the same person should be assigned to related tasks.
- ● The most critical tasks should be assigned to the most responsible people.

The evaluation process in a project environment is difficult for an employee at the functional–project interface, especially if hostilities develop between the functional and project managers. In this situation, the interfacing employee almost always suffers owing to a poor rating by either the project manager or his supervisor. Unless the employee continually keeps his superior abreast of his performance and achievements, the supervisor must rely solely on the input (often flawed) received from project office personnel.

Three additional questions must be answered with regard to employee evaluation:

- Of what value are job descriptions?
- How do we maintain wage and salary grades?
- Who provides training and development, especially under conditions where variable manloading can exist?

If each project is, in fact, different from all others, then it becomes an almost impossible task to develop accurate job descriptions. In many cases, wage and salary grades are functions of a unit manning document that specifies the number, type, and grade of all employees required on a given project. Although this might be a necessity in order to control costs, it also is difficult to achieve because variable manloading changes project priorities. Variable manloading creates several difficulties for project managers, especially if new employees are included. Project managers like to have seasoned veterans assigned to their activities because there generally does not exist sufficient time for proper and close supervision of the training and development of new employees. Functional managers, however, contend that the training has to be accomplished on someone's project, and sooner or later all project managers must come to this realization.

On the manager level, the two most common problems involve personal values and conflicts. Personal values are often attributed to the "changing of the guard." New managers have a different sense of values from that of the older, more experienced managers. Miner identifies some of these personal values attributed to new managers[11]:

- Less trust, especially of people in positions of authority.
- Increased feelings of being controlled by external forces and events, and thus belief that they cannot control their own destinies. This is a kind of change that makes for less initiation of one's own activities and a greater likelihood of responding in terms of external pressures. There is a sense of powerlessness, although not necessarily a decreased desire for power.
- Less authoritarian and more negative attitudes toward persons holding positions of power.
- More independence, often to the point of rebelliousness and defiance.
- More freedom, less control in expressing feelings, impulses, and emotions.
- Greater inclination to live in the present and to let the future take care of itself.
- More self-indulgence.
- Moral values that are relative to the situation, less absolute, and less tied to formal religion.
- A strong and increasing identification with their peer and age groups, with the youth culture.

---

11. John B. Miner, "The OD-Management Development Conflict." Reprinted with permission from *Business Horizons,* December 1973, p. 32. Copyright © 1973 by the Board of Trustees at Indiana University.

- Greater social concern and greater desire to help the less fortunate.
- More negative attitude toward business, the management role in particular. A professional position is clearly preferred to managing.
- A desire to contribute less to an employing organization and to receive more from the organization.

Previously, we defined one of the attributes of a project manager as liking risks. Unfortunately, the amount of risk that today's managers are willing to accept varies not only with their personal values but also with the impact of current economic conditions and top management philosophies. If top management views a specific project as vital for the growth of the company, then the project manager may be directed to assume virtually no risks during the execution of the project. In this case the project manager may attempt to pass all responsibility to higher or lower management claiming that "his hands are tied." Wilemon and Cicero identify problems with risk identification[12]:

- The project manager's anxiety over project risk varies in relation to his willingness to accept final responsibility for the technical success of his project. Some project managers may be willing to accept full responsibility for the success or failure of their projects. Others, by contrast, may be more willing to share responsibility and risk with their superiors.
- The greater the length of stay in project management, the greater the tendency for project managers to remain in administrative positions within an organization.
- The degree of anxiety over professional obsolescence varies with the length of time the project manager spends in project management positions.

The amount of risk that managers will accept also varies with age and experience. Older, more experienced managers tend to take few risks, whereas the younger, more aggressive managers may adopt a risk-lover policy in hopes of achieving a name for themselves.

Conflicts exist at the project–functional interface regardless of how hard we attempt to structure the work. According to Cleland and King, this interface can be defined by the following relationships[13]:

- Project Manager
  - *What* is to be done?
  - *When* will the task be done?
  - *Why* will the task be done?
  - *How much* money is available to do the task?
  - *How well* has the total project been done?

---

12. D. L. Wilemon and John P. Cicero, "The Project Manager: Anomalies and Ambiguities," *Academy of Management Journal,* Vol. 13, 1970, pp. 269–282.

13. From David I. Cleland and William Richard King, *Systems Analysis and Project Management* (New York: McGraw-Hill), p. 237. Copyright © 1968, 1975 by McGraw-Hill, Inc. Used with permission of McGraw-Hill Book Company.

- Functional Manager
  - *Who* will do the task?
  - *Where* will the task be done?
  - *How* will the task be done?
  - *How well* has the functional input been integrated into the project?

The result of these differing views is inevitable conflict between the functional and project manager, as described by William Killian[14]:

> The conflicts revolve about items such as project priority, manpower costs, and the assignment of functional personnel to the project manager. Each project manager will, of course, want the best functional operators assigned to his project. In addition to these problems, the accountability for profit and loss is much more difficult in a matrix organization than in a project organization. Project managers have a tendency to blame overruns on functional managers, stating that the cost of the function was excessive. Whereas functional managers have a tendency to blame excessive costs on project managers with the argument that there were too many changes, more work required than defined initially, and other such arguments.

Major conflicts can also arise during problem resolution sessions because the time constraints imposed on the project often prevent both parties from taking a logical approach. One of the major causes of prolonged problem-solving is a lack of pertinent information. The following information should be reported by the project manager[15]:

- The problem
- The cause
- The expected impact on schedule, budget, profit, or other pertinent area
- The action taken or recommended and the results expected of that action
- What top management can do to help

10.12 MANAGEMENT PITFALLS

The project environment offers numerous opportunities for project managers and team members to get into trouble. Common types of management pitfalls are:

- Lack of self-control (knowing oneself)
- Activity traps
- Managing versus doing
- People versus task skills

---

14. William P. Killian, "Project Management—Future Organizational Concepts," *Marquette Business Review,* Vol. 2, 1971, pp. 90–107.

15. Russell D. Archibald, *Managing High-Technology Programs and Projects* (New York: Wiley, 1976), p. 230.

- Ineffective communications
- Time management
- Management bottlenecks

Knowing oneself, especially one's capabilities, strengths, and weaknesses, is the first step toward successful project management. Too often, managers will assume that they are jacks-of-all-trades, will "bite off more than they can chew," and then find that insufficient time exists for training additional personnel.

The following lines illustrate self-concept:

Four Men

It chanced upon a winter's night
Safe sheltered from the weather.
The board was spread for only one,
Yet four men dined together.
There sat the man I meant to be
In glory, spurred and booted.
And close beside him, to the right
The man I am reputed.
The man I think myself to be
His seat was occupying
Hard by the man I really am
To hold his own was trying.
And all beneath one roof we met
Yet none called his fellow brother
No sign of recognition passed
They knew not one another.

Author unknown

Activity traps result when the means become the end, rather than the means to achieve the end. The most common activity traps are team meetings, customer–technical interchange meetings, and the development of special schedules and charts that cannot be used for customer reporting but are used to inform upper-level management of project status. Sign-off documents are another activity trap and managers must evaluate whether all this paperwork is worth the effort.

We previously defined a characteristic of poor leadership as the inability to obtain a balance between management functions and technical functions. This can easily develop into an activity trap where the individual becomes a doer rather than a manager. Unfortunately, there often exists a very fine line between managing and doing. As an example, consider a project manager who was asked by one of his technical people to make a telephone call to assist him in solving a problem. Simply making the phone call is doing work that should be done by the project team members or even the functional manager. However, if the person being called requires that someone in absolute authority be included in the conversation, then this can be considered managing instead of doing.

There are several other cases where one must become a doer in order to be an effective manager and command the loyalty and respect of subordinates. Assume a special situation where you must schedule subordinates to work overtime on holidays or weekends.

By showing up at the plant during these times, just to make a brief appearance, you can create a better working atmosphere and understanding with the subordinates.

Another major pitfall is the decision to utilize either people skills or task skills. Is it better to utilize subordinates with whom you can obtain a good working relationship or to employ highly skilled people simply to get the job done? Obviously, the project manager would like nothing better than to have the best of both worlds, but this is not always possible. Consider the following situations:

- There is a task that will take three weeks to complete. John has worked for you before, but not on such a task as this. John, however, understands how to work with you. Paul is very competent but likes to work alone. He can get the job done within constraints. Should you employ people or task skills? (Would your answer change if the task were three months instead of three weeks?)
- There exist three tasks, each one requiring two months of work. Richard has the necessary people skills to handle all three tasks, but he will not be able to do so as efficiently as a technical specialist. The alternate choice is to utilize three technical specialists.

Based on the amount of information given, the author prefers task skills so as not to hinder the time or performance constraints on the project. Generally speaking, for long-duration projects that require constant communications with the customer, it might be better to have permanently assigned employees who can perform a variety of tasks. Customers dislike seeing a steady stream of new faces.

It is often said that a good project manager must be willing to work sixty to eighty hours a week to get the job done. This might be true if he is continually fighting fires or if budgeting constraints prevent employing additional staff. The major reason, however, is the result of ineffective time management. Prime examples might include the continuous flow of paperwork, unnecessary meetings, unnecessary phone calls, and acting as a tour guide for visitors.

- To be effective, the project manager must establish time management rules and then ask himself four questions:
  - What am I doing that I don't have to be doing at all?
  - What am I doing that can be done better by someone else?
  - What am I doing that could be done sufficiently well by someone else?
  - Am I establishing the right priorities for my activities?
- Rules for time management
  - Conduct a time analysis (time log)
  - Plan solid blocks for important things
  - Classify your activities
  - Establish priorities
  - Establish opportunity cost on activities
  - Train your system (boss, subordinate, peers)
  - Practice delegation
  - Practice calculated neglect
  - Practice management by exception
  - Focus on opportunities—not on problems

10.13 COMMUNICATIONS

PMBOK® Guide, 2004
Chapter 10 Project
Communications Management

Effective project communications ensure that we get the right information to the right person at the right time and in a cost-effective manner. Proper communication is vital to the success of a project. Typical definitions of effective communication include:

● An exchange of information
● An act or instance of transmitting information
● A verbal or written message
● A technique for expressing ideas effectively
● A process by which meanings are exchanged between individuals through a common system of symbols

The communications environment can be regarded as a network of channels. Most channels are two-way channels. The number of two-way channels, N, can be calculated from the formula

$$N = \frac{X(X - 1)}{2}$$

In this formula, X represents the number of people communicating with each other. For example, if four people are communicating (i.e., $X = 4$), then there are six two-way channels.

When a breakdown in communications occurs, disaster follows, as Figure 10–12 demonstrates.

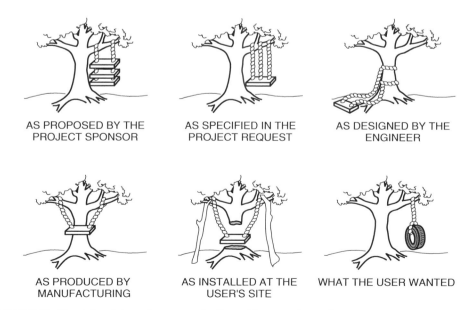

AS PROPOSED BY THE
PROJECT SPONSOR

AS SPECIFIED IN THE
PROJECT REQUEST

AS DESIGNED BY THE
ENGINEER

AS PRODUCED BY
MANUFACTURING

AS INSTALLED AT THE
USER'S SITE

WHAT THE USER WANTED

FIGURE 10–12. A breakdown in communications. (Source unknown)

Figures 10–13 and 10–14 show typical communications patterns. Some people consider Figure 10–13 "politically incorrect" because project managers should not be identified as talking "down" to people. Most project managers communicate laterally, whereas line managers communicate vertically downward to subordinates. Figure 10–15 shows the complete communication model. The screens or barriers are from one's perception, personality, attitudes, emotions, and prejudices.

PMBOK® Guide, 2004
Sender–Receiver Models

- *Perception barriers* occur because individuals can view the same message in different ways. Factors influencing perception include the individual's level of education and region of experience. Perception problems can be minimized by using words that have precise meaning.
- *Personality and interests,* such as the likes and dislikes of individuals, affect communications. People tend to listen carefully to topics of interest but turn a deaf ear to unfamiliar or boring topics.
- *Attitudes, emotions, and prejudices* warp our sense of interpretation. Individuals who are fearful or have strong love or hate emotions will tend to protect themselves by distorting the communication process. Strong emotions rob individuals of their ability to comprehend.

Typical barriers that affect the encoding process include:

- Communication goals

PMBOK® Guide, 2004
10.1 Communications Planning

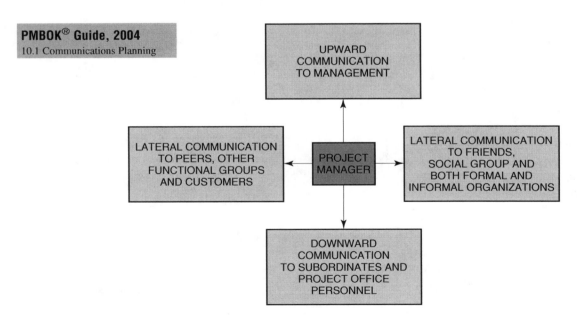

FIGURE 10–13. Communication channels. *Source:* D. I. Cleland and H. Kerzner, *Engineering Team Management* (Melbourne, Florida: Krieger, 1986), p. 39.

PMBOK® Guide, 2004

10.1 Communications Planning

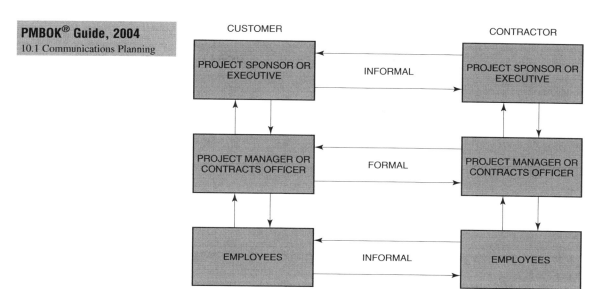

FIGURE 10–14. Customer communications. *Source:* D. I. Cleland and H. Kerzner, *Engineering Team Management* (Melbourne, Florida: Krieger, 1986), p. 64.

PMBOK® Guide, 2004

10.2.2 Information Distribution
10.2.2.1 Communications Skills

- Communication skills
- Frame of reference
- Sender credibility
- Needs
- Personality and interests
- Interpersonal sensitivity

PMBOK® Guide, 2004

Figure 10–3 Communications
   Basic Model

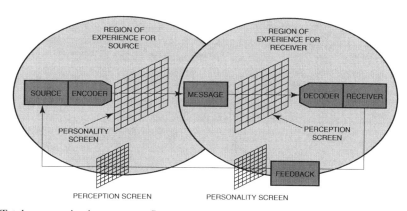

FIGURE 10–15. Total communication process. *Source:* D. I. Cleland and H. Kerzner, *Engineering Team Management* (Melbourne, Florida: Krieger, 1986), p. 46.

- Attitude, emotion, and self-interest
- Position and status
- Assumptions (about receivers)
- Existing relationships with receivers

Typical barriers that affect the decoding process include:

- Evaluative tendency
- Preconceived ideas
- Communication skills
- Frame of reference
- Needs
- Personality and interest
- Attitudes, emotion, and self-interest
- Position and status
- Assumptions about sender
- Existing relationship with sender
- Lack of responsive feedback
- Selective listening

The receiving of information can be affected by the way the information is received. The most common ways include:

- Hearing activity
- Reading skills
- Visual activity
- Tactile sensitivity
- Olfactory sensitivity
- Extrasensory perception

The communications environment is controlled by both the internal and external forces, which can act either individually or collectively. These forces can either assist or restrict the attainment of project objectives.

Typical internal factors include:

- Power games
- Withholding information
- Management by memo
- Reactive emotional behavior
- Mixed messages
- Indirect communications
- Stereotyping
- Transmitting partial information
- Blocking or selective perception

Typical external factors include:

- The business environment
- The political environment
- The economic climate
- Regulatory agencies
- The technical state-of-the-art

The communications environment is also affected by:

- Logistics/geographic separation
- Personal contact requirements
- Group meetings
- Telephone
- Correspondence (frequency and quantity)
- Electronic mail

Noise tends to distort or destroy the information within the message. Noise results from our own personality screens, which dictate the way we present the message, and perception screens, which may cause us to "perceive" what we thought was said. Noise therefore can cause ambiguity:

- Ambiguity causes us to hear what we want to hear.
- Ambiguity causes us to hear what the group wants.
- Ambiguity causes us to relate to past experiences without being discriminatory.

In a project environment, a project manager may very well spend 90 percent or more of his or her time communicating. Typical functional applications include:

- Providing project direction
  - Decision-making
  - Authorizing work
  - Directing activities
  - Negotiating
  - Reporting (including briefings)
- Attending meetings
- Overall project management
- Marketing and selling
- Public relations
- Records management
  - Minutes
  - Memos/letters/newsletters
  - Reports
  - Specifications
  - Contract documents

PMBOK® Guide, 2004
10.2.3 Information Distribution
10.2.3 Outputs

Project managers are required to provide briefings for both internal and external customers. Visual aids can greatly enhance a presentation. Their advantages include:

- Enlivening a presentation, which helps to capture and hold the interest of an audience.
- Adding a visual dimension to an auditory one, which permits an audience to perceive a message through two separate senses, thereby strengthening the learning process.
- Spelling out unfamiliar words by presenting pictures, diagrams, or objects, and by portraying relations graphically, which helps in introducing material that is difficult or new.
- Remaining in view much longer than oral statements can hang in the air, which can serve the same purpose as repetition in acquainting an audience with the unfamiliar and bringing back listeners who stray from the presentation.

Meetings can be classified according to their frequency of occurrence:

- The daily meeting where people work together on the same project with a common objective and reach decisions informally by general agreement.
- The weekly or monthly meeting where members work on different but parallel projects and where there is a certain competitive element and greater likelihood that the chairman will make the final decision himself or herself.
- The irregular, occasional, or special-project meeting, composed of people whose normal work does not bring them into contact and whose work has little or no relationship to that of the others. They are united only by the project the meeting exists to promote and motivated by the desire that the project succeed. Though actual voting is uncommon, every member effectively has a veto.

There are three types of written media used in organizations:

PMBOK® Guide, 2004
10.2.2 Information Distribution

- Individually oriented media: These include letters, memos, and reports.
- Legally oriented media: These include contracts, agreements, proposals, policies, directives, guidelines, and procedures.
- Organizationally oriented media: These include manuals, forms, and brochures.

Because of the time spent in a communications mode, the project manager may very well have as his or her responsibility the process of *communications management*. Communications management is the formal or informal process of conducting or supervising the exchange of information either upward, downward, laterally or diagonally. There appears to be a direct correlation between the project manager's ability to manage the communications process and project performance.

The communications process is more than simply conveying a message; it is also a source for control. Proper communications let the employees in on the act because employees need to know and understand. Communication must convey both information and motivation. The problem, therefore, is how to communicate. Below are six simple steps:

- Think through what you wish to accomplish.
- Determine the way you will communicate.
- Appeal to the interest of those affected.
- Give playback on ways others communicate to you.
- Get playback on what you communicate.
- Test effectiveness through reliance on others to carry out your instructions.

Knowing how to communicate does not guarantee that a clear message will be generated. There are techniques that can be used to improve communications. These techniques include:

- Obtaining feedback, possibly in more than one form
- Establishing multiple communications channels
- Using face-to-face communications if possible
- Determining how sensitive the receiver is to your communications
- Being aware of symbolic meaning such as expressions on people's faces
- Communicating at the proper time
- Reinforcing words with actions
- Using a simple language
- Using redundancy (i.e., saying it two different ways) whenever possible

With every effort to communicate there are always barriers. The barriers include:

- Receiver hearing what he wants to hear. This results from people doing the same job so long that they no longer listen.
- Sender and receiver having different perceptions. This is vitally important in interpreting contractual requirements, statements of work, and proposal information requests.
- Receiver evaluating the source before accepting the communications.
- Receiver ignoring conflicting information and doing as he pleases.
- Words meaning different things to different people.
- Communicators ignoring nonverbal cues.
- Receiver being emotionally upset.

The scalar chain of command can also become a barrier with regard to in-house communications. The project manager must have the authority to go to the general manager or counterpart to communicate effectively. Otherwise, filters can develop and distort the final message.

Three important conclusions can be drawn about communications techniques and barriers:

PMBOK® Guide, 2004

Chapter 10 Communications
Skills

- Don't ssume that the message you sent will be received in the form you sent it.
- The swiftest and most effective communications take place among people with common points of view. The manager who fosters good relationships with his associates will have little difficulty in communicating with them.
- Communications must be established early in the project.

In a project environment, communications are often filtered. There are several reasons for the filtering of upward communications:

- Unpleasantness for the sender
- Receiver cannot obtain information from any other source
- To embarrass a superior
- Lack of mobility or status for the sender
- Insecurity
- Mistrust

Communication is also listening. Good project managers must be willing to listen to their employees, both professionally and personally. The advantages of listening properly are that:

- Subordinates know you are sincerely interested
- You obtain feedback
- Employee acceptance is fostered.

The successful manager must be willing to listen to an individual's story from beginning to end, without interruptions, and to see the problem through the eyes of the subordinate. Finally, before making a decision, the manager should ask the subordinate for his solutions to the problem.

Project managers should ask themselves four questions:

- Do I make it easy for employees to talk to me?
- Am I sympathetic to their problems?
- Do I attempt to improve human relations?
- Do I make an extra effort to remember names and faces?

The project manager's communication skills and personality screen often dictates the communication style. Typical communication styles include:

PMBOK® Guide, 2004

Chapter 10 Communications
Skills

- Authoritarian: gives expectations and specific guidance
- Promotional: cultivates team spirit
- Facilitating: gives guidance as required, noninterfering
- Conciliatory: friendly and agreeable, builds compatible team
- Judicial: uses sound judgment
- Ethical: honest, fair, by the book
- Secretive: not open or outgoing (to project detriment)

TABLE 10—4. COMMUNICATIONS POLICY

Program Manager	Functional Manager	Relationship
The program manager utilizes existing authorized communications media to the maximum extent rather than create new ones.		Communications up, down, and laterally are essential elements to the success of programs in a multiprogram organization, and to the morale and motivation of supporting functional organizations. In principle, communication from the program manager should be channeled through the program team member to functional managers.
Approves program plans, subdivided work description, and/or work authorizations, and schedules defining specific program requirements.	Assures his organization's compliance with all such program direction received.	Program definition must be within the scope of the contract as expressed in the program plan and work breakdown structure.
Signs correspondence that provides program direction to functional organizations. Signs correspondence addressed to the customer that pertains to the program except that which has been expressly assigned by the general manager, the function organizations, or higher management in accordance with division policy.	Assures his organization's compliance with all such program direction received. Functional manager provides the program manager with copies of all "Program" correspondence released by his organization that may affect program performance. Ensures that the program manager is aware of correspondence with unusual content, on an exception basis, through the cognizant program team member or directly if such action is warranted by the gravity of the situation.	In the program manager's absence, the signature authority is transferred upward to his reporting superior unless an acting program manager has been designated. Signature authority for correspondence will be consistent with established division policy.
Reports program results and accomplishments to the customer and to the general manager, keeping them informed of significant problems and events.	Participates in program reviews, being aware of and prepared in matters related to his functional specialty. Keeps his line or staff management and cognizant program team member informed of significant problems and events relating to any program in which his personnel are involved.	Status reporting is the responsibility of functional specialists. The program manager utilizes the specialist organizations. The specialists retain their own channels to the general manager but must keep the program manager informed.

- Disruptive: breaks apart unity of group, agitator
- Intimidating: "tough guy," can lower morale
- Combative: eager to fight or be disagreeable

Team meetings are often used to exchange valuable and necessary information. The following are general guides for conducting more effective meetings:

PMBOK® Guide, 2004
Chapter 10
10.3 Performance Reporting

- Start on time. If you wait for people, you reward tardy behavior.
- Develop agenda "objectives." Generate a list and proceed; avoid getting hung up on the order of topics.
- Conduct one piece of business at a time.
- Allow each member to contribute in his own way. Support, challenge, and counter; view differences as helpful; dig for reasons or views.
- Silence does not always mean agreement. Seek opinions: "What's your opinion on this, Peggy?"
- Be ready to confront the verbal member: "Okay, we've heard from Mike on this matter; now how about some other views?"
- Test for readiness to make a decision.
- Make the decision.
- Test for commitment to the decision.
- Assign roles and responsibilities (only after decision-making).
- Agree on follow-up or accountability dates.
- Indicate the next step for this group.
- Set the time and place for the next meeting.
- End on time.
- Ask yourself if the meeting was necessary.

Many times, company policies and procedures can be established for the development of communications channels. Table 10–4 illustrates such communications guidelines.

10.14 PROJECT REVIEW MEETINGS

Project review meetings are necessary to show that progress is being made on a project. There are three types of review meetings:

- Project team review meetings
- Executive management review meetings
- Customer project review meetings

Most projects have weekly, bimonthly, or monthly meetings in order to keep the project manager and his team informed about the project's status. These meetings are flexible and should be called only if they will benefit the team.

Executive management has the right to require monthly status review meetings. However, if the project manager believes that other meeting dates are better (because they occur at a point where progress can be identified), then he should request them.

Customer review meetings are often the most critical and most inflexibly scheduled. Project managers must allow time to prepare handouts and literature well in advance of the meeting.

10.15 PROJECT MANAGEMENT BOTTLENECKS

Poor communications can easily produce communications bottlenecks. The most common bottleneck occurs when all communications between the customer and the parent organization must flow through the project office. Requiring that all information pass through the project office may be necessary but slows reaction times. Regardless of the qualifications of the project office members, the client always fears that the information he receives will be "filtered" prior to disclosure.

Customers not only like firsthand information, but also prefer that their technical specialists be able to communicate directly with the parent organization's technical specialists. Many project managers dislike this arrangement, for they fear that the technical specialists may say or do something contrary to project strategy or thinking. These fears can be allayed by telling the customer that this situation will be permitted if, and only if, the customer realizes that the remarks made by the technical specialists do not, in any way, shape, or form, reflect the position of the project office or company.

For long-duration projects the customer may require that the contractor have an established customer representative office in the contractor's facilities. The idea behind this

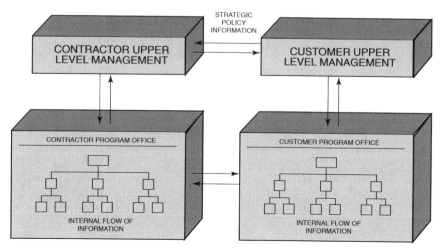

FIGURE 10–16.   Information flow pattern from contractor program office.

is sound in that all information to the customer must flow through the customer's project office at the contractor's facility. This creates a problem in that it attempts to sever direct communications channels between the customer and contractor project managers. The result is the establishment of a local project office to satisfy contractual requirements, while actual communications go from customer to contractor as though the local project office did not exist. This creates an antagonistic local customer project office.

Another bottleneck occurs when the customer's project manager considers himself to be in a higher position than the contractor's project manager and, therefore, seeks some higher authority with which to communicate. Project managers who seek status can often jeopardize the success of the project by creating rigid communications channels.

Figure 10–16 identifies why communications bottlenecks such as these occur. There almost always exist a minimum of two paths for communications flow to and from the customer, which can cause confusion.

10.16 COMMUNICATION TRAPS

PMBOK® Guide, 2004
Chapter 10
10.1.2 Communications Planning

Projects are run by communications. The work is defined by the communications tool known as the work breakdown structure. Actually, this is the easy part of communications, where everything is well defined. Unfortunately, project managers cannot document everything they wish to say or relate to other people, regardless of the level in the company. The worst possible situation occurs when an outside customer loses faith in the contractor. When a situation of mistrust prevails, the logical sequence of events would be:

- More documentation
- More interchange meetings
- Customer representation on your site

In each of these situations, the project manager becomes severely overloaded with work. This situation can also occur in-house when a line manager begins to mistrust a project manager, or vice versa. There may suddenly appear an exponential increase in the flow of paperwork, and everyone is writing "protection" memos. Previously, everything was verbal.

Communication traps occur most frequently with customer–contractor relationships. The following are examples of this:

- Phase I of the program has just been completed successfully. The customer, however, was displeased because he had to wait three weeks to a month after all tests were completed before the data were presented. For Phase II, the customer is insisting that his people be given the raw data at the same time your people receive it.
- The customer is unhappy with the technical information that is being given by the project manager. As a result, he wants his technical people to be able to communicate with your technical people on an individual basis without having to go through the project office.
- You are a subcontractor to a prime contractor. The prime contractor is a little nervous about what information you might present during a technical interchange

meeting where the customer will be represented, and therefore wants to review all material before the meeting.

● Functional employees are supposed to be experts. In front of the customer (or even your top management) an employee makes a statement that you, the project manager, do not believe is completely true or accurate.

● On Tuesday morning, the customer's project manager calls your project manager and asks him a question. On Tuesday afternoon, the customer's project engineer calls your project engineer and asks him the same question.

Communication traps can also occur between the project office and line managers. Below are several examples:

● The project manager holds too many or too few team meetings.

● People refuse to make decisions, and ultimately the team meetings are flooded with agenda items that are irrelevant.

● Last month, Larry completed an assignment as an assistant project manager on an activity where the project manager kept him continuously informed as to project status. Now, Larry is working for a different project manager who tells him only what he needs to know to get the job done.

In a project environment, the line manager is not part of any project team; otherwise he would spend forty hours per week simply attending team meetings. Therefore, how does the line manager learn of the true project status? Written memos will not do it. The information must come firsthand from either the project manager or the assigned functional employee. Line managers would rather hear it from the project manager because line employees have the tendency to censor bad news from the respective line manager. Line managers must be provided true status by the project office.

Sometimes, project managers expect too much from their employees during problem-solving or brainstorming sessions, and communications become inhibited. There are several possible causes for having unproductive team meetings:

● Because of superior–subordinate relationships (i.e., pecking orders), creativity is inhibited.

● All seemingly crazy or unconventional ideas are ridiculed and eventually discarded. Contributors do not wish to contribute anything further.

● Meetings are dominated by upper-level management personnel.

● Many people are not given adequate notification of meeting time and subject matter.

10.17 PROVERBS AND LAWS

Below are twenty project management proverbs that show you what can go wrong[16]:

● You cannot produce a baby in one month by impregnating nine women.

● The same work under the same conditions will be estimated differently by ten different estimators or by one estimator at ten different times.

---

16. Source unknown.

- The most valuable and least used word in a project manager's vocabulary is "NO."
- You can con a sucker into committing to an unreasonable deadline, but you can't bully him into meeting it.
- The more ridiculous the deadline, the more it costs to try to meet it.
- The more desperate the situation, the more optimistic the situatee.
- Too few people on a project can't solve the problems—too many create more problems than they solve.
- You can freeze the user's specs but he won't stop expecting.
- Frozen specs and the abominable snowman are alike: They are both myths, and they both melt when sufficient heat is applied.
- The conditions attached to a promise are forgotten, and the promise is remembered.
- What you don't know hurts you.
- A user will tell you anything you ask about—nothing more.
- Of several possible interpretations of a communication, the least convenient one is the only correct one.
- What is not on paper has not been said.
- No major project is ever installed on time, within budget, with the same staff that started it.
- Projects progress quickly until they become 90 percent complete; then they remain at 90 percent complete forever.
- If project content is allowed to change freely, the rate of change will exceed the rate of progress.
- No major system is ever completely debugged; attempts to debug a system inevitably introduce new bugs that are even harder to find.
- Project teams detest progress reporting because it vividly demonstrates their lack of progress.
- Parkinson and Murphy are alive and well—in your project.

There are thousands of humorous laws covering all subjects, including economics, general business, engineering, management, and politics. The list below shows some of these laws that are applicable to project management:

- **Abbott's Admonitions**
  1. If you have to ask, you're not entitled to know.
  2. If you don't like the answer, you shouldn't have asked the question.
- **Acheson's Rule of the Bureaucracy:** A memorandum is written not to inform the reader but to protect the writer.
- **Anderson's Law:** I have yet to see any problem, however complicated, which, when you looked at it in the right way, did not become still more complicated.
- **Benchley's Law:** Anyone can do any amount of work provided it isn't the work he or she is supposed to be doing at that moment.
- **Bok's Law:** If you think education is expensive—try ignorance.
- **Boling's Postulate:** If you're feeling good, don't worry. You'll get over it.
- **Brook's First Law:** Adding manpower to a late software project makes it later.
- **Brook's Second Law:** Whenever a system becomes completely defined, some damn fool discovers something which either abolishes the system or expands it beyond recognition.

- **Brown's Law of Business Success:** Our customer's paperwork is profit. Our own paperwork is loss.
- **Chisholm's Second Law:** When things are going well, something will go wrong. *Corollaries*
  1. When things just can't get any worse, they will.
  2. Anytime things appear to be going better, you have overlooked something.
- **Cohn's Law:** The more time you spend reporting what you are doing, the less time you have to do anything. Stability is achieved when you spend all your time doing nothing but reporting on the nothing you are doing.
- **Connolly's Law of Cost Control:** The price of any product produced for a government agency will be not less than the square of the initial firm fixed-price contract.
- **Cooke's Law:** In any decisive situation, the amount of relevant information available is inversely proportional to the importance of the decision.
- **Mr. Cooper's Law:** If you do not understand a particular word in a piece of technical writing, ignore it. The piece will make perfect sense without it.
- **Cornuelle's Law:** Authority tends to assign jobs to those least able to do them.
- **Courtois's Rule:** If people listened to themselves more often, they'd talk less.
- **First Law of Debate:** Never argue with a fool. People might not know the difference.
- **Donsen's Law:** The specialist learns more and more about less and less until, finally, he or she knows everything about nothing; whereas the generalist learns less and less about more and more until, finally, he knows nothing about everything.
- **Douglas's Law of Practical Aeronautics:** When the weight of the paperwork equals the weight of the plane, the plane will fly.
- **Dude's Law of Duality:** Of two possible events, only the undesired one will occur.
- **Economists' Laws**
  1. What men learn from history is that men do not learn from history.
  2. If on an actuarial basis there is a 50–50 chance that something will go wrong, it will actually go wrong nine times out of ten.
- **Old Engineer's Law:** The larger the project or job, the less time there is to do it.
- **Nonreciprocal Laws of Expectations**
  1. Negative expectations yield negative results.
  2. Positive expectations yield negative results.
- **Fyffe's Axiom:** The problem-solving process will always break down at the point at which it is possible to determine who caused the problem.
- **Golub's Laws of Computerdom**
  1. Fuzzy project objectives are used to avoid the embarrassment of estimating the corresponding costs.
  2. A carelessly planned project takes three times longer to complete than expected; a carefully planned project takes only twice as long.
  3. The effort required to correct the course increases geometrically with time.
  4. Project teams detest weekly progress reporting because it so vividly manifests their lack of progress.
- **Gresham's Law:** Trivial matters are handled promptly; important matters are never resolved.

- **Hoare's Law of Large Programs:** Inside every large program is a small program struggling to get out.
- **Issawi's Law of Cynics:** Cynics are right nine times out of ten; what undoes them is their belief that they are right ten times out of ten.
- **Johnson's First Law:** When any mechanical contrivance fails, it will do so at the most inconvenient possible time.
- **Malek's Law:** Any simple idea will be worded in the most complicated way.
- **Patton's Law:** A good plan today is better than a perfect plan tomorrow.
- **Peter's Prognosis:** Spend sufficient time in confirming the need and the need will disappear.
- **Law of Political Erosion:** Once the erosion of power begins, it has a momentum all its own.
- **Pudder's Law:** Anything that begins well ends badly. Anything that begins badly ends worse.
- **Putt's Law:** Technology is dominated by two types of people—those who understand what they do not manage and those who manage what they do not understand.
- **Truman's Law:** If you cannot convince them, confuse them.
- **Von Braun's Law of Gravity:** We can lick gravity, but sometimes the paperwork is overwhelming.

10.18 MANAGEMENT POLICIES AND PROCEDURES

Although project managers have the authority and responsibility to establish project policies and procedures, they must fall within the general guidelines established by top management. Table 10–5 identifies sample top-management guidelines. Guidelines can also be established for planning, scheduling, controlling, and communications.

10.19 STUDYING TIPS FOR THE PMI® PROJECT MANAGEMENT CERTIFICATION EXAM

This section is applicable as a review of the principles to support the knowledge areas and domain groups in the PMBOK® Guide. This chapter addresses:

- Human Resources Management
- Communications Management
- Closure

Understanding the following principles is beneficial if the reader is using this text to study for the PMP® Certification Exam:

TABLE 10–5. PROJECT GUIDELINES

Program Manager	Functional Manager	Relationship
The program manager is responsible for overall program direction, control, and coordination; and is the principal contact with the program management of the customer.	The functional organization managers are responsible for supporting the program manager in the performance of the contract(s) and in accordance with the terms of the contract(s) and are accountable to their cognizant managers for the total performance.	The program manager determines what will be done: he obtains, through the assigned program team members, the assistance and concurrence of the functional support organizations in determining the definitive requirements and objectives of the program.
To achieve the program objectives, the program manager utilizes the services of the functional organizations in accordance with the prescribed division policies and procedures affecting the functional organizations.		The functional organizations determine *how* the work will be done.
The program manager establishes program and technical policy as defined by management policy.	The functional support organizations perform all work within their functional areas for all programs within the cost, schedule, quality, and specifications established by contract for the program so as to assist the program manager in achieving the program objectives.	The program manager operates within prescribed division policies and procedures except where requirements of a particular program necessitate deviations or modifications as approved by the general manager. The functional support organizations provide strong, aggressive support to the program managers.
The program manager is responsible for the progress being made as well as the effectiveness of the total program.		
Integrates research, development, production, procurement, quality assurance, product support, test, and financial and contractual aspects.	The functional support organization management seeks out or initiates innovations, methods, improvements, or other means that will enable that function to better schedule commitments, reduce cost, improve quality, or otherwise render exemplary performance as approved by the program manager.	The program manager relies on the functional support program team members for carrying out specific program assignments.
Approves detailed performance specifications, pertinent physical characteristics, and functional design criteria to meet the program's development or operational requirements.		Program managers and the functional support program team members are jointly responsible for ensuring that unresolved conflicts between requirements levied on functional organizations by different program managers are brought to the attention of management.
Ensures preparation of, and approves, overall plan, budgets, and work statements essential to the integration of system elements.		
Directs the preparation and maintenance of a time, cost, and performance schedule to ensure the orderly progress of the program.		

(continues)

301

TABLE 10–5. PROJECT GUIDELINES (*Continued*)

Program Manager	Functional Manager	Relationship
Coordinates and approves subcontract work statement, schedules, contract type, and price for major "buy" items. Coordinates and approves vendor evaluation and source selections in conjunction with procurement representative to the program team. Program decision authority rests with the program manager for all matters relating to his assigned program, consistent with division policy and the responsibilities assigned by the general manager.		Program managers do not make decisions that are the responsibility of the functional support organizations as defined in division policies and procedures and/or as assigned by the general manager. Functional organization managers do not request decisions of a program manager that are not within the program manager's delineated authority and responsibility and that do not affect the requirements of the program. Functional organizations do not make program decisions that are the responsibility of the program manager. Joint participation in problem solution is essential to providing satisfactory decisions that fulfill overall program and company objectives, and is accomplished by the program manager and the assigned program team members. In arriving at program decisions, the program manager obtains the assistance and concurrence of cognizant functional support managers, through the cognizant program team member, since they are held accountable for their support of each program and for overall division functional performance.

- How the various management theories relate to project management
- Various leadership styles
- Different types of power
- Different types of authority
- Need to document authority
- Contributions of Maslow, McGregor, Herzberg, and Ouchi
- Importance of human resources management in project management
- Need to clearly identify each team member's role and responsibility
- Various ways to motivate team members
- That both the project manager and the team are expected to solve their own problems
- That team development is an ongoing process throughout the project life cycle
- Barriers to encoding and decoding
- Need for communication feedback
- Various communication styles
- Types of meetings

The following multiple-choice questions will be helpful in reviewing the principles of this chapter:

1. Which of the following is not one of the sources of authority for a project manager?
   A. Project charter
   B. Job description for a project manager
   C. Delegation from senior management
   D. Delegation from subordinates

2. Which form of power do project managers that have a command of technology and are leading R&D projects most frequently use?
   A. Reward power
   B. Legitimate power
   C. Expert power
   D. Referent power

3. If a project manager possesses penalty (or coercive) power, he or she most likely also possesses:
   A. Reward power
   B. Legitimate power
   C. Expert power
   D. Referent power

4. A project manager with a history of success in meeting deliverables and in working with team members would most likely possess a great deal of:
   A. Reward power
   B. Legitimate power
   C. Expert power
   D. Referent power

5. Most project managers are motivated by which level of Maslow's hierarchy of human needs?
   A. Safety
   B. Socialization
   C. Self-esteem
   D. Self-actualization

6. You have been placed in charge of a project team. The majority of the team members have less than two years of experience working on project teams and most of the people have never worked with you previously. The leadership style you would most likely select would be:
   A. Telling
   B. Selling
   C. Participating
   D. Delegating

7. You have been placed in charge of a new project team and are fortunate to have been assigned the same people that worked for you on your last two projects. Both previous projects were very successful and the team performed as a high-performance team. The leadership style you would most likely use on the new project would be:
   A. Telling
   B. Selling
   C. Participating
   D. Delegating

8. Five people are in attendance in a meeting and are communicating with one another. How many two-way channels of communication are present?
   A. 4
   B. 5
   C. 10
   D. 20

9. A project manager provides a verbal set of instructions to two team members on how to perform a specific test. Without agreeing or disagreeing with the project manager, the two employees leave the project manager's office. Later, the project manager discovers that the tests were not conducted according to his instructions. The most probable cause of failure would be:
   A. Improper encoding
   B. Improper decoding
   C. Improper format for the message
   D. Lack of feedback on instructions

10. A project manager that allows workers to be actively involved with the project manager in making decisions would be using which leadership style.
    A. Passive
    B. Participative/democratic
    C. Autocratic
    D. Laissez-faire

11. A project manager that dictates all decisions and does not allow for any participation by the workers would be using which leadership style.
    A. Passive
    B. Participative/democratic

C. Autocratic
D. Laissez-faire

12. A project manager that allows the team to make virtually all of the decisions without any involvement by the project manager would be using which leadership style.
    A. Passive
    B. Participative/democratic
    C. Autocratic
    D. Laissez-faire

ANSWERS

1. D
2. C
3. A
4. D
5. D
6. A
7. D
8. C
9. D
10. B
11. C
12. D

PROBLEMS

10–1 A project manager finds that he does not have direct reward power over salaries, bonuses, work assignments, or project funding for members of the project team with whom he interfaces. Does this mean that he is totally deficient in reward power? Explain your answer.

10–2 For each of the remarks made below, what types of interpersonal influences could exist?

a. "I've had good working relations with department X. They like me and I like them. I can usually push through anything ahead of schedule."

b. A research scientist was temporarily promoted to project management for an advanced state-of-the-art effort. He was overheard making the following remark to a team member: "I know it's contrary to department policy, but the test must be conducted according to these criteria or else the results will be meaningless."

10–3 Do you agree or disagree that scientists and engineers are likely to be more creative if they feel that they have sufficient freedom in their work? Can this condition backfire?

10–4 Should the amount of risk and uncertainty in the project have a direct bearing on how much authority is granted to a project manager?

10–5 Some projects are directed by project managers who have only monitoring authority. These individuals are referred to as influence project managers. What kind of projects would be under their control? What organizational structure might be best for this?

10–6 As a project nears termination, the project manager may find that the functional people are more interested in finding a new role for themselves than in giving their best to the current situation. How does this relate to Maslow's hierarchy of needs, and what should the project manager do?

10–7 Richard M. Hodgetts ("Leadership Techniques in the Project Organization," *Academy of Management Journal,* June 1968, pp. 211–219) conducted a survey on aerospace, chemical, construction, and state government workers as to whether they would rate the following leadership techniques as very important, important, or not important:

- Negotiation
- Personality and/or persuasive ability
- Competence
- Reciprocal favors

How do you think each industry answered the questionnaires?

10–8 In a project environment, time is a constraint rather than a luxury, and this creates a problem for the project manager who has previously never worked with certain team members. Some people contend that the project manager must create some sort of test to measure, early on, the ability of people to work together as a team.

Is such a test possible for people working in a project environment? Are there any project organizational forms that would be conducive for such testing?

10–9 Project managers consider authority and funding as being very important in gaining support. Functional personnel, however, prefer friendship and work assignments. How can these two outlooks be related to the theories of Maslow and McGregor?

10–10 On large projects, some people become experts at planning while others become experts at implementation. Planners never seem to put on another hat and see the problems of the people doing the implementation whereas the people responsible for implementation never seem to understand the problems of the planners. How can this problem be resolved on a continuous basis?

10–11 What kind of working relationships would result if the project manager had more reward power than the functional managers?

10–12 For each of the following remarks, state the possible situation and accompanying assumptions that you would make.

a. "A good project manager should manage by focusing on keeping people happy."
b. "A good project manager must be willing to manage tension."
c. "The responsibility for the success or failure rests with upper-level management. This is their baby."
d. Remarks by functional employee: "What if I fail on this project? What can he (the project manager) do to me?"

10–13 Can each of the following situations lead to failure?

    a. Lack of expert power
    b. Lack of referent power
    c. Lack of reward and punishment power
    d. Not having sufficient authority

10–14 One of your people comes into your office and states that he has a technical problem and would like your assistance by making a phone call.

    a. Is this managing or doing?
    b. Does your answer depend on who must be called? (That is, is it possible that authority relationships may have to be considered?)

10–15 On the LRC, can we structure the responsibility column to primary and secondary responsibilities?

10–16 Discuss the meaning of each of the two poems listed below:

> We shall have to evolve
> Problem solvers galore
> Since each problem they solve
> Creates ten problems more.
> *Author unknown*

> Jack and Jill went up the hill
>   To fetch a pail of water
> Jack fell down and broke his crown
>   And Jill came tumbling after.

> Jack could have avoided this awful lump
>   By seeking alternative choices
> Like installing some pipe and a great big pump
>   And handing Jill the invoices.[17]

10–17 What is the correct way for a project manager to invite line managers to attend team meetings?

10–18 Can a project manager sit and wait for things to happen, or should he cause things to happen?

10–19 The company has just hired a fifty-four-year-old senior engineer who holds two masters degrees in engineering disciplines. The engineer is quite competent and has worked well as a loner for the past twenty years. This same engineer has just been assigned to the R&D phase of your project. You, as project manager or project engineer, must make sure that this engineer works as a team member with other functional employees, not as a loner. How do you propose to accomplish this? If the individual persists in wanting to be a loner, should you fire him?

---

17. Stacer Holcomb, OSD (SA), as quoted in *The C/E Newsletter*, publication of the cost effectiveness section of the Operations Research Society of America, Vol. 2, No. 1, January 1967.

10–20 Suppose the linear responsibility chart is constructed with the actual names of the people involved, rather than just their titles. Should this chart be given to the customer?

10–21 How should a functional manager handle a situation where the project manager:

    a. Continually cries wolf concerning some aspect of the project when, in fact, the problem either does not exist or is not as severe as the project manager makes it out to be?

    b. Refuses to give up certain resources that are no longer needed on the project?

10–22 How do you handle a project manager or project engineer who continually tries to "bite off more than he can chew?" If he were effective at doing this, at least temporarily, would your answer change?

10–23 A functional manager says that he has fifteen people assigned to work on your project next week (according to the project plan and schedule). Unfortunately, you have just learned that the prototype is not available and that these fifteen people will have nothing to do. Now what? Who is at fault?

10–24 Manpower requirements indicate that a specific functional pool will increase sharply from eight to seventeen people over the next two weeks and then drop back to eight people. Should you question this?

10–25 Below are several sources from which legal authority can be derived. State whether each source provides the project manager with sufficient authority from which he can effectively manage the project.

    a. The project or organizational charter
    b. The project manager's position in the organization
    c. The job description and specifications for project managers
    d. Policy documents
    e. The project manager's "executive" rank
    f. Dollar value of the contract
    g. Control of funds

10–26 Is this managing or doing?[18]

MANAGING	DOING	
_____	_____	1. Making a call with one of your people to assist him in solving a technical problem.
_____	_____	2. Signing a check to approve a routine expenditure.
_____	_____	3. Conducting the initial screening interview of a job applicant.
_____	_____	4. Giving one of your experienced people your solution to a new problem without first asking for his recommendation.
_____	_____	5. Giving your solution to a recurring problem that one of your new people has just asked you about.
_____	_____	6. Conducting a meeting to explain to your people a new procedure.

18. From Raymond O. Leon, *Manage More by Doing Less* (New York: McGraw-Hill), p. 4. Copyright © 1971 by McGraw-Hill, Inc., New York. Used with permission of McGraw-Hill Book Company.

————	————	7. Phoning a department to request help in solving a problem that one of your people is trying to solve.
————	————	8. Filling out a form to give one of your people a pay increase.
————	————	9. Explaining to one of your people why he is receiving a merit pay increase.
————	————	10. Deciding whether to add a position.
————	————	11. Asking one of your people what he thinks about an idea you have that will affect your people.
————	————	12. Transferring a desirable assignment from employee A to employee B because employee A did not devote the necessary effort.
————	————	13. Reviewing regular written reports to determine your people's progress toward their objectives.
————	————	14. Giving a regular progress report by phone to your supervisor.
————	————	15. Giving a tour to an important visitor from outside of your organization.
————	————	16. Drafting an improved layout of facilities.
————	————	17. Discussing with your key people the extent to which they should use staff services during the next year.
————	————	18. Deciding what your expense-budget request will be for your area of responsibility.
————	————	19. Attending a professional or industrial meeting to learn detailed technical developments.
————	————	20. Giving a talk on your work activities to a local community group.

10–27 Below are three broad statements describing the functions of management. For each statement, are we referring to upper-level management, project management, or functional management?

    a. Acquire the best available assets and try to improve them.

    b. Provide a good working environment for all personnel.

    c. Make sure that all resources are applied effectively and efficiently such that all constraints are met, if possible.

10–28 Decide whether you agree or disagree that, in the management of people, the project manager:

- Must convert mistakes into learning experiences.
- Acts as the lubricant that eases the friction (i.e., conflicts) between the functioning parts.

10–29 Functional employees are supposed to be the experts. A functional employee makes a statement that the project manager does not believe is completely true or accurate. Should the project manager support the team member? If so, for how long? Does your answer depend on to whom the remarks are being addressed, such as upper-level management or the customer? At what point should a project manager stop supporting his team members?

10–30 Below are four statements: two statements describe a function, and two others describe a purpose. Which statements refer to project management and which refer to functional management?

- Function
  - Reduce or eliminate uncertainty
  - Minimize and assess risk
- Purpose
  - Create the environment (using transformations)
  - Perform decision-making in the transformed environment

10–31 Manager A is a department manager with thirty years of experience in the company. For the last several years, he has worn two hats and acted as both project manager and functional manager on a variety of projects. He is an expert in his field. The company has decided to incorporate formal project management and has established a project management department. Manager B, a thirty-year-old employee with three years of experience with the company, has been assigned as project manager. In order to staff his project, manager B has requested from manager A that manager C (a personal friend of manager B) be assigned to the project as the functional representative. Manager C is twenty-six years old and has been with the company for two years. Manager A agrees to the request and informs manager C of his new assignment, closing with the remarks, "This project is yours all the way. I don't want to have anything to do with it. I'll be too busy with paperwork as the result of our new organizational structure. Just send me a memo once in a while telling me what's happening."

During the project kickoff meeting it became obvious to both manager B and manager C that the only person with the necessary expertise was manager A. Without the support of manager A, the time duration for project completion could be expected to double.

This situation is ideal for role playing. Put yourself in the place of managers A, B, and C and discuss the reasons for your actions. How can this problem be overcome? How do you get manager A to support the project? Who should inform upper-level management of this situation? When should upper-level management be informed? Would any of your answers change if manager B and manager C were not close friends?

10–32 Is it possible for a product manager to have the same degree of tunnel vision that a project manager has? If so, under what circumstances?

10–33 Your company has a policy that employees can participate in an educational tuition reimbursement program, provided that the degree obtained will benefit the company and that the employee's immediate superior gives his permission. As a project manager, you authorize George, your assistant project manager who reports directly to you, to take courses leading to an MBA degree.

Midway through your project, you find that overtime is required on Monday and Wednesday evenings, the same two evenings that George has classes. George cannot change the evenings that his classes are offered. You try without success to reschedule the overtime to early mornings or other evenings. According to company policy, the project office must supervise all overtime. Since the project office consists of only you and George, you must perform the overtime if George does not. How should you handle this situation? Would your answer change if you thought that George might leave the company after receiving his degree?

10–34 Establishing good interface relationships between the project manager and functional manager can take a great deal of time, especially during the conversion from a traditional to a project organizational form. Below are five statements that represent the different stages in the development of a good interface relationship. Place these statements in the proper order and discuss the meaning of each one.

a. The project manager and functional manager meet face-to-face and try to work out the problem.
b. Both the project and functional managers deny that any problems exist between them.
c. The project and functional managers begin formally and informally to anticipate the problems that can occur.
d. Both managers readily admit responsibility for several of the problems.
e. Each manager blames the other for the problem.

10–35 John is a functional support manager with fourteen highly competent individuals beneath him. John's main concern is performance. He has a tendency to leave scheduling and cost problems up to the project managers. During the past two months, John has intermittently received phone calls and casual visits from upper-level management and senior executives asking him about his department's costs and schedules on a variety of projects. Although he can answer almost all of the performance questions, he has experienced great difficulty in responding to time and cost questions. John is a little apprehensive that if this situation continues, it may affect his evaluation and merit pay increase. What are John's alternatives?

10–36 Projects have a way of providing a "chance for glory" for many individuals. Unfortunately, they quite often give the not-so-creative individual an opportunity to demonstrate his incompetence. Examples would include the designer who always feels that he has a better way of laying out a blueprint, or the individual who intentionally closes a door when asked to open it, or vice versa. How should a project manager handle this situation? Would your answer change if the individual were quite competent but always did the opposite just to show his individuality? Should these individuals be required to have close supervision? If close supervision is required, should it be the responsibility of the functional manager, the project office, or both?

10–37 Are there situations in which a project manager can wait for long-term changes instead of an immediate response to actions?

10–38 Is it possible for functional employees to have performed a job so long or so often that they no longer listen to the instructions given by the project or functional managers?

10–39 On Tuesday morning, the customer's project manager calls the subcontractor's project manager and asks him a question. On Tuesday afternoon, the customer's project engineer calls the contractor's project engineer and asks him the same question. How do you account for this? Could this be "planned" by the customer?

10–40 Below are eight common methods that project and functional employees can use to provide communications:

a. Counseling sessions
b. Telephone conversation
c. Individual conversation
d. Formal letter
e. Project office memo
f. Project office directive
g. Project team meeting
h. Formal report

For each of the following actions, select one and only one means of communication from the above list that you would utilize in accomplishing the action:

1. Defining the project organizational structure to functional managers
2. Defining the project organizational structure to team members
3. Defining the project organizational structure to executives
4. Explaining to a functional manager the reasons for conflict between his employee and your assistant project managers
5. Requesting overtime because of schedule slippages
6. Reporting an employee's violation of company policy

MANAGEMENT FUNCTIONS

7. Reporting an employee's violation of project policy
8. Trying to solve a functional employee's grievance
9. Trying to solve a project office team member's grievance
10. Directing employees to increase production
11. Directing employees to perform work in a manner that violates company policy
12. Explaining the new indirect project evaluation system to project team members
13. Asking for downstream functional commitment of resources
14. Reporting daily status to executives or the customer
15. Reporting weekly status to executives or the customer
16. Reporting monthly or quarterly status to executives or the customer
17. Explaining the reason for the cost overrun
18. Establishing project planning guidelines
19. Requesting a vice president to attend your team meeting
20. Informing functional managers of project status
21. Informing functional team members of project status
22. Asking a functional manager to perform work not originally budgeted for
23. Explaining customer grievances to your people
24. Informing employees of the results of customer interchange meetings
25. Requesting that a functional employee be removed from your project because of incompetence

10–41 Last month, Larry completed an assignment as chief project engineering on project X. It was a pleasing assignment. Larry, and all of the other project personnel, were continually kept informed (by the project manager) concerning all project activities. Larry is now working for a new project manager who tells his staff only what they have to know in order to get their job done. What can Larry do about this situation? Can this be a good situation?

10–42 Phase I of a program has just been completed successfully. The customer, however, was displeased because he always had to wait three weeks to a month after all tests were complete before data were supplied by the contractor.

For Phase II of the program, the customer is requiring that advanced quality control procedures be adhered to. This permits the customer's quality control people to observe all testing and obtain all of the raw data at the same time the contractor does. Is there anything wrong with this arrangement?

10–43 You are a subcontractor to company Z, who in turn is the prime contractor to company Q. Before any design review or technical interchange meeting, company Z requires that they review all material to be presented both in-house and with company Q prior to the meeting. Why would a situation such as this occur? Is it beneficial?

10–44 Referring to Problem 10–43, during contract negotiations between company Q and company Z, you, as project manager for the subcontractor, are sitting in your office when the phone rings. It is company Q requesting information to support its negotiation position. Should you provide the information?

10–45 How does a project manager find out if the project team members from the functional departments have the authority to make decisions?

10–46 One of your functional people has been assigned to perform a certain test and document the results. For two weeks you "hound" this individual only to find out that he is continually procrastinating on work in another program. You later find out from one of his co-workers that he hates to write. What should you do?

10–47 During a crisis, you find that all of the functional managers as well as the team members are writing letters and memos to you, whereas previously everything was verbal. How do you account for this?

10–48 Below are several problems that commonly occur in project organizations. State, if possible, the effect that each problem could have on communications and time management:

    a. People tend to resist exploration of new ideas.
    b. People tend to mistrust each other in temporary management situations.
    c. People tend to protect themselves.
    d. Functional people tend to look at day-to-day activities rather than long-range efforts.
    e. Both functional and project personnel often look for individual rather than group recognition.
    f. People tend to create win-or-lose positions.

10–49 How can executives obtain loyalty and commitments from horizontal and vertical personnel in a project organizational structure?

10–50 What is meant by polarization of communications? What are the most common causes?

10–51 Many project managers contend that project team meetings are flooded with agenda items, many of which may be irrelevant. How do you account for this?

10–52 Paul O. Gaddis ("The Project Manager," *Harvard Business Review,* May–June 1959, p. 90, copyright © 1959 by the President and Fellows of Harvard College. All rights reserved) has stated that:

> In learning to manage a group of professional employees, the usual boss–subordinate relationship must be modified. Of special importance, the how—the details or methods of work performance by a professional employee—should be established by the employee. It follows that he must be given the facts necessary to permit him to develop a rational understanding of the why of tasks assigned to him.

How would you relate this information to the employee?

10–53 The customer has asked to have a customer representative office set up in the same building as the project office. As project manager, you put the customer's office at the opposite end of the building from where you are, and on a different floor. The customer states that he wants his office next to yours. Should this be permitted, and, if so, under what conditions?

10–54 During an interchange meeting from the customer, one of the functional personnel makes a presentation stating that he personally disagrees with the company's solution to the particular problem under discussion and that the company is "all wet" in its approach. How do you, as a project manager, handle this situation?

10–55 Do you agree or disagree with the statement that documenting results "forces" people to learn?

10–56 Should a project manager encourage the flow of problems to him? If yes, should he be selective in which ones to resolve?

10–57 Is it possible for a project manager to hold too few project review meetings?

10–58 If all projects are different, should there exist a uniform company policies and procedures manual?

10–59 Of the ten items below, which are considered as part of directing and which are controlling?

    a. Supervising
    b. Communicating
    c. Delegating
    d. Evaluating
    e. Measuring
    f. Motivating
    g. Coordinating
    h. Staffing
    i. Counseling
    j. Correcting

10–60 Which of the following items is not considered to be one of the seven Ms of management?

    a. Manpower
    b. Money
    c. Machines
    d. Methods
    e. Materials
    f. Minutes
    g. Mission

10–61 Match the following leadership styles (source unknown):

1. Management by inaction _____	a. Has an executive who manages with flair, wisdom, and vision. He listens to his people, prods them, and leads them.
2. Management by detail _____	
3. Management by invisibility _____	
4. Management by consensus _____	
5. Management by manipulation _____	b. Grows out of fear and anxiety.
6. Management by rejection _____	c. Can be fair or unfair, effective or ineffective, legitimate or illegitimate. Some people are manipulators of others for power. People are not puppets.
7. Management by survival _____	
8. Management by depotism _____	
9. Management by creativity _____	
10. Management by leadership _____	
_____	d. Is the roughly negative style. Executive always has ideas; devil's advocate. Well-prepared proponents can win—so such a boss can be stimulating.
_____	e. Has an executive who needs every conceivable fact; is methodical and orderly; often is timid, inappropriate, or late.
_____	f. Is good as long as it is based on reality. The executive has a trained instinct.

_____ g. Has an executive who will do anything to survive—the jungle fighter. If
it is done constructively, the executive will build instead of destroy.

_____ h. Is totalitarian. There are no clashes of
ideas. The organization moves. Crea-
tive people flee. Employees always
know who is boss.

_____ i. Has an executive who is not around,
has good subordinates, and works in
an office, offstage.

_____ j. Can be important in dealing with the
unknown (R&D projects). Subordinates are independent and powerful.
This style could be a substitute for
decision-making. It is important for
setting policy.

CASE STUDIES

THE TROPHY PROJECT

The ill-fated Trophy Project was in trouble right from the start. Reichart, who had been an assistant project manager, was involved with the project from its conception. When the Trophy Project
was accepted by the company, Reichart was assigned as the project manager. The program schedules started to slip from day one, and expenditures were excessive. Reichart found that the functional managers were charging direct labor time to his project but working on their own "pet"
projects. When Reichart complained of this, he was told not to meddle in the functional manager's
allocation of resources and budgeted expenditures. After approximately six months, Reichart was
requested to make a progress report directly to corporate and division staffs.

Reichart took this opportunity to bare his soul. The report substantiated that the project
was forecasted to be one complete year behind schedule. Reichart's staff, as supplied by the line
managers, was inadequate to stay at the required pace, let alone make up any time that had already been lost. The estimated cost at completion at this interval showed a cost overrun of at
least 20 percent. This was Reichart's first opportunity to tell his story to people who were in a
position to correct the situation. The result of Reichart's frank, candid evaluation of the Trophy
Project was very predictable. Nonbelievers finally saw the light, and the line managers realized
that they had a role to play in the completion of the project. Most of the problems were now
out in the open and could be corrected by providing adequate staffing and resources. Corporate
staff ordered immediate remedial action and staff support to provide Reichart a chance to bail
out his program.

The results were not at all what Reichart had expected. He no longer reported to the project office; he now reported directly to the operations manager. Corporate staff's interest in the

project became very intense, requiring a 7:00 A.M. meeting every Monday morning for complete review of the project status and plans for recovery. Reichart found himself spending more time preparing paperwork, reports, and projections for his Monday morning meetings than he did administering the Trophy Project. The main concern of corporate was to get the project back on schedule. Reichart spent many hours preparing the recovery plan and establishing manpower requirements to bring the program back onto the original schedule.

Group staff, in order to closely track the progress of the Trophy Project, assigned an assistant program manager. The assistant program manager determined that a sure cure for the Trophy Project would be to computerize the various problems and track the progress through a very complex computer program. Corporate provided Reichart with twelve additional staff members to work on the computer program. In the meantime, nothing changed. The functional managers still did not provide adequate staff for recovery, assuming that the additional manpower Reichart had received from corporate would accomplish that task.

After approximately $50,000 was spent on the computer program to track the problems, it was found that the program objectives could not be handled by the computer. Reichart discussed this problem with a computer supplier and found that $15,000 more was required for programming and additional storage capacity. It would take two months for installation of the additional storage capacity and the completion of the programming. At this point, the decision was made to abandon the computer program.

Reichart was now a year and a half into the program with no prototype units completed. The program was still nine months behind schedule with the overrun projected at 40 percent of budget. The customer had been receiving his reports on a timely basis and was well aware of the fact that the Trophy Project was behind schedule. Reichart had spent a great deal of time with the customer explaining the problems and the plan for recovery. Another problem that Reichart had to contend with was that the vendors who were supplying components for the project were also running behind schedule.

One Sunday morning, while Reichart was in his office putting together a report for the client, a corporate vice president came into his office. "Reichart," he said, "in any project I look at the top sheet of paper and the man whose name appears at the top of the sheet is the one I hold responsible. For this project your name appears at the top of the sheet. If you cannot bail this thing out, you are in serious trouble in this corporation." Reichart did not know which way to turn or what to say. He had no control over the functional managers who were creating the problems, but he was the person who was being held responsible.

After another three months the customer, becoming impatient, realized that the Trophy Project was in serious trouble and requested that the division general manager and his entire staff visit the customer's plant to give a progress and "get well" report within a week. The division general manager called Reichart into his office and said, "Reichart, go visit our customer. Take three or four functional line people with you and try to placate him with whatever you feel is necessary." Reichart and four functional line people visited the customer and gave a four-and-a-half-hour presentation defining the problems and the progress to that point. The customer was very polite and even commented that it was an excellent presentation, but the content was totally unacceptable. The program was still six to eight months late, and the customer demanded progress reports on a weekly basis. The customer made arrangements to assign a representative in Reichart's department to be "on-site" at the project on a daily basis and to interface with Reichart and his staff as required. After this turn of events, the program became very hectic.

The customer representative demanded constant updates and problem identification and then became involved in attempting to solve these problems. This involvement created many changes in the program and the product in order to eliminate some of the problems. Reichart had trouble with the customer and did not agree with the changes in the program. He expressed his disagreement vocally when, in many cases, the customer felt the changes were at no cost. This caused a deterioration of the relationship between client and producer.

One morning Reichart was called into the division general manager's office and introduced to Mr. "Red" Baron. Reichart was told to turn over the reins of the Trophy Project to Red immediately. "Reichart, you will be temporarily reassigned to some other division within the corporation. I suggest you start looking outside the company for another job." Reichart looked at Red and asked, "Who did this? Who shot me down?"

Red was program manager on the Trophy Project for approximately six months, after which, by mutual agreement, he was replaced by a third project manager. The customer reassigned his local program manager to another project. With the new team the Trophy Project was finally completed one year behind schedule and at a 40 percent cost overrun.

LEADERSHIP EFFECTIVENESS (A)

Instructions   This tabulation form on page 321 is concerned with a comparison of personal supervisory styles. Indicate your preference to the two alternatives after each item by writing appropriate figures in the blanks. Some of the alternatives may seem equally attractive or unattractive to you. Nevertheless, please attempt to choose the alternative that is relatively more characteristic of you. For each question given, you have three (3) points that you may distribute in any of the following combinations:

A. If you agree with alternative (a) and disagree with (b), write 3 in the top blank and 0 in bottom blank.
   a. 3
   b. 0

B. If you agree with (b) and disagree with (a), write:
   a. 0
   b. 3

C. If you have a slight preference for (a) over (b), write:
   a. 2
   b. 1

D. If you have a slight preference for (b) over (a), write:
   a. 1
   b. 2

Important—Use only the combinations shown above. Try to relate each item to your own personal experience. Please make a choice from every pair of alternatives.

   1. On the job, a project manager should make a decision and . . .

   a. _____ tell his team to carry it out.

   b. _____ "tell" his team about the decision and then try to "sell" it.

2. After a project manager has arrived at a decision . . .

   a. _____ he should try to reduce the team's resistance to his decision by indicating what they have to gain.

   b. _____ he should provide an opportunity for his team to get a fuller explanation of his ideas.

3. When a project manager presents a problem to his subordinates . . .

   a. _____ he should get suggestions from them and then make a decision.

   b. _____ he should define it and request that the group make a decision.

4. A project manager . . .

   a. _____ is paid to make all the decisions affecting the work of his team.

   b. _____ should commit himself in advance to assist in implementing whatever decision his team selects when they are asked to solve a problem.

5. A project manager should . . .

   a. _____ permit his team an opportunity to exert some influence on decisions but reserve final decisions for himself.

   b. _____ participate with his team in group decision-making but attempt to do so with a minimum of authority.

6. In making a decision concerning the work situation, a project manager should . . .

   a. _____ present his decision and ideas and engage in a "give-and-take" session with his team to allow them to fully explore the implications of the decision.

   b. _____ present the problem to his team, get suggestions, and then make a decision.

7. A good work situation is one in which the project manager . . .

   a. _____ "tells" his team about a decision and then tries to "sell" it to them.

   b. _____ calls his team together, presents a problem, defines the problem, and requests they solve the problem with the understanding that he will support their decision(s).

8. A well-run project will include . . .

   a. _____ efforts by the project manager to reduce the team's resistance to his decisions by indicating what they have to gain from them.

   b. _____ "give-and take" sessions to enable the project manager and team to explore more fully the implications of the project manager's decisions.

9. A good way to deal with people in a work situation is . . .

   a. _____ to present problems to your team as they arise, get suggestions, and then make a decision.

   b. _____ to permit the team to make decisions, with the understanding that the project manager will assist in implementing whatever decision they make.

10. A good project manager is one who takes . . .

    a. _____ the responsibility for locating problems and arriving at solutions, then tries to persuade his team to accept them.

    b. _____ the opportunity to collect ideas from his team about problems, then he makes his decision.

11. A project manager . . .

    a. _____ should make the decisions in his organization and tell his team to carry them out.

    b. _____ should work closely with his team in solving problems, and attempt to do so with a minimum of authority.

12. To do a good job, a project manager should . . .

    a. _____ present solutions for his team's reaction.

    b. _____ present the problem and collect from the team suggested solutions, then make a decision based on the best solution offered.

13. A good method for a project manager is . . .

    a. _____ to "tell" and then try to "sell" his decision.

    b. _____ to define the problem for his team, then pass them the right to make decisions.

14. On the job, a project manager . . .

    a. _____ need not give consideration to what his team will think or feel about his decisions.

    b. _____ should present his decisions and engage in a "give-and-take" session to enable everyone concerned to explore, more fully, the implications of the decisions.

15. A project manager . . .

    a. _____ should make all decisions himself.

    b. _____ should present the problem to his team, get suggestions, and then make a decision.

16. It is good . . .

    a. _____ to permit the team an opportunity to exert some influence on decisions, but the project manager should reserve final decisions for himself.

    b. _____ for the project manager to participate with his team in group decision-making with as little authority as possible.

17. The project manager who gets the most from his team is the one who . . .

    a. _____ exercises direct authority.

    b. _____ seeks possible solutions from them and then makes a decision.

18. An effective project manager should . . .

a. _____ make the decisions on his project and tell his team to carry them out.

b. _____ make the decisions and then try to persuade his team to accept them.

19. A good way for a project manager to handle work problems is to . . .

a. _____ implement decisions without giving any consideration to what his team will think or feel.

b. _____ permit the team an opportunity to exert some influence on decisions but reserve the final decision for himself.

20. Project managers . . .

a. _____ should seek to reduce the team's resistance to their decisions by indicating what they have to gain from them.

b. _____ should seek possible solutions from their team when problems arise and then make a decision from the list of alternatives.

LEADERSHIP QUESTIONNAIRE
Tabulation Form

	1	2	3	4	5
1	a	b			
2		a	b		
3				a	b
4	a				b
5			a		b
6			a	b	
7		a			b
8		a	b		
9				a	b
10	a		b		
11	a				b
12			a	b	
13		a			b
14	a		b		
15	a			b	
16			a		b
17	a			b	
18	a	b			
19	a		b		
20		a		b	
TOTAL					

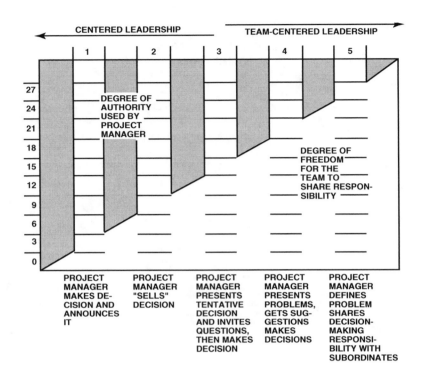

LEADERSHIP EFFECTIVENESS (B)

The Project

PMBOK® Guide, 2004

Chapter 9 Human Resources
Management

Chapter 10 Communications
Management

Domain of Professional
Responsibility

Your company has just won a contract for an outside customer. The contract is for one year, broken down as follows: R&D: six months; prototype testing: one month; manufacturing: five months. In addition to the risks involved in the R&D stage, both your management and the customer have stated that there will be absolutely no trade-offs on time, cost, or performance.

When you prepared the proposal six months ago, you planned and budgeted for a full-time staff of five people, in addition to the functional support personnel. Unfortunately, due to limited resources, your staff (i.e., the project office) will be as follows:

Tom: An excellent engineer, somewhat of a prima donna, but has worked very well with you on previous projects. You specifically requested Tom and were fortunate to have him assigned, although your project is not regarded as a high priority. Tom is recognized as both a technical leader and expert, and is considered as perhaps the best engineer in the company. Tom will be full-time for the duration of the project.

Bob: Started with the company a little over a year ago, and may be a little "wet behind the ears." His line manager has great expectations for him in the future but, for the time being, wants you to give him on-the-job-training as a project office team member. Bob will be full-time on your project.

Carol: She has been with the company for twenty years and does an acceptable job. She has never worked on your projects before. She is full-time on the project.

George: He has been with the company for six years, but has never worked on any of your projects. His superior tells you that he will be only half-time on your project until he finishes a crash job on another project. He should be available for full-time work in a month or two. George is regarded as an outstanding employee.

Management informs you that there is nobody else available to fill the fifth position. You'll have to spread the increased workload over the other members. Obviously, the customer may not be too happy about this.

In each situation that follows, circle the best answer. The grading system will be provided later.

Remember: These staff individuals are "dotted" to you and "solid" to their line manager, although they are in your project office.

Situation 1: The project office team members have been told to report to you this morning. They have all received your memo concerning the time and place of the kickoff meeting. However, they have not been provided any specific details concerning the project except that the project will be at least one year in duration. For your company, this is regarded as a long-term project. A good strategy for the meeting would be:

A. The team must already be self-motivated or else they would not have been assigned. Simply welcome them and assign homework.
B. Motivate the employees by showing them how they will benefit: esteem, pride, self-actualization. Minimize discussion on specifics.
C. Explain the project and ask them for their input. Try to get them to identify alternatives and encourage group decision-making.
D. Identify the technical details of the project: the requirements, performance standards, and expectations.

Situation 2: You give the team members a copy of the winning proposal and a "confidential" memo describing the assumptions and constraints you considered in developing the proposal. You tell your team to review the material and be prepared to perform detailed planning at the meeting you have scheduled for the following Monday. During Monday's planning meeting, you find that Tom (who has worked with you before) has established a take-charge role and has done some of the planning that should have been the responsibility of other team members. You should:

A. Do nothing. This may be a beneficial situation. However, you may wish to ask if the other project office members wish to review Tom's planning.
B. Ask each team member individually how he or she feels about Tom's role. If they complain, have a talk with Tom.
C. Ask each team member to develop his or her own schedules and then compare results.
D. Talk to Tom privately about the long-term effects of his behavior.

Situation 3: Your team appears to be having trouble laying out realistic schedules that will satisfy the customer's milestones. They keep asking you pertinent questions and seem to be making the right decisions, but with difficulty.

A. Do nothing. If the team is good, they will eventually work out the problem.
B. Encourage the team to continue but give some ideas as to possible alternatives. Let them solve the problem.

C. Become actively involved and help the team solve the problem. Supervise the planning until completion.

D. Take charge yourself and solve the problem for the team. You may have to provide continuous direction.

Situation 4: Your team has taken an optimistic approach to the schedule. The functional managers have reviewed the schedules and have sent your team strong memos stating that there is no way that they can support your schedules. Your team's morale appears to be very low. Your team expected the schedules to be returned for additional iterations and trade-offs, but not with such harsh words from the line managers. You should:

A. Take no action. This is common to these types of projects and the team must learn to cope.

B. Call a special team meeting to discuss the morale problem and ask the team for recommendations. Try to work out the problem.

C. Meet with each team member individually to reinforce his or her behavior and performance. Let members know how many other times this has occurred and been resolved through trade-offs and additional iterations. State your availability to provide advice and support.

D. Take charge and look for ways to improve morale by changing the schedules.

Situation 5: The functional departments have begun working, but are still criticizing the schedules. Your team is extremely unhappy with some of the employees assigned out of one functional department. Your team feels that these employees are not qualified to perform the required work. You should:

A. Do nothing until you are absolutely sure (with evidence) that the assigned personnel cannot perform as needed.

B. Sympathize with your team and encourage them to live with this situation until an alternative is found.

C. Assess the potential risks with the team and ask for their input and suggestions. Try to develop contingency plans if the problem is as serious as the team indicates.

D. Approach the functional manager and express your concern. Ask to have different employees assigned.

Situation 6: Bob's performance as a project office team member has begun to deteriorate. You are not sure whether he simply lacks the skills, cannot endure the pressure, or cannot assume part of the additional work that resulted from the fifth position in the project being vacant. You should:

A. Do nothing. The problem may be temporary and you cannot be sure that there is a measurable impact on the project.

B. Have a personal discussion with Bob, seek out the cause, and ask him for a solution.

C. Call a team meeting and discuss how productivity and performance are decreasing. Ask the team for recommendations and hope Bob gets the message.

D. Interview the other team members and see if they can explain Bob's actions lately. Ask the other members to assist you by talking to Bob.

Situation 7: George, who is half-time on your project, has just submitted for your approval his quarterly progress report for your project. After your signature has been attained, the report is sent to senior management and the customer. The report is marginally acceptable and not at all what you would have expected from George. George apologizes to you for the report and blames it on his other project, which is in its last two weeks. You should:

    A. Sympathize with George and ask him to rewrite the report.
    B. Tell George that the report is totally unacceptable and will reflect on his ability as a project office team member.
    C. Ask the team to assist George in redoing the report since a bad report reflects on everyone.
    D. Ask one of the other team members to rewrite the report for George.

Situation 8: You have completed the R&D stage of your project and are entering phase II: prototype testing. You are entering month seven of the twelve-month project. Unfortunately, the results of phase I R&D indicate that you were too optimistic in your estimating for phase II and a schedule slippage of at least two weeks is highly probable. The customer may not be happy. You should:

    A. Do nothing. These problems occur and have a way of working themselves out. The end date of the project can still be met.
    B. Call a team meeting to discuss the morale problem resulting from the slippage. If morale is improved, the slippage may be overcome.
    C. Call a team meeting and seek ways of improving productivity for phase II. Hopefully, the team will come up with alternatives.
    D. This is a crisis and you must exert strong leadership. You should take control and assist your team in identifying alternatives.

Situation 9: Your rescheduling efforts have been successful. The functional managers have given you adequate support and you are back on schedule. You should:

    A. Do nothing. Your team has matured and is doing what they are paid to do.
    B. Try to provide some sort of monetary or nonmonetary reward for your team (e.g., management-granted time off or a dinner team meeting).
    C. Provide positive feedback/reinforcement for the team and search for ideas for shortening phase III.
    D. Obviously, your strong leadership has been effective. Continue this role for the phase III schedule.

Situation 10: You are now at the end of the seventh month and everything is proceeding as planned. Motivation appears high. You should:

    A. Leave well enough alone.
    B. Look for better ways to improve the functioning of the team. Talk to them and make them feel important.
    C. Call a team meeting and review the remaining schedules for the project. Look for contingency plans.
    D. Make sure the team is still focusing on the goals and objectives of the project.

Situation 11: The customer unofficially informs you that his company has a problem and may have to change the design specifications before production actually begins. This would be a catastrophe for your project. The customer wants a meeting at your plant within the next seven days. This will be the customer's first visit to your plant. All previous meetings were informal and at the customer's facilities, with just you and the customer. This meeting will be formal. To prepare for the meeting, you should:

A. Make sure the schedules are updated and assume a passive role since the customer has not officially informed you of his problem.
B. Ask the team to improve productivity before the customer's meeting. This should please the customer.
C. Call an immediate team meeting and ask the team to prepare an agenda and identify the items to be discussed.
D. Assign specific responsibilities to each team member for preparation of handout material for the meeting.

Situation 12: Your team is obviously not happy with the results of the customer interface meeting because the customer has asked for a change in design specifications. The manufacturing plans and manufacturing schedules must be developed anew. You should:

A. Do nothing. The team is already highly motivated and will take charge as before.
B. Reemphasize the team spirit and encourage your people to proceed. Tell them that nothing is impossible for a good team.
C. Roll up your shirt sleeves and help the team identify alternatives. Some degree of guidance is necessary.
D. Provide strong leadership and close supervision. Your team will have to rely on you for assistance.

Situation 13: You are now in the ninth month. While your replanning is going on (as a result of changes in the specifications), the customer calls and asks for an assessment of the risks in cancelling this project right away and starting another one. You should:

A. Wait for a formal request. Perhaps you can delay long enough for the project to finish.
B. Tell the team that their excellent performance may result in a follow-on contract.
C. Call a team meeting to assess the risks and look for alternatives.
D. Accept strong leadership for this and with *minimum,* if any, team involvement.

Situation 14: One of the functional managers has asked for your evaluation of all of his functional employees currently working on your project (excluding project office personnel). Your project office personnel appear to be working more closely with the functional employees than you are. You should:

A. Return the request to the functional manager since this is not part of your job description.
B. Talk to each team member individually, telling them how important their input is, and ask for their evaluations.
C. As a team, evaluate each of the functional team members, and try to come to some sort of agreement.
D. Do not burden your team with this request. You can do it yourself.

Situation 15: You are in the tenth month of the project. Carol informs you that she has the opportunity to be the project leader for an effort starting in two weeks. She has been with the company for twenty years and this is her first opportunity as a project leader. She wants to know if she can be released from your project. You should:

A. Let Carol go. You do not want to stand in the way of her career advancement.
B. Ask the team to meet in private and conduct a vote. Tell Carol you will abide by the team vote.
C. Discuss the problem with the team since they must assume the extra workload, if necessary. Ask for their input into meeting the constraints.
D. Counsel her and explain how important it is for her to remain. You are already short-handed.

Situation 16: Your team informs you that one of the functional manufacturing managers has built up a brick wall around his department and all information requests must flow through him. The brick wall has been in existence for two years. Your team members are having trouble with status reporting, but always get the information after catering to the functional manager. You should:

A. Do nothing. This is obviously the way the line manager wants to run his department. Your team is getting the information they need.
B. Ask the team members to use their behavioral skills in obtaining the information.
C. Call a team meeting to discuss alternative ways of obtaining the information.
D. Assume strong leadership and exert your authority by calling the line manager and asking for the information.

Situation 17: The executives have given you a new man to replace Carol for the last two months of the project. Neither you nor your team have worked with this man before. You should:

A. Do nothing. Carol obviously filled him in on what he should be doing and what is involved in the project.
B. Counsel the new man individually, bring him up to speed, and assign him Carol's work.
C. Call a meeting and ask each member to explain his or her role on the project to the new man.
D. Ask each team member to talk to this man as soon as possible and help him come on board. Request that individual conversations be used.

Situation 18: One of your team members wants to take a late-afternoon course at the local college. Unfortunately, this course may conflict with his workload. You should:

A. Postpone your decision. Ask the employee to wait until the course is offered again.
B. Review the request with the team member and discuss the impact on his performance.
C. Discuss the request with the team and ask for the team's approval. The team may have to cover for this employee's workload.
D. Discuss this individually with each team member to make sure that the task requirements will still be adhered to.

Situation 19: Your functional employees have used the wrong materials in making a production run test. The cost to your project was significant, but absorbed in a small "cushion" that you saved for emergencies such as this. Your team members tell you that the test will be rerun without any slippage of the schedule. You should:

A. Do nothing. Your team seems to have the situation well under control.
B. Interview the employees that created this problem and stress the importance of productivity and following instructions.
C. Ask your team to develop contingency plans for this situation should it happen again.
D. Assume a strong leadership role for the rerun test to let people know your concern.

Situation 20: All good projects must come to an end, usually with a final report. Your project has a requirement for a final report. This final report may very well become the basis for follow-on work. You should:

A. Do nothing. Your team has things under control and knows that a final report is needed.
B. Tell your team that they have done a wonderful job and there is only one more task to do.
C. Ask your team to meet and provide an outline for the final report.
D. You must provide some degree of leadership for the final report, at least the structure. The final report could easily reflect on your ability as a manager.

Fill in the table below. The answers appear in Appendix B.

Situation	*Answer*	*Points*	*Situation*	*Answer*	*Points*
1			11		
2			12		
3			13		
4			14		
5			15		
6			16		
7			17		
8			18		
9			19		
10			20		
				Total	

MOTIVATIONAL QUESTIONNAIRE

On the next several pages, you will find forty statements concerning what motivates you and how you try to motivate others. Beside each statement, circle the number that corresponds to your opinion. In the example below, the choice is "Slightly Agree."

−3	Strongly Disagree
−2	Disagree
−1	Slightly Disagree
0	No Opinion
(+1)	Slightly Agree
+2	Agree
+3	Strongly Agree

Part 1

The following twenty statements involve *what motivates you*. Please rate each of the statements as honestly as possible. Circle the rating that you think is correct, *not* the one you think the instructor is looking for:

1. My company pays me a reasonable salary for the work that I do. —3 —2 —1 0 +1 +2 +3

2. My company believes that every job that I do can be considered as a challenge. —3 —2 —1 0 +1 +2 +3

3. The company provides me with the latest equipment (i.e., hardware, software, etc.) so I can do my job effectively. —3 —2 —1 0 +1 +2 +3

4. My company provides me with recognition for work well done. —3 —2 —1 0 +1 +2 +3

5. Seniority on the job, job security, and vested rights are provided by the company. —3 —2 —1 0 +1 +2 +3

6. Executives provide managers with feedback of strategic or long-range information that may affect the manager's job. —3 —2 —1 0 +1 +2 +3

7. My company provides off-hour clubs and organizations so that employees can socialize, as well as sponsoring social events. —3 —2 —1 0 +1 +2 +3

8. Employees are allowed to either set their own work/performance standards or to at least approve/review standards set for them by management. —3 —2 —1 0 +1 +2 +3

9. Employees are encouraged to maintain membership in professional societies and/or attend seminars and symposiums on work-related subjects.

   | −3 | −2 | −1 | 0 | +1 | +2 | +3 |

10. The company often reminds me that the only way to have job security is to compete effectively in the marketplace.

11. Employees who develop a reputation for "excellence" are allowed to further enhance their reputation, if job related.

    | −3 | −2 | −1 | 0 | +1 | +2 | +3 |

12. Supervisors encourage a friendly, cooperative working environment for employees.

    | −3 | −2 | −1 | 0 | +1 | +2 | +3 |

13. My company provides me with a detailed job description, identifying my role and responsibilities.

    | −3 | −2 | −1 | 0 | +1 | +2 | +3 |

14. My company gives *automatic* wage and salary increases for the employees.

    | −3 | −2 | −1 | 0 | +1 | +2 | +3 |

15. My company gives me the opportunity to do what I do best.

    | −3 | −2 | −1 | 0 | +1 | +2 | +3 |

16. My job gives me the opportunity to be truly creative, to the point where I can solve complex problems.

    | −3 | −2 | −1 | 0 | +1 | +2 | +3 |

17. My efficiency and effectiveness is improving because the company provided me with better physical working conditions (i.e., lighting, low noise, temperature, restrooms, etc.)

    | −3 | −2 | −1 | 0 | +1 | +2 | +3 |

18. My job gives me constant self-development.

    | −3 | −2 | −1 | 0 | +1 | +2 | +3 |

19. Our supervisors have feelings for employees rather than simply treating them as "inanimate tools."

    | −3 | −2 | −1 | 0 | +1 | +2 | +3 |

20. Participation in the company's stock option/retirement plan is available to employees.

    | −3 | −2 | −1 | 0 | +1 | +2 | +3 |

Part 2

Statements 21–40 involve how project managers motivate team members. Again, it is important that your ratings honestly reflect the way you think that *you,* as project manager, try to motivate employees. Do *not* indicate the way others or the instructor might recommend motivating the employees. Your thoughts are what are important in this exercise.

21. Project managers should encourage employees to take advantage of company benefits such as stock option plans and retirement plans.

    −3   −2   −1   0   +1   +2   +3

22. Project managers should make sure that team members have a good work environment (i.e., heat, lighting, low noise, restrooms, cafeteria, etc.).

    −3   −2   −1   0   +1   +2   +3

23. Project managers should assign team members work that can enhance each team member's reputation.

    −3   −2   −1   0   +1   +2   +3

24. Project managers should create a relaxed, cooperative environment for the team members.

    −3   −2   −1   0   +1   +2   +3

25. Project managers should *continually* remind the team that job security is a function of competitiveness, staying within constraints, and good customer relations.

    −3   −2   −1   0   +1   +2   +3

26. Project managers should try to convince team members that each new assignment is a challenge.

    −3   −2   −1   0   +1   +2   +3

27. Project managers should be willing to reschedule activities, if possible, around the team's company and out-of-company social functions.

    −3   −2   −1   0   +1   +2   +3

28. Project managers should continually remind employees of how they will benefit, monetarily, by successful performance on your project.

    −3   −2   −1   0   +1   +2   +3

29. Project managers should be willing to "pat people on the back" and provide recognition where applicable.   −3   −2   −1   0   +1   +2   +3

30. Project managers should encourage the team to maintain constant self-development with each assignment.   −3   −2   −1   0   +1   +2   +3

31. Project managers should allow team members to set their own standards, where applicable.   −3   −2   −1   0   +1   +2   +3

32. Project managers should assign work to functional employees according to seniority on the job.   −3   −2   −1   0   +1   +2   +3

33. Project managers should allow team members to use the informal, as well as formal, organization to get work accomplished.   −3   −2   −1   0   +1   +2   +3

34. As a project manager, I would like to control the salaries of the full-time employees on my project.   −3   −2   −1   0   +1   +2   +3

35. Project managers should share information with the team. This includes project information that may not be directly applicable to the team member's assignment.   −3   −2   −1   0   +1   +2   +3

36. Project managers should encourage team members to be creative and to solve their own problems.   −3   −2   −1   0   +1   +2   +3

37. Project managers should provide detailed job descriptions for team members, outlining the team member's role and responsibility.   −3   −2   −1   0   +1   +2   +3

38. Project managers should give each team member the opportunity to do what the team member can do best.   −3   −2   −1   0   +1   +2   +3

39. Project managers should be willing to interact informally with the team members and get to know them, as long as there exists sufficient time on the project.   −3   −2   −1   0   +1   +2   +3

40. Most of the employees on my project earn a salary commensurate with their abilities.   −3   −2   −1   0   +1   +2   +3

Part 1 Scoring Sheet (What Motivates You?)

Place your answers (the numerical values you circled) to questions 1–20 in the corresponding spaces in the chart below.

Basic Needs	*Safety Needs*	*Belonging Needs*
#1 _____	#5 _____	#7 _____
#3 _____	#10 _____	#9 _____
#14 _____	#13 _____	#12 _____
#17 _____	#20 _____	#19 _____
Total _____	Total _____	Total _____

Esteem/Ego Needs	*Self-Actualization Needs*
#4 _____	#2 _____
#6 _____	#15 _____
#8 _____	#16 _____
#11 _____	#18 _____
Total _____	Total _____

Transfer your total score in each category to the table on the following page by placing an "X" in the appropriate area for motivational needs.

Part 2 Scoring Sheet (How Do You Motivate?)

Place your answers (the numerical values you circled) to questions 21–40 in the corresponding spaces in the chart below.

Basic Needs	*Safety Needs*	*Belonging Needs*
#22 _____	#21 _____	#24 _____
#28 _____	#25 _____	#27 _____
#34 _____	#32 _____	#33 _____
#40 _____	#37 _____	#39 _____
Total _____	Total _____	Total _____

Esteem/Ego Needs	*Self-Actualization Needs*
#23 _____	#26 _____
#29 _____	#30 _____
#31 _____	#36 _____
#35 _____	#38 _____
Total _____	Total _____

Transfer your total score in each category to the table on the following page by placing an "X" in the appropriate area for motivational needs.

QUESTIONS 1–20

Points																									
Needs	-12	-11	-10	-9	-8	-7	-6	-5	-4	-3	-2	-1	0	+1	+2	+3	+4	+5	+6	+7	+8	+9	+10	+11	+12
Self-Actualization																									
Esteem/Ego																									
Belonging																									
Safety																									
Basic																									

QUESTIONS 21–40

Points																									
Needs	-12	-11	-10	-9	-8	-7	-6	-5	-4	-3	-2	-1	0	+1	+2	+3	+4	+5	+6	+7	+8	+9	+10	+11	+12
Self-Actualization																									
Esteem/Ego																									
Belonging																									
Safety																									
Basic																									

Management of Your Time and Stress

Related Case Studies (from Kerzner/*Project Management Case Studies,* 2nd Edition)	Related Workbook Exercises (from Kerzner/*Project Management Workbook and PMP®/CAPM® Exam Study Guide,* 9th Edition)	PMBOK® Guide, 3rd Edition, Reference Section for the PMP® Certification Exam
• The Reluctant Workers* • Time Management Exercise	• Multiple Choice Exam	• Human Resource Management • Risk Management

11.0 INTRODUCTION

PMBOK® Guide, 2004
Human Resources Management
Project Time Management

Managing projects within time, cost, and performance is easier said than done. The project management environment is extremely turbulent, and is composed of numerous meetings, report writing, conflict resolution, continuous planning and replanning, communications with the customer, and crisis management. Ideally, the effective project manager is a manager, not a doer, but in the "real world," project managers often compromise their time by doing both.

Disciplined time management is one of the keys to effective project management. It is often said that if the project manager cannot control his own time, then he will control nothing else on the project.

---

*Case Study also appears at end of chapter.

11.1 UNDERSTANDING TIME MANAGEMENT[1]

For most people, time is a resource that, when lost or misplaced, is gone forever. For a project manager, however, time is more of a constraint, and effective time management principles must be employed to make it a resource.

Most executives prefer to understaff projects, in the mistaken belief that the project manager will assume the additional workload. The project manager may already be heavily burdened with meetings, report preparation, internal and external communications, conflict resolution, and planning/replanning for crises. And yet, most project managers somehow manipulate their time to get the work done. Experienced personnel soon learn to delegate tasks and to employ effective time management principles. The following questions should help managers identify problem areas:

- Do you have trouble completing work within the allocated deadlines?
- How many interruptions are there each day?
- Do you have a procedure for handling interruptions?
- If you need a large block of uninterrupted time, is it available? With or without overtime?
- How do you handle drop-in visitors and phone calls?
- How is incoming mail handled?
- Do you have established procedures for routine work?
- Are you accomplishing more or less than you were three months ago? Six months ago?
- How difficult is it for you to say no?
- How do you approach detail work?
- Do you perform work that should be handled by your subordinates?
- Do you have sufficient time each day for personal interests?
- Do you still think about your job when away from the office?
- Do you make a list of things to do? If yes, is the list prioritized?
- Does your schedule have some degree of flexibility?

The project manager who can deal with these questions has a greater opportunity to convert time from a constraint to a resource.

11.2 TIME ROBBERS

The most challenging problem facing the project manager is his inability to say no. Consider the situation in which an employee comes into your office with a problem. The employee may be sincere when he says that he simply wants your advice but, more often

---

1. Sections 11.1, 11.2, and 11.3 are adapted from David Cleland and Harold Kerzner, *Engineering Team Management* (Melbourne, Florida: Krieger, 1986), Chapter 8.

PMBOK® Guide, 2004
Chapter 11 Time Management
Chapter 11 Risk Management
1.5.4 General Management
Knowledge and Skills

than not, the employee wants to take the monkey off of his back and put it onto yours. The employee's problem is now *your* problem.

To handle such situations, first screen out the problems with which you do not wish to get involved. Second, if the situation does necessitate your involvement, then you must make sure that when the employee leaves your office, he realizes that the problem is still his, not yours. Third, if you find that the problem will require your continued attention, remind the employee that all future decisions will be joint decisions and that the problem will still be on the employee's shoulders. Once employees realize that they cannot put their problems on your shoulders, they learn how to make their own decisions.

There are numerous time robbers in the project management environment. These include:

- Incomplete work
- A job poorly done that must be done over
- Telephone calls, mail, and email
- Lack of adequate responsibility and commensurate authority
- Changes without direct notification/explanation
- Waiting for people
- Failure to delegate, or unwise delegation
- Poor retrieval systems
- Lack of information in a ready-to-use format
- Day-to-day administration
- Union grievances
- Having to explain "thinking" to superiors
- Too many levels of review
- Casual office conversations
- Misplaced information
- Shifting priorities
- Indecision at any level
- Procrastination
- Setting up appointments
- Too many meetings
- Monitoring delegated work
- Unclear roles/job descriptions
- Executive meddling
- Budget adherence requirements
- Poorly educated customers
- Not enough proven managers
- Vague goals and objectives

- Lack of a job description
- Too many people involved in minor decision-making
- Lack of technical knowledge
- Lack of authorization to make decisions
- Poor functional status reporting
- Work overload
- Unreasonable time constraints
- Too much travel
- Lack of adequate project management tools
- Departmental "buck passing"
- Company politics
- Going from crisis to crisis
- Conflicting directives
- Bureaucratic roadblocks ("ego")
- Empire-building line managers
- No communication between sales and engineering
- Excessive paperwork
- Lack of clerical/administrative support
- Dealing with unreliable subcontractors
- Personnel not willing to take risks
- Demand for short-term results
- Lack of long-range planning
- Learning new company systems
- Poor lead time on projects
- Documentation (reports/red tape)
- Large number of projects
- Desire for perfection

- Lack of project organization
- Constant pressure
- Constant interruptions

- Shifting of functional personnel
- Lack of employee discipline
- Lack of qualified manpower

11.3 TIME MANAGEMENT FORMS

There are two basic forms that project managers and project engineers can use for practicing better time management. The first form is the "to do" pad as shown in Figure 11–1. The project manager or secretary prepares the list of things to do. The project manager then decides which activities he must perform himself and assigns the appropriate priorities.

The activities with the highest priorities are then transferred to the "daily calendar log," as shown in Figure 11–2. The project manager assigns these activities to the appropriate time blocks based on his own energy cycle. Unfilled time blocks are then used for unexpected crises or for lower-priority activities.

If there are more priority elements than time slots, the project manager may try to schedule well in advance. This is normally not a good practice, because it creates a backlog of high-priority activities. In addition, an activity that today is a "B" priority could easily become an "A" priority in a day or two. The moral here is do not postpone until tomorrow what you or your team can do today.

Date _____				
Activities	Priority	Started	In Process	Completed

FIGURE 11–1. "To-do" pad.

Date ________

Time	Activity	Priority
8:00-9:00		
9:00-10:00		
10:00-11:00		
11:00-12:00		
12:00-1:00		
1:00-2:00		
2:00-3:00		
3:00-4:00		
4:00-5:00		

FIGURE 11–2. Daily calendar log.

11.4 EFFECTIVE TIME MANAGEMENT

There are several techniques that project managers can practice in order to make better use of their time[2]:

- Delegate.
- Follow the schedule.
- Decide fast.
- Decide who should attend.
- Learn to say no.
- Start now.
- Do the tough part first.
- Travel light.
- Work at travel stops.
- Avoid useless memos.
- Refuse to do the unimportant.
- Look ahead.
- Ask: Is this trip necessary?
- Know your energy cycle.

2. Source unknown.

- Control telephone and email time.
- Send out the meeting agenda.
- Overcome procrastination.
- Manage by exception.

As we learned in Chapter 10, the project manager, to be effective, must establish time management rules and then ask himself four questions:

- Rules for time management
  - Conduct a time analysis (time log).
  - Plan solid blocks for important things.
  - Classify your activities.
  - Establish priorities.
  - Establish opportunity cost on activities.
  - Train your system (boss, subordinate, peers).
  - Practice delegation.
  - Practice calculated neglect.
  - Practice management by exception.
  - Focus on opportunities—not on problems.
- Questions
  - What am I doing that I don't have to do at all?
  - What am I doing that can be done better by someone else?
  - What am I doing that could be done as well by someone else?
  - Am I establishing the right priorities for my activities?

11.5 STRESS AND BURNOUT

The factors that serve to make any occupation especially stressful are responsibility without the authority or ability to exert control, a necessity for perfection, the pressure of deadlines, role ambiguity, role conflict, role overload, the crossing of organizational boundaries, responsibility for the actions of subordinates, and the necessity to keep up with the information explosions or technological breakthroughs. Project managers have all of these factors in their jobs.

A project manager has his resources controlled by line management, yet the responsibilities of bringing a project to completion by a prescribed deadline are his. A project manager may be told to increase the work output, while the work force is simultaneously being cut. Project managers are expected to get work out on schedule, but are often not permitted to pay overtime. One project manager described it this way: "I have to implement plans I didn't design, but if the project fails, I'm responsible."

Project managers are subject to stress due to several different facets of their jobs. This can manifest itself in a variety of ways, such as:

1. *Being tired.* Being tired is a result of being drained of strength and energy, perhaps through physical exertion, boredom, or impatience. The definition here applies more to a short-term, rather than long-term, effect. Typical causes for feeling tired include meetings, report writing, and other forms of document preparation.

2. *Feeling depressed.* Feeling depressed is an emotional condition usually characterized by discouragement or a feeling of inadequacy. It is usually the result of a situation that is beyond the control or capabilities of the project manager. There are several sources of depression in a project environment: Management or the client considers your report unacceptable, you are unable to get timely resources assigned, the technology is not available, or the constraints of the project are unrealistic and may not be met.

3. *Being physically and emotionally exhausted.* Project managers are both managers and doers. It is quite common for project managers to perform a great deal of the work themselves, either because they consider the assigned personnel unqualified to perform the work or because they are impatient and consider themselves capable of performing the work faster. In addition, project managers often work a great deal of "self-inflicted" overtime. The most common cause of emotional exhaustion is report writing and the preparation of handouts for interchange meetings.

4. *Burned out.* Being burned out is more than just a feeling; it is a condition. Being burned out implies that one is totally exhausted, both physically and emotionally, and that rest, recuperation, or vacation time may not remedy the situation. The most common cause is prolonged overtime, or the need thereof, and an inability to endure or perform under continuous pressure and stress. Burnout can occur almost overnight, often with very little warning. The solution is almost always a change in job assignment, preferably with another company.

5. *Being unhappy.* There are several factors that produce unhappiness in project management. Such factors include highly optimistic planning, unreasonable expectations by management, management cutting resources because of a "buy-in," or simply customer demands for additional data items. A major source of unhappiness is the frustration caused by having limited authority that is not commensurate with the assigned responsibility.

6. *Feeling trapped.* The most common situation where project managers feel trapped is when they have no control over the assigned resources on the project and feel as though they are at the mercy of the line managers. Employees tend to favor the manager who can offer them the most rewards, and that is usually the line manager. Providing the project manager with some type of direct reward power can remedy the situation.

7. *Feeling worthless.* Feeling worthless implies that one is without worth or merit, that is, valueless. This situation occurs when project managers feel that they are managing projects beneath their dignity. Most project managers look forward to the death of their project right from the onset, and expect their next project to be more important, perhaps twice the cost, and more complex. Unfortunately, there are always situations where one must take a step backwards.

8. *Feeling resentful and disillusioned about people.* This situation occurs most frequently in the project manager's dealings (i.e., negotiations) with the line managers.

During the planning stage of a project, line managers often make promises concerning future resource commitments, but renege on their promises during execution. Disillusionment then occurs and can easily develop into serious conflict. Another potential source of these feelings is when line managers appear to be making decisions that are not in the best interest of the project.

9. *Feeling hopeless.* The most common source of hopelessness are R&D projects where the ultimate objective is beyond the reach of the employee or even of the state-of-the-art technology. Hopelessness means showing no signs of a favorable outcome. Hopelessness is more a result of the performance constraint than of time or cost.

10. *Feeling rejected.* Feeling rejected can be the result of a poor working relationship with executives, line managers, or clients. Rejection often occurs when people with authority feel that their options or opinions are better than those of the project manager. Rejection has a demoralizing effect on the project manager because he feels that he is the "president" of the project and the true "champion" of the company.

11. *Feeling anxious.* Almost all project managers have some degree of "tunnel vision," where they look forward to the end of the project, even when the project is in its infancy. This anxious feeling is not only to see the project end, but to see it completed successfully.

Stress is not always negative, however. Without certain amounts of stress, reports would never get written or distributed, deadlines would never be met, and no one would even get to work on time. But stress can be a powerful force resulting in illness and even fatal disease, and must be understood and managed if it is to be controlled and utilized for constructive purposes.

The mind, body, and emotions are not the separate entities they were once thought to be. One affects the other, sometimes in a positive way, and sometimes in a negative way. Stress becomes detrimental when it is prolonged beyond what an individual can comfortably handle. In a project environment, with continually changing requirements, impossible deadlines, and each project being considered as a unique entity in itself, we must ask, How much prolonged stress can a project manager handle comfortably?

The stresses of project management may seem excessive for whatever rewards the position may offer. However, the project manager who is aware of the stresses inherent in the job and knows stress management techniques can face this challenge objectively and make it a rewarding experience.

11.6 STUDYING TIPS FOR THE PMI® PROJECT MANAGEMENT CERTIFICATION EXAM

This section is applicable as a review of the principles to support the knowledge areas and domain groups in the PMBOK® Guide. This chapter addresses:

- Human Resources Management
- Risk Management
- Execution

Understanding the following principles is beneficial if the reader is using this text to study for the PMP® Certification Exam:

● How stress can affect the way that the project manager works with the team
● How stress affects the performance of team members

The following multiple-choice questions will be helpful in reviewing the principles of this chapter:

1. Which of the following leadership styles most frequently creates "additional" time robbers for a project manager?
   A. Telling
   B. Selling
   C. Participating
   D. Delegating

2. Which of the following leadership styles most frequently creates "additional" time robbers for the project team?
   A. Telling
   B. Selling
   C. Participating
   D. Delegating

3. Which of the following time robbers would a project manager most likely want to handle by himself or herself rather than through delegation to equally qualified team members?
   A. Approval of procurement expenditures
   B. Status reporting to a customer
   C. Conflicting directives from the executive sponsor
   D. Earned-value status reporting

ANSWERS

1. A
2. D
3. C

PROBLEMS

11–1 Should time robbers be added to direct labor standards for pricing out work?

11–2 Is it possible for a project manager to improve his time management skills by knowing the "energy cycle" of his people? Can this energy cycle be a function of the hour of the day, day of the week, or whether overtime is required?

CASE STUDY

THE RELUCTANT WORKERS

Tim Aston had changed employers three months ago. His new position was project manager. At first he had stars in his eyes about becoming the best project manager that his company had ever seen. Now, he wasn't sure if project management was worth the effort. He made an appointment to see Phil Davies, director of project management.

Tim Aston: "Phil, I'm a little unhappy about the way things are going. I just can't seem to motivate my people. Every day, at 4:30 P.M., all of my people clean off their desks and go home. I've had people walk out of late afternoon team meetings because they were afraid that they'd miss their car pool. I have to schedule morning team meetings."

Phil Davies: "Look, Tim. You're going to have to realize that in a project environment, people think that they come first and that the project is second. This is a way of life in our organizational form."

Tim Aston: "I've continually asked my people to come to me if they have problems. I find that the people do not think that they need help and, therefore, do not want it. I just can't get my people to communicate more."

Phil Davies: "The average age of our employees is about forty-six. Most of our people have been here for twenty years. They're set in their ways. You're the first person that we've hired in the past three years. Some of our people may just resent seeing a thirty-year-old project manager."

Tim Aston: "I found one guy in the accounting department who has an excellent head on his shoulders. He's very interested in project management. I asked his boss if he'd release him for a position in project management, and his boss just laughed at me, saying something to the effect that as long as that guy is doing a good job for him, he'll never be released for an assignment elsewhere in the company. His boss seems more worried about his personal empire than he does in what's best for the company.

"We had a test scheduled for last week. The customer's top management was planning on flying in for firsthand observations. Two of my people said that they had programmed vacation days coming, and that they would not change, under any conditions. One guy was going fishing and the other guy was planning to spend a few days working with fatherless children in our community. Surely, these guys could change their plans for the test."

Phil Davies: "Many of our people have social responsibilities and outside interests. We encourage social responsibilities and only hope that the outside interests do not interfere with their jobs.

"There's one thing you should understand about our people. With an average age of forty-six, many of our people are at the top of their pay grades and have no place to go. They must look elsewhere for interests. These are the people you have to work with and motivate. Perhaps you should do some reading on human behavior."

Conflicts

Related Case Studies (from Kerzner/*Project Management Case Studies,* 2nd Edition)	Related Workbook Exercises (from Kerzner/*Project Management Workbook and PMP®/CAPM® Exam Study Guide,* 9th Edition)	PMBOK® Guide, 3rd Edition, Reference Section for the PMP® Certification Exam
• Facilities Scheduling at Mayer Manufacturing* • Scheduling the Safety Lab • Telestar International* • The Problem with Priorities	• Multiple Choice Exam	• Human Resource Management

12.0 INTRODUCTION

PMBOK® Guide, 2004
9.4 Manage Project Team
9.4.2.3 Conflict Management

In discussing the project environment, we have purposely avoided discussion of what may be its single most important characteristic: conflicts. Opponents of project management assert that the major reason why many companies avoid changeover to a project management organizational structure is either fear or an inability to handle the resulting conflicts. Conflicts are a way of life in a project structure and can generally occur at any level in the organization, usually as a result of conflicting objectives.

*Case Study also appears at end of chapter.

The project manager has often been described as a conflict manager. In many organizations the project manager continually fights fires and crises evolving from conflicts, and delegates the day-to-day responsibility of running the project to the project team members. Although this is not the best situation, it cannot always be prevented, especially after organizational restructuring or the initiation of projects requiring new resources.

The ability to handle conflicts requires an understanding of why they occur. Asking and answering these four questions may help handle and prevent conflicts.

- What are the project objectives and are they in conflict with other projects?
- Why do conflicts occur?
- How do we resolve conflicts?
- Is there any type of analysis that could identify possible conflicts before they occur?

12.1 OBJECTIVES

Each project must have at least one objective. The objectives of the project must be made known to all project personnel and all managers, at every level of the organization. If this information is not communicated accurately, then it is entirely possible that upper-level managers, project managers, and functional managers may all have a different interpretation of the ultimate objective, a situation that invites conflicts. As an example, company X has been awarded a $100,000 government contract for surveillance of a component that appears to be fatiguing. Top management might view the objective of this project to be discovering the cause of the fatigue and eliminating it in future component production. This might give company X a "jump" on the competition. The division manager might just view it as a means of keeping people employed, with no follow-on possibilities. The department manager can consider the objective as either another job that has to be filled, or a means of establishing new surveillance technology. The department manager, therefore, can staff the necessary positions with any given degree of expertise, depending on the importance and definition of the objective.

Project objectives must be:

- Specific, not general
- Not overly complex
- Measurable, tangible, and verifiable
- Appropriate level, challenging
- Realistic and attainable
- Established within resource bounds
- Consistent with resources available or anticipated
- Consistent with organizational plans, policies, and procedures

Some practitioners use the more simplistic approach of defining an objective by saying that the project's objective must follow the SMART rule, whereby:

- S = specific
- M = measurable

- A = attainable
- R = realistic or relevant
- T = tangible or time bound

Unfortunately, the above characteristics are not always evident, especially if we consider that the project might be unique to the organization in question. As an example, research and development projects sometimes start out general, rather than specific. Research and development objectives are reestablished as time goes on because the initial objective may not be attainable. As an example, company Y believes that they can develop a high-energy rocket-motor propellant. A proposal is submitted to the government, and, after a review period, the contract is awarded. However, as is the case with all R&D projects, there always exists the question of whether the objective is attainable within time, cost, and performance constraints. It might be possible to achieve the initial objective, but at an incredibly high production cost. In this case, the specifications of the propellant (i.e., initial objectives) may be modified so as to align them closer to the available production funds.

Many projects are directed and controlled using a management-by-objective (MBO) approach. The philosophy of management by objectives:

- Is proactive rather than reactive management
- Is results oriented, emphasizing accomplishment
- Focuses on change to improve individual and organizational effectiveness

Management by objectives is a systems approach for aligning project goals with organizational goals, project goals with the goals of other subunits of the organization, and project goals with individual goals. Furthermore, management by objectives can be regarded as a:

- Systems approach to planning and obtaining project results for an organization
- Strategy of meeting individual needs at the same time that project needs are met
- Method of clarifying what each individual and organizational unit's contribution to the project should be

Whether or not MBO is utilized, project objectives must be set.

12.2 THE CONFLICT ENVIRONMENT

In the project environment, conflicts are inevitable. However, as described in Chapter 10, conflicts and their resolution can be planned for. For example, conflicts can easily develop out of a situation where members of a group have a misunderstanding of each other's roles and responsibilities. Through documentation, such as linear responsibility charts, it is possible to establish formal organizational procedures (either at the project level or company-wide). Resolution means collaboration in which people must rely on one another. Without this, mistrust will prevail.

The most common types of conflicts involve:

- Manpower resources
- Equipment and facilities
- Capital expenditures
- Costs
- Technical opinions and trade-offs
- Priorities
- Administrative procedures
- Scheduling
- Responsibilities
- Personality clashes

Each of these conflicts can vary in relative intensity over the life cycle of a project. However, project managers believe that the most frequently occurring conflicts are over schedules but the potentially damaging conflicts can occur over personality clashes. The relative intensity can vary as a function of:

- Getting closer to project constraints
- Having only two constraints instead of three (i.e., time and performance, but not cost)
- The project life cycle itself
- The person with whom the conflict occurs

Sometimes conflict is "meaningful" and produces beneficial results. These meaningful conflicts should be permitted to continue as long as project constraints are not violated and beneficial results are being received. An example of this would be two technical specialists arguing that each has a better way of solving a problem, and each trying to find additional supporting data for his hypothesis.

Conflicts can occur with anyone and over anything. Some people contend that personality conflicts are the most difficult to resolve. Below are several situations. The reader might consider what he or she would do if placed in the situations.

- Two of your functional team members appear to have personality clashes and almost always assume opposite points of view during decision-making. They are both from the same line organization.
- Manufacturing says that they cannot produce the end-item according to engineering specifications.
- R&D quality control and manufacturing operations quality control argue as to who should perform a certain test on an R&D project. R&D postulates that it is their project, and manufacturing argues that it will eventually go into production and that they wish to be involved as early as possible.
- Mr. X is the project manager of a $65 million project of which $1 million is subcontracted out to another company in which Mr. Y is the project manager. Mr. X does not consider Mr. Y as his counterpart and continually communicates with the director of engineering in Mr. Y's company.

Ideally, the project manager should report high enough so that he can get timely assistance in resolving conflicts. Unfortunately, this is easier said than done. Therefore, project managers must plan for conflict resolution. As examples of this:

- The project manager might wish to concede on a low-intensity conflict if he knows that a high-intensity conflict is expected to occur at a later point in the project.
- Jones Construction Company has recently won a $120 million effort for a local company. The effort includes three separate construction projects, each one beginning at the same time. Two of the projects are twenty-four months in duration, and the third is thirty-six months. Each project has its own project manager. When resource conflicts occur between the projects, the customer is usually called in.
- Richard is a department manager who must supply resources to four different projects. Although each project has an established priority, the project managers continually argue that departmental resources are not being allocated effectively. Richard now holds a monthly meeting with all four of the project managers and lets them determine how the resources should be allocated.

Many executives feel that the best way of resolving conflicts is by establishing priorities. This may be true as long as priorities are not continually shifted around. As an example, Minnesota Power and Light established priorities as:

- Level 0: no completion date
- Level 1: to be completed on or before a specific date
- Level 2: to be completed in or before a given fiscal quarter
- Level 3: to be completed within a given year

This type of technique will work as long as there are not a large number of projects in any one level.

The most common factors influencing the establishment of project priorities include:

- The technical risks in development
- The risks that the company will incur, financially or competitively
- The nearness of the delivery date and the urgency
- The penalties that can accompany late delivery dates
- The expected savings, profit increase, and return on investment
- The amount of influence that the customer possesses, possibly due to the size of the project
- The impact on other projects or product lines
- The impact on affiliated organizations

The ultimate responsibility for establishing priorities rests with top-level management. Yet even with priority establishment, conflicts still develop. David Wilemon has identified several reasons why conflicts still occur[1]:

- The greater the diversity of disciplinary expertise among the participants of a project team, the greater the potential for conflict to develop among members of the team.

---

1. David L. Wilemon, "Managing Conflict in Temporary Management Situations," *The Journal of Management Studies,* 1973, pp. 282–296.

- The lower the project manager's degree of authority, reward, and punishment power over those individuals and organizational units supporting his project, the greater the potential for conflict to develop.
- The less the specific objectives of a project (cost, schedule, and technical performance) are understood by the project team members, the more likely it is that conflict will develop.
- The greater the role of ambiguity among the participants of a project team, the more likely it is that conflict will develop.
- The greater the agreement on superordinate goals by project team participants, the lower the potential for detrimental conflict.
- The more the members of functional areas perceive that the implementation of a project management system will adversely usurp their traditional roles, the greater the potential for conflict.
- The lower the percent need for interdependence among organizational units supporting a project, the greater the potential for dysfunctional conflict.
- The higher the managerial level within a project or functional area, the more likely it is that conflicts will be based upon deep-seated parochial resentments. By contrast, at the project or task level, it is more likely that cooperation will be facilitated by the task orientation and professionalism that a project requires for completion.

12.3 CONFLICT RESOLUTION

PMBOK® Guide, 2004
9.4.2.3 Conflict Management

Although each project within the company may be inherently different, the company may wish to have the resulting conflicts resolved in the same manner. The four most common methods are:

1. The development of company-wide conflict resolution policies and procedures
2. The establishment of project conflict resolution procedures during the early planning activities
3. The use of hierarchical referral
4. The requirement of direct contact

Many companies have attempted to develop company-wide policies and procedures for conflict resolution, but this method is often doomed to failure because each project and conflict is different. Furthermore, project managers, by virtue of their individuality, and sometimes differing amounts of authority and responsibility, prefer to resolve conflicts in their own fashion.

A second method for resolving conflicts, and one that is often very effective, is to "plan" for conflicts during the planning activities. This can be accomplished through the use of linear responsibility charts. Planning for conflict resolution is similar to the first method except that each project manager can develop his own policies, rules, and procedures.

Hierarchial referral for conflict resolution, in theory, appears as the best method because neither the project manager nor the functional manager will dominate. Under this arrangement, the project and functional managers agree that for a proper balance to exist their common superior must resolve the conflict to protect the company's best interest. Unfortunately, this is not realistic because the common superior cannot be expected to continually resolve lower-level conflicts and it gives the impression that the functional and project managers cannot resolve their own problems.

The last method is direct contact in which conflicting parties meet face-to-face and resolve their disagreement. Unfortunately, this method does not always work and, if continually stressed, can result in conditions where individuals will either suppress the identification of problems or develop new ones during confrontation.

Many conflicts can be either reduced or eliminated by constant communication of the project objectives to the team members. This continual repetition may prevent individuals from going too far in the wrong direction.

12.4 UNDERSTANDING SUPERIOR, SUBORDINATE, AND FUNCTIONAL CONFLICTS[2]

PMBOK® Guide, 2004
9.4.2.3 Conflict Management

In order for the project manager to be effective, he must understand how to work with the various employees who interface with the project. These employees include upper-level management, subordinate project team members, and functional personnel. Quite often, the project manager must demonstrate an ability for continuous adaptability by creating a different working environment with each group of employees. The need for this was shown in the previous section by the fact that the relative intensity of conflicts can vary in the life cycle of a project.

The type and intensity of conflicts can also vary with the type of employee, as shown in Figure 12–1. Both conflict causes and sources are rated according to relative conflict intensity. The data in Figure 12–1 were obtained for a 75 percent confidence level.

In the previous section we discussed the basic resolution modes for handling conflicts. The specific mode that a project manager will use might easily depend on whom the conflict is with, as shown in Figure 12–2. The data in Figure 12–2 do not necessarily show the modes that project managers would prefer, but rather identify the modes that will increase or decrease the potential conflict intensity. For example, although project managers consider, in general, that withdrawal is their least favorite mode, it can be used quite effectively with functional managers. In dealing with superiors, project managers would rather be ready for an immediate compromise than for face-to-face confrontation that could favor upper-level management.

Figure 12–3 identifies the various influence styles that project managers find effective in helping to reduce potential conflicts. Penalty power, authority, and expertise are considered as strongly unfavorable associations with respect to low conflicts. As expected, work challenge and promotions (if the project manager has the authority) are strongly favorable.

---

2. The majority of this section, including the figures, was adapted from *Seminar in Project Management Workbook,* © 1977 by Hans J. Thamhain. Reproduced by permission of Dr. Hans J. Thamhain.

FIGURE 12–1. Relationship between conflict causes and sources.

FIGURE 12–2. Association between perceived intensity of conflict and mode of conflict resolu-

(The figure shows only those associated which are statistically significant at the 95 percent level)

INTENSITY OF CONFLICT PERCEIVED BY PROJECT MANAGER (P.M.)	INFLUENCE METHODS AS PERCEIVED BY PROJECT MANAGERS						
	EXPERTISE	AUTHORITY	WORK CHALLENGE	FRIENDSHIP	PROMOTION	SALARY	PENALTY
BETWEEN P.M. AND HIS PERSONNEL	■	■	▲		▲		■
BETWEEN P.M. AND HIS SUPERIOR			▲				■
BETWEEN P.M. AND FUNCTIONAL SUPPORT DEPARTMENTS		■					■

▲ STRONGLY FAVORABLE ASSOCIATION WITH REGARD TO LOW CONFLICT ($-\tau$)

■ STRONGLY UNFAVORABLE ASSOCIATION WITH REGARD TO LOW CONFLICT ($+\tau$)

• KENDALL τ CORRELATION

FIGURE 12–3. Association between influence methods of project managers and their perceived conflict intensity.

12.5 THE MANAGEMENT OF CONFLICTS[3]

PMBOK® Guide, 2004
9.4.2.3 Conflict Management

Good project managers realize that conflicts are inevitable, but that good procedures or techniques can help resolve them. Once a conflict occurs, the project manager must:

- Study the problem and collect all available information
- Develop a situational approach or methodology
- Set the appropriate atmosphere or climate

If a confrontation meeting is necessary between conflicting parties, then the project manager should be aware of the logical steps and sequence of events that should be taken. These include:

- Setting the climate: establishing a willingness to participate
- Analyzing the images: how do you see yourself and others, and how do they see you?
- Collecting the information: getting feelings out in the open
- Defining the problem: defining and clarifying all positions
- Sharing the information: making the information available to all
- Setting the appropriate priorities: developing working sessions for setting priorities and timetables

---

3. See note 2.

- Organizing the group: forming cross-functional problem-solving groups
- Problem-solving: obtaining cross-functional involvement, securing commitments, and setting the priorities and timetable
- Developing the action plan: getting commitment
- Implementing the work: taking action on the plan
- Following up: obtaining feedback on the implementation for the action plan

The project manager or team leader should also understand conflict minimization procedures. These include:

- Pausing and thinking before reacting
- Building trust
- Trying to understand the conflict motives
- Keeping the meeting under control
- Listening to all involved parties
- Maintaining a give-and-take attitude
- Educating others tactfully on your views
- Being willing to say when you were wrong
- Not acting as a superman and leveling the discussion only once in a while

Thus, the effective manager, in conflict problem-solving situations:

- Knows the organization
- Listens with understanding rather than evaluation
- Clarifies the nature of the conflict
- Understands the feelings of others
- Suggests the procedures for resolving differences
- Maintains relationships with disputing parties
- Facilitates the communications process
- Seeks resolutions

12.6 CONFLICT RESOLUTION MODES _____

PMBOK® Guide, 2004
9.4.2.3 Conflict Management

The management of conflicts places the project manager in the precarious situation of having to select a conflict resolution mode (previously defined in Section 12.4). Based upon the situation, the type of conflict, and whom the conflict is with, any of these modes could be justified.

Confronting (or Collaborating)

With this approach, the conflicting parties meet face-to-face and try to work through their disagreements. This approach should focus more on solving the problem and less on being combative. This approach is collaboration and integration where both parties need to win. This method should be used:

- When you and the conflicting party can both get at least what you wanted and maybe more
- To reduce cost
- To create a common power base
- To attack a common foe
- When skills are complementary
- When there is enough time
- When there is trust
- When you have confidence in the other person's ability
- When the ultimate objective is to learn

Compromising

To compromise is to bargain or to search for solutions so both parties leave with some degree of satisfaction. Compromising is often the result of confrontation. Some people argue that compromise is a "give and take" approach, which leads to a "win-win" position. Others argue that compromise is a "lose-lose" position, since neither party gets everything he/she wants or needs. Compromise should be used:

- When both parties need to be winners
- When you can't win
- When others are as strong as you are
- When you haven't time to win
- To maintain your relationship with your opponent
- When you are not sure you are right
- When you get nothing if you don't
- When stakes are moderate
- To avoid giving the impression of "fighting"

Smoothing (or Accommodating)

This approach is an attempt to reduce the emotions that exist in a conflict. This is accomplished by emphasizing areas of agreement and de-emphasizing areas of disagreement. An example of smoothing would be to tell someone, "We have agreed on three of the five points and there is no reason why we cannot agree on the last two points." Smoothing does not necessarily resolve a conflict, but tries to convince both parties to remain at the bargaining table because a solution is possible. In smoothing, one may sacrifice one's own goals in order to satisfy the needs of the other party. Smoothing should be used:

- To reach an overarching goal
- To create obligation for a trade-off at a later date
- When the stakes are low
- When liability is limited
- To maintain harmony
- When any solution will be adequate

- To create goodwill (be magnanimous)
- When you'll lose anyway
- To gain time

Forcing (or Competing, Being Uncooperative, Being Assertive)   This is what happens when one party tries to impose the solution on the other party. Conflict resolution works best when resolution is achieved at the lowest possible levels. The higher up the conflict goes, the greater the tendency for the conflict to be forced, with the result being a "win-lose" situation in which one party wins at the expense of the other. Forcing should be used:

- When you are right
- When a do-or-die situation exists
- When stakes are high
- When important principles are at stake
- When you are stronger (never start a battle you can't win)
- To gain status or to gain power
- In short-term, one-shot deals
- When the relationship is unimportant
- When it's understood that a game is being played
- When a quick decision must be made

Avoiding (or Withdrawing)   Avoidance is often regarded as a temporary solution to a problem. The problem and the resulting conflict can come up again and again. Some people view avoiding as cowardice and an unwillingness to be responsive to a situation. Avoiding should be used:

- When you can't win
- When the stakes are low
- When the stakes are high, but you are not ready yet
- To gain time
- To unnerve your opponent
- To preserve neutrality or reputation
- When you think the problem will go away
- When you win by delay

12.7 STUDYING TIPS FOR THE PMI® PROJECT MANAGEMENT CERTIFICATION EXAM

This section is applicable as a review of the principles to support the knowledge areas and domain groups in the PMBOK® Guide. This chapter addresses:

- Human Resources Management
- Execution

Understanding the following principles is beneficial if the reader is using this text to study for the PMP® Certification Exam:

- Components of an objective
- What is meant by a SMART criteria for an objective
- Different types of conflicts that can occur in a project environment
- Different conflict resolution modes and when each one should be used

The following multiple-choice questions will be helpful in reviewing the principles of this chapter:

1. When talking about SMART objectives, the "S" stands for:
   A. Satisfactory
   B. Static
   C. Specific
   D. Standard

2. When talking about SMART objectives, the "A" stands for:
   A. Accurate
   B. Acute
   C. Attainable
   D. Able

3. Project managers believe that the most commonly occurring conflict is:
   A. Priorities
   B. Schedules
   C. Personalities
   D. Resources

4. The conflict that generally is the most damaging to the project when it occurs is:
   A. Priorities
   B. Schedules
   C. Personalities
   D. Resources

5. The most commonly preferred conflict resolution mode for project managers is:
   A. Compromise
   B. Confrontation
   C. Smoothing
   D. Withdrawal

6. Which conflict resolution mode is equivalent to problem-solving?
   A. Compromise
   B. Confrontation
   C. Smoothing
   D. Withdrawal

7. Which conflict resolution mode avoids a conflict temporarily rather than solving it?
   A. Compromise
   B. Confrontation

C. Smoothing

D. Withdrawal

ANSWERS

1. C
2. C
3. B
4. C
5. B
6. B
7. D

PROBLEMS

12–1 Is it possible to establish formal organizational procedures (either at the project level or company-wide) for the resolution of conflicts? If a procedure is established, what can go wrong?

12–2 Under what conditions would a conflict result between members of a group over misunderstandings of each other's roles?

12–3 Is it possible to have a situation in which conflicts are not effectively controlled, and yet have a decision-making process that is not lengthy or cumbersome?

12–4 If conflicts develop into a situation where mistrust prevails, would you expect activity documentation to increase or decrease? Why?

12–5 If a situation occurs that can develop into meaningful conflict, should the project manager let the conflict continue as long as it produces beneficial contributions, or should he try to resolve it as soon as possible?

12–6 Consider the following remarks made by David L. Wilemon ("Managing Conflict in Temporary Management Situations," *Journal of Management Studies,* October 1973, p. 296):

> The value of the conflict produced depends upon the effectiveness of the project manager in promoting beneficial conflict while concomitantly minimizing its potential dysfunctional aspects. A good project manager needs a "sixth sense" to indicate when conflict is desirable, what kind of conflict will be useful, and how much conflict is optimal for a given situation. In the final analysis he has the sole responsibility for his project and how conflict will impact the success or failure of his project.

Based upon these remarks, would your answer to Problem 12–5 change?

12–7 Mr. X is the project manager of a $65 million project of which $1 million is subcontracted out to another company in which Mr. Y is project manager. Unfortunately, Mr. X does not consider Mr. Y as his counterpart and continually communicates with the director of engineering in Mr. Y's company. What type of conflict is that, and how should it be resolved?

12–8 Contract negotiations can easily develop into conflicts. During a disagreement, the vice president of company A ordered his director of finance, the contract negotiator, to break off contract negotiations with company B because the contract negotiator of company B did not report directly to a vice president. How can this situation be resolved?

12–9 For each part below there are two statements; one represents the traditional view and the other the project organizational view. Identify each one.

   a. Conflict should be avoided; conflict is part of change and is therefore inevitable.
   b. Conflict is the result of troublemakers and egoists; conflict is determined by the structure of the system and the relationship among components.
   c. Conflict may be beneficial; conflict is bad.

12–10 Using the modes for conflict resolution defined in Section 12.6, which would be strongly favorable and strongly unfavorable for resolving conflicts between:

   a. Project manager and his project office personnel?
   b. Project manager and the functional support departments?
   c. Project manager and his superiors?
   d. Project manager and other project managers?

12–11 Which influence methods should increase and which should decrease the opportunities for conflict between the following:

   ● Project manager and his project office personnel?
   ● Project manager and the functional support departments?
   ● Project manager and his superiors?
   ● Project manager and other project managers?

12–12 Would you agree or disagree with the statement that "Conflict resolution through collaboration needs trust; people must rely on one another."

12–13 Davis and Lawrence (*Matrix,* © 1977. Adapted by permission of Pearson Education Inc., Upper Saddle River, New Jersey) identify several situations common to the matrix that can easily develop into conflicts. For each situation, what would be the recommended cure?

   a. Compatible and incompatible personnel must work together
   b. Power struggles break the balance of power
   c. Anarchy
   d. Groupitis (people confuse matrix behavior with group decision-making)
   e. A collapse during economic crunch
   f. Decision strangulation processes
   g. Forcing the matrix organization to the lower organizational levels
   h. Navel-gazing (spending time ironing out internal disputes instead of developing better working relationships with the customer)

12–14 Determine the best conflict resolution mode for each of the following situations:

   a. Two of your functional team members appear to have personality clashes and almost always assume opposite points of view during decision-making.
   b. R&D quality control and manufacturing operations quality control continually argue as to who should perform testing on an R&D project. R&D postulates that it's their project, and manufacturing argues that it will eventually go into production and that they wish to be involved as early as possible.

    c. Two functional department managers continually argue as to who should perform a certain test. You know that this situation exists, and that the department managers are trying to work it out themselves, often with great pain. However, you are not sure that they will be able to resolve the problem themselves.

12–15 Forcing a confrontation to take place assures that action will be taken. Is it possible that, by using force, a lack of trust among the participants will develop?

12–16 With regard to conflict resolution, should it matter to whom in the organization the project manager reports?

12–17 One of the most common conflicts in an organization occurs with raw materials and finished goods. Why would finance/accounting, marketing/sales, and manufacturing have disagreements?

12–18 Explain how the relative intensity of a conflict can vary as a function of:

    a. Getting closer to the actual constraints
    b. Having only two constraints instead of three (i.e., time and performance, but not cost)
    c. The project life cycle
    d. The person with whom the conflict occurs

12–19 The conflicts shown in Figure 12–1 are given relative intensities as perceived in project-driven organizations. Would this list be arranged differently for non–project-driven organizations?

12–20 Consider the responses made by the project managers in Figures 12–1 through 12–3. Which of their choices do you agree with, and which do you disagree with? Justify your answers.

12–21 As a good project manager, you try to plan for conflict avoidance. You now have a low-intensity conflict with a functional manager and, as in the past, handle the conflict with confrontation. If you knew that there would be a high-intensity conflict shortly thereafter, would you be willing to use the withdrawal mode for the low-intensity conflict in order to lay the groundwork for the high-intensity conflict?

12–22 Jones Construction Company has recently won a $120 million effort for a local company. The effort includes three separate construction projects, each one beginning at the same time. Two of the projects are eighteen months in duration and the third one is thirty months. Each project has its own project manager. How do we resolve conflicts when each project may have a different priority but they are all for the same customer?

12–23 Several years ago, Minnesota Power and Light established priorities as follows:

    Level 0: no priority
    Level 1: to be completed on or before a specific date
    Level 2: to be completed in or before a given fiscal quarter
    Level 3: to be completed within a given year

How do you feel about this system of establishing priorities?

12–24 Richard is a department manager who must supply resources to four different projects. Although each project has an established priority, the project managers continually argue that departmental resources are not being allocated effectively. Richard has decided to have a monthly group meeting with all four of the project managers and to let them determine how the resources should be allocated. Can this technique work? If so, under what conditions?

CASE STUDIES

FACILITIES SCHEDULING AT MAYER MANUFACTURING

Eddie Turner was elated with the good news that he was being promoted to section supervisor in charge of scheduling all activities in the new engineering research laboratory. The new laboratory was a necessity for Mayer Manufacturing. The engineering, manufacturing, and quality control directorates were all in desperate need of a new testing facility. Upper-level management felt that this new facility would alleviate many of the problems that previously existed.

The new organizational structure (as shown in Exhibit 12–1) required a change in policy over use of the laboratory. The new section supervisor, on approval from his department manager, would have full authority for establishing priorities for the use of the new facility. The new policy change was a necessity because upper-level management felt that there would be inevitable conflict between manufacturing, engineering, and quality control.

After one month of operations, Eddie Turner was finding his job impossible, so Eddie has a meeting with Gary Whitehead, his department manager.

Eddie: "I'm having a hell of a time trying to satisfy all of the department managers. If I give engineering prime-time use of the facility, then quality control and manufacturing say that I'm playing favorites. Imagine that! Even my own people say that I'm playing favorites with other directorates. I just can't satisfy everyone."

Gary: "Well, Eddie, you know that this problem comes with the job. You'll get the job done."

Eddie: "The problem is that I'm a section supervisor and have to work with department managers. These department managers look down on me like I'm their servant. If I were a department manager, then they'd show me some respect. What I'm really trying to say is that I would like you to send out the weekly memos to these department managers telling them of the new priorities. They wouldn't argue with you like they do with me. I can supply you with all the necessary information. All you'll have to do is to sign your name."

Exhibit 12–1. Mayer Manufacturing organizational structure

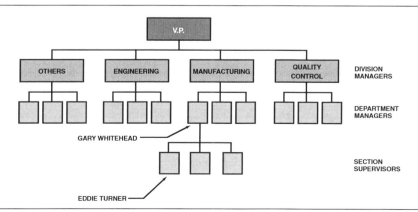

Gary: "Determining the priorities and scheduling the facilities is your job, not mine. This is a new position and I want you to handle it. I know you can because I selected you. I do not intend to interfere."

During the next two weeks, the conflicts got progressively worse. Eddie felt that he was unable to cope with the situation by himself. The department managers did not respect the authority delegated to him by his superiors. For the next two weeks, Eddie sent memos to Gary in the early part of the week asking whether Gary agreed with the priority list. There was no response to the two memos. Eddie then met with Gary to discuss the deteriorating situation.

Eddie: "Gary, I've sent you two memos to see if I'm doing anything wrong in establishing the weekly priorities and schedules. Did you get my memos?"

Gary: "Yes, I received your memos. But as I told you before, I have enough problems to worry about without doing your job for you. If you can't handle the work let me know and I'll find someone who can."

Eddie returned to his desk and contemplated his situation. Finally, he made a decision. Next week he was going to put a signature block under his for Gary to sign, with carbon copies for all division managers. "Now, let's see what happens," remarked Eddie.

TELESTAR INTERNATIONAL

On November 15, 1978, the Department of Energy Resources awarded Telestar a $475,000 contract for the developing and testing of two waste treatment plants. Telestar had spent the better part of the last two years developing waste treatment technology under its own R&D activities. This new contract would give Telestar the opportunity to "break into a new field"—that of waste treatment.

The contract was negotiated at a firm-fixed price. Any cost overruns would have to be incurred by Telestar. The original bid was priced out at $847,000. Telestar's management, however, wanted to win this one. The decision was made that Telestar would "buy in" at $475,000 so that they could at least get their foot into the new marketplace.

The original estimate of $847,000 was very "rough" because Telestar did not have any good man-hour standards, in the area of waste treatment, on which to base their man-hour projections. Corporate management was willing to spend up to $400,000 of their own funds in order to compensate the bid of $475,000.

By February 15, 1979, costs were increasing to such a point where overrun would be occurring well ahead of schedule. Anticipated costs to completion were now $943,000. The project manager decided to stop all activities in certain functional departments, one of which was structural analysis. The manager of the structural analysis department strongly opposed the closing out of the work order prior to the testing of the first plant's high-pressure pneumatic and electrical systems.

Structures Manager: "You're running a risk if you close out this work order. How will you know if the hardware can withstand the stresses that will be imposed during the test? After all, the test is scheduled for next month and I can probably finish the analysis by then."

Project Manager: "I understand your concern, but I cannot risk a cost overrun. My boss expects me to do the work within cost. The plant design is similar to one that we have tested before, without any structural problems being detected. On this basis I consider your analysis unnecessary."

Structures Manager: "Just because two plants are similar does not mean that they will be identical in performance. There can be major structural deficiencies."

Project Manager: "I guess the risk is mine."

Structures Manager: "Yes, but I get concerned when a failure can reflect on the integrity of my department. You know, we're performing on schedule and within the time and money budgeted. You're setting a bad example by cutting off our budget without any real justification."

Project Manager: "I understand your concern, but we must pull out all the stops when overrun costs are inevitable."

Structures Manager: "There's no question in my mind that this analysis should be completed. However, I'm not going to complete it on my overhead budget. I'll reassign my people tomorrow. Incidentally, you had better be careful; my people are not very happy to work for a project that can be canceled immediately. I may have trouble getting volunteers next time."

Project Manager: "Well, I'm sure you'll be able to adequately handle any future work. I'll report to my boss that I have issued a work stoppage order to your department."

During the next month's test, the plant exploded. Postanalysis indicated that the failure was due to a structural deficiency.

    a. Who is at fault?
    b. Should the structures manager have been dedicated enough to continue the work on his own?
    c. Can a functional manager, who considers his organization as strictly support, still be dedicated to total project success?

HANDLING CONFLICT IN PROJECT MANAGEMENT

The next several pages contain a six-part case study in conflict management. Read the instructions carefully on how to keep score and use the boxes in the table on page 308 as the worksheet for recording your choice and the group's choice; after the case study has been completed, your instructor will provide you with the proper grading system for recording your scores.

Part 1: Facing the Conflict   As part of his first official duties, the new department manager informs you by memo that he has changed his input and output requirements for the MIS project (on which you are the project manager) because of several complaints by his departmental employees. This is contradictory to the project plan that you developed with the previous manager and are currently working toward. The department manager states that he has already discussed this with the vice president and general manager, a man to whom both of you report, and feels that the former department manager made a poor decision and did not get sufficient input from the employees who would be using the system as to the best system specifications. You telephone him and try to convince him to hold off on his request for change until a later time, but he refuses.

Changing the input–output requirements at this point in time will require a major revision and will set back total system implementation by three weeks. This will also affect other department managers who expect to see this system operational according to the original schedule. You can explain this to your superiors, but the increased project costs will be hard to absorb. The potential cost overrun might be difficult to explain at a later date.

At this point you are somewhat unhappy with yourself at having been on the search committee that found this department manager and especially at having recommended him for this position. You know that something must be done, and the following are your alternatives:

- A. You can remind the department manager that you were on the search committee that recommended him and then ask him to return the favor, since he "owes you one."
- B. You can tell the department manager that you will form a new search committee to replace him if he doesn't change his position.
- C. You can take a tranquilizer and then ask your people to try to perform the additional work within the original time and cost constraints.
- D. You can go to the vice president and general manager and request that the former requirements be adhered to, at least temporarily.
- E. You can send a memo to the department manager explaining your problem and asking him to help you find a solution.
- F. You can tell the department manager that your people cannot handle the request and his people will have to find alternate ways of solving their problems.
- G. You can send a memo to the department manager requesting an appointment, at his earliest convenience, to help you resolve your problem.
- H. You can go to the department manager's office later that afternoon and continue the discussion further.
- I. You can send the department manager a memo telling him that you have decided to use the old requirements but will honor his request at a later time.

Line	Part	Personal		Group	
		Choice	Score	Choice	Score
1	1. Facing the Conflict				
2	2. Understanding Emotions	////		////	
3	3. Establishing Communications				
4	4. Conflict Resolution	////		////	
5	5. Understanding Your Choices				
6	6. Interpersonal Influences				
	TOTAL	////		////	

Although other alternatives exist, assume that these are the only ones open to you at the moment. Without discussing the answer with your group, record the letter representing your choice in the appropriate space on line 1 of the worksheet under "Personal."

As soon as all of your group have finished, discuss the problem as a group and determine that alternative that the group considers to be best. Record this answer on line 1 of the worksheet under "Group." Allow ten minutes for this part.

Part 2: Understanding Emotions

Never having worked with this department manager before, you try to predict what his reactions will be when confronted with the problem. Obviously, he can react in a variety of ways:

A. He can *accept* your solution in its entirety without asking any questions.
B. He can discuss some sort of justification in order to *defend* his position.
C. He can become extremely annoyed with having to discuss the problem again and demonstrate *hostility*.
D. He can demonstrate a willingness to *cooperate* with you in resolving the problem.
E. He can avoid making any decision at this time by *withdrawing* from the discussion.

	Your Choice					Group Choice				
	Acc.	Def.	Host.	Coop.	With.	Acc.	Def.	Host.	Coop.	With.
A. I've given my answer. See the general manager if you're not happy.										
B. I understand your problem. Let's do it your way.										
C. I understand your problem, but I'm doing what is best for my department.										
D. Let's discuss the problem. Perhaps there are alternatives.										
E. Let me explain to you why we need the new requirements.										
F. See my section supervisors. It was their recommendation.										
G. New managers are supposed to come up with new and better ways, aren't they?										

In the table above are several possible statements that could be made by the department manager when confronted with the problem. Without discussion with your group, place a check mark beside the appropriate emotion that could describe this statement. When each member of the group has completed his choice, determine the group choice. Numerical values will be assigned to your choices in the discussion that follows. Do not mark the worksheet at this time. Allow ten minutes for this part.

Part 3: Establishing Communications

Unhappy over the department manager's memo and the resulting follow-up phone conversation, you decide to walk in on the department manager. You tell him that you will have a problem trying to honor his request. He tells you that he is too busy with his own problems of restructuring his department and that your schedule and cost problems are of no concern to him at this time. You storm out of his office, leaving him with the impression that his actions and remarks are not in the best interest of either the project or the company.

The department manager's actions do not, of course, appear to be those of a dedicated manager. He should be more concerned about what's in the best interest of the company. As you contemplate the situation, you wonder if you could have received a better response from him had you approached him differently. In other words, what is your best approach to opening up communications between you and the department manager? From the list of alternatives shown below, and working alone, select the alternative that best represents how you would handle this situation. When all members of the group have selected their personal choices, repeat the process and make a group choice. Record your personal and group choices on line 3 of the worksheet. Allow ten minutes for this part.

A. Comply with the request and document all results so that you will be able to defend yourself at a later date in order to show that the department manager should be held accountable.

B. Immediately send him a memo reiterating your position and tell him that at a later time you will reconsider his new requirements. Tell him that time is of utmost importance, and you need an immediate response if he is displeased.

C. Send him a memo stating that you are holding him accountable for all cost overruns and schedule delays.

D. Send him a memo stating you are considering his request and that you plan to see him again at a later date to discuss changing the requirements.

E. See him as soon as possible. Tell him that he need not apologize for his remarks and actions, and that you have reconsidered your position and wish to discuss it with him.

F. Delay talking to him for a few days in hopes that he will cool off sufficiently and then see him in hopes that you can reopen the discussions.

G. Wait a day or so for everyone to cool off and then try to see him through an appointment; apologize for losing your temper, and ask him if he would like to help you resolve the problem.

Part 4: Conflict Resolution Modes

Having never worked with this manager before, you are unsure about which conflict resolution mode would work best. You decide to wait a few days and then set up an appointment with the department manager without stating what subject matter will be discussed. You then try to determine what conflict resolution mode appears to be dominant based on the opening remarks of the department manager. Neglecting the fact that your conversation with the department manager might already be considered as confrontation, for each statement shown below, select the conflict resolution mode that the *department manager* appears to prefer. After each member of the group has recorded his personal choices in the table on page 365, determine the group choices. Numerical values will be attached to your answers at a later time. Allow ten minutes for this part.

 A. *Withdrawal* is retreating from a potential conflict.
 B. *Smoothing* is emphasizing areas of agreement and de-emphasizing areas of disagreement.
 C. *Compromising* is the willingness to give and take.
 D. *Forcing* is directing the resolution in one direction or another, a win-or-lose position.
 E. *Confrontation* is a face-to-face meeting to resolve the conflict.

	Personal Choice					Group Choice				
	With.	Smooth.	Comp.	Forc.	Conf.	With.	Smooth.	Comp.	Forc.	Conf.
A. The requirements are my decision, and we're doing it my way.										
B. I've thought about it and you're right. We'll do it your way.										
C. Let's discuss the problem. Perhaps there are alternatives.										
D. Let me again explain why we need the new requirements.										
E. See my section supervisors; they're handling it now.										
F. I've looked over the problem and I might be able to ease up on some of the requirements.										

Part 5: Understanding Your Choices

Assume that the department manager has refused to see you again to discuss the new requirements. Time is running out, and you would like to make a decision before the costs and schedules get out of hand. From the list below, select your personal choice and then, after each group member is finished, find a group choice.

 A. Disregard the new requirements, since they weren't part of the original project plan.
 B. Adhere to the new requirements, and absorb the increased costs and delays.
 C. Ask the vice president and general manager to step in and make the final decision.
 D. Ask the other department managers who may realize a schedule delay to try to convince this department manager to ease his request or even delay it.

Record your answer on line 5 of the worksheet. Allow five minutes for this part.

Part 6: Interpersonal Influences

Assume that upper-level management resolves the conflict in your favor. In order to complete the original work requirements you will need support from this department manager's organization. Unfortunately, you are not sure as to which type of interpersonal influence to use. Although you are considered as an expert in your field, you fear that this manager's functional employees may have a strong allegiance to the department manager and may not want to adhere to your requests. Which of the following interpersonal influence styles would be best under the given set of conditions?

A. You threaten the employees with penalty power by telling them that you will turn in a bad performance report to their department manager.

B. You can use reward power and promise the employees a good evaluation, possible promotion, and increased responsibilities on your next project.

C. You can continue your technique of trying to convince the functional personnel to do your bidding because you are the expert in the field.

D. You can try to motivate the employees to do a good job by convincing them that the work is challenging.

E. You can make sure that they understand that your authority has been delegated to you by the vice president and general manager and that they must do what you say.

F. You can try to build up friendships and off-work relationships with these people and rely on referent power.

Record your personal and group choices on line 6 of the worksheet. Allow ten minutes for completion of this part.

The solution to this exercise appears in Appendix A.

Special Topics

Related Case Studies (from Kerzner/*Project Management Case Studies*, 2nd Edition)	Related Workbook Exercises (from Kerzner/*Project Management Workbook and PMP®/CAPM® Exam Study Guide*, 9th Edition)	PMBOK® Guide, 3rd Edition, Reference Section for the PMP® Certification Exam
• American Electronics International • The Tylenol Tragedies • Photolite Corporation (A) • Photolite Corporation (B) • Photolite Corporation (C) • Photolite Corporation (D) • First Security Bank of Cleveland • Jackson Industries	• The Potential Problem Audit • The Situational Audit • Multiple Choice Exam	• Integration Management • Human Resource Management • Project Management Roles and Responsibilities

13.0 INTRODUCTION

There are several situations or special topics that deserve attention. These include:

- Performance measurement
- Compensation and rewards
- Managing small projects

- Managing mega projects
- Morality, ethics and the corporate culture
- Internal partnerships
- External partnerships
- Training and education
- Integrated project teams

13.1 PERFORMANCE MEASUREMENT

PMBOK® Guide, 2004
9.4.2 Manage Project Team

A good project manager will make it immediately clear to all new functional employees that if they perform well in the project, then he (the project manager) will inform the functional manager of their progress and achievements. This assumes that the functional manager is not providing close supervision over the functional employees and is, instead, passing on some of the responsibility to the project manager—a common situation in project management organization structures.

Many good projects as well as project management structures have failed because of the inability of the system to evaluate properly the functional employee's performance. In a project management structure, there are basically six ways that a functional employee can be evaluated on a project:

- *The project manager prepares a written, confidential evaluation and gives it to the functional manager.* The functional manager will evaluate the validity of the project manager's comments and prepare his own evaluation. Only the line manager's evaluation is shown to the employee. The use of confidential forms is not preferred because it may be contrary to government regulations and it does not provide the necessary feedback for an employee to improve.
- *The project manager prepares a nonconfidential evaluation and gives it to the functional manager.* The functional manager prepares his own evaluation form and shows both evaluations to the functional employee. This is the technique preferred by most project and functional managers. However, there are several major difficulties with this technique. If the functional employee is an average or below-average worker, and if this employee is still to be assigned to this project after his evaluation, then the project manager might rate the employee as above average simply to prevent any sabotage or bad feelings downstream. In this situation, the functional manager might want a confidential evaluation instead, knowing that the functional employee will see both evaluation forms. Functional employees tend to blame the project manager if they receive a below-average merit pay increase, but give credit to the functional manager if the increase is above average. The best bet here is for the project manager periodically to tell the functional employees how well they are doing, and to give them an honest appraisal. Several companies that use this technique allow the project manager to show the form to the line manager first (to avoid conflict later) and then show it to the employee.
- *The project manager provides the functional manager with an oral evaluation of the employee's performance.* Although this technique is commonly used, most

functional managers prefer documentation on employee progress. Again, lack of feedback may prevent the employee from improving.

- *The functional manager makes the entire evaluation without any input from the project manager.* In order for this technique to be effective, the functional manager must have sufficient time to supervise each subordinate's performance on a continual basis. Unfortunately, most functional managers do not have this luxury because of their broad span of control and must therefore rely heavily on the project manager's input.

- *The project manager makes the entire evaluation for the functional manager.* This technique can work if the functional employee spends 100 percent of his time on one project, or if he is physically located at a remote site where he cannot be observed by his functional manager.

- *All project and functional managers jointly evaluate all project functional employees at the same time.* This technique should be limited to small companies with fewer than fifty or so employees; otherwise the evaluation process might be time-consuming for key personnel. A bad evaluation will be known by everyone.

Evaluation forms can be filled out either when the employee is up for evaluation or after the project is completed. If it is to be filled out when the employee is eligible for promotion or a merit increase, then the project manager should be willing to give an *honest*

PERFORMANCE FACTORS	EXCELLENT (1 OUT OF 15)	VERY GOOD (3 OUT OF 15)	GOOD (8 OUT OF 15)	FAIR (2 OUT OF 15)	UNSATISFACTORY (1 OUT OF 15)
	FAR EXCEEDS JOB REQUIREMENTS	EXCEEDS JOB REQUIREMENTS	MEETS JOB REQUIREMENTS	NEEDS SOME IMPROVEMENT	DOES NOT MEET MINIMUM STANDARDS
QUALITY	LEAPS TALL BUILDINGS WITH A SINGLE BOUND	MUST TAKE RUNNING START TO LEAP OVER TALL BUILDING	CAN ONLY LEAP OVER A SHORT BUILDING OR MEDIUM ONE WITHOUT SPIRES	CRASHES INTO BUILDING	CANNOT RECOGNIZE BUILDINGS
TIMELINESS	IS FASTER THAN A SPEEDING BULLET	IS AS FAST AS A SPEEDING BULLET	NOT QUITE AS FAST AS A SPEEDING BULLET	WOULD YOU BELIEVE A SLOW BULLET?	WOUNDS HIMSELF WITH THE BULLET
INITIATIVE	IS STRONGER THAN A LOCOMOTIVE	IS STRONGER THAN A BULL ELEPHANT	IS STRONGER THAN A BULL	SHOOTS THE BULL	SMELLS LIKE A BULL
ADAPTABILITY	WALKS ON WATER CONSISTENTLY	WALKS ON WATER IN EMERGENCIES	WASHES WITH WATER	DRINKS WATER	PASSES WATER IN EMERGENCIES
COMMUNICATIONS	TALKS WITH GOD	TALKS WITH ANGELS	TALKS TO HIMSELF	ARGUES WITH HIMSELF	LOSES THE ARGUMENT WITH HIMSELF

FIGURE 13–1. Guide to performance appraisal.

appraisal of the employee's performance. Of course, the project manager should not fill out the evaluation form if he has not had sufficient time to observe the employee at work.

The evaluation form can be filled out at the termination of the project. This, however, may produce a problem in that the project may end the month after the employee is considered for promotion. The advantage of this technique is that the project manager may have been able to find sufficient time both to observe the employee in action and to see the output.

Figure 13–1 represents, in a humorous way, how project personnel perceive the evaluation form. Unfortunately, the evaluation process is very serious and can easily have a severe impact on an individual's career path with the company even though the final evaluation rests with the functional manager.

Figure 13–2 shows a simple type of evaluation form on which the project manager identifies the best description of the employee's performance. This type of form is generally used whenever the employee is up for evaluation.

Figure 13–3 shows another typical form that can be used to evaluate an employee. In each category, the employee is rated on a subjective scale. In order to minimize time and pa-

EMPLOYEE'S NAME	DATE
PROJECT TITLE	JOB NUMBER
EMPLOYEE ASSIGNMENT	
EMPLOYEE'S TOTAL TIME TO DATE ON PROJECT	EMPLOYEE'S REMAINING TIME ON PROJECT

TECHNICAL JUDGMENT:				
☐ Quickly reaches sound conclusions	☐ Usually makes sound conclusions	☐ Marginal decision-making ability	☐ Needs technical assistance	☐ Makes faulty conclusions
WORK PLANNING:				
☐ Good planner	☐ Plans well with help	☐ Occasionally plans well	☐ Needs detailed instructions	☐ Cannot plan at all
COMMUNICATIONS:				
☐ Always understands instructions	☐ Sometimes needs clarification	☐ Always needs clarifications	☐ Needs follow-up	☐ Needs constant instruction
ATTITUDE:				
☐ Always job interested	☐ Shows interest most of the time	☐ Shows no job interest	☐ More interested in other activities	☐ Does not care about job
COOPERATION:				
☐ Always enthusiastic	☐ Works well until job is completed	☐ Usually works well with others	☐ Works poorly with others	☐ Wants it done his/her way
WORK HABITS:				
☐ Always project oriented	☐ Most often project oriented	☐ Usually consistent with requests	☐ Works poorly with others	☐ Always works alone

ADDITIONAL COMMENTS: ______________________________

____

____

FIGURE 13–2. Project work assignment appraisal.

	EXCELLENT	ABOVE AVERAGE	AVERAGE	BELOW AVERAGE	INADEQUATE
TECHNICAL JUDGMENT					
WORK PLANNING					
COMMUNICATIONS					
ATTITUDE					
COOPERATION					
WORK HABITS					
PROFIT CONTRIBUTION					

EMPLOYEE'S NAME — DATE
PROJECT TITLE — JOB NUMBER
EMPLOYEE ASSIGNMENT
EMPLOYEE'S TOTAL TIME TO DATE ON PROJECT — EMPLOYEE'S REMAINING TIME ON PROJECT

ADDITIONAL COMMENTS: _____

FIGURE 13–3. Project work assignment appraisal.

perwork, it is also possible to have a single evaluation form at project termination for evaluation of all employees. This is shown in Figure 13–4. All employees are rated in each category on a scale of 1 to 5. Totals are obtained to provide a relative comparison of employees.

Obviously, evaluation forms such as that shown in Figure 13–4 have severe limitations, as a one-to-one comparison of all project functional personnel is of little value if the employees are from different departments. How can a project engineer be compared to a cost accountant?

Several companies are using this form by assigning coefficients of importance to each topic. For example, under a topic of technical judgment, the project engineer might have a coefficient of importance of 0.90, whereas the cost accountant's coefficient might be 0.25. These coefficients could be reversed for a topic on cost consciousness. Unfortunately, such comparisons have questionable validity, and this type of evaluation form is usually of a confidential nature.

Even though the project manager fills out an evaluation form, there is no guarantee that the functional manager will believe the project manager's evaluation. There are always situations in which the project and functional managers disagree as to either quality or direction of work.

Another problem may exist in the situation where the project manager is a "generalist," say at a grade-7 level, and requests that the functional manager assign his best

PROJECT TITLE   JOB NUMBER

EMPLOYEE ASSIGNMENT   DATE

CODE:

EXCELLENT = 5
ABOVE AVERAGE = 4
AVERAGE = 3
BELOW AVERAGE = 2
INADEQUATE = 1

NAMES	TECHNICAL JUDGMENT	WORK PLANNING	COMMUNICATIONS	ATTITUDE	COOPERATION	WORK HABITS	PROFIT CONTRIBUTION	SELF MOTIVATION	TOTAL POINTS

FIGURE 13–4. Project work assignment appraisal.

employee to the project. The functional manager agrees to the request and assigns his best employee, a grade-10 specialist. One solution to this problem is to have the project manager evaluate the expert only in certain categories such as communications, work habits, and problem-solving, but not in the area of his technical expertise.

As a final note, it is sometimes argued that functional employees should have some sort of indirect input into a project manager's evaluation. This raises rather interesting questions as to how far we can go with the indirect evaluation procedure.

From a top-management perspective, the indirect evaluation process brings with it several headaches. Wage and salary administrators readily accept the necessity for using different evaluation forms for white-collar and blue-collar workers. But now, we have a situation in which there can be more than one type of evaluation system for white-collar workers alone. Those employees who work in project-driven functional departments will be evaluated directly and indirectly, but based on formal procedures. Employees who charge their time to overhead accounts and non–project-driven departments might simply be evaluated by a single, direct evaluation procedure.

Many wage and salary administrators contend that they cannot live with a white-collar evaluation system and therefore have tried to combine the direct and indirect evaluation forms into one, as shown in Figure 13–5. Some administrators have even gone so far

I. EMPLOYEE INFORMATION:

1. NAME _____ 2. DATE OF EVALUATION _____

3. JOB ASSIGNMENT _____ 4. DATE OF LAST EVALUATION _____

5. PAY GRADE _____

6. EMPLOYEE'S IMMEDIATE SUPERVISOR _____

7. SUPERVISOR'S LEVEL: ☐ SECTION ☐ DEPT. ☐ DIVISION ☐ EXECUTIVE

II. EVALUATOR'S INFORMATION:

1. EVALUATOR'S NAME _____

2. EVALUATOR'S LEVEL: ☐ SECTION ☐ DEPT. ☐ DIVISION ☐ EXECUTIVE

3. RATE THE EMPLOYEE ON THE FOLLOWING:

	EXCELLENT	VERY GOOD	GOOD	FAIR	POOR
ABILITY TO ASSUME RESPONSIBILITY					
WORKS WELL WITH OTHERS					
LOYAL ATTITUDE TOWARD COMPANY					
DOCUMENTS WORK WELL AND IS BOTH COST AND PROFIT CONSCIOUS					
RELIABILITY TO SEE JOB THROUGH					
ABILITY TO ACCEPT CRITCISM					
WILLINGNESS TO WORK OVERTIME					
PLANS JOB EXECUTION CAREFULLY					
TECHNICAL KNOWLEDGE					
COMMUNICATIVE SKILLS					
OVERALL RATING					

4. RATE THE EMPLOYEE IN COMPARISON TO HIS CONTEMPORARIES:

LOWER 10%	LOWER 25%	LOWER 40%	MIDWAY	UPPER 40%	UPPER 25%	UPPER 10%

5. RATE THE EMPLOYEE IN COMPARISON TO HIS CONTEMPORARIES:

SHOULD BE PROMOTED AT ONCE	PROMOTABLE NEXT YEAR	PROMOTABLE ALONG WITH CONTEMPORARIES	NEEDS TO MATURE IN GRADE	DEFINITELY NOT PROMOTABLE

6. EVALUATOR'S COMMENTS: _____

_____

_____

SIGNATURE _____

III. CONCURRENCE SECTION:

1. NAME _____

2. POSITION: ☐ DEPARTMENT ☐ DIVISION ☐ EXECUTIVE

3. CONCURRENCE ☐ AGREE ☐ DISAGREE

4. COMMENTS: _____

_____

_____

_____

SIGNATURE _____

IV. PERSONNEL SECTION: (to be completed by the Personnel Department only)

V. EMPLOYEE'S SIGNATURE: _____ DATE: _____

FIGURE 13–5. Job evaluation.

as to adopt a single form company-wide, regardless of whether an individual is a white- or blue-collar worker.

The design of the employee's evaluation form depends on what evaluation method or procedure is being used. Generally speaking, there are nine methods available for evaluating personnel:

- Essay appraisal
- Graphic rating scale
- Field review
- Forced-choice review
- Critical incident appraisal
- Management by objectives
- Work standards approach
- Ranking methods
- Assessment center

Descriptions of these methods can be found in almost any text on wage and salary administration. Which method is best suited for a project-driven organizational structure? To answer this question, we must analyze the characteristics of the organizational form as well as those of the personnel who must perform there. An an example, project management can be described as an arena of conflict. Which of the above evaluation procedures can best be used to evaluate an employee's ability to work and progress in an atmosphere of conflict? Figure 13–6 compares the above nine evaluation procedures against the six most common project conflicts. This type of analysis must be carried out for all variables and characteris-

	Essay Appraisal	Graphic Rating Scale	Field Review	Forced-Choice Review	Critical Incident Appraisal	Management By Objectives	Work Standards Approach	Ranking Methods	Assessment Center
Conflict over schedules	●	●		●	●		●	●	
Conflict over priorities	●	●		●	●		●	●	
Conflict over technical issues	●			●			●		
Conflict over administration	●	●	●	●			●	●	●
Personality conflict	●	●		●			●		
Conflict over cost	●		●	●	●		●	●	●

Circles define areas where evaluation technique may be difficult to implement.

FIGURE 13–6. Rating evaluation techniques against types of conflict.

tics that describe the project management environment. Most compensation managers would agree that the management by objectives (MBO) technique offers the greatest promise for a fair and equitable evaluation of all employees. Although MBO implies that functional employees will have a say in establishing their own goals and objectives, this may not be the case. In project management, maybe the project manager or functional manager will set the objectives, and the functional employee will be told that he has to live with that. Obviously, there will be advantages and disadvantages to whatever evaluation procedures are finally selected.

13.2 FINANCIAL COMPENSATION AND REWARDS

Proper financial compensation and rewards are important to the morale and motivation of people in any organization. However, there are several issues that often make it necessary to treat compensation practices of project personnel separately from the rest of the organization:

- *Job classification and job descriptions* for project personnel are usually not compatible with those existing for other professional jobs. It is often difficult to pick an existing classification and adapt it to project personnel. Without proper adjustment, the small amount of formal authority of the project and the small number of direct reports may distort the position level of project personnel in spite of their broad range of business responsibilities.
- *Dual accountability* and dual reporting relationships of project personnel raise the question of who should assess performance and control the rewards.
- *Bases for financial rewards* are often difficult to establish, quantify, and administer. The criteria for "doing a good job" are difficult to quantify.
- *Special compensations* for overtime, extensive travel, or living away from home should be considered in addition to bonus pay for preestablished results. Bonus pay is a particularly difficult and delicate issue because often many people contribute to the results of such incentives. Discretionary bonus practices can be demoralizing to the project team.

Some specific guidelines are provided here to help managers establish compensation systems for their project organizations. The foundations of these compensation practices are based on four systems: (1) job classification, (2) base pay, (3) performance appraisals, and (4) merit increases.

Job Classifications and Job Descriptions   Every effort should be made to fit the new classifications for project personnel into the existing standard classification that has already been established for the organization.

The first step is to define job titles for various project personnel and their corresponding responsibilities. Titles are noteworthy because they imply certain responsibilities, position power, organizational status, and pay level. Furthermore, titles may indicate certain functional responsibilities, as does, for example, the title of task manager.[1] Therefore, titles should be carefully selected and each of them supported by a formal job description.

The job description provides the basic charter for the job and the individual in charge of it. A good job description is brief and concise, not exceeding one page. Typically, it is broken down into three sections: (1) overall responsibilities, (2) specific duties, and (3) qualifications. A sample job description is given in Table 13–1.

Base-Pay Classifications and Incentives

After the job descriptions have been developed, one can delineate pay classes consistent with the responsibilities and accountabilities for business results. If left to the personnel specialist, these pay scales may slip toward the lower end of an equitable compensation. This is understandable because, on the surface, project positions look less senior than their functional counterparts, as formal authority over resources and direct reports are often less necessary for project positions than for traditional functional positions. The impact of such a skewed compensation system is that the project organization will attract less qualified personnel and may be seen as an inferior career path.

Many companies that have struggled with this problem have solved it by (1) working out compensation schemes as a team of senior managers and personnel specialists, and (2) applying criteria of responsibility and business/profit accountability to setting pay scales for project personnel in accord with other jobs in their organization. Managers who are hiring can choose a salary from the established range based on their judgment of actual position responsibilities, the candidate's qualifications, the available budget, and other considerations.

Performance Appraisals

Traditionally, the purpose of the performance appraisal is to:

- Assess the employee's work performance, preferably against preestablished objectives
- Provide a justification for salary actions
- Establish new goals and objectives for the next review period
- Identify and deal with work-related problems
- Serve as a basis for career discussions

In reality, however, the first two objectives are in conflict. As a result, traditional performance appraisals essentially become a salary discussion with the objective to justify sub-

---

1. In most organizations the title of task manager indicates being responsible for managing the technical content of a project subsystem within a functional unit, having dual accountabilities to the functional superior and the project office.

TABLE 13–1. SAMPLE JOB DESCRIPTION

**Job Description: Lead Project
Engineer of Processor Development**

Overall Responsibility
Responsible for directing the technical development of the new Central Processor including managing the
technical personnel assigned to this development. The Lead Project Engineer has dual responsibility, (1) to
his/her functional superior for the technical implementation and engineering quality and (2) to the project
manager for managing the development within the established budget and schedule.

Specific Duties and Responsibilities
1. Provide necessary program direction for planning, organizing, developing and integrating the engineering
   effort, including establishing the specific objectives, schedules, and budgets for the processor subsystem.
2. Provide technical leadership for analyzing and establishing requirements, preliminary designing, designing,
   prototyping, and testing of the processor subsystem.
3. Divide the work into discrete and clearly definable tasks. Assign tasks to technical personnel within the
   Lead Engineer's area of responsibility and other organizational units.
4. Define, negotiate, and allocate budgets and schedules according to the specific tasks and overall program
   requirements.
5. Measure and control cost, schedule, and technical performance against program plan.
6. Report deviations from program plan to program office.
7. Replan trade-off and redirect the development effort in case of contingencies such as to best utilize the
   available resources toward the overall program objectives.
8. Plan, maintain, and utilize engineering facilities to meet the long-range program requirements.

Qualifications
1. Strong technical background in state-of-the-art central processor development.
2. Prior task management experience with proven record for effective cost and schedule control of multidisciplinary technology-based task in excess of SIM.
3. Personal skills to lead, direct, and motivate senior engineering personnel.
4. Excellent communication skills, both orally and in writing.

---

sequent managerial actions.[2] In addition, discussions dominated by salary actions are usually not conducive for future goal setting, problem-solving, or career planning.

In order to get around this dilemma, many companies have separated the salary discussion from the other parts of the performance appraisal. Moreover, successful managers
have carefully considered the complex issues involved and have built a performance appraisal system solidly based on content, measurability, and source of information.

The first challenge is in content, that is, to decide "what to review" and "how to measure performance." Modern management practices try to individualize accountability as
much as possible. Furthermore, subsequent incentive or merit increases are tied to profit
performance. Although most companies apply these principles to their project organizations, they do it with a great deal of skepticism. Practices are often modified to assure balance and equity for jointly performed responsibilities. A similar dilemma exists in the area

---

2. For detailed discussions, see The Conference Board, *Matrix Organizations of Complex Businesses,* 1979; plus
some basic research by H. H. Meyer, E. Kay, and J. R. P. French, "Split Roles in Performance Appraisal,"
Harvard Business Review, January–February 1965.

of profit accountability. The comment of a project manager at the General Electric Company is typical of the situation faced by business managers: "Although I am responsible for business results of a large program, I really can't control more than 20 percent of its cost." Acknowledging the realities, organizations are measuring performance of their *project managers,* in at least two areas:

- *Business results* as measured by profits, contribution margin, return on investment, new business, and income; also, on-time delivery, meeting contractual requirements, and within-budget performance.
- *Managerial performance* as measured by overall project management effectiveness, organization, direction and leadership, and team performance.

The first area applies only if the project manager is indeed responsible for business results such as contractual performance or new business acquisitions. Many project managers work with company-internal sponsors, such as a company-internal new product development or a feasibility study. In these cases, producing the results within agreed-on schedule and budget constraints becomes the primary measure of performance. The second area is clearly more difficult to assess. Moreover, if handled improperly, it will lead to manipulation and game playing. Table 13–2 provides some specific measures of project management performance. Whether the sponsor is company-internal or external, project managers are usually being assessed on how long it took to organize the team, whether the project is moving along according to agreed-on schedules and budgets, and how closely they meet the global goals and objectives set by their superiors.

| **PMBOK® Guide, 2004**
9.4.2 Manage Project Team
9.4.2.2 Project Performance Appraisals | **TABLE 13–2. PERFORMANCE MEASURES FOR PROJECT MANAGERS** |

Who Performs Appraisal
    Functional superior of project manager

Source of Performance Data
    Functional superior, resource managers, general managers

Primary Measures
    1. Project manager's success in leading the project toward preestablished global objectives
        • Target costs
        • Key milestones
        • Profit, net income, return on investment, contribution margin
        • Quality
        • Technical accomplishments
        • Market measures, new business, follow-on contract
    2. Project manager's effectiveness in overall project direction and leadership during all phases, including establishing:
        • Objectives and customer requirements
        • Budgets and schedules
        • Policies
        • Performance measures and controls
        • Reporting and review system

(continues)

TABLE 13–2. PERFORMANCE MEASURES FOR PROJECT MANAGERS
(*Continued*)

Secondary Measures
1. Ability to utilize organizational resources
   - Overhead cost reduction
   - Working with existing personnel
   - Cost-effective make-buy decisions
2. Ability to build effective project team
   - Project staffing
   - Interfunctional communications
   - Low team conflict complaints and hassles
   - Professionally satisfied team members
   - Work with support groups
3. Effective project planning and plan implementation
   - Plan detail and measurability
   - Commitment by key personnel and management
   - Management involvement
   - Contingency provisions
   - Reports and reviews
4. Customer/client satisfaction
   - Perception of overall project performance by sponsor
   - Communications, liaison
   - Responsiveness to changes
5. Participation in business management
   - Keeping mangement informed of new project/product/business opportunities
   - Bid proposal work
   - Business planning, policy development

Additional Considerations
1. Difficulty of tasks involved
   - Technical tasks
   - Administrative and orgnizational complexity
   - Multidisciplinary nature
   - Staffing and start-up
2. Scope of the project
   - Total project budget
   - Number of personnel involved
   - Number of organizations and subcontractors involved
3. Changing work environment
   - Nature and degree of customer changes and redirections
   - Contingencies

On the other side of the project organization, resource managers or project personnel are being assessed primarily on their ability to direct the implementation of a specific project subsystem:

- *Technical implementation* as measured against requirements, quality, schedules, and cost targets
- *Team performance* as measured by ability to staff, build an effective task group, interface with other groups, and integrate among various functions

Specific performance measures are shown in Table 13–3. In addition, the actual project performance of both project managers and their resource personnel should be assessed on the conditions under which it was achieved: the degree of task difficulty, complexity, size, changes, and general business conditions.

TABLE 13–3. PERFORMANCE MEASURES FOR PROJECT PERSONNEL

Who Performs Appraisal
  Functional superior of project person

Source of Performance Data
  Project manager and resource managers

Primary Measures
  1. Success in directing the agreed-on task toward completion
     • Technical implementation according to requirements
     • Quality
     • Key milestones/schedules
     • Target costs, design-to-cost
     • Innovation
     • Trade-offs
  2. Effectiveness as a team member or team leader
     • Building effective task team
     • Working together with others, participation, involvement
     • Interfacing with support organizations and subcontractors
     • Interfunctional coordination
     • Getting along with others
     • Change orientation
     • Making commitments

Secondary Measures
  1. Success and effectiveness in performing functional tasks in addition to project work in accordance with functional charter
     • Special assignments
     • Advancing technology
     • Developing organization
     • Resource planning
     • Functional direction and leadership
  2. Administrative support services
     • Reports and reviews
     • Special task forces and committees
     • Project planning
     • Procedure development
  3. New business development
     • Bid proposal support
     • Customer presentations
  4. Professional development
     • Keeping abreast in professional field
     • Publications
     • Liaison with society, vendors, customers, and educational institutions

Additional Considerations
  1. Difficulty of tasks involved
     • Technical challenges
     • State-of-the-art considerations
     • Changes and contingencies
  2. Managerial responsibilities
     • Task leader for number of project personnel
     • Multifunctional integration
     • Budget responsibility
     • Staffing responsibility
     • Specific accountabilities
  3. Multiproject involvement
     • Number of different projects
     • Number and magnitude of functional task and duties
     • Overall workload

Finally, one needs to decide who is to perform the performance appraisal and to make the salary adjustment. Where dual accountabilities are involved, good practices call for inputs from both bosses. Such a situation could exist for project managers who report functionally to one superior but are also accountable for specific business results to another person. While dual accountability of project managers is an exception for most organizations, it is common for project resource personnel who are responsible to their functional superior for the quality of the work and to their project manager for meeting the requirements within budget and schedule. Moreover, resource personnel may be shared among many projects. Only the functional or resource manager can judge overall performance of resource personnel.

Merit Increases and Bonuses

Professionals have come to expect merit increases as a reward for a job well done. However, under inflationary conditions, pay adjustments seldom keep up with cost-of-living increases. To deal with this salary compression and to give incentive for management performance, companies have introduced bonuses. The problem is that these standard plans for merit increases and bonuses are based on individual accountability while project personnel work in teams with shared accountabilities, responsibilities, and controls. It is usually very difficult to credit project success or failure to a single individual or a small group.

Most managers with these dilemmas have turned to the traditional remedy of the performance appraisal. If done well, the appraisal should provide particular measures of job performance that assess the level and magnitude at which the individual has contributed to the success of the project, including the managerial performance and team performance components. Therefore, a properly designed and executed performance appraisal that includes input from all accountable management elements, and the basic agreement of the employee with the conclusions, is a sound basis for future salary reviews.

13.3 EFFECTIVE PROJECT MANAGEMENT IN THE SMALL BUSINESS ORGANIZATION

The definition of a small project could be:

- Total duration is usually three to twelve months.
- Total dollar value is $5,000 to $1.5 million (upper limit is usually capital equipment projects).
- There is continuous communication between team members, and no more than three or four cost centers are involved.
- Manual rather than computerized cost control may be acceptable.
- Project managers work closely with functional personnel and managers on a daily basis, so time-consuming detail reporting is not necessary.
- The work breakdown structure does not go beyond level three.

Here, we are discussing project management in both small companies and small organizations within a larger corporation. In small organizations, major differences from large companies must be accounted for:

● *In small companies, the project manager has to wear multiple hats and may have to act as a project manager and line manager at the same time.* Large companies may have the luxury of a single full-time project manager for the duration of a project. Smaller companies may not be able to afford a full-time project manager and therefore may require that functional managers wear two hats. This poses a problem in that the functional managers may be more dedicated to their own functional unit than to the project, and the project may suffer. There is also the risk that when the line manager also acts as project manager, the line manager may keep the best resources for his own project. The line manager's project may be a success at the expense of all the other projects that he must supply resources for.

In the ideal situation, the project manager works horizontally and has project dedication, whereas the line manager works vertically and has functional (or company) dedication. If the working relationship between the project and functional managers is a good one, then decisions will be made in a manner that is in the best interest of both the project and the company. Unfortunately, this may be difficult to accomplish in small companies when an individual wears multiple hats.

● *In a small company, the project manager handles multiple projects, perhaps each with a different priority.* In large companies, project managers normally handle only one project at a time. Handling multiple projects becomes a serious problem if the priorities are not close together. For this reason, many small companies avoid the establishment of priorities for fear that the lower-priority activities will never be accomplished.

● *In a small company, the project manager has limited resources.* In a large company, if the project manager is unhappy with resources that are provided, he may have the luxury of returning to the functional manager to either demand or negotiate for other resources. In a small organization, the resources assigned may be simply the only resources available.

● *In a small company, project managers must generally have a better understanding of interpersonal skills than in a larger company.* This is a necessity because a project manager in the small company has limited resources and must provide the best motivation that he can.

● *In the smaller company, the project manager generally has shorter lines of communications.* In small organizations project managers almost always report to a top-level executive, whereas in larger organizations the project managers can report to any level of management. Small companies tend to have fewer levels of management.

● *Small companies do not have a project office.* Large companies, especially in aerospace or construction, can easily support a project office of twenty to thirty people, whereas in the smaller company the project manager may have to be the entire project office. This implies that the project manager in a small company may be required to have more general and specific information about all company activities, policies, and procedures than his counterparts in the larger companies.

● *In a small company, there may be a much greater risk to the total company with the failure of as little as one project.* Large companies may be able to afford the loss of a multimillion-dollar program, whereas the smaller company may be in serious financial trouble. Thus many smaller companies avoid bidding on projects that would necessitate hiring additional resources or giving up some of its smaller accounts.

● *In a small company, there might be tighter monetary controls but with less sophisticated control techniques.* Because the smaller company incurs greater risk with the failure (or cost overrun) of as little as one project, costs are generally controlled much more tightly and more frequently than in larger companies. However, smaller companies generally rely on manual or partially computerized systems, whereas larger organizations rely heavily on sophisticated software packages.

● *In a small company, there is usually more upper-level management interference.* This is expected because in the small company there is a much greater risk with the failure of a single project. In addition, executives in smaller companies "meddle" more than executives in larger companies, and quite often delegate as little as possible to project managers.

● *Evaluation procedures for individuals are usually easier in a smaller company.* This holds true because the project manager gets to know the people better, and, as stated above, there exists a greater need for interpersonal skills on the horizontal line in a smaller company.

● *In a smaller company, project estimating is usually more precise and based on either history or standards.* This type of planning process is usually manual as opposed to computerized. In addition, functional managers in a small company usually feel obligated to live up to their commitments, whereas in larger companies, much more lip service is given.

13.4 MEGA PROJECTS

Mega projects may have a different set of rules and guidelines from those of smaller projects. For example, in large projects:

● Vast numbers of people may be required, often for short or intense periods of time.
● Continuous organizational restructuring may be necessary as each project goes through a different life-cycle phase.
● The matrix and project organizational form may be used interchangeably.
● The following elements are critical for success.
  ● Training in project management
  ● Rules and procedures clearly defined
  ● Communications at all levels
  ● Quality front-end planning

Many companies dream of winning mega project contracts only to find disaster rather than a pot of gold. The difficulty in managing mega projects stems mainly from resource restraints:

● Lack of available on-site workers (or local labor forces)
● Lack of skilled workers

- Lack of properly trained on-site supervision
- Lack of raw materials

As a result of such problems, the company immediately assigns its best employees to the mega project, thus creating severe risks for the smaller projects, many of which could lead to substantial follow-on business. Overtime is usually required, on a prolonged basis, and this results in lower efficiency and unhappy employees.

As the project schedule slips, management hires additional home-office personnel to support the project. By the time that the project is finished, the total organization is overstaffed, many smaller customers have taken their business elsewhere, and the company finds itself in the position of needing another mega project in order to survive and support the existing staff.

Mega projects are not always as glorious as people think they are. Organizational stability, accompanied by a moderate growth rate, may be more important than quantum steps to mega projects. The lesson here is that mega projects should be left to those companies that have the facilities, expertise, resources, and management know-how to handle the situation.

13.5 MORALITY, ETHICS, AND THE CORPORATE CULTURE _____

> **PMBOK® Guide, 2004**
> 1.3 Domain of Professional
> Responsibility and the PMP®
> Code of Conduct

Companies that promote morality and ethics in business usually have an easier time developing a cooperative culture than those that encourage unethical or immoral behavior. The adversity generated by unethical acts can be either internally or externally driven. Internally driven adversity occurs when employees or managers in your own company ask you to take action that may be in the best interest of your company but violates your own moral and ethical beliefs. Typical examples might include:

- You are asked to lie to the customer in a proposal in order to win the contract.
- You are asked to withhold bad news from your own management.
- You are asked to withhold bad news from the customer.
- You are instructed to ship a potentially defective unit to the customer in order to maintain production quotas.
- You are ordered to violate ethical accounting practices to make your numbers "look good" for senior management.
- You are asked to cover up acts of embezzlement or use the wrong charge numbers.
- You are asked to violate the confidence of a private personal decision by a team member.

External adversity occurs when your customers ask you to take action that may be in the customer's best interest (and possibly your company's best interest), but once again violates your personal moral and ethical beliefs. Typical examples might include:

- You are asked to hide or destroy information that could be damaging to the customer during legal action against your customer.
- You are asked to lie to consumers to help maintain your customer's public image.

- You are asked to release unreliable information that would be damaging to one of your customer's competitors.
- The customer's project manager asks you to lie in your proposal so that he/she will have an easier time in approving contract award.

Project managers are often placed in positions where an action must be taken for the best interest of the company and its customers, and yet the same action could be upsetting to the workers. Consider the following example as a positive way to handle this:

- A project had a delivery date where a specific number of completed units had to be on the firm's biggest customer's receiving dock by January 5. This customer represented 30% of the firm's sales and 33% of its profits. Because of product development problems and slippages, the project could not be completed early. The employees, many of whom were exempt, were informed that they would be expected to work 12-hour days, including Christmas and New Year's, to maintain the schedule. The project manager worked the same hours as his manufacturing team and was visible to all. The company allowed family members to visit the workers during the lunch and dinner hours during this period. After delivery was accomplished, the project manager arranged for all of the team members to receive two weeks of paid time off. At completion of the project, the team members were volunteering to work again for this project manager.

The project manager realized that asking his team to work these days might be viewed as immoral. Yet, because he also worked, his behavior reinforced the importance of meeting the schedule. The project manager's actions actually strengthened the cooperative nature of the culture within the firm.

Not all changes are in the best interest of both the company and the workers. Sometimes change is needed simply to survive, and this could force employees to depart from their comfort zones. The employees might even view the change as immoral. Consider the following example:

- Because of a recession, a machine tool company switched from a non–project-driven to a project-driven company. Management recognized the change and tried to convince employees that customers now wanted specialty products rather than standard products, and that the survival of the firm may be at stake. The company hired a project management consulting company to help bring in project management since the business was now project-driven. The employees vigorously resisted both the change and the training with the mistaken belief that, once the recession ended, the customers would once again want the standard, off-the-shelf products and that project management was a waste of time. The company is no longer in business and, as the employees walked out of the plant for the last time, they blamed project management for the loss of employment.

Some companies develop "Standard Practice Manuals" that describe in detail what is meant by ethical conduct in dealing with customers and suppliers. Yet, even with the existence of these manuals, well-meaning individuals may create unintended consequences that wreak havoc.

Consider the following example:

- The executive project sponsor on a government-funded R&D project decided to "massage" the raw data to make the numbers look better before presenting the data to a customer. When the customer realized what had happened, their relationship, which had been based upon trust and open communications, was now based upon mistrust and formal documentation. The entire project team suffered because of the self-serving conduct of one executive.

Sometimes, project managers find themselves in situations where the outcome most likely will be a win-lose position rather than a win-win situation. Consider the following three situations:

- An assistant project manager, Mary, had the opportunity to be promoted and manage a new large project that was about to begin. She needed her manager's permission to accept the new assignment, but if she left, her manager would have to perform her work in addition to his own for at least three months. The project manager refused to release her, and the project manager developed a reputation of preventing people from being promoted while working on his project.
- In the first month of a twelve-month project, the project manager realized that the end date was optimistic, but he purposely withheld information from the customer in hopes that a miracle would occur. Ten months later, the project manager was still withholding information waiting for the miracle. In the eleventh month, the customer was told the truth. People then labeled the project manager as an individual who would rather lie than tell the truth because it was easier.
- To maintain the customer's schedule, the project manager demanded that employees work excessive overtime, knowing that this often led to more mistakes. The company fired a tired worker who inadvertently withdrew the wrong raw materials from inventory, resulting in a $55,000 manufacturing mistake.

In all three situations, the project manager believed that his decision was in the best interest of the company at that time. Yet the final result in each case was that the project manager was labeled as unethical or immoral.

It is often said that "money is the root of all evil." Sometimes companies believe that recognizing the achievements of an individual through a financial reward system is appropriate without considering the impact on the culture. Consider the following example:

- At the end of a highly successful project, the project manager was promoted, given a $5,000 bonus and a paid vacation. The team members who were key to the project's success and who earned minimum wage, went to a fast food restaurant to celebrate their contribution to the firm and their support of each other. The project manager celebrated alone.

The company failed to recognize that project management was a team effort. The workers viewed management's reward policy as immoral and unethical because the project manager was successful due to the efforts of the entire team.

Moral and ethical conduct by project managers, project sponsors, and line managers can improve the corporate culture. Likewise, poor decisions can destroy a culture, often in much less time than it took for the culture to be developed.

13.6 PROFESSIONAL RESPONSIBILITIES

PMBOK® Guide, 2004
1.3 Domain of Professional Responsibility and the PMP® Code of Conduct

Professional responsibilities for project managers have become increasingly important in the last few years because of the unfavorable publicity on the dealings of corporate America. These professional responsibilities have been with us for some time, especially in dealing with government agencies. Professional responsibilities for a project manager are both broad-based and encompassing. PMI® released a Project Management Professional (PMP®) Role Delineation Study in 2000 that emphasizes the professional responsibilities of the project manager. The Professional Responsibilities Domain Area in the PMBOK®Guide is based upon the Role Delineation Study and The PMI® Code of Conduct. There are five tasks emphasized under Professional Responsibilities Domain Area of the PMBOK® Guide:

- **Ensure Individual Integrity and Professionalism:** The project manager is expected to act in a professional manner at all times. This includes adhering to all legal requirements, maintaining moral and ethical standards, and protecting the community and all stakeholders even though there may be some conflicting interests among the shareholders. The project manager must be knowledgeable about legal requirements (including professional standards legal requirements), as well as multinational, ethnic, ethical, and cultural standards at both the project's location and within the team. Understanding the values set forth by the stakeholders is also necessary.

- **Contribute to the Project Management Knowledge Base:** Project managers are expected to contribute to the project management knowledge base by sharing project management knowledge on such topics as current research, best practices, lessons learned, and continuous improvement efforts. The intent of this contribution is to advance the profession, improve the quality of project management, and improve the capabilities of one's colleagues. Contributions can take the form of articles, presentations, books, and various other media.

- **Enhance Individual Competence:** Project managers are expected to enhance their own individual competencies in the same manner as they contribute to the profession. Usually, project managers that contribute to the profession enhance their own competencies at the same time.

- **Balance Stakeholder Interests:** All stakeholders may have different values and interests. These competing interests mandate that project managers not only

understand stakeholder needs and objectives but also possess strong conflict resolution skills, negotiation skills, and communication skills.

- **Interact with the Team and Stakeholders in a Professional and Cooperative
Manner:** Project managers are expected to understand the ethnic and cultural
norms of both the team members and the stakeholders. This leads to the category
of cultural diversity and socioeconomic influences such as political differences,
national holidays, communication preferences, religious practices, ethical and
moral beliefs, and other demographic considerations. Project managers must be
willing to embrace diversity, be open-minded, exercise self-control, exhibit empathy, and exercise tolerance with a willingness to compromise.

In addition to the five tasks described under professional responsibility, PMI® has developed a Code of Professional Conduct that reinforces these five tasks. The code applies
to everyone working in a project environment, not merely the project manager. As such,
the code emphasizes that PMP®s must function as "role models" and exhibit characteristics such as honesty, morality, and ethical behavior.

The code has two major sections:

- Responsibilities to the Profession
- Responsibilities to the Customers and the Public

There are numerous situations that can create problems for project managers in dealing with professional responsibilities expectations. These situations include:

- Maintaining professional integrity
- Adhering to ethical standards
- Recognizing diversity
- Avoiding/reporting conflicts of interest
- Not making project decisions for personal gains
- Receiving gifts from customers and vendors
- Providing gifts to customers and vendors
- Truthfully reporting information
- Willing to identify violations
- Balancing stakeholder needs
- Succumbing to stakeholder pressure
- Managing your firm's intellectual property
- Managing your customer's intellectual property
- Adhering to security and confidentiality requirements
- Abiding by the Code of Professional Conduct

Several of these topics are explained below.

Conflict of Interest   A conflict of interest is a situation where the individual is placed in a
compromising position where the individual can gain personally based
upon the decisions made. This is also referred to as personal enrichment. There are nu-

merous situations where a project manager is placed in such a position. Examples might be:

- Insider knowledge that the stock will be going up or down
- Being asked to improperly allow employees to use charge numbers on your project even though they are not working on your project
- Receiving or giving inappropriate (by dollar value) gifts
- Receiving unjustified compensation or kickbacks
- Providing the customer with false information just to keep the project alive

Project managers are expected to abide by the PMI® Code of Professional Conduct, which makes it clear that project managers should conduct themselves in an ethical manner. Unjust compensation or gains not only are frowned upon but are unacceptable. Unless these conflict-of-interest situations are understood, the legitimate interests of both the customer and the company may not be forthcoming.

Inappropriate Connections   Not all stakeholders are equal in their ability to influence the decisions made by the project manager. Some stakeholders can provide inappropriate influence/compensation, such as:

- A loan with a very low interest rate
- Ability to purchase a product/service at a price that may appear equivalent to a gift
- Ability to receive free gifts such as airline tickets, tickets to athletic events, free meals and entertainment, or even cash

Another form of inappropriate connections would be with family or friends. These individuals may provide you with information or influence by which you could gain personally in a business situation. Examples of affiliation connections might be:

- Receiving insider information
- Receiving privileged information
- Opening doors that you could not open by yourself, at least without some difficulty

Acceptance of Gifts   Today, all companies have rules concerning the acceptance of gifts and their disclosure. While it may be customary in some countries to give or accept gifts, the standard rule is usually to avoid all gifts. Some companies may stipulate limits on when gifts are permitted and the appropriateness of the gift. The gifts might be cash, free meals, or other such items.

Responsibility to Your Company (and Stakeholders)   Companies today, more than ever before, are under pressure to maintain ethical practices with customers and suppliers. This could be interpreted as a company code of ethics that stipulates the professional behavior expected from the project manager and the team members. This applies specifically to the actions of both the project manager as well as the team members. Some companies even go so far as to develop "standard practice manuals" on how to act in a professional manner. Typical sections of such manuals might be:

- Truthful representation of all information
- Full disclosure of all information
- Protection of company-proprietary information
- Responsibility to report violations
- Full compliance with groups auditing violations
- Full disclosure, and in a timely manner, of all conflicts of interest
- Ensure that all of the team members abide by the above items

13.7 INTERNAL PARTNERSHIPS

A partnership is a group of two or more individuals working together to achieve a common objective. In project management, maintaining excellent, working relations with internal partners is essential. Internally, the critical relationship is between the project and line manager.

In the early days of project management, the selection of the individual to serve as the project manager was most often dependent upon who possessed the greatest command of technology. The result, as shown in Figure 13–7, was a very poor working relationship between the project and line manager. Line managers viewed project managers as a threat, and their relationship developed into a competitive, superior-subordinate relationship. The most common form of organizational structure was a very strong matrix where the project

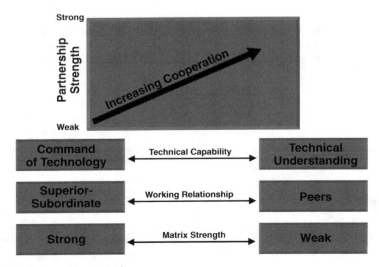

FIGURE 13–7. Partnership strength.

manager, perceived as having a command of technology, had a greater influence over the assigned employees than did their line manager.

As the magnitude and technical complexity of the projects grew, it became obvious that the project managers could not maintain a command of technology in all aspects of the project. Project managers were viewed as possessing an understanding of rather than command of technology. They became more dependent upon line managers for technical support. The project manager then found himself in the midst of a weak matrix where the employees were receiving the majority of their technical direction from the line managers.

As the partnership between the project and line managers developed, management recognized that partnerships worked best on a peer-to-peer basis. Project and line managers began to view each other as equals and share in the authority, responsibility, and accountability needed to assure project success. Good project management methodologies emphasize the cooperative working relationship that must exist between the project and line managers.

13.8 EXTERNAL PARTNERSHIPS

Project management methodologies also emphasize the working relationships with external organizations such as suppliers. Outsourcing has become a major trend because it allows companies to bring their products and services to the market faster and often at a more competitive price. Therefore, external partnerships can become beneficial for both the suppliers and the customers.

There are three categories of suppliers:

- **An External Supplier:** These are suppliers that you may or may not have worked with previously. There has been no investment into a relationship with these suppliers. If they win a contract, and even if they perform well, there is no guarantee that they will receive another contract. Usually an external supplier must go through all of the requirements of the competitive bidding process for each project.
- **An Approved Supplier:** This is usually considered the lowest level of external partnering. Approved suppliers are part of an approved supplier-bidding list and are invited to bid on selected projects. If the approved supplier wins a contract, there is no guarantee that any additional contracts will be forthcoming. Some minimal relationship between the customer and supplier may exist, but the supplier may still be required to go through all of the standard protocols of competitive bidding.
- **A Preferred Supplier:** These suppliers usually get the first chance at receiving a contract but may still have to go through the entire competitive bidding process, but with a minimum amount of paperwork. Proposal information on previous history, past experience with the customer or the type of project, and other such information may not be required as part of the contractual bidding process in order to reduce time and cost. A relationship between the customer and the supplier exists. Information on lessons learned, best practices, and technological changes are often exchanged freely.

- **A Strategic Partnership Supplier:** A strong relationship exists between the customer and supplier, and they freely exchange information, especially strategic information. Each views the relationship as a long-term partnership with long-term benefits. Strategic suppliers often receive sole-source contracts without having to prepare a formal proposal, thus generating cost savings for both companies. Strategic suppliers may not be the lowest cost suppliers, but the customer's cost savings of not having to perform competitive bidding is well worth the effort.

External partnerships, if properly managed, can provide significant long-term benefits to both the customer and supplier.

The Department of Defense has been conducting research into what constitutes an effective supplier relationship.[3] Each Chrysler supplier had a Chrysler person knowledgeable about the supplier's business to contact for all supplier dealings for that commodity. These companies also interacted with key suppliers in close teaming arrangements that facilitated sharing information. Commonly called integrated product teams (IPTs), members worked together so that design, manufacturing, and cost issues were considered together. Team members were encouraged to participate as partners in meeting project goals and to interact frequently. In addition, some companies collocated suppliers with their own people or set up central working facilities with suppliers for working out issues such as how a product might be improved or be made less expensive. Motorola and Xerox saw such teams as a key vehicle for facilitating early supplier involvement in their products—one of their primary strategies. Motorola said key suppliers had building access and came in many times during a week to work with Motorola engineers.

These companies also asked suppliers to meet high standards, then differentiated the types of relationships within their pool of suppliers. Many treated key suppliers—those contributing the most to their product, such as critical parts or unique processes—differently than suppliers for noncritical or standard parts. For example, one Corning division categorized suppliers and developed relationships with them based on the extent of their impact on the customer and performance. Level 1 suppliers have a direct impact on customer satisfaction, level 2 suppliers are important to day-to-day operations, and level 3 suppliers provided commonly available products. DuPont differentiated between alliance partners—suppliers with similar goals and objectives that wish to work with DuPont for mutual benefit—and all other suppliers.

Perhaps more significantly, Chrysler's relationships with its suppliers had evolved to the point that it no longer needed to make large investments in some key technology areas. Instead, the suppliers made the technology investment themselves and had enough confidence in their relationship with Chrysler that they did not fear the long-term commitment that this entailed. For its part, Chrysler trusted the suppliers to make investments that would help keep their vehicles competitive. In this case, both supplier and product developer saw their success as that of the final product and a continuing mutually beneficial relationship.

---

3. *DoD Can Help Suppliers Contribute More to Weapon System Programs,* Best Practices Series, GAO/NSIAD-98-87, Government Accounting Office, March 1998, pp. 38, 48, 51.

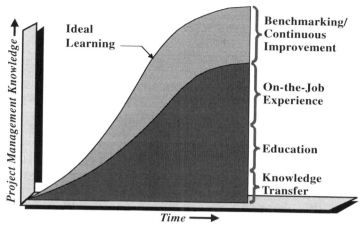

FIGURE 13–8. Project management learning curve.

13.9 TRAINING AND EDUCATION

PMBOK® Guide, 2004
Task 3 of Professional
Responsibility—Enhance
Individual Competence

Given that most companies use the same basic tools as part of their methodology, what makes one company better than another? The answer lies in the execution of the methodology. Training and education can accelerate not only the project management maturity process but also the ability to execute the methodology.

Actual learning takes place in three areas, as shown in Figure 13–8: on-the-job experience, education, and knowledge transfer. Ideal project management knowledge would be obtained by allowing each employee to be educated on the results of the company's lessons learned studies including risk management, benchmarking, and continuous improvement efforts. Unfortunately, this is rarely done and ideal learning is hardly ever reached. To make matters worse, actual learning is less than most people believe because of lost knowledge. This lost knowledge is shown in Figure 13–9 and will occur even in companies that maintain low employee turnover ratios. These two figures also illustrate the importance of maintaining the same personnel on the project for the duration of the effort.

Companies often find themselves in a position of having to provide a key initiative for a multitude of people, or simply specialized training to a program team about to embark upon a new long-term effort. In such cases, specialized training is required, with targeted goals and results that are specifically planned for. The elements common to training on a key initiative or practice include[4]:

- A front-end analysis of the program team's needs and training requirements
- Involvement of the program teams in key decisions

---

4. Adapted from *DoD Training Can Do More to Help Weapon System Programs Implement Best Practices,* Best Practices Series, GAO/NSIAD-99-206, Government Accounting Office, August 1999, pp. 40–41, 51.

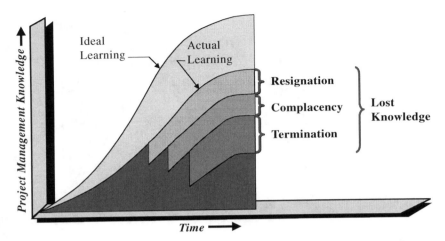

FIGURE 13–9. Project management learning curve.

- Customized training to meet program team's specific needs
- Targeted training for the implementation of specific practices
- Improved training outcomes, including better course depth, timeliness, and reach

The front-end analysis is used to determine the needs and requirements of the program office implementing the practice. The analysis is also used to identify and address barriers each program office faces when implementing new practices. According to the director of the benchmarking forum for the American Society of Training and Development, this type of analysis is crucial for an organization to be able to institute performance-improving measures. Using information from the front-end analysis, the training organizations customize the training to ensure that it directly assists program teams in implementing new practices. To ensure that the training will address the needs of the program teams, the training organizations involve the staff in making important training decisions. Program staff help decide the amount of training to be provided for certain job descriptions, course objectives, and depth of course coverage. Companies doing this believe their training approach, which includes program staff, has resulted in the right amount of course depth, timeliness, and coverage of personnel.

Officials at Boeing's Employee Training and Development organization state that their primary goal is to support their customers, the employees assigned to the Commercial Airplane Group. The training representatives develop a partnership with the staff from the beginning of the program to design and manufacture a new airplane. The training representatives form "drop teams" to collate with the program to conduct a front-end analysis and learn as much as possible about the business process and the staff's concerns. The analysis allows the drop team to determine what training is needed to support the staff implementing the new practice.

Boeing training officials said they worked side by side with the program staff to create a training program that provided team building and conflict resolution techniques and technical skills training that specifically focused on improving work competencies that would change as a result of the 777's new digital environment. To ensure all 777 staff was equally trained, employees were required to complete training before they reported to the program. For example, the professional employees—engineers and drafters—were required to complete 120 hours of start-up training on several key 777 practices, including design build teams and computer-aided three-dimensional interactive applications software.[5] Teams were often trained together at the work location. Boeing officials stated that training was instrumental to the implementation of key practices on the 777 program, such as design build teams—essentially integrated program teams (IPTs). The officials stated that design build teams were at odds with the company's culture because employees were not accustomed to working in a team environment and sharing information across functional areas.

Boeing's director of learning program development summarized the corporate training strategy for implementing new practices as one that includes a clearly stated vision or mission statement, well-defined goals, and enablers, such as training and good processes, to support the implementers. This philosophy enabled Boeing to take a year to develop the training program tailored to the 777 program—which was intended to change the corporate culture and encourage employees to rethink how they did their jobs. Both Boeing training and program officials believe that the training investment resulted in the successful implementation of the key 777 practices.

While the company officials acknowledged that training was instrumental in the implementation of the key practices, everyone also stated that training was just one of the necessary components. Creating the right environment is also key to the successful implementation of new practices, and the quality of the training was dependent on the environment. Boeing officials stressed that strong leadership is often another key force. At the inception of key programs at IBM, top leaders provide sufficient funding for training, well-defined expectations, clear direction, oversight, continued interest, and incentives to ensure that the new practices are possible to implement. The manager for the 777 program stated that Boeing's management works in teams—a key practice. He believed that it was management's ability to lead by example that helped prevent a return to the former functional way of operating. These companies believe that other factors, such as an accommodating organizational structure, good internal communication, consistent application, and supportive technology, are needed to foster the implementation of key new practices.

13.10 INTEGRATED PRODUCT/PROJECT TEAMS

PMBOK® Guide, 2004
Chapter 4 Integration Management
Chapter 9 Human Resources Management

In recent years, there has been an effort to substantially improve the formation and makeup of teams required to develop a new product or implement a new practice. These teams have membership from across the entire organization and are called integrated product/project teams (IPTs).

---

5. This application is a computer-based design tool that allows designers the opportunity to view design drawings and the interface of millions of airplane parts as three-dimensional.

The IPT consists of a sponsor, program manager, and the core team. For the most part, members of the core team are assigned full-time to the team but may not be on the team for the duration of the entire project.

The skills needed to be a member of the core team include:

- Self-starter ability
- Work without supervision
- Good communication skills
- Cooperative
- Technical understanding
- Willing to learn backup skills
- Able to perform feasibility studies and cost/benefit analyses
- Able to perform or assist in market research studies
- Able to evaluate asset utilization
- Decision-maker
- Knowledgeable in risk management
- Understand the need for continuous validation

Each IPT is given a project charter that identifies the project's mission and identifies the assigned project manager. However, unlike traditional charters, the IPT charter can also identify the key members of the IPT by name or job responsibility.

Unlike traditional project teams, the IPT thrives on sharing information across the team and collective decision-making. IPTs eventually develop their own culture and, as such, can function in either a formal or informal capacity.

Since the concept of an IPT is well suited to large, long-term projects, it is no wonder that the Department of Defense has been researching best practices for an IPT.[6] The government looked at four projects, in both the public and private sectors, which were highly successful using the IPT approach and four government projects that had less than acceptable results. The successful IPT projects are shown in Table 13–4. The unsuccessful IPT

TABLE 13–4. EFFECTIVE IPTS

Program	Cost Status	Schedule Status	Performance Status
Daimler-Chrysler	Product cost was lowered	Decreased development cycle months by 50 percent	Improved vehicle designs
Hewlett-Packard	Lowered cost by over 60 percent	Shortened development schedule by over 60 percent	Improved system integration and product design
3M	Outperformed cost goals	Product deliveries shortened by 12 to 18 months	Improved performance by 80 percent
Advanced Amphibious Assault Vehicle	Product unit cost lower than original estimate	Ahead of original development schedule	Demonstrated fivefold increase in speed

6. *DoD Teaming Practices Not Achieving Potential Results,* Best Practices Series, GOA-01-501, Government Accounting Office, April 2001.

TABLE 13–5. INEFFECTIVE IPTS

Program	Cost Status	Schedule Status	Performance Status
CH-60S Helicopter	Increased cost but due to additional purchases	Schedule delayed	Software and structural difficulties
Extended Range Guided Munitions	Increases in development costs	Schedule slipped three years	Redesigning due to technical difficulties
Global Broadcast Service	Experiencing cost growth	Schedule slipped 1.5 years	Software and hardware design shortfalls
Land Warrior	Cost increase of about 50 percent	Schedule delayed four years	Overweight equipment, inadequate battery power and design

projects are shown in Table 13–5. In analyzing the data, the government came up with the results shown in Figure 13–10. Each vertical line in Figure 13–10 is a situation where the IPT must go outside of its own domain to seek information and approvals. Each time this happens, it is referred to as a "hit." The government research indicated that the greater the number of hits, the more likely it is that the time, cost, and performance constraints will not be achieved. The research confirmed that if the IPT has the knowledge necessary to make decisions, and also has the authority to make the decisions, then the desired performance would be achieved. Hits will delay decisions and cause schedule slippages.

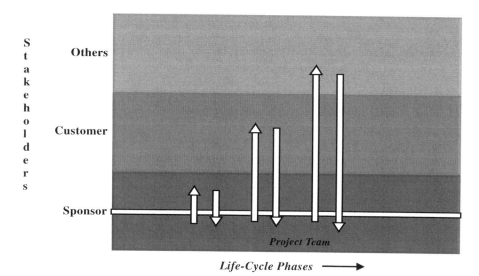

FIGURE 13–10. Knowledge and authority.

13.11 STUDYING TIPS FOR THE PMI® PROJECT MANAGEMENT CERTIFICATION EXAM

This section is applicable as a review of the principles to support the knowledge areas and domain groups in the PMBOK® Guide. This chapter addresses:

- Human Resources Management
- Professional Responsibility
- Planning
- Execution

Understanding the following principles is beneficial if the reader is using this text to study for the PMP® Certification Exam:

- Principles and tasks included under professional responsibility
- Factors that affect professional responsibility such as conflicts of interest and gifts
- PMI® Code of Professional Conduct (this can be downloaded from the PMI® web site, pmi.org)
- That personnel performance reviews, whether formal or informal, are part of a project manager's responsibility
- Differences between project management in a large company and project management in a small company

The following multiple-choice questions will be helpful in reviewing the principles of this chapter:

1. You have been sent on a business trip to visit one of the companies bidding on a contract to be awarded by your company. You are there to determine the validity of the information in its proposal. They take you to dinner one evening at a very expensive restaurant. When the bill comes, you should:
   A. Thank them for their generosity and let them pay the bill
   B. Thank them for their generosity and tell them that you prefer to pay for your own meal
   C. Offer to pay for the meal for everyone and put it on your company's credit card
   D. Offer to pay the bill, put it on your company's credit card, and make the appropriate adjustment in the company's bid price to cover the cost of the meals

2. You are preparing a proposal in response to a Request for Proposal (RFP) from a potentially important client. The salesperson in your company working on the proposal tells you to "lie" in the proposal to improve the company's chance of winning the contract. You should:
   A. Do as you are told
   B. Refuse to work on the proposal
   C. Report the matter to your superior, the project sponsor, or the corporate legal group
   D. Resign from the company

3. You are preparing for a customer interface meeting and your project sponsor asks you to lie to the customer about certain test results. You should:
   A. Do as you are told
   B. Refuse to work on the project from this point forth

    C. Report the matter to either your superior or the corporate legal group for advice

    D. Resign from the company

4. One of the project managers in your company approaches you with a request to use some of the charge numbers from your project (which is currently running under budget) for work on their project (which is currently running over budget). Your contract is a cost-reimbursable contract for a client external to your company. You should:

    A. Do as you are requested

    B. Refuse to do this unless the project manager allows you to use his charge numbers later on

    C. Report the matter to your superior, the project sponsor, or the corporate legal group

    D. Ask the project manager to resign from the company

5. You have submitted a proposal to a client as part of a competitive bidding effort. One of the people evaluating your bid informs you that it is customary to send them some gifts in order to have a better chance of winning the contract. You should:

    A. Send them some gifts

    B. Do not send any gifts and see what happens

    C. Report the matter to your superior, the project sponsor, or the corporate legal group for advice

    D. Withdraw the proposal

6. You just discovered that the company in which your brother-in-law is employed has submitted a proposal to your company. Your brother-in-law has asked you to do everything possible to make sure that his company will win the contract because his job may be in jeopardy. You should:

    A. Do what your brother-in-law requests

    B. Refuse to look into the matter and pretend it never happened

    C. Report the conflict of interest to your superior, the project sponsor, or the corporate legal group

    D. Hire an attorney for advice

7. As part of a proposal evaluation team, you have discovered that the contract will be awarded to Alpha Company and that a formal announcement will be made in two days. The price of Alpha Company's stock may just skyrocket because of this contract award. You should:

    A. Purchase as much Alpha Company stock as you can within the next two days

    B. Tell family members to purchase the stock

    C. Tell employees in the company to purchase the stock

    D. Do nothing about stock purchases until after the formal announcement has been made

8. Your company has decided to cancel a contract with Beta Company. Only a handful of employees know about this upcoming cancellation. The announcement of the cancellation will be made in about two days. You own several shares of Beta Company stock and know full well that the stock will plunge on the bad news. You should:

    A. Sell your stock as quickly as possible

    B. Sell your stock and tell others whom you know own the stock to do the same thing

    C. Tell the executives to sell their shares if they are stockowners

    D. Do nothing until after the formal announcement is made

9. You are performing a two-day quality audit of one of your suppliers. The supplier asks you to remain a few more days so that they can take you out deep-sea fishing and gambling at the local casino. You should:

    A. Accept as long as you complete the audit within two days

    B. Accept but take vacation time for fishing and gambling

C. Accept their invitation but at a later time so that it does not interfere with the audit

D. Gracefully decline their invitation

10. You have been assigned as the project manager for a large project in the Pacific Rim. This is a very important project for both your company and the client. In your first meeting with the client, you are presented with a very expensive gift for yourself and another expensive gift for your husband. You were told by your company that this is considered an acceptable custom when doing work in this country. You should:

A. Gracefully accept both gifts

B. Gracefully accept both gifts but report only your gift to your company

C. Gracefully accept both gifts and report both gifts to your company

D. Gracefully refuse both gifts.

11. Your company is looking at the purchase of some property for a new plant. You are part of the committee making the final decision. You discover that the owner of a local auto dealership from whom you purchase family cars owns one of the properties. The owner of the dealership tells you in confidence that he will give you a new model car to use for free for up to three years if your company purchases his property for the new plant. You should:

A. Say thank you and accept the offer

B. Remove yourself from the committee for conflict of interest

C. Report the matter to your superior, the project sponsor, or the corporate legal group for advice

D. Accept the offer as long as the car is in your spouse's name

12. Your company has embarked upon a large project (with you as project manager) and as an output from the project there will be some toxic waste as residue from the manufacturing operations. A subsidiary plan has been developed for the containment and removal of the toxic waste and no environmental danger exists. This information on toxic waste has not been made available to the general public as yet, and the general public does not appear to know about this waste problem. During an interview with local newspaper personnel you are discussing the new project and the question of environmental concerns comes up. You should:

A. Say there are no problems with environmental concerns

B. Say that you have not looked at the environmental issues problems as yet

C. Say nothing and ask for the next question

D. Be truthful and reply as delicately as possible

13. As a project manager, you establish a project policy that you, in advance of the meeting, review all handouts presented to your external customer during project status review meetings. While reviewing the handouts, you notice that one slide contains company confidential information. Presenting this information to the customer would certainly enhance good will. You should:

A. Present the information to the customer

B. Remove the confidential information immediately

C. Discuss the possible violation with senior management and the legal department before taking any action

D. First discuss the situation with the team member that created the slide and then discuss the possible violation with senior management and the legal department before taking any action

14. You are managing a project for an external client. Your company developed a new testing procedure to validate certain properties of a product and the new testing procedure was developed entirely with internal funds. Your company owns all of the intellectual property

rights associated with the new test. The workers that developed the new test used one of the components developed for your current customer as part of the experimental process. The results using the new test showed that the component would actually exceed the customer's expectations. You should:

A. Show the results to the customer but do not discuss the fact that it came from the new test procedure

B. Do not show the results of the new test procedure since the customer's specifications call for use of the old test procedures

C. First change the customer's specifications and then show the customer the results

D. Discuss the release of this information with your legal department and senior management before taking any action

15. Using the same scenario as in the previous question, assume that the new test procedure that is expected to be more accurate than the old test procedure indicates that performance will not meet customer specifications whereas the old test indicates that customer specifications will be barely met. You should:

A. Present the old test results to the customer showing that specification requirements will be met

B. Show both sets of test results and explain that the new procedure is unproven technology

C. First change the customer's specifications and then show the customer the results

D. Discuss the release of this information with your legal department and senior management before taking any action

16. Your customer has demanded to see the "raw data" test results from last week's testing. Usually the test results are not released to customers until after the company reaches a conclusion on the meaning of the test results. Your customer has heard through the grapevine that the testing showed poor results. Management has left the entire decision up to you. You should:

A. Show the results and explain that it is simply raw data and that your company's interpretation of the results will be forthcoming

B. Withhold the information until after the results are verified

C. Stall for time even if it means lying to the customer

D. Explain to the customer your company's policy of not releasing raw data

17. One of your team members plays golf with your external customer's project manager. You discover that the employee has been feeding the customer company-sensitive information. You should:

A. Inform the customer that project information from anyone other than the project manager is not official until released by the project manager

B. Change the contractual terms and conditions and release the information

C. Remove the employee from your project team

D. Explain to the employee the ramifications of his actions and that he still represents the company when not at work; then report this as a violation

18. Your company has a policy that all company-sensitive material must be stored in locked filing cabinets at the end of each day. One of your employees has received several notices from the security office for violating this policy. You should:

A. Reprimand the employee

B. Remove the employee from your project

C. Ask the Human Resources Group to have the employee terminated

D. Counsel the employee as well as other team members on the importance of confidentiality and the possible consequences for violations

19. You have just received last month's earned-value information that must be shown to the customer in the monthly status review meeting. Last month's data showed unfavorable variances that exceeded the permissible threshold limits on time and cost variances. This was the result of a prolonged power outage in the manufacturing area. Your manufacturing engineer tells you that this is not a problem and next month you will be right on target on time and cost as you have been in the last five months. You should:

A. Provide the data to the customer and be truthful in the explanation of the variances

B. Adjust the variances so that they fall within the threshold limits since this problem will correct itself next month

C. Do not report any variances this month

D. Expand the threshold limits on the acceptable variances but do not tell the customer

20. You are working in a foreign country where it is customary for a customer to present gifts to the contractor's project manager throughout the project as a way of showing appreciation. Declining the gifts would be perceived by the customer as an insult. Your company has a policy on how to report gifts received. The *best* way to handle this situation would be to:

A. Refuse all gifts

B. Send the customer a copy of our company's policy on accepting gifts

C. Accept the gifts and report the gifts according to policy

D. Report all gifts even though the policy says that some gifts need not be reported

21. You are interviewing a candidate to fill a project management position in your company. On her resume, she states that she is a PMP®. One of your workers who knows the candidate informs you that she is not a PMP® yet but is planning to take the test next month and certainly expects to pass. You should:

A. Wait until she passes the exam before interviewing her

B. Interview her and ask her why she lied

C. Inform PMI® of the violation

D. Forget about it and hire her if she looks like the right person for the job

22. You are managing a multinational project from your office in Chicago. Half of your project team are from a foreign country but are living in Chicago while working on your project. These people inform you that two days during next week are national religious holidays in their country and they will be observing the holiday by not coming into work. You should:

A. Respect their beliefs and say nothing

B. Force them to work because they are in the United States where their holiday is not celebrated

C. Tell them that they must work noncompensated overtime when they return to work in order to make up the lost time

D. Remove them from the project team if possible

23. PMI® informs you that one of your team members who took the PMP® exam last week and passed may have had the answers to the questions in advance provided to him by some of your other team members who are also PMP®s and were tutoring him. PMI® is asking for your support in the investigation. You should:

A. Assist PMI® in the investigation of the violation

B. Call in the employee for interrogation and counseling

C. Call in the other team members for interrogation and counseling

D. Tell PMI® that it is their problem, not your problem

24. One of your team members has been with you for the past year since her graduation from college. The team member informs you that she is now a PMP® and shows you her certificate from PMI® acknowledging this. You wonder how she was qualified to take the exam since she had no prior work experience prior to joining your company one year ago. You should:

A. Report this to PMI® as a possible violation
B. Call in the employee for counseling
C. Ask the employee to surrender her PMP® credentials
D. Do nothing

25. Four companies have responded to your RFP. Each proposal has a different technical solution to your problem and each proposal states that the information in the proposal is company-proprietary knowledge and not to be shared with anyone. After evaluation of the proposals, you discover that the best technical approach is from the highest bidder. You are unhappy about this. You decide to show the proposal from the highest bidder to the lowest bidder to see if the lowest bidder can provide the same technical solution but at a lower cost. This situation is:

A. Acceptable since once the proposals are submitted to your company, you have unlimited access to the intellectual property in the proposals
B. Acceptable since all companies do this
C. Acceptable as long as you inform the high bidder that you are showing their proposal to the lowest bidder
D. Unacceptable and is a violation of the Code of Professional Conduct

ANSWERS

1. B
2. C
3. C
4. C
5. C
6. C
7. D
8. D
9. D
10. C
11. C
12. D
13. D
14. D
15. D
16. A
17. D

18. D
19. A
20. D
21. C
22. A
23. A
24. A
25. D

PROBLEMS

13–1 Beta Company has decided to modify its wage and salary administration program whereby line managers are evaluated for promotion and merit increases based on how well they have lived up to the commitments that they made to the project managers. What are the advantages and disadvantages of this approach?

13–2 How should a project manager handle a situation in which the functional employee (or functional manager) appears to have more loyalty to his profession, discipline, or expertise than to the project? Can a project manager also have this loyalty, say, on an R&D project?

13–3 Most wage and salary administrators contend that project management organizational structures must be "married" to the personnel evaluation process because personnel are always concerned with how they will be evaluated. Furthermore, converting from a traditional structure to a project management structure cannot be accomplished without first considering performance evaluation. What are your feelings on this?

13–4 As part of the evaluation process for functional employees, each project manager submits a written, confidential evaluation report to the employee's department manager who, in turn, makes the final judgment. The employee is permitted to see only the evaluation from his department manager. Assume that the average department merit increase is 7 percent, and that the employee could receive the merit increases shown in the following table. How would he respond in each case?

Project Manager's Evaluation	Merit Increase, %	Credit or Blame to		Reason
		P.M.	**Fct. Mgr.**	
Excellent	5			
Excellent	7			
Excellent	9			
Average	5			
Average	7			
Average	9			
Poor	5			
Poor	7			
Poor	9			

13–5 Should the evaluation form in Figure 13–4 be shown to the employees?

13–6 Does a functional employee have the right to challenge any items in the project manager's nonconfidential evaluation form?

13–7 Some people contend that functional employees should be able to evaluate the effectiveness of the project manager after project termination. Design an evaluation form for this purpose.

13–8 Some executives feel that evaluation forms should not include cooperation and attitude. The executives feel that a functional employee will always follow the instructions of the functional manager, and therefore attitude and cooperation are unnecessary topics. Does this kind of thinking also apply to the indirect evaluation forms that are filled out by the project managers?

13–9 Consider a situation in which the project manager (a generalist) is asked to provide an evaluation of a functional employee (a specialist). Can the project manager effectively evaluate the functional employee on technical performance? If not, then on what information can the project manager base his evaluation? Can a grade-7 generalist evaluate a grade-12 specialist?

13–10 Gary has been assigned as a part-time, assistant project manager. Gary's duties are split between assistant project management and being a functional employee. In addition, Gary reports both vertically to his functional manager and horizontally to a project manager. As part of his project responsibilities, Gary must integrate activities between his department and two other departments within his divison. His responsibilities also include writing a nonconfidential performance evaluation for all functional employees from all three departments that are assigned to his project. Can Gary effectively and honestly evaluate functional employees in his own department—people with whom he will be working side by side when the project is over? Should the project manager come to his rescue? Suppose Gary is a part-time project manager instead of a part-time assistant project manager. Can anyone come to his rescue now?

13–11 The following question was asked of executives: How do you know when to cut off research? The answers given: That's a good question, a very good question, and some people don't know when to cut it off. You have to have a feel; in some cases it depends on how much resource you have and whether you have enough resources to take a chance on sustaining research that may appear to be heading for a dead end. You don't know sometimes whether you're heading down the wrong path or not; sometimes it's pretty obvious you ought to shift directions—you've gone about as far as you can or you've taken it far enough that you can demonstrate to your own satisfaction that you just can't get there from here, or it's going to be very costly. You may discover that there are more productive ways to get around the barrier; you're always looking for faster ways. And it depends entirely on how creative the person is, whether he has tunnel vision, a very narrow vision, or whether he is fairly flexible in his conceptual thinking so that he can conceive of better ways to solve the problem. Discuss the validity of these remarks.

13–12 In a small company, can a functional manager act as director of engineering and director of project management at the same time?

13–13 In 1982, an electrical equipment manufacturer decentralized the organization, allowing each division manager to set priorities for the work in his division. The division manager of the R&D division selected as his number one priority project the development of low-cost methods for manufacturing. This project required support from the manufacturing division. The division manager for manufacturing did not assign proper resources, claiming that the results of such a project would not be realized for at least five years, and that he (the manufacturing manager) was worried only about the immediate profits. Can this problem be resolved and divisional decentralization still be maintained?

13–14 The executives of a company that produces electro-optical equipment for military use found it necessary to implement project management using a matrix. The project managers reported to corporate sales, and the engineers with the most expertise were promoted to project engineering. After the first year of operation, it became obvious to the executives that the engineering functional managers were not committed to the projects. The executives then made a critical decision. The functional employees selected by the line managers to serve on projects would report as a solid line to the project engineer and dotted to the line manager. The project engineers, who were selected for their technical expertise, were allowed to give technical direction and monetary rewards to the employees. Can this situation work? What happens if an employee has a technical question? Can he go to his line manager? Should the employees return to their former line managers at project completion? What are the authority/responsibility problems with this structure? What are the long-term implications?

13–15 Consider the four items listed on page 123 that describe what happens when a matrix goes out of control. Which of these end up creating the greatest difficulty for the company? for the project managers? for the line managers? for executives?

13–16 As a functional employee, the project manager tells you, "Sign these prints or I'll fire you from this project." How should this situation be handled?

13–17 How efficient can project management be in a unionized, immobile manpower environment?

13–18 Corporate salary structures and limited annual raise allocations often prevent proper proj-ect management performance rewards. Explain how each of the following could serve as a motivational factor:

   a. Job satisfaction
   b. Personal recognition
   c. Intellectual growth

Modern Developments in Project Management

Related Case Studies (from Kerzner/*Project Management Case Studies,* 2nd Edition)	Related Workbook Exercises (from Kerzner/*Project Management Workbook and PMP®/CAPM® Exam Study Guide,* 9th Edition)	PMBOK® Guide, 3rd Edition, Reference Section for the PMP® Certification Exam
• Lakes Automotive • Ferris HealthCare, Inc. • Clark Faucet Company	• Project Management Maturity Questionnaire • Multiple Choice Exam	None

14.0 INTRODUCTION

PMBOK® Guide, 2004
PMBOK Chapters 1, 2, and 3 (inclusive)

As more industries accept project management as a way of life, the change in project management practices has taken place at an astounding rate. But what is even more important is the fact that these companies are sharing their accomplishments with other companies during benchmarking activities.

Eight recent interest areas are included in this chapter:

● The project management maturity model (PMMM)
● Developing effective procedural documentation
● Project management methodologies
● Continuous improvement
● Capacity planning
● Competency models

- Managing multiple projects
- End-of-phase review meetings

14.1 THE PROJECT MANAGEMENT MATURITY MODEL (PMMM)

All companies desire excellence in project management. Unfortunately, not all companies recognize that the time frame can be shortened by performing strategic planning for project management. The simple use of project management, even for an extended period of time, does *not* lead to excellence. Instead, it can result in repetitive mistakes and, what's worse, learning from your own mistakes rather than from the mistakes of others.

Companies such as Motorola, Nortel, Ericsson, and Compaq perform strategic planning for project management, and the results are self-explanatory. What Nortel and Ericsson have accomplished from 1992 to 1998, other companies have not achieved in twenty years of using project management.

Strategic planning for project management is unlike other forms of strategic planning in that it is most often performed at the middle-management level, rather than by executive management. Executive management is still involved, mostly in a supporting role, and provides funding together with employee release time for the effort. Executive involvement will be necessary to make sure that whatever is recommended by middle management will not result in unwanted changes to the corporate culture.

Organizations tend to perform strategic planning for new products and services by laying out a well-thought-out plan and then executing the plan with the precision of a surgeon. Unfortunately, strategic planning for project management, if performed at all, is done on a trial-by-fire basis. However, there are models that can be used to assist corporations in performing strategic planning for project management and achieving maturity and excellence in a reasonable period of time.

The foundation for achieving excellence in project management can best be described as the project management maturity model (PMMM), which is comprised of five levels, as shown in Figure 14–1. Each of the five levels represents a different degree of maturity in project management.

- *Level 1—Common Language:* In this level, the organization recognizes the importance of project management and the need for a good understanding of the basic knowledge on project management, along with the accompanying language/terminology.
- *Level 2—Common Processes:* In this level, the organization recognizes that common processes need to be defined and developed such that successes on one project can be repeated on other projects. Also included in this level is the recognition that project management principles can be applied to and support other methodologies employed by the company.
- *Level 3—Singular Methodology:* In this level, the organization recognizes the synergistic effect of combining all corporate methodologies into a singular methodology, the center of which is project management. The synergistic effects also make process control easier with a single methodology than with multiple methodologies.

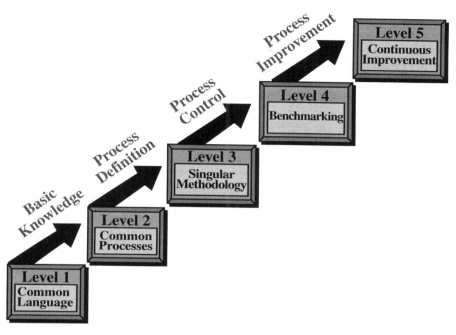

FIGURE 14–1. The five levels of maturity.

- *Level 4—Benchmarking:* This level contains the recognition that process improvement is necessary to maintain a competitive advantage. Benchmarking must be performed on a continuous basis. The company must decide whom to benchmark and what to benchmark.
- *Level 5—Continuous Improvement:* In this level, the organization evaluates the information obtained through benchmarking and must then decide whether or not this information will enhance the singular methodology.

When we talk about levels of maturity (and even life-cycle phases), there exists a common misbelief that all work must be accomplished sequentially (i.e., in series). This is not necessarily true. Certain levels can and do overlap. The magnitude of the overlap is based upon the amount of risk the organization is willing to tolerate. For example, a company can begin the development of project management checklists to support the methodology while it is still providing project management training for the workforce. A company can create a center for excellence in project management before benchmarking is undertaken.

Although overlapping does occur, the order in which the phases are completed cannot change. For example, even though Level 1 and Level 2 can overlap, Level 1 *must* still be completed before Level 2 can be completed. Overlapping of several of the levels can take place, as shown in Figure 14–2.

- *Overlap of Level 1 and Level 2:* This overlap will occur because the organization can begin the development of project management processes either while refinements are being made to the common language or during training.

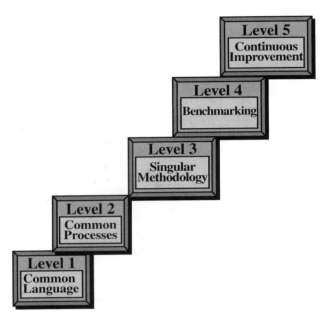

FIGURE 14–2. Overlapping levels.

- *Overlap of Level 3 and Level 4:* This overlap occurs because, while the organization is developing a singular methodology, plans are being made as to the process
  for improving the methodology.
- *Overlap of Level 4 and Level 5:* As the organization becomes more and more
  committed to benchmarking and continuous improvement, the speed by which the
  organization wants changes to be made can cause these two levels to have significant overlap. The feedback from Level 5 back to Level 4 and Level 3, as shown
  in Figure 14–3, implies that these three levels form a continuous improvement cycle, and it may even be possible for all three of these levels to overlap.

Level 2 and Level 3 generally do not overlap. It may be possible to begin some of the
Level 3 work before Level 2 is completed, but this is highly unlikely. Once a company is
committed to a singular methodology, work on other methodologies generally terminates.
Also, companies can create a Center for Excellence in project management early in the
life-cycle process, but will not receive the full benefits until later on.

Risks can be assigned to each level of the PMMM. For simplicity's sake, the risks can
be labeled as low, medium, and high. The level of risk is most frequently associated with
the impact on the corporate culture. The following definitions can be assigned to these
three risks:

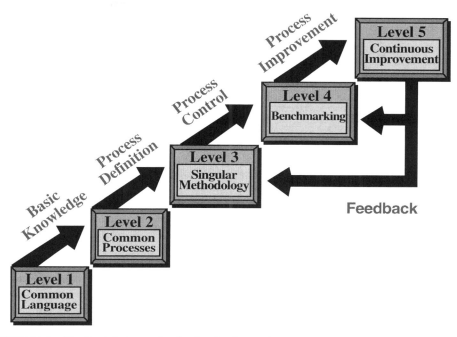

FIGURE 14–3. Feedback between the five levels of maturity.

- *Low Risk:* Virtually no impact upon the corporate culture, or the corporate culture is dynamic and readily accepts change.
- *Medium Risk:* The organization recognizes that change is necessary but may be unaware of the impact of the change. Multiple-boss reporting would be an example of a medium risk.
- *High Risk:* High risks occur when the organization recognizes that the changes resulting from the implementation of project management will cause a change in the corporate culture. Examples include the creation of project management methodologies, policies, and procedures, as well as decentralization of authority and decision-making.

Level 3 has the highest risk and degree of difficulty for the organization. This is shown in Figure 14–4. Once an organization is committed to Level 3, the time and effort needed to achieve the higher levels of maturity have a low degree of difficulty. Achieving Level 3, however, may require a major shift in the corporate culture.

These types of maturity models will become more common in the future, with generic models being customized for individual companies. These models will assist management in performing strategic planning for excellence in project management.

Level	Description	Degree of Difficulty
1	Common Language	Medium
2	Common Processes	Medium
3	Singular Methodology	High
4	Benchmarking	Low
5	Continuous Improvement	Low

FIGURE 14–4. Degrees of difficulty of the five levels of maturity.

14.2 DEVELOPING EFFECTIVE PROCEDURAL DOCUMENTATION

Good procedural documentation will accelerate the project management maturity process, foster support at all levels of management, and greatly improve project communications. The type of procedural documentation selected is heavily biased on whether we wish to manage formally or informally, but it should show how to conduct project-oriented activities and how to communicate in such a multidimensional environment. The project management policies, procedures, forms, and guidelines can provide some of these tools for delineating the process, as well as a format for collecting, processing, and communicating project-related data in an orderly, standardized format. Project planning and tracking, however, involve more than just the generation of paperwork. They require the participation of the entire project team, including support departments, subcontractors, and top management, and this involvement fosters unity. Procedural documents help to:

- Provide guidelines and uniformity
- Encourage useful, but minimum, documentation
- Communicate information clearly and effectively
- Standardize data formats
- Unify project teams
- Provide a basis for analysis
- Ensure document agreements for future reference
- Refuel commitments
- Minimize paperwork
- Minimize conflict and confusion

- Delineate work packages
- Bring new team members on board
- Build an experience track and method for future projects

Done properly, the process of project planning must involve both the performing and the customer organizations. This leads to visibility of the project at various organizational levels, and stimulates interest in the project and the desire for success.

The Challenges

Even though procedural documents can provide all these benefits, management is often reluctant to implement or fully support a formal project management system. Management concerns often center around four issues: overhead burden, start-up delays, stifled creativity, and reduced self-forcing control. First, the introduction of more organizational formality via policies, procedures, and forms might cost money, and additional funding may be needed to support and maintain the system. Second, the system is seen as causing start-up delays by requiring additional project definition before implementation can start. Third and fourth, the system is often perceived as stifling creativity and shifting project control from the responsible individual to an impersonal process. The comment of one project manager may be typical: "My support personnel feel that we spend too much time planning a project up front; it creates a very rigid environment that stifles innovation. The only purpose seems to be establishing a basis for controls against outdated measures and for punishment rather than help in case of a contingency." This comment illustrates the potential misuse of formal project management systems to establish unrealistic controls and penalties for deviations from the program plan rather than to help to find solutions.

How to Make It Work

Few companies have introduced project management procedures with ease. Most have experienced problems ranging from skepticism to sabotage of the procedural system. Many use incremental approaches to develop and implement their project management methodology. Doing this, however, is a multifaceted challenge to management. The problem is seldom one of understanding the techniques involved, such as budgeting and scheduling, but rather is a problem of involving the project team in the process, getting their input, support, and commitment, and establishing a supportive environment.

The procedural guidelines and forms of an established project management methodology can be especially useful during the project planning/definition phase. Not only does project management methodology help to delineate and communicate the four major sets of variables for organizing and managing the project—(1) tasks, (2) timing, (3) resources, and (4) responsibilities—it also helps to define measurable milestones, as well as report and review requirements. This provides project personnel the ability to measure project status and performance and supplies the crucial inputs for controlling the project toward the desired results.

Developing an effective project management methodology takes more than just a set of policies and procedures. It requires the integration of these guidelines and standards into the culture and value system of the organization. Management must lead the overall efforts and foster an environment conducive to teamwork. The greater the team spirit, trust, commitment, and quality of information exchange among team members, the more likely the team will be to develop effective decision-making processes, make individual and group commitments, focus on problem-solving, and operate in a self-forcing, self-correcting control mode.

Established Practices   Although project managers may have the right to establish their own policies and procedures, many companies design project control forms that can be used uniformly on all projects. Project control forms serve two vital purposes by establishing a common framework from which:

- The project manager will communicate with executives, functional managers, functional employees, and clients.
- Executives and the project manager can make meaningful decisions concerning the allocation of resources.

Some large companies with mature project management structures maintain a separate functional unit for forms control. This is quite common in aerospace and defense, but is also becoming common practice in other industries and in some smaller companies.

Large companies with a multitude of different projects do not have the luxury of controlling projects with three or four forms. There are different forms for planning, scheduling, controlling, authorizing work, and so on. It is not uncommon for companies to have 20 to 30 different forms, each dependent upon the type of project, length of project, dollar value, type of customer reporting, and other such arguments. Project managers are often allowed to set up their own administration for the project, which can lead to long-term damage if they each design their own forms for project control.

The best method for limiting the number of forms appears to be the task force concept, where both managers and doers have the opportunity to provide input. This may appear to be a waste of time and money, but in the long run provides large benefits.

To be effective, the following ground rules can be used:

- Task forces should include managers as well as doers.
- Task force members must be willing to accept criticism from other peers, superiors, and especially subordinates who must "live" with these forms.
- Upper-level management should maintain a rather passive (or monitoring) involvement.
- A minimum of signature approvals should be required for each form.
- Forms should be designed so that they can be updated periodically.
- Functional managers and project managers must be dedicated and committed to the use of the forms.

Categorizing the Broad   The dynamic nature of project management and its multifunctional in-
Spectrum of Documents   volvement create a need for a multitude of procedural documents to guide a project through the various phases and stages of integration.

Especially for larger organizations, the challenge is not only to provide management guidelines for each project activity, but also to provide a coherent procedural framework within which project leaders from all disciplines can work and communicate with each other. Specifically, each policy or procedure must be consistent with and accommodating to the various other functions that interface with the project over its life cycle. This complexity of intricate relations is illustrated in Figure 14–5.

One simple and effective way of categorizing the broad spectrum of procedural documents is by utilizing the work breakdown concept, as shown in Figure 14–6. Accordingly, the principal procedural categories are defined along the principal project life-cycle phases. Each category is then subdivided into (1) general management guidelines, (2) policies, (3) procedures, (4) forms, and (5) checklists. If necessary, the same concept can be carried forward one additional step to develop policies, procedures, forms, and checklists for the various project and functional sublevels of operation. Although this might be needed for very large programs, an effort should be made to minimize "layering" of policies and procedures to avoid new problems and costs. For most projects, a single document covers all levels of project operations.

As We Mature . . .

As companies become more mature in executing the project management methodology, project management policies and

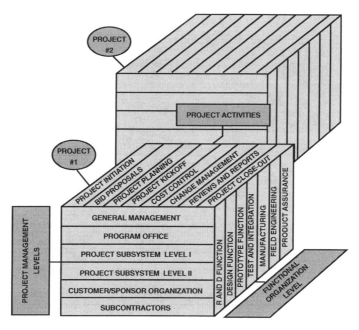

FIGURE 14–5. Interrelationship of project activities with various functional/organizational levels and project management levels.

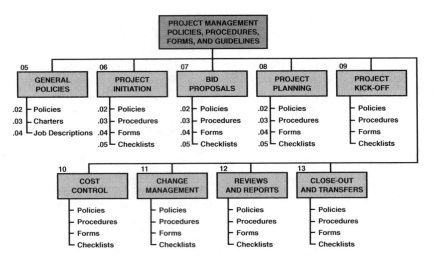

FIGURE 14–6.　Categorizing procedural documents within a work breakdown structure.

procedures are disregarded and replaced with guidelines, forms, and checklists. More flexibility is provided the project manager. Unfortunately, this takes time because executives must have faith in the ability of the project management methodology to work without the rigid controls provided by policies and procedures. Yet all companies seem to go through the evolutionary stages of policies and procedures before they get to guidelines, forms, and checklists.

14.3 PROJECT MANAGEMENT METHODOLOGIES

The ultimate purpose of any project management system is to increase the likelihood that your organization will have a continuous stream of successfully managed projects. The best way to achieve this goal is with good project management methodologies that are based upon guidelines and forms rather than policies and procedures. Methodologies must have enough flexibility that they can be adapted easily to each and every project.

Methodologies should be designed to support the corporate culture, not vice versa. It is a fatal mistake to purchase a canned methodology package that mandates that you change your corporate culture to support it. If the methodology does not support the culture, it will not be accepted. What converts any methodology into a world-class methodology is its adaptability to the corporate culture. There is no reason why companies cannot develop their own methodology. Companies such as Compaq Services, Ericsson, Nortel Networks, Johnson Controls, and Motorola are regarded as having world-class methodologies for project management and, in each case, the methodology was developed internally. Developing your own methodology internally to guarantee a fit with the corporate culture usually provides a much greater return on investment than purchasing canned packages that require massive changes.

Even the simplest methodology, if accepted by the organization and used correctly, can increase your chances of success. As an example, Matthew P. LoPiccolo, Director of I.S. Operations for Swagelok Company, describes the process Swagelok went through to develop its methodology:

> We developed our own version of an I.S. project management methodology in the early 90s. We had searched extensively and all we found were a lot of binders that we couldn't see being used effectively. There were just too many procedures and documents. Our answer was a simple checklist system with phase reviews. We called it Checkpoint.
>
> As strategic planning has become more important in our organization, the need for improved project management has risen as well. Project management has found its place as a key tool in executing tactical plans.
>
> As we worked to improve our Checkpoint methodology, we focused on keeping it simple. Our ultimate goal was to transform our methodology into a one-page matrix that was focused on deliverables within each project phase and categorized by key project management areas of responsibility. The key was to create something that would provide guidance in daily project direction and decision making. In order to gain widespread acceptance, the methodology needed to be easy to learn and quick to reference. The true test of its effectiveness is our ability to make decisions and take actions that are driven by the methodology.
>
> We also stayed away from the temptation to buy the solution in the form of a software package. Success is in the application of a practical methodology not in a piece of software. We use various software products as a tool set for scheduling, communicating, effort tracking, and storing project information such as time, budget, issues and lessons learned.

The summary description of the methodology developed by Swagelok is shown in Table 14–1. Swagelok also realized that training and education would be required to support both the methodology and project management in general. Table 14–2 shows the training plan created by Swagelok Company.

14.4 CONTINUOUS IMPROVEMENT

All too often complacency dictates the decision-making process. This is particularly true of organizations that have reached some degree of excellence in project management, become complacent, and then realize too late that they have lost their competitive advantage. This occurs when organizations fail to recognize the importance of continuous improvement.

Figure 14–7 illustrates why there is a need for continuous improvement. As companies begin to mature in project management and reach some degree of excellence, they achieve a sustained competitive advantage. The sustained competitive advantage might

TABLE 14–1. SWAGELOK COMPANY'S CHECKPOINT METHODOLOGY, VERSION 3

Project Management	Assessment	Initiate Define/Plan	Design Specify	Deliver Construct/Integrate	Close Deploy/Transition
Key deliverables	Feasibility report	Project charter Business requirements Technical requirements	Detailed business rqmts. Systems analysis Design prototype	System construction System integration pilot test Implementation plan	Project deliverables evaluation Operational transition Vendor performance report Project performance report
Approval	Feasibility report review Assessment approval	Project approval	Design approval Prototype approval	Construct integrate approval Deployment approval	Project audit Completion approval
Scope	Scope boundaries	Scope/deliverables Benefits/value Assumptions & alternatives Strategic & tactical: impact/ priority/alignment	Change request procedures Issue management procedure	Change management Issue management	Manage delivered value
Human resource	Resource identification	Roles and responsibilities General resource capacity Training requirements Business sponsors	Resource impact & assignment Team training	Resource management Resource performance Knowledge transfer End-customer training	Resource performance evaluation
Time	"Window of opportunity"	Preliminary project schedule Time reporting database	Work breakdown structure Project plan	Execute & monitor plan	Verify activity/completion Close time buckets

420

Cost	Cost projections	Capital budget Operating budget Return on investment	Budget details	Execute & monitor budget	Close cost centers
Procurement	Alternatives evaluation	Hardware Software Consulting services Vendor RFPs	Vendor selection Contract finalization	Purchase hardware & software Vendor performance report	Ongoing maintenance agreements Vendor performance evaluation
Quality	Vendor assessment Quality requirements	Quality plan Previous lessons learned	Test approach Config. management approach Review lessons learned Walkthroughs/reviews	Test plans Test (i.e., unit, integration, system, acceptance)	Process review Post-implementation review Capture to lessons learned
Risk	"Opportunity costs"	Risk assessment	Risk management plan	Risk mitigation	Capture to lessons learned
Technology	Architecture alignment	Architecture requirements	Architecture verification	Technology architecture	Architecture review
Communication	Inter- and intra-program coordination	Communication requirements project site	Progress reports Meetings schedule Project site update	Project site update	Administrative closure

TABLE 14-2. SWAGELOK COMPANY'S TRAINING PLAN

Project Management Toolset	Training Programs			
	Project Manager	Line Manager	Project Team Member	Executive Managment
1) Project management concepts	PMP class PMP certification PMO overview	PM 101 PM 102 — Small project management	PM 101	Executive overview
2) Checkpoint (methodology)	Teaching level	Basic understanding	Basic understanding	Overview
3) MS project (scheduling)	Knowledgeable to expect	Basic understanding	Not required	Not required
4) TSP (effort tracking)	Management level	Management level	Time entry	Not required
5) Budget DB (budget tracking)	Management of project budget	Owner of department budget	Not required	Not required
6) SICL DB (issues/changes/lessons management)	Owner	How to view	How to view	Not required
7) Netmosphere (project communication)	Owner, publisher	How to view	How to view	How to view

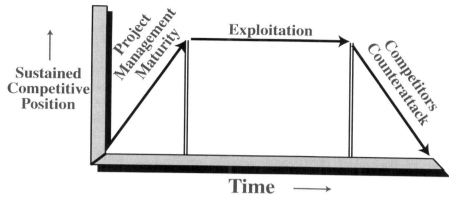

FIGURE 14–7. Why there is a need for continuous improvement.

very well be the single most important strategic objective of the firm. The firm will then begin the exploitation of its sustained competitive advantage.

Unfortunately, the competition is not sitting by idly watching you exploit your sustained competitive advantage. As the competition begins to counterattack, you may lose a large portion, if not all, of your sustained competitive advantage. To remain effective and competitive, the organization must recognize the need for continuous improvement, as shown in Figure 14–8. Continuous improvement allows a firm to maintain its competitive advantage even when the competitors counterattack.

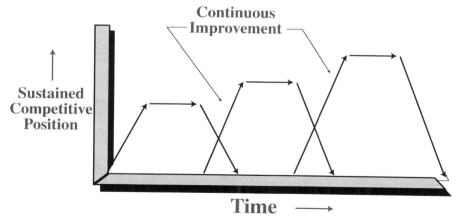

FIGURE 14–8. The need for continuous improvement.

14.5 CAPACITY PLANNING

As companies become excellent in project management, the benefits of performing more work in less time and with fewer resources becomes readily apparent. The question, of course, is how much more work can the organization take on? Companies are now struggling to develop capacity planning models to see how much new work can be undertaken within the existing human and nonhuman constraints.

Figure 14–9 illustrates the classical way that companies perform capacity planning. The approach outlined in this figure holds true for both project- and non–project-driven organizations. The "planning horizon" line indicates the point in time for capacity planning. The "proposals" line indicates the manpower needed for approved internal projects or a percentage (perhaps as much as 100 percent) for all work expected through competitive bidding. The combination of this line and the "manpower requirements" line, when compared against the current staffing, provides us with an indication of capacity. This technique can be effective if performed early enough such that training time is allowed for future manpower shortages.

The limitation to this process for capacity planning is that only human resources are considered. A more realistic method would be to use the method shown in Figure 14–10, which can also be applied to both project-driven and non–project-driven organizations. From Figure 14–10, projects are selected based upon such factors as strategic fit, profitability, who the customer is, and corporate benefits. The objectives for the projects selected are then defined in both business and technical terms, because there can be both business and technical capacity constraints.

The next step is a critical difference between average companies and excellent companies. Capacity constraints are identified from the summation of the schedules and plans.

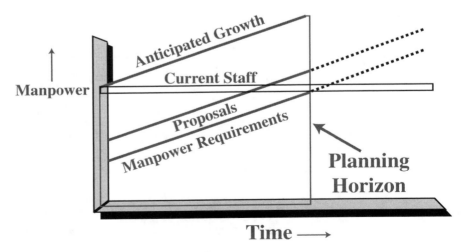

FIGURE 14–9. Classical capacity planning.

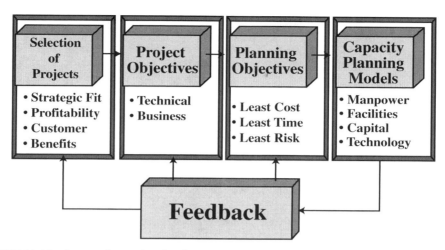

FIGURE 14–10. Improved capacity planning.

In excellent companies, project managers meet with sponsors to determine the objective of the plan, which is different than the objective of the project. Is the objective of the plan to achieve the project's objective with the least cost, least time, or least risk? Typically, only one of these applies, whereas immature organizations believe that all three can be achieved on every project. This, of course, is unrealistic.

The final box in Figure 14–10 is now the determination of the capacity limitations. Previously, we considered only human resource capacity constraints. Now we realize that the critical path of a project can be constrained not only by time but also by available manpower, facilities, cash flow, and even existing technology. It is possible to have multiple critical paths on a project other than those identified by time. Each of these critical paths provides a different dimension to the capacity planning models, and each of these constraints can lead us to a different capacity limitation. As an example, manpower might limit us to taking on only four additional projects. Based upon available facilities, however, we might only be able to undertake two more projects, and based upon available technology, we might be able to undertake only one new project.

14.6 COMPETENCY MODELS

In the twenty-first century, companies will replace job descriptions with competency models. Job descriptions for project management tend to emphasize the deliverables and expectations from the project manager, whereas competency models emphasize the specific skills needed to achieve the deliverables.

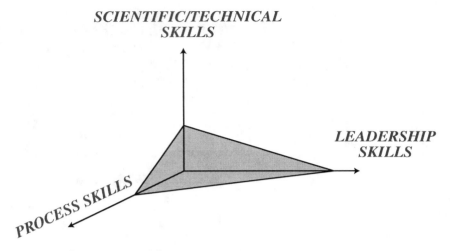

FIGURE 14–11. Competency model.

Figure 14–11 shows the competency model for Eli Lilly. Project managers are expected to have competencies in three broad areas[1]:

- Scientific/technical skills
- Leadership skills
- Process skills

For each of the three broad areas, there are subdivisions or grade levels. A primary advantage of a competency model is that it allows the training department to develop customized project management training programs to satisfy the skill requirements. Without competency models, most training programs are generic rather than customized.

Competency models focus on specialized skills in order to assist the project manager in making more efficient use of his or her time. Figure 14–12, although argumentative, shows that with specialized competency training, project managers can increase their time effectiveness by reducing time robbers and rework.

Competency models make it easier for companies to develop a complete project management curriculum, rather than a singular course. This is shown in Figure 14–13. As companies mature in project management and develop a company-wide core competency model, an internal, custom-designed curriculum will be developed. Companies, especially large ones, will find it necessary to maintain a course architecture specialist on their staff.

---

1. A detailed description of the Eli Lilly competency model and the Ericsson competency model can be found in Harold Kerzner, *Applied Project Management* (New York: Wiley, 1999), pp. 266–283.

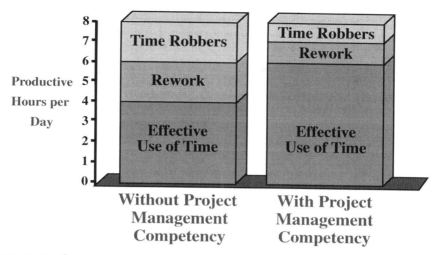

FIGURE 14–12. Core competency analysis.

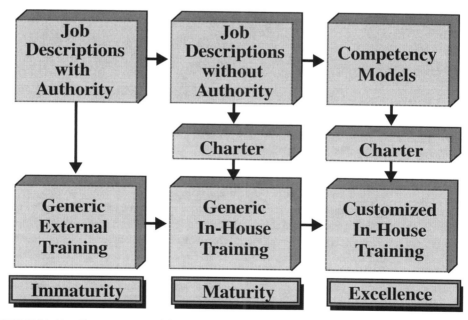

FIGURE 14–13. Competency models and training.

14.7 MANAGING MULTIPLE PROJECTS

As organizations mature in project management, there is a tendency toward having one person manage multiple projects. The initial impetus may come either from the company sponsoring the projects or from project managers themselves. There are several factors supporting the managing of multiple projects. First, the cost of maintaining a full-time project manager on all projects may be prohibitive. The magnitude and risks of each individual project dictate whether a full-time or part-time assignment is necessary. Assigning a project manager full-time on an activity that does not require it is an overmanagement cost. Overmanagement of projects was considered an acceptable practice in the early days of project management because we had little knowledge on how to handle risk management. Today, methods for risk management exist.

Second, line managers are now sharing accountability with project managers for the successful completion of the project. Project managers are now managing at the template levels of the WBS with the line managers accepting accountability for the work packages at the detailed WBS levels. Project managers now spend more of their time integrating work rather than planning and scheduling functional activities. With the line manager accepting more accountability, time may be available for the project manager to manage multiple projects.

Third, senior management has come to the realization that they must provide high-quality training for their project managers if they are to reap the benefits of managing multiple projects. Senior managers must also change the way that they function as sponsors. There are six major areas where the corporation as a whole may have to change in order for the managing of multiple projects to succeed.

- *Prioritization:* If a project prioritization system is in effect, it must be used correctly such that employee credibility in the system is realized. One risk is that the project manager, having multiple projects to manage, may favor those projects having the highest priorities. It is possible that no prioritization system may be the best solution. Not every project needs to be prioritized, and prioritization can be a time-consuming effort.
- *Scope Changes:* Managing multiple projects is almost impossible if the sponsors/customers are allowed to make continuous scope changes. When using multiple projects management, it must be understood that the majority of the scope changes may have to be performed through enhancement projects rather than through a continuous scope change effort. A major scope change on one project could limit the project manager's available time to service other projects. Also, continuous scope changes will almost always be accompanied by reprioritization of projects, a further detriment to the management of multiple projects.
- *Capacity Planning:* Organizations that support the management of multiple projects generally have a tight control on resource scheduling. As a result, the organization must have knowledge of capacity planning, theory of constraints, resource leveling, and resource limited planning.
- *Project Methodology:* Methodologies for project management range from rigid policies and procedures to more informal guidelines and checklists. When manag-

ing multiple projects, the project manager must be granted some degree of freedom. This necessitates guidelines, checklists, and forms. Formal project management practices create excessive paperwork requirements, thus minimizing the opportunities to manage multiple projects. The project size is also critical.

● *Project Initiation:* Managing multiple projects has been going on for almost 40 years. One thing that we have learned is that it can work well as long as the projects are in relatively different life-cycle phases because the demands on the project manager's time are different for each life-cycle phase.

● *Organizational Structures:* If the project manager is to manage multiple projects, then it is highly unlikely that the project manager will be a technical expert in all areas of all projects. Assuming that the accountability is shared with the line managers, the organization will most likely adopt a weak matrix structure.

14.8 END-OF-PHASE REVIEW MEETINGS

For more than 20 years, end-of-phase review meetings were simply an opportunity for executives to "rubber stamp" the project to continue. As only good news was presented the meetings were used to give the executives some degree of comfort concerning project status.

Today, end-of-phase review meetings take on a different dimension. First and foremost, executives are no longer afraid to cancel projects, especially if the objectives have changed, if the objectives are unreachable, or if the resources can be used on other activities that have a greater likelihood of success. Executives now spend more time assessing the risks in the future rather than focusing on accomplishments in the past.

Since project managers are now becoming more business-oriented rather than technically oriented, the project managers are expected to present information on business risks, reassessment of the benefit-to-cost ratio, and any business decisions that could affect the ultimate objectives. Simply stated, the end-of-phase review meetings now focus more on business decisions, rather than on technical decisions.

Critical Chain Project Management[1]

Related Case Studies (from Kerzner/*Project Management Case Studies*, 2nd Edition)	Related Workbook Exercises (from Kerzner/*Project Management Workbook and PMP®/CAPM® Exam Study Guide*, 9th Edition)	PMBOK® Guide, 3rd Edition, Reference Section for the PMP® Certification Exam
None	None	• Time Management

15.0 INTRODUCTION

PMBOK® Guide, 2004
6.5.2.6 Schedule Development—
Critical Chain Method

The selection and completion of enough projects to improve an organization is often a matter of survival for executives. Witness the statistic by outplacement firm Drake, Beam, Morin stating that 57 percent of the 367 large corporations surveyed have replaced their CEOs in the past three years.[2] Executives use projects as a primary means to meet their goals. Therefore, we can assume that many of these CEOs were unable to complete enough projects successfully in the measurement time period to keep their jobs.

---

1. Chapter author Gerald I. Kendall, PMP, Principal, TOC International, www.tocinternational.com, email Gerryikendall@cs.com, 850-939-9006.

2. *USA Today,* April 8, 2002, page B1, "Scandals, Setbacks Topple CEOs" Formerly Golden Image."

In trying to meet their goals, executives often describe three major challenges in project management:

- Choosing the right projects from among a large pool
- Getting each project to completion more quickly
- Funneling more projects through the organization without adding resources

Critical Chain is a project management methodology designed to address the latter two goals. Critical Chain is based upon a general improvement methodology called the Theory of Constraints, which addresses the first executive goal—choosing the right projects. Choosing the right projects is part of strategic planning, which is discussed in depth in other books.[3]

As executives attempt to release new projects into the organization, they often hear complaints that people are overloaded. Inevitably, they face a conflict between moving resources to the new project and allowing resources to continue working on existing projects. People in the organization may also urge the executive to delay the start of the new project while the executive feels compelled to move ahead.

Most executives accept this conflict as a fact of life. They believe that their role is to push people as hard as they can to perform to high standards. As a result, the reaction of many executives to the resource conflict is to demand that existing projects be finished earlier so that their new projects can begin sooner. These demands leave project managers with their own huge conflict. In order to finish a project sooner, most project managers find that they are forced to either reduce scope or quality or add resources, which will exceed the budget. None of these alternatives is acceptable to executives.

The resulting behavior, which is now prevalent in many organizations, is the fodder for a new approach called Critical Chain Project Management. When project and resource managers fail to convince executives to delay the start of a new project, they often take three actions that lead to many other negative effects:

- Multitasking of resources
- Working toward cutting task estimates
- Managing people very closely to ensure that they meet their due dates

Since executives are a major part of the system of projects inside organizations, Critical Chain recognizes that executives are part of the problem. To solve the problem and have a major impact on project results, executives must therefore be part of the solution.

The Critical Chain solution to scheduling and managing projects was derived from a methodology called "The Theory of Constraints." Dr. Eliyahu M. Goldratt is the individual most often credited with the creation and advancement of this methodology over the past twenty-five years. To derive the Critical Chain solution, Goldratt applied the five focusing steps, identified in his writings.[4] These steps are:

1. *Identify* the system's constraint.
2. Decide how to *exploit* the constraint.
3. *Subordinate* everything else to the above decision.
4. *Elevate* the system's constraint.
5. If, in a previous step, the system's constraint has been broken, *go back* to step 1.

Within any project, the Critical Chain is defined as the longest chain of dependent events where the dependency is either task or resource related. This definition assumes that the longest chain is the one that is most likely

---

3. See Gerald I. Kendall, *Viable Vision* (Boca Raton, FL: J. Ross Publishing, 2004).

4. Eliyahu M. Goldratt, *Theory of Constraints* (Croton-on-Hudson, NY: North River Press, 1990).

to impact negatively the overall duration of the project. The Critical Chain is not necessarily equivalent to the project duration since, sometimes, there are noncritical tasks that begin before the Critical Chain tasks begin.

The Critical Chain solution recognizes the Critical Chain as the leverage point for reducing the project's duration. The first focusing step, *identify*, recognizes that managers put practices into place that block the reduction of the Critical Chain. The *exploit* and *subordinate* steps implement changes to condense the Critical Chain (in other words, to shorten the amount of time it takes to complete a project).

Critical Chain implements major behavioral changes in project managers, resource managers, team members, and executives. The only way that so many people in an organization can accept such fundamental changes is through a deep understanding of the current behaviors, the new behaviors required, and the benefits. This is usually accomplished through education of executives, project managers, resource managers, and team members, followed by policy and measurement changes. These changes include:

- An end to the practice of measuring people in any way on the accuracy of their estimates
- An end to the practice of measuring people on meeting due dates for individual project tasks
- A replacement of the above two practices by "the relay runner work ethic," explained later in this chapter
- A system, agreed to by all executives and senior managers, of allowing new projects to start only when a "strategic resource" is available
- The recognition of the need to strategically protect projects from task time variations, by using properly placed buffers. This imbeds the philosophy of W. Edwards Deming, the great quality advocate, regarding the handling of "common cause" and "special cause" variation and predictability.
- The significant reduction of the practice of multitasking by moving toward dedicated work on project tasks
- The implementation of multiproject software with the data actually being used by executives, resource managers, and project managers. Critical Chain reports present a common and accurate picture of the organization's projects and a systematic and logical way to manage variances.
- The implementation of buffer management as a key management and executive process for identifying project problems during execution

The successful implementation of Critical Chain has resulted in major improvements in organizations, examples of which are documented in the case studies in this chapter. In order to understand the magnitude of the cultural change and the problems to be overcome, this chapter explains the fundamentals of the Critical Chain approach, in both individual project environments and throughout an organization.

15.1 ANATOMY OF A TASK ESTIMATE

In order to illustrate how Critical Chain works, a simple project will be used. While the example is specific, it has general attributes that apply to every project.

In this example, a company that builds the huge towers that house communications equipment has just received a contract for a new tower. Each tower is unique since it is built to meet the specific requirements of county and state government regarding height and durability in severe weather. Other project variables include the capacity of the tower to house various communications carriers, ground preparation, fencing, wiring, and on-site staging and testing. Although unique, every tower has some components with the same basic underlying design as previous towers, so only minor modifications to design drawings are required. A highly summarized version of the project appears in Figure 15–1.

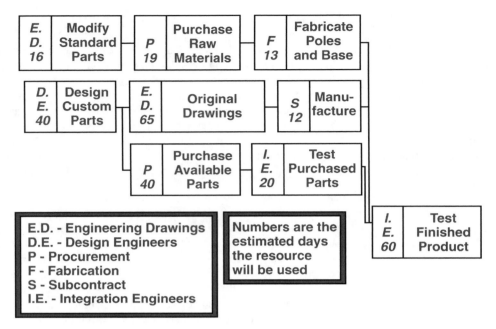

FIGURE 15–1. Build a tower project.

The first task is to "modify standard parts." It is estimated to take sixteen days elapsed time, and is being done by the resources in the Engineering Drawings department.

Every theory or methodology is based upon assumptions. Critical Chain is no exception. One of the assumptions in Critical Chain is that a task time, such as the first task described above, is not a deterministic number. It is an estimate. What this means is that any task that is part of a project cannot be predetermined to take an exact amount of time. By the very nature of projects, each task is unique and somewhat unpredictable in terms of how long it will take. Even if the same person were to do an almost identical task as before, the time to perform the task can vary widely. Is the person's mental state the same? Is he using the identical computer and software as before? Are all of the conditions identical (team members, bosses, external contractors, communications facilities, etc.)?

In this section, we will explore how the task time varies in execution, and how this impacts the estimate. In most companies, people take pride in reliable estimates. It is not good for anyone's career, especially an engineer's career, to repeatedly be way off on estimates. Considering that an engineer can never predict exactly what kinds of problems he or she may run into, and considering that this project is not the only work that the engineer is doing, the engineer provides an estimate that takes all of these considerations into account.

The engineer knows that this is not the only project the company is working on. Some work is far more urgent than other work, and the urgency itself is unpredictable. What happens is that a contractor or a community decides to build towers to offer new or improved communications services within the community. Many residents who live in the community consider the towers ugly and do not want them erected near where they live, so locations for a tower are limited. Further, the approval of a particular location requires preliminary surveys, including a geological survey to check soil conditions, and some political investigation to determine which locations are likely to be approved by the zoning commission.

Therefore, it is quite unpredictable when a location will be found and approved. Once a location is approved, the contractor often wants the project work done as soon as possible, before people change their minds.

This is all part of the engineer's uncertainty when providing an estimate. In this case, assume that the task could be realistically done in ten days if the engineer could dedicate himself to this one task. However, this rarely happens. If other project work is authorized, the engineer will either be working substantial overtime to meet the ten-day estimate or will be late.

Therefore, the engineer does not give an estimate of ten days. The engineer protects his reputation by committing to a date that gives him flexibility. In other words, there is a difference between the due-date he would commit to if dedicated to the one task (a "dedicated" estimate) versus the due date he actually commits to ("elapsed time" estimate). Another way to protect his reputation is to add safety or padding time directly into the task estimate. This is more common where the amount of individual effort on tasks is closely watched or tracked.

So far, we have discussed only the first task, which has relatively little variability. The engineers are taking existing drawings and doing minor modifications. The amount of protection on this type of task is likely to be small.

Now let us consider the last task in the project, which we have called "testing the finished product." This task usually has a very high degree of uncertainty. This is where all of the previous tasks must come together. If any one of the previous tasks is not finished on time, this task cannot start on time. If any one of the previous tasks was done without perfect quality, this task will discover the problem. Fixing the problem might require sending parts back to an outside vendor and waiting for rework, or trying to free up resources inside the organization to do rework. Under most circumstances, resources in organizations are very heavily scheduled, and it is not easy to free them up.

There are two types of dependencies that can cause a task to be late. One type is called a "logical task dependency." For example, you cannot purchase raw materials (task 2 in Figure 15–1) until the engineering drawings are ready (task 1). Another type of dependency is called "resource dependency." For example, assume that there is only one person who is capable of doing the engineering drawings. The same engineering drawing resource is used in two places—once to modify existing drawings and once to complete new drawings. The chance of having new drawings available for the subcontractors to manufacture (task 6 in Figure 15–1) depends not only on those new drawings being completed on time, but also on the previous task for the engineering drawing resource being completed on time so that the same engineer(s) can work on the next task.

Resource dependencies, compounded with task dependencies, further decrease the probability that a task will finish on time. At the final stages of a project (usually involving some type of integration or testing), there are usually a lot of task and resource dependencies. This implies a high degree of uncertainty in these tasks. A large amount of protection is usually put into these types of tasks.

In order to understand how much protection is included in an estimate, consider the task duration profile shown in Figure 15–2. The exact nature of this profile for any task in any organization can never be known. However, the general shape of the curve is commonly observed in any organization.

This curve shows, on the vertical axis, the probability of a task finishing within the duration shown on the bottom of the graph. There are three points that we can identify immediately on any such curve. For any task that is expected to take ten days, for example, we know that there is a zero percent probability that this task will finish in zero days. The minimum time duration is some number greater than zero. This starting point would appear at the left side of the curve. Chances are very slim that this task will finish in the shortest duration.

For this task, there is another number on the curve, which is the longest amount of time we might expect a ten-day task to take. This number might be 2.5 or 3 times the normal expectation. In other words, in rare cases, a ten-day task might take us twenty-five or thirty days. The probability of such an occurrence is also rare, and appears on the right side of the curve.

There is another number, which is the most likely time. This number is somewhere between the lowest duration and the highest duration. The peak in the curve represents this most likely duration.

The curve shown in Figure 15–2 is skewed to the right. If correct, it suggests that project tasks are likely to take much longer than expected, and less likely to take a shorter time. Critical Chain claims this is true for several reasons, explained in detail in Dr. Goldratt's book, *Critical Chain*.[5]

One reason that tasks typically do not finish in shorter durations than planned is the effect of dependencies. Some of the work that is needed to finish the task does not show up on time, either because a resource was tied up on a previous task or because a previous task did not finish on time.

Another reason that tasks are often skewed to the late side is multitasking, which is discussed more extensively below. Briefly, multitasking exists when an organization has a project resource that is assigned to do multiple tasks at the same time. Organizations often have more projects than they have resources to dedicate to these projects. As a result, people often start their tasks later than planned. The multiple tasks may be on the same project or on different projects.

People sometimes start tasks late due to "Student Syndrome." This behavior is similar to what happens in a classroom when a professor announces that there will be a test tomorrow on all of the material covered during the semester. The students complain bitterly that this is not fair, since they did not have enough time to study for the test. A kind professor might change the test date, moving it back two weeks. Do the students rush out of the class and begin studying immediately? Not typically. Their attitude usually is, "We have plenty of time. Why rush?" They begin studying the night before the test.

When people give elapsed time estimates or estimates with padding, they realize that there is no urgency to start working on this task. Since they are multitasked, they pick the most urgent tasks to work on, and delay the start of work on other tasks.

This behavior relates directly to the skewed curve. Often, the major difficulties in completing a task are not discovered until the person is very involved in the task. This usu-

---

5. Eliyahu M. Goldratt, *Critical Chain* (Great Barrington, MA: North River Press, 1997).

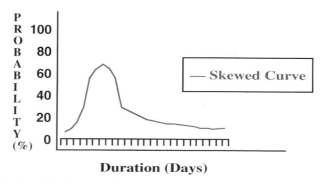

FIGURE 15–2. Profile of the duration of a task.

ally happens in the latter part of working on the task. At this stage, it may be too late to finish the task within the time estimate. Student Syndrome wastes the protection that was embedded in the original task time estimate. As a result, the actual time to complete the task moves toward the right side of the skewed curve.

The reason that the concept of the skewed curve is important, relative to task time estimates, is that it impacts the estimate that a person will give. If somewhere toward the middle of the curve, the task has a 50/50 chance of being late, this is not the likely estimate that a person will provide. An engineer who wants to be considered reliable will not take a 50/50 chance of being late. To be considered reliable (i.e., 80 percent chance or better), he will estimate toward the right side of the curve. On a skewed curve, the 80 percent chance of meeting the estimate is often 2–2.5 times the 50/50 duration, according to the statistical distribution of a skewed curve.

Therefore, on tasks that are considered by team members to be more risky or more difficult to predict, a ten-day task may well be estimated at twenty to twenty-five days. However, even with such an estimate, the protection is often wasted due to Student Syndrome and multitasking.

These task estimates are not created in a vacuum. Often, there is extensive discussion about the estimates, with managers pushing back on what they consider to be unreasonably protected estimates. On the other hand, team members expecting management to push back often inflate their estimates to take this into account. The end result is that estimates often are distorted based on the individual experiences and negotiating skills of management and team members. Further, two estimates for the same task, done by different people, will likely vary widely.

15.2 TASK EXECUTION

The above discussion centered on task estimates that occur primarily during the planning phase of a project. What happens during the execution of a project, when a task is estimated as described above?

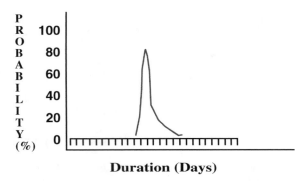

FIGURE 15–3. Observed duration of a task during execution.

Most project managers know their ability to meet project goals is tied to each team member meeting his task deadlines. In project-driven companies where an individual's time is charged to the budget of the project, the project managers will do everything they can to hold people accountable for their estimates.

Depending on the level of accountability and the amount of tracking, individuals often work toward due dates. In project-driven companies where individuals' time is tracked, they will try to charge as much of their time as possible to billable projects. Therefore, even if they do finish a task much earlier than estimated, if they do not immediately have another billable project to move to, they often will prolong their task until the target date is reached or their estimated time is consumed.

As a result, even when individuals finish tasks early, it is not common to see them pass on their tasks early to the next resource who must work on it. In some organizations, you can witness early finishes in one or two departments, but rarely across the entire project.

Often, even when someone does finish and pass on a task early, the next resource is not flexible enough to start working on it immediately because he has other work to do. The extra protection from an early finish of one task is thus wasted.

Therefore, the observed duration of actual task times is a very different curve than a statistical analysis would lead a person to expect. The difference in the curve shown in Figure 15–3, as compared to Figure 15–2, is that it is much narrower. Also, the shortest duration is very close to the estimated duration. There is a much higher probability of finishing at the estimated duration or very close to it. This curve is explained by the practice of leaving enough room in an estimate to take contingencies into account, and not reporting early finishes on a task.

15.3 PROTECTION IN A CRITICAL CHAIN PROJECT

In a Critical Chain project, management accepts that task times are not deterministic. This means that during planning, a person cannot state that the task will take exactly 3.2 days, for example. Task times are guesses. Therefore, it is perfectly normal for task times to take longer than estimated.

Management does not worry about whether or not a task finishes on time. They focus on finishing the project on time. In Critical Chain environments, organizations quote annual project on-time percentages typically above 95 percent. This section examines the way in which projects are protected to achieve these results.

W. Edwards Deming taught management the importance of having a system that stays in control. By this, Deming refers to the "predictability" of a system, relative to its goals. In describing such a system, Deming refers to two types of "problems" that any system can encounter. He calls these problems "variations."[6] Every system is subject to a type of problem called "common cause" variation. These types of problems are absolutely normal, and management should do nothing about them. In fact, if a manager tries to do something about a common cause variation, it often causes the system to go into chaos.

For example, in any organization, it is perfectly natural and expected that some people occasionally will not show up to work on time or will report in sick. It is perfectly natural for machines to break down from time to time. A person, designing the procedures for an organization, should expect these "common cause variations." Deming insists that the correct procedure, when a common cause variation is encountered, is to do nothing.

In any system, "common cause" variation (in which managers should expect the variations and take no action) and "special cause" variation (in which managers always take action) must be defined.

To arrive at a project plan that will stay in control throughout the entire execution, the following steps are necessary:

- *Start with the best schedule that you can derive in the traditional manner. Take task estimates and cut them in half. Add half of this protection back into the project strategically as a project buffer and feeding buffers, as described below.* This step is intended to remove "Student Syndrome" behavior. At the same time, it is fully expected that many such estimates will be exceeded during execution. This is taken into account with protection placed strategically within the project plan.
- *Resource level the project.* Do not schedule the project assuming that resource contention will magically take care of itself. In Critical Chain, resource contention is resolved up front.
- *Don't measure people on completing their tasks on time or on the accuracy of their estimates.* If management wants to reward team members, the reward should be based on finishing the project on time or early.
- *Allow people to work on a Critical Chain task in a "dedicated" manner.* This is part of the second focusing step, "Exploit the system's constraint." Dedicated behavior implies that once a person begins to work on a task, he will work only on that task until either it is complete, or he has progressed far enough on the task to turn it over to the next resource to work on it. Further, dedicated behavior implies that if the task is turned over to the next resource, but will be returned to the current

---

6. An excellent explanation is contained in Donald J. Wheeler, *Understanding Variation, The Key to Managing Chaos,* 2nd ed. (Knoxville, TN: SPC Press, 2000).

resource within a very short period of time for more work, the current resource will wait for the return of the task, rather than begin work on a new task. This is true if the new tasks will take up substantially more time than waiting for the current task to be returned.

- *Change the organization's resource management approach to implement the paradigm that resources on the Critical Chain have more flexibility to accept work earlier than expected.* This is usually accomplished through an early warning system, called the resource buffer. The resource buffer does not take up any time on a schedule. It simply acts as an alarm clock, warning resources that they are *X* days away from receiving a new task.

- *Implement a project buffer to protect the project's Critical Chain.* It sits at the end of a project and is calculated as a percentage of the length of the Critical Chain, typically 30–50 percent. This buffer is protecting the collection of tasks on the Critical Chain from any common cause variation.

- *Implement feeding buffers on each feeding path, to protect the Critical Chain from variances on any feeding path.*

We will use the same example as shown in Figure 15–1 to illustrate how this works.

Figure 15–4 shows what the project looks like, after the protection has been removed from each task. For example, the first task, "Modify Standard Parts," was changed from the sixteen-day estimate shown in Figure 15–1 to a ten-day estimate. The task "Design Custom Parts" was changed from a forty-day estimate to a fifteen-day estimate.

The next step is to perform resource leveling. Since the same resources from the Engineering Drawings area and the Procurement area will be working on all of these tasks, we will not allow them to do two tasks at the same time.

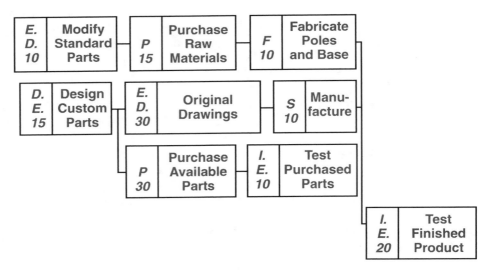

FIGURE 15-4. Build a tower project with dedicated effort (no padding).

Figure 15–5 shows the project after resources are leveled.

The next step is to identify the Critical Chain—the longest chain of dependent events, where the dependency is either task or resource related. Looking at Figure 15–5, we can identify several possible paths. In considering which path is the most critical, Critical Chain looks at two possible paths for every task.

One path asks, "What is the next task that is logically dependent on this task?" For example, after the second task, "Purchase Raw Materials" in Figure 15–5, the next task that is logically dependent on purchasing raw materials is task 3, Fabricating the Poles and Base. You cannot fabricate without purchasing.

Another path asks, "What is the next task that uses the same resource as the current task where the dependency is therefore a resource dependency?" In the above example, after "Purchase raw materials," which uses the Procurement resource, the next task using Procurement is "Purchase available Parts."

Based on this analysis, Critical Chain examines the duration of each of the possible paths and picks out the longest path based on task or resource dependency. In this example, Figure 15–6 identifies the Critical Chain, shown in shaded format.

To finish the Critical Chain schedule, the project and feeding buffers must be inserted. Buffers are illustrated in Figure 15–7 with bold text. The buffers were calculated at 40 percent of the length of the paths.

Every task is now attached either to a feeding buffer or to the project buffer. In this example, there are three paths that feed into the Critical Chain. Therefore, there are three feeding buffers. The task "Design Custom Parts" feeds the Critical Chain directly and also feeds another task, "Original Drawings" on a feeding path.

With the protection now accumulated, the effect of individual task time deviations during execution are insulated by the buffers. In effect, the buffers act as shock absorbers.

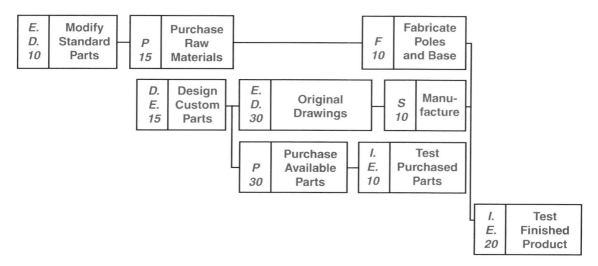

FIGURE 15-5. Resource-leveled project.

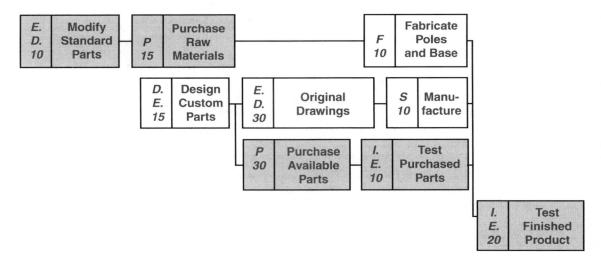

FIGURE 15–6. The Critical Chain identified.

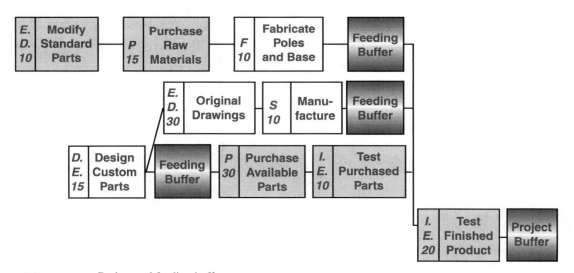

FIGURE 15–7. Project and feeding buffers.

15.4 BUFFER MANAGEMENT

Buffer management is the key to managing a Critical Chain project. The Critical Chain methodology does not work without it. Project and resource managers examine buffer reports daily or weekly to determine what actions, if any, they must take. The time frame varies, according to the length of the projects. Buffer reports for short projects (e.g., less than one month) are examined more frequently. Senior management examines buffers weekly or monthly to determine if projects are in control or out of control.

Every task in a Critical Chain project is connected either to a project buffer or a feeding buffer. When a task takes longer than estimated, it eats into the buffer that it is connected to. Buffer penetration reports indicate when the project is in danger. They also indicate which current task is causing the problem.

The comparison of the percentage of the project buffer consumed to the percentage of the Critical Chain completed gives a partial picture. For example, if the project shows that 50 percent of the Critical Chain is completed, while only 20 percent of the project buffer has been consumed, the project is considered to be in excellent shape.

Looking at Figure 15–7, the first task is scheduled to take ten days. If the task takes fifteen days to complete, it has eaten five days from the project buffer. The status is then ten out of eighty-five days complete, or 12 percent. At the same time, we have eaten five out of the thirty-four days of buffer, or 15 percent. On the surface, this is close to normal. However, trends help the interpretation, as we will see below.

Since feeding buffers are shock absorbers on the noncritical paths, only after a feeding buffer is 100 percent consumed does the project buffer get impacted. Therefore, feeding buffers are watched, but are always a lower priority than a project buffer. For example, looking at Figure 15–7, the last task on the first path is to fabricate poles and bases, estimated to take ten days. This task will only begin to impact the Critical Chain after all four days of the feeding buffer are consumed.

The trend of buffer consumption compared to Critical Chain completion over time gives another key part of the picture. For example, consider the data in Figure 15–8.

Looking exclusively at one set of figures, for week 4, you observe that the project has eaten away 15 percent of the project buffer, while only 8 percent of the Critical Chain is complete. On the basis of this one set of figures, it looks like a crisis—something worthy of intervention. However, the trend shows exactly the opposite.

In week 1 of the project, 10 percent of the project buffer was consumed while only 2 percent of the Critical Chain was completed. One figure, by itself, should not alarm the project manager. However, it certainly is worth investigating.

By week 2, the project trend is rapidly deteriorating. We see that 20 percent of the project buffer is gone while only 3 percent of the project's critical chain is complete. This

	Week 1	Week 2	Week	Week 4
Percent project buffer consumed	10	20	20	15
Percent critical chain complete	2	3	5	8

FIGURE 15–8. Buffer consumption trend.

shows the situation is getting worse, not by a little bit, but by a lot. This might be a sign of what Deming refers to as "special cause variation." Certainly, it is worth further investigation, and possibly action.

By the third week, the situation is beginning to improve. The project buffer is no longer being penetrated while the project's critical chain is progressing.

By week 4, the situation is much better. Due to one or more tasks on the Critical Chain finishing earlier than expected, the project has gotten some of its safety back. The project buffer is only 15 percent consumed, as the Critical Chain completion percentage grows.

Note that any task on the Critical Chain that is completed earlier than expected adds that amount of safety back to the project buffer. Any task on a feeding path that finishes earlier than expected adds that amount of safety to the feeding buffer. This assumes that the next resource on the path is flexible enough to take advantage of an early finish from a previous task.

As reinforced by the case studies, buffer management is key to the success of any Critical Chain implementation. Senior managers who have implemented Critical Chain also advise that buffer status should rigidly dictate priorities. From a project manager's perspective, the first priority is the task currently penetrating the project buffer. The next priority is the task or tasks penetrating the feeding buffer(s).

For organizations with critical milestones, where either bonuses or penalties depend on meeting them, the second priority is another buffer, called the "milestone" buffer. It behaves almost identically to the project buffer. In effect, the milestone buffer protects a subset of the project. That subset is like a mini-project. In this case, the milestone buffer is a subset of the overall project buffer, and is used to monitor and give early warning to a milestone date that may be at risk.

15.5 MANAGING THE EXECUTION OF A CRITICAL CHAIN PROJECT

The resource manager looks at all the tasks that a given resource pool is performing and sets priorities according to the task that is most penetrating a project buffer. For example, suppose that the resource pool can work on two different tasks. One task is on a feeding path and is currently penetrating a feeding buffer. The other task is on the Critical Chain and the task is not penetrating the buffer. The priority is still on the Critical Chain task.

The information to generate the Critical Chain reports comes from the reporting, by resource, of three key pieces of information: When a task is initiated; how many days are left to complete the task; and when a task is complete. As long as senior management is performing weekly reviews, based on the up-to-date data, the resource managers become very proficient at keeping their data updated. In many Critical Chain environments, updates are performed daily with formal management reports being generated weekly.

The project manager looks at the buffer reports to quickly identify whether they are dealing with common cause or special cause variation. Any individual task that is taking longer than estimated is still within the realm of common cause variation. However, a series of tasks that have all taken much longer than expected are in the realm of special cause variation.

One rule of thumb for special cause variation deals with situations where the probability of occurrence is less than 5 percent. In Critical Chain, the assumption is that any single task has about a 50 percent probability of finishing on time. Since the probabilities are very subjective, when three or four tasks in a row are all significantly exceeding their estimates, other factors, such as risk and variability in those specific types of tasks, must also be considered.

In environments that use both Critical Chain and earned value reporting, the reporting should still be done only once, but should feed both databases.

15.6 CRITICAL CHAIN MULTIPROJECT PROBLEM AND SOLUTION

Many organizations do not have resources that are dedicated full time to a single project for the project's duration. In fact, it is a common practice for management to initiate more and more projects with the result that resources are multitasked. Either they are working on more than one project at a time, or they are splitting their time between a project and other responsibilities.

The idea of multitasking has become so embedded in management practices that most managers believe it is a very positive practice. By multitasking, managers believe that resources are more effectively utilized and that work flow is not negatively impacted. These are assumptions that the Critical Chain multi-project solution challenges.

The practice of multitasking originates with the demands of senior functional managers to initiate new projects immediately. A functional manager needs projects to be completed in order to meet his goals. The belief is that the sooner the project is initiated, the sooner it will be complete.

Typically, organizations do not formally measure the load on the various resources coming from the combination of projects that the organization is working on. While some project plans show resource loading, the information is often too detailed to enable serious resource planning.

With each functional executive thinking his project is "the most important," the common practice is to push work into the system to get his projects moved forward. This is what leads to multitasking. Managers, faced with conflicting demands for the same resource, from various executives or senior managers, try to satisfy all demands by having resources work on multiple projects. In this environment, the priority system is "who is screaming the loudest." In effect, there is no priority system.

Multitasking is not always bad. For example, if a resource begins work on Project 1 and has to wait for a week for an approval or some other task completion, it would be good to take advantage of that gap in time with multitasking. As long as he is able to get back to the work he was doing without delay when the approval comes through, this is good multitasking. But if the other task requires a month, this becomes bad multitasking. Bad multitasking is illustrated in Figure 15–9.

In Figure 15–9, a resource has three tasks to complete on three different projects. Each task is approximately three weeks work. Multitasking implies that task *X* is started, worked

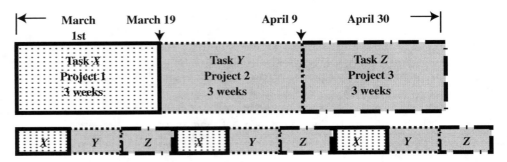

FIGURE 15–9. Effect of bad multitasking.

on for a few hours or days, and then the work is stopped. The resource works for a period of time on task *Y*, and then on task *Z*. This rotation of work continues until each task is complete.

There is an obvious impact on the time that it now takes to complete each task. Even if this resource, by magic, could start each task without any start-up time, the first task would not finish until mid-April. The cycle time of that task is no longer three weeks—it is now seven weeks, or more, because people cannot start immediately where they left off. With some types of work, such as computer programming or engineering design, the impact of start-up time can be severe.

However, there is sometimes a more devastating effect in terms of quality, and that is rework. Bad multitasking may impinge so heavily on concentration that people start making mistakes. The implication in Figure 15–9 is that nine weeks of total work will actually take twelve to fifteen weeks in a multitasking environment.

Simulation exercises show that the effect of bad multitasking is to increase project cycle times by more than 100 percent. In the Critical Chain case studies, the effects were even worse.

In the multiproject environment, the system's constraint can be stated as the management practice of pushing work into the system irrespective of the capacity of the resources to perform the work. The system's arteries are clogged.

Dr. Goldratt states "The more complex the problem, the simpler the solution must be, or it will not work." It would be far too complex, and probably futile, to try to schedule all of an organization's resources across projects and other work. However, a simple solution is to schedule multiple projects according to one resource—the most heavily loaded resource across all projects. This resource is the one most likely to impact the cycle time of the entire collection of an organization's projects.

In Critical Chain, this resource is called the "drum." The analogy is soldiers marching in battle. In order to keep the soldiers together, marching at the same pace, a soldier beats a drum to set the pace. In Critical Chain, the capacity of the organization's critical resource sets the pace of all projects. That resource beats the drum.

Project start dates are staggered according to the capacity of the drum resource. The top management of the company reaches consensus on the organization's drum and subsequently, the priority (i.e., which project is staggered first, second, third, etc.). If some projects do not use the drum resource at all, those projects can be scheduled at any time.

Usually, when senior managers are educated on Critical Chain, they are able to identify a few candidates for a drum resource. Sometimes, it is not obvious which candidate is the best choice. In this case, the process can be facilitated by doing Critical Chain project plans for some or all active projects, loading the information into a Critical Chain software package, and looking at the resulting reports on resource loading.

One important piece of information is the percentage of projects that the different resources are utilized on. The other piece of information is the percentage utilization of each resource. In combination, these data help identify the drum resource.

To begin staggering projects according to the capacity of the drum resource, some current projects must be deactivated or the drum resource must be given additional capacity. Typically, many projects are deactivated.

A significant example comes from an aircraft maintenance group. A country was given several defense aircraft as a gift. The aircraft were overdue for their major maintenance cycle. Each aircraft had dozens of problems that required the expertise of a small group of highly trained engineers. On average, each problem required 135 days to resolve. Over a period of several years, the maintenance function had been unsuccessful in getting a single aircraft back into operation.

The expert engineers were allowed to work unlimited overtime, but this did not change the results. On average, each engineer had several dozen problems he was working on.

Upon implementation of Critical Chain, each engineer was limited to a maximum of three open problems. Considering each problem as a project, several dozen projects per engineer were deactivated.

The results were published. Over a five-month period, the average lead time per problem (from the time the problem was identified until complete) went from 135 days to fewer than 30 days. Overtime declined to almost zero.

In most cases, the resource that appears to be the most heavily loaded across projects in fact has huge excess capacity. The excess capacity is masked by bad multitasking caused by too many concurrently active projects in the system. Once the projects are staggered, the organization is able to flow many more projects through the same resource pool.

In combination with implementing buffers and buffer management, the staggering of projects provides predictability in the project management environment. Managers are able to separate planning from execution without having to replan projects whenever Murphy's law hits.

To further insulate projects from each other, implementers use a buffer called the strategic resource buffer. This buffer simply puts gaps between the date that the strategic resource is due to be released from one project and their scheduled start date on the next project. In this way, if the strategic resource is late finishing one project, it has no or little impact on the schedules of all following projects. The rule of thumb for the size of this buffer is 30–50 percent of the size (in days) of the tasks that the strategic resource is performing.

One other buffer is designed to protect the critical resource from wasting its time. When the critical resource arrives on a project, the organization wants to ensure that the work is there waiting for them and not vice versa. Therefore, any tasks that feed work to the drum resource are scheduled to be completed ahead of when the work is needed.

15.7 IMPLEMENTING MULTIPROJECT CRITICAL CHAIN

In order for top management, project and resource managers to support a multiproject implementation, the project information must be visible to everyone, current, and accurate at all times. Most often, this is accomplished using Critical Chain software. At the time of writing, the following three software packages support multiproject Critical Chain:

- Concerto, by SpeedtoMarket—see www.speedtomarket.com
- PS8, by Scitor—see www.scitor.com
- ProChain and ProChain Plus, by ProChain Solutions—see www.prochain.com

Concerto is an Oracle-based solution, using Microsoft Project for both data entry and display. PS8 uses its own SQL database. ProChain is an add-on to Microsoft Project.

A successful implementation consists of at least the following prerequisites:

- Identification and consensus on the drum resource(s) for the projects being implemented using Critical Chain
- Consensus on the method of staggering the projects, on the priority system. This usually implies deactivating some or many currently active projects.
- Appointment of one person to be the master scheduler to help determine the options for staggering new projects, and to keep all project and resource managers informed about the status of the drum resource
- Consensus on changes to any schedules of any currently active projects
- Executive buy-in to the process, especially that no new projects will be initiated without following the staggering process
- Comprehensive education and procedures for all project and resource managers, including not just the "how to," but also the "why" aspects of Critical Chain

15.8 HOW CRITICAL CHAIN EXTENDS CRITICAL PATH

Critical Chain assumes a good critical path network that has been effectively resource leveled. Starting from that point, Critical Chain enhances the ability to optimize the schedule and sets the stage for improved project monitoring and control. It should be noted that some of the actions needed to implement Critical Chain successfully might be significant changes for an organization. Following are specific ways that the Critical Chain approach works and adds value.

1. Using the Critical Chain approach, team members are asked to dedicate themselves to a project task, to complete it as quickly as possible, and to periodically report how many days are remaining. When planning a project, task times should be estimated much closer to how long the task will take with dedicated resources, rather than elapsed times assuming the organization's current practice of assign-

ing resources to work on several tasks at once. This also significantly reduces behaviors called "Student Syndrome" and "Parkinson's Law."

2. Bad multitasking is significantly reduced, permanently. This goes hand in hand with reducing task estimates to dedicated elapsed times and having people complete tasks before starting new ones.

3. In executing a project, people are not measured and are not held accountable for completing their tasks on time. People are asked to pass on their outputs to the next resource as quickly as possible. Use of intermediate due dates is limited. This is sometimes called the "relay runner ethic."

4. By taking resource dependency and logical task dependency into account, the longest sequence of dependent tasks can be seen more clearly. This longest sequence, the Critical Chain, may cross logical paths in the network.

5. Buffers are a key part of the schedule and how it is managed. The ability to increase the certainty of project completion dates is closely related to the use of buffers. The use of buffers, strategically placed in the plan, allows the planner to clearly accommodate all common cause variations (variations in duration that predictably occur because they are part of the system within which projects are performed). Buffer types include project buffers, feeding buffers, resource buffers, drum buffers, and strategic resource buffers.

6. Critical Path uses a concept of slack time or float to determine how much flexibility there is in noncritical path tasks. Critical Chain approach assumes that slack times often do not provide real flexibility due to behaviors such as "Student Syndrome." Critical Chain approach groups tasks on each noncritical (or feeding) path entering into the Critical Chain and "protects" the Critical Chain with a feeding buffer. The feeding buffer is equivalent to a schedule contingency reserve that is local to a part of the project. The Critical Chain approach is explicit and systematic about the use of feeding buffers throughout the task network.

7. This buffering allows for noncritical tasks to be scheduled at their latest possible start times to discourage costly early investment of work in process. This also significantly reduces behaviors called "Student Syndrome" and "Parkinson's Law." Early starts are discouraged unless there is a major strategic reason for doing so.

8. Often, the Critical Path changes during execution because there is no buffer to absorb the variation in task times. If implemented correctly, the Critical Chain plan and the Critical Chain itself do not change throughout the life of the project because the buffers absorb the uncertainties in task duration.

9. Critical Chain recognizes that there are multiproject environments in which projects have resource-based interdependencies. In other words, projects share a common resource pool for at least some tasks.

10. The Critical Chain approach identifies the critical resource (called a drum resource) across a collection of projects. When overloaded or not available, this resource is the one most likely to impact the project cycle time of all projects.

11. The staggered introduction of projects into the system is used to improve the flow of projects, to increase the predictability in each project outcome, and to increase the effectiveness of critical resources by minimizing the effect of bad multitasking.

A shorter project cycle time and an increase of the number of projects that can be pushed through the system without increasing resources result from staggering the release of new projects.

12. Similar to vertical traceability in Critical Path, the Critical Chain plan and detailed schedules are linked entities. Any logic at the detailed levels must be reflected in the summary level(s).

PROBLEMS

15-1 Describe the five types of buffers used by the Critical Chain methodology, and the unique purpose of each one.

15-2 How should a resource manager decide which task a resource should work on, when there is a conflict?

15-3 In what ways does a Critical Chain plan address Deming's concerns about common cause variation?

15-4 Is a Critical Chain schedule more useful to people planning and managing tasks, or to people actually performing the tasks? Explain.

15-5 Describe the primary role of the "drum" manager.

15-6 Describe four ways that Critical Chain is different from (extends) the Critical Path approach (as Critical Path is traditionally applied)?

15-7 How could a buffer report alert a manager to a schedule problem?

15-8 The following are different measurements used by organizations for project managers and team members. Which two represent a Critical Chain philosophy?

    a. Accuracy of task time estimates
    b. Do your work as fast as possible and pass it on to the next resource as early as possible.
    c. Finish your task by the due date
    d. Finish the project on time or early

15-9 From an executive perspective, which of the following are the major benefits of a Critical Chain approach?

    a. Improved cash flow
    b. Less time to review major projects, with better reporting
    c. More projects completed each year using the same resources
    d. Better performance to milestones

15-10 Two project managers are looking for the same resource to perform work on their projects. In one project, the work is on a task on a feeding path, in which the feeding buffer is 95 percent consumed. In the other project, the work is on the Critical Chain, in which the Critical Chain is 50 percent complete and the project buffer is 0 percent consumed. Which task should the resource be assigned to first? Why?

15-11 Critical Chain is a methodology to help managers plan projects and manage their execution to deliver the projects on time, on budget, and within scope. In each case below, given the two choices, identify which choice best fits with a Critical Chain approach.

a. Plan has 10,000 tasks or plan has 300 tasks.
b. Resources are identified by individual name or resources are identified by pool name.
c. In a multiproject environment, there is one master scheduler or each project manager determines when his project will start.
d. Team members know the estimated effort for a task or team members do not know the estimated effort for a task.

15-12   Why must executives buy into the multiproject Critical Chain approach?

15-13   There are three major software products that support Critical Chain. One product is an "add-on" to Microsoft Project. Describe one major advantage of being linked to Microsoft Project and one major disadvantage.

15-14   One of the software products that supports Critical Chain is based on the Oracle database. Describe one major advantage of having a project management product use the Oracle database and one major disadvantage.

15-15   One of the software products that supports Critical Chain has its own proprietary database. Describe one major advantage of having a project management product use its own database and one major disadvantage.

15-16   Why does the Critical Chain methodology claim that individual tasks cannot be protected by inflated estimates or due dates? How does buffering a project and feeding paths provide greater predictability in a project outcome?

15-17   If you were a project manager in your first Critical Chain project, how would you convince team members to pass their work on early to the next resource?

15-18   As a resource manager, what information do you need from your resources daily or weekly in order to keep the Critical Chain database up to date?

15-19   In the multiproject environment, the drum becomes the anchor according to which new projects are released into the system. From the case studies, is the drum typically a resource used close to the beginning of a project or closer to the end of a project? Why?

15-20   For each buffer category below, indicate how many buffers you would expect to find in any single project?

a. Project buffer
b. Feeding buffer
c. Resource buffer
d. Strategic resource buffer
e. Drum buffer

CASE STUDIES

LUCENT TECHNOLOGIES

Lucent Technologies, Inc., is a $33 billion manufacturer and service provider in the communications industry, headquartered in New Jersey. With about 100,000 employees in more than 65 countries, Lucent's focus is in the mobile Internet and high-speed broadband markets for all types of communications networks. This includes Internet, e-business, wireless, optical, data, and voice communications products and services.

In this highly innovative and competitive industry, the speed to market is very important. To ensure rapid development, Lucent uses the services of its Bell Labs R&D community, which operates in thirty different countries. Lucent invests about 12 percent of revenues in R&D each year, making these labs the birthplace of innovative products in use by many millions of people around the globe.

One of the first divisions of Lucent to employ Critical Chain methodology was the Optical Fiber Solutions group. This group is headquartered out of Norcross, GA. It is a pioneer in the development and manufacture of optical fiber and fiber components. Optical fiber is rapidly growing in communications applications, due to its combination of high speed and reliability.

The Optical Fiber Solutions unit consists of several thousand employees, including several hundred scientists and engineers. A Bell Laboratories director of this group, Dr. William J. Baron, describes the project environment before Critical Chain implementation as constantly changing.

Within this division, there are some large projects with dedicated resources. However, many projects use resources that are shared between projects, characteristic of the multiproject environment. Before Critical Chain implementation, project priorities were constantly changing. About 40 percent of the projects finished on schedule. Project cycle times, according to benchmarks, appeared to be on par or shorter, compared to similar companies.

To make a Critical Chain implementation successful, Mr. Baron describes the change process as "99 percent culture change and 1 percent theory." He indicates that getting the business unit president and senior executives to understand the buffers, and buffer management is critical to success. At Lucent, Dr. Richard Franks, CEO of Oak Hill Consulting, accomplished this with an executive training program using simulations of three projects to reinforce the understanding. According to Dr. Franks, "Simulations are critical to holding the attention of senior executives and gaining their buy-in to the changes."

During the transition, one of the big questions was how to handle projects that were already started. Dr. Baron decided that if projects were "well-enough along," the implementation team would allow them to complete without converting their schedules to Critical Chain. The team began the process taking two very high priority projects, deciding on their drum resource, and scheduling them using Critical Chain.

Initially, their drum revolved around an incoming material used in development projects. After six months, they found that projects were still experiencing logjams. As a result, the drum was changed to later in their development process and has continued to prove effective as a staggering mechanism over several years.

This division of Lucent uses software called ProChain (a Microsoft Project add-on) to figure out their Critical Chain schedules. Projects are tracked using weekly buffer updates and tracking meetings.

In the initial two years of implementation, the following results were achieved:

- In the Premise Cable Products group (inside-building cables), 100 percent of the sixteen projects scheduled using Critical Chain were completed on time. Cycle times were reduced by 50 percent in the first year.
- In the Outside Plant Cable Products group, development capacity tripled, with no increase in staffing. Cycle times in this division were also reduced by 50 percent the first year.
- Over the two-year period, over 95 percent of all projects were delivered on time.

Mr. Baron credits Critical Chain methodology with having a major impact on new product introduction. Multitasking is no longer a way of life. Morale is also higher, with the feeling that when a commitment is given, the Critical Chain plan helps make it a reality. As noted by David and Suzan Bergland, the consulting team from TOC Solutions, LLC, who worked with Dr. Franks in a follow-on implementation at Lucent, "Bill Baron and his team have reaped huge gains by cutting away the old rules that bound them. Now their project commitments are predictable and with predictability comes the information they need to manage expectations as well as their work."

The increase in capacity to complete more projects has allowed the division to shift its mix of projects. As Dr. Baron describes, "The work has shifted to much more forward looking projects. Less work is of a trivial nature."

Critical Chain implementations within Lucent have spread to other divisions, where the competitive pressures are also driving the demand for both faster R&D and a higher volume of project completions.

ELBIT SYSTEMS LTD.

Elbit Systems Ltd. (ESL) is a public company, headquartered in Haifa, Israel with subsidiaries worldwide, employing about 4400 people. ESL develops, manufactures and integrates advanced, high-performance defense electronic and electro-optic systems for customers throughout the world including the U.S., Europe, Israel, Latin America and the Far East. Elbit Systems focuses on upgrade programs for airborne, ground and naval defense platforms, often as a prime contractor. The company also focuses on designing, developing, manufacturing and integrating command, control and communication (C3) systems as well as electronic and electro-optic systems and products.

ESL main areas of business are:

- Fixed-wing and helicopter upgrades and systems;
- Pilot helmet-mounted systems;
- Combat vehicle upgrades and systems;
- C3 and battlefield information upgrades and systems and unmanned air vehicle (UAV) platforms
- Electro-optic and space systems and products;

ESL tailors and adapts its technologies, integration skills, market knowledge and battle-proven systems to each customer's individual requirements in both existing and new platforms. ESL's projects are diverse, covering innovations in systems deployed in the air, on the sea, on land and in space. Projects can last up to five years. The company is organized in SBU's (Strategic Business Units) organized each as a matrix operation.

Program managers use people for the active projects, many of which are common across projects. As a rapidly growing company, ESL's internal competition for people was also growing over time.

Prior to implementing Critical Chain in ESL's multi-project SBU's, ESL experienced to different degrees the common problems encountered by project oriented industries:

- Due dates not met
- Too many changes
- Resources and information not available when needed
- Conflicts on priorities between projects
- Budget overruns
- To much rework

Since ESL operates in a very competitive environment, the sales team often puts pressure on the engineering resources to reduce their estimates and make very aggressive promises. As Guy Brill, ESL's Chief Operating Officer describes, "Customers demand shorter and shorter cycle times". The engineering groups often believe that their estimates are already too aggressive. Knowing that sales will make demands to deliver earlier than engineering can promise, engineers sometimes inflate their estimates, expecting to be asked to cut back.

To try to satisfy everyone's demands for people, the company's resources began significant multitasking (splitting their time between projects). Multitasking, in turn, created great confusion and fights over priorities. As Mr. Brill describes, "this created the effect of making all program managers equally unhappy".

To resolve these issues, ESL began a Critical Chain implementation in April of 1997. After an initial 2-day workshop, the effort began with two pilot projects. However, ESL quickly discovered that in a matrix organization, this approach was deficient. The key issue was in resource management—being able to get resources when you need them, without major conflicts between projects. These efforts early in the history of Critical Chain multi-project implementation became the foundation of the multi-project approach.

By July of 1997, ESL was able to hold a workshop for top management. With their buy-in and support of the new project management methodology, the company held a kick-off meeting in September of 1997 for 400 people. The CEO was there to endorse the new way of managing project resources. By November, the infrastructure and software was in place and transitions to Critical Chain were well underway. Multi-project Critical Chain software did not exist prior to this effort. Software required to support the multi-project approach, called Concerto, was developed as part of this effort at ESL. The key was to provide a synchronized view of the entire company's project resources. As a result, bad multitasking was significantly reduced. Avionic programs were converted to Critical Chain in 1997, and other programs were converted in 1998.

The approach that the company took in implementing was to train project and resource managers on the Critical Chain basics in a 2-day workshop. Following the workshop, these managers took 3 days to build their Critical Chain plans and resolve conflicts. Any obstacles, which could not be resolved by individual project managers, were brought to a steering committee.

One of the significant issues that emerged during implementation was how to measure and reward people on projects. Previously, team members had been rewarded based on meeting or beating their task due dates. Since this measurement is counterproductive to Critical Chain, the steering committee decided to reward people based on overall company and project performance.

However, a critical motivation issue remained. Critical Chain requires the "relay runner" work ethic. ESL is a project company, which means that much of their revenue comes directly from project work. Therefore, it was considered very negative for any person to not have a real project (job number) on which to charge their time. The implementation of the "relay runner" work ethic meant that from time to time, many team members would have "idle" time—time that would not be spent on an active project, and that was OK with ESL's management. However, there would still be the problem of the perception and worry of team members, concerned about how they would be viewed by management.

To solve this problem, ESL went through several iterations of approaches. Their first thought was to have an "idling" job number, but the terminology of "idling" was negative. This was changed to R&D job numbers, with the strong assurance that management would not be looking at individual idle time or individual reporting to the R&D job numbers.

One of the biggest challenges in implementing the multi-project changes was in deciding how to stagger and prioritize the projects. ESL first selected one of the software groups as their

Drum resource. Projects were scheduled so as to not overload this software group. While multitasking was significantly reduced, there was still a major obstacle. Too many projects were ending up at the integration stage at the same time.

Engineers working at the integration stage were among the company's best. They had to be familiar with the entire project specifications and customer requirements. They had to be knowledgeable enough to integrate and test the entire product thoroughly.

At integration, if a component of a system meets its specifications standalone, but fails during integration testing, arguments can easily occur between different departments over who owns the problem. At the integration stage, so close to project completion, the engineers sometimes believe that they are wasting their time by working on a problem that could belong to one of the user departments. Therefore, the attitude often was "Prove that this is our problem, not yours". To resolve these difficult problems often required a collection of resources from different departments, resources that were not always readily available. Since integration took so long, teams were often split up before integration was complete. The result was that projects were often delayed in integration. Contention between projects still significantly delayed the ability of the projects to move through integration quickly enough to meet schedules.

At a result, the company pioneered a solution in conjunction with Dr. Goldratt, called "Virtual Drum". This solution uses a policy, rather than the loading of a physical resource, as a means to stagger projects. At ESL, the policy is that only 1-2 projects are allowed to move through integration at one time. With this policy in place, and with teams not broken up during this phase, the integration engineers and other departmental resources work together with no conflict in priorities. This solution has now been in place for several years.

As reflected by Guy Brill, "there are three major issues for Critical Chain multi-project success":

- Preparation of viable work plans with a Critical Chain and a properly sized buffer (30% for ESL). Having such a buffer is sacred to any ESL project plan.
- Implementation of buffer management, as a way of prioritizing tasks during execution of the multiple projects. Tasks must be prioritized according to the percentage penetration of the various buffers
- Limiting the multitasking. At ESL, the virtual Drum concept was successful in making this happen.

At ESL, with daily reporting of task starts and completions, and overnight updating, the "real-time" management of projects is in place. ESL implemented another type of buffer, called the milestone buffer, due to the types of contracts they undertake. Often, payments or penalties are associated with meeting certain critical milestones, especially in the longer-term projects. The milestone buffer is similar to a project completion buffer. Task priorities are decided based on penetration of the project completion buffers, the milestone buffers, and lastly the feeding buffers, in that order.

ESL limits the number of tasks in each Critical Chain plan to 200–300. More detailed plans are developed, tied to the individual tasks in the Critical Chain plan. Where it used to take greater than one hour for senior management to review each project, now the entire collection of 30–40 projects can be reviewed effectively in 1.5 hours total time.

ESL claims that Critical Chain has eliminated the negative effects described at the beginning of the case study. There is excellent synchronization of program teams, based on a common language, reporting that is visible to everyone and due to the Drum approach to scheduling. Plans are better constructed, with a major improvement in meeting schedule dates. Problems are identified on a timely basis, with milestone problems visible far enough in advance to take appropriate action. Priorities are clear to everyone.

ESL has not yet educated all of their suppliers on Critical Chain. However, they are able to identify any suppliers that cause problems in the Critical Chain. With this information, they are able to selectively offer incentives to specific suppliers to reduce risk and encourage early delivery.

ESL does show the Critical Chain work plan and buffers to their customers. However, this is done with a full explanation, developed by ESL, of the meaning of the buffers and how they are used to protect the project. In addition, ESL is able to use this explanation to reinforce the important role that the customer plays in meeting critical milestones.

For the future, ESL would like to use their increased reliability and shorter lead times to gain a stronger competitive edge. Internally, they believe that they can use the Pareto principal in buffer penetration to identify and remove the most frequent causes of buffer penetration, and subsequently reduce both cycle time and buffer sizes.

Critical Chain is now being implemented worldwide, across the ESL subsidiaries.

SEAGATE TECHNOLOGY

Seagate Technology is a multibillion-dollar manufacturer of storage devices for PCs, networks, and other media requiring permanent, safe, accessible information. Headquartered in California, the company's manufacturing and design facilities exist across the United States and around the world. The company began operations in 1979, primarily making disc drives. While the revenues today are still primarily from disc storage devices, the storage hosts have expanded from PCs to other devices such as video recorders, televisions, and games.

Seagate was one of the pioneers in implementing the Critical Chain methodology. Speed to market, with new technology, is very important in Seagate's strategy. Generally, the first supplier to deliver an innovative new product to a market enjoys the combination of high margins and high volume, until the competitors catch up. To meet the competitive challenges to Seagate's market leadership position, Brent King, executive director, Business Process Development, began to investigate Critical Chain in 1999.

Mr. King assists Seagate's chief technical officer in new product development in the Drive division (disc products). In this role, he helps to facilitate core teams, which take new product development into product launch after handoff from research and advanced concepts groups. In May of 1999, one of the core development teams, located in Minnesota, was given a challenge—read Dr. Goldratt's *Critical Chain* book and implement the concepts. One month later, this team accepted the challenge and began to build its network using Critical Chain.

By August 1999, the Critical Chain challenge was forwarded to senior product center management—"Don't think in terms of reducing cycle times from 15 months to 14.5 months. Think about how to cut cycles in half!' This challenge was accepted, and by September of 1999, the second Minnesota core team began its network build. By March 2000, core teams in Oklahoma City and Longmont, CO, were also live with Critical Chain networks.

At this time, the approach to product development was to use dedicated core teams. Therefore, it made sense to begin using Critical Chain in projects that were near the beginning of their development cycle. Since development cycles take from several months up to about a year to complete, the transition period for all projects within one location to be on the Critical Chain approach required about one year.

Within Seagate, program managers are the ones who determine the product development schedules. While there are relatively few program managers (typically one at each site), there are many resource managers. Approximately 200 of these resource managers have been receiving ongoing training in the Critical Chain approach.

Mr. King describes how one of the big changes with Critical Chain came from "Eliminating all buffers from individual tasks and consolidating these into one project buffer." This recognition of the advantage of project predictability is helping overcome resistance to change. In addition, the support of Seagate's chief technical officer and the use of Critical Chain reports by senior management speeds up acceptance. As Mr. King describes, every manager "Has legacy methods of managing projects and resources. We have not forced every manager to use Critical Chain, but the acceptance is increasing. The de facto standard is becoming Critical Chain with Concerto software."

While most core teams have some resources dedicated to the single project, resources still get multitasked. In Seagate's environment, some engineers have unique talents. Therefore, if an engineer with such unique talent finishes a task and moves on to another project, there is still a good chance that he could be called back to do maintenance work on prior tasks. This multitasking problem has not yet been completely resolved.

However, one of the major mechanisms for staggering projects according to a drum resource has remained stable and has worked very well. At Seagate, the drum is the group responsible for servo algorithm design. These algorithms are closely linked to drive rotational speed, mechanical reliability, and functionality. The servo group is therefore involved in product development at the up-front design stage, during the development and testing of the drive, and toward the end of the project at integration time.

Many problems in meeting overall specifications at integration time can be overcome by designing a work-around through a servo firmware modification. Therefore, it is very important for overall development cycle times to ensure that this resource can be very responsive throughout the project life cycle. The Critical Chain staggering approach helps to ensure this responsiveness. This means that new programs are scheduled according to the availability of this resource. As well, senior management reviews loading and progress weekly using the Critical Chain reports from Concerto software.

Seagate is continuing to improve processes using its own methodology called SLAM II (Sustained Leadership All Markets). This methodology looks at all program management activities, including market needs, product portfolio, quality, technology, and project management tools. In this respect, project management and Critical Chain together form one part of the total picture. SLAM is akin to the main gearbox, with Critical Chain being one gear.

In conclusion, Mr. King advises anyone who is new to Critical Chain and wanting to implement to "Be ready for the nuances of different cultures." He explains that people come to Seagate from different organizations and backgrounds. "It's much better to have one way to do engineering work [throughout the organization], not two or three. The reality is that Critical Chain needs the involvement and support of all management. Senior management endorsement is a really important thing." Two years after it began the Critical Chain journey, Seagate is continuing to spread the new culture of planning and managing projects to other internal suppliers and eventually to external suppliers, to complete the culture change.

UNIT 4

The Discipline of Teams

The material within this unit has been excerpted from the following textbook:

Jon R. Katzenbach & Douglas K. Smith
The Discipline of Teams:
A Mindbook-Workbook for Delivering Small Group Performance

Copyright 2001 by Jon R. Katzenbach and Douglas K. Smith
ISBN: 0-471-38254-X

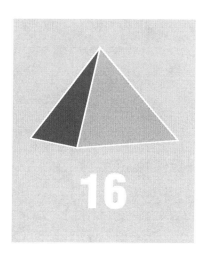

Discipline Is Wisdom

The most important characteristic of teams is discipline; not bonding, togetherness, or empowerment. Perhaps the finest examples of small group of performance are in the U.S. Marine Corps (USMC). Some of the small groups qualify as teams and some do not. But whatever small group configuration is required, the USMC invariably uses the right one at the right time. The reason is discipline. Discipline is a three-dimensional concept for the USMC. Top-down command and control is alive and well, but it is no match for the peer discipline and self-discipline that create value-driven marines. (Figure 16–1 illustrates the true dimensions of performance discipline.)

It is this three-dimensional discipline that ensures that the leadership role in a USMC fire team will shift, depending on who has the high ground. This same discipline motivates rifle platoon leadership teams, where a gunnery sergeant might tell his captain to change the intended tactical maneuver because he, the gunny, perceives a better way. It is this discipline that motivates every rifleman to act on the intent of leaders two levels up, since intent always takes precedence over any direct command to the contrary. Moreover, the USMC can apply real-team discipline with the same conviction and facility as they apply the single-leader discipline, for which they are better known. Marines are masters of team performance because they are proficient at not one, but two disciplines that create versatile, powerful performance units.

It is not happenstance that this unit is entitled *The Discipline of Teams,* the sequel and companion to our earlier work, *The Wisdom of Teams.* In fact, for the first book, we might have easily chosen *discipline* for the title instead of *wisdom,* since we certainly recognized its importance at the time. We even called our definition of teams a *discipline.* What we failed to appreciate fully, however, is the difficulty many would encounter in differentiating and integrating the team and single-leader disciplines. That difficulty, more than anything else, warrants this sequel, which we sincerely hope will provide additional help to

FIGURE 16–1 The three dimensions of performance discipline

the readers of and believers in *The Wisdom of Teams* as they work hard to get real teams in the right places at the right times for the right reasons.

Nearly a decade has passed since our initial work on *The Wisdom of Teams*. Since its initial publication in 1993, the book has been translated into over fifteen languages and serves as a standard text in the curriculum of several leading universities, indicating that the book has stood the test of time. Over the years, we have continued to work with and learn about small groups (from all sectors of the economy and all parts of the globe) whose performance increasingly distinguishes those organizations that succeed from those that don't.

In his review of *The Wisdom of Teams,* John Byrne of *Business Week* called teams "the essential building block of the organization of the future." Clearly, that organization of the future is the organization of today. And, unlike a decade ago, few argue with the critical role and contribution of teams. The concept of teaming was still relatively fresh, if not controversial, in the late 1980s. When mentioned in top management circles, teaming elicited cynical smirks just as often as enthusiastic smiles. In fact, one of our purposes in writing *The Wisdom of Teams* was to help line managers and executives make better use of teams as performance units rather than as human resource ploys to promote involvement and empowerment. The situation is markedly different today. Teams and teaming are as much a fixture in good management practice as planning, budgeting, personnel performance reviews, strategy, information technology, and other elements of organizational design. We find it hard to imagine a thriving, successful enterprise with no experience or use of teams.

So, why a sequel? For two reasons: First, we believe we have gained significant experience and insight about what groups can do to ensure they apply the right discipline at the right time; second, the world of teams has evolved over the past ten years in ways that increase both the importance of and challenges to achieving team performance. Virtual teaming is perhaps the single, most indicative development in that regard. Groups all over the world now can utilize countless new technological tools for working together more effectively. These tools permit people to interact across far greater geographic, cultural, language, and time-zone barriers than ever before. At the same time, new *groupware,* both hardware and software, complicates, confuses, and subverts efforts to apply the team discipline. We believe these challenges are worthy of thoughtful exploration and commentary.

Despite the rapid spread of teaming for performance purposes, we have little trouble identifying organizations and people who flounder in their use of teams. Understanding the value and potential of teams has proved to be much easier than applying the discipline required in achieving team performance. As a result, far too many people still think of *team* as a name for an organizational unit or a set of companionable feelings. Yet, as we suggested in *The Wisdom of Teams* and will further explore and provide guidance for in this unit, teaming works best when treated as a discipline for small group performance. Moreover, teaming is only one of the two essential disciplines for achieving small group performance. The other is the *single-leader discipline,* a clarifying label change from *The Wisdom of Teams* where we called it *working-group discipline.* With the single-leader discipline, a formal leader is in control and responsible for the direction and success of the group. This is not so with the team discipline. When small groups apply the team discipline appropriately, only the team can succeed, and only the team can fail. Of course individual accountability still matters, but unless it is combined with mutual accountability and common levels of commitment to achieve collective results, teams cannot perform.

Disciplines are not checklists of best practices, but according to *Webster's Collegiate Dictionary,* they do imply "orderly or prescribed conduct and patterns of behavior." More important, disciplines are grounded in fundamental principles, and those who would benefit from applying those disciplines must continually adhere to the underlying principles. For example, there is a discipline for practicing yoga, piano, and golf. There is even a discipline for losing weight. Consequently, if you wish to lose weight, you must eat less, eat more wisely, and exercise more. If you do each of those three things only once and check them off your list, you will not lose weight. Only through repeated and persistent application of all three can you expect to meet significant weight loss goals.

So, too, with both the team and single-leader disciplines for small group performance. Certainly, it is critical to distinguish one from the other. It is also important to recognize how these disciplined performance units differ from the more common effective groups that are so often labeled *teams,* but produce little more than congenial interaction and effective group dynamics. In Chapter 17, we will review the principles and behavior patterns for each of the *performance disciplines.* In Chapter 18, we explore the impact of *virtual teaming.* In Chapter 19, we suggest how your small group can use specific performance challenges to choose when to use one versus the other. If you apply these disciplines consistently, your group can expect to advance well beyond that of an effective group in terms of performance results. Conversely, if you use either discipline sporadically or merely as a checklist, your performance will fall short. The key point, however, is that these are time-tested disciplines that result in higher levels of small group performance. They are not names for types of groups; nor are they labels for feelings of togetherness or individual versus group identity.

Every small group we have ever been part of or privy to has had to figure out how to get along and communicate with one another well enough to deliver performance. Getting along, that is, effective group dynamics, is certainly important. But getting along is as critical to the single-leader discipline as it is to the team discipline. Far too many people, including experts, speak, act, manage, lead, and advise as though getting along, or improving group dynamics, is the same thing as teaming. It is not.

By contrast, when small groups emphasize performance as their touchstone, they not only achieve significant performance results, but they also learn to respect and like each other. We are not arguing against the value of bonding, trust, and mutual respect for small groups. In fact, one of our fundamental beliefs is that *a common performance objective is much more motivating for effective teams than the desire to be a team.* The same applies to the single-leader discipline: *performance objectives linked to individual accountability motivate small group performance much more than the desire for individual opportunity and distinction.* Small groups that emphasize performance will differentiate goals that warrant the single-leader approach from those that warrant the team approach. As a result, the members of the small group are much more likely to build and sustain trust-based working relationships than groups who obsess on relationships, feelings, and roles.

Of course, to use performance effectively as a guide in choosing between and applying the two disciplines, your group must be clear about performance. Your group must first decide that you want and need to be more than an effective group. Does performance matter or not? Following the publication of *The Wisdom of Teams,* perhaps nothing surprised us more than the difficulties people in organizations have in articulating specific performance goals. With the sometime exception of financial goals, people in most organizations chase after activity-based goals, or goals that describe the activities to be done, instead of the performance impacts or outcomes those activities are supposed to produce. Chapter 19 introduces you to the critical distinction between *outcome-based goals* and *activity-based goals.* Chapter 20 discusses how your small group can create and manage itself according to a *performance agenda* that specifies the outcomes and helps you match those outcomes with disciplines and resources.

If your group carefully distinguishes goals best approached through teaming from those best accomplished through the single-leader discipline, you will greatly increase your performance potential. Moreover, when your group chooses the team discipline, your attention to performance will guide you in applying the six basic principles of the team discipline as defined in *The Wisdom of Teams:* " . . . a small number of people with complementary skills who are committed to a common purpose, performance goals, and approach for which they hold themselves mutually accountable."

Chapter 21 offers guidance regarding the application of the principles to your team performance challenges, and discusses how you can know whether you have integrated mutual accountability with individual accountability and, if not, what to do about it. Finally, Chapter 22 returns to virtual teaming to explore the obstacles and opportunities it creates.

In supplying detailed guidance, plus dozens of exercises for small groups, the unit is a direct response to countless requests for a companion or sequel workbook to *The Wisdom of Teams.* To that end, this unit offers new background, frameworks, tools, and exercises for converting broad purposes into specific, outcome-based performance goals. Moreover, we also illustrate how to use those goals to choose between the team and single-leader disciplines. In so doing, the unit drives home a central point that we took for granted in *The Wisdom of Teams.* Understanding the differences between effective groups and disciplined performance units is a lot easier than integrating the two different disciplines to achieve significantly higher performance results.

This unit, however, has an important additional purpose: to shed new light on the rapidly expanding world of *virtual teaming.* Specifically, we want to help groups who use information and communications technology to accomplish group work and performance.

In the years since publishing *The Wisdom of Teams,* there has been an explosion in virtual teaming and virtual work. People now regularly collaborate through the medium of technology across geographic, organizational, and time-zone boundaries. It is difficult to identify an organization anywhere in the world that is not experiencing this shift. And there have been hundreds of books and articles written to guide people toward more effective use of the technology.

Our purpose here is to discuss the opportunities and effects of the new technology on the challenge of using the two disciplines for small-group performance. In Chapter 18, we stress that while technology can enable the two disciplines, it does not change them or the value of rigorously applying them. Two extreme claims are often made about group work technology. One contends that groupware actually prevents real teams; the other contends that groupware greatly enables team performance. Both oversimplify the likely impact of this rapidly evolving arena. In addition, far too many observers have implied that technology revolutionizes or supplants management disciplines. It does not. The two key management disciplines for small performance units, team and single leader, remain the same, whether your group works in the same room or across many time zones and geographic locations. Nonetheless, both teaming and single-leader efforts are increasingly affected by group work technology. As we discuss in Chapter 22, this technology makes applying the team discipline both easier and harder. And, in our opinion, the underlying character of the technology reinforces a bias within small groups that inadvertently favors, often unwisely, the single-leader discipline. Nonetheless, the value of choosing and rigorously applying the two disciplines remains unchanged.

Chapters 18 and 22 are focused exclusively on how virtual groups can best use technology to achieve performance, as well as several critical pitfalls to avoid. However, throughout the unit, we also highlight if and when virtual work and virtual teaming are truly different from nonvirtual efforts.

To summarize, this unit has several purposes and objectives. First, there is a growing need to distinguish effective, congenial groups from disciplined performance units. More important, the unit distinguishes, clarifies, and assists you in applying the two essential disciplines for small group performance: the team and single-leader. And, it will provide the direction and help small groups need to convert ambiguous, activity-based objectives into specific, outcome-based goals. We explore ways that small groups and their leaders can use performance goals as the basis for choosing and applying the two disciplines. For groups applying the team discipline, each chapter offers detailed advice, tools, and exercises to help ensure success. Most important, perhaps, every exercise in this unit can be done by the members of the small groups themselves, without the aid of outside facilitators. Finally, we have tried to distinguish the most critical aspects of technology and virtual teaming so that groups can apply the time-tested disciplines for small group performance across multiple locations and time zones.

Once again, however, we are sure that we address a moving target. By the time you read this unit, the organizational and technological context for teams and single-leader units will have evolved. New challenges, new approaches, and new dimensions of teaming continually emerge. Nonetheless, we believe the best way to deal with these subjects continues to be a relentless focus on the performance challenge you face and rigorous application of the appropriate discipline. The wisdom of teams continues to be the discipline of teams.

Mastering Two Disciplines—
Not One

IT IS MORE THAN INSTINCT ALONE . . .

We have all been part of a small group that somehow came together to accomplish unexpected feats as a team. The personal chemistry was right, the circumstances were compelling, and the group jelled. We have all also been part of small-group efforts that fell apart because of a misplaced concern about becoming a team, when, instead, the situation called for one clear leader to take charge. So how can you get team performance when it counts, without losing the power of single leadership and individual accountability when they count? This is a matter of applying the right discipline at the right time against the right challenge.

There are two key disciplines of small-group performance: the team discipline and the single-leader discipline. The *team discipline* promises a great deal of versatility and collective power when deployed against a challenge that warrants and demands a team. Many important performance challenges, however, do not benefit from teaming. For example, a half dozen salespeople, assigned to separate territories, typically will maximize sales results through the sum of their individual efforts. Challenges like this are best achieved through the *single-leader discipline,* which is defined as the sum of separate, individual contributions directed and managed by a single leader. (Please note: In *The Wisdom of Teams,* we called this the "working group" discipline. Over the past decade, we and those we consult with have found "single leader" to be a more useful descriptor.)

Members of small groups must be conscious and deliberate about when, where, and how to use the team discipline versus the single-leader discipline. Not surprisingly, both disciplines are effective if used in the right situations, and a balanced leadership approach will integrate the two, rather than constantly favoring one over the other. Unfortunately, too many leaders neither integrate nor balance these two disciplines. Instead, they instinctively, if not blindly, follow the single-leader approach, as though it were the *only* way to manage. Also, they may put more or less emphasis on teamwork, in the sense of togetherness, depending on the leader's personal style.

Leaders with this unfortunate habit and mind-set, together with the groups they lead, increasingly fail because performance results in today's fast-moving and challenging environment demand mastery of both disciplines. Intentionally or not, such leaders foster what we call *compromise units,* small groups who fail to grasp and apply either of the two disciplines, and become dysfunctional.

People in compromise units do not recognize that team performance requires the team discipline. Instead, members of such groups and their leaders never get beyond inadequate appeals to teamwork. They cry out to "be more of a team" and complain about "not getting along" or being insufficiently "empowered." Leaders of such groups often go hot and cold in their approaches, first commanding members to "Be a team!" then backing off with the hope that a real team will somehow coalesce. They seldom do. Yet, when leaders retreat, and the group fails to apply the discipline of team basics, a confused and leaderless gang inevitably results. Compromise units are the worst of both worlds, allowing performance to deteriorate because the leader and members of the group have neglected to apply the two key disciplines of small-group performance.

Learning how and when to apply the two disciplines for small-group performance begins with recognizing that each discipline supports *the five basic elements of effective group work.* It is important to remember that an effective group is a significant step below a performance unit. Nonetheless, neither of the two small-group performance units, real team or single-leader group, can realize its performance potential unless the five elements are in place. First, the group has or develops *an understandable charter* that provides the group with a reason and purpose for working together; however, the charter is not necessarily focused on performance. Second, the members of the group *communicate and coordinate effectively* to allow constructive interactions involving all of the members. Third, the members of the group establish *clear roles and areas of responsibility,* which allow them to work individually or collectively. Fourth, the members create *a time-efficient process,* minimizing wandering discussions and wasted time. And, finally, the group develops *a sense of accountability* helping each member understand individual contributions to the success of the group; hence, progress can be monitored and evaluated accordingly. Figure 17–1 illustrates how these elements of effective group work provide the base on which performance units develop. The essential difference between an effective group and the two performance units is in the clarity of the group's focus on performance and the rigor with which the members of the group apply the appropriate discipline required by the performance challenge.

The team discipline and the single-leader discipline are two distinctly different managerial approaches. Both are required for an effective group to become a performance unit. Leaders and the other members of small groups must master all three branches of the Y: (1) the elements of effective group work; (2) the discipline of single-leader groups, and (3) the basics of real-team performance. Optimizing the value of small-group work requires understanding each of the branches and knowing how to use performance as a guide for deciding when to branch left (single leader) versus right (team).

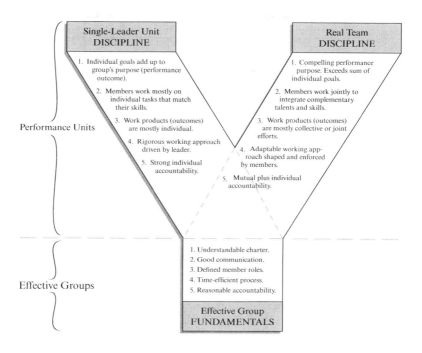

FIGURE 17–1 Climbing the Y

Source: Copyright by Katzenbach Partners LLC.

17.1 THE SINGLE-LEADER DISCIPLINE

The single-leader discipline revolves around one leader. The leader, often in consultation with the group, determines the performance-based reason and purpose for group work, makes the decisions, establishes the required individual contributions and group pattern of communications, and determines the requirements of success and how and when to evaluate progress. In the single-leader discipline, the formal leader:

1. Makes and communicates decisions for the group. The members of the group respect the decisions because the leader has the required formal authority, as well as recognized experience, proven judgment, and relevant knowledge of the performance situation. Indeed, members of the group *expect* the leader to make the decisions. While consultation can be a part of the decision process, the leader makes the final decision.

2. Sets the performance goals and determines individual responsibilities. While the goal-setting process often involves open communication and two-way negotiation, the leader has the final say about what constitutes an appropriate goal for each member, as well as for the group as a whole. Members often provide important input in this process, but the leader establishes the goals.

3. Sets the pace and determines the working approach. The leader monitors the progress and pace of each person's effort and motivates individuals, as well as the group as a whole. The leader determines the overall working approach, which reflects a series of individual contributions based on stable, well-defined, individual roles for each member of the group. The leader accelerates or slows the pace by setting deadlines for the group and its members.

4. Evaluates the results. The leader assesses individual results, as well as overall group progress, and makes adjustments as needed. The leader is responsible for achieving group results that are acceptable to higher-level managers. Throughout the process, the leader recognizes and rewards the contributions and results of individuals.

5. Establishes benchmarks and standards. The leader fosters sharing of ideas among the members and encourages best practices both within and outside the group, ensuring effective group communication between members and outsiders. In most cases, the leader makes the final determination of the best standards for the group.

6. Maintains control of the group effort by clarifying individual accountability and emphasizes consequence management. As a result, the members of the group are clear about their roles, specific goals, expected end-products, manner of interaction with others, and deadlines. The leader determines the measures that apply to individuals and to the group as a whole. In the final analysis, the leader is in control. Furthermore, the members of the group, as well as senior management outside the group, expect the leader to be in control.

The single-leader discipline is a familiar and essential part of all well-managed organizations. Throughout history, most organizational departments and business units have been led primarily in this mode. Team gurus and enthusiasts aside, we believe most leaders and employees are more comfortable working within the single-leader discipline because each team member knows what is expected and how performance will be assessed. Perhaps what is more revealing is that being accountable for your own, individual goals and actions is preferable, clearer, and easier than the shared responsibility that characterizes the team discipline. With every good intention, we may advocate teamwork, but our actions all too often favor the single-leader discipline mind-sets and behaviors.

17.2 THE TEAM DISCIPLINE

As useful, valuable, and time-honored as the single-leader discipline is to small-group performance, it is not the only way, or always the best way, to manage small groups. The team discipline, which demands shared leadership and mutual accountability is the alternative. When groups effectively apply the team discipline, the group, not the formal leader, determines the performance rationale and purpose for group work, and the group establishes the required individual and collective contributions and pattern of communications. The group also sets the requirements for success and how and when to evaluate progress.

The team discipline requires peer- and self-enforcement and is described in *The*

Wisdom of Teams as "a small number of people with complementary skills who are committed to a common purpose, performance goals, and approach for which they hold themselves mutually accountable." These elements are reviewed in Chapter 21 (mutual accountability). Instead of elaborating element by element at this point, the following paragraphs highlight how the team discipline differs from the single-leader discipline.

1. In the team discipline, decisions are made by the appropriate people. Sometimes the decision-maker is, in fact, the designated team leader and sometimes it is the whole group. But, far more often, decisions are made by the person or people whose skills and experience best qualify them to decide. This is why team basics require a set of complementary skills. Groups who apply the team discipline do not require consensus decisions. In fact, the group rarely even votes. Instead, decisions get made by those the group believes best positioned to do so, usually as a result of talent, skill, experience, and assigned work task. The leader only intervenes when group members are incapable or unwilling to reach a decision. In contrast to the clear, unvarying, decision-making authority that characterizes the single-leader discipline, leadership and choice making shifts and is shared among the members in groups using the team discipline.

2. Goals of groups using the team discipline are set and affirmed individually and collectively by the group. While the designated leader may argue persuasively for certain goals, the goals are not set until the members of the group have explored the implications, wrestled with the trade-offs, and developed a shared understanding and mutual sense of commitment. This process differs from the characteristic, one-on-one negotiation between each member and the leader in the single-leader discipline. Moreover, in the team discipline the group clearly differentiates between individual goals and collective goals. (In fact, the achievement of collective goals is the joint responsibility of two or more members.) When groups are using the team discipline, the number and value of collective goals invariably outweigh the number and value of individual goals.

3. In the team discipline, the pace and working approach are set by the group, making the approach a matter of shared commitment. The team chooses the best way to distribute and integrate work, manage logistics and administration, and establish and enforce norms for each other. More important, the roles and contributions of the members shift to fit different performance-task needs, instead of remaining predictable, stable, and relatively inflexible as in the single-leader approach.

4. In the team discipline, the group rigorously and consistently evaluates its own results. Because the purpose and goals of the team require similar levels of commitment from all of the members, the group assesses its progress *as a team*. The team is its own toughest critic, and members are less forgiving of performance shortfalls than their sponsors or even the leader. Members of a team hold each other accountable to a greater degree than they are held accountable by either the leader or the sponsoring authority. Furthermore, when teams evaluate progress, the dialogue is open, nonhierarchical, and more focused on performance progress and the entire effort of the group than on individual performance.

5. In the team discipline, the members of the group set high standards. These demanding standards arise from the compelling performance purpose to which all members are committed. Because of their shared commitment, the members of the group seek out tough standards and high comparisons for themselves. The group is seldomly satisfied with the standards or benchmarks used elsewhere in the organization. It is not uncommon for a team to establish a set of goals that exceeds the goals set in its charter from the sponsoring authority. Groups using the team discipline thrive on clearing a bar that others would not attempt.

6. Members of groups using the team discipline hold themselves individually and mutually accountable. With groups applying the team discipline, it is very difficult (if not impossible) for any one member to fail—only the team can succeed or fail. Team members are not easy on one another in this respect. Yet, they are extremely flexible and adaptable in helping each other to contribute to the fullest extent possible and to develop new skill levels in the process. In marked contrast, the single-leader discipline almost exclusively emphasizes individual accountability and development. Indeed, mutual accountability for shared purpose and goals may be *the* hallmark of the team discipline.

Read the preceding two sections on the single-leader discipline and the team discipline again in conjunction with the Y chart in the first section of this chapter. Note how each discipline builds upon and extends the five basics of effective group work: (1) a clearly understood purpose and rationale for group work—though not necessarily performance focused; (2) open communication and coordination among all of the members—though always within a predictable meeting agenda; (3) clear roles and areas of responsibility as to how work will get done—though seldom differentiated by individual versus collective work product needs; (4) a time-efficient process that minimizes "group groping"—though seldom variable by group task; and (5) a sense of who is accountable for what and what success looks like and how to evaluate progress—though seldom rigorously enforced. In short, these fundamentals enable groups to work effectively, but not to perform exceptionally.

Yet, as you reread these two sections, we urge you to learn the distinctions between these two separate performance disciplines for small groups as well as the fundamentals of effective group work. The two disciplines should feel different. For example, if you consider a small group in which you currently participate, you ought to find it easy to use the above descriptions to identify which of these two management disciplines is being used and if your efforts are best characterized as an effective group or worse, a compromise unit.

Table 17–1 provides a model to highlight the key differences between effective groups who merely interact well, and performance units who apply discipline to achieve success.

A balanced approach to small-group effectiveness starts with the conscious choice of which discipline will work best for a particular performance challenge. *Note:* these two disciplines lead to performance unit results—they are not simply the names for two types of work groups. We are not suggesting or encouraging leaders and groups to choose between being a team or being a single-leader group. In fact, we strongly warn against that mindset. Leaders and groups must look at each separate performance challenge they face, decide if they really need a performance unit, and then choose the best discipline for their

Table 17–1 Effective group fundamentals versus the single-leader or team disciplines

Effective Work Group: That Interacts Well	Single-Leader Discipline: Performance Unit	Real-Team Discipline: Performance Unit
Clearly understood charter or purpose (not necessarily related to enterprise performance).	Strong performance charter and purpose comprised mostly of individual contributions.	Compelling performance challenge comprised of many collective work products.
Hierarchical leader promotes open communication and coordination.	Focused, single leader applies relevant experience and know-how to create performance focus.	Leadership role shifted/shared among members to reflect and exploit performance potential.
Individual goals seldom add up to a clear performance purpose for the group. The goals are not outcome-based.	Individual outcome-based goals and work products that add up to the performance purpose.	Outcome-based goals include both individual and collective work products (the latter predominates).
Clear roles and areas of responsibility remain constant throughout the group effort.	Stable roles and contributions reflect talents and skills of members.	Shifting roles and contributions to match varying performance tasks, as well as exploiting and developing member skills/talents.
Accountability is understood, but consequence management principles seldom prevail.	Individual accountability enforced primarily by leader; consequence management usually prevails.	Both individual and mutual accountability, largely peer- and self-enforced. However, only the team can "fail."

situation. The two key disciplines are ways to achieve demanding performance results, not arbitrary names for types of groups.

17.3 LINKING WORK PRODUCTS TO PERFORMANCE

Whenever a small group can deliver performance through the combined sum of individual contributions, then the single-leader discipline is the most effective choice. This choice is fast, efficient, and comfortable, since most organizational units have followed the single-leader model for decades. However, if there must be collective contributions in addition to individual efforts, then the group should apply the team discipline. We choose to call such contributions work products. As illustrated in Figure 17–2, many group performance challenges can be achieved through the sum of individual work products. Other challenges demand the extra, team-based performance that arises from collective work products. Such products add an important dimension of performance that simply cannot be achieved primarily by individuals working on their own; hence, the value of the collective work product can be significant. The collective work product is the reason why teams outperform single-leader units.

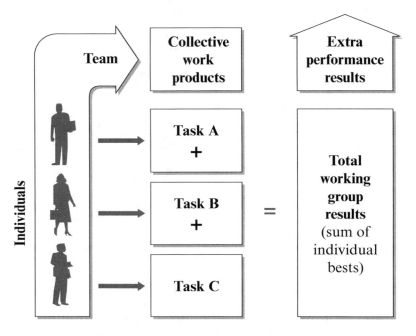

FIGURE 17–2 Collective work potential

Collective work products come from the hands-on work of two or more people, each with different skills, talents, and perspectives, who collaborate to produce value not achievable by any one of them alone. For example, a market researcher who collaborates with a product designer and a sales representative to design, set up, conduct, and debrief a focus group creates value from their joint or collective work effort. The skills, effort, and talent of all three combine to produce the focus group and what is to be learned from it. The different perspectives of the three people working together result in a better set of focus-group questions and interactions, as well as a richer interpretation of the response. If one of the three people conducts the focus group, or even if each of them conducts a separate focus group, the value of their merging perspectives would be largely lost.

A collective work product requires the skills, talents, and melded perspectives of several members of the group working together. One person working independently cannot produce the same quality product. Also, the leader cannot create the product by simply combining the individual work efforts of several people. Members have to roll up their sleeves and work together (either around the table, over the phone, or across the Internet). When performance demands collective-work products through real-time collaboration and integration of multiple skills and perspectives, the sum of individual work products and contributions falls short, and the single-leader approach will under-perform.

Individual work products come from individual effort, talent, and skill. Sounds obvious, and it is. The value created derives primarily from the hands-on work of one person. For example, a market researcher who designs, sets up, conducts, and debriefs a focus group by herself creates an individual work product. The researcher might ask an assistant to make phone calls, get help from an audio-visual technician in recording the focus group, or ask an editor to review the draft of the conclusions for clarity. But the researcher is doing the essential value-added work.

The distinction here is one of common sense. Yet, it is a distinction far too often ignored. In this case, four people are doing the work: the market researcher, the assistant, the technician, and the editor. However, most of the value in the work product from the focus group comes primarily from one person: the market researcher. It is the market researcher's individual work product. In the case of the jointly designed and conducted focus group in the preceding example, the collective interactions of the market researcher, the product designer, and the sales representative create the value.

People sometimes confuse work products with decisions. Work products, whether individual or collective, are more about work than decisions. Work products involve more than reviewing, deciding, and delegating—the actions so often associated with the job of manager. For example, steering committees that review, discuss, decide, and delegate are not producing collective work products. They are, as a committee, performing the classic management role of making decisions. But decisions—even though they often create value in and of themselves—are not the work products that define small group disciplines. The work leading to such decisions, as well as the work that such decisions require, may warrant performance unit levels of effort. Thus the decision event itself may dictate performance unit work. As a consequence, steering committees can seldom be classified as teams, although they may sponsor or stimulate group actions that warrant performance unit action.

In choosing between the single-leader and the team disciplines, groups must determine if their goals require significant and essential collective work products, or if the performance challenge is best achieved through the sum of individual work products and contributions. If the group cannot identify important, *required* collective work products, the team-approach should not be applied.

In the previous sentence, the word "*required*" is important. In our experience, most small groups can imagine many possibilities for collective work products. For example, the market researcher could easily approach the focus group in either of the ways described above. The key question, therefore, is not whether your group can imagine one or more meaningful and important collective work products, but whether the specific performance challenge at hand *requires* and benefits from collective work products.

Consider, then, these two examples of different performance challenges:

Challenge 1: "We need to know if our core consumer segments will respond favorably or unfavorably to emphasizing 'healthy' and 'natural' in our upcoming ad campaign."

Challenge 2: "We must understand if we can grow our customer base significantly by redesigning our product line that currently sells so well to the 'fifty-plus crowd' in ways that will appeal to people in their teens and twenties."

A market researcher could imagine approaching Challenge 1 through delivering the kind of collective work product described earlier. But, in our experience, performance does not necessarily require that approach. Neither product designers nor sales representatives are needed to assist the market researcher in designing, conducting, or learning from a series of focus groups whether 'healthy' and 'natural' will benefit or hurt sales. On the other hand, it is difficult to imagine anyone succeeding against Challenge 2 without collective work products. There are too many uncertainties and open questions, all of which would benefit significantly from the real-time combination of the differing skills, experiences, and perspectives of the market researcher, product designer, and sales representative.

EXERCISE 17.1
LEARN FROM YOUR OWN EXPERIENCE

Gather one or more groups of people. Ask them to take a few minutes to write down at least one prior experience when they believed they were part of a really effective team versus one when they felt the group was ineffective. When everyone has completed this task, give them another five minutes to identify the characteristics that distinguished the two situations. Once people have completed this assignment, ask the whole group to divide itself into subgroups of four to eight people, with some groups focusing only on the characteristics of effective teams and others on the characteristics of ineffective teams. Give these groups twenty minutes to discuss their insights before asking each subgroup to share feedback with the whole group.

When you have gathered the feedback, ask the group to compare the findings and insights they have generated with the material in Chapter 17: (1) the five basic elements of all effective groups, (2) the team discipline, (3) the single-leader discipline, and (4) "compromise units."

EXERCISE 17.2
TEST YOUR UNDERSTANDING

Use the true/false test in Table 17–2 to evaluate your understanding of the two key disciplines and related concepts.

Table 17–2 Test your understanding

		True	False
1.	A team approach is better than a leader-led approach only if significant collective work products are needed.		
2.	A team approach is likely to be more effective than a leader-led effort when the number of members exceeds twenty-five.		
3.	In groups larger than twenty, the most practical way to achieve team levels of performance is to utilize subgroups.		
4.	Leader-led groups achieve results faster than teams.		
5.	Once a team has mastered the basics, their results are just as fast as a leader-led group.		
6.	At the start of a project, it is important for every small group to decide to be a team and then figure out how best to adhere to that discipline.		
7.	A small group can sometimes function as a team and sometimes as a single leader unit, provided the group applies the right discipline in the right places at the right times.		
8.	The best way for a group to achieve team levels of performance is for the formal leader to back off and empower the group to manage itself.		
9.	Teaming is nothing more than getting along and helping each other.		
10.	People in groups will only respect decisions if they are made by the boss.		
11.	Sometimes my group will perform best if the leader will just make decisions, assign each of us our individual jobs, and just get on with it.		
12.	Most people are more comfortable with clearly defined responsibilities and roles, as well as individual accountability.		
13.	Teaming is required whenever it is possible to imagine any collective work product.		
14.	Teams typically set higher standards and goals than what the chain of command expects.		
15.	Clear and compelling performance goals are what create great teams, instead of the desire to team up.		

Answers: 1. T; 2. F; 3. T; 4. T; 5. T; 6. F; 7. T; 8. F; 9. F; 10. F; 11. T; 12. T; 13. F; 14. T; 15. T

EXERCISE 17.3
ASSESS AND REACT _____

Gather your group together. Ask each person to answer the questions in Table 17–3 on a 1 to 5 scale, with 1 being *strongly agree,* and 5 indicating *strongly disagree.* When you have completed your answers, compare notes. Discuss whether your group balances the single-leader discipline with the team discipline, or perhaps habitually uses only one of these disciplines. Also, discuss whether your group is a compromise unit. Finally, ask yourselves whether there are any specific performance challenges your group faces that would benefit from a different approach from the one usually taken.

Table 17–3 Assess and react

		1	2	3	4	5
1.	Our working approach is determined by the way in which the leader assigns tasks and runs the meetings.					
2.	We hold one another accountable for higher collective results than our leaders and sponsors expect of us.					
3.	We all participate in evaluating each other's efforts instead of leaving that up to our leader.					
4.	Most members of our group are not comfortable in leading the group.					
5.	Members of our group are very clear about their roles, and we maintain those roles in all meetings and interactions.					
6.	We need clearer decisions and less time spent on touchy-feely stuff.					
7.	Most of the real work required is best done by each member working on his/her assignment in his/her area of competence.					
8.	We spend a lot of time between meetings collaborating on work that couldn't get done individually.					
9.	Our leader delegates effectively to others and only supervises and monitors individual progress.					
10.	When we set our goals, we seldom distinguish between individual goals and joint or collective goals.					
11.	We learn a lot from one another because we often shift roles and share work tasks.					
12.	We seldom take time to discuss and decide on our purpose and aspirations as a group; these are clearly specified by our leader.					
13.	When new members of our group are added, we spend quality time as a group incorporating their views into our purpose, goals, and working approach.					

Table 17–3 Assess and react *(continued)*

		1	2	3	4	5
14.	All of our meetings are conducted very efficiently by the leader, and the topics and agendas are clear in advance.					
15.	It is more important that we get along with one another than achieve extraordinary results.					
16.	All members of the group feel comfortable suggesting changes in the group's goals and working approach.					
17.	Our group is too big to function effectively as a team; hence, most of the real work is done by individual and subgroups, only some of which work as performance teams.					
18.	We are each held accountable by the leader for individual goals and contributions that add to our group's purpose.					
19.	Time is clearly more important to our purpose than collective work products; hence, most of the work is individually driven.					
20.	Members are primarily respected by the others for their skills rather than personality.					

EXERCISE 17.4
MATCH YOUR PERFORMANCE CHALLENGES TO THE TWO DISCIPLINES _____

Gather your group and spend whatever time is needed to list the most pressing performance challenges that you currently face. Refine this list until you have five to ten particular challenges. Pick one challenge from the list. Review Figure 17–1 and Table 17–1. Now, ask half of your group to make the best possible arguments in favor of applying the single-leader discipline to the selected performance challenge. Ask the other half of the group to argue in favor of the team discipline. When you have completed this debate, move on to a second specific challenge from your list, then a third, and so on.

EXERCISE 17.5
DOES PERFORMANCE REQUIRE COLLECTIVE WORK PRODUCTS? _____

Again, start by identifying one or more specific performance challenges facing your group. Pick one of those challenges to discuss. Ask the group to brainstorm regarding the kind of work that must get done to succeed. Convert this description of work into a series of specific work products. Identify and discuss among yourselves whether the work products are individual or collective. Then, using Figure 17–2, discuss whether your group's performance *requires* or benefits from collective work products. Remember that the question here is not whether you can identify collective work products, or whether any particular collective work product is a good idea or potentially valuable. Instead, the question is whether the performance objectives and goals demand such work products.

18

Virtual Teaming

Does your team include members who must work together from separate physical locations across different time zones? If yes, then it is likely you need "virtual team" capability, both human and technological. To some extent, virtual teaming has always been with us. For example, groups have long used teleconferencing to connect team members whose logistical constraints precluded their physical presence at a key work session. Increasingly, however, virtual teaming is becoming an integral part of most small group work, primarily as a consequence of technology that has evolved way beyond mere teleconferencing. Today, organizations are no longer confined to team efforts that assemble people from the same location or the same time zone. Indeed, small groups of people from two or more locations and time zones routinely convene for collaborative purposes. Such groups are expected to take advantage of hardware such as intranets, Internet, video and teleconferencing, and fax, as well as software that supports activities like project management, document sharing, and executive management information synthesis. For purposes of this book, we categorize all such technologies, both hardware and software, as *groupwork technology,* or more simply, *groupware.*

The growing diversity and capacity of groupware help make virtual teaming possible and practical, if not inevitable. But technology alone does not explain the rapid rise in virtual teaming. As people-intensive sources of competitive advantage have gained importance, organizations, from commercial to government to nonprofit, have shifted how and where work is done. In short, the workplace of today is a far cry from the assembly lines and offices of yesteryear. In fact, twenty years ago, most work done by people in organizations was a function of routine processes dictated by formal structures, rules, and programs. Today, a lot of work still reflects such formal elements but just as often work occurs in the context of more flexible, ad hoc, and nonroutine special projects.

Project work has become as important to the success of organizations as process work. Short- to medium-term efforts that seek performance improvements in many different arenas, such as quality, customer care, reengineering, product development, strategy formulation, and innovation, consume more labor than ever before. Such projects are usually staffed by small groups of people who apply a constantly changing mix of the team and single-leader disciplines.

The many challenges that require project work has increased the *demand* for work done in small groups. At the same time, technology has increased the *supply* of project workers because organizations are not limited to workers located in the same place or time zone. If, for example, you were asked to assemble a group to tackle a significant strategic alliance project, you would not need to limit your choices to people located in the same building as yourself. Instead, you and your organization could select people from among your company's various facilities throughout the world. In fact, you could staff your small group with people who are not even part of your company, such as outside experts, special researchers, and alliance partner resources. Consequently, if your headquarters, plant, or office complex houses two-hundred people, but your company, its critical alliance partners, and professional advisors number in the thousands, the choices for your effort are vastly expanded.

Of the dozens of teams we researched during the writing of *The Wisdom of Teams,* only a handful had membership from multiple locations. By contrast, in the decade since publishing the book, we have witnessed an explosion in the number of such teams. Virtual teaming efforts now pervade all kinds of organizations and institutions. Yet, this phenomenon is only part of a much more fundamental change, the rapidly expanding amount of *virtual work.*

Virtual work consists of tasks and activities that occur within today's vast network of electronics, telecommunications, and information technology. The computer, with all its attendant software and hardware, continues to redefine where and how work is done. Even co-located, non-virtual teams, where all members work down the hall from one another, increasingly interact over the same technology as virtual teams. This technology makes all communication quicker and easier. As a result, the vast majority of office workers rely on user-friendly computers, e-mail, project management, document sharing, and other software. Therefore, even co-workers *literally sitting next to one another in the same team room* will have many virtual moments, interacting and collaborating through groupware. Groupwork technology permits interactions to take place within time frames that fit the convenience and different work patterns of workers.

In short, small groups increasingly work virtually even when not involved in virtual teams. Their work across a crowded room through the medium of computers is similar to the work of virtual teams using computers across larger spans of time and geography. In each case, the groups face the challenge of making the best use of groupware in their continuing efforts to deliver performance in new and different ways.

18.1 VIRTUAL TEAMING: SAME DISCIPLINES IN NEW CONTEXT _____

Not surprisingly, virtual work and teaming efforts pose challenges that differ markedly from co-located work. (See Chapter 22 for further discussion of these challenges.) None of the challenges, however, are as significant as what we believe to be the most critical issue: Are the two disciplines that are essential for small group performance—team and single-leader—different for virtual teams?

Our answer is, "No." The two disciplines are the same for virtual and non-virtual teams, as well as for virtual and non-virtual work. Having participated in, observed, and reviewed dozens of virtual teams over many years, we remain convinced that choosing and applying the right discipline is the most significant difference between the virtual groups who deliver performance versus those that fall short. To validate this belief, as well as expand our range of examples for this book, we worked with associates from Katzenbach Partners LLC to research the efforts of over a dozen virtual teams from different industries and global dispersions.

The results of this research were not surprising, but they did convince us that the world of virtual teaming deserves special attention. Fortunately, some of the most effective teams reviewed during our work on *The Wisdom of Teams* were virtual teams. For example, the McKinsey Rapid Response Team members were located in Atlanta, New York, and San Francisco. The Rapid Response Team faced challenges in applying the team discipline that differed in important ways from those confronted by physically co-located teams. For example, the Rapid Response Team could not have performed as well without spending time in face-to-face meetings. The time together toward the beginning of the effort and again when critical issues or challenges required face-to-face meeting was of particular value to the team. But basic team discipline consisting of a small number of people with complementary skills holding themselves mutually accountable to a common purpose, common performance goals, and commonly agreed upon working approach, did not change. Nor did the three litmus tests for identifying when to use the team discipline: (1) performance goals that demanded collective work products, (2) shifting member and leadership roles, and (3) mutual plus individual accountability. These imperatives stand the tests of time, distance, and technology.

Over the years, we have observed that virtual groups, relying on the single-leader discipline, succeed when that discipline is the best choice. The research provided current evidence of our initial hypotheses, and expanded our insights about how virtual groups work differently in applying the appropriate discipline, single-leader or real-team. In one of many examples, a small group of managers at KPMG Peat Marwick was asked to oversee the move of hundreds of people from one building to another. This building transition group relied heavily on e-mail, document sharing, simple project management, and other collaboration software. While the members of the group practiced good teamwork behavior, such as effective communications, sharing of best practices, and mutual support, they relied primarily on the single-leader discipline. The group leader was in control: making the critical decisions, allocating individual tasks and responsibility, facilitating group communications, evaluating and monitoring task progress, and holding people accountable for individual contributions. Under the group leader's command and with the contributions of the individuals involved, the group met all the performance challenges they faced—and their use of groupwork technology helped a lot.

In contrast, when virtual teams misapply, confuse, or lose sight of the two basic disciplines, they fail. For example, a group of five people from Boston and New York were charged with designing and delivering a key feature in a suite of software products. These five people had the necessary programming, software architecture, business knowledge, and marketing skills. Success clearly warranted the team discipline because collective work products, mutual accountability, and shared leadership were essential in achieving the group's performance purpose. Instead, the group relied on the single-leader approach, and, consequently, fell short of their goal. This software group and the KPMG building transition group actually used the same groupware. In fact, the software group's expertise and familiarity with the technology far exceeded that of the building transition group. Therefore, it is the choice of discipline, and not the software, that matters.

Our point is simple: *Technology is an enabler of both disciplines, not a substitute for either.* With respect to groupwork technology, it does not matter whether groups are comprised of novices or experts. The basics of small-group performance remain the same. You must learn when to use the single-leader discipline to achieve your goals and when to use the team discipline. Leading-edge technology, no matter how well applied, will not compensate for choosing the wrong discipline, or applying it poorly.

Indeed, this was the central conclusion reached by KPMG, following experimentation with groupware among several teams. The small group that oversaw the building move successfully used the technology to enable the single-leader discipline. Other groups also succeeded in using the technology to support the team discipline. Yet, not surprisingly, every single group who fell into the trap of hoping that the groupware would substitute for managerial discipline failed.

If your small group must do virtual work, the most important lesson in this book is that of choosing and using the discipline that fits your particular performance need. You cannot rely on technology, any more than you can natural instinct, for making the appropriate choice. In both disciplines, technology can help the work, but it cannot replace using the right discipline at the right time and place. So, focus clearly on your performance challenges and learn when and how best to use the team or single-leader approach. Do not assume that the basic disciplines of performance will fit merely because you are employing advanced technology or specially designed groupware. And do not make the mistake of assuming that technology will somehow provide the necessary discipline.

18.2 GROUPWORK TECHNOLOGY: KEY FEATURES AND FUNCTIONALITY

A variety of groupwork technologies now permit you to collaborate with others across different time zones and in different places. As noted earlier, some of these technologies have been around for decades, for example, fax, telephone, teleconferencing, and video conferencing. Other groupware has emerged in the past decade with the growing use of computers and the Internet, including e-mail and various collaboration, project management, and software applications. There are hundreds of technological options from which to choose.

This section introduces the most relevant and important features and discusses how virtual teams can take advantage of them. Specific obstacles and difficulties posed by the technology are discussed in Chapter 22.

1. *Video, chatroom, and teleconferencing* devices permit groups who are not in the same location or time zones to hold meetings and discussions. Those who have used this type of groupware already know how this experience differs when contrasted with face-to-face meetings. In chatrooms and teleconferencing, there is no body language or facial expressions to help interpret meaning and intent; in video conferencing, the sound and image can include awkward hesitations. Jokes, for example, are often difficult to follow because of the pauses. Groups quickly learn that all three technologies work best when the interactions are confined to need-to-know information or issues that everyone must understand and resolve together. As one person with experience in virtual teaming told us, "Using these technologies just to get status reports from each individual is really boring and a waste of time." Participants also recognize that establishing some working rules or etiquette norms up front helps ensure better interactions and minimizes the discourteous behavior of not paying attention. For example, people using this technology instead of face-to-face meetings often find it easier to tune out (one popular form of tuning out is when a presumed participant is actually doing other work). Finally, many groups have learned how to use two of these technologies simultaneously: chatroom, plus either video or teleconferencing. By doing so, people within the group can choose to express themselves by speaking or in writing, an option that often produces both richer discussions and input and dialogues with fewer interruptions. Why? Because when only one means of communication is available, people compete for the floor. When two means are available, people can log in their comments without disrupting the flow of conversation.

2. *Email:* The good news and bad news about e-mail are increasingly well known and obvious. Used well, e-mail permits members of groups to communicate critical information, challenges, and issues. But without careful attention to when and how to rely on e-mail, groups add to the proliferation of e-mail that increasingly is the bane of so many. Worst of all, carelessly composed e-mail messages can insult, embarrass, and alienate receivers. More subtly, e-mail is a poor substitute for the following threaded discussions feature described below. Groups who rely on e-mail instead of threaded discussions encounter more frustration than progress in raising, discussing, and resolving issues critical to the performance of the group. As one person told us, "When I read a lengthy e-mail, it sparks hundreds of thoughts and questions. But unlike in face-to-face team meetings, I can't ask them or engage in a discussion about them."

3. *Threaded discussions* permit groups to raise, discuss, and resolve issues in orderly, comprehensible, and controlled ways. They work as follows: Let's say I raise Issue A and post it to the team. You respond to my comment. I respond back to your comment. A third member of our team responds to my original comment. And a fourth member of the team responds to your response to my original comment. Finally, the fourth member of our team raises a completely different issue, Issue B. Exhibit 18–1 shows what each of the members of our team sees when they use their mouse

Exhibit 18–1 Threaded discussions

When you log on to your team's groupware, this is what you see:

Issue A (raised by me)

    Your response to Issue A

        My response to your response

        Fourth team member's response to your response

    Third team member's response to Issue A

Issue B (raised by fourth team member)

---

to click on this threaded discussion. As you can see, anyone can follow the discussion from start to finish and, in doing so, see who is responding to whom and what is being said about each issue. Threaded discussions, then, offer the opportunity for teams to create and record a repository and history of their thinking and work. Used wisely, this feature of groupwork is invaluable to teams.

4. *Document management* provides teams a library for their written and visual work. Reports, presentations, brochures, memos, training materials, sales materials —any document can be stored and accessed by members of the team. Moreover, team members can check documents out of the library and return modified documents. As long as the software includes version control, teams can be assured that no version of the document is ever lost. Consequently, if I modify your draft, and, later, the team decides your draft was better or wants to access it for other reasons, your unmodified version remains easily retrievable.

5. *People profiles,* background information, skill and experience descriptions, contact information, calendars, roles, responsibilities, and tasks can be stored using groupwork technology. While this information can be retained in paper files, the ease of access, extraction, and modification is often enhanced by well-designed groupware.

6. *Metrics and goals* can be posted. Moreover, the group can track progress, directly or by linking the groupwork software to other information systems in the company. Metrics and goals can be modified without losing the initial version. Most important, the technology can help enforce discipline and ensure outcome-based goals by tracking the groups progress against those goals.

7. *Project management* starts with project definition. Our group can define our project in terms of purpose and goals. As we progress, we can subdivide the project into subprojects, as well as tasks. Each of these tasks, including the deadlines and metrics, can be assigned to members of our group. Moreover, we can use project management software to identify which subprojects and tasks are most critical and dependent on one another. By understanding such interdependencies, we can establish the most efficient and effective overall project plan and timeline for completion. We can also subdivide goals into individual and collective work products,

ensuring team effort in the right places. If we are disciplined, we can also differentiate subprojects to fit team or single-leader approaches.

8. *Groupwork technology can provide executive/management information:* who in the group is getting their work done on time, who participates in threaded discussions; who read or provided input to critical documents, and what progress is being made toward goals, metrics, and other milestones. Thus, leaders can more readily pinpoint members who need special attention and what type of attention is appropriate.

EXERCISE 18.1
ARE YOU A VIRTUAL TEAM? WILL YOU DO
SIGNIFICANT VIRTUAL WORK? SO WHAT?

Consider the members of your group; that is, the people who must work together to achieve some performance purpose and challenge. Are a significant number located in different locations and time zones? If so, you warrant virtual team consideration. Even if you are not a virtual team, will you do significant amounts of virtual work? That is, will it benefit you to interact routinely with one another through the medium of groupware?

If you are a virtual team or will do significant amounts of virtual work, you should take time out to discuss the implications of how virtual teaming and work compare with normal, co-located efforts.

EXERCISE 18.2
WHAT GROUPWARE TECHNOLOGY WILL YOU USE?

If you are a virtual team or will do significant amounts of virtual work, discuss and decide which of the basic features of groupwork technology shown in Table 18–1 you plan to use on a regular basis.

EXERCISE 18.3
NOVICES AND/OR EXPERTS: PERSONAL EXPERIENCES/
BEST PRACTICES WITH GROUPWARE

Once you have selected the groupware features and functions you plan to utilize, take an hour or two with your group to discuss your individual knowledge and experience levels with each feature. Are you novices or experts? What best practices do you know from personal experience? If, as a group, you have few to no members with deep expertise, how will you obtain relevant skills or assistance? What specific expectations will you set for learning and using the features you have selected? If, on the other hand, most or all of you have relevant experience, how will you avoid misunderstandings and miscommunications as you move forward?

Table 18–1 Groupwork technology

	Regularly	Once in A While	Never
Videoconferencing			
Teleconferencing			
Chatroom			
E-mail			
Threaded discussions			
Document management			
People profiles and contact			
Metrics and goals			
Project management			
Executive/management information			
Other: _____			

If you cannot meet face-to-face to have this discussion, you should use features such as videoconferencing or threaded discussion for the same purpose.

EXERCISE 18.4
PRACTICE, PRACTICE, PRACTICE: THREADED DISCUSSION

For each feature you select, design an initial experiment in which all members can practice using the feature as well as deliver on a specific set of expectations. For example, use threaded discussions. Pick an issue facing your team and, over a set period of time, such as two days, use the threaded discussion feature to dialogue and interact with one another about that issue. Any issue will do. For example, you might conduct Exercise 17.5, about collective work products, through the medium of a threaded discussion. *Require all members to participate in this discussion.* At the end of the two-day trial, have a follow-up discussion about what worked, what didn't, and the implications of future group use of threaded discussions. Again, you should design and conduct a similar exercise for each separate feature your group intends to utilize.

EXERCISE 18.5
PRACTICE, PRACTICE, PRACTICE: CONFERENCING PLUS CHAT _____

Schedule a teleconference or videoconference call. Arrange for everyone attending to log on to the team's chatroom. Pick an issue you would like to discuss. Appoint someone as moderator and someone else to monitor the input to the chatroom. Set the expectation that each person will experiment with two different ways of providing input to the discussion: (1) by speaking and (2) by typing in comments to the chatroom feature. When your group has thoroughly discussed the issue at hand, turn the attention of the group to debriefing what worked, what didn't, and the implications of using these combined features of groupware.

EXERCISE 18.6
PRACTICE, PRACTICE, PRACTICE: DOCUMENT MANAGEMENT _____

Agree about the use of the document management feature of your groupware technology. Make sure each person is familiar with the application's rules regarding checking out, modifying, reposting, and checking in documents, as well as saving distinct versions of each document. Once you have familiarized yourselves with the application, select a document that is important to the work of your group. Assign someone the job of creating and posting the document in your relevant groupware application. Mandate that every person in the group experiment with checking out, modifying, and reposting the document, as well as helping to ensure that the group saves each distinct version of the document. Assign a limited time frame for this experiment; we suggest one week. At the end of the week, discuss what worked, what didn't, and the implications of making the best use of document management as you move forward.

EXERCISE 18.7 CUSTOMIZE TRAINING _____

If your group chooses to get training on groupware technology, work diligently with the trainer or facilitator to customize the training, so that:

1. You are trained only on those features and functions you will regularly use.
2. You have the discussion included in Exercise 18.3 as part of the training.
3. The training includes a hands-on version of Exercises 18.4, 18.5, 18.6, or similar exercises for other features and functions.
4. The training includes "next steps" discussions and agreements about how your group will and will not use the various groupware features emphasized.

19

Outcomes—Not Activities—
Shape Your Choice

> *YOU HAVE TO KNOW WHAT SUCCESS LOOKS LIKE . . .*

The core message in Chapter 17 is *make conscious choices.* Small-group effectiveness starts with consciously choosing which performance challenges are best suited to the team discipline and which warrant the single-leader discipline. Chapter 18 argues that virtual teams and non-virtual teams must make the same basic choices. To reiterate, the two approaches to small-group performance are not arbitrary names for labeling groups themselves: they are two distinct management disciplines. Groups should not choose to "be a team" or "be a single-leader group" based upon personal preference, an executive mandate, or the misperception that one discipline always works better than the other. Instead, groups seeking to optimize performance should base the selection of discipline on the requirements of the performance situation or task at hand. The best performing groups excel at integrating both disciplines.

In this chapter, we focus on gaining clarity and rigor in your articulation and understanding of performance. *In our experience, the more specifically small groups describe and characterize their performance challenges and goals, the better they are at making the best choice between the team and single-leader disciplines.* For example, a small group in an e-commerce company, seeking to improve the experience of users on the company website, will have a more productive discussion about the team versus the single-leader discipline with regard to Performance Statement 1 than Performance Statement 2:

Performance Statement 1: Reduce average user access time from 5.9 seconds to 1.5 seconds within six weeks.

Performance Statement 2: Figure out ways to improve the user experience of our web site.

Both of these statements offer compelling challenges. And, Performance Statement 2 might better resemble the charter or purpose statement with which many small groups begin their journey to success. In fact, Performance Statement 1 represents one of several distinct performance challenges within the overall aspiration captured by Statement 2, making our point: To achieve significant performance results, groups must convert broad aspirations, such as Performance Statement 2, into specific performance goals and objectives, as in Performance Statement 1, so that the groups are in the position to decide when to apply the team discipline or when the single-leader discipline would work best.

When small groups lose sight of their performance rationale, they fall prey to personality conflicts, poor communications, and bad feelings. Too often, they reach out for soft-side facilitators or fall back on bonding exercises that seldom work. It is sufficiently difficult to resolve subjective and messy issues, even with the aid of clear, compelling performance goals to guide the group. But without such goals, groups become rudderless; and, neither facilitation nor bonding nor leader exhortation can replace the missing focus on performance. Instead, the standards for resolution typically become hierarchy, power, personality, favoritism, and other troubling and divisive criteria.

The most troublesome misstep down this path occurs when leaders view the purpose of collaboration in terms of *activities rather outcomes*. Organizations make this mistake over and over again, e.g.:

1. Enterprise visions emphasize becoming a "team-based organization" without reference to what that means or why it matters, i.e., *the team's the thing!*
2. Change initiatives stress the number of teams created as the measure of their success. If you are not a member of a team, you somehow feel guilty! Everyone claims team affiliation, i.e., *more is better!*
3. Team training programs become mired down as every aspect of empowerment, feelings, and togetherness is explored. Content centers on team building and bonding. Trainers simply assume that participants understand the connection between such exercises and work, i.e., *empowerment is what it's all about!*
4. Culture change efforts highlight the values of team and teamwork in the absence of any link to specific goals or challenges. Well-intended leaders perpetuate the notion that teamwork (certainly an admirable value) will somehow lead to team performance (a rigorous discipline), i.e., *creating a team environment becomes an objective in itself!*

In each of these cases, the performance foundation for why groups must team is obscure, and disappointment, frustration, and wasted effort are the inevitable results. The people involved assume that teaming is necessary and good: a lazy assumption that leads to trouble. When there is no rationale behind teaming, people act as though there is no distinction between the two disciplines. This quickly leads to compromise units: small groups who do not effectively apply the team discipline or the single-leader discipline. To avoid this trap, groups must work hard to clarify, specify, and enrich their understanding and articulation of performance, as well as the outcomes and metrics that determine success.

19.1 ARTICULATING OUTCOME-BASED PERFORMANCE GOALS _____

We urge you to articulate and then use *outcome-based goals* instead of *activity-based goals* in making your choice between team and single-leader disciplines. (For a complete discussion of using outcome-based goals as the foundation for managing performance and change throughout an organization, see Doug Smith's book entitled *Make Success Measurable!* Another Mindbook/Workbook.) As the terms imply, outcome-based goals describe the specific outcomes by which success will be determined, while activity-based goals describe the activities believed necessary to achieve that success. Outcomes are the results, consequences, end products, or impacts of actions. You can usually see, sometimes touch, and always do something with them: they are clearly identifiable and frequently tangible. Outcomes can be measured in different ways, including time, speed, cost, revenue, profit, defects, errors, volume, and number, among others. In the system for Marriott International Hotels, for example, one of the most critical measurable outcomes for all employees is the scores of their Guest Service Index. Each month that index reports highly credible customer feedback and is calibrated to reflect both individual and team efforts. Whatever the measurement, outcomes answer the question, "How would you know success?" for the challenge at hand.

The following are examples of outcome-based goals:

1. Win three new accounts in the next quarter.
2. Reduce the average duration of patient-days by one day over the next five months.
3. Halve the time it takes to process and approve new software licenses by March 30.
4. Improve the retention rate among top-rated performers by 20% this year without incurring any additional salary or benefit expense.
5. Convert at least half of our franchisees to company-owned stores this year, while simultaneously improving store-based service quality scores among company-owned stores by twofold.
6. Triple the number of product line extensions brought to market over the next six months.
7. Within six weeks, eliminate the top three causes of customer-defined defects on our automated voice response system, while decreasing the average response time by at least half.
8. Raise first-round venture capital financing by October without giving up more than 30% of the company.

In contrast to outcome-based goals, activity-based goals describe the activities and actions at the heart of the performance challenge in question. For the preceding series of examples, the following illustrate activity-based goal statements:

1. Develop a plan for winning new accounts.
2. Save money through reducing patient days.
3. Reengineer the new software license process.
4. Make this company the best place to work.
5. Implement our new customer quality strategy through company-owned stores.

6. Build a culture of innovation.
7. Improve customer service by fixing the automated response system.
8. Find the investors we need.

Look closely at the difference between the activity-based goals and outcome-based goals. When goals are stated as activities, small groups have a difficult time determining which performance discipline is required. Is it necessary to have real-time collaboration? How do we benefit from the integration of multiple skills through shifting roles and shared leadership, collective work products, and mutual accountability? Activity-based goals make it extremely difficult to articulate whether the sum of individual-best contributions will produce the appropriate results. Outcome-based goals facilitate purposeful group dialogue. You can more easily explore whether individual contributions will deliver the required results versus the collective contributions that come from collaboration, shifting roles, shared leadership, and collective work products.

Unfortunately, with the exception of revenue and cost goals, most goal statements in organizations are activity-based. Most annual plans, personal performance plans, project or initiative plans, and other forms of goal commitments feature statements such as "research what customers want," "develop a strategy for hiring," "improve communications," "build a market-driven culture," and "reorganize into teams." There may or may not be dates attached to these goals. But even if accompanied by dates, activity-based goals never answer the question, "How would we know we succeeded?" Instead, activity-based goals assume the pursuit of the given activity will somehow create the desired results.

Answering the question "How will you know success?" is one of the most powerful ways your group can convert activity-based goals into outcome-based goals (see Exercise 19.2). Think, for example, about the common desire to improve communications. How would we know we succeeded? If we answer, "We will know we have improved communications when communications improve," all of us would laugh. Another good test is whether the obverse of a goal statement sounds foolish (e.g., "get worse at communications"). Such absurdity is a good sign that activities, instead of outcomes, are being discussed. In this example, success has more to do with performance results that currently elude us because of poor communication.

Perhaps we are falling short in customer satisfaction because we permit engineers and technologists to design and build products that result in significant numbers of customer complaints. We may choose to reverse that trend *by seeking to reduce customer complaints on our four most critical product lines by 20% by the year's end*. We intend to succeed by asking engineers, technologists, customer service representatives, and marketing and sales to communicate more effectively with one another about customer product needs. Such communication could result in a reworking of the new product or product line extension process to increase both the quality of current products and the flow of new products to the markets. At the same time, we seek to reduce the number, frequency, and response time of customer complaints. In each case, we are trying to accomplish specific outcomes that matter to customers, instead of merely improving communications for the sake of improving communications.

Exhibit 19–1 maps the various activities in this example to desired outcomes. You will note that improved communications is an activity that we must get better at as part of re-

Exhibit 19–1 Activities lead to outcomes

> The activity, "improve communications"→ leads to → the activity of "better understanding customer's product needs" → leads to → the activity of "reengineering the new product development process → leads to → an outcome of "better products in shorter time" → which can be expressed as a specific outcome-based goal such as: "By year's end, reduce customer complaints by at least 20% through the introduction of new products in our four main product categories."

working or reengineering the new product process. Reworking the new product process is also an activity we must pursue in order to deliver outcome-based performance results measured by more new products, as well as a reduced number of customer complaints. These activities are necessary to success; but unlike outcomes, activities are not a good set of goals for success. Outcomes are.

The discipline of team basics is itself an activity. So is the single-leader discipline. Just as improving communications and reengineering might produce outcomes that matter, so can teams and single-leader units. But, as demonstrated in Exhibit 19–1, it rarely helps groups to set activities as goals. While being a team might help with group cohesion, being a team rarely serves as a useful performance goal.

19.2 MAKE YOUR OUTCOME-BASED GOALS SMART

To ensure your group is working with outcome-based goals, use the five criteria in the SMART acronym:[1]

1. *Specific:* Goals are specific when they answer what the group seeks to get better at and for whose benefit. The more specific the goal, the better. For example, in the preceding illustration with respect to new accounts, the group wants to improve new accounts. Yet, that example could be even more specific by describing the kind of new accounts. Instead of three new accounts, the goal might specify three new accounts in the emerging web-based business sector that demand alliance-based sales effort.

   When groups clearly specify what kind of work, process, or effort they hope to improve, as well as who will benefit from the effort, they make better choices. They become clearer about the extent to which collective work products versus individual best performances are required. Outcomes can be categorized as collective or individual work products, whereas activities cannot. In this example, a small group

---

1. See Make Success Measurable by Douglas K. Smith

from two or more alliance partners could easily answer why the team discipline was needed to get better at alliance-based sales to new web-based business accounts. Without the collective effort of people with different skill-sets and from different companies, the group would be unlikely to succeed. Indeed, merely assigning one individual from each company the task of signing up more new accounts would probably fail because each individual would lack the full skills and experience required to demonstrate to customers the value of a combined offering. In contrast, if the goal were to "acquire three new accounts for our traditional line of grocery products," the sales group is likely to find that the single-leader discipline with strong individual accountability's sufficient for success, since all members of the group are equally knowledgeable in the traditional product offering.

2. *Measurable:* Goals are measurable when they provide the yardstick for evaluating success and answering the question, "By how much?" Every performance challenge uses one or more of the following four categories of success measurement:

   ■ *Time/speed:* This measures the time or speed it takes something to happen or be completed. Note that such measures might reflect a customer expectation (for example, customer service calls answered in less than one second), or indicate the amount of effort or investment demanded (for example, no more than five person-months of project effort).

   ■ *Cost:* This measures the cost of an input or activity as well as the investment required for a new product, capital, project, strategy, or other major purpose.

   ■ *Quality in terms of customer-defined defects or errors:* This measures how well products or services compare with company-imposed specifications (for example, there will never be more than four customers in any check-out line) or customer expectations (we will never have more than ten customer complaints per month, regardless of what the complaint is because the customer is always right). Most often, the number or frequency of defects, errors, or failures is used here.

   ■ *Positive yields:* This is a miscellaneous and large category that reflects positive expressions of what your group is attempting to accomplish. It typically includes financial metrics such as revenue, profit, or return on investment, as well as nonfinancial metrics such as number of new products or services, number of new or retained key hires, customer satisfaction, employee satisfaction, and so forth.

As your group considers each of these four categories, notice that the first two, time and cost, measure the effort or input required to produce some output that is best measured by one or both of the second two: quality or positive yields. Often, the best goals contain measurable improvements in productivity, that is, more output for less input. For example, "within 6 weeks, eliminate the top three causes of customer-defined defects on our automated voice response system, while decreasing the average response time by at least half" contains an improved output, reduced defects, plus a reduced amount of input and average speed. In addition, this goal statement answers the all-important question, "By how much?"

Metrics aid in the choice between the two disciplines. When the chosen metrics fit their performance challenges and convert to measurable goals, small groups usually find it easier to choose between team and single-leader disciplines. For example, in the preceding automated voice response goal, someone in the group might know about an off-the-shelf technology solution that could dramatically reduce response time without any extensive training or other change. If so, that challenge could best be solved using the single-leader discipline. On the other hand, the group might lack any good ideas about how to deliver the promised performance beyond getting customer service representatives and others to do a lot of team-based problem solving and improvement.

3. *Aggressive yet achievable:* The most effective goals make us aim high. Only by creating challenging goals will we get the most out of our capabilities. Aiming high applies to both individual and team goals. Yet, goals must also be credible if we expect people to persist. For example, a hospital that has incurred one to two million dollar deficits on a budget of one hundred million for five straight years could hardly expect to produce a twenty million dollar surplus in the coming year, without some dramatic windfall. Setting such a goal certainly would qualify as aggressive; it would also be unachievable. A leadership team might lay claim to such a goal, but most people throughout the institution would find it overly demanding, if not absurd, and soon give up trying. If, by contrast, the leadership team set a goal to reach breakeven or create a small surplus, team members and people throughout the institution would likely see the goal as both aggressive and achievable.

4. *Relevant:* Goals and metrics should directly relate to the challenge at hand. This sounds simple enough, but far too often, people set goals, particularly financial goals, that only measure success indirectly or over extended time frames. Decades of orientation toward revenue, costs, profits, and investments have caused most people in most organizations to quickly settle on financial goals as the standard for success against all challenges. Yet, over the past fifteen to twenty years, we have witnessed a profusion of challenges that do not translate directly into dollars and cents. Such aspirations as time to market, reengineering, war for talent, customer service, and customer-defined quality usually do not lend themselves to direct or near-term financial measurement. While favorable economic results *lag* achievement against these challenges, the connections are not obvious. Hence, the best, most direct, and relevant goals and metrics for such efforts are better expressed with non-financial yardsticks. For example, speed, time, defects, errors, and user satisfaction are not financial, but they do measure performance results. Groups should spend time trying to articulate goals and metrics that directly track achieving the challenge at hand, rather than adhering to financial metrics that lag or are only indirectly indicative of performance. The more direct and relevant the metrics and goals selected, the more productive the feedback when the group reviews what is working, what is not working, and how to do better.

5. *Time-bound:* Goals without deadlines or milestones are not goals. They may be aspirations, values, and visions; but, they are not goals. By committing ourselves to a time frame, we ensure focus and accountability. And, to the extent that the overall time frame can be interspersed with milestones that track progress, so much the better.

Often, the selected time frame determines which discipline to use. Sometimes accelerated time pressures create an imperative for team performance. For example, consider the new software licensing process mentioned earlier. The stated goal was to cut the time of licensing in half by March 30. If a small group of lawyers, accountants, and sales managers set this goal ten or eleven months ahead of March 30, they could probably achieve the goal through the sum of their individual contributions since they would have plenty of time to work separately on individual pieces which could be integrated sequentially by the leader. However, if they set the goal only one month ahead, that is, on March 1 of the year in question, the shorter time frame for achievement could make the team discipline an imperative as the only way to ensure simultaneous collective efforts by all members rather than relying on sequential integration by the leader.

Most of the time, however, the single-leader discipline is faster because an experienced leader "knows best" how to proceed and need not spend much time bringing the group up-to-speed in shaping goals, working approach, and milestones. Between the single-leader and team disciplines, however, time frame can be a two-edged sword. On the one hand, most groups will operate much more efficiently in single-leader mode, particularly those with an experienced leader or with members who are unfamiliar or unpracticed at the team discipline. They will certainly accomplish individual work product results faster and with less bother. Consequently, many groups choose the single-leader discipline because "they don't want to waste time becoming a team."

On the other hand, this time efficiency comes with a limitation: the single-leader discipline will not produce the extra performance of teams. If that extra performance demands moving slower at first, then so be it. Most teams, by the way, work just as fast as single-leader groups once the team discipline has been mastered.

Armed with SMART goals, groups can confidently determine when real-time collaboration and collective work products are critical to their performance challenge. They can decide between the incremental, extra performance demanded of the team discipline versus the more expedient, sum of individual bests, characteristic of the single-leader discipline (see Figure 17–2 in Chapter 17).

Consider the following example. A branded clothing company has historically organized functionally around product, merchandising, sales, and sourcing. The CEO believes the company's poor performance arises from too few people with general management skills, so she decides to create five new strategic business units (SBUs). The five new general managers, the CEO, CFO, and head of Human Resources go off-site to discuss the new organization. Should this group apply the single-leader or the team discipline?

The activity-based aspiration, build general management skills, is no help in answering the question. Assume, then, the group works hard to answer the question, "How will we determine our success at building general management skills?" Among other things, they agree that general managers must become skilled at making trade-offs across different functions with the larger business in mind. The following two versions of a goal emerges from their deliberations:

1. *Version 1:* Each new general manager must deliver a budget within two months. The budgets must have at least 20% year-over-year revenue, 10% profit growth, re-

sulting in a return on invested capital of 16%. In addition, the plan must identify at least three major trade-offs, describe alternative rationales for making trade-off decisions, and defend the choice made in terms of each GM's own business.

2. *Version 2:* The five general managers working together with the CFO and head of HR must deliver a budget for the entire company in two months. This overall budget will encompass the budgets for each of the five separate SBUs. Both the overall and the separate business budgets must show year-over-year 20% revenue and 10% profit growth, resulting in an ROI of 16%. In addition, the group must identify key trade-offs, both within and across SBUs, as well as alternative rationales and choices made.

In Version 1, it is far more likely that the five new general managers can achieve the goal, as well as develop important new skills, through the sum of individual best performances. Remember, both the single-leader discipline and team discipline benefit from effective group behaviors, such as sharing best practices, constructive criticism, active listening, and positive reinforcement. Thus, the five people would gain from discussing and sharing what they were learning, although the degree to which they might do so would, in most organizations, undoubtedly suffer from the competition for resources and recognition among senior executives in charge of different businesses.

In Version 2, however, the group of seven people almost certainly needs to apply the team discipline. The identification of key trade-offs, as well as rationales for making choices are the kind of collective work products and incremental outcome that demands real-time integration of the multiple skills and perspectives within the group. For example, the budget for the whole business *must* be a collective work product. In this case, it is also likely that the overall budget will achieve more ambitious performance results because of the team potential that is invoked.

Please note: The senior executives at this company might responsibly choose either Version 1 or Version 2 as their goal. Each will advance their overall aspiration. Without the hard work of articulating these outcome-based goals, however, they really have no basis, other than instinct, for selecting between team and single-leader discipline. And, if they discuss teaming only in the context of their activity-based goal, of "building general management skills," they will fall into the trap of exclaiming to one another, "We have to really be a team to make this happen!"

EXERCISE 19.1
OUTCOMES VERSUS ACTIVITIES

Ask your group to list the goals currently being pursued. If these are already written down, use the statements as described. If they are not in writing, then ask the group to articulate and write them down. Once you have a list of goal statements, discuss among yourselves whether and why you believe the goals are activity-based or outcome-based. For any you agree are activity-based, try to rewrite them as outcome-based.

EXERCISE 19.2
HOW WOULD YOU KNOW SUCCESS?

Gather your group and take fifteen to thirty minutes to review the challenges you face and how you are trying to meet them. Ask someone to keep a list of key objectives and phrases on a flip chart. Once you have finished this, ask yourselves the following critical questions: *How will you know you were successful? What will you measure, assess, or calibrate against?*

As you brainstorm and agree upon possible answers to this question, remember to avoid circular statements such as, "We would know we succeeded because we succeeded!" (e.g., "We will know we are communicating better when we are communicating better"). Also, be careful to recognize and acknowledge when your answers indicate activities, such as "We will succeed when we all understand the problem," versus outcomes, for example, "We will have succeeded when we have at least three new paying customers."

EXERCISE 19.3
CHOOSE YOUR YARDSTICKS

Consider a performance challenge facing your group. Use Exercises 19.1 and 19.2 to help you begin to identify and articulate outcomes that would indicate success. Now brainstorm a list of metrics you might use to articulate your outcomes with greater specificity. Use the following columns to help:

Time/Speed	Cost	Defects/Errors	Positive Yields
_____	_____	_____	_____
_____	_____	_____	_____
_____	_____	_____	_____

Remember to think hard about both financial and non-financial metrics and try to identify leading and lagging indicators. When you have generated a good list, try to agree on one or more metrics that do the best job of reflecting success in a concurrent and direct manner. Then, try to articulate SMART, outcome-based goals using the selected metrics.

EXERCISE 19.4
GET SMART

Use the SMART criteria to construct outcome-based goals for your performance challenges. Use Table 19–1 to refine your goal statements.

Table 19–1 SMART criteria

	Yes, because:	No, because:
Specific?		
Measurable?		
Aggressive, yet achievable?		
Relevant to the challenge at hand?		
Time-bound?		

EXERCISE 19.5
INDIVIDUAL VERSUS COLLECTIVE WORK PRODUCTS

Armed with SMART outcome-based goals, ask your group to discuss and decide whether success will require collective work products in addition to individual work products. Use Exercise 17.5 to help, only this time with your more specific goals in mind.

EXERCISE 19.6
CHOOSE YOUR DISCIPLINES

Ask your group to list the most pressing parts of the overall performance challenge at hand and convert each of those parts into one or more outcome-based goals. You might want to prioritize the top three, five, or seven goals. However you choose to approach your list, use the material in this chapter and Chapter 17 to discuss whether to use the team versus the single-leader discipline to accomplish each of the goals in front of you.

Note to Virtual Teams   Your group can do each of these exercises in a face-to-face meeting or with the help of groupware technology, such as threaded discussions, tele and videoconferencing, or chatrooms. In our experience, if you are doing these exercises near the beginning of your effort, you will gain more from them in a face-to-face meeting because it will help members interpret, know, and develop respect for one another's skills and talents. Having said that, groups often face logistical and resource constraints that force them to debate and discuss the issues raised here through groupware, even toward the beginning of their efforts. If that is the case, please use the results of the exercises in Chapter 2 to guide your discussions. In particular, set rules and expectations regarding participation, time frames, use of questions whenever anyone fails to fully understand, and other particular requirements to be sure your dialogues are productive and that the absence of body language and other cues do not derail or mislead your discussions.

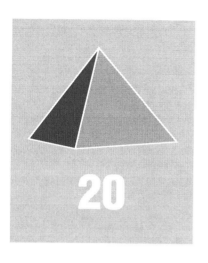

20

Performance Agendas for Applying Both Disciplines

Many members of small groups in pursuit of increased performance capability tell us they are confronted with a wide variety of ongoing challenges *against which they must deploy themselves and others.* The groups cannot succeed without the flexibility and determination to deploy the single-leader and the team disciplines as needed to fit different performance tasks. The key, once again, is learning to balance the two disciplines within an integrated approach, not to sacrifice one for the other or compromise in ways that nullify full performance potential. By contrast, other groups have purposes, goals, and actions more concentrated on a single target and requiring effort only from the group members themselves. Unlike the more complex situation, these latter groups find it straightforward to choose between either the single-leader or team disciplines and pursue that choice rigorously.

Which of these two descriptions best characterizes the situation and challenge facing your group? In our experience, the following patterns often prevail:

1. Pattern 1:
   - If your group's challenge is near to frontline, operating work,
   - If impact is expected and required within a short time frame,
   - If the impact of your group's performance narrowly affects the entire organization's success,
   - If it is likely that members within your group will do all the work without assistance from others,
   Then
   - It is more likely your group can make a one-time choice between the two disciplines and move forward confidently until your performance challenge changes and requires choosing again.

2. Pattern 2:
   - ■ If the effort of your group is further away from daily work,
   - ■ If the time frame required to produce a significant performance impact is long,
   - ■ If your group's performance impact has a broad and large effect on the entire organization's success,
   - ■ If people beyond your group must participate and contribute,

   Then
   - ■ It is more likely that your group must simultaneously and continuously integrate and rely on both the single-leader and team disciplines.

Pattern 1 often characterizes self-managing plant floor teams, sales teams, groups of customer service representatives in phone centers, and other functionally oriented and day-to-day operating groups who must produce similar results over reasonably short time frames ranging from an hour to a month or so. These groups must convert their purpose and challenge into one or more SMART outcome-based goals and consciously choose which of the two disciplines is most likely to produce success.

Teams assembled to recommend and implement changes with important but narrow impacts on the entire organization also fall in Pattern 1. For example, a cross-functional team seeking to reduce the time it takes to get promotion materials into the hands of salespeople might set a goal such as "cutting the time it takes to get salespeople new brochures from twenty-six weeks to eight weeks." This dramatic increase in performance will probably benefit from the team discipline approach. Once that is clear, the members can use the team discipline to meet their goal. A group pursuing a one-time, analytically driven challenge to "reduce the cost of issuing and sending accounts payable checks from four dollars to three dollars" is similarly situated, as is a group chartered with "developing recommendations for closing at least two new accounts over the next six weeks."

Groups finding themselves in Pattern 2 face more complex, longer-term, and broader performance challenges. Consider, for example, a team seeking to reengineer the entire process of sales generation through fulfillment. This team includes six executives from sales, marketing, operations, finance, customer service, and human resources. These six people will confront dozens of challenges well beyond getting brochures into salespeople's hands faster or doubling the number of new accounts in a sales region over the next six weeks. They should set an overall aspiration for accelerating the entire process. At the same time, they must improve revenue, profits, and customer satisfaction by a specified, significant amount. Such an overall SMART goal for their effort might be, "within four months, cut the cycle time of sales generation through fulfillment by two-thirds while generating 50% gains in revenues and profits and improving customer satisfaction at least 20%."

This ambitious reengineering target requires considering a wide range of required actions, both individual and group, many of which demand the articulation of sub-goals, as well as assigning responsibilities to individuals or sub-teams. Such critical to-dos include:

1. *Process mapping:* The reengineering team must get help to do both an "as is" and "should be" detailed diagram of all the activities and people involved in the entire sales generation through fulfillment process.
2. *Root cause analyses:* As the extended group (core team and helpers) considers the differences and critical gaps between what is and what should be, they need to de-

termine the root causes. These are the fundamental determinants of things like cycle times, revenue generation, profitability, and customer satisfaction. A good root cause analysis is based on facts and figures, rather than opinions and anecdotes.

3. *Hypotheses and experiments:* The team must also conduct a variety of experimental efforts aimed at performance improvement. Given the seniority of the team members, most of these efforts involve people closer to the actual work of the sales generation through fulfillment process.

4. *Communications and involvement:* The team must find ways to keep all the affected employees and customers informed of progress and the implications of findings and actions. They will also need assistance from many of those same people throughout the reengineering effort.

5. *New organizational approaches:* No reengineering effort of this magnitude succeeds without significant shifts in both the formal and informal organization. Changes are required in formal elements, like job responsibilities, reporting relationships, information systems, compensation and reward approaches, and skillsets. Changes are also required in informal elements like networks, relationships, ad hoc interactions, and flexible units. As the team works to identify and then implement such changes, a variety of sub-challenges will emerge.

6. *Implementation planning and delivery* that integrates with existing patterns and budgets: As the extended group carries out their implementation plans, the core team will want to limit disruption to others, employees as well as customers. They must strive to minimize any negative impact on shareholder results during the transition period. Again, this challenge produces a number of sub-challenges and sub-goals.

In this context, the six leaders will want to explore opportunities to apply both the team and single-leader disciplines, depending on the specific sub-goal and action at hand. They need to manage themselves and others to take full advantage of these flexible units because:

1. They cannot succeed by themselves; many other people have important contributions to make, sometimes as individuals and sometimes as sub-teams.

2. They cannot succeed if all six of members and outside contributors insist on participating in all aspects of the work; instead work must be allocated among the members and outside contributors in ways that are doable.

3. They cannot succeed if they assign themselves work strictly according to their own, respective functional expertise and hierarchical position. They need to use the team discipline to ensure cross-functional problem solving, creativity, and execution. And this cross-functional norm applies to others who get involved and make contributions.

4. They cannot succeed if they fail to take advantage of the functional experience, intrinsic talent, and skill represented in their group. They also need to use the single-leader or individual-accountability discipline when sub-goals and actions can best be achieved that way.

In addition, the reengineering team has to accomplish all of the above within realistic resource and time constraints. They operate within limits of time, money, people, and opportunity. They must plan, prioritize, and make wise resource trade-offs. Thus, conserving and growing the resources available to them is crucial, as is making the best use of those resources against tasks at hand. If an individual can accomplish a particular task, the team wastes time and resources by assigning it to a team. Conversely, if only a sub-team's multiple talents and skill-mix can succeed, the reengineering leaders squander resources and sacrifice performance by strictly adhering to individual accountability. Finally, if the reengineering team cannot prioritize in a credible way, the effort risks failure as people lose heart when they try to do everything at once because everything is top priority.

This reengineering team illustrates a common managerial challenge that confronts leadership teams with broad aspirations and responsibilities, be they teams at the very top or those who run single-business units, strategic alliances, joint ventures, shared services, major functions, or complex change initiatives. All such groups confront a complex, moving target of multiple challenges and goals. They cannot succeed by reducing the team versus single-leader choice to a once-only discussion or a personal favorite choice. They must break into sub-groups, involving others beyond the team, and capitalize on the diversity of the flexible units by choosing and applying both disciplines. The ultimate challenge is in learning to apply both disciplines as needed by each particular performance challenge and goal at hand. (For more on the unique challenges of leadership teams, see Jon Katzenbach's *Teams At The Top.*)

20.1 PERFORMANCE AGENDAS FOR LEADERSHIP TEAMS

We have developed and successfully applied a simple management tool we call the *performance agenda,* designed to help small groups with multiple challenges gain clarity about goals and priorities. Properly used, this agenda enables any group to apply both disciplines as they manage themselves and others through the effort required by the challenges they face. Figure 20–1 presents the blank form of a performance agenda. Using it effectively requires the following steps:

Articulate Your Team's Overall Aspiration

Assemble your team and devote the time needed to clarify and agree on the challenges you face, as well as the goals that will measure success (henceforth, our references to goals assume they meet the SMART conditions detailed in Chapter 19). Most teams confronted with broad challenges have experience articulating a vision, mission, charter, or purpose. That is what we mean by articulating your team's overall aspiration. Such statements are brief, convey a sense of urgency and importance, and usually identify a few themes that capture how the team's work will deliver value to customers, shareholders, employees, and others. More important, such statements are best when they are expressed in words that are simple, clear, and meaningful to each group member or participant in the effort. Katzenbach's book, *Real Change Leaders,* provides a number of illustrations of such statements that he describes as *working visions* because their simple messages work to capture the emotional commitment of those who both shape and pursue them.

Few teams, however, have much experience translating such statements into outcome-based goals. The Mindbook and Workbook sections of Chapters 17 and 19 will help such

Challenges we are resourcing	SMART outcome-based goals	Which discipline?	Responsibility (names)

Other challenges we face, but are not resourcing	Illustrative outcomes that would indicate success

FIGURE 20–1 Performance agenda for a small group

teams. In the above example, the reengineering team's original vision was to redesign the sales generation through fulfillment process to increase greatly the value delivered to customers and shareholders. The team converted this working vision into a goal statement that reads, "Within the next four months, cut the cycle time of sales generation through fulfillment by two-thirds while simultaneously generating 50% gains in revenues and profits and at least 20% improvement in customer satisfaction."

Break Aspirations into Sub-Challenges

Use brainstorming and other problem-solving techniques to answer the question, "What are the things we must do to accomplish our purpose and achieve our desired outcomes?"

The more complete the list, the better. A useful technique for compiling and categorizing such a list is called *clustering*. Give each person in your team a pad of adhesive-backed notes and, working singly or in pairs, spend the time needed to identify the specific tasks required to achieve your working vision and goals. Place the notes on a wall and let the group study and move all the notes into cohesive clusters of similar challenges and activities. This clustering effort rapidly eliminates redundancies, clarifies meanings, and generates a realistic list of what it will take to accomplish the overall aspiration and goals.

Identify What Contributions are Required from Others

Once you have produced a first-cut list of the key challenges and activities required for success, determine who else needs to get involved. If your group must lead a coordinated effort toward some aspiration with broad impact on the organization, its achievement is likely to warrant contributions from others. Potential contributors should be identified, whenever possible, by name and job type. Be sure to include people from supplier, partner, and customer organizations whenever they represent the skills best suited to the task. You want to end up with a specific list of who can best contribute to each key activity and challenge. At this point, however, do not concern yourselves with whether the people you identify have the time or permission to help.

Convert the List into Smart Goal(s)

Using the tools, techniques, and exercises in Chapters 17 and 19, a group can translate each major sub-challenge and activity into one or more outcome-based goals. In this way, team members and others can determine what work needs to be done, by whom, and toward what end. Such goals also put your team in a position to choose between the single-leader and the team discipline on a performance goal by performance goal basis. (See Chapter 17.) Finally, once the major sub-challenges are expressed as clear goals, a group can better assess whether the full impact of achieving those goals will produce the success required by the overall aspiration. If not, it's back to the drawing board to add goals or change aspirations. In other words, you need to determine whether and when it all adds up to the kind of total performance you want to accomplish.

Decide Which Challenges You Will Staff

Most groups approach this aspect of their effort through prioritization grounded in some notion of relative "importance." This approach can be a trap. While there are always gradations of importance among the various sub-challenges, many of the distinctions become difficult to make and are not that useful. Most of the sub-challenges a team identifies as essential are important to achieving its aspiration and goals. Thus, groups who pursue the "relative importance path" to prioritization often end up declaring their intention to do everything in ways that neither they nor others find credible. Having committed to prioritize, they actually end up not doing so. As a result, the expectations about who is responsible for what become completely unrealistic. Hence, they build in failure, not success.

Rather than launching into subjective and indeterminate debates about relative importance, we urge a review of your full list of challenges and aspirations and ask you to answer two questions:

1. First, will you assign responsibility and resources against the explicit goals associated with each sub-challenge and activity in question?
2. Second, will you demand and expect those assigned to devote the time and effort required for achievement of the outcome-based goal(s) within the expected time frames? In other words, *will specific people actually be identified, assigned, and held accountable* within specified time frames?

The first of these two questions is straightforward. Either you are able to assign resources, or you are not. The availability of the people you hope will make contributions is the most practical indicator of priority. A particular person or team who might be the best choice for help also might not be available. The group has the option of deferring the effort against the relevant sub-challenge until such resources become available. The second question is more difficult and demands candor. Do not mislead yourselves and others by bold-sounding but clearly unrealistic claims about what people are expected to contribute. Such bravado is an all too common mistake of ambitious groups; it wastes the time, energy, and scarce resources of everyone involved. It also destroys credibility and commitment.

Answering these two questions assists groups in setting priorities that reflect pragmatic realities about resources and capacity, rather than engaging in theoretical debates about relative importance. Regardless of how important any particular sub-challenge or activity may be to your overall aspiration, if you cannot resource the effort you will not achieve it. That is reality. If a group is unwilling to assign the necessary resources, for whatever reasons, or if the person(s) assigned cannot devote the time and effort to deliver against the goal(s), relative priorities are meaningless. In short, focus on what is doable, not what is theoretically desirable.

Finally, this step requires the group to decide how they will deploy themselves against the various sub-challenges and goals they identify. In other words, this step produces team member commitment. Most teams benefit from direct participation and contribution to the real work ahead. Members of the dreaded compromise units invariably position themselves solely as decision-makers and reviewers of the work of others. Do not make this mistake. Instead, figure out which of the sub-challenges and goals can best benefit from the personal effort of the people on your team, either individually or in combination with others, and hold yourselves accountable for those contributions and results.

Draw a Clear Line Between *Resourced* and *Not Resourced*

This simple line clearly separates what is being worked upon versus not worked upon. The line signals the group to concentrate on the challenges that we will call *above the line;* that is, those they will staff and set credible expectations for, versus those *below the line;* that is, those they cannot staff or set credible expectations for. But, challenges that go unresourced and are below the line are still important. Thus, false distinctions about relative importance are avoided. Teams can freely talk about all of the things required for their success without confusing themselves or others about what is currently being tackled versus what is being deferred. And, when sub-challenges and SMART outcomes that are above the line are achieved, the team can address something important below the line by resourcing it and setting realistic expectations regarding its accomplishment.

Choose the Best Discipline for Each Challenge Above the Line

For each sub-challenge and its related outcomes above the line, decide whether the goals are more likely to be achieved through the single-leader or the team discipline. Use what you have learned in Chapters 17 and 19 to determine whether the outcomes in question will benefit most from the sum of individual work products and accountability with a context of stable roles and single leadership. Or, decide whether they demand an incremental, extra collective performance that comes from the real-time application of team basics. Remember that this choice can be made either by the entire group or by the specific people responsible for each sub-challenge.

This step completes the initial performance agenda. If your team has completed the initial template shown in Figure 20–1, you understand the working vision, what outcomes will produce success at that vision, as well as the required detailed set of sub-challenges and goals. You also have determined which of those sub-challenges and goals will be currently resourced, above the line, and who is responsible for making those contributions, both within and beyond your core team. Most important, you will have decided which discipline is best suited to achieve each of those contributions.

Monitor Performance and Make Adjustments

Use your performance agenda as the basis for reviewing progress against the achievement of your vision and goals. When individuals and/or teams succeed at various sub-challenges, decide which of the additional challenges that are below the line should now get resourced. As new and unexpected demands appear, convert those into clear goals and choose whether to resource them and what people and which disciplines make most sense. As you and others succeed against the full list of challenges and goals, remember to recognize, celebrate, and communicate the sense of progress and accomplishment.

Preparing for Meetings and Work Sessions

The way a group prepares for and conducts meetings and work sessions makes a considerable difference to performance. Different approaches produce different behavior patterns and results. Unfortunately, most small groups and their leaders make the serious mistake of conducting all meetings in the same way. This leads to two different meeting patterns, neither of which is consistently productive.

The first pattern concentrates too much attention on the efficient use of time. Agendas, topics, and time frames are determined beforehand, and the leader tightly manages the session against those requirements. Many people prefer this approach because it minimizes meeting time, thereby conserving their personal time. The watchword of too many leaders seems to be that of "leveraging my time." When the primary purpose of the meeting is to share information, review progress, or syndicate decisions, a time-efficient meeting certainly makes sense. Such sessions, however, are not effective when groups must do real work together that goes beyond updates, approvals, and progress reviews. For example, if a group meets to make advances against a collective work product or to discuss and debate fundamental purposes, goals, or working approaches, the time-efficient agenda interferes with essential work. If all your meetings are leader-led, agenda-tight sessions, team levels of performance are highly unlikely.

The second pattern is worse. When there is no stated purpose or agenda for the meeting, discussions wander aimlessly in search of togetherness, communication, and empowerment. Decisions are seldom made, and end products rarely emerge, and, then, only by happenstance. Such sessions are completely undisciplined and frustrate all but those few members who use them to further personal agendas and dominate the discussion. Many committee meetings fall into this pattern, particularly when no clear performance purpose or goals are discussed or established.

The answer, of course, is to design meetings and work sessions to fit different tasks and performance imperatives. Simply put, you need different kinds of work sessions for different kinds of work products. As obvious as this may sound, few groups do this with any rigor or consistency. The following steps can help groups to design and conduct meetings that make the most sense for whatever job is at hand:

1. Define the purpose of the meeting in performance terms. Group sessions should rarely be held for the purpose of bonding or togetherness; those are byproducts of performance. Instead, such sessions should have a clear purpose that directly relates to the performance results required. Even the initial meeting of the group can have a performance purpose, that is, to clarify the charter, to gain commitment to a set of goals, to determine the working approach that will bring the right skill sets to bear at the right time, or to develop a performance agenda.

   If the purpose of the meeting requires real work by the group, it is a good idea to ask some or all of the members to define that purpose, specifying the desired end products. On the other hand, if a meetings is needed to update each other, clarify individual work assignments, or provide leadership guidance, then schedule and efficiently run the meeting.

   For any meeting or work session of the group, it is a good exercise for the leader or members responsible for the meeting to answer the following questions:
   - What do we need to accomplish by the end of the meeting?
   - Who needs to contribute to the set of accomplishments, and what kinds of contributions do we expect from various participants?
   - What kinds of resistance or obstacles are we likely to encounter?
   - How will we handle attempts to divert the meeting from its primary purpose?
   - Who should lead the overall meeting, and who should lead the discussion/work on particular topics? Do we need to break into sub-groups for parts of the discussion? If so, what is the purpose of those sub-group sessions?
   - Are we scheduling topics that are similar in their work requirements?
   - Does the meeting require any special facilitation? If so, who should provide it?
   - What kind of advance preparation is required, and who should be responsible for the preparation? Will the work be shared with all members prior to the meeting? If yes, will members be expected to contribute responses or otherwise demonstrate understanding?

2. Maintain a *two-bucket inventory* of issues and topics. Over the course of their efforts, small groups address many different kinds of issues and topics. It helps if both the leader and the members have established a consistent way of categorizing such issues and challenges to reflect time-efficiency needs versus open-ended, problem-solving needs. Groups benefit when the criteria for categorizing work in this way are clearly spelled out and understood by all. It is an important part of the discipline required for optimizing performance of the group. To that end, the following questions deserve the attention of the leader and/or the members:

- Does this issue/topic require the skills of several members of the group, or does one individual know most of what is required to deal with it?
- Can the required skills be applied best through each member working his/her part of the problem, or does it require two or more people working together?
- If the issue/topic requires both individual and collective work, how important are the collective efforts?
- What kind of skill/experience profile would best fit the collective work product portions of the issue/ topic?
- Do we need to be able to shift the leadership role during work session?

The first step toward addressing these questions is to plan a brainstorming session that produces a list of issues. It is helpful to limit the list to ten or twelve issues. If a large list emerges, however, you can employ any of several simple techniques to prioritize it. One easy approach is to give each member three different colored stick-on tabs, and allow them to apply the tabs to the list in order of their preference approach.

Once you have a list of reasonable size, ask the members to record and submit their answers to the above questions for each issue. Based upon the answers to the questions, the group should be able to categorize each issue. Members can also challenge particular categorizations as an issue that can be discussed in a time-efficient way versus a problem-solving, open-ended way. Ask one or two people to be *keepers of the buckets* as a way of forcing this categorization. The bucket-keepers play a valuable role in screening issue/topic candidates and can also maintain a rough prioritization of the topics within their bucket. At the end of the initial categorization exercise, you should have created a simple process whereby the bucket-keepers provide repositories for different kinds of issues as they emerge.

EXERCISE 20.1
HOW COMPLEX IS YOUR CHALLENGE? _____

Gather your group to discuss the relative importance of simultaneously applying both the single-leader and team disciplines to your overall performance challenge. To do this, first spend time discussing and articulating the overall challenge ahead of you. Then, ask yourselves to assess the requirements and character of that challenge against the following criteria:

1. *Characteristics of work:* Closer or further from front-line, operating, day-to-day work? What is the relative proportion of the work time that will be spent on collective versus individual work products?

2. *Time to performance impact and completion:* Shorter term, completed within a day to several weeks, versus longer term, completed within several months to a year or longer? What is the time required to learn and apply team basics, and how does that compare with the time urgency of completing the task?

3. *Breadth of performance impact:* Narrower, performance outcomes represent a small impact on overall organization results, versus broader, performance impact represents major piece of overall organization results?

4. *Participation by others:* Only team members need to do work for success? Versus success will demand contributions from many people beyond your team?

5. *Stability of working approach:* Tasks are predictable and recurring? Leadership role should be relatively constant and filled by a person who knows what is required?

Use your discussion of these questions to determine whether your small group's challenge is more like Pattern 1 or Pattern 2 reviewed early in this chapter.

EXERCISE 20.2
ARTICULATING A VISION

If your discussions indicate that you are a leadership team whose success depends on significant contributions from other people beyond your team, use this exercise to shape and articulate a working vision, mission, or purpose statement for the overall challenge. Such a statement of purpose, or working vision, will meet the following criteria:

1. Capture the essence of the difference you are trying to bring about and why it is critical to the organization and those who will help you.
2. Emphasize no more than one to four basic themes.
3. Provide a rallying cry and basis for enthusiasm, as well as focus.
4. Be brief, memorable, and in words meaningful to all members of the group; avoid getting mired down in wordsmithing, but make the meanings clear.

In our experience, groups are most successful when they move back and forth between (1) discussing the key themes, challenges, and performance differences they hope to make; and, (2) converting those discussions into phrases and statements. Groups can begin with either of these steps, go to the other, and then return to the first, and so on until the group is clear and coherent about what is the nature of its challenge; what kind of performance impacts it hopes to achieve; and how the language of its vision or purpose statement will convey the needed direction, themes, and inspiration to others.

EXERCISE 20.3
CONVERT VISION INTO SMART OUTCOME-BASED GOALS _____

Once your group has a true working vision, or purpose statement, that meets the criteria in Exercise 20.2, work together to convert that vision into one or more overall clear goals that answer the question, "How will you know success?" You can use Exercises 19.2, 19.3, and 19.4 to help.

EXERCISE 20.4
IDENTIFYING SUB-CHALLENGES AND DEVELOPING A PLAN _____

Gather your group for a half-day session to convert your vision and overall goals into a plan of action for success. Start by asking yourselves, "What are all the things we and/or others must do to accomplish our purpose and achieve our desired outcomes?" You should probably devote up to three-fourths of the half-day session to brainstorming, identifying, making sense of, and agreeing upon these key sub-challenges and activities.

You can use any number of brainstorming techniques to get started. We suggest using the clustering technique. Specifically, pair off, use adhesive-backed notes to identify as many sub-challenges and activities as possible, post those on a wall, and then spend time clustering similar ideas and themes. Other brainstorming techniques could also work. The key, however, is to avoid the trap of discussing possible sub-challenges as an entire team at the beginning. Such discussions inevitably reduce the number of possible ideas instead of expanding them.

Once you have put together a list of the major sub-challenge and activities, organize them into a coherent plan of action. The plan, at least at first blush, should meet the needs of your group's working vision and goals. The key question here is, "If our extended team were to successfully accomplish all the critical steps and actions indicated in this plan, would we be likely to achieve our vision and goals?"

EXERCISE 20.5
CREATE AND USE PERFORMANCE AGENDAS _____

Apply the following steps to create, and then use a performance agenda to manage the effort of your team and others:

1. Articulate your team's overall aspiration.
2. Break aspirations into sub-challenges.
3. Identify what will be required from others.
4. Convert the list into SMART goal(s).
5. Decide which challenges you will staff.
6. Draw a clear line between "resourced" and "not resourced."
7. Choose the right discipline for each challenge above the line.
8. Monitor performance, make adjustments.

EXERCISE 20.6
PREPARING FOR FACE-TO-FACE MEETINGS

Avoid the bad habit of running every meeting the same way. Instead, ask yourselves whether the purpose of the upcoming meeting is to update one another on progress and information, hear relevant, organization information from the group leader, discuss and resolve some logistical or administrative issues, and/or hear about decisions the group leader must make. If so, schedule a time-efficient meeting and respect everyone's time.

On the other hand, if the purpose of the meeting is to probe and explore ideas, and problem-solve, consider a more open-ended meeting. Also, consider thoughtful advance preparation to position topics and issues. Answer the following questions:

1. What do we need to accomplish by the end of the meeting?
2. Who needs to contribute to that set of accomplishments, and what kinds of contributions do we expect from various participants?
3. What kinds of resistance or obstacles are we likely to encounter?
4. How will we handle attempts to divert the meeting from its primary purpose?
5. Who should lead the overall meeting, and who should lead the discussion/work on particular topics? Do we need to break into sub-groups for parts of the discussion? If so, what is the purpose of those sub-group sessions?
6. Are we scheduling topics that are similar in their work requirements?
7. Does the meeting require any special facilitation? If so, who should provide it?
8. What kind of advance preparation is required, and who should be responsible for doing it? Will the work be shared with all members prior to the meeting? If yes, will members be expected to contribute responses or otherwise demonstrate understanding?

EXERCISE 20.7
PREPARING FOR VIRTUAL MEETINGS

If your group anticipates a virtual meeting, using a teleconference call or other groupware features, ask the same series of questions described in Exercise 20.6. However, be sure to tailor your answers and approaches to fit the differences between face-to-face sessions and virtual sessions. (See Chapters 18 and 22.) If the best approach to accomplishing the purpose of your meeting requires a time-efficient agenda, be sure to schedule the topics, updates, and discussions accordingly. Insofar as possible, ensure that everyone connected to the meeting is paying attention at all times.

Conversely, if the meeting has an open-ended, problem-solving purpose that will require the group to do real work, make sure that everyone is fully prepared and pay careful attention to how best to gain contributions. You might, for example, simultaneously use both the chatroom and teleconference features of groupware to carry on a virtual meeting.

Applying the Team Discipline

Mutual and Individual Accountability

I WANT TO KNOW WHO IS ACCOUNTABLE!!

How many times have we heard an admonishment for the sound management principle of clear accountability? No self-respecting supervisory, managerial, or executive leader would argue against it. Nor would any member of a small group underrate the importance of being accountable for individual contributions to the group's results. This is more than a fundamental precept of consequence management: it is common sense.

The problem is that many of today's most critical performance challenges cannot be accomplished through the sum of individual best efforts and skills. Instead, collective work products are needed.

Collective work products demand important work contributions that have three attributes: (1) two or more people with multiple skills working together, (2) leadership roles that shift, and (3) joint, or mutual, accountability for results that cannot be obtained without more than one person being held responsible. A collective work product also requires some measure of individual accountability. Again, we see the wisdom and relevance of a *both/and* point of view, instead of an *either/or* point of view. (See *Taking Charge of Change* by Doug Smith.) Both individual accountability and mutual accountability produce team performance. Conversely, acting as though you must have either individual accountability or mutual accountability prevents team performance. While one of the core litmus tests of a real team is its sense of mutual accountability, team performance does not occur without each member taking on individual responsibility for many tasks, including the contribution of their skill to collective work products. A team effort depends on both, whereas a leader-led effort can mostly rely on individual work products.

21.1 RESISTANCE TO INTEGRATION

As obvious as the integration of mutual and individual accountability may seem, many leaders find it difficult to blend them. They are more comfortable with consequence management grounded in individual accountability. Most managerial experiences, habits, and practices more easily relate to holding someone responsible for doing their job, delivering an end product, and meeting a deadline. In this way, we make sure that one person has the responsibility for every single outcome of value, provided, of course, we can anticipate every single outcome. Classic hierarchy itself is an attempt to create discrete lines and boxes that clearly pinpoint individual responsibility and division of labor. In fact, advancement in any organization goes to individuals, not groups or teams. If you want to get ahead in your organization, the best way is to be sure that your individual accomplishments are recognized by the boss. If everyone in an organization could only know who and what belongs in every box, life would be a lot simpler.

Conversely, by resisting the integration of mutual and individual accountability, we avoid the apparent "fuzziness" of mutual accountability, i.e., when no one person is clearly accountable and, therefore, everyone is "off the hook" if things don't work out. There is no question that individual accountability is a more comfortable notion for the control-minded leader. Leaders want to put the "monkey on someone else's back," since it creates constructive anxiety, clarity, and pressure for getting results. Having one person to look to for getting the job done is a lot cleaner than relying on a group. And, there is little doubt that it takes more discipline and hard work to ensure that mutual accountability does not, in fact, let everyone off the hook. Like most things that are worthwhile, however, the extra work required to integrate individual with mutual accountability really pays off when it comes to team performance challenges.

21.2 BUILDING A SENSE OF MUTUAL ACCOUNTABILITY

Building a sense of mutual accountability within a group that already has a compelling performance purpose is far easier in practice than most people believe. In fact, gaining commitment to a common purpose and a set of clear goals is half the battle. At the same time, mutual accountability requires more than bonding exercises and mutual expressions of support within the group. Feeling good about one another is not the same as holding one another mutually accountable for specific and demanding outcomes.

Implicit in a sense of mutual accountability is careful attention to language, as well as metrics and outcomes. Again, the U.S. Marines provide a powerful example of the importance of language in building individual and the team discipline. From the first moment USMC recruits set foot on Parris Island, they are prohibited from referring to themselves in the first person. For twelve weeks, they must use the term *this recruit* in all personal references, rather than the more natural *I* or *me*. The explanation given to any outsider about this rather odd rule is simply *there is no I in team.* Of course, the language rules for recruits extends beyond the I-rule and reflects the USMC's unique insight into the importance of language in influencing behaviors. With respect to teams, if you are undisciplined in language, you are likely to be undisciplined in ensuring the behavior that team performance demands. Small groups with team performance opportunities must develop a common language around the key elements of team basics. Careless language promotes careless and undisciplined behavior.

Of course, language alone will not produce mutual accountability. Just like individual accountability, the concept requires clarity regarding performance outcomes, along with clarity regarding metrics used to track progress and the milestones used to determine pace. People cannot hold themselves accountable for collective performance unless they agree on goals and time frames. As simple as this sounds, it is too easy for a small group to harbor different views about outcomes, measures, and schedules. Small groups should be rigorous about goals, measures, and deadlines, and they must do so on a firm foundation of demonstrable, shared understanding. (See Chapter 6.)

Recognition and reward are also an integral part of mutual accountability. But, most recognition and reward systems are individually conceived and implemented. Compensation systems are designed to reward individuals, and gainsharing programs are designed to reward large groups. Small-group achievements seldom fit into these programs. Hence, it falls upon the group itself, occasionally assisted by wise and perceptive sponsors, to recognize and celebrate team accomplishments. The more a group pays attention to joint achievements, the stronger the sense of mutual accountability. In particular, recognizing the completion of collective work products and goals is at the heart of what mutual accountability is all about. "We are all in this together. We hold ourselves jointly accountable for our achievements."

How your group handles failures and setbacks is also relevant to building a sense of mutual accountability. In a real team effort, based on mutual respect among all members, individuals do not fail; only the team can fail. Pointing the finger of blame at one person invariably diminishes mutual accountability and promotes devisiveness. As a result, finger-pointing is a rare occurrence among real teammates. This is not to say that members do not have important individual responsibilities and tasks for which they are accountable to the group. Nor does it mean an absence of constructive feedback to one another. What it does say, however, is that for those important collective work products that determine team levels of performance, blame, and credit are a collective, not individual, matter. Needless to say, of course, any member of the team who consistently falls short of group expectations and performance requirements will invariably be excluded from key work product assignments. If the shortfalls continue, that person will be dropped or otherwise excluded from the team.

What Not To Do   If your group aspires to team performance there are a number of things to avoid because they seriously erode the sense of mutual accountability.

1. Do not perpetuate inflexible roles. In a group performance situation, there is a strong temptation to want to create clear, stable roles for each of the members. In some cases, this makes sense, especially where each member brings a special set of skills and experience to the group that can be best captured in a clearly defined role that exploits those skills. Certainly, a real team benefits from a membership

that is comprised of complementary skill-sets deployed in ways that fit the group's performance purpose. However, a powerful advantage of being a team is the capacity to use different talents and skill-sets in multiple ways that are seldom best-defined by permanent or inflexible roles. For members to capitalize on role shifts, it is essential for them to have a sense of mutual accountability that causes the group to seek out creative ways to use their innate talents and acquired skills in multiple roles without eroding the performance discipline.

2. Do not allow *share of voice* to become a function of hierarchy. If dialogue and problem-solving exchanges are dominated by those at the top of the formal hierarchy, the opportunity for each member to contribute in different ways is severely hampered. Teams invariably find ways to open discussions to every member and ensure that equivalent weight is accorded to everyone's point of view, regardless of seniority, title, job, or function. The merit, rather than the source of the idea, is what should determine the attention it receives. Moreover, the more ideas that are encouraged, the richer the knowledge base of the group becomes; any hierarchical filtering of ideas reduces that base. It also reduces the members' sense of mutual accountability because it suggests that seniority and position are controlling the output of the group.

3. Do not assign work based on job title. Working skills are much more important than formal titles in achieving team levels of performance. Members of the group immediately recognize when assignments are determined by job title or position in the hierarchy, and they will feel little accountability for one anothers' efforts if they believe tasks are assigned suboptimally relative to working skills and intrinsic talents. Another, even more discouraging pattern is when the grunt work of the team is always delegated to the junior members, with senior members as overseers or in advisory roles. When the higher titled members never get their hands dirty, team performance suffers. Mutual accountability requires members to believe that work assignments go the people best able to deliver results and that everyone on the team does equivalent amounts of real work.

4. Do not create special member immunities. No member of the group, including the formal leader, should be immune from the real work of the team. Nor should any member be immune from the more difficult or mundane tasks or agreed upon norms of behavior. Members feel mutual accountability only when they believe that each person is equally sharing the unskilled or tedious tasks. The reverse is also true: no member should be immune from leading the group when the task warrants it. In fact, the work assignments should be made in ways that help each member develop new skills and attain higher levels of existing skills. As the members see their personal growth become a reality, feelings of confidence, commitment, and mutual accountability strengthen.

5. Do not look to the leader to make all key decisions. It is not surprising that many group members like to avoid the burden of decision-making, particularly on controversial or difficult decisions. The nondecision-making role is the more comfortable position to be in; groups that fall into this pattern, however, are missing three very powerful factors that contribute to strong mutual accountability: (1) the opportunity to optimize the leadership capability within the group, (2) the opportu-

nity for all members to build their own decision-making confidence, and (3) the sense of accountability for the decisions made.

6. Do not allow strong personalities to dominate. Every group has two or three people whose style and personality lead them to dominate discussions, dialogues, and decisions. Left to their natural instincts, these members will take over the group process while the less outgoing personalities tend to allow that to happen. Again, this kind of imbalance can result in a loss of ideas, experience, judgment, and overall leadership capacity. It often requires conscious action either by the group, the team leader, or sponsoring authority to counter this tendency by the way in which agendas are constructed, assignments developed, and interactions encouraged. The purpose here is to integrate the best that both dominant and shy people offer, not to exclude the input of either.

7. Do not permit shy members to hang back. Equally unfortunate is the group whose shy members remain quietly in the background. Many potentially significant contributors are not comfortable stepping out in front of a group. Some would rather work on their own, let others influence and decide, and respond rather than initiate in a group setting. Such members, however, represent hidden potential that the team process is intended to uncover. The beauty of a well-functioning real team is the capacity of the group to stimulate, encourage, and motivate reticent members to seize the initiative and contribute in ways that exceed their own expectations, not to mention the expectations of others.

8. Do not fail to discipline disruptive or noncontributing members. Too often, well-intended groups who aspire to perform as a team are reluctant to discipline members whose actions are counterproductive. They assume that tough, no-nonsense prohibitions on disruptions or punitive actions against persistent non-contributors are somehow inconsistent with teaming. In fact, some of our descriptions of mutual accountability can be interpreted in that way. However, the basic notion of mutual accountability requires that the group must discipline its own nonperformers, as well as recognize, enable, and encourage the better performers. Mutual accountability does not mean covering up for the disrupters and noncontributors; it means dealing with them in a way that yields the desired performance result. Sometimes that requires replacing team members, sometimes it requires punishing them, and sometimes it requires working with them. The real team does whatever it takes to eliminate disruptive behavior and ensure productive contributions from all of its members.

The above list of what not-to-do is important. In fact, this list is as important as the establishment of clear goals, metrics, and milestones. Goals, metrics, and milestones are only the first step in ensuring mutual accountability; elimination of these accountability killers is also imperative.

How to Know If You're Mutually Accountable

So what exactly does mutual accountability look and feel like? How can a group sense the level of mutual accountability among its members? Unfortunately, there is no magical screening mechanism that lights up when mutual accountability is working. There are, however, a number of questions to ask and conditions to look for that signify that mutual accountability is *alive and well*. Conversely, there are a number of red flags to watch for that signify weak or nonexistent mutual accountability. Let's first look at some of the best indicators of alive and well.

Alive-and-Well Indicators   The first place to look, or listen, is in the team's language. Whenever a group's actions and results reflect a strong sense of mutual accountability, members invariably use *we* or *our,* in reference to the group's goals, tasks, and targets. As described earlier, new USMC recruits are not allowed to use the terms *I* or *me* at any time during their entire twelve weeks of boot camp. Perhaps the USMC is the extreme, but, the trade-off *me* or *you* is seldom used when members of a real team are talking about their purpose, goals, and working approach.

Reflecting this same attitude, we observe a notable absence of finger-pointing in the group's interactions. Even when groups get stuck and frustrations and pressures become intense, team members seldom single one another out for blame; instead they focus forward on what needs to be done collectively "by us." Rather than fixate on who did what wrong, they talk about how multiple members can step up the pace or take up the slack by working *together* in different ways. At the same time, this emphasis on collective terminology does not prevent them from bringing pressure to bear on dysfunctional members. While it is true that no one person can fail in a real team, it is also true that no one person is allowed to cause the team to fail.

Common metrics or indicators of success are another important indicator. Each member has a common view of success, and how the group's accomplishments will be measured or determined. Not every desired outcome will be numerically measurable, but each should have clearly recognizable conditions of achievement. Each member of the group will describe those conditions in the same way, often using the same words. In the case of the Sony Dream Team that penetrated 20% of the Japanese market for engineering work stations in record time, success was described in product characteristics. In the case of the Tallahassee Democrat's Elite Team, success evolved from "eliminating advertising errors" to "creating a new level of customer service." Different metrics, each of which were clearly articulated by every member of these high-performing teams. If the members of your team cannot articulate the indicators of success in agreed-upon terms, mutual accountability is unlikely to be alive and well.

A final important indicator of mutual accountability is the relative weight, number, and clarity of collective work products versus individual work products. Do all members of the team recognize the difference between the outcomes or products that must be delivered jointly versus those that can be delivered individually? And are those joint deliverables of high priority and of greater importance to the team's mission or overall purpose than those that are deliverable by individual members working on their own? The relative importance of collective work products is a critical litmus test for choosing the appropriate discipline; it is also an excellent indicator of the need for and the existence of mutual accountability.

Red Flags

The following six items are red flags, or early warning signs, of trouble:

1. Most work assignments go to individuals singly. It is normal and natural to want to put someone's name beside each task, goal, and outcome. In that way, the group can ensure that the job will be completed, and the leader can know who is responsible for what. This is the heart of individual consequence management and is second nature to most good managers. Unfortunately, it precludes mutual accountability. Unless important tasks and outcomes require multiple names, you will not deliver the collective work products that are critical to team levels of performance.

2. One-on-one discussions dominate meetings. Good managers like to talk directly to the person responsible for a task. That attitude will produce meetings in which each member of the team has a specified topic and time to report, and any issues will be discussed largely between that topic leader and the formal group leader. Hence, for most of the time in most meetings, most of the members are but an audience asking occasional questions. They are neither active participants nor responsible problem solvers or contributors. Mutual accountability fades quickly in this kind of meeting.

3. The group's only metrics are budget-like financial numbers. The group is defined by its budget. Outcomes are expressed in either increased revenues or reduced costs, and resources are prescribed by numerical calculus (headcount × compensation × time). Every task of the group can easily be translated into financial numbers. Again, this signifies the kind of consequence management that precludes mutual accountability. It lacks the flexibility for the group to determine how it wants to hold itself accountable, and what will constitute meaningful indicators of success including nonfinancial outcomes. Strictly by-the-numbers accountability also lacks motivational content.

4. All meetings adhere to tight agendas and schedules. We all abhor meetings that wander aimlessly from topic to topic, reaching no actionable conclusions and wasting valuable time on side issues. To avoid such agonies, well-meaning leaders strive for clear agendas and predetermined time frames. A good meeting is often defined as one that begins on time, ends on time, and covers all the topics on the agenda. Unfortunately, such meetings allow no time for the kind of open dialogue, joint problem solving, and group design work that real team performance requires. As a result, there is no need or opportunity for mutual accountability to prevail.

5. The formal leader does little real work. Good leaders are good at delegating. They are also masters of leveraging their own time, sometimes at the expense of others' time. Some say that the best leader will have little to do because of the ability to delegate the real work to others. In a single leader-led group, this attitude is appropriate and effective; in a team, it is corrosive. Team leaders must be resourceful gap-fillers. They need to always be on the alert for work that isn't being done effectively and quick to step into the breach to make things happen. In that role, team leaders are the catalysts for mutual accountability because they shoulder some of the load, rather than exclusively directing others to do all the work.

6. The group has added nothing to the charter supplied by the sponsor. If a group

exerts no influence on outcomes, the members will feel little or no mutual accountability. Rather, they quickly gravitate to clarifying their individual roles or work assignments and getting that job done. If the group believes time spent *purposing,* or reshaping, group goals and metrics is time wasted, because the sponsor has prescribed the results, no mutual accountability will emerge.

Much of the challenge in integrating mutual and individual accountability comes from being clear about what the mutual and individual goals or outcomes and tasks really are. Hence, the exercises that we suggest for establishing mutual accountability and keeping it alive and well have to do with sorting out the tasks and metrics. Nonetheless, since the natural mind-set in most well-run enterprises favors individual accountability, the following six exercises are worth the effort.

EXERCISE 21.1
IDENTIFYING COLLECTIVE WORK PRODUCTS
VERSUS INDIVIDUAL WORK PRODUCTS

Determine the relative importance and urgency of collective work products relative to the group's mission and purpose. Exercise 3.5 is an excellent starting point. Categorize expected outcomes or work products as either collectively or individually delivered. Then you can readily assess the relative importance of the contents of each to the achievement of the overall group purpose and definition of success.

EXERCISE 21.2
RECASTING COLLECTIVE WORK PRODUCTS AS
INDIVIDUAL WORK PRODUCTS, AND VICE VERSA

Identify three collective work products and change the conditions so that they become individual work products, and vice versa. Note the trade-offs. This exercise usually works best when two breakout groups work separately, but simultaneously, on the same sets of products. However, one of the groups is instructed to craft a set of conditions that favor individual products, while the second group focuses its attention on shaping collective products and outcomes. Then, the two groups reverse roles so that both groups have a chance at shaping individual, as well as collective outcomes. Finally, the breakout groups reconvene and discuss their conclusions in an attempt to come to joint convictions about when collective work products make more sense than individual ones.

EXERCISE 21.3
WORKING OUT DIFFERENT METRICS FOR ASSESSING OUTCOMES

Explore different ways to evaluate progress and success against specific collective work products, with respect to the overall mission and purpose of the team. Again, use breakout groups to expand on the ideas and increase the number of different options that could be effective tracking and measurement mechanisms.

EXERCISE 21.4
DESIGNING AND CONDUCTING DIFFERENT
MEETINGS FOR DIFFERENT PURPOSES

Design and conduct a meeting that is focused entirely on individual reports and efficient use of time. Design and conduct a meeting that is focused entirely on collective work products, problem solving, and solution design. Design and conduct a meeting that can serve both purposes. Draw on some of the ideas and approaches detailed in Chapter 4.

EXERCISE 21.5
TESTING THE MEMBERS' UNDERSTANDING OF DESIRED OUTCOMES

Ask the members to describe the overall mission and purpose of the group and the most important end products and outcomes. Evaluate those descriptions with respect to terminology, time frames, and metrics. Identify inconsistencies, confusion, and disagreements. Break into subgroups and discuss ways to close the gaps.

EXERCISE 21.6
EVALUATE THE LANGUAGE USED BY THE GROUP

Ask different members of the group to keep track of the language that is used in meetings. Evaluate that language with respect to how people refer to goals, tasks, and activities. How often are the terms *we* and *us* employed versus *me, you,* or *they*? Use breakout groups to construct a common language dictionary of critical terms that capture important meanings and behavior patterns. Identify and discuss whether the group falls into "either/or," "win/lose" debates versus "both/and" integrated dialogue and discussion.

22 Obstacles and Opportunities for Virtual Teaming

There is good news and bad news for virtual performance units. On the positive side, groupware can help people in multiple locations and time zones collaborate more effectively with one another without creating insurmountable logistical, expense, travel, and scheduling difficulties. Groups can also save their work more easily than ever before. They can introduce new members and ad hoc contributors to the group's purpose, goals, approach, and progress. Members from anywhere in the world can link into *virtual team rooms* that embody and enhance the quality, effectiveness, and efficiency of the group's work.

On the other hand, groupware poses many new and different challenges. In fact, just getting members to make use of the appropriate groupware options can be a challenge in itself. And, there is a potential dark side to the technology. Horrendous stories of e-mail proliferation are perhaps the most familiar illustration of what can happen to human interaction when technology gets out of hand. Other challenges exist as well. Foremost among them, as reviewed in Chapter 18, is acting as if groupware replaces or changes the two basic disciplines of team and single leader for effective small group performance. In addition, small groups that rely so much on groupware that they fail to meet with one another physically can sacrifice the emotional commitment, shared understanding, and mutual respect critical to team performance. Last, but not least, there are the challenges of keeping conversations private so that they are open and constructive, and keeping the number of participants small enough so that members do real work together.

Both the positive and negative effects of groupware arise from three fundamental characteristics of the technology: (1) expanded access, (2) asynchronous participation, and (3) disembodied communication. When combined, these realities make the work of virtual groups both easier and harder at the same time. Clearly, the most important point we make in this section is how groupwork technology reinforces natural biases toward the single-leader, instead of the team, discipline, often at the expense of performance results.

The rest of this chapter divides the positive and the negative aspects of the three technology characteristics cited above into two parts: (1) the consequences of expanded access, and (2) the consequences of asynchronous participation and disembodied communication. We conclude the chapter by describing the impact of globalization on all three characteristics.

22.1 EXPANDED ACCESS

Groupwork technology enables greatly expanded access to people, documents, discussions, metrics, and even access to the past. As long as the hookups are in place, your team can tap into the knowledge, expertise, and participation of anyone inside or beyond your company; and anyone can tap into the work of your team, both as it is happening and as it is saved. It is possible, in fact relatively easy, for everyone involved to read documents, participate in discussions, calibrate progress and metrics, and stay abreast of whatever work the team can capture and do within the medium of the technology.

On the positive side, this vastly expanded access is effective, efficient, and powerful. More information, awareness, and participation stimulate better performance. For example, we know a team that was responsible for developing and implementing a new strategy in a global enterprise. In the course of writing their plan, they sought help from a consultant familiar with their company's culture. Without groupwork technology, this team would have had to spend days briefing the consultant prior to meeting with him. The effectiveness of the briefings would have depended on the respective memories and rough notes of the team members about what they were trying to accomplish and what work they had already done.

With groupware, however, the consultant could easily access and read through the saved work of the team, including threaded discussions, documents, metrics, and other materials collected at the team's site. (For a review of groupware, see Chapter 18.) When combined with phone conversations, groupware permitted the consultant to learn how the team had approached their challenge. Moreover, the consultant could use the groupware to post comments in threaded discussions and make suggestions regarding critical issues and documents, all prior to any face-to-face meeting with the team.

In other words, the interaction between the consultant and the team was immediate, comprehensive, and time-efficient. Critical, shared understanding was developed before the consultant ever met with the team. The consultant customized his advice in ways that would not have been possible without groupware and within a fraction of the time it would have otherwise taken to do so. When the consultant finally met face-to-face with the team, everyone had a richer understanding and perspective about the challenge at hand. Hence, the whole group focused their time together on the most critical issues. As one member commented, "The meeting was half as long and three times more effective. . . ." This was because of groupware.

What happened in this example can and should happen regularly with teams who seek counsel or input from others through the medium of groupwork technology. Teams often must seek help from ad hoc contributors, sponsors, or other people who do not have to become fully committed members of the team to make meaningful contributions. Groupware facilitates the assistance of such people.

At the same time, however, expanded access poses difficulties. To begin with, large numbers of people complicate and hinder *both* of the small group disciplines we are discussing in this book. With such unlimited access, small groups must be careful not to get too large. When groups are too large the single-leader and the team disciplines do not work well. The team discipline demands a small number; teams that get much larger than ten or twelve rarely succeed unless they work in subgroups. Groupwork technology too easily causes teams to collapse under the strain of involving too many people.

The negative impacts on the single-leader discipline are also apparent. Decades of organizational behavior and effectiveness research have shown that the ability of one leader to stay in control breaks down as the number of direct reports gets up into double digits. In such instances, leaders delegate responsibility to others to hold the span of control to a manageable size. But as authority gets delegated, organization complexity grows. And while manageable spans can vary considerably under different conditions, there is always a limit to the number of people one leader can oversee. Groups that deploy groupwork technology in ways that precipitate excessive growth in the size of the group are well advised to consider sub-teaming options, or "rules of engagement" that clearly differentiate between core team members and ancillary contributors. Large groups of people need to move beyond the scope of the two performance unit disciplines in order to accomplish their objectives.

In addition to size, groupware has a number of other, less obvious impacts on small group effectiveness. True performance units, especially those applying the team discipline, always develop an ethic of accepted and unaccepted behaviors for collaboration. For example, many teams emphasize fact-based discussions that are open to all ideas, but not personalized toward anyone on the team. This kind of ethic emerges through trial by fire—the "storming" well known to anyone that has teamed with others. "Storming" leads to "norming" as key, behavioral expectations and rules are set by the group. Effective teams conclude that: "We can and should disagree constructively within the team. But we need to keep our disagreements and 'dirty laundry' inside the team."

Keeping disagreements "in the team" is jeopardized when the discussions of the team are available to others. Teams that use advanced groupware and fail to discuss an approach for dealing with this difficulty run two serious risks. First, a person who is not a mutually respected, legitimate member of the team can gain access to storming discussions. Intentionally or unintentionally, this access can spread negative controversy and mistrust within and beyond the team. Second, people on the team lose their candor in groupware discussions because they question the security of the arrangements.

Consequently, groups must openly ask and answer questions about the role, contributions, and access to the team's work by ad hoc contributors and others beyond the team. Think for a moment about working in a familiar, physically co-located team. You would not invite every ad hoc contributor to every team discussion. Yet, unless virtual teams are careful, this is what happens with groupware. Members are strongly inclined toward inclusion and openness for the sake of broadening the information base. As valuable as such broadening may be for information purposes, it can easily inhibit team performance when it weakens or threatens mutual trust among the core members. It is critical to ask such questions as, "Will this person be a fully committed and mutually respected member of the group? And, if not, what restrictions do we impose regarding access to the team's ongoing and saved work? What restrictions, if any, will be imposed on his or her participation in the team's current and future discussions? What norms or rules must he or she follow? And how can those norms be enforced without losing valuable inputs?" It is often constructive to engage the ad hoc contributors in answering these questions.

22.2 ASYNCHRONOUS PARTICIPATION AND DISEMBODIED COMMUNICATION

When small groups meet face-to-face or over the phone, they participate synchronously, that is, they interact at the same time. Much of groupwork technology, however, allows for asynchronous participation, i.e., most members working at different times from different locations. To illustrate, let's say that on Tuesday afternoon you post the draft of a document for an upcoming operating review, and on Wednesday morning I e-mail comments to you. Later on Wednesday, you review my comments, make a few changes to the document and repost it. I scan the document for your changes on Thursday. This is purely asynchronous participation, that is, you and I are never discussing the document together at the same time.

Moreover, in this example, our communication is entirely in writing; we are not talking with one another. Our communication is disembodied, literally stripped of body language, facial expression, and vocal tones. I read and responded to your document and you similarly responded to mine. At no point do we discuss your document while we are together in the same place or at the same time. My input is limited to what I read in your words and vice versa. If I should misread your tone or intent, our reactions can get off track and become dysfunctional. Even if we add telephone interactions to this situation, we are still handicapped in our ability to interpret important thoughts, feelings, and meanings that are not carefully and explicitly articulated.

The effects of asynchronous participation and disembodied communications are best understood in combination. The good news is that efficiency rises when you and I are not tied down by the logistical necessity of working on the document at the same time and place. Even more important than the costs and inconveniences associated with logistics (e.g., scheduling a time and place when we are both available, which, if we work in different cities, might mean expensive travel) are the increased possibilities for more constructive reflection and input. In the synchronous case, you and I would review your document at the same time in one anothers' presence. One or both of us might do a less thoughtful job because of pressures surrounding our moment of interaction. Perhaps I am running to catch an airplane or have just left a difficult meeting. Perhaps one or both of us cannot absorb all the implications of the document in one sitting. Perhaps we only think of important comments later when it might be too late or inconvenient to contribute them.

Groupwork technology also enhances the contributions by people who might not feel entirely comfortable or confident in group settings. Remember that e-mail, threaded discussions, and electronic data dissemination are relatively stripped of status. As a result, people who might not speak up for reasons of hierarchy, job role, or personality in synchronous meetings often feel comfortable doing so within the protection of groupware. Moreover, the body language and facial expressions present in physical meetings can reduce participation. How many times have you or a colleague been inhibited from speaking by the combined tonal and facial grimace of another group member making it clear that "this is not the best time to speak up"?

Finally, input from group members can receive a fairer hearing when read by others asynchronously and without the attendant body language of the group. This is one of the most commented-upon phenomena in the World Wide Web: when we consider comments without knowledge of status, position, hierarchy, gender, race, ethnicity, age, or other criteria, we focus more on content and substance. We are less inhibited by extraneous factors and find ourselves being more open-minded. In such cases groupware clearly enhances the possibilities of better thinking, better decisions, and better work.

Yet, in addition to the many advantages of asynchronous participation and disembodied communication, there are three serious disadvantages:

1. Groupwork technology can limit group creativity. Teams that fail to have face-to-face interactions diminish their chances for spontaneous collaboration. We have all attended sessions when people built on one another's ideas in exciting and unexpected ways. *This kind of group creativity arises from being physically present.* Groupwork technology enhances the possibilities in two important ways: (1) each individual's contribution will reflect his or her individual very best thinking, unimpeded by pressures of time, place, or presence of others; and (2) each person will receive the best, fairest hearing from other members of the group. Yet, it comes at a cost. Groups often do their most creative and critical work *as groups* rather than as individuals. Through working together in the same room at the same time, they generate insights and creative solutions not likely to emerge from asynchronous, individual contributions.

   As we pointed out in *The Wisdom of Teams,* the stories of successful teams invariably turn on some critical juncture or moment when the team—*as a team*—jelled around an idea or an event or a possibility. The odds of such creative and vital moments decrease when all the work and interactions of the group happen in cyberspace. With groupware, you each may interact well and work constructively with each others' words and documents, but that is not the same thing as working and collaborating with the entire group present.

2. Groupware can subtly convert collective work products into individual work products. To understand how, we need to look closely at co-location. Even though the word literally means *same place,* co-location actually involves two aspects: place and time. Obviously, if you and I are working together in the same room, we are collaborating at the same time. But, you and I might be connected over the phone or in a chatroom and be working together at the same time, even if not in the same place. In each of these two cases, we are doing work together. But when we rely strictly on asynchronous features of groupware, for example, see the document revision process discussed earlier, we are not performing co-located, collaborative work together. We are more like relay runners, each taking the baton from the other

before doing our individual work, and passing the baton back. Groupware may shorten the time intervals between baton passes. But asynchronous individual effort, regardless of how often and efficient, cannot replace working together when simultaneous interaction and nonverbal communication is required.

Teams that ignore this subtle distinction between working together versus working individually do so at their own peril. They discover too late that their collective work products have become a series of individual work products.

For example, a team from STMicroelectronics set a goal of breaking company records for the time it took to bring new products to market. They used groupware to assemble programmers, designers, and others from India, France, and California. The team assigned collective work products to programmers and designers from all three locations, which spanned more than ten time zones.

They learned that merely calling something a collective work product, however, did not lead to true collaboration through the medium of groupware technology. Because of the radical time zone differences, those assigned to the group tended to rely on groupware to the exclusion of face-to-face or even synchronous voice interactions. It is extremely difficult to schedule and hold teleconference calls spanning the time zones that stretch from India to California. As a result, essential aspects of collaboration became impossible. For example, the programmers from India literally had coding conventions that went unexplained to their colleagues in France and California.

The team eventually recognized that collective work products demanded co-location. At critical junctures, they chose to fly people from India to France and California and station them there until the needed progress happened. A rough rule of thumb emerged around the question, "How many times must team members interact with one another during the day in order to make progress?" If the answer were greater than one or two, it was a sure sign that co-location, or at least reasonably finite time zone differences, had to be established.

3. Groupware technology endangers mutual accountability. Asynchronous participation and disembodied communication combine to threaten the shared understanding and emotional commitment demanded by the team discipline's requirement of *common* purpose, *common* goals, and *commonly* agreed upon working approach. *Common* requires a demonstrable, shared understanding of purpose, goals, and approach; in contrast, *compromising* to achieve consensus too often reflects some ill-founded imperative for 100% agreement. Shared understanding, without 100% agreement, typically requires a lot of group work that comes from effort as a group instead of only from a series of one-to-one interactions with each others' written words and documents. Of the dozens of virtual teams we have participated in or observed, it is not surprising that none could succeed without meeting early on as a group to discuss team basics. Nor was it surprising to find that such discussions were equally necessary whenever the team got stuck or faced a particularly difficult challenge.

The aforementioned elements of expanded access, asynchronous participation, and disembodied communication are all increasingly common in today's global environment. Seldom do we encounter a company with any significant growth potential that is not giving a high priority to operating in multiple parts of the world. Manufacturing operations find lower-cost labor abroad, sales efforts cannot resist new markets overseas, and investors are constantly seeking the untapped potential of global resources. As a result, small groups of all kinds are working across global boundaries with a regularity and diversity seldom experienced just a decade ago.

Simply put, there is no other way for such groups to perform without dealing in some way with the elements of expanded access, asynchronous participation, and disembodied communication. Added to that is the complexity of different language and cultural barriers that must be overcome. English may have emerged as the "language of business." But, while many Europeans, Asians, Africans, South Americans, Middle Easterners, and others from around the globe are articulate in English, their cultures are very different, making nonverbal communications difficult to interpret even in face-to-face situations. Moreover, unique cultural heritages can dramatically affect small group performance. In Germany, for example, there really is not a commonly used term for *team;* hence, the English version is usually applied. In Japan, the importance of a strong leader is a cultural norm that literally defies team basics.

Most groups that aspire to team performance among members from different cultures find they need to create a *team culture* of their own, rather than try to get all members to subordinate their behaviors to reflect any single cultural way (e.g., the "American" way or the "German" way or the "Japanese" way). The emergence of such team cultures is more common within global organizations where strong values already cut across national boundaries. McKinsey and Company is an excellent example of a truly global enterprise that has a set of values that enables multicultural groups to work together effectively.

Still, performance units in any culture or nationality are primarily a matter of applying the right discipline to the performance task at hand. In those countries where strong leader behavior is more firmly ingrained in a national culture, you are more likely to encounter single-leader units within that country's enterprises. At the same time, however, the potential value of team performance is real, although the effort required to achieve it may be much harder.

It is no accident that *The Wisdom of Teams* has been translated into fifteen languages and has continued to be a best seller overseas for nearly ten years. Nor is it any accident that we continue to receive unsolicited testimonials from members of teams all over the globe. Virtual teaming technology merely accentuates the importance of multi-cultural groups becoming proficient at the two performance unit disciplines. But, multicultural groups must pay especially close attention to the concerns we cite regarding the effects of expanded access, asynchronous participation, and disembodied communication.

22.3 BIAS TOWARD THE SINGLE-LEADER DISCIPLINE—THE DISTORTION OF "WORKING TOGETHER"

The expanded access, asynchronous participation, and disembodied communication characteristics of groupware bias groups toward the single-leader discipline. Whenever the performance goals of the group are best achieved through the single-leader discipline, this bias is constructive. But if your group faces challenges that demand the team discipline, then you must be careful to recognize and deal with the bias of groupwork technology.

Ironically, most groupwork technology claims to contain "tools for teams." Yet, a careful look at project management, threaded discussions, document management, and executive management features reveals their bias toward individual work and individual accountability. Think about your own experience with such technology. When you are working—whether responding to email, posting a discussion item, reviewing a document, checking progress on metrics and goals, or making or receiving a task assignment—you are working *alone*. You may be interacting with the words of others. Unfortunately, interacting with another person's words is not the same as interacting with the whole person in real time. Without the benefit of body language, facial expressions, and tonal innuendo, you can easily miss the intent, if not the entire point, of an important communication.

As discussed in Chapters 17 through 20, collective work products constitute a powerful litmus test for identifying team performance situations. The need for the team discipline is high when tangible results must be delivered by two or more people collaborating in real time. But, there is a bias in groupware technology toward using the single-leader approach. If we are not careful, we expect people to collaborate on a collective work product, but, like the STMicroelectronics team, encourage the opposite. The way they conduct their actual work tends more toward individual work, responsibility, and accountability. In an all too typical response, one person with long experience with virtual work efforts clearly indicated that, on reflection, he had rarely worked in virtual groups that assigned two or more people joint accountability for work products and goals; a telling illustration of the bias of this technology toward individual accountability. Instead, he said, the prevailing pattern was "one person, one task."

This systematic inclination toward individual work and individual accountability reinforces the biases of consequence management. As discussed at length in *The Wisdom of Teams,* most managers have much more experience and confidence in using the single-leader discipline than the team discipline. Effectively using groupware to apply the team discipline, then, demands more rigor and conscious deliberation about when to team. Otherwise, you will not avoid the traps associated with the bias toward individual work products.

22.4 WHAT TO DO: PRACTICAL POINTERS ON VIRTUAL TEAMING AND VIRTUAL WORK

Before reviewing best practices in virtual teaming, let us repeat our central message: *Do not take your collective eyes off performance and how best to choose and use the single-leader and team disciplines to achieve it.* As you move forward, here are some critical steps you and your group should consider:

1. Use face-to-face meetings to build and develop shared understanding and commitment, as well to get unstuck. Such meetings are important early on when the group is beginning to develop the mutual respect and understanding required to succeed.

Equally important, however, are those times in a virtual effort when things are not working and the group is stuck or becalmed. Often the best, and sometimes the only, way to get back on track is to work together in the same room at the same time. Groupwork technology can certainly reduce, but rarely eliminates, the need for face-to-face interactions over the entire course of a demanding performance challenge. One comment echoes many we have heard: "We bonded [only] when we met in person." Effective team performance, of course, is not primarily about bonding. But without meaningful, face-to-face interactions and doing real work *together*, it is extremely difficult to build understanding, respect, and accountability for a team's purpose, goals, and working approach. Yes, in that unusual instance when a group of people are well-known to one another and have worked together a number of times, we can imagine effective teaming without any face-to-face interactions. In fact, we encountered such a situation at General Electric's electric motors business in Fort Wayne, Indiana. A key member of a leadership team in Fort Wayne was physically located in Singapore where the unit's manufacturing operations were concentrated. Many virtual team efforts by the group were successful without his physical presence, but largely because he was so well-known to his other teammates. Such circumstances are the exception rather than the rule in today's workplace. And the more complex the group challenge becomes, in terms of both performance results and location/time zone diversity, the more frequently face-to-face sessions make sense.

2. Avoid the illusion of collaborative groupware meetings. To some extent, this is a corollary of the point just made. Whenever teams gather through groupware to advance, they need to recognize and adjust for the key differences between face-to-face and groupware interactions. In Chapter 20, we cautioned against approaching all meetings in the same way. We encouraged readers to recognize when meetings would benefit from a concern for time-efficiency versus providing for a more open-ended, problem-solving approach. Groupware interactions work well for the first, but are problematic for the second. Nonetheless, in the course of a virtual team effort the group must often use groupware to enable open-ended, problem-solving sessions. Accordingly, we encourage teams to recognize the constraints imposed by technology and consider the following aids: (1) explicitly appoint facilitators, (2) use chat features simultaneously with voice or video, (3) carefully poll members whenever a particularly critical subject arises, and (4) apply any other technique the group can imagine to make sure that dialogue remains open-ended.

3. Do not swamp yourselves with high numbers. From the beginning, your group should discuss what it means to be a full member of the group versus a partial member or contributor. Unlimited involvement is not the name of this game! You must choose deliberately and consciously who will have access to what. You need to establish special protocols or access codes to implement these decisions. You should establish clear criteria to delineate core group members, and thereby enable you to control the size of your group. As the number of people making contributions to your team grows with the passage of time, you need to regularly review the status of each person as *core group member* versus *partial contributor*. Make whatever changes are merited, including limiting or eliminating access to the groupwork tech-

nology by those whose roles are no longer core or who have completed their assignments on your behalf. Finally, if the number of ad hoc contributors gets too large for the group leader to oversee, create subgroups and divide up the oversight responsibility among other core members of your group.

4. Discuss and decide which features of groupware you will use and how you will use them. Like most software and hardware, groupwork technology continually improves, with more and more features and functions added all the time. Today, your group has access to hundreds of features and functions. As a result, far too many groups make two critical mistakes. First, they fail to deliberately discuss and choose which of the features to use and exactly how to use them. Second, they overestimate the number of features and functions the group can effectively master in the early phases of teaming, and, as a result, create frustrating and confusing technological interactions. (Even in the writing of this book, for example, the authors utilized incompatible software for several weeks before appropriate modifications could eliminate the frustration.)

Instead of careful deliberation and choice, groups too often participate in broad, generalized training or install groupwork technology with vague and unrealistic expectations about skill, knowledge, and familiarity. For example, you assume I am familiar with threaded discussions and post a comment. When I don't respond, you get frustrated. When this happens, groups quickly learn to use only those features with which each person is already familiar (e.g., e-mail alone). This lowest common denominator approach seriously underutilizes the technology. And the attendant frustrations and confusions delay the effort. In contrast, groups who deliberately choose which features they will use tend to ensure common understanding and shared learning about those features.

If you are relatively new to groupwork technology, start with only a handful of features. That way, your group can develop skills, usage, and familiarity together. As a few features are mastered, others can be added. Do not, however, force a shift in groupware without full group support, assuming that the advanced capability will somehow carry the day. Use the exercises in Chapter 18 to help your group learn to pick and practice the groupware features that make the most sense to your performance challenge.

5. Discuss and choose your own *netiquette*. You need to meet face-to-face early on to agree on several things: (1) how you will divide up the work itself; (2) how you will administer yourselves and deal with logistics; (3) what approaches should be used for decision-making and evaluating progress; and, finally, (4) what behavioral norms, or rules of the road, will be required. Your group should discuss each of these with reference to groupwork technology. If you will rely extensively on groupware, an explicit discussion of the expectations and anticipated use regarding that technology ought to be an integral part of your working approach.

For example, you need to deliberately choose whether everyone connected with your effort or only core group members receives e-mail or are otherwise included in threaded discussions and document sharing. What are your expectations regarding input? Must you hear from all members on each critical document and issue, or only some members? What about language? Will your group welcome jokes?

Will you tolerate *flaming* (i.e., harsh invectives aimed at people inside or beyond the group)? What about participation itself? Will your group set an expectation regarding usage of the groupware technology? Or, will you permit usage to rise and fall without any expectation?

When your group faces a critical choice or decision, how will you work together? It's a good idea to identify some conditions that will signal the need for face-to-face work. For example, what kinds of collective work products are likely to require face-to-face participation? Since you probably cannot meet face-to-face for every decision, what kind of participation will you encourage or expect prior to decisions? Who will make the decisions and on what basis or with what contribution from others? How will you communicate those decisions to one another? Will you communicate them to ad hoc contributors or other people beyond the extended group in you organization?

6. Discuss and assign monitoring and guiding roles regarding the group's use of group-work technology. Groupware demands new leadership roles, especially with regard to project management, document management, and threaded discussions. In each case, someone should be formally assigned to pay attention to whether the work of the moment, for example, discussing and resolving an issue or reviewing and improving a document, is getting done in the manner best suited to performance.

In some ways, this required role is analogous to a facilitator, gatekeeper, or leader in face-to-face meetings. For example, imagine that six of us are assembled to review a document. We would ensure the document has been read before the meeting and is reviewed thoroughly by all of us at the meeting. We would seek comments from everyone at the meeting, trying to ensure we took advantage of our individual and collective best thinking. As the meeting drew to a close, we would agree on next steps and responsibilities for any required redrafting of the document and set a time for the next review.

This approach is clearly familiar, but as with so much in groupwork technology, it takes on a different spin when the meeting is not face-to-face. One or two people in your group must take responsibility for ensuring that the document in question receives comparable input, agreement about what might be changed, and assignment of next-step responsibilities. If such roles are not explicitly assigned and communicated, the required work often falls through the cracks.

Put differently, your group needs to assign people to be discussion guides and administrators. Someone must pay attention to whether group members are using the groupwork technology, participating in document management and threaded discussions, responding to e-mail and other alerts, getting their tasks done, submitting needed metrics and other information, and so forth. And if anyone is falling short, the guide or administrator needs to communicate on-line or off-line to find out why and what can be done to improve participation and contribution.

Do not assume that the person assigned this role must be the group leader. Nor should you always give this role to the same person. Groupwork technology permits your group a lot of flexibility in assigning such roles. Like the other suggestions made in this chapter, however, you must make such choices and assignments explicitly and self-consciously. Again, this is best done face-to-face. Groups who assume that groupwork technology will run itself are heading for trouble.

7. Pay particular attention to when and how to shift the leadership role in situations that require team performance. One of the great strengths of the team approach lies in shifting leadership to fit the task at hand. Doing so, however, is challenging for any small group aspiring to team performance. But it can be even more difficult in virtual teaming because of the strong bias towards the single-leader discipline.

For that reason, it is critical that the formal leader of a virtual team situation engage the core team actively and extensively on this topic. Develop clear guidelines for when and how to shift the leadership role. A performance agenda, like that discussed in Chapter 4, can guide virtual teams through the thickets of shared leadership.

Review and use the exercises in Chapter 18 after reading Chapter 22. In addition, consider the following:

EXERCISE 22.1
ROLE DEFINITION AND ACCESS

Once your group has selected the features and functions of groupware you will use, spend time distinguishing the access to your group work that will be given to full members versus partial members. You might need the help of technologists to implement the decisions you make. Once you have put your decisions into practice, review how effectively they are working and make the needed adjustments. Also, schedule a regular review of who has what access so that you can prune, add, and modify scope of access whenever needed.

EXERCISE 22.2
NETIQUETTE

Once near the beginning and then again after a few weeks or so of experience, your group should set netiquette rules of behavior and expectations. These include answering the following questions:

1. Are people expected to check the team's site regularly? If so, how regularly?
2. Are there time limits for responding to people? If so, what are they, and are they limited to only certain kinds of issues or alerts?
3. Is there any limit to the kind of language your group wishes to impose?
4. Who gets alerted on what kind of issues?
5. Will you monitor usage of groupware by team members? If people are falling short of usage, what are the consequences, if any?

EXERCISE 22.3
CALLING FOR A FACE-TO-FACE SESSION

In advance, your group should fully explore the circumstances under which anyone in the team can suggest or call for a face-to-face session. By identifying the parameters for calling them and formally discussing and reviewing such sessions, you will learn when and how to use these critical moments for group progress.

EXERCISE 22.4
NEW MEMBER INTRODUCTION

Whenever a new member or ad hoc contributor gets introduced, ask one or two people from the team to prepare an appropriate introduction guide and package. This package ought to include a description of the group's performance challenge, goals, and work plan; a description of the kind of contribution expected from the new person; access to the people and backgrounds of people on the team; and, most important, access to the *relevant* saved work of the team that is critical to the role of the new person. For example, ad hoc contributors should have access to those particular threaded discussions, documents, and other work that will quickly and effectively provide them the background they need.

EXERCISE 22.5
GUIDE FOR GUIDES

If you are assigned the task of guiding discussions and other aspects of groupwork, then you need to choose how you will perform each of the following critical tasks:

1. Monitoring threaded discussions and other forms of participation.
2. Posing questions to relevant members on relevant subjects.
3. Polling group members on key issues and decisions.
4. Ensuring that people have read and responded to documents.
5. Attending to disagreements and ensuring they become enlightened instead of un-enlightened.
6. Contacting members either on-line or off-line when their participation and contributions fall short.

EXERCISE 22.6
COLLECTIVE WORK PRODUCTS AND CO-LOCATION _____

Using Exercises 17.5 and 19.5, identify and assign collective work products critical to the performance of your group. Now ask those assigned to determine the opportunities and impediments they foresee in applying groupware technology to their work. Ask them to pay particular attention to the number and nature of daily interactions required for success. Determine if the number of interactions is significant and/or if the nature of their collaborative work demands face-to-face approaches to working together. If so, ask the group to figure out a work plan that builds in the appropriate co-location, together with a budget for the related logistical expenses.

Solutions to the Project Management Conflict Exercise

Part One: Facing the Conflict

After reading the answers that follow, record your score on line 1 of the worksheet on page 365.

A. Although many project managers and functional managers negotiate by "returning" favors, this custom is not highly recommended. The department manager might feel some degree of indebtedness at first, but will surely become defensive in follow-on projects in which you are involved, and might even get the idea that this will be the only way that he will be able to deal with you in the future. If this was your choice, allow one point on line 1.

B. Threats can only lead to disaster. This is a surefire way of ending a potentially good arrangement before it starts. Allow no points if you selected this as your solution.

C. If you say nothing, then you accept full responsibility and accountability for the schedule delay and increased costs. You have done nothing to open communications with the department manager. This could lead into additional conflicts on future projects. Enter two points on line 1 if this was your choice.

D. Requesting upper-level management to step in at this point can only complicate the situation. Executives prefer to step in only as a last resort. Upper-level management will probably ask to talk to the department manager first. Allow two points on line 1 if this was your choice.

E. Although he might become defensive upon receiving your memo, it will become difficult for him to avoid your request for help. The question, of course, is when he will give you this help. Allow eight points on line 1 if you made this choice.

F. Trying to force your solution on the department manager will severely threaten him and provide the basis for additional conflict. Good project managers will always try to predict emotional reactions to whatever decisions they might be forced to make. For this choice, allow two points on line 1 of the worksheet.

G. Making an appointment for a later point in time will give both parties a chance to cool off and think out the situation further. He will probably find it difficult to refuse your request for help and will be forced to think about it between now and the appointment. Allow ten points for this choice.

H. An immediate discussion will tend to open communications or keep communication open. This will be advantageous. However, it can also be a disadvantage if emotions are running high and sufficient time has not been given to the selection of alternatives. Allow six points on line 1 if this was your choice.

I. Forcing the solution your way will obviously alienate the department manager. The fact that you do intend to honor his request at a later time might give him some relief especially if he understands your problem and the potential impact of his decision on other departments. Allow three points on line 1 for this choice.

Part Two: Understanding Emotions

Using the scoring table shown on page 549, determine your total score. Record your total in the appropriate box on line 2 of the worksheet on page 365. There are no "absolutely" correct answers to this problem, merely what appears to be the "most" right.

Part Three: Establishing Communications

A. Although your explanations may be acceptable and accountability for excess costs may be blamed on the department manager, you have not made any attempt to open communications with the department manager. Further conflicts appear inevitable. If this was your choice, allow a score of zero on line 3 of the worksheet.

B. You are offering the department manager no choice but to elevate the conflict. He probably has not had any time to think about changing his requirements and it is extremely doubtful that he will give in to you since you have now backed him into a corner. Allow zero points on line 3 of the worksheet.

C. Threatening him may get him to change his mind, but will certainly create deteriorating working relationships both on this project and any others that will require that you interface with his department. Allow zero points if this was your choice.

D. Sending him a memo requesting a meeting at a later date will give him and you a chance to cool down but might not improve your bargaining position. The department manager might now have plenty of time to reassure himself that he was right because you probably aren't under such a terrible time constraint as you led him to believe if you can wait several days to see him again. Allow four points on line 3 of the worksheet if this was your choice.

E. You're heading in the right direction trying to open communications. Unfortunately, you may further aggravate him by telling him that he lost his cool and should have apologized to you when all along you may have been the one who lost your cool. Expressing regret as part of your opening remarks would benefit the situation. Allow six points on line 3 of the worksheet.

F. Postponing the problem cannot help you. The department manager might consider the problem resolved because he hasn't heard from you. The confrontation should not be postponed. Your choice has merit in that you are attempting to open up a channel for communications. Allow four points on line 3 if this was your choice.

G. Expressing regret and seeking immediate resolution is the best approach. Hopefully, the department manager will now understand the importance of this conflict and the need for urgency. Allow ten points on line 3 of the worksheet.

	Reaction	Personal or Group Score
A. I've given you my answer. See the general manager if you're not happy.	Hostile or Withdrawing	4
B. I understand your problem. Let's do it your way.	Accepting	4
C. I understand your problem, but I'm doing what is best for my department.	Defensive or Hostile	4
D. Let's discuss the problem. Perhaps there are alternatives.	Cooperative	4
E. Let me explain to you why we need the new requirements.	Cooperative or Defensive	4
F. See my section supervisors. It was their recommendation.	Withdrawing	4
G. New managers are supposed to come up with new and better ways, aren't they?	Hostile or Defensive	4
	Total: Personal	
	Total: Group	

Part Four: Conflict Resolution

Use the table shown on page 550 to determine your total points. Enter this total on line 4 of the worksheet on page 365.

Part Five: Understanding Your Choices

A. Although you may have "legal" justification to force the solution your way, you should consider the emotional impact on the organization as a result of alienating the department manager. Allow two points on line 5 of the worksheet.

B. Accepting the new requirements would be an easy way out if you are willing to explain the increased costs and schedule delays to the other participants. This would certainly please the department manager, and might even give him the impression that he has a power position and can always resolve problems in this fashion. Allow four points on line 5 of your worksheet.

C. If this situation cannot be resolved at your level, you have no choice but to request upper-level management to step in. At this point you must be pretty sure that a compromise is all but impossible and are willing to accept a go-for-broke position. Enter ten points on line 5 of the worksheet if this was your choice.

	Mode	Personal or Group Score
A. The requirements are my decision and we're doing it my way.	Forcing	4
B. I've thought about it and you're right. We'll do it your way.	Withdrawal or Smoothing	4
C. Let's discuss the problem. Perhaps there are alternatives.	Compromise or Confrontation	4
D. Let me explain why we need the new requirements.	Smoothing, Confrontation, or Forcing	4
E. See my section supervisors; they're handling it now.	Withdrawal	4
F. I've looked over the problem and I might be able to ease up on some of the requirements.	Smoothing or Compromise	4
	Total: Personal	
	Total: Group	

D. Asking other managers to plead your case for you is not a good situation. Hopefully upper-level management will solicit their opinions when deciding on how to resolve the conflict. Enter six points on line 5 if this was your choice, and hope that the functional managers do not threaten him by ganging up on him.

Part Six: Interpersonal Influences

A. Threatening the employees with penalty power will probably have no effect at all because your conflict is with the department manager, who at this time probably could care less about your evaluation of his people. Allow zero points on line 6 of the worksheet if you selected this choice.

B. Offering rewards will probably induce people toward your way of thinking provided that they feel that you can keep your promises. Promotions and increased responsibilities are functional responsibilities, not those of a project manager. Performance evaluation might be effective if the department manager values your judgment. In this situation it is doubtful that he will. Allow no points for this answer and record the results on line 6 of the worksheet.

C. Expert power, once established, is an effective means of obtaining functional respect provided that it is used for a relatively short period of time. For long-term efforts, expert power can easily create conflicts between project and functional managers. In this situation, although relatively short term, the department manager probably will not consider you as an expert, and this might carry on down to his functional subordinates. Allow six points on line 6 of the worksheet if this was your choice.

D. Work challenge is the best means of obtaining support and in many situations can overcome personality clashes and disagreements. Unfortunately, the problem occurred because of complaints by the functional personnel and it is therefore unlikely that work challenge would be effective here. Allow eight points on line 6 of the worksheet if this was your choice.

E. People who work in a project environment should respect the project manager because of the authority delegated to him from the upper levels of management. But this does not mean that they will follow his directions. When in doubt, employees tend to follow the direction of the person who signs their evaluation form, namely, the department manager. However, the project manager has the formal authority to "force" the line manager to adhere to the original project plan. This should be done only as a last resort, and here, it looks as though it may be the only alternative. Allow ten points if this was your answer and record the result on line 6 of the worksheet.

F. Referent power cannot be achieved overnight. Furthermore, if the department manager feels that you are trying to compete with him for the friendship of his subordinates, additional conflicts can result. Allow two points on line 6 of the worksheet if this was your choice.

APPENDIX B

Solution to Leadership Exercise

Situation 1
   A. This technique may work if you have proven leadership credentials. Since three of these people have not worked for you before, some action is necessary.
   B. The team should already be somewhat motivated and reinforcement will help. Team building must begin by showing employees how they will benefit. This is usually the best approach on long-term projects. (5 points)
   C. This is the best approach if the employees already understand the project. In this case, however, you may be expecting too much out of the employees this soon. (3 points)
   D. This approach is too strong at this time, since emphasis should be on team building. On long-term projects, people should be given the opportunity to know one another first. (2 points)

Situation 2
   A. Do nothing. Don't overreact. This may improve productivity without damaging morale. See the impact on the team first. If the other members accept Tom as the informal leader, because he has worked for you previously, the results can be very favorable. (5 points)
   B. This may cause the team to believe that a problem exists when, in fact, it does not.
   C. This is duplication of effort and may reflect on your ability as a leader. Productivity may be impaired. (2 points)
   D. This is a hasty decision and may cause Tom to overreact and become less productive. (3 points)

Situation 3
   A. You may be burdening the team by allowing them to struggle. Motivation may be affected and frustration will result. (1 point)
   B. Team members expect the project manager to be supportive and to have ideas. This will reinforce your relationship with the team. (5 points)

C. This approach is reasonable as long as your involvement is minimum. You must allow the team to evolve without expecting continuous guidance. (4 points)

D. This action is premature and can prevent future creativity. The team may allow you to do it all.

Situation 4

A. If, in fact, the problem does exist, action must be taken. These types of problems do not go away by themselves.

B. This will escalate the problem and may make it worse. It could demonstrate your support for good relations with your team, but could also backfire. (1 point)

C. Private meetings should allow you to reassess the situation and strengthen employee relations on a one-on-one basis. You should be able to assess the magnitude of the problem. (5 points)

D. This is a hasty decision. Changing the team's schedules may worsen the morale problem. This situation requires replanning, not a strong hand. (2 points)

Situation 5

A. Crisis management does not work in project management. Why delay until a crisis occurs and then waste time having to replan?

B. This situation may require your immediate attention. Sympathizing with your team may not help if they are looking toward you for leadership. (2 points)

C. This is the proper balance: participative management and contingency planning. This balance is crucial for these situations. (5 points)

D. This may seriously escalate the problem unless you have evidence that performance is substandard. (1 point)

Situation 6

A. Problems should be uncovered and brought to the surface for solution. It is true that this problem may go away, or that Bob simply does not recognize that his performance is substandard.

B. Immediate feedback is best. Bob must know your assessment of his performance. This shows your interest in helping him improve. (5 points)

C. This is not a team problem. Why ask the team to do your work? Direct contact is best.

D. As above, this is your problem, not that of the team. You may wish to ask for their input, but do not ask them to perform your job.

Situation 7

A. George must be hurting to finish the other project. George probably needs a little more time to develop a quality report. Let him do it. (5 points)

B. Threatening George may not be the best situation because he already understands the problem. Motivation by threatening normally is not good. (3 points)

C. The other team members should not be burdened with this unless it is a team effort.

D. As above, this burden should not be placed on other team members unless, of course, they volunteer.

Situation 8

A. Doing nothing in time of crisis is the worst decision that can be made. This may frustrate the team to a point where everything that you have built up may be destroyed.

      B. The problem is the schedule slippage, not morale. In this case, it is unlikely that they are related.

      C. Group decision making can work but may be difficult under tight time constraints. Productivity may not be related to the schedule slippage. (3 points)

      D. This is the time when the team looks to you for strong leadership. No matter how good the team is, they may not be able to solve all of the problems. (5 points)

Situation 9
    A. A pat on the back will not hurt. People need to know when they are doing well.

    B. Positive reinforcement is a good idea, but perhaps not through monetary rewards. (3 points)

    C. You have given the team positive reinforcement and have returned authority/responsibility to them for phase III. (5 points)

    D. Your team has demonstrated the ability to handle authority and responsibility except for this crisis. Dominant leadership is not necessary on a continuous basis.

Situation 10
    A. The best approach. All is well. (5 points)

    B. Why disturb a good working relationship and a healthy working environment? Your efforts may be counterproductive.

    C. If the team members have done their job, they have already looked for contingencies. Why make them feel that you still want to be in control? However, if they have not reviewed the phase III schedule, this step may be necessary. (3 points)

    D. Why disturb the team? You may convince them that something is wrong or about to happen.

Situation 11
    A. You cannot assume a passive role when the customer identifies a problem. You must be prepared to help. The customer's problems usually end up being your problems. (3 points)

    B. The customer is not coming into your company to discuss productivity.

    C. This places a tremendous burden on the team, especially since it is the first meeting. They need guidance.

    D. Customer information exchange meetings are *your* responsibility and should not be delegated. You are the focal point of information. This requires strong leadership, especially during a crisis. (5 points)

Situation 12
    A. A passive role by you may leave the team with the impression that there is no urgency.

    B. Team members are motivated and have control of the project. They should be able to handle this by themselves. Positive reinforcement will help. (5 points)

    C. This approach might work but could be counterproductive if employees feel that you question their abilities. (4 points)

    D. Do not exert strong leadership when the team has already shown its ability to make good group decisions.

Situation 13
    A. This is the worst approach and may cause the loss of both the existing and follow-on work.

    B. This may result in overconfidence and could be disastrous if a follow-on effort does not occur.

C. This could be very demoralizing for the team, because members may view the existing program as about to be canceled. (3 points)

D. This should be entirely the responsibility of the project manager. There are situations where information may have to be withheld, at least temporarily. (5 points)

Situation 14   A. This is an ideal way to destroy the project-functional interface.

B. This consumes a lot of time, since each team member may have a different opinion. (3 points)

C. This is the best approach, since the team may know the functional personnel better than you do. (5 points)

D. It is highly unlikely that you can accomplish this.

Situation 15   A. This is the easiest solution, but the most dangerous if it burdens the rest of the team with extra work. (3 points)

B. The decision should be yours, not your team's. You are avoiding your responsibility.

C. Consulting with the team will gain support for your decision. It is highly likely that the team will want Carol to have this chance. (5 points)

D. This could cause a demoralizing environment on the project. If Carol becomes irritable, so could other team members.

Situation 16   A. This is the best choice. You are at the mercy of the line manager. He may ease up some if not disturbed. (5 points)

B. This is fruitless. They have obviously tried this already and were unsuccessful. Asking them to do it again could be frustrating. Remember, the brick wall has been there for two years already. (3 points)

C. This will probably be a wasted meeting. Brick walls are generally not permeable.

D. This will thicken the brick wall and may cause your team's relationship with the line manager to deteriorate. This should be used as a last resort *only* if status information cannot be found any other way. (2 points)

Situation 17   A. This is a poor assumption. Carol may not have talked to him or may simply have given him her side of the project.

B. The new man is still isolated from the other team members. You may be creating two project teams. (3 points)

C. This may make the new man uncomfortable and feel that the project is regimented through meetings. (2 points)

D. New members feel more comfortable one-on-one, rather than having a team gang up on them. Briefings should be made by the team, since project termination and phaseout will be a team effort. (5 points)

Situation 18   A. This demonstrates your lack of concern for the growth of your employees. This is a poor choice.

B. This is a personal decision between you and the employee. As long as his performance will not be affected, he should be allowed to attend. (5 points)

C. This is not necessarily a problem open for discussion. You may wish to informally seek the team's opinion. (2 points)

D. This approach is reasonable but may cause other team members to feel that you are showing favoritism and simply want their consensus.

Situation 19 A. This is the best choice. Your employees are in total control. Do nothing. You must assume that the employees have already received feedback. (5 points)

B. The employees have probably been counseled already by your team and their own functional manager. Your efforts can only alienate them. (1 point)

C. Your team already has the situation under control. Asking them for contingency plans at this point may have a detrimental effect. They may have already developed contingency plans. (2 points)

D. A strong leadership role now may alienate your team.

Situation 20 A. A poor choice. You, the project manager, are totally accountable for all information provided to the customer.

B. Positive reinforcement may be beneficial, but does nothing to guarantee the quality of the report. Your people may get overcreative and provide superfluous information.

C. Soliciting their input has some merit, but the responsibility here is actually yours. (3 points)

D. Some degree of leadership is needed for all reports. Project teams tend to become diffused during report writing unless guided. (5 points)

Index _____

Abbott's admonitions, 298
Above the line. *See* Resourced, not
    resourced vs.
Accolade, 105–106
Accommodating, 355–356
Accountability:
    small-group performance and, 468
    See also Individual accountability,
        Mutual Acceptability
Accountability dual, 377
    for task estimates, 438
Acheson's rule of the bureaucracy, 298
Action planning, in Stage-Gate
    framework, 85–86
Activities:
    conflict between: 173–174
Activity-based goals, 464, 465
    changing to outcome-based goals,
        494–495
    choosing outcome-based rather than,
        493
    examples of, 493–494
    outcome-based vs., 491–492, 493–494
    problems with, 492–493

Activity traps, 283
Actual Cost (AC) or Actual Cost of Work
    Performed (ACWP), 29, 76–77,
    78–79
Actual cost of work performed
    effects of staffing methods on,
        150–151
Ad hoc contributors:
    groupwork technology and,154, 528,
        530
    subgroups and, 179
    virtual teaming and, 161
Administrative skills (of project
    manager), 206–207
"Aggressor" (employee role), 236
America Online, Inc. (AOL), 31
Ambiguity, 289
American Productivity and Quality
    Center (APQC), 82, 83, 90, 91–92,
    115–116
Analytic hierarchy process (AHP), 5–6
    for project selection and prioritization,
        39, 43
Anderson's law, 298

Anxiety, 270–271, 342
Applications Pathway gate, 102, 104
Appraisals:
    performance, 382
    project work assignment, 372–374
Apple, H.P., 220, 240
Approved suppliers, 393
Argyis, Chris, 252
Archibald, Russell, D., 200–201, 225, 282
Assignments, work:
    mutual accountability and individual, 522–523
Audit, of current process, 104
Authoritarian communication style, 292
Authorization document, 26
Authority, 262
    communications bottlenecks, involving, 295–296
    effect of staffing methods on, 150–151
    project, 254–262
Autocratic leadership, 276
Avoiding, 356
AXA/Equitable Financial, 47

Balance:
    in new product development portfolio, 107,108,109,114–116,123–128
    in ranking, 38–39
    portfolio, 25, 66–67
    resource, risk and, 25, 62–63
Balanced scorecard approach, 23–24, 38–39
    for new product development, 117, 122–125
Base pay, 378
Basic needs, 251
BCG Strategy Model, 123, 125
Behavioral norms:
    building mutual accountability and, 520–521
Behaviors, changes in, 433
Behavioral relationships, 275–276

Behavioral school of management, 248
Below the line. *See* Resourced, not resourced vs
Benchley's law, 298
Benefits:
    evaluating and ranking, 23, 24, 25, 38–39
    of transformation projects, 69
    prequalification for, 58–61
Best practices:
    in Stage-Gate framework, 83–84, 86–88
Blanchard, Kenneth, 274–275
"Blocker" (employee role), 237
Boeing, 396–397
Bok's law, 298
Boling's postulate, 298
Bonuses, 383
Bounding box approach, 27, 30–31
Bread-and-butter projects, 125–127
Brook's first law, 298
Brook's second law, 298
Brown's law of business success, 298
Bubble diagrams, 6, 39, 113–114, 115, 123–128, 129
Buckets, 6, 39, 113–114, 115, 123–128, 129
Bucket-keepers, 518 *See also Two-bucket inventory*
Budget at Completion (BAC), 28, 75–76, 77, 78
Budgeted Cost of Work Performed (BCWP),
    see also Earned Value (EV), 22–29, 76–77, 78
    See also Planned Value (PV)
Budgeted Cost of Work Scheduled (BCWS) 28–29, 76, 77–78
    See also Planned Value (PV)
Buffers, 447, 449
Burnout, 341
Business analysis, 6–7
Business case, 49, 62
    building, in Stage-Gate framework, 83–84, 95–96

Business objectives, *See* Objectives,
business, Strategic alignment,
Strategic plan; Strategy
Business planning, project portfolio
management, and, 6–7, 34–35
Business position, 123, 125
Business Week, 462
Byrne, John, 462

Capacity planning, 424–425, 428
C/S Solutions, 67–68
Case Studies:
    Conflict in Project Management,
        363–368
    Leadership Effectiveness, 317–328
    Mayer Manufacturing, 361–362
    Motivational questionnaire, 328–334
    Reluctant Workers, 344
    Telstar International, 362–363
    Trophy Project, 315–317
Cash flow, 24–25, 34, 35, 127–128
Ceiling price, 417
Chain of command, 291
Change:
    resistance to, 196
    uncertainty and, 63
Change initiatives, 492
Changepoint, 45
Charters, 473
    outcome-based performance goals and,
        491–492
    problems with mutual accountability
        and, 523–524
    small-group performance and, 468
    work sessions / meetings and, 511
Charters: governance, 33–34
    projects, 26
Chatrooms:
    groupwork technology and, 485
    practical pointers, 535
Checklists, popularity and effectiveness
    of, 128, 129
Chief executive officer (CEO), 16, 32
    responsibilities of, 33, 48, 50
    See also Senior executives,

Chief financial officer (CFO), 16, 32
Chief information officer (CIO):
    in project portfolio management
        governance, 16, 32–33
    in traditional project management
        organizations, 12, 14
Chief operating officer (COO), 16, 17, 32
Chief project officer (CPO):
    in project portfolio management
        governance, 16
    in traditional project management, 36
    organizations, 12, 14
Chisholm's second law, 298
Chrysler, 394, 101
Cicero, J.P. 210, 273, 281
"Clarifer" (employee role), 238
Clarity, 7, 45–46
Classical management, 219, 248
Cleland, David I., 228, 240, 256–257,
    266, 281–282, 286–287, 336
Clustering:
    definition of, 508
Cobra, 44–45
Code of Professional Conduct, 390
Cohn's law, 299
Collective decision-making, 251
Collective work products:
    attributes of, 517
    co-location and, 532
    explanation of, 474
    face-to-face participation and,
        536–537
    group performance and, 473–474
    groupwork technology and, 531–532
    outcome-based goals and, 495–497
    required, 475
    steering committees and, 475
Co-location:
    collective work products and, 532
    explanation of, 532
Combative communication style, 294
Commands, direct, vs. intent, 461–462
Commercialization, 84–85, 97–98, 99
Commitment(s):
    of team members, 267, 269

Common cause variations, 439
Common, compromise and consensus vs.: groupwork technology and, 532–533
Communications:
    formal leader and importance of, 469–470
    groupwork technology and increased, 530–531
    importance of allowing more than one means of, 485
    improving, example of 494–495
    in project management, 34–35, 68
    in Stage-Gate process, 104–105
    performance agendas and, 505
    small group performance and, 463, 468
    with gorilla projects, 68
    with senior executives, 34–35, 39–40, 41, 48, 50
Communication(s), 285–297
    and listening, 292
    and team development, 267, 270–271
    as network of channels, 285
    barriers to, 286–291, 296–297
    bottlenecks in, 295–296
    effective, 285, 290–291
    environment for, 288–289
    filtering of, 297
    functional application of, 289
    patterns of, 286
    policy for, 293
    receiving of, 288
    steps for effective, 291
    styles of, 292, 294
    techniques for improving, 291
    with customers, 210, 287
    with visual aids, 290
    written, 290
Communications management, 290
Company, responsibilities to, 391–392
Compaq, 410, 418
Compaq-HP merger. See Hewlett-Packard (HP)
Compensation, 377–383

and base pay, 378
and job classification, 377–378
and performance appraisals, 378–382
bonuses, 383
merit increases, 383
Competence, 389
Competency models, 425–427
Competitive product analysis, 88, 90, 94, 95, 111–112
Compromise, groupwork technology and, 532–533
Compromising, 355
Compromise units, 472
    definition of, 467–468
    development of, 493
    explanation of, 493
    poor performance and, 468
Computer IT Governance by Changepoint, 45–46
Concept tests, 88, 90, 95–96
Concerto (software), 448
Conciliatory communication style, 292
Conflict:
    between projects, 174
Conflict(s), 345–356
    and project objectives, 346–347
    between line and project managers, 281–282
    classification of, 351–353
    intensity of, 351–353
    meaningful, 348
    most common types of, 347–348
    personality, 348
    realitive intensity of, 348
    reasons for occurrence of, 349–350
    schedule, 348
    within project teams, 265
Conflicts of interest, 390–391
Conflict in Project Management (case study), 363–368
Conflict management/resolution
    confrontation meetings for, 353–354
    and establishment of priorities, 349–350
    methods of, 350–351

modes of, 351, 352, 354–356
  problems arising during, 282
  project manager and, 204–205
  role of project managers in, 348–349
Confrontation meetings, 353–354
Connolly's law of cost control, 299
"Consensus taker" (employee role) 238
Consensus, groupwork technology and,
  532–533
Consultants, 226
Consultants, groupwork technology and,
  528–529
Constraints: expected commercial value
  (ECV) and, 122
  productivity index and, 118, 121, 122
  project selection and, 24–25, 118, 121,
  122
  See also Theory of constraints
Constraints theory of, 432
Contingencies, 74–75
Continuous improvement, 419–423
Controling, 249
Cooke's law, 299
Cooper, R. G., 29–30, 105–106, 130
Cooperative cultures, 386
Coordinating, 250
Core group member, partial contributor
  vs., 535–536
Corning, 394
Cornuell's law, 299
Corporate Culture, morality/ethics and,
  386–389
Cost-benefit analyses, 202
Cost escalation, 71, 73
Cost performance analysis:
  earned value analysis (EVA) for, 28,
  29, 31, 41–42, 75–79
  traditional, 77–79
  See also Earned value analysis (EVA)
Cost measurable success and, 496
Cost Performance Index (CPI), 77, 78
Cost/Schedule Control Systems, Criteria
  (C/SCSC), 75–76
Cost Variance (CV), 29, 41, 76–77,
  78–79

Counseling, 250
Courtois's rule, 299
Credibility, unrealistic expectations and,
  509
Critical Chain Project Management,
  431–457
  and behavioral changes, 433
  and multitasking, 445–447
  and Theory of Constraints, 432
  as extension of critical path network
  448–450
  buffer management in, 493–494
  (CCPM), 42–43, 68
  definition of, 432
  Elbit Systems Ltd. (case study),
  453–456
  Lucent Technologies (case study),
  451–453
  project execution in, 444–445
  project protection in, 438–442
  Seagate Technology (case study),
  456–457
  task estimates in, 433–437
  task execution in, 437–438
  task times in, 438–440
  with multiple projects, 445–448
Critical path method (CPM), 176
  see also Network
Critical path scheduling (CPM) tools and
  techniques, 28, 42–43, 67–68, 79
Cross-functional problem solving,
  505–506
Cross-functional teams, 504
  at AOL, in Stage-Gate framework, 84,
  90–91, 95–96, 104
Culture:
  for excising poor projects, 49
  guidelines for 49–50
Currency exchange rate risk, 71, 73
Customers communication with, 210,
  296–297
  unethical/immoral requests by, 386–387
Customer relations management (CRM),
  43–44
Customer review meetings, 295

Daily calendar log, 339
Daily meetings, 290
Dashboards, 39–40
Data presentation tools, 39–41, 44
    See also Tools (software)
Davis, Keith, 242
Davis, S., 359
Deadlines, SMART goals and, 497–498
Debate, first law of, 299
Decision analysis methodologies, 39
Decision points, for gorilla projects,
    67–68
Decision making: factors contributing to
    mutual accountability, 520–521
    by teams, 271
    formal leader vs. team leaders, 471
    inappropriate influences on, 391
    styles of, 276
    work products vs., 475
Decision theory school of management,
    248
Decoding, 287
De facto authority, 262
De jure authority, 262
Delay, project, 16, 19–20
Delegation and directing, 249
    and overtime, 336
    factors affecting, 261
Deliverables, in Stage-Gate, 85–86
Deployment, 109–110, 111–113
Deming, W. Edwards, 439–444
Democratic leadership, 276
Department of Defense, (DOD), 394,
    398, 399
Dependencies, task, 435
Depression, 341
Detailed investigation stage, 102, 104
Development funnels, 86–88
Development stage, 84–85, 96–97, 99,
    101
Development stage, resource allocation
    by, 114–115
"Devil's advocate" (employee role),
    236
Diminishing float or slack, 28

Directing, 249–254
    and hierarchy of needs, 251–252
    and motivation, 250–254
    and professional needs, 253
    and Theory X/Theory Y, 250–251
    difficulty of, 250
    steps of, 249–250
Discipline:
    building mutual accountability and,
        521–522
    three-dimensional, 461
    See also Single-leader discipline,
        Team discipline
Discovery stage, 84, 92–94
Disillusionment, 341–342
Display methods, of portfolio balances,
    123, 125–128
    of project selection data, 40–41
    See also Documentation Reporting
Disruptive communication style, 294
Disruptive technologies, 101
Document management:
    assigning monitoring / guiding roles
        and, 537–538
    bias toward single-leader discipline,
        533–534
    groupwork technology and, advantages
        of, 486–487
Documentation, 104–106
    procedural, 414–418
    See also display methods; Reporting
Documentation of project manager's
    authority, 261
Document sharing: netiquette and ,
    536–537
    virtual teaming and , 481, 482
DOD, *see* Department of Defense
Doing, managing vs., 283–284
"Dominator" (employee role), 236
Donsen's law, 299
Douglas's law of practical aeronautics, 299
Drum resources, 446–447
Dual accountability, 377
Dude's law of duality, 299
DuPont, 394

Early adopters, 5

Earned Value, (EV), 76, 77, 78
  See also Budgeted Cost of Work
    Performed (BCWP)

Earned Value analysis, (EVA), 16, 54
  applications of, 75–76, 79
  baseline for, 39, 75–76
  for project performance evaluation,
    28–29, 31, 41–42
  glossary of terms, 27–28
  primer on, 75–79
  software tools for, 41, 42–43, 44–45
  summarization in, 78–79

Earned value management, 75

EBIT, (earnings before interest and
    taxes), 118

Economists' laws, 299

Education, 395–397

Efficiency: in Stage-Gate framework,
  91

Efficient Frontier, 39, 40

Eli, Lilly, 426

Elbit Systems Ltd. (ESL) (case study),
  453–456

Electronic data dissemination, increased
    communications and, 530–531

E-mail:
  assigning monitoring/guiding roles
    and, 537–538
  bias toward single-leader discipline,
    533–534
  groupwork technology and, 151, 485
  increased communications and,
    530–531
  netiquette and, 536–537
  virtual work and, 482, 483

Emotional exhaustion, 341

Empirical school of management, 248

Employees :
  assignment of responsibilities to, 230
  evaluation of, 279–280
  hard-nosed tactics with, 209
  performance measurement with,
    370–377
  problems with, 279–282

project manager and performance of,
    278
  readiness of, 275
  "roles" of, 236–238
  "star", 230
  training new, 233, 234

Encoding, 284, 287

"Encourager" (employee role), 238

End-of-phase review meetings, 429

Enhancement projects. *See* Growth or
    enhancement projects

Enterprise project management (EPM),
    3, 10–11
  project portfolio management *verses*,
    15

Enterprise resource-planning (ERP)
    systems, 17, 37, 42–44, 45

Enterprise services automation (ESA),
    43–44, 45–46

Entrepreneurial skills (of project
    manager), 206

Environment(s):
  communications, 288–289
  dynamic project, 265, 268
  for conflict, 347–350
  problems in project, 279
  staffing, 196–198

Erickson, T.J., 107

Ericsson, 410, 418

ESL Case Study, *See* Elbit Systems LTD.
    (case study)

Esteem, 252

Estimates:
  accountability for, 438
  of tasks (Critical Chain), 433–437

Ethics, 386–389

Ethical communication style, 292

Evaluation, *See* Performance evaluation;
    Project selection

Evaluations, employee, 370–377
  and program managers, 207
  and projects as means to meeting
    goals, 431
  and project office, 228
  and project team, 229

Evaluations, employee, (*continued*)
  as project managers, 208
  selection of project manager by,
      198–202
  support of, for teams, 267–268, 270
Exhaustion, 341
Expectancy theory, 252
Export power, 263
External partnerships, 393–394
External suppliers, 393
Event (s):
  definition, 187–190
  interface, control of, 190, 192
Etiquette, groupwork technology and,
      485
Excercises:
  assessing and reacting, 478–479
  collective work products, co-location
      and, 539–540
  complexity of the challenge,
      determining the, 512–513
  conferencing and chatrooms, 489
  converting vision into SMART
      outcome-based goals, 514
  customized training, 489
  desired outcomes, testing
      understanding of, 525
  discipline, choosing a, 501
  document management,489
  experience, learning from, 476
  experience with, 487–488
  face-to-face sessions, 539
  for assessing outcomes, 525
  groupware determining use of,
      487–488
  guide for guides, 540
  identifying, 524
  individual vs. collective work
      products, 501
  language, evaluating, 525
  matching performance challenges to
      disciplines, 479–480
  meetings, preparing for, 515
  metrics, 500
  netiquette, 538–539

new member introduction, 538–539
  outcomes vs. activities, 499–500
  performance agendas, creating and
      using, 514
  performance requirements,
      determining, 479
  recasting collective work products as
      individual work products,
      524–525
  role definition and access, 538
  SMART, 500–501
  sub-challenges, identifying, 514
  success, recognizing, 499–500
  suiting the meeting to the purpose, 525
  threaded discussions, 488
  understanding, testing, 476–477
  virtual meetings, preparing for, 515
  virtual team, identifying a, 487
  vision, articulating a, 513–514
Execution:
  of project portfolio management,
      32–35
  quality of, 88–90
Executive dashboards, 39–40
Executives guide to PPM, 7
Expected commercial value, (ECV),
      121–122
Experiments, performance agendas and,
      511
Expert Choices, 45–46
ExxonMobil Chemicals, 99, 101, 102

Facilitating communication style, 292
Facilitators:
  assigning monitoring/guiding roles for
      virtual work and, 537
  exercises independent of, 465
  performance problems and, 491–492
Failure, project:
  causes of, 3–4, 88
  in new product development, 81–82,
      88
  project selection and rates of, 81–82
Familiarity matrix bubble diagram,
      113–114

Fax, virtual teaming and, 481
Flaming, netiquette and, 537
Feasibility studies, 202
Feeding Buffers, 440, 442, 443
Field trials, 97–98
Filtering, 292
Financial analysis:
    for new product development, 94–95,
        96, 97, 98, 117–123, 125
    in Stage-Gate framework, 94–95, 96,
        97, 98
    popularity versus effectiveness of,
        127–130
    See also Earned value analysis (EVA),
        Expected commercial value
        (ECV), Net
present value, (NVP), Return on
    Investment (ROI)
Financial officers, 16–17, 32–33
Financial reports, 34–35
Financial valuation techniques, 5–6, 23,
    38
    See also Earned value analysis (EVA),
        Expected commercial value
        (ECV), Net value, (NVP), Return
        on Investment (ROI)
    Net Present value (NPV), Return on
        investment (ROI)
First law of debate, 299
First-year sales metrics, 92
Fleming, Q. W., 75–76
Float, 28
Focus:
    in Stage-Gate framework 86–88
Forcasting, 7, 16–17, 34–35
Forcing, 356
Formal authority-oriented leadership
    techniques, 274
Formal leader:
    building mutual accountability and,
        523–524
    duties of, 469–470
    single-leader discipline and, 463
French, J.R.P., 379
Front-end analysis, 396

Functional managers, *see* Line
    manager(s)
Functional organizations, 197
Future, the project managers in, 212–213
Fyffe's axiom, 299

Gaddis, Paul O., 313
Galbraith, Jay R., 264
Gates: Applications Pathway, 102, 104
    criteria, 85–86, 87, 88
    flexible, 91–92
    format of, 85–86
    for new product development,
        116–117
    Gate 1 (Idea Screen), 94–95
    Gate 2 (Second Screen), 95
    Gate 3 (Go to Development), 95–97
    Gate 4 (Go to Testing), 97
    Gate 5 (Go to Launch), 97–99
    overview of, 82–83, 84–92
Gate-based approaches, *See* Stage-Gate
    process
"Gate keeper: (employee role), 238
Gatekeepers, assigning
    monitoring/guiding roles for virtual
    work and, 537
Gatekeepers, 86–87, 102, 104
Gate meetings, 86
General Electric, 535
Geographical mix, 113–114, 115
Gifts, acceptance of, 391
Go/kill decision points, 84–92, 116–117,
    128–129
    See also Gates
Goals:
    building mutual accountability and,
        523
    collective vs. individual work
        products, 475
    cost, 494
    financial, 464
    formal leader and setting, 469–470
    groupwork technology and, advantages
        of, 487
    individual vs. collective, 471–472

Goals (*continued*)
  performance, problems articulating,
    463–464
  revenue, 493–494
  setting aggressive but achievable, 497
  SMART and, 497, 504–505
  See also Activity based goals;
    Outcome based goals
Goldratt, Eliyahu, 432, 436, 446
Golub's laws of computerdom, 299
Gorilla projects, 66–69
  See also Transformation projects
Governance:
  overview of, 16–17, 32–33, 34–35, 36,
    49
  participants in, 16–17, 32–33, 36
  project portfolio life span and, 14
  See also Information technology (IT)
    project governance
Governance council or team:
composition of, 16–17
  defined, 19–20
  project management office
    coordination with, 33–35
  project pipeline maintenance and,
    29–30, 31
  project prequalification and, 57, 58
  project selection and, 22–23, 48
  roles and responsibilities of, 33–34, 35
Gresham's law, 299
Grinnell, S.K., 222, 240
Groupware, *See* Groupwork technology
Groupwork technology:
  challenges of difficulty in keeping
    conversations private, 527–528
  discipline, 533–534
  drawbacks of, 462
  e-mail proliferation, 485, 527
  endangering performance as a team,
    527–528
  expanded access, 527–530
  explanation of, 481–484
  key features and functionality of,
    484–487

participation and communication,
  530–533
positive and negative effects bias
  toward single-leader team
  performance and, 464–465
Growth or enhancement projects:
  prequalification of, 59–60
  prioritization of, 66–67
Gullett, C.Ray, 223, 241
GTE, 114–115

Handoff, 90–91
Hard-nosed tactics, 209
Hardware, *See* Groupwork technology
"Harmonizer" (employee role), 238
Hawthorne experiments, 5–6
Hersey, Paul, 274–275
Herzberg, Frederick, 252
Hewlett-Packard (HP),
  Compaq merger with, 30, 47
Hierarchy(ies) of needs, 251–252
Hierarchy: building mutual
  accountability, 519–520
  division of labor and individual
    accountability, 518
Hierarchical referral, 350–351
Histograms, 127–128
Hoare's law of large programs, 300
Hodgetts, Richard M., 273–274, 306
Homework, in Stage-Gate framework,
  90, 94–95, 99, 101
Honeywell, 112–113
Hopeless, felling, 342
Human relations-oriented leadership
  techniques, 274
Human Resources, misuse of teams by,
  462
Hygiene factors, 252
Hypotheses, performance agendas and,
  505

IBM, 397
I-rule, 518–519, 522
Idea screen, 94–95

Idea-to-launch framework, 82–106
See also Stage-Gate process
Ideas:
    channels for, 94
    generating and capturing, 92–94
Implementation, of project portfolio
        management, 46, 47–51
    checklist for, 48, 49, 50
Implementation, performance agendas
    and, 505
In-house product tests, 97–98
Incompetency, 222
Incremental product changes, 114–116
Individual accountability, 463, 464, 473
    formal leader and , 470
    integration and, 518
    reengineering teams and, 506
    single-leader disciplines and, 472
    technology and, 533–534
    See also Single-leader discipline
Individual work products:
    activity-based goals and, 495–496
    explanation of, 474–475
    group performance and, 473
    groupwork technology and, 531–532
    technology and, 533–534
Influence, 391
"Information giver" (employee role),
    238
"Information seeker" (employee role),
    237
Information synthesis, 481
Information system support:
    for project portfolio management,
        16–17
    for Stage-Gate process, 104–106
    See also Tools
Information technology (IT)businesses:
    CIO in, 32–33
    project portfolio management
        governance in, 33
    tools for, 45, 46
Information technology (IT) project
    governance, 16–17, 32 33

Infrastructure support processes, 16–17,
    49–50
Initiative plans, 500
"Initiator: (employee role), 237
Innovation, product. *See* New product
    development
Input / output analysis, 187–189
Integration:
    areas of, 34–35
    project portfolio management for, 3–4,
        36, 42
    project portfolio management tools
        and, 42–46
    resistance to, 518
    single-leader / team disciplines and,
        467–468
Intent, direct commands vs., 461–462
Interdependencies between and within
    projects, 177
Interface(s):
    agreements, 186
    communicating, 192
    event, scheduling, 191–192
    events, types of, 190
    event control, 192
    event definition, 188–190
    event documentation, 190–191
    event identification, 188–190
    management, 185–193
    performance, 187–189
    physical, 187–189
    product, 188–189
    project, 189–190
Internet:
    content vs. status, 530–531
    virtual teaming and, 481–482
    See also Chatrooms
Integrated product/project teams (IPTs),
    394, 397–399
Integrity, 389
Internal partnerships, 392–393
International projects, exchange rate risk
    in, 71, 73
Interpersonal Influences, 262–265

Intimidating communication style, 294
Intranet, virtual teaming and, 481–482
Inventory: of existing projects, 47–48
Investment portfolios, 25, 38, 61
Involvement:
    in project portfolio management,
        16–17, 32–33
    in traditional project management,
        32–33
    See also Participants; Senior
        executives
Issawi's law of cynics, 300
Iterative product development, 96–97
ITT Industries, 113

Jaeger, A.M., 251
Japan, 251
Job classification, 377–378
Job descriptions, 280, 377–378
Job reassignment, 218
Johnson's first law, 300
Joint accountability *See* Mutual
    accountability
Judicial communication style, 292

Karger, D.W., 259
Katzenbach, Jon, 506
Katzenbach Partners LLC, 483
Kay, E., 380
Kendall, Gerald, I., 431–432
Kerzner, Harold, 286–287, 336, 426
Killer variables, 95
Killian, William, P., 226–227, 282
King, William Richard, 256–257, 266,
    281–282
KISS rule, 250
Knock-out questions, 86
KPMG Peat Marwick, groupwork
    technology and, 483–484

Language: building discipline and,
    518–519
    cultural barriers and, 162–163
    indicators, 528
Laissez-faire leadership, 276

Large projects, 385–386
Launch-Commercialization stage, 84–85,
    97–98
Laws, management, 297–300
Lawson, 45–46
Lawrence, P., 359
Leadership, 273–279
    by project manager, 203–204,
        264–265, 273–274, 277–279
    definition of, 273
    elements of, 273
    life-cycle, 274–277
    of team, 265, 269
    organizational impact of, 277–279
    techniques for, 273–274
    See Governance; Governance council
        or team
Leadership Effectiveness (case studies),
    317–328
Learning, 395–397
Legitimate power, 262
Leon, Raymond O., 308
Levine, H.A., 10
Life-cycle leadership, 274–277
Limited resource re-scheduling, 177–178
Limits, 26, 27, 30–31
Linear responsibility charts (LRCs),
    256–261
Line manager(s) authority of, 255–256
    and communications policy, 293
    and employee evaluations, 370–371,
        373–374
    and project managers, 218, 281–282,
        392–393
    and project office personnel, 226–227
    and selection of project staff, 230
    and training of employees, 233
    communication traps between project
        managers and, 297
    leadership by, 209
    multiple responsibilities of, 234–235
    viewpoints of project managers, vs.,
        266
Listening, 292
Logical task dependency, 435

Lucent Technologies (case study),
110–111, 451–453

Make Success Measurable!, 493,
494–495n1
outcome-based performance goals and,
492–493
Maintenance or utility projects:
prequalification of, 58–60
prioritization of, 66–67
Maintenance phase. *See* Project pipeline
maintenance
Malek's law, 300
Management of buffers, 443–444
classical, 219, 248
communications, 234
schools of, 248
Management:
interface, 185–192
Management-by-exception, 30–31, 79
Management-by-objective (MBO), 347,
377
Management. *See* Operations
management; Project management;
Project pipeline maintenance
Management pitfalls, 282–284
Management policies and procedures,
300–302
Management proverbs and laws, 297–300
Manager of project management,
139–140, 141–147, 167
Market attractiveness, 123, 125
Market function involvement, 16–17,
34–35
Market newness, 125, 126, 127
Market orientation, 88–90
Market research, 88, 90, 94–95, 111–112
Market tests, 88, 90, 97–98
Market trends assessment, 111–112
Maslow, Abraham, 251
Maslow's hierarchy of needs, 252
Master schedule, 165
Mausner, B., 252
Matrix, management, 140–141
task responsibility, 154–155

Maturity, 275, 276
of project manager, 208–209
Mayer Manufacturing (case study),
361–362
McGregor, Douglas, 250
McKinsey-GE model, 123, 125
McKinsey Rapid Response Team, 483,
533
Meaningful conflict, 348
Measurement, success, 496–497
Measurement:
factors in, 26, 40, 41
See also Performance evaluation;
Performance metrics
Meetings: 290
building mutual accountability, 523
confrontation, 353–354
effective, 294
end-of-phase review meetings, 429
face-to-face, 535–536
one-on-one discussions and, 523
portfolio review, 86
preparing for, 510–511
project review, 294–295
unproductive, 297
Mega projects, 385–386
Mercedes Benz star method for resource
allocation, 112–113
Mercury Interactive, 45–46
Mergers, 29–30, 31
See also Hewlett-Packard (HP)
Merit increases, 383
Methodologies, project management,
418–419, 428–429
Metrics:
as indicators of mutual accountability,
522
assigning monitoring /guiding roles
and, 537
choosing a discipline and, 496–497
groupwork technology and, advantages
of, 487
relevance of, 497–498
Meyer, H. H., 379
Microsoft Access, 45–46

Microsoft Project, 44–45, 46
Milestones, 29–30, 96–97
Miner, John B., 280–281
Mr. Cooper's law, 299
Monte Carlo techniques, 42–43, 67–68, 122
Monthly meetings, 290
Moore, G. A., 66–67, 68, 69
Morality, 386–389
Motivation, 222, 249–254
Motivational Questionnaire (case study), 328–334
Motorola, 394, 410, 418
Multiple projects(s):
    central planning for, 178–179
    large versus small, 176
    management, 175–177
    managing, 428–429
    objectives, 164
    operations planning and control, 178–181
Multiproject Critical Chain, 445–448
Multitasking, 436, 445–447
Murdick, R.G., 259
Must-meet criteria, 86, 94–95, 96–97, 102, 104
Mutual accountability, 463, 464, 473
    building a sense of, 518
    clear performance outcomes and, 518–519
    groupware technology and, 532–533
    indicators of, 521–522
    handling failures and setbacks, 519
    language and, 518–519
    recognition and reward, 518–519
    red flags and, 523–524
    recognizing, 521–522
    resistance to integration, 517–518
    team discipline and, 472, 517
    things to avoid, 519–522
    See Also Team discipline

Netiquette, 536–537
Net-present value (NVP):
    in Stage-Gate framework, 95–96

probability-adjusted, 122
productivity index based on, 118, 121, 122
project prequalification for, 59–60
project selection for, 38, 39, 117–121
risk and, 62–63
Network:
    based planning and control systems, 176
Networks of channels, 285
New product development (NPD):
    best practices for, 86–92
    defined, 81
    failure rate of, 81–82
    financial analysis for, 94–95,96, 97, 98, 117–123, 125
    portfolio balance in, 114–116
    portfolio reviews in, 116, 117, 118–128
    project portfolio management for, 81, 106–130
    Stage-Gate process for, 29–31, 81, 82–106, 110–111
    strategic portfolio development for, 128, 129
    technology and technology platform, 99, 101, 102, 104, 113–114, 115
    types of, 113–114, 115, 116, 127
    uncertainty in, 63–64
New-to-the-business products, 115–116
New-to-the-world products, 115–116
Newness:
    bubble diagram of, 125, 126, 127
    dimensions of, 125, 126, 127
    levels of, 113–114, 115, 116
Niku, 45–46
Noise, 289
Nonreciprocal laws of expectations, 299
Nortel, 410, 418

Objectives
    characteristics of good, 346
    management-by-objective, 347
    unclear, 265 , 267

Objectives, business:
  project management for, 16, 19–20,
    27–31, 34
  strategic new product development
    and, 27–28
  traditional project management and,
    12–13
  See also Strategic plan; Strategy
Objectives, project:
  project management for, 15–16,
    27–28
Old Engineer's law, 299
On-the-spot decision making, 295
On-time performance metrics, 92
Open Plan, 44–45
Operations management:
  in project portfolio management
    governance, 16–17
  project portfolio management as
    bridge for, 11–13, 54–55, 56
  project portfolio management as hub
    for, 54–57
  roles and responsibilities of, 12,
    54–55
Operations planning and control,
  178–183
Opportunity management:
  tools for, 37, 38–39, 43–44
Oracle, 45
Organization:
  matrix, 140–141
  of program/project management
    function (*see* Project
    management)
  of project participants, 148, 150 (*see
    also* Project office)
  of project support services (*see* Project
    office)
  relationships, 154–155
Organization breakdown structures
  (OBS), 69
Organization(s) impact of leadership on,
  277–279
Organization, performance agendas and,
  505

Organization, project portfolio
    management:
  execution and, 32–35
  overview of, 16–17
  See also Governance; Governance
    council
Organizational chart, project, 230–233
Organizational skills, (of project
    manager) 206
Ouchi, William G., 251
Outcome-based goals, 464, 465, 473
  activity based vs., 491–492, 493–494
  articulating, 493–495
  changing activity-based goal to,
    494–495
  examples of, 493
  SMART, 495–499, 504
Outputs, of gates, 85–86
Outsourcing, 393
Overtime, 336
Oyster projects, 125, 126, 127

Pairwise comparisons, 39, 43–44
Palisade, 67–68
Parallel processing, 90–91
Parameters, critical:
  establishing, 26, 30–31
  for high-uncertainty projects, 30–31
  for pre-existing projects, 47–48
  for project prequalification, 58–61
  measuring, 26, 27, 28–29, 30–31,
    47–48
  tools for controlling, 40–41
  updating, 29–30, 40–41, 42, 47, 48
Partial contributor, core group member
  vs., 535–536
Participants:
  hierarchical levels of, 32–33
  in project portfolio management,
    32–33
  in Stage-Gate process, 104–105
  in traditional project management,
    32–33
  See also involvement, Senior
    executives

Participative leadership, 276
Partnerships external, 393–394
 internal, 392–393
 strategic, 394
Part-time project managers, 208
Patton's law, 300
Payback criteria, 118
Pay classes/grades, 226–227, 230, 378
Pearl projects, 125, 126, 127
Penalty conditions, 71, 73
PeopleSoft, 45, 46
Penalty power, 263
People skills, task skills, vs, 284
Perception barriers to communication, 286
Performance agenda, 463–464
 applying both disciplines and, 503–506
 articulating team aspirations, 506–507
 choosing the best discipline, 510
 converting challenges in SMART goals, 508
 deciding which challenges to staff, 508–509
 example of, 507
 identifying required contributions, 508
 monitoring performance, 510
 patterns in, 503–505
 preparing for work sessions and, 510–512
 resourced vs. not resourced, 509–510
 steps toward the initial, 506
 turning aspirations into sub-challenges, 508
Performance appraisals, 378–382
Performance challenges, examples of, 475–476
Performance dashboards, 39–40
Performance evaluation, earned value analysis (EVA) for, 28–29, 31, 41–42, 75–79
 factors in, 26, 40–41
 financial reporting and, 34–35

guidelines for, 49–50
 in maintenance phase, 16, 26–31, 40–42
 in traditional project management organizations, 12–13
 of pre-existing projects, 47–48
 process of, techniques of, 16
 techniques of, 16
 tools for, 40–42
 uncertainty and, 64–66
 also Project pipeline maintenance
Performance measurement with employees, 370–377
 with project managers, 380–381
 with project personnel, 382
Performance metrics:
 in Stage-Gate framework, 91–92
Performance, personnel, 196, 278–279
Performance plans, personal, 494
Performance results, communication and, 494
Performance statements, examples of, 491–492
Performance units *See* Teaming performance vs.
Permissiveness, 222
Personality conflicts, 348
Personnel, *see* Staffing
Personal values, 280–281
PERT approach, 42–43
Pertmaster, 67–68
Peter's Prognosis, 300
Phased baselining, 30
Phases:
 of project portfolio management, 15–16, 19–20, 36–37
 See also Project pipeline maintenance;
  Project selection; Stage-Gate process,
 Stages
Physical exhaustion, 341
Physiological needs, 251
Pie charts, 127–128
Pilot production, 97–99
Pilot program, 48, 50

Pipelining. *See* Project pipeline maintenance, Project pipelining
Planned Value (PV), 76, 77, 78
See also Budgeted Cost of Work Scheduled (BCWS)
Planning. *See* Business planning, Investment planning; Portfolio planning
Project planning; Schedule planning, Strategic plan, Tactical plans
Planning by project manager, 205–206, 213–214
Plan View, 45–46
Platform projects, 99, 101, 102–104, 113–114, 115
POs, *see* Project offices
Policy:
  communications, 293
  conflict-resolution, 350–351
  management, 300–302
  personnel, 197
Political erosion, law of, 300
Portfolio management. *See* Project portfolio management
Portfolio maps, 123, 125, 128–129
Portfolio planning, 6–7
See also Project selection and prioritization
Portfolio reviews, in new product development, 116, 117, 118–128
See also Performance evaluation
Postlaunch review, 92, 98–99
Power, 262–265
Positive yields, measurable success and, 496
Precedence Diagram Method (PDM), 189
"Predictability" of a system, 439
Preferred suppliers, 393
Prequalification. *See* Project prequalification
Pretesting, 97–98
Price ceiling:
  in smaller companies, 385
Primavera, 46

Priorities:
  conflict resolution and establishment of, 349–350
  factors influencing, 172–173
  of projects, 172–174
  project, 428
  rules, 173–174
Prioritization decision points, 85–86
See Project selection and prioritization
PRISMS for IT Governance and Resource Management, 46
Process manager, 104–105
Problem-solving by management, 278
Procedures, management, 300–302
ProChain (software), 448
Procedural documentation, 414–418
Process mapping, performance agendas and, 504–505
Process work. *See* Project work
Produceability, 429
Product:
  interfaces, 188–190
Product definition, 90
Product Development and Management Association (PDMA), 82, 83
Product lines, 113–114
Product profitability metrics, 92
Product road map, 109–112
Product superiority, 87–88
Productivity index, 118, 119–122
Professional services automation (PSA), 4, 43–44, 45–46
Professionalism, 389
Professional needs, 253
Profiles groupwork technology and advantages of people, 486
Program:
  managing, 174–175
Programs, problems with team training, 492
Program Evaluation and Review Technique (PERT), 176
see also Network
Progressive evaluation, 481

Project(s)
  mega, 385–386
  organizational chart for, 230–233
Project Buffer, 440, 442, 443
Project charter, 26
Project charter authority, 262
Project-driven organizations, 197
Projects(s):
  approved list, 191
  communication systems, selection,
    168–169
  coordination list, 190–191
  factors affecting, 172–173
  high-uncertainty, 30–31, 63
  identification, 189–190
  information systems, selection,
    169–170
  interface(s), 151–152, 186
  management, 185–192
  mega, 385–386
  models, 173
  multiple (*see* Multiple project(s)
  multiproject, 163
  objectives, defining, multiproject,
    163–164
  office, 147–151
  organizational chart for, 230–233
  portfolio types, 164–165
  priorities, 164–165, 172–174
  project manager responsibilities, 167
  resource management, 177–178
  revision list, 191
  rules, 173–174
  schedule(s), 165
  selection, 167–171
  selection, new product, 170–171
  selection of, 198–202, 208–211
  skill requirements for, and stress,
    340–342
  sponsor, 167
  staffing of, 147–148
  successful, 197
  taskforce, 141
  types of, 20–21, 53–54, 58, 66–67,
    113–114, 115, 116, 127

Project life cycle, 26, 30
Project managager(s):
  administrative skills of, 206–207
  and communications policy, 293
  and conflict resolution, 348–349
  and employee evaluations, 307–373
  and line managers, 218, 281–282,
    392–393
  and project authority, 254–262
  and risk, 281
  and stress, 340–342
  assigning monitoring / guiding roles
    and, 537–538
  availability of, 209
  bias toward single-leader discipline,
    533–534
  communication traps between line
    managers and, 297
  conflict resolution skills of, 204–205
  controlling function of, 249
  Critical Chain, 431–457
  directing function of, 249–254
  duties of, 213–217
  employees, problems with, 279–282
  entrepreneurial skills of, 206, 279–282
  executives as, 208
  groupwork technology and advantages
    of, 487
  leadership skills of, 203–204,
    264–265, 273–274, 277–279
  manager of, 164–166, 167
  management support building skills of,
    207
  maturity of, 208–209
  multiple projects under single, 208
  next generation of, 212–213
  of multiprojects, 163–183
  of responsibilities of the PM office,
    (PMO), 142–147
  office / PMO, 142–143
  organization, of the function, 139–161
  organizational skills of, 206
  part-time, 208
  performance measurement for,
    380–381

personal attributes of, 197–198,
200–201
planning skills of, 205–206
professional responsibilities, 389–392
project staffing alternatives, 147–148
project versus matrix, 140–141
qualifications of, 217–219
resource allocation skills of, 207
responsibilities of, 199–200, 213–217
selection of, 198–202, 208–211
skill requirements for, 202–207
support services, 151 154
team building skills of, 203
technical expertise of, 198, 205,
209–210
time management by, 339–340
to manage individual projects, 139,
147–151
to manage multiple projects, 139
163–183
training of, 202–211
use of interpersonal influences by,
262–265
viewpoints of line managers, vs., 266
Project manager, 167
administrative skill of, 206–207
as interface manager, 186–188
organizational location of, 141–142
reporting location, 141–142, 146
responsibilities, 167
virtual teaming and, 481–482
virtual work and, 482, 483
Project management, communication in,
34–35
in traditional organizations, 12–14,
32–33
project portfolio management as bridge
for, 11–13, 54–55, 56
project portfolio management *versus*,
11–14
success measures for, 10–11
tools of, 38, 42–44, 46
See also project pipeline maintenance
Project Management Knowledge Base,
389

Project Management Institute (PMI),
75–76
Project management maturity model
(PMMM), 410–414
Project management methodologies,
418–419, 428–429
Project management office (PMO):
defined, 19
governance council coordination with,
33–35
project pipeline maintenance and,
29–30, 31
project prequalification and, 57–58, 60
roles and responsibilities of, 12,
33–34, 35
tool-set responsibilities of, 19–20
traditional organizations, 12–13, 14,
32–33
Project office:
alternate staffing methods for,
147–148
assignment of persons to, 147–148
organization of, 148–149
relationship of data processing
function with, 154
Project offices (POs), 219–220, 223–229,
384
communications bottleneck in, 295–296
size of, 148
Project pipeline maintenance, 5, 26–31
guidelines for, 49–50
objectives for, 15–16, 19–20
phase of, 15–16, 40–42
techniques for, 30–31
tools for, 40–42
uncertainty and, 63–66
See also Performance evaluation;
Project management
Project plans, 494
Project planning, 67
Project portfolio life span (PPLS), 9,
13–14
Project portfolio management, 164–167
process, 165–166
steering group, 166–167

Project portfolio management (PPM):
  applicability of, 5–7, 21
  as bridge between operations and
      projects management, 11–13, 53,
      54–55, 56
  as hub, 53, 54–55, 57
  components of, 5, 51
  conditions for, 19–20, 48, 49–50
  definitions of, 3, 14–15, 41–42, 54–57
  effectiveness of, 5, 7, 127–130
  enterprise project management *versus*,
      15
  execution of, 32–35
  executive's guide to, 7
  for new product development, 81–130
  fundamentals of, 14–17, 36–37
  goals of, 107–108, 190
  governance and organization of,
      16–17, 32–35
  historical background of, 3, 11
  impact of, 46, 45–51
  implementation, 46, 47–51
  levels of, 107–108
  misconceptions about, 3
  phases of, 15–16, 19–20, 21, 36–37
  popularity of, by method, 127–129
  project management *versus,* 11–14
  rational for, 3–4, 10–14, 107–108, 109
  supporting processes for, 16–17, 49–50
  tactical level of, 109, 116–128
  tools (software) for, 41–43
Project prequalification, 5, 53–54, 57–60
  criteria for, 58–61
  process of, 57–58, 59
  template for, 58
Project review meetings, 294–295
Project selection and prioritization, 5,
      21–26
  analytic hierarchy process (AHP) for,
      39, 43–44
  conditions for, 19–20, 48, 49–50
  data display for, 39–41, 12, 125,
      127–128
  Efficient Frontier model for, 39,40
  factors in, 22–23, 24, 25, 37

for new product development,
      106–130
for strategic alignment, 107–108,
      109–116
in traditional project management
      organizations, 12–13, 21–22
initiation of, 47–51
phase of, 15–16
prequalification for, 53–54, 57–60
project inventory for, 47–48, 247, 327
reevaluation and, 26–31
Stage-Gate framework for, 86–88
structured process for, 25–26
tools for, 37–41
See also Ranking
Project work:
  process work vs., 482
  supply and demand, 482–483
Promotional communication style, 292,
      294
Promotional or package changes, 116
ProSight, 45–46
Protocept tests, 88, 90
Proverbs, management, 297–300
PS8 (software), 448
Pudder's law, 300
Pure project management, 276, 277
Putt's law, 300
Purposing, problems with mutual
      accountability and charters,
      523–524

Quality control checkpoints, 85–86
  see also Gates
Quality of execution, 88, 90
Quotas, 48

Radical innovations, 101, 115–116
Ranking:
  balanced and weighted, 38–39,
      66–67
  factors in, 38–39
  new product development, 117–128
  of value and benefits, 23–25, 38–39
  phase of, 15, 16, 38, 39

risk and, 24–25, 37, 38–39, 61–63
See also Project selection and
prioritization
R&D *see* Research and development
Readiness (of employees), 275
Reassignment, job, 218
Readiness-check criteria, 86, 95, 96–97,
102,104
"Recognition seeker: (employee role),
236–237
Recruitment, 221
Reduction, project, 48, 86–88
Reeser, Clayton, 221
Referent power, 264, 276
Relationship behavior, 275–276
Reluctant workers (case study), 344
Reports/reporting with Critical Chain
management, 445
Reporting:
financial, 34–35
of ranking and selection data, 39–41
on project performance, 41–42
to senior executives, 34–35, 39–41, 42
See also Display methods,
Documentation
Research and development (R&D)
project management, 210, 348
Resentfulness, 341–342
Resource allocation in Critical Chain
management, 446–447
program managers and, 207
Resource availability and allocation:
balance in, 25
in new product development, 106, 107,
108, 109
in traditional project management
organizations, 12–13
product selection and, 22–23, 24–25,
37, 48
product termination and, 31
tools for evaluating, 37
Resource breakdown charts, 127–128
Resource breakdown structures (RBS),
69
Return on investment (ROI):

project prequalification for, 59, 60
project selection for, 23, 38, 118
Resource Buffer, 440
Resource dependency, 435
Resources, management, 177–178
Responsibility(ies):
matrix, 155
multiproject operation planning and
control, 178–182
of manager of project management,
164–165, 167
of multiproject manager, 167
of portfolio steering group, 166–167
of program manager, 167
of project manager, 167
of project sponsor, 167
professional, 389–392
task matrix, 155
to company/stakeholders, 391–392
Responsibility assignment matrix
(RAM), 256, 258
Revenue flow, 34–35
Review meetings, 429
Revisions, major product, 114–116
Rewards, financial, 388–389
Reward power, 262
Risk, 61–66
disclosure of, 62–63
expected commercial value (ECV)
and, 121–122
of transformation projects, 60
of high-uncertainty projects, 30–31,
63–64
policy for, 62–63
Quality, measurable success and, 496
work breakdown structures, 71, 73–75
See also Uncertainty
Real Change Leaders, 506
Recognition, mutual accountability and,
518–519
Resourced, not resourced vs., 509–510
Responsibility, clear roles and areas of,
468
Results, evaluation of:
formal leader and, 470

Results, evaluation of (*continued*)
single-leader vs. team discipline,
471–472
Reward, mutual accountability and,
518–519
Risk-adjusted discount rates, 117, 118
Risk assessment and management
(RAM), 61–66
in project maintenance, 63–66
in project selection, 22–23, 24–25, 37,
38–39, 61–63
for technical risk, 38–39
for transformation (gorilla) projects,
67–68
tools for, 37, 38–39,42–43,44,45
work breakdown structures (WBS) for,
71, 73–75
See also Uncertainty
Risk management, and project
management, skills, 212
Risk reward bubble diagrams, 125, 126,
127
Road maps, 109–112
Roles:
building mutual accountability and
shifts in, 519–520
Roles and responsibilities, 3, 13, 19–20,
32–34, 35, 48, 50
See also Governance; Governance
council; Participant; Project
management office; Senior
executives
Role conflicts, with project teams, 265
Root cause analyses, performance
agendas and, 504–505
Roussel, P., 107
Ryan, William G., 255

Saad, K.N., 107
SAP, 45
Scalar chain of command, 291
Schedule conflicts, 348
Schedule master:
portfolio, 165

Schedule Performance Index (SPI), 29,
77, 78–79
Schedule risk, 67–68
Schedule slippage:
earned value analysis of, 28–29,
41–42, 77
Schedule Variance (SV), 29, 41, 76–77,
78, 79
Sciforma, 46
Scope changes, 428
Scoping stage, 84, 94–95, 102
Scoring models:
popularity and effectiveness of, 128,
129
Selection. *See* Project selection
Selection criteria. *See* Parameters,
critical;
Project prequalification, Project
selection
Seagate Technology (case study),
456–457
Secretive-communication style, 292
Self-actualization, 252
Self-concept, 283
Self-esteem, 252
Self-regulation, 57–58
Senior executives:
communicating with, 34–35, 39–41
involvement of, 36
language of, 34–35
project portfolio management and,
6–7, 14
project success measures and, 10–11
support and communications of, 48, 50
Sensitivity analysis, 95–96
Sequential processing, 90–91
SG-Navigator, 104–105, 106
Should-meet criteria, 86, 87, 94–95,
96–97, 102, 104
Simulation models, 122
Single-leader discipline, 461–462
common performance objectives, 464
definition of, 467–468
explanation of, 463

general discussion of, 469–470

performance agendas for applying team and, 503–512

performance and discipline decisions, 468–469

performance statements and, 491–492

team discipline vs., 462–463, 471–473

time-efficiency and, 497–498

See also Formal leader Team discipline

Situational Leadership Model, 275–276

Six Sigma, 4–5

Size of project pipeline, 22–23, 25, 37, 48

Skills, people vs. task, 284

Slack, 28

Slice-and-dice software, 42–43, 44

Small companies, effective project management in, 383–385

Small-group performance, five basic elements of effective, 468–469, 472–473

SMART:
outcome-based goals and, 495–499, 504

SMART rule, 346–347

Smith, Doug, 493, 495n1, 517

Snyderman, B.B., 252

Social needs, 251
supporting Critical Chain, 448

Software, *See* Groupwork technology

Software, *See* Tools

Sony Dream Team, 522

SPCs, *see* Statistical process controls

Special cause variations, 439, 444, 445

Special-project meetings, 290

Speed, in Stage-Gate framework, 91–92

Speed, measurable success and, 496

Spending breakdown, 107, 108, 109

Sponsers: 32, 48
problems with mutual accountability and charters, 523–524

Staffing:
and directing, 249
and employee "roles," 236–238
environment for, 196–198

process of, 217–223
of teams, 267, 269
special problems with, 233–235
understaffing, 336

Stage-Gate process, 16, 81, 130
abbreviated version of, for low-risk projects, 83–84, 86–92

best practices in, 99, 100, 101

cross-functional approach of, 84

effectiveness of, 90–91,95–96, 104

for new product development, 81–106, 110–111

for project performance-evaluation, 29–31, 64–65, 66

for technology development projects, 99, 101, 102–104

for technology platform projects, 99, 101

idea-to-launch framework of, 82–83

implementation of, 81–106

overview of, 84–85

structure of, 16–17, 32–33

tools for, 104–106

walk-through of, 92–99

See also Gates, Stages

Stage-Gate- TD, 102–104

Stages, in Stage-Gate framework, 82–83, 84, 92–99

Discovery, 84, 92–94

flexible, 91–92

overview of, 84–85

Stage 1 (Build the Business Case), 83–84, 95–96, 99, 101

Stage 2 (Scoping), 84, 94–95, 99, 101, 102

Stage 3 (Development), 84, 99, 101

Stage 4 (Testing and Validation), 84–85,97–98,99,101

Stage 5 (Launch: Commercialization), 84–85, 97–99

Stake holder:
balancing interests of, 390–391
interacting with, 390
responsibilities to, 391–392

Standard Practice Manuals, 387–388
Standards, setting:
    formal leader and, 470
    single-leader vs. team discipline, 471–472
"Star" employees, 230
Statement of work (SOW), 207
Strategic alignment:
    need for, 321
    project portfolio management for, 322–333
Strategic arenas, 109–110, 111, 113, 114
Strategic assessment, 110–111
Strategic buckets, 71, 73, 111–115
Strategic plan:
    project pipeline maintenance and, 29–30, 34–35
    project selection and, 22–23, 34–35
    See also Business planning;
        Objectives, business
Strategic partnerships, 394
Strategic Portfolio Management, 107–109, 128, 129
Strategic road maps, 109–112
Strategic Resource Buffer, 447
Stragegic Portfolio
Strategic road maps, 109–112
Strategy:
    See also Objectives, business
    work breakdown structures (WBS) for, 69, 71–73
Steering committees, 475
ST Microelectronics, 160–161
    individual accountability, 534
Steiner, George A., 255
Stewart, John M., 198–199
Stress, 340–342
    in project management, 340–342
    manifestations of, 340–342
    positive aspects of, 342
Stoner, James A.F. , 277
Storming, 529
Strategic business units, (SBU), SMART
    example and, 498–499

Structured objectives planning software, 43–44
Stuckenbruck, Linn, 242
Student Syndrome, 436–437, 449
Subgroups:
    ad hoc contributors and, 536–537
    large groups and groupwork technology, 528–529
Sub-teaming: options, 529
Success measures, project, 10–11
    See also Parameters, critical
Success, measurement of, 496–497
Supervising, 249
Suppliers, 393
Swagelok Company, 419–422
"Swing" design (communication analogy), 285
Systems, multiproject, 178–182
Systems theory, 248

Tactical plans:
    project portfolio management and, 34–35
    project selection and, 22–23
Tactical portfolio decisions, 116
Tactics:
    for new product development portfolio management, 109, 116–128
Taking Charge of Change, 517
    Elite Team, 522
Targets, 26, 27, 30–31
    See also paramenters, critical
Task behavior, 275–276
Task estimates (Critical Chain), 433–437
Task skills, people skills vs., 284
Task times, 438–440
Taylor, W.J. 242
Teams. *See* Cross-functional teams;
        Governance
    council or team; Portfolio management teams
Team culture, 533
Team discipline, 461–462
    accountability and, 517–525

advantages / disadvantages of, 467–468

common performance objectives, 463–464

performance agendas for applying single-leader and, 503–512

performance and discipline decisions, 468–469

performance statements and, 491–492

single-leader discipline vs., 463, 471–473

six basic element of team discipline, 464, 470–471

testing when to use, 483

See also Single leader discipline, Team performance

Teaming: misconception of, 463

performance units vs., 463

Team performance, 462–463

Teams at the Top, 512

Teams, project, 197, 223, 229–230

and project manager, 203, 219

anxiety in, 270–271

barriers to development of, 265–270

communication within, 267, 270–271

conflicts within, 265

decision making by, 271

effective vs. ineffective, 272

leadership of, 265, 269

management of newly formed, 270–271

ongoing process of building, 272–273

performance measurement for, 381

support of senior management for, 267–268, 270

Team members, interacting with, 398

Technical assessment, 94–95, 96, 102, 104

Technical expertise, 198, 205, 209–210

Technology:

bias toward single-leader discipline, 464–465

security breaches and, 529–530

Technology development (TD) projects:

Stage-Gate process for, 99, 101, 102, 104

strategic portfolio management of 113–114, 115

Technology newness, 125–127

Technology platform development:

Stage-Gate process for, 99, 101, 102, 104

strategic portfolio management for, 113–114, 115

Technology road map, 110–111

Technology trend assesment, 111–112

Teleconferencing:

groupwork technology and, advantages/disadvantages of, 485–487

virtual teaming and, 481–482

Telstar International (case study), 362–363

Temporary assignments, 196

Termination, project:

in evaluation and maintenance phase, 16, 19–20, 29–30, 31, 41–42

in Stage-Gate framework, 86–88

in traditional project management organizations, 12–13

success through, 31

Testing and Validation stage, 84–85, 97–98, 99, 101

Thamhain, Hans J. 263, 352–353

Theory of Constraints, (TOC), 68, 432

See also Constraints; Critical chain project management (CCPM)

Theory X, 250

Theory Y, 250–251

Theory Z, 251

Threaded discussions: assigning monitoring/guiding roles and, 537–538

bias toward single-leader discipline, 533–534

groupwork technology and, advantages / disadvantages of, 485–486

increased communications and, 531

netiquette and, 536–537

Thresholds, 26, 27
Time-efficient process, small-group
    performance and, 468
Time management, 284, 335–342
    and stress/burnout, 340–342
    barriers to effective, 336–337
    forms for, 338–339
    identification of, as problem area, 336
    techniques for effective, 339–340
Time to market, 68–69
Time wasting, 91
Timing:
    of gorilla projects, 67
    portfolio balance and, 127–128
Tired, being, 341
"To do" pad, 338
Tools (software), 35–46
    data presentation, 39–41, 44
    for analytic hierarchy process, 43–44
    for critical path scheduling (CPM), 42
    for earned value analysis (EVA), 41,
        42–43, 44–45, 79
    for enterprise resource planning
        (ERP), 42–43
    for new product development,
        110–125
    for professional services automation
        (PSA),43–44
    for project pipeline maintenance,
        40–42
    for project portfolio
        management,41–46
    for project risk, 42–43
    for project selection and prioritization,
        37–41
    for schedule risk, 42–43, 67–68
    for Stage-Gate process, 104–106
    integrated examples of, 44–46
    project management, 38, 42–44, 46
    project management office and, 19–20
    vendors of, 43–46
Tools for gates and portfolio reviews,
    117–123, 125
Tools, specific products:
    Accolade, 105–106

Changepoint, 45–46
Clarity, 45–46
Cobra, 44–45
Compuware IT Governance by
    Changepoint, 45, 46
Expert Choice, 45–46
Lawson, 45–46
Mercury Interactive, 45–46
Microsoft Access, 45–46
Microsoft Project, 44–45, 46
Niku, 45–46
Open plan, 44–45
Oracle, 45
Palisade, 45–46
People Soft, 45–46
Plan View, 45–46
Primavera, 46
PRISMS for IT, Governance and
    Resource Management, 46
Sciforma, 46
SG-Navigator, 104–106
WelcomPortfolio, 44–45
WelcomRisk, 44–45
Welcom tool set, 44–45
"Topic jumper" (employee role), 236
Training, 316, 395–397
    and directing, 395–397
    on key initiatives/practices, 395–396
    of new employees, 233, 234
    of project manager, 211
Transformation projects:
    as gorillas, 66–69
    defined, 66–67
    management of, 67–68
    prequalification of, 60
    time-to-market for, 68–69
Travel expenses, efficiency of groupware
    and, 530
Trends in project management,
    409–429
    capacity planning, 424–425
    competency models, 425–427
    continuous improvement, 419–423
    do-it-yourself methodologies, 419
    end-of-phase review meetings, 429

multiple projects, management of, 428–429

procedural documentation, development of, 414–418

project management maturity model, 410–414

Trophy Project (case study), 315–317

Truman's law, 300

Trust, 218, 296

Two-bucket inventory, 512

Uncertainty:
  change and, 63
  in new product development, 106–107
  managing, 53–54, 61–66
  projects with high,30–31, 63–64
  review and action for, 64–66
  See also Risk; Risk assessment and management

Understaffing, 336

Unhappy, being, 341

United Management Technologies (UMT), 45–46, 48, 50

U.S. Department of Defense, 75–76

U.S. Marine Corps three dimensional discipline and, 461–462

Utility projects. *See* Maintenance or utility projects

Values, personal, 280–281

Value:
  and prioritiaztion
  defining, 22–23, 38–39, 107, 108, 109
  for new product development projects, 117–123, 125
  for transformation projects, 69
  prequalification for, 58–61
  ranking, 23–25, 38–39
  See also Earned value analysis (EVA); Project selection Value-in-use analysis, 88, 90

Very large projects, 385–386

Video conferencing:
  groupwork technology and, advantages/ disadvantages of,
481–482, 485

Virtual teaming, 462, 463, 464, 465, 481–483
  application of, 483–484
  assigning, monitoring / guiding roles, 537–538
  avoiding high numbers, 535–536
  avoiding the illusion of collaborative groupware meetings, 535
  bias toward single-leader discipline, 533–534
  expanded access, 527–528
  face-to-face meetings, 534–535
  information synthesis and, 481
  multicultural groups and, 533–534
  netiquette, 536–537
  obstacles and opportunities, 527–528
  participation and communication, 530–533
  practical pointers, 534–535
  selecting features of groupware, 536
  team performance and shifting leadership roles, 537–538
  the right discipline for, 483–484
  workbook excercises and, 501

Virtual team rooms, 527

Virtual work:
  definition of, 482
  See also Virtual teaming

Visual aids, 290

Visual displays, 5–6, 39–41, 123–128

Voice-of-customer inputs, 88, 90, 94–95

Von Braun's law of gravity, 300

Voting groups, 39, 43–44

Watling, T. F., 242

Weekly meetings, 290

WelcomPortfolio, 44–45

WelcomRisk, 44–45

Welcomtool set, 44–45

Wheeler, Donald J., 445

White elephants, 125, 126, 127

Wideman, R. M., 13–14

Wilemon, David L., 210, 273, 281, 349–350, 358

Withdrawl, proposal, 57–58
"Withdrawer" (employee role), 237
Withdrawing, 356
Wisdom of Teams, The: discipline in, 461–462
    six basic elements of team discipline and, 470–471
    teams as performance units in, 462
Workbench Results Management, 45
Work breakdown structures (WBS), 29, 42–43, 69–75
    earned value analysis and, 78–79
    for risk, 71, 73–75
    for strategies, 69–71, 73
    using, as checklists, 73–74
Working approach, 510–511
    formal leader and, 469–470
    single-leader vs., team discipline, 471–472
Workforce constraints, 24–25
Working group discipline, *See* Single-leader discipline

Working skill: building mutual accountability and, 520
Workplace, changes in, 481–482
Work products, 473–474
    decisions, vs., 474–475
    See also Collective work products: Individual work products
Work sessions:
    defining the purpose, 511–512
    maintaining a two-bucket inventory, 512
    preparing for, 510–511
Worthlessness, feelings of, 341
"Wow!" factor, 87–88
Written communications, 290
Written media, 290
Xerox, 394

Y, the, 472
    three branches of, 468–469

Zero defects, 4–5